THE HIDDEN PLACES OF
ENGLAND

By Peter Long

© Travel Publishing Ltd.

Published by: Travel Publishing Ltd, 7a Apollo House, Calleva Park, Aldermaston, Berks, RG7 8TN

ISBN 1-904-434-40-1

© Travel Publishing Ltd

First published 1998, second edition 2000, third edition 2002, fourth edition 2004, fifth edition 2006

Printing by: Scotprint, Haddington

Maps by: © Maps in Minutes ™ (2006)
© Crown Copyright, Ordnance Survey 2006

Editor: Peter Long

Cover Design: Lines and Words, Aldermaston

Cover Photograph: Bolton Priory and the River Wharfe, Yorkshire © www.picturesofbritain.co.uk

Text Photographs: Text photos have been kindly supplied by the Pictures of Britain photo library
© www.picturesofbritain.co.uk

Foreword

This is the 5th edition of the *Hidden Places of England* and it has been fully updated. In this respect we would like to thank the many Tourist Information Centres in England for helping us update the editorial content. Regular readers will note that the pages of the guide have been extensively redesigned to allow more information to be presented on the many interesting places to visit in each county. In addition, although you will still find details of places of interest and advertisers of places to stay, eat and drink included under each village, town or city, these are now cross referenced to more detailed information contained in a separate, easy-to-use section of the book.

The Hidden Places of England contains a wealth of interesting information on the history, the countryside, the towns and villages and the more established places of interest. But it also promotes the more secluded and little known visitor attractions and places to stay, eat and drink many of which are easy to miss unless you know exactly where you are going.

We include hotels, bed & breakfasts, restaurants, pubs, bars, teashops and cafes as well as historic houses, museums, gardens and many other attractions throughout England, all of which are comprehensively indexed. Most places are accompanied by an attractive photograph and are easily located by using the map at the beginning of each chapter. We do not award merit marks or rankings but concentrate on describing the more interesting, unusual or unique features of each place with the aim of making the reader's stay in the local area an enjoyable and stimulating experience.

Whether you are travelling around England on business or for pleasure we do hope that you enjoy reading and using this book. We are always interested in what readers think of places covered (or not covered) in our guides so please do not hesitate to use the reader reaction form provided to give us your considered comments. We also welcome any general comments which will help us improve the guides themselves. Finally if you are planning to visit any other corner of the British Isles we would like to refer you to the list of other *Hidden Places* titles to be found to the rear of the book and to the Travel Publishing website.

Travel Publishing

Did you know that you can also search our website for details of thousands of places to see, stay, eat or drink throughout Britain and Ireland? Our site has become increasingly popular and now receives over 160,000 hits per day. Try it!

website: www.travelpublishing.co.uk

Location Map

Contents

Bedfordshire

The often overlooked county of Bedfordshire is one of charming typically English villages and small market towns surrounded by a rich rural landscape. Despite their modern appearance, the towns of Luton and Dunstable, in the south of the county, have their roots firmly in the past and it was at Dunstable that Archbishop Cranmer held court in 1533 to dissolve the marriage of Henry VIII and Catherine of Aragon. The county town of Bedford also has a long history and has strong associations with John Bunyan, who was born nearby. The county is littered with stately homes and old country houses, including the splendid Houghton House, which is widely believed to be the inspiration for the House Beautiful in *Pilgrim's Progress*, and magnificent Woburn Abbey, the seat of the Dukes of Bedford, which is famous for its superb art collection and its Wild Animal Kingdom and Leisure Park. The Abbey is certainly one of the county's finest attractions, but Bedfordshire is also home to Whipsnade Wild Animal Park, the largest centre of conservation in Europe, and the headquarters of the Royal Society for the Protection of Birds.

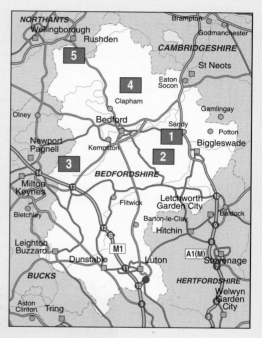

FOOD & DRINK

1	The Kings Arms, Girtford	p 2, 336
3	The Swan Inn, Cranfield	p 4, 337
4	The Plough at Bolnhurst, Bolnhurst	p 4, 336
5	The New Inn, Wymington	p 4, 338

ACCOMMODATION

1	The Kings Arms, Girtford	p 2, 336

PLACES OF INTEREST

2	The Swiss Garden, Old Warden	p 3, 336

I   THE KINGS ARMS

Nr Sandy

The **Kings Arms** combines traditional pub qualities of good food, good beer and good company with comfortable, practical B&B accommodation.

see page 336

BEDFORD

Bedford was already a thriving market place before the Norman Conquest but it is for its association with John Bunyan that the town is best known. Born in Elstow, just to the south, Bunyan went into the same trade as his father, a tinsmith, and during the Civil War he was drafted into the Parliamentarian Army. In the 1650s he met John Gifford, the then pastor of the Independent Congregation, and it was their lengthy discussions that led to Bunyan's conversion; he was baptised by Gifford in a backwater leading off the Great Ouse. It was while preaching in the villages of Bedfordshire that Bunyan came into conflict with authority and he served two terms at the County Gaol. During his imprisonment, between 1660-72 he wrote many of his works including his most famous, *Pilgrim's Progress*.

Following his release in 1672, he was elected pastor of the Independent Congregation and built a meeting house that was finally completed in 1707. The church seen today dates from 1849 and now houses the **Bunyan Museum**.

For a greater insight into the history of the town and surrounding area the Bedford Museum is well worth a visit, as is the adjoining **Cecil Higgins Art Gallery** with its internationally renowned collection.

Immediately southeast of Bedford is the village of **Cardington**, home of the Whitbread family of brewing fame. The skyline is dominated by the two giant hangars that were built to house the airships, including the R100 and R101, that were once thought to be the future of flying.

Canopied Village Pump, Old Warden

The Church of St Mary contains the Whitbread family vault, and across the road from the church is the tomb of the victims of the R101 disaster.

AROUND BEDFORD

BIGGLESWADE

9½ miles SE of Bedford on the A6001

Biggleswade was the home of Dan Albone, the inventor of the modern bicycle and designer of the first practical tandem and a ladies cycle with a low crossbar and a skirt guard. He developed a racing cycle, which in 1888 set speed and endurance records with the doughty CP Mills in the saddle. He was also responsible for the Ivel Agricultural Tractor, forerunner of the modern tractor.

To the west of Biggleswade lies **Old Warden**, an enchanting village which was developed in the early 19th century by Sir Robert Ongley who also created the **Swiss Garden**, a romantic fantasy with a tiny thatched Swiss style cottage and arches of creepers. In the grounds of this Jacobean style mansion house, is the fantastic **Shuttleworth Collection** of historic aircraft.

North of Biggleswade is the headquarters of the **Royal Society for the Protection of Birds**, **The Lodge**, which is also home to a nature reserve of open heath, woodland and formal gardens.

LUTON

18 miles S of Bedford on the A6

The largest town in Bedfordshire

and perhaps best known for its Airport and Vauxhall cars, Luton first prospered in the 17th century on the strength of its straw plaiting and hat making industries. The **Stockwood Craft Museum and Gardens**, housed in a Georgian stable block, provides the opportunity to step back in time and also here is the **Mossman Collection** of over 60 horse-drawn vehicles.

Close by is the magnificent house of **Luton Hoo**, which now houses a superb art collection. Its parkland was landscaped by Capability Brown. To the west of Luton lies **Dunstable**, an important centre in Roman Britain and a busy market town for around 1,000 years. Close by, at **Whipsnade**, is the **Tree Cathedral** (National Trust), where, after World War I, trees were planted in the shape of a cathedral complete with nave, transepts and chancel. **Whipsnade Wild Animal Park** is the country home of the Zoological Society of London and one of Europe's largest wildlife conservation centres.

AMPTHILL

7½ miles SW of Bedford off the A507

A historic town that was a great favourite with Henry VIII but its castle was replaced by Ampthill Park in 1694 and the parkland, landscaped by Capability Brown, is now the **Ampthill Deer Park**. To the east lies **Maulden Woods**, an area of mixed woodland and open meadows with muntjac deer and badgers, while, just to the north is

2 THE SWISS GARDEN

Old Warden, nr Biggleswade

The Swiss Garden takes you back to the early 19th century and an era of ornamental gardening and picturesque architecture.

 see page 336

3

3 THE SWAN INN

Cranfield

The Swan offers a fine choice of food and drink and high-quality accommodation in a country setting with ready access from the M1.

 see page 337

4 THE PLOUGH

Bolnhurst

Outstanding modern British cooking brings patrons from miles around to the **Plough at Bolnhurst**.

 see page 336

5 THE NEW INN

Wymington, nr Rushden

New tenants (Dec 2005) are winning many friends with the genuine hospitality and the fine food they provide at the **New Inn**.

 see page 338

Moot Hall, Ampthill

Houghton House, reputed to have been the inspiration for the House Beautiful in *Pilgrim's Progress*.

A little further afield is **Silsoe** and Wrest Park, whose gardens are a living history of English gardening from 1700-1850.

LEIGHTON BUZZARD

17½ miles SW of Bedford on the A4012

A prosperous market town where visitors can take a steam train journey on the **Leighton Buzzard Railway** on tracks laid in 1919 to carry sand from the local quarries. The town lies at one end of the **Greensand Ridge Walk**, which extends for some 40 miles across Bedfordshire to Gamlingay, Cambridgeshire.

WOBURN

12 miles SW of Bedford on the A4012

This originally Saxon hamlet is best known as the home of **Woburn Abbey**, the seat of the Dukes of Bedford. Along with the fantastic art collection and superb furniture in the house, Woburn has an antiques centre and a deer park that is also home to the **Wild Animal Kingdom and Leisure Park**.

Berkshire

The eastern region of the Royal County of Berkshire has been graced for over 900 years by the royal presence at Windsor. The Castle is a magnificent royal residence and Windsor Great Park is what remains of an ancient royal hunting ground. The River Thames, too, plays a part in forming the landscape here, as well as acting as the county border between Oxfordshire, and there are many delightful riverside towns and villages to explore. To the west, at the ancient town of Reading, the county's other principle river, the Kennet, joins the Thames, closely accompanied by the Kennet and Avon Canal. Further westwards is the prosperous old wool town of Newbury, to the north of which are the Berkshire Downs, a rolling area of grassland that contains many prehistoric remains and is also a training ground for racehorses.

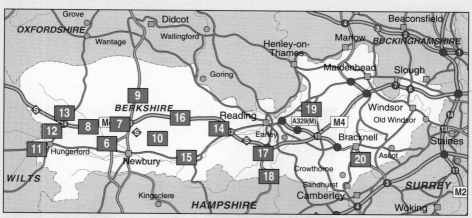

FOOD & DRINK

ACCOMMODATION

PLACES OF INTEREST

NEWBURY

A prosperous wool town in the Middle Ages, evidence of which can be seen in the splendid 'wool' **Church of St Nicholas** built in the 16th century. The town will be forever linked with the legend of Jack o' Newbury, a wool merchant who was asked to raise two horsemen with footmen for Henry VIII's campaign against the Scots. Jack raised 50 of each and led them himself, but they only got as far as Buckinghamshire before news of the victory at Flodden reached them and they returned home. Two centuries later, Newbury became a busy coaching stop on the route between London and Bath and in 1810 came the opening of the **Kennet and Avon Canal**. **Newbury Lock**, built in 1796, was the first lock to be built along the canal and is also the only lock to have lever-operated ground paddles.

Back in the town centre and housed in a 17th century cloth hall is **Newbury Museum** which, among its many displays, tells the story of the two battles fought nearby during the Civil War.

To the north lies **Donnington**, home to 18th century Grove House, the childhood home of Beau Brummel, and to **Donnington**

Kennet & Avon Canal, Newbury

Castle, of which only the imposing twin-towered gatehouse survives.

AROUND NEWBURY

EAST ILSLEY

8½ miles N of Newbury on the A34

Along with its neighbour, **West Ilsley**, the village is associated with racehorses that use the gallops on the downs as their training grounds.

Closer to Newbury, near **Hampstead Norreys** on the B4009, is **Wyld Court Rainforest**, a fascinating World Land Trust conservation centre where visitors can walk through several indoor tropical rainforests viewing a unique collection of spectacular and rare plants along with rainforest animals.

COMBE

7½ miles SW of Newbury off the A343

This isolated hamlet is overlooked by **Walbury Hill** which, at 974 feet, is the highest point in Berkshire. A popular place with walkers, it has an Iron Age hill fort on the summit, from where there are superb panoramic views. Close to the hill lies **Combe Gibbet**, one of the last public hanging places in the country. To the north is **Inkpen Common**, a Site of

Town Hall, Hungerford

Special Scientific Interest where, along with the heath and woodland, a wet valley bog and pond have been created in an old clay pit.

HUNGERFORD

8½ miles W of Newbury on the A338

The town's heyday came in the 18th century, when the turnpike road from London to Bath was built, and the good times continued with the opening of the **Kennet and Avon Canal**. Several of the old coaching inns have survived and it was in 1688 at The Bear Hotel that a meeting took place between William of Orange and representatives of James II that culminated in the end of the House of Stuart and James's flight to France.

---

10   THE CASTLE INN

Cold Ash, nr Thatcham

Long-standing landlords keep the customers at the **Castle Inn** happy with a great choice of super home cooking and real ales.

🍴 *see page 339*

---

11   THE THREE SWANS HOTEL

High Street, Hungerford

High standards of food, drink and accommodation are maintained at the **Three Swans Hotel** on Hungerford's main street.

🛏 *see page 340*

---

12   TALLY HO!

Hungerford Newtown, nr Hungerford

Just minutes from J14 of the M4, the **Tally Ho!** is a popular choice for lovers of good home cooking.

🍴 *see page 340*

7

13 THE PHEASANT INN

Shefford Woodlands, nr Hungerford

This is horseracing territory, but it's not just followers of the turf who vote the **Pheasant** a winner for its superb hospitality, great cooking and top-class accommodation.

see page 341

14 THE RED LION

Theale, nr Reading

The **Red Lion** is a roaring success, open all day for drinks and every session except Sunday evening for popular home-cooked food.

see page 342

15 THE RISING SUN

Woolhampton

Home-made savoury pies and puddings are among the favourite dishes served at the **Rising Sun**.

see page 342

LAMBOURN

11½ miles NW of Newbury on the B4000

Situated up on the Berkshire Downs, this village is best known as a centre for the training of racehorses. The **Lambourn Trainer's Association** organises guided tours of the village's famous stables and also trips up to the gallops to see the horses going through their paces.

To the north of the village are the **Lambourn Seven Barrows**, one of the most impressive Bronze Age burial sites in the country.

READING

The town grew up around its **Abbey**, which was founded in 1121 by Henry I and became one of the most important religious houses in the country. Reading is also one of only a handful of towns where kings of England have been laid to rest - Henry I was buried in the Abbey. Adjacent to the ruins of the Abbey is **Reading Prison**, where Oscar Wilde was imprisoned and where he wrote *De Profundis*. His confinement inspired him to compose the epic poem *The Ballad of Reading Gaol* while in exile in Paris in 1898.

With the building of roads and the opening of the canal, Reading really began to boom and to become linked with great names such as Sutton Seeds, Huntley & Palmer biscuits and the brewing industry. **Reading Museum** tells the story of the town from its earliest beginnings. Situated on the banks of the River Kennet and housed in a range of canal buildings, **Blake's Lock Museum** concerns itself with the life of the town in the 19th and early 20th century.

AROUND READING

ALDERMASTON

9 miles SW of Reading on the A340

It was in this tranquil village that in 1840 the William Pear was first propagated by schoolmaster John Staid; it was first known as the Aldermaston pear, and a cutting of the plant is believed to have been taken to Australia, where it is now called the Bartlett pear. The lovely **Church of St Mary** provides the atmospheric setting for the **York Mystery Cycle**, 14th century nativity plays that are performed here each year.

Close to the village there is a delightful walk along the Kennet and Avon Canal to **Aldermaston Wharf**, a beautifully restored 18th century building that houses the Kennet and Avon Canal Visitor Centre.

PANGBOURNE

4½ miles NW of Reading on the A329

Situated at the confluence of the Rivers Pang and Thames, the town grew up in the late 19th and early 20th centuries as a fashionable place to reside, and the numerous attractive villas that have survived include a row of ornate Victorian houses known as the Seven Deadly Sins. It was to Pangbourne and **Church Cottage** that the author Kenneth Graham retired and wrote *The Wind in the Willows*, based on the original bedtime stories he invented for his son. An elegant iron bridge links the town with **Whitchurch**, on the opposite bank of the River Thames; it was at **Whitchurch Lock** that the characters in Jerome K Jerome's *Three Men in a Boat* abandoned their craft after a series of mishaps and returned to London.

SONNING

3½ miles NE of Reading off the A4

An attractive little village on the banks of the River Thames, this was once home to a palace belonging to the Bishops of Salisbury. Behind the wall of the old palace is Deanery Gardens, a well-hidden house built to the design of Lutyens. To the southeast, on the site of Woodley airfield, is the **Museum of Berkshire Aviation** which chronicles the history of this once thriving centre of the aircraft industry.

WARGRAVE

6½ miles NE of Reading on the A321

The peace of this charming riverside village was shattered in 1914 when suffragettes burnt down the church in protest that the vicar refused to remove the word 'obey' from the marriage service. In the churchyard stands the **Hannen Mausoleum**, a splendid family

monument designed by Lutyens in 1906.

Nearby **Druid's Temple** stands in the garden of **Temple Combe**, close to a house designed by the architect Frank Lloyd Wright. The only house of his in England, it was built in 1958 on an elaborate U-shaped design, and its many unusual features include suede-panelled interior walls.

COOKHAM

14 miles NE of Reading on the A4094

This small town on the River Thames was the birthplace of Sir Stanley Spencer, who used it as the setting for many of his paintings. The **Stanley Spencer Gallery**, housed in a converted Victorian chapel, has a permanent exhibition of his work. He was born here, spent most of his life here, and is buried in the churchyard of Holy Trinity.

BRACKNELL

10 miles SE of Reading on the A322

It was designated a New Town in 1948, but Bracknell dates back to the 10th century when the community stood at the junction of two major routes through Windsor Forest.

What now remains of the great royal hunting ground of Windsor Forest (also called Bracknell Forest) lies to the south and in this vast area of parks and nature reserves is the **Lookout Discovery Park**, an interactive science centre that brings to life the mysteries of both science and nature.

16 THE POT KILN

Frilsham, nr Yattendon

The superb food takes centre stage at the **Pot Kiln**, which enjoys a delightful setting in picturesque countryside.

 see page 343

17 THE SWAN

Three Mile Cross, nr Reading

The Swan originated as 17th century timber-framed workers cottages and now serves real ales and a selection of meals.

 see page 344

18 BULL AT RISELEY

Riseley, nr Reading

The **Bull at Riseley** is on target with its well-kept real ales and locally sourced food.

 see page 345

19 THE DUKE OF WELLINGTON

Twyford

The **Duke of Wellington** richly deserves its far-reaching reputation for well-kept real ales and super food.

see page 343

9

20 LOOK OUT DISCOVERY CENTRE

Bracknell

A fun day out for all the family, enjoying the hands-on science and nature exhibition, as well as the surrounding woodland.

see page 345

•

Windsor Castle is not just a defensive structure but also an ecclesiastical centre and within its walls lies the magnificent St George's Chapel which was started by Edward IV in 1478. It is the last resting place of ten monarchs, from Edward IV himself to Henry VIII with his favourite wife Jane Seymour, Charles I, George V with Queen Mary, and George VI, beside whom the ashes of his beloved daughter Princess Margaret were laid in February 2002. It is also the Chapel of the Most Noble Order of the Garter, Britain's highest order of chivalry.

•

SANDHURST

11 miles SE of Reading on the A3095

The town is the home of the **Royal Military Academy**, the training place for army officers for almost a century, and the academy's Staff College Museum tells the history of officer training from its inception to the present day.

WINDSOR

The largest castle in the country and a royal residence for over 900 years, **Windsor Castle** was built by William the Conqueror in the late 11th century as one of a chain of defences on the approaches into London. Down the centuries several monarchs have added to the Norman structure, most notably Henry VIII, Charles II and George IV. Various parts of the Castle are open to the public, including 16 state apartments that house a remarkable collection of furniture, porcelain and armour. Also here is **Queen Mary's Dolls' House**, which was designed by Lutyens and has both electric lights and running water. In November 1992, a massive fire swept through the northeast corner of the castle but, after much restoration, the affected rooms, including St George's Hall, are now once again open to the public.

Frogmore House, a modest early 18th century manor house standing in Home Park, has acted as a second, more relaxed royal residence than the nearby castle. In the **Royal Mausoleum** Queen Victoria is buried beside her beloved husband.

The charming town grew up beneath the walls of the castle and there is plenty here to interest the visitor. The grand central station in the heart of the town dates from 1897 and is now home to the fascinating **Royalty and Empire** exhibition that charts the life and times of Queen Victoria, and at the **Town and Crown Exhibition** the development of Windsor is explained. Windsor is the home of the Household Cavalry, at Combermere Barracks, and here there is the superb **Household Cavalry Museum** while **The Dungeons of Windsor** tells stories of crime and punishment from as far back as the 13th century. To the south of the town lies **Windsor Great Park**, the remains of the extensive royal hunting forest.

AROUND WINDSOR

ETON

1 mile N of Windsor on the A355

Situated just across the River Thames from Windsor, the town has grown up around **Eton College**, the famous public school that was founded in 1440 by Henry VI and was originally intended for the education of 70 poor and worthy scholars.

ASCOT

6 miles SW of Windsor on the A329

This was a small village until 1711 when Queen Anne moved the original Windsor race meeting here and founded the world famous **Ascot Racecourse**.

Buckinghamshire

South Buckinghamshire, with the River Thames as its southern county boundary, lies almost entirely within the Chiltern Hills and is a charming and delightful area that has, over the years inspired many writers and artists, including Milton, Shakespeare and Roald Dahl. Though many of the towns and villages here have histories going back well before the Norman Conquest, the influence of London is never far away and several have been linked with the capital for many years by the Metropolitan Railway. The links with London have also seen many famous and wealthy people make their homes here and, tucked away in the rolling countryside, can be found two fabulous former residences of the Rothschild family, Waddesdon Manor and Mentmore Towers. Buckinghamshire is also home to the country retreat of the Prime Minister, Chequers. The north of the county is dominated by the New Town of Milton Keynes

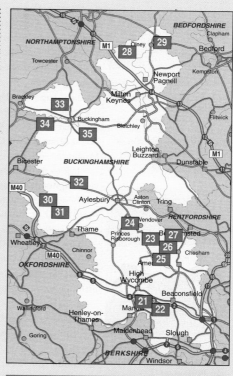

FOOD & DRINK

ACCOMMODATION

HIGH WYCOMBE

The largest town in Buckinghamshire and originally an old Chilterns Gap market town, High Wycombe is traditionally known for its manufacture of chairs and, in particular, the Windsor design. Several old buildings survive today, including the Little Market House of 1761, and what is now the **Wycombe Local History and Chair Museum**.

Just to the north of the town lies **Hughenden Manor**, which was bought by Benjamin Disraeli shortly after the publication of his novel *Tancred* and was his home until his death in 1881. Today, the remodelled 18th century house displays an interesting collection of memorabilia of Disraeli's life; the great Victorian Prime Minister lies buried in the estate church.

To the west of Wycombe lies the charming estate village of **West Wycombe** and **West Wycombe Park**, the home of the Dashwood family until the 1930s. The house dates from the early 18th century, and the grounds and parkland, landscaped by a pupil of Capability Brown, contain temples and an artificial lake shaped like a swan. Hewn out of the nearby hillside are **West Wycombe Caves** which were created by Sir Francis Dashwood, who employed his estate workers on the task after a series of failed harvests. Along with his passion for remodelling old buildings, Sir

Francis had a racier side to his character and was a founder member of the Hellfire Club, a group of rakes who engaged in highly colourful activities.

AROUND HIGH WYCOMBE

PRINCES RISBOROUGH

7½ miles NW of High Wycombe on the A4010

Once home to a palace belonging to the Black Prince, the eldest son of Edward III, this attractive place has a host of 17th and 18th century cottages. Nearby is **Princes Risborough Manor House** (National Trust), which is an early example of a redbrick building – it dates from 1670.

One of the most famous residences in the country lies at nearby **Great Kimble**: the 16th century mansion, **Chequers**, has been the country house of the British Prime Minister since 1920.

GREAT MISSENDEN

5 miles N of High Wycombe on the A4128

This attractive village is home to the early 15th century **Old Court House**, one of only two court houses in the Chiltern Hundreds, and the home of Roald Dahl, the author of much loved children's books. His grave is in the churchyard of St Peter and St Paul.

WENDOVER

9½ miles N of High Wycombe on the B4009

A delightful old market town situated in a gap in the Chiltern Hills, Wendover has several half-timbered, thatched houses and cottages, the best example of which are **Anne Boleyn's Cottages**. Close by, on the edge of the Chiltern escarpment, lie **Wendover Woods**, created for recreational pursuits as well as for conservation and timber production by the Forestry Commission.

AMERSHAM

6 miles NE of High Wycombe on the A404

The town's main street has a good mix of fine old buildings, notably the 17th century Market Hall and **Amersham Museum**, housed in part of a medieval hall. Amersham was a staging post for coaches and many of the old inns remain, including the **Crown Hotel** that many will recognise from the film *Four Weddings and a Funeral*.

To the east of Amersham is the picturesque village of **Chenies**, home to the fascinating 15th century **Chenies Manor** house. Originally the home of the earls of Bedford (before they moved to Woburn), the house was built by the architect who enlarged Hampton Court for Henry VIII.

CHALFONT ST GILES

7 miles E of High Wycombe off the A413

The most famous building in this typical English village is the 16th century **Milton's Cottage**, where the poet stayed in 1665 to escape the plague in London. Though he only lived here a short time, the blind poet wrote *Paradise Lost* and began *Paradise Regained* before moving back to London. The cottage and its garden are now a

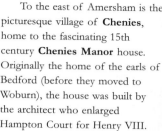

24 THE RED LION HOTEL

Wendover

The **Red Lion** is a distinguished 17th century hotel offering high standards of cooking and 26 very comfortable bedrooms.

🛏 see page 347

25 THE PLOUGH INN

Hyde Heath, nr Amersham

Overlooking the village green, the **Plough Inn** serves excellent home-cooked food up to 10 o'clock every evening.

🍴 see page 347

Amersham High Street

Museum dedicated to the poet. A fascinating place in the nearby Newland Park is the **Chiltern Open Air Museum**, dedicated to rescuing vernacular architecture.

BEACONSFIELD

5 miles SE of High Wycombe on the A40

The old part of this town is known for its literary connections: the 17th century poet Edmund Waller was a resident (and is buried in the churchyard of St Mary and All Saints), and GK Chesterton, poet Robert Frost and the children's author Enid Blyton all made Beaconsfield their home. Here, too, is **Bekonscot**, a rural model village which was created by Roland Callingham, a London accountant, in the 1920s and 30s.

To the southeast lies **Stoke Poges**, whose churchyard provided Thomas Gray with the inspiration to write his famous *Elegy Written in a Country Churchyard*. The poet is buried in the church; to the east stands the massive **Gray Monument**, built in 1799 by John Penn, grandson of William Penn, founder of Pennsylvania.

Just south of Beaconsfield lies **Burnham Beeches**, an area that has long been a place of leisure and relaxation for Londoners.

MARLOW

4 miles S of High Wycombe on the A4155

An attractive commuter town on the banks of the River Thames. It was at a riverside pub, the Two Brewers, that Jerome K Jerome wrote his masterpiece *Three Men in a Boat*. Today, Marlow is probably best known for its annual June **Regatta**.

To the west lies the much-filmed village of **Hambleden** which was given to the National Trust by the family of the bookseller WH Smith (later Viscount Hambleden).

MILTON KEYNES

One of the town's most notable buildings is **Christ Church**, built in the style of Christopher Wren, which is the first purpose-built ecumenical church in Britain. The rural heritage of the villages that are now incorporated into its suburbs has not been forgotten and the **Museum of Industry and Rural Life** has a large collection of industrial, domestic and agricultural bygones; in the **Exhibition Gallery**, displays of art, crafts and local history can be seen.

AROUND MILTON KEYNES

OLNEY

8 miles N of Milton Keynes on the A509

This pretty town on the banks of the River Ouse is associated with William Cowper, reformed slave-trader, preacher and hymn-writer, who lived here between 1768 and 1786; his house is now the **Cowper and Newton Museum**, which not only concentrates on Cowper's life and work but also houses a nationally important Lace Collection. The town's recent claim to fame is the Pancake Race held each Shrove Tuesday.

BLETCHLEY

3 miles SE of Milton Keynes on the A5

Now virtually a suburb of Milton Keynes, Bletchley is famous as the home of **Bletchley Park**, the Victorian mansion that housed the country's wartime code breakers.

MENTMORE

12 miles SE of Milton Keynes off the B488

The village is home to the first of the Rothschild mansions, **Mentmore Towers**, which was built for Baron Meyer Amschel de Rothschild in the mid 19th century. A splendid building in the Elizabethan style and a superb example of grandiose Victorian extravagance, the house was sold in the 1970s and is now the headquarters of the University of Natural Law. To the southeast lies

Ivinghoe Beacon, an Iron Age hill fort which provides a wonderful viewpoint on the edge of the Chiltern Hills. The Beacon is at one end of Britain's oldest road, the **Ridgeway National Trail** - the other end is at the World Heritage site of Avebury in Wiltshire.

AYLESBURY

15½ miles S of Milton Keynes on the A413

The county town of Buckinghamshire since the 18th century, this ancient town sheltered by the Chiltern Hills is famous for its Aylesbury ducks. The old part of the town (now a conservation area) is centred on the market square and here, amongst the sleepy lanes, is the **King's Head Inn** where Henry VIII is said to have wooed Anne Boleyn. During the Civil War, Aylesbury was a base for both Cromwell and the King, depending on how well the conflict

29 THE ROBIN HOOD

Clifton Reynes

The **Robin Hood** – a prince among pubs – welcomes friends old and new with classic English cooking, plus a few surprises.

 see page 349

30 THE PHEASANT INN

Brill, nr Aylesbury

The **Pheasant Inn** enjoys a pleasant country setting in which to enjoy good food and comfortable accommodation.

 see page 348

31 THE PUB IN CHILTON

Chilton

The **Pub in Chilton** is an immaculate inn open all day for food and drink.

see page 349

32 THE LION INN

Waddesdon

A warm welcome, a good choice of drinks and a wide-ranging menu bring locals and visitors to the **Lion Inn**.

 see page 349

Waddesdon Manor, nr Aylesbury

33 THE QUEENS HEAD

Chackmore

The **Queens Head** is a charming village pub open every lunchtime and evening for a good choice of food and drink.

 see page 350

34 THE RED LION

Little Tingewick, Finmere

Chef-patron Nigel Jones has put the **Red Lion** on the gastronomic map with his superb dishes of worldwide inspiration.

 see page 350

35 THE OLD THATCHED INN

Adstock

A picturesque setting, relaxed atmosphere, fine food and drink and luxurious guest bedrooms – all to be found at the **Old Thatched Inn**.

see page 350

was progressing and, nearby, at Holman's Bridge, Prince Rupert suffered a crushing defeat. Housed in a splendid Georgian building, the **County Museum** has an excellent section on Louis XVIII of France, who lived at Hartwell House during his years of exile.

To the northwest, near the village of **Waddesdon**, is another of the county's magnificent country houses, **Waddesdon Manor**, built between 1874 and 1889 for Baron Ferdinand de Rothschild in the style of a French Renaissance château. The house contains one the best collections of 18th century French decorative arts in the world. Close by, at **Quainton**, is the **Buckinghamshire Railway Centre**, a working museum with one of the largest collections of steam and diesel locomotives in the country.

At Boarstall, close to the village of Brill, are two interesting NationalTrust properties. **Boarstall Duck Decoy** is a rare working example of an ingenious contraption for catching ducks that was common in the 17th century. **Boarstall Tower** is a superb moated gatehouse and the only part that remains of Boarstall House, which was built in 1312.

MIDDLE CLAYDON

11 miles SW of Milton Keynes off the A413

Close to the village lies 17th century **Claydon House**, best remembered for its associations with Florence Nightingale who stayed here for long periods, especially during her old age (her sister had married into the Verney family, who owned the house). 'Florrie's Lorry', the carriage used by Florence in the Crimea, is one of the many fascinating exhibits on display.

BUCKINGHAM

10 miles W of Milton Keynes on the A413

Dating back to Saxon times, Buckingham was a prosperous place in the Middle Ages, though few old buildings survived a disastrous fire in 1725. As a consequence many of the buildings here are Georgian and the **Old Gaol Museum** is a fine example of mid 18th century architecture. One building that did survive the flames is the **Buckingham Chantry Chapel**, built in 1475 on the site of a Norman building. A more recent addition to this delightful market town is the University of Buckingham that was granted its charter in 1983.

To the north of Buckingham lies Stowe School, a leading public school that occupies an 18th century mansion that was once the home of the Dukes of Buckingham. The grounds of the house, **Stowe Landscape Gardens**, were created in the 18th century by Earl Temple and his nephew and they remain one of the most original and finest landscape gardens in Europe.

Cambridgeshire

The southeast of the county is dominated by the county town, Cambridge, one of the leading academic centres of the world and a place that needs plenty of time to explore. The surrounding countryside is fairly flat and ideal for walking or cycling; it contains a surprising variety of habitats along with stately homes and windmills - a particular feature of East Anglia.

Extending over much of the county from The Wash are the flat fields of The Fens that contain some of the richest soil in England. Here, too, villages and small towns such as Ely were originally island settlements in the days when this was a misty landscape of marshes and bogs. The massive project of draining this land has spanned the centuries, starting with the Romans, who were the first to construct embankments and drains to lessen the frequency of flooding. Throughout the Middle Ages large areas of marsh and bog were reclaimed, and after the Civil War, the New Bedford River was cut to provide more drainage. First windmills and then steam and finally electric pumping engines have been used to remove the water from the fields. The Fens offer unlimited opportunities for exploration on foot, by car, by bicycle or by boat.

The old county of Huntingdonshire lies at the heartland of the rural heritage of Cambridgeshire and the former county town, Huntingdon, is famous as the birthplace and home of Oliver Cromwell. Places associated with the great Parliamentarian abound but there are also many ancient market towns and villages to discover along with numerous nature reserves and prehistoric sites.

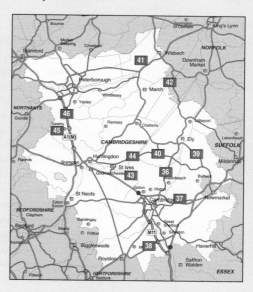

36 FARMLAND MUSEUM & DENNY ABBEY

Waterbeach

Set in the remains of a beautifully restored 12th century Benedictine Abbey is the fascinating Farmland Museum.

 see page 351

37 THE WHITE SWAN

Stow-cum-Quy

The **White Swan** enjoys a fine reputation for the quality of its beer and its food.

see page 353

CAMBRIDGE

One of the world's leading university cities, Cambridge was an important market town centuries before the scholars arrived, as it stood at the point where the forest met the fenlands, at the lowest fording point of the River Cam. The oldest college is **Peterhouse**, founded by the Bishop of Ely in 1284, and in the next century Clare, Pembroke, Gonville and Caius, Trinity Hall and Corpus Christi followed.

The colleges reflect a variety of architectural styles but the grandest and most beautiful is undoubtedly **King's College**. Among the many university and college buildings to explore there are some that simply should not be missed, including King's College Chapel, with its glorious stained glass and Rubens' *Adoration of the Magi*; **Pepys Library** in Magdalene College; and Trinity's wonderful Great Court. A trip by punt along the **Backs** of the River Cam gives a unique view to many of the colleges and the waterway also passes under six bridges including the **Bridge of Sighs** and the extraordinary Mathematical Bridge.

Apart from the colleges, Cambridge has plenty of other grand buildings and some of the country's leading museums, including the **Fitzwilliam Museum**, renowned for its art collection and ancient world antiquities. One of the city's greatest treasures is the **University Library**, one of the world's greatest research libraries, with six million books, a million maps and 350,000 manuscripts. For many, the most interesting place to visit is the **Botanic Gardens**, not really a museum, but a wonderful collection of plants that rivals the gardens at Kew and Edinburgh

Among the city's many fine churches is the **Church of the Holy Sepulchre**, always known as the Round Church, one of only four surviving round churches in England.

The village of **Grantchester**, where Rupert Brooke lived for two happy years at The Orchards, can be reached by a pleasant walk from the city or a leisurely punt along the River Cam.

AROUND CAMBRIDGE

LODE

6 miles NE of Cambridge off the B1102

This attractive and peaceful village is home to **Anglesey Abbey**, an early 17th century mansion house that was built on the site of an Augustinian priory. It holds Lord Fairhaven's magnificent collection of paintings, furnishings, tapestries and clocks, and its garden is a charming place for a peaceful stroll. To the south is the village of **Bottisham**, whose Holy Trinity Church was described by John Betjeman as 'perhaps the best in the county'.

Further afield, to the north, is **Denny Abbey**, which was founded in the 12th century by the Benedictine order but has also been

Anglesey Abbey, Lode

38 IMPERIAL WAR MUSEUM DUXFORD

Duxford

A branch of the **Imperial War Museum**, Duxford is Europe's premier aviation museum.

 see page 351

the home of the Knights Templar, Franciscan nuns and the Countess of Pembroke. After the Dissolution of the Monasteries the abbey became a farmhouse and is now home to the **Farmland Museum**.

BURWELL

10 miles NE of Cambridge on the B1102

A sad sight in the churchyard of St Mary's is a gravestone that marks the burial place of some 78 people of Burwell who all died in a barn fire while watching a travelling Punch and Judy Show. The **Devil's Dyke**, thought to have been built to keep out Danish invaders, runs through Burwell on its route from Reach to Woodditton.

To the southwest lies **Swaffham Prior** where there are two churches in the same graveyard and two fine old windmills, one of which, an 1850 tower mill, has been restored and still produces flour.

DUXFORD

8 miles S of Cambridge off the A505

To the west of the village lies **Duxford Aviation Museum**, now part of the Imperial War Museum, with an outstanding collection of over 150 historic aircraft.

Between Duxford and Cambridge, close to **Stapleford**, there is some great walking, in parkland, where there are traces of an Iron Age hill fort, and on Magog Downs. To the west, near

19

39 THE SOHAM
LODGE HOTEL &
WINDMILL
RESTAURANT

Soham, nr Ely

The Soham Lodge offers quality accommodation and a wide range of food and drink in very comfortable modern surroundings.

 see page 352

40 THE CHERRY TREE

Haddenham, nr Ely

The **Cherry Tree** is a friendly village inn with home cooking and a pleasant beer garden.

 see page 353

the village of **Shepreth**, is the **Shepreth L Moor Nature Reserve**, an important area of wet meadowland that is home to birds and many rare plants.

ARRINGTON

10 miles SW of Cambridge off the A1198

This village is home to the spectacular **Wimpole Hall**, one of the best examples of an 18th century country mansion in England. The lovely interiors contain fine collections of furniture and paintings, while the magnificent, formal gardens include a Victorian parterre and a rose garden.

MADINGLEY

2 miles W of Cambridge off the A1303

Madingley is home to one of the most peaceful and evocative places in the region, the **American Cemetery**. A place of pilgrimage for the families of American service men who operated from the many wartime bases in the county, the cemetery commemorates 3,800 dead and 5,000 missing in action in World War II.

ELY

The jewel in the crown of the Fens, the city owes its existence to St Etheldreda, Queen of Northumbria, who founded a monastery on the Isle of Ely in AD 673. However, it was not until 1081 that work on the present **Cathedral** began and it was completed more than a century later. The most outstanding feature

is the Octagon, built to replace the original Norman tower that collapsed in 1322, but there are many other delights, including the 14th century Lady Chapel, the Prior's Door and St Ovin's Cross, the only piece of Saxon stonework in the building. Ely's Tourist Information Centre is housed in a pretty black and white timbered building that is the only known surviving house, apart from Hampton Court, where Cromwell and his family are known to have lived.

AROUND ELY

SOHAM

5½ miles SE of Ely off the A142

Downfield Windmill was built in 1726 as a smock mill and then rebuilt as a tower mill in 1890 after it had been destroyed by gales. To the southwest lies **Wicken Fen**, the oldest nature reserve in the country, famous for its rich variety of plant, insect and bird life.

HADDENHAM

6 miles SW of Ely on the A1123

At 120 feet above sea level, Haddenham is the highest village in the Fens and, not surprisingly, it too has a windmill – **Haddenham Great Mill** which was built in 1803, has four sails and three sets of grinding stones. Last worked commercially in 1946, it was restored in the 1990s.

To the north, at **Sutton**, is a great family attraction, the **Mepal Outdoor Centre** that includes a children's play park, an adventure play area and boats for hire. Providing a unique insight into Fenland history and industrial archaeology, the **Stretham Old Engine**, at **Stretham**, is a fine example of a land drainage steam engine.

SOMERSHAM

11 miles W of Ely on the B1050

Once the site of a palace for the Bishops of Ely, Somersham is now home to the **Raptor Foundation** where owls and other birds of prey find refuge. This is a very popular attraction, with regular flying and falconry displays.

MARCH

13 miles NW of Ely on the B1101

This settlement once occupied the second largest island in the great level of the Fens, and as the land was drained March grew as a trading and religious centre and, later, as a market town and hub of the railway. The **March and District Museum** tells the story of the people and history of the town and surrounding area. Meanwhile, **St Wendreda's** uniquely dedicated church was described by John Betjeman as "worth cycling 40 miles into a headwind to see." Its roof, adorned with over 100 carved angels, is certainly a stirring sight

WISBECH

19 miles NW of Ely on the A1101

This town also lies at the centre of a thriving agricultural region and the 18th century saw many fine buildings constructed along the river. The finest of these is

undoubtedly **Peckover House**, built in 1722 and bought at the end of the 18th century by Jonathan Peckover, a member of the Quaker banking family. Behind its elegant façade are charming panelled rooms and ornate plaster decorations.

The town was the birthplace in 1838 of Octavia Hill, co-founder of the National Trust, and the house in which she was born is now the **Octavia Hill Museum** where her work is commemorated.

The **Wisbech and Fenland Museum** is one of the oldest purpose-built museums in the country, and its numerous displays include the manuscript of Charles Dickens' *Great Expectations* and Napoleon's Sèvres breakfast set captured at Waterloo.

HUNTINGDON

First settled by the Romans and the former county town of Huntingdonshire, Huntingdon was the birthplace, in 1599, of Oliver Cromwell. He attended Huntingdon Grammar School, where Samuel Pepys was also a pupil, before becoming the MP for Huntingdon in the Parliament of 1629. His school is now the **Cromwell Museum** and it houses the only public collection relating specifically to him. Opposite the museum stands **All Saints' Church** which contains the Cromwell burial vault. On the Market Square, the 16th century **Falcon Inn** was Cromwell's headquarters during the Civil War.

41 THE CHEQUERS INN

Tholomas Drove, nr Wisbech

The **Chequers** is a charming hamlet pub with a growing reputation for its excellent food and interesting ales.

see page 353

42 THE RED HART

Three Holes, nr Wisbech

The **Red Hart** offers a choice of English and Danish cuisine, plus four rooms for overnight guests.

see page 355

Cowper House, with its impressive early 18th century frontage, was the home of the poet William Cowper from 1765 to 1767, and a former coaching inn, The George Hotel, is reputed to have been used by the highwayman Dick Turpin.

At nearby **Hemingford Abbots** stands **Hemingford Grey**, a manor that is one of the oldest continuously inhabited houses in England – it was built in around 1130.

Linked to Huntingdon by a 14th century bridge across the River Ouse, **Godmanchester** was a Roman settlement and has continued in importance down the centuries. There are several grand houses here including **Island Hall**, a mid 18th century mansion that was built for John Jackson, the Receiver General for Huntingdon. A footpath leads from the famous **Chinese Bridge** (1827) to **Port Holme Meadow**, one of the largest meadows in England and the site of Roman remains as well as being home to a huge diversity of botanical and bird species.

AROUND HUNTINGDON

RAMSEY

7 miles N of Huntingdon on the B1040

It was in this pleasant market town in AD 969 that Earl Ailwyn founded **Ramsey Abbey**, which by the 12th century had become one of the most important in England. However, after the Dissolution the Abbey and its lands were sold to Sir Richard Williams, great-grandfather of Oliver Cromwell. Most of the buildings were demolished and, in 1938, the house was converted for use as a school – which it remains today.

Housed in an 18th century farm building and several barns is the **Ramsey Rural Museum**, where the exhibits include restored farm and traditional craftsmen's equipment.

To the southwest of Ramsey is the scattered village of **Upwood** and **Woodwalton Fen Nature Reserve**.

WHITTLESEY

15 miles N of Huntingdon on the A605

This market town, where brick-making was a local industry, was the birthplace of the writer LP Hartley, author of *The Go-Between,* and of the soldier Sir Harry Smith, a hero of many 19th century Indian campaigns. The highlight of the year here is the ancient **Straw Bear Procession** when a man clad in a suit of straw dances through streets during a four-day January festival.

To the southeast lies **Flag Fen Bronze Age Excavation**, comprising massive 3,000-year-old timbers that were part of a major settlement and have been preserved in the peaty ground. A Roman road, re-creations of a Bronze Age settlement, a museum of artefacts and rare breed animals can also be seen here.

To the north is **Thorney Abbey**, though what stands today is only a small part of this once great Benedictine Abbey.

St Ives

ST IVES

4 miles E of Huntingdon on the A1123

Oliver Cromwell lived in St Ives in the 1630s and a statue of him stands on Market Hill – the statue was erected here in 1901 after it was rejected by Huntingdon. Other notable townsfolk include Sir Clive Sinclair, who developed his pocket calculators in the town, and the Victorian rower John Goldie, whose name is remembered by the second Cambridge boat.

ST NEOTS

8½ miles SW of Huntingdon on the B1428

The first bridge over the River Great Ouse was built in 1180 in the town, which takes its name from the Cornish saint whose remains

were interred in the priory before the Norman Conquest. The priory was demolished with the Dissolution of the Monasteries and in the early 17th century the old bridge was replaced by a stone one which became the scene of a battle during the Civil War.

GRAFHAM

5 miles SW of Huntingdon off the B661

Created in the 1960s as a reservoir, **Grafham Water** offers a wide range of sports facilities in its 1,500 acres. The area is a Site of Special Scientific Interest, and a nature reserve at the western edge is run jointly by Anglian Water and the Wildlife Trust.

To the west lies **Kimbolton**, a place with plenty of history and

43   THE WHITE HORSE INN

Swavesey, nr Cambridge

The **White Horse Inn** is a great pub for hospitality, food and drink and a meeting place for locals and for many sporting and other clubs and societies.

see page 354

44   THE CROWN

Earith, nr St Ives

A large garden leading down to the Great Ouse is an additional attraction to the fine food and ales served at **The Crown**.

see page 355

23

several interesting buildings, including **Kimbolton Castle** where parts of the original Tudor building can still be seen.

PETERBOROUGH

15 miles NW of Huntingdon on the A1339

Cambridgeshire's second city, Peterborough has a long and interesting history that dates back to the Bronze Age. In 1967 it was designated a New Town, and modern development and expansion have increased its facilities without, thankfully, destroying its historic heart. Henry VIII elevated the 12th century church to a **Cathedral** and his first wife Catherine of Aragon is buried here as, for a while, was Mary, Queen of Scots after her execution at Fotheringhay. Railway enthusiasts are in their element here with the twin attractions of **Railworld**, a hands-on exhibition dealing with modern rail travel, and the wonderful **Nene Valley Railway**, which operates between the city and its Museum at Wansford. Close by is the **Thorpe Meadows Sculpture Park**, one of several open spaces in and around the city.

Also on the outskirts of the city are **Longthorpe Tower**, part of a fortified manor house which is graced by some very fine 14th century domestic wall paintings, and **Peakirk Waterfowl Gardens**, home to hundreds of birds.

Cheshire

There are many aspects to Cheshire: the rural landscape of the Cheshire Plains, the textile towns in the east, the ancient salt towns and the grand stately homes. Chester, the prosperous county town, was first established by the Romans, who built a fort here to protect against invasions from Wales. Salt had been mined in Cheshire long before the Romans arrived but the particular need for brine for the fledgling chemical manufacturers along the River Mersey saw a great increase in activity. Further east is the famous silk town of Macclesfield, while Styal was created as a model village for one of the first cotton mills in the area, Quarry Bank Mill.

Cheshire is also home to some of the country's grandest country houses, including Tatton Park, Arley Hall, Tabley Hall and Dunham Massey Hall.

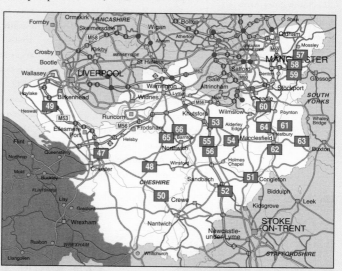

FOOD & DRINK

ACCOMMODATION

PLACES OF INTEREST

47 THE SHREWSBURY ARMS

Mickle Trafford, nr Chester

The **Shrewsbury Arms** is a superb country pub offering old-fashioned standards of hospitality and some of the very best food in the region.

see page 356

CHESTER

It was in AD 70 that the famous 20th Legion, the Valeria Victrix, established its headquarters and took full advantage of Chester's strategic position on the River Dee, close to the Welsh border. During this period the **City Walls** were first built; today they remain the most complete in the country and provide an excellent 2-mile walk as well as fine views of the River Dee, Chester's glorious buildings and the Welsh mountains in the distance. At one point, the wall runs alongside St John Street, which was in Roman times the main thoroughfare between the fortress and the **Amphitheatre**, the largest such construction to be uncovered in Britain and one that was capable of seating 7,000 spectators.

The Normans began the construction of what is now **Chester Cathedral**, a majestic building of weathered pink stone on a site that has been a place of worship for 1,000 years. It was originally an abbey – one of the very few to survive Henry VIII's closure of the monasteries in the 1540s – and the cloisters are regarded as the finest in England. It was at Chester Cathedral, in 1742, that George Frederick Handel personally conducted rehearsals for his oratorio *The Messiah* before its first performance in Dublin.

During the Civil War Chester supported the Royalist cause but it was while watching from the city's walls that Charles I saw his troops heavily defeated at nearby Rowton Moor. Chester has many museums telling the city's story from Roman times through the dark days of the Civil War to the present day. Visitors can also enjoy a unique shopping experience – two-tiered galleries of reconstructed medieval shops under covered walkways known as **The Rows**.

The city has some ancient sporting links: **Chester Regatta** hosts the oldest rowing races in the world, and

Eastgate, Chester

Chester Races are held on the oldest **Racecourse** in the country, The Roodeye. Finally, no visit to Chester is complete without a trip to **Chester Zoo**, at Upton-by-Chester on the city's northern outskirts, and where, surrounded by landscaped gardens, over 500 different species can be seen in near natural enclosures.

AROUND CHESTER

ASHTON

6½ miles E of Chester on the B5393

Maintained by the Forestry Commission since the early 1900s, **Delamere Forest**, once a hunting ground for royalty and the nobility, lies just a couple of miles northeast of Ashton and although it is an excellent place for walking and picnicking it remains a working forest of some 4,000 acres.

TARPORLEY

9 miles E of Chester off the A49

At the time when most of the surrounding area was part of Delamere Forest, Tarporley was the headquarters of the forest wardens (the verderers) who meted out rough justice to offenders of the forest laws from their own courts. One such court was at **Utkinton**, just north of the town, and in an old farmhouse is the trunk of an ancient forest tree with its roots still in the ground. When the court was in session, the wardens placed the Hunting Horn of Delamere – their symbol of authority – on the tree.

BEESTON

9½ miles SE of Chester off the A49

Rising some 500 feet from the Cheshire Plain, the craggy cliff of Beeston Hill is one of the most dramatic sights in the county and it is made all the more impressive by the ruins of **Beeston Castle** (the 'Castle of the Rock') on the summit. Although it was built in around 1220, the castle did not see military action until the Civil War when a Royalist captain and just eight musketeers captured the fortress and its garrison of 60 soldiers – without even firing a shot! Later, Cromwell ordered the castle to be partially destroyed but it is still very imposing with walls 30 feet thick and a well 366 feet deep. An exhibition tells the 4,000-year story of the site.

Seen clearly from the top of Beeston Hill is another of Cheshire's fortifications, **Peckforton Castle**. Further south again from Beeston is another marvellous mock medieval construction, **Cholmondeley Castle**, built in the early 19th century and particularly noted for its gardens.

FARNDON

7 miles S of Chester off the B5130

During the Civil War, Farndon's strategic position, between Royalist North Wales and Parliamentarian Cheshire, along with its bridge, led to many skirmishes and these events are depicted in the stained glass windows of the parish church.

48 THE FOX & BARREL

Cotebrook, nr Tarporley

The **Fox & Barrel** is one of the best eating places in Cheshire, offering great food, fine wines, well-kept ales and convivial company.

see page 357

49 THE COUNTRY MOUSE RESTAURANT

Brimstage, Wirral

The **Country Mouse Restaurant** is open every day for a wonderful array of home cooking, including the best baking for many miles around.

see page 358

Farndon's most famous son, the cartographer John Speed, was born in the village in 1542. Speed followed his father's trade as a tailor, married, had 18 children and was nearly 50 before he began to devote his time to researching and producing his beautifully drawn maps.

NESTON

10 miles NW of Chester on the B5135

Right up until the early 19th century, Neston was the most significant town on The Wirral, the once desolate and wind swept peninsula that, following the rise of shipbuilding and other industries in the 19th century, has not only become a desirable place to live but has also been justifiably dubbed the 'Leisure Peninsula' by tourism officials.

One of the Wirral's major attractions is **Ness Botanic Gardens**, just to the southeast of Neston and situated on the banks of the Dee Estuary. Now run by the University of Liverpool as an Environmental and Horticultural Research Station, the 64-acre gardens have been planned to provide magnificent displays all year round.

After Neston became useless as a port, maritime traffic moved along the Dee estuary to **Parkgate** and, as the new gateway to Ireland, this still attractive village saw some notable visitors: John Wesley preached here while waiting for favourable winds to take him to Ireland, Handel landed here after conducting his first performance of *The Messiah* in Dublin, and Turner came here to sketch the panoramic views across the estuary of the Flintshire hills.

To the east of Neston, centrally placed between the Dee and Mersey estuaries, is the village of **Willaston**, the home of **Hadlow Road Station**. Although a train has not run through here since 1962, the station, along with its signal box and ticket office, has been restored to appear as it would have done in the early 1950s. This is one of the more intriguing features of the **Wirral Way**, a nature reserve and walk that follows the track bed of the old railway between Hooton and West Kirkby. On the Mersey side of the Wirral peninsula lies **Eastham Woods Country Park**, an area of woodland that is home to all three species of native woodpecker.

Further up the Mersey lies **Ellesmere Port**, situated at the point where the Shropshire Union Canal meets the River Mersey. The canal basin is now home to **The Boat Museum**, where the world's largest collection of historic narrow boats and barges has been assembled.

NANTWICH

This attractive market town surrounded by the rich dairy farmlands of south Cheshire was once second only in importance in the county to Chester, its prosperity built on the mining of salt.

The most disastrous event in Nantwich's long history was its great fire in 1583 that saw some 600 thatched and timber-framed buildings destroyed. The most striking building to survive the fire, probably because it was surrounded by a moat, is the lovely black and white house in Hospital Street that is known as **Churche's Mansion** after the merchant, Richard Churche, who built it in 1577. The upper floor has been furnished in the Elizabethan style and is open to the public during the summer. Another building spared from the fire is the town's impressive 14th century church that is often called the **Cathedral of South Cheshire**.

During the Civil War Nantwich supported Cromwell's Parliamentarian army and, after several weeks of fighting, the Royalist forces were finally defeated on 25th January 1644 and the townspeople celebrated the victory by wearing sprigs of holly in their hair. There are records of the Civil War in the **Nantwich Museum**, which also contains exhibitions on the town's long history and its salt, dairy and cheese-making industries.

AROUND NANTWICH

CREWE

4 miles NE of Nantwich on the A534

Crewe is very much a product of the railway age and it was only when the Grand Junction Railway arrived here in 1837 and, five years later, moved all its construction and repair workshops to this site that the town was founded. The **Railway Age Museum**, re-opened

Easter 2006, offers a fascinating insight into Crewe's place in railway history.

CONGLETON

14½ miles NE of Nantwich on the A534

In the foothills of the Pennines, the land around Congleton has been inhabited since the Stone Age and the remains of a 5,000-year-old chambered tomb, known as **The Bridestones**, can be seen beside the road running eastwards from the town towards Leek. In Elizabethan times, the people of the town had such a passion for bear baiting that it became known locally as the Bear Town, and Congleton was the very last town in England to outlaw this cruel practice.

The town developed as an important textile centre during the 18th century with many of its mills

Little Moreton Hall

29

involved in silk manufacturing, cotton spinning and ribbon weaving. In **Mill Green**, near the River Dane, part of the very first silk mill to operate here still stands.

Just a couple of miles south of Congleton lies the pretty village of **Astbury** set around a triangular village green. Black and white half-timbered houses have almost become a symbol for the county of Cheshire and one of the most stunning examples of all is **Little Moreton Hall**, the 'wibbly wobbly' house that provided the memorable location for the television adaptation of *Moll Flanders*.

Further south again lies the famous folly, **Mow Cop**, which was built by Randle Wilbraham in the 18th century on his Rode Hall estate to enhance the view from his house. This mock ruin stands on a rocky hill, some 1,100 feet above sea level and, from its summit, on a clear day, there are magnificent views across the Pennines to the northeast, Cheshire to the west, and northwards to Alderley Edge.

SANDBACH

8½ miles NE of Nantwich on the A534

The handsome market square of this former important coaching town is dominated by its two famous stone crosses. Although only the superbly carved shafts have survived, the crosses were created sometime in the 9th century and the striking scenes they depict are believed to represent the conversion of Mercia to Christianity during the reign of King Penda.

KNUTSFORD

The Knutsford of the 19th century that Elizabeth Gaskell wrote about so vividly has expanded a great deal, but its centre still evokes the intimacy of a small Victorian town with its narrow streets and cobbled alleyways. More recent is the **Gaskell Memorial Tower**, a tall blank-walled building that was erected in her memory by entrepreneur and glove manufacturer Richard Harding Watt in 1907.

It was back in 1262 that Edward I granted the town a charter and the **Knutsford Heritage Centre**, housed in a timber-framed 17th century former smithy, is an ideal place to discover more of the town's long history.

Close by is an unusual exhibition, the **Penny Farthing Museum**. These curious machines were in fashion for just 20 years before the last model was manufactured in 1892, and the collection here includes a replica of the famous 'Starley Giant' with a front wheel that is seven feet in diameter!

Just north of Knutsford is **Tatton Park**, a historic country estate that is centred on a magnificent Georgian mansion. A short walk from the grand house is Home Farm, the heart of the estate, where there are the old estate offices and many original farm animal breeds to be seen. Surrounding the mansion is a vast deer park that has a history stretching back to 8000 BC when the deer here were hunted for meat and clothing.

Another grand Georgian mansion, **Tabley House**, lies to the west of Knutsford. Designed by John Carr for the 1st Lord de Tabley in 1761, the house today is home to a wonderful collection of English paintings, including works by Turner, Reynolds and Opie, that were put together by Lord Tabley and his son, who were the founders of London's National Gallery.

Tatton Park

To the south of Knutsford is the charming Cheshire village of **Lower Peover** and the delightful old coaching inn the Bells of Peover, which flies not only the Union Flag but also the American Stars and Stripes to commemorate the visit made here by General Patton and Eisenhower during World War II. For a time, in those dark days, General Patton lived at nearby **Peover Hall**.

AROUND KNUTSFORD

WILMSLOW

6 miles NE of Knutsford on the A538

Just to the north of the bustling commuter town of Wilmslow and surrounded by the 150-acre Styal Country Park is **Quarry Bank Mill**, a grand old building dating from 1784 that was one of the first generation of cotton mills. Visitors can follow the history of the mill through a series of museum displays, see weaving and spinning demonstrations and discover what life was like for the children who lived at the Apprentice House. Also within the park is the delightful factory village of **Styal**, which was established by the mill's original owner, Samuel Greg, a philanthropist and pioneer of the factory system.

To the south of Wilmslow lies the long wooded escarpment, **Alderley Edge**, nearly two miles long, that rises to 600 feet and culminates in sandy crags overlooking the Cheshire Plain. Walkers can roam through the woods along the many footpaths, one of which leads to **Hare Hill Gardens**, whose Victorian grounds include fine woodland and a walled garden themed in blue, white and yellow flowers.

---

56 THE COTTAGE RESTAURANT & LODGE

Allostock, nr Knutsford

The **Cottage** offers a range of traditional and modern cuisine and 12 well-equipped bedrooms in a delightful rural setting.

see page 360

57 THE MILLBROOK

Millbrook

The **Millbrook** is a handsome mid-Victorian pub/restaurant serving a wide selection of home-cooked dishes.

see page 361

STALYBRIDGE

6 miles E of Manchester on the A57

Set beside the River Tame and with the North Pennine Moors stretching for miles to the east, Stalybridge was one of the earliest cotton towns. One of the cotton workers' most prominent leaders was the Rev Joseph Rayner Stephens, and a granite obelisk in his memory stands in the town's Stamford Park.

BOLLINGTON

11 miles E of Knutsford on the B5091

A striking feature of this former cotton town is the splendid 20-arched viaduct that once carried the railway over the River Dean and which today is part of the **Middlewood Way**, a 10-mile country trail that follows a scenic, traffic-free route from Macclesfield to Marple. Just as remarkable as the viaduct is **White Nancy**, a round stone tower that stands on the 900-ft summit of **Kerridge Hill**; it was built to commemorate the Battle of Waterloo.

MACCLESFIELD

11 miles SE of Knutsford on the A523

The town nestles below the High Peak, and it was on this rock that Edward I and Queen Eleanor founded a church. Reached via a gruelling flight of 108 steps, the Church of St Michael and All Angels was extended in the 1890s, but its early core remains, including the **Legh Chapel** that was built in 1422 to receive the body of Piers Legh, who had fought at Agincourt and died at the Siege of Meaux.

It was in Macclesfield in 1743 that Charles Roe built the first silk mill beside the River Bollin. The industry flourished and, 150 years later, it had become known as the Silk Town. Several excellent museums tell the story of the town's connection with silk. On the northwestern edge of the town is the **West Park Museum**, whose exhibits include a collection of Egyptian antiquities and a gallery devoted to the work of Charles Tunnicliffe.

To the east of the town centre runs the **Macclesfield Canal**, one of the highest waterways in England, that was opened in 1831 and which links with the Trent and Mersey and the Peak Forest canals. Between Macclesfield and Congleton, the canal descends over 100 feet in a spectacular series of 12 locks before crossing the River Dane by Thomas Telford's handsome iron viaduct. Another unusual feature of this superbly engineered canal are the two 'roving bridges' south of Congleton that swing from one bank to the other, where the towpath changes sides, and enable horses to cross over without having to unhitch the towrope.

Close to the village of **Warren**, a couple of miles southwest of Macclesfield, is the black and white half-timbered **Gawsworth Hall** that was built in 1480 by the Fitton family. The celebrated beauty Mary Fitton is believed to be the 'Dark Lady' of Shakespeare's sonnets. Gawsworth's famous open-air theatre stages a summer programme that ranges from Shakespeare to Gilbert and Sullivan opera.

LOWER WITHINGTON

6½ miles SE of Knutsford on the B5392

To the northwest of this village, and visible from miles around, is the huge white dish of the world famous **Jodrell Bank** radio telescope that first came into service in 1957. The Science Centre here offers visitors a wonderful array of hands-on exhibits, and a superb 35-acre Arboretum is planted with 2,500 species of trees and shrubs. It houses the National Collections of *Sorbus* and *Malus*.

NORTHWICH

7 miles SW of Knutsford on the A559

Although salt production in Cheshire began even before the Roman occupation, its extraction and processing at Northwich began on a major scale in 1670 when rock salt was discovered in nearby Marston. Its extraction from the Keuper marl of the Cheshire Plain has had some spectacular side effects – in Elizabethan times, John Leland recorded that a hill at Combermere suddenly disappeared into underground workings! Northwich later became notorious for the number of its buildings leaning at crazy angles due to the subsidence - the White Lion Inn lies a complete storey lower than its original height.

Cheshire's and Northwich's long involvement with salt is vividly recorded at the **Salt Museum** which is housed in what used to be the Northwich Workhouse, a handsome Georgian building designed by the architect of Arley Hall.

To the north of the town is one of the most impressive feats of engineering of the canal age and one of the country's most fascinating attractions – the **Anderton Boat Lift**, constructed

Anderton Boat Lift

62   SUTTON HALL

Sutton, nr Macclesfield

Sutton Hall is a magnificent baronial hall offering the best features of a sumptuous hotel, fine restaurant and friendly public house.

   see page 364

63   THE CAT & FIDDLE

Macclesfield Forest

The **Cat & Fiddle** is a renowned inn located in Macclesfield Forest. Real ales come from Robinson's Brewery, and excellent food is served all day.

   see page 363

64   THE BRIDGE HOTEL & RESTAURANT

Prestbury

The **Bridge Hotel** offers comfortable, well-equipped accommodation and fine food in a picturesque setting.

   see page 365

An interesting curiosity at Bridge Foot, near Warrington, is a combined telephone kiosk and letter box. These were quite common in the early 1900s, but Warrington's is one of the few survivors. The comedian and ukelele player George Formby is buried in the town's cemetery.

in 1875 to transfer boats from the Trent and Mersey Canal to the Weaver Navigation 50 feet below. It was designed by Edward Leader Williams, the engineer behind the Manchester Ship Canal, and is now fully restored; two barges could enter the lift's upper tanks, two the lower, and, by pumping water out of the lower tank, the boats exchanged places and canals.

About a mile north of Anderton, **Marbury Country Park** was formerly part of a large country estate but the area is now managed by Cheshire County Council whose wardens have created a variety of habitats for plants, trees and animals.

In Victorian times, the **Old Salt Mine** at **Marston**, just northeast of Northwich, was a huge tourist attraction: in 1844, the Tsar of Russia sat down to dinner, along with eminent members of the Royal Society, in a huge cavern that was lit by 10,000 lamps. The village is home to the **Lion Salt Works Museum**, where volunteers keep alive the only surviving open-pan saltworks in the country.

GREAT BUDWORTH
6 miles W of Knutsford off the A559

To the north of this village of attractive old cottages lies another of Cheshire's great estates, **Arley Hall and Gardens**, where visitors can find one of its grandest houses in perfect harmony with one of the county's finest gardens. Along with the sumptuous stately home that had all the latest state-of-the-art innovations, the conservationist Squire Egerton-Warburton and his wife masterminded the magnificent gardens; he is credited with creating what is believed to be the first herbaceous border in England.

WARRINGTON

Warrington is North Cheshire's largest town – an important industrial centre since Georgian and Victorian times and with substantial buildings of those days to prove it. Its imposing **Town Hall** was built in 1750 in very grand style with windows framed in painfully expensive copper, and elaborately designed entrance gates. A major Victorian contribution to the town is its excellent **Museum and Art Gallery** in Bold Street, one of the earliest municipal museums. The exhibits are remarkably varied: among them are shrunken heads, a unique china teapot collection, a scold's bridle, Egyptian mummies, Roman artefacts and some very fine Victorian watercolours and oils.

AROUND WARRINGTON

WIDNES
6 miles SW of Warrington on the A557

Widnes stands on the north shore of the Mersey, linked to Runcorn by a remarkably elegant road bridge. A popular attraction is **Spike Island**, which provides a landscaped walk from which the superstructures of ships passing along the Manchester Ship Canal can be seen gliding past.

DARESBURY

5 miles SW of Warrington on the A558

All Saints Church in Daresbury has a unique stained glass window: there are panels depicting a Gryphon and a Cheshire Cat, others show a Mock Turtle, a March Hare and a Mad Hatter. This is of course the **Lewis Carroll Memorial Window**, commemorating the author of *Alice in Wonderland*. Carroll himself is shown at one side, dressed in clerical garb and kneeling. His father was Vicar of Daresbury when Carroll was born here in 1832 and baptised as Charles Lutwidge Dodgson. The boy enjoyed an apparently idyllic childhood at Daresbury until his father moved to another parish when Charles/Lewis was eleven years old.

RUNCORN

7 miles SW of Warrington on the A557

Runcorn is one of Britain's best known post-war new towns, developed around a much older town bearing the same name. Here, **Norton Priory** is always a delightful and intriguing place for a family outing, whatever the weather. The Augustinian priory was built in 1134 as a retreat for just 12 'black canons', so named because they wore a cape of black woollen cloth over a white linen surplice. Work by the Norton Priory Museum Trust has uncovered the remains of the church, chapter house, cloisters and dormitory, and these finds are informatively explained in an audio-visual presentation. The Museum is open every afternoon, all year; the Gardens, which include a charming walled garden, are open from April to October.

LYMM

4 miles SE of Warrington on the A56

During the stage coach era, Eagle Brow was notorious, a dangerously steep road that dropped precipitously down the hillside into the village of Lymm. To bypass this hazard, a turnpike was built (now the A56), so preserving the heart of this ancient village with its half-timbered houses and well preserved village stocks. Lymm Dam, popular with anglers and bird-watchers, is part of a lovely woodland centre which is linked to the surrounding countryside and the canal towpath by a network of footpaths and bridleways.

DUNHAM MASSEY

4 miles E of Lymm on B5160

Dunham Massey Hall and Park (National Trust) has 250 acres of parkland where fallow deer roam freely and noble trees planted in the late 1700s still flourish. A restored water mill is usually in operation every Wednesday, and there are splendid walks in every direction. The Hall, once the home of the Earls of Stamford and Warrington, is a grand Georgian mansion of 1732 that boasts an outstanding collection of furniture, paintings and Huguenot silver. The Hall is open most days from April to October; the Park is open every day.

Lymm stands on the sides of a ravine and its streets have actually been carved out of the sandstone rock. The same rock was used to construct Lymm's best-known landmark, the ancient cross crowned with a huge cupola that stands at the top of the High Street.

Cornwall

An isolated beauty that contains some of the most dramatic and spectacular scenery in the country. This is an apt description of Cornwall, a land of strong Celtic heritage and ancestry, a place dotted with monuments such as crosses, holy wells and prehistoric sights and where legends of old, particularly those surrounding King Arthur, still have a strong romantic appeal among the Cornish people and to visitors. Surrounded by rugged coastline, Cornwall has often been referred to as the English Riviera, encompassing pretty little fishing ports, secluded picturesque villages, narrow winding lanes and romantic seafaring traditions. While the northern coastline is dramatic, the southern Cornish coast is one of sheltered coves. Here, too, is one of the country's largest natural harbours, at Falmouth, but many of the fishing villages expanded to manage the exportation of the vast quantities of mineral ore and

china clay that were extracted from inland Cornwall. Finally, there is Land's End, the westernmost tip of England, where the granite of Cornwall meets the Atlantic Ocean in a dramatic series of steep cliffs.

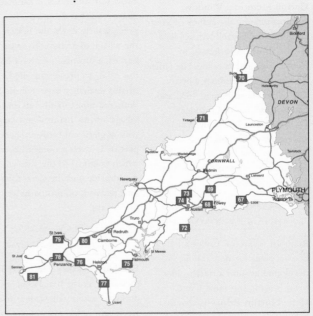

LAUNCESTON

Situated on the eastern edge of Bodmin Moor and close to the county border with Devon, it was here, shortly after the Norman Conquest, that William I's half-brother, Robert of Mortain, built the massive **Launceston Castle** overlooking the River Kensey. Although now in ruins, the 12-feet thick walls of the keep and tower can still be seen. Launceston also had a powerful Augustinian priory, founded beside the river in 1136; the main buildings have gone, but its chapel of ease remains.

To the west of the town, the **Launceston Steam Railway** takes visitors on a scenic trip through the beautiful Kensey Valley.

Launceston is also the start of the **Tamar Valley Discovery Trail**, a 30-mile footpath from here to Plymouth that takes in many of the villages that litter the Cornwall-Devon border. At **St Ann's Chapel**, near Gunnislake, stands the **Tamar Valley Donkey Park**, Cornwall's only donkey sanctuary and home to more than two dozen donkeys and other rescued animals.

AROUND LAUNCESTON

CALSTOCK
12 miles SE of Launceston off the A390

Well known for its splendid views of the Tamar valley, this village was an important river port in the 19th century and

its decline came with the construction of the huge Railway Viaduct which carries the picturesque Tamar Valley Line southwards to Plymouth.

Just to the southwest of Calstock is one of the best preserved medieval estates in the West Country – **Cotehele House** (National Trust), built between 1485 and 1624. Along with its Great Tudor Hall, fabulous tapestries and period furniture, the fortified granite house incorporates some charming features such as the secret spy-hole in the Great Hall and a tower clock with a bell but no face or hands. Surrounding the house are, firstly, the grounds, containing exotic and tender plants that thrive in the mild valley climate, and beyond that the estate

Launceston Castle

East Looe

Inside the restaurant or out in the sun-trap courtyard, the **Grapevine** will delight visitors with its top-class cooking.

see page 366

with its ancient network of pathways that allow exploration of the valley.

The River Tamar runs through the estate and close to an old cider house and mill is **Cotehele Quay**, a busy river port in Victorian times and now home to an outstation of the National Maritime Museum, an art and craft gallery and a licensed tea room. The restored Tamar sailing barge *Shamrock* is moored alongside the museum.

SALTASH

17 miles SE of Launceston on the A38

The 'Gateway to Cornwall', here the River Tamar is spanned by two mighty bridges. Designed by Isambard Kingdom Brunel in 1859, the iron-built **Royal Albert Bridge** carries the railway, while alongside is the much more slender **Tamar Bridge**, a suspension road bridge that was opened in 1961. To the south of Saltash lies **Mount Edgcumbe House**, to where the Earls of Edgcumbe moved when they left Cotehele House; it is surrounded by a country park that encompasses a stretch of heritage coast, numerous follies and one of Cornwall's greatest gardens. The southernmost point of the country park takes in **Rame Head**, 400 feet cliffs that guard the entrance into Plymouth Sound. Also on this peninsula is 18th century **Antony House**, home to a wonderful collection of paintings (many by Sir Joshua Reynolds), tapestries and furniture. Surrounding the house are the gardens and grounds landscaped by Humphry Repton.

LISKEARD

13½ miles SW of Launceston on the B3254

Although it is a small town, Liskeard boasts some grand Victorian public buildings, including the Guildhall and the Public Hall, home to a local museum. In Well Street, lies one of Liskeard's most curious features – an arched grotto that marks the site of **Pipe Well**, a medieval spring reputed to have curative powers.

Another well lies to the southwest: **St Keyne's Well** is named after the daughter of a Welsh king who settled here in the 5th century. The nearby village is also named after the saint and is home to **Paul Corin's Magnificent Music Machines**, a wonderful collection of mechanical musical instruments.

LOOE

20 miles SW of Launceston on the A387

The tidal harbour at Looe, created by the two rivers the East Looe and West Looe, made this an important fishing and seafaring port and it is still Cornwall's second most important port with fish auctions taking place at East Looe's famous **Banjo Pier**. East Looe is the older part, and housed in the 16th century **Old Guildhall** is the town's Museum.

To the southwest of Looe is **Polperro**, many people's idea of a typical Cornish fishing village, its steep, narrow streets and alleyways filled with picturesque fisherman's cottages.

FOWEY

24½ miles SW of Launceston on the A3082

A lovely old seafaring town, with steep, narrow streets, Fowey has one of the most beautiful natural harbours along the south coast. The town's **Museum** is an excellent place to discover Fowey's colourful past and its literary connections: Daphne du Maurier lived at Gribbin Head and Sir Arthur Quiller-Couch lived for over 50 years at The Haven, on the Esplanade.

To the south of Fowey lies **St Catherine's Castle**, part of a chain of fortifications that were built by Henry VIII to protect the harbours along the south coast.

Just up the River Fowey is **Golant** and the Iron Age lookout point of **Castle Dore Earthworks**, while further upstream is **Lostwithiel**, a small market town that was the capital of Cornwall in the 13th century. The strategic crossing point of the River Fowey here is protected by the surprisingly complete remains of 12th century **Restormel Castle**.

BODMIN

19½ miles SW of Launceston on the A389

Situated midway between Cornwall's two coasts and at the junction of two ancient trade routes, Bodmin has always been an important town, and **Castle Canyke** was built during the Iron Age to defend this important route. To the south is **Lanhydrock House**, one of the most fascinating late 19th century houses in England, surrounded by wonderful formal gardens, woodland and parkland.

BOLVENTOR

10½ miles SW of Launceston on the A30

Situated at the heart of Bodmin Moor, this scenic village is home to the former coaching inn that was immortalised by Daphne du Maurier in her famous novel, *Jamaica Inn*. Structurally little changed today, **Jamaica Inn** still welcomes visitors who come here not only seeking refreshment and accommodation but also to discover the secrets of the moors and the life and works of du Maurier.

Bodmin Moor is the smallest of the three great West Country moors; at 1,377 feet, Brown Willy is the highest point on the moor, while, just to the northwest, lies Rough Tor, the moor's second highest point. Throughout this wild and beautiful moorland there are remains of early occupiers, including Bronze Age hut circles and field enclosures and Iron Age hill forts.

To the south of Bolventor is the mysterious natural tarn, **Dozmary Pool**, a place that is strongly linked with the legend of King Arthur and said by some to be the place where the Lady of the Lake received the dying King's sword, Excalibur.

To the southeast lies the one-time mining village of **Minions**, and close by are the impressive Bronze Age **Hurlers Stone Circle** and **Trethevy Quoit**, an impressive enclosed chamber tomb that

68 THE SHIP INN

Trafalgar Square, Fowey

The maritime connection is strong at the **Ship Inn**, a great spot for food, drink or a stay in pleasant, convivial surroundings.

see page 367

69 RESTORMEL CASTLE

Nr Lostwithiel

Overlooking the River Fowey, the 11th century ruins of Restormel Castle were once the stronghold of the Earls of Cornwall.

see page 366

70 SUNRISE

Burn View, Bude

Sunrise is a beautifully maintained Victorian house providing a comfortable, stylish Bed & Breakfast base in the centre of Bude.

 see *page 367*

71 TINTAGEL CASTLE

Tintagel

Tintagel Castle has long been associated with the legend of King Arthur and, although the ruins date from the 12th century, the site has been inhabited for much longer.

see *page 367*

originally formed the core of a vast earthwork mound.

BUDE

15 miles NW of Launceston off the A39

A traditional seaside resort with sweeping expanses of sand, rock pools and Atlantic breakers, Bude has also developed into a popular surfing centre. Completed in 1820, the **Bude Canal** was an ambitious project that aimed to connect the Atlantic with the English Channel via the River Tamar. However, the only stretch to be finished was that between Bude and Launceston and it is now the Bude Canal Trail footpath.

Close to the canal's entrance stands **Bude Castle**, designed by the local 19th century physician and brilliant inventor, Sir Goldsworthy Gurney. What makes this building (now an office) particularly interesting is that it is thought to have been the first building in Britain to be constructed on sand. To celebrate the new millennium, Carole Vincent and Anthony Fanshawe designed the **Bude Light 2000**, the first large-scale public sculpture to combine coloured concrete with fibre optic lighting. To the south of Bude is one of the most dramatic places along this stretch of coastline, **Crackington Haven**, a tiny port overlooked by towering 400ft cliffs.

TINTAGEL

17 miles W of Launceston on the B3263

Tintagel Castle, set on a wild and windswept headland, is forever linked with the legend of King

Arthur, and the village naturally owes much of its popularity to its Arthurian connections; one of its many interesting attractions on this theme is **King Arthur's Great Hall**. Also worth seeing here is the weather-beaten **Old Post Office**, a 14th century manor house that became a Post Office in the 19th century. Purchased by the National Trust in 1903 for £100, the building still has its original stone-paved medieval hall and ancient fireplace along with the ground floor office of the postmistress.

To the south lies the most famous slate quarry in Cornwall, **Delabole Slate Quarry**.

TRURO

The administrative and ecclesiastical centre of Cornwall, this elegant small city was once a fashionable place to rival Bath. The foundation stone of **Truro Cathedral** was laid in 1880 and this splendid Early English style building, with its celebrated Victorian stained glass window, was finally completed in 1910. To the northeast lies **Probus**, a large village that is home to the 'really useful garden' – **Probus Gardens**. Here, too, is **Trewithen House and Gardens**, which were laid out in the early 20th century.

AROUND TRURO

NEWQUAY

10 miles N of Truro on the A392

A traditional English seaside resort, with all the usual trappings,

Newquay also has a long history and for centuries was an important pilchard fishing village. On the Towan Headland stands a **Huer's Hut** from where the Huer would scan the sea looking for shoals of pilchards and, once spotted, he would cry 'hevva' to alert the awaiting fishing crews. Today, its beautiful rocky coastline and acres of golden sands have seen it develop into a popular seaside resort famous throughout the world for its surfing.

Inland are the imposing engine house and chimney stack of **East Wheal Rose** mine, Cornwall's richest lead mine, and close by is the delightful small Elizabeth manor house, **Trerice**, which is also home to a Mower Museum.

PADSTOW

19½ miles NE of Truro on the A389

It was here that the Welsh missionary St Petroc landed in the 6th century and founded a Celtic Minster. Beginning at the door of the town's 13th century parish Church of St Petroc, the **Saints Way** is a middle-distance footpath that follows the route that was taken by travellers and pilgrims crossing Cornwall on their way from Brittany to Ireland.

Although the River Camel silted up in the 19th century, the Harbour remains the town's focal point and here are many of Padstow's older buildings, including **Raleigh Cottage**, where Sir Walter Raleigh lived while he was Warden of Cornwall, and the tiny Harbour Cottage. The harbour is also home to the **Shipwreck Museum**.

On the other side of the Camel Estuary are the small resorts of **Polzeath** and **New Polzeath** and a beautiful coastal path that takes in the cliffs and farmland of Pentire Point and Rumps Point. The **Church of St Enodoc** is a Norman building that has, on several occasions, been virtually submerged by windblown sand. The beautiful churchyard contains the graves of many shipwrecked mariners and that of the poet Sir John Betjeman, who is buried here along with his parents. Betjeman spent many of his childhood holidays in the villages and coves around the Camel Estuary, and his affection for the local people and places was the inspiration for many of his works. The church is reached across a golf course that is

Padstow

41

72 LLAWNROC INN

Gorran Haven, nr St Austell

The **Llawnroc** Inn is a friendly pub very near the coast, with two cheerful bars, a fine selection of food and drink and attractive sea-facing bedrooms.

 see page 368

73 THE BUGLE INN

Bugle

Friendly village pub with a selection of freshly prepared food and comfortable accommodation.

 see page 368

74 WHEAL MARTYN CHINA CLAY MUSEUM

Carthew, St Austell

A fascinating day out for the family where visitors can discover the history of china clay production.

see page 368

regarded as one of the most scenic links courses in the country.

WADEBRIDGE

20 miles NE of Truro on the A39

Standing at the historic lowest bridging point on the River Camel, this ancient port and busy market town is now a popular holiday centre. The town is also home to **Bridge on Wool**, which was constructed on bridge piers that were sunk on foundation of woolsacks; the bridge still carries the main road that links the town's two ancient parishes. The town's former railway station is now home to the **John Betjeman Centre**.

ST AUSTELL

12½ miles NE of Truro on the A390

When William Cookworthy discovered large deposits of kaolin, or china clay, in 1748, this old market town, a centre of tin and copper mining, was transformed. Over the years, the waste material from the clay pits to the north and west of the town has been piled up into conical spoil heaps that have led to the area being nicknamed the **Cornish Alps**. More recently, action has been taken to soften the countryside and the heaps and disused pits have been landscaped with planting, undulating footpaths and nature trails.

In the heart of the Cornish Alps lies Wheal Martyn, an old clay works that is now home to the **Wheal Martyn China Clay Museum**. To the northeast, in the heart of the china clay area, lies the wonderful **Eden Project**, an ambitious undertaking that aims to "promote the understanding and responsible management of the vital relationship between plants, people and resources."

To the southeast lies **Charlestown**, a small fishing village that developed into a harbour for exporting china clay. Close to the docks is the **Charlestown Shipwreck, Rescue and Heritage Centre** which offers an insight into the town's history, local shipwrecks and the various devices that have been developed over the years for rescuing and recovering those in peril at sea

MEVAGISSEY

11½ miles E of Truro on the B3273

The largest fishing village in St Austell Bay. Housed in a harbour building dating from 1745 are the **Mevagissey Folk Museum**, the **World of Model Railway Exhibition** and **The Aquarium**. In the 1750s, when John Wesley first came to Mevagissey to preach, he was greeted with a barrage of rotten eggs and old fish and had to be rescued from the crowd and taken to safety. In return for their hospitality, Wesley gave his hosts James and Mary Lelean his silver shoe buckles.

To the northwest of Mevagissey lie the famous **Lost Gardens of Heligan**, one of the country's most interesting gardens that was originally laid out in 1780 but lay undisturbed for 70 years before being rediscovered in 1990. Today, this beautiful and intriguing place is once again attracting visitors from all over the world.

ST MAWES

7½ miles S of Truro on the A3078

This charming town in the shelter of Carrick Roads is dominated by its artillery fort, **St Mawes Castle**, which was built in the 1540s as part of Henry VIII's coastal defences.

FALMOUTH

8 miles SW of Truro on the A39

A spectacular deep-water anchorage that is the world's third largest natural harbour, Falmouth lies in Britain's Western Approaches and guards the entrance into Carrick Roads. Standing on a 200 feet promontory overlooking the entrance to Carrick Roads, Henry VIII's **Pendennis Castle** is one of Cornwall's great fortresses and, along with St Mawes Castle, it has protected Britain's shores from attack ever since its construction.

Falmouth's nautical and notorious past is revealed at the **National Maritime Museum Cornwall**.

To the north lies **Feock**, one of the prettiest small villages in Cornwall and to the south lies **Restronguet Point**. It was from **Tolverne**, just north of Feock, that Allied troops left for the Normandy coast during the D-day landings and on the shingle beach the remains of the concrete honeycombed mattresses can still be seen. Close by lies the estate of **Trelissick**, a privately owned 18th century house that is surrounded by marvellous gardens

and parkland that offer wonderful views over Carrick Roads.

HELFORD

12½ miles SW of Truro off the B3293

A picture postcard village on the southern banks of the Helford estuary, Helford was once the haunt of smugglers, but today it is a popular sailing centre. From the village, the five-mile **Helford River Walk** takes in several isolated hamlets and a 200-year-old fig tree that grows in the churchyard at **Manaccan**.

On the northern banks of the River Helford are two glorious gardens: **Glendurgan Garden**, created in the 1820s, and **Trebah Garden** that has often been called the 'garden of dreams'.

LIZARD

22 miles SW of Truro on the A3038

The most southerly village in mainland Britain, Lizard is a place of craft shops, cafés and art galleries that lends its name to the **Lizard Peninsula**, an area that is physically separate from mainland Cornwall. The Lizard is known for its unique serpentine rock, a green mineral that became fashionable in the 19th century after Queen Victoria visited Cornwall and ordered many items made from the stone for her house, Osborne, on the Isle of Wight.

To the south of the village lies **Lizard Point**, the tip of the peninsula, whose three sides are lashed by waves whatever the season.

To the northwest of Lizard,

75 MEUDON HOTEL

Mawnan Smith, nr Falmouth

Comfort, service, fine food and unrivalled amenities put **Meudon Hotel** among the very finest in the Southwest.

🛏 see page 369

76 THE GARDENS

Ashton

A picturesque B&B with 3 guest rooms and home-cooked breakfasts.

🛏 see page 370

Trebah Gardens, Helford

former town house of the Godolphin family.

To the northwest lie **Trevarno Estate and Gardens**, and close by is the **Poldark Mine Heritage Complex**, with its underground tour of tunnels and the famous 18th century Poldark village.

To the east of the town is another interesting family attraction, **Flambards**, which is based around a faithful re-creation of a Victorian street. Nearby is the Royal Navy's land and sea rescue headquarters at **Culdrose**, one of the largest and busiest helicopter bases in Europe.

REDRUTH

8½ miles SW of Truro on the A393

This market town owes its past prosperity to its location – at the heart of Cornwall's mining industry – and some pockets of Victorian, Georgian and earlier buildings can still be found. In the 19th century the land around **Camborne** was the most intensely mined in the world with, in the 1850s, over 300 mines producing some two thirds of the world's copper! With such a history of mining it is not surprising that Camborne is home to the world famous **School of Mining** and its Geological Museum.

Immediately south of Redruth lies dramatic **Carn Brea**, a granite hill that rises some 738 feet above sea level and is crowned by a 90 feet monument to Francis Basset, a local benevolent mine and land owner. Nearby is the mysterious **Gwennap Pit**, a round, grass-

77 NANPLOUGH FARM

Cury, nr Helston

Nanplough Farm welcomes guests with a choice of self-catering and B&B holiday accommodation in a lovely quiet setting on the Lizard Peninsula.

see page 370

close to **Mullion**, is the popular sandy beach of **Poldhu Cove**, from where in 1901 Guglielmo Marconi transmitted the first wireless message from the clifftops and across the Atlantic. A granite column commemorates the event. A couple of miles inland, on **Goonhilly Downs**, is a monument to the very latest in telecommunications – the Earth Satellite Station.

HELSTON

15 miles SW of Truro on the A394

Dating back to Roman times, this ancient stannary town also developed as a port but, today, it is best known for the famous Festival of the Furry, or **Flora Dance**, a colourful festival of music and dance with ancient pagan connections. Among the town's surprising number of Georgian, Regency and Victorian buildings are the **Helston Folk Museum** and 16th century Angel House, the covered amphitheatre that is thought to have been created by the collapse of a subterranean mine shaft.

To the north, along the coast, lie the two thriving holiday centres of **Porthtowan** and **Portreath**, which, although they developed as a copper mining village and ore exporting port respectively, are now the summer preserve of holidaymakers and surfers.

ST AGNES

8 miles NW of Truro on the B3285

Once known as the source of the finest tin in Cornwall, this old village still retains many of its original miners' cottages while, surrounding the village, are the ruins of old mine workings including the clifftop buildings of one of Cornwall's best known mines – **Wheal Coates**. The mine operated between 1860 and 1890 and the derelict Engine House is one of the more exceptional landmarks along this stretch of coast. The remains of **Wheal Kitty** provides panoramic views over this once industrial area. The tin production processes is explained on guided tours around **Blue Hills Tin Streams** at nearby **Trevellas**.

Just up the coast lies the holiday resort of **Perranporth** whose Celtic heritage is kept alive during the annual **Lowender Peran Festival** of music and dance.

From the village of St Agnes a footpath takes walkers out to St Agnes Head and St Agnes Beacon, an area of land that not only provides spectacular views over the old mine workings but where there are remains from both the Bronze and Iron Age.

Wheal Coates, St Agnes

78 MOUNT VIEW HOTEL

Longrock, nr Penzance

Mount View Hotel attracts both local customers and visitors with its warm, welcoming air, good food, comfortable accommodation and great views.

see page 371

79 HALSETOWN INN

Halsetown, nr St Ives

Halsetown Inn is a warm, friendly pub serving excellent food and a wide range of beers and other drinks. It also has 5 rooms for B&B guests.

see page 372

80 TREVASKIS FARMSHOP & RESTAURANT

Gwinear, nr Hayle

Trevaskis Farm is one of the West Country's leading centres of top-quality farm produce, where visitors can enjoy superb food and learn about the farm's activities.

see page 373

PENZANCE

Cornwall's only promenade stretches from here to Newlyn, and other interesting buildings include the exotic **Egyptian House** created from two cottages in the 1830s, and The Union Hotel, where the first announcement in mainland England of the victory of Trafalgar and the death of Nelson was made. Penzance's links with the sea are remembered at the Maritime Museum and the **Trinity House Lighthouse Centre**.

To the southwest lies **Newlyn**, the largest fish landing port in England. As well as being home to the **Pilchard Works Heritage Museum**, the town is known for its artistic associations: it was here in the late 19th century that the **Newlyn School** of art was founded.

AROUND PENZANCE

ZENNOR

5½ miles N of Penzance on the B3306

This delightful ancient village shows evidence of Bronze Age settlers and the **Wayside Folk Museum** has numerous exhibits that tell of this region's industrial past. DH Lawrence lived here with his wife Frieda during World War I and it was during his stay here, under police surveillance, that Lawrence wrote *Women in Love*. However, his pacifist tendencies and Frieda's German heritage (her cousin was the flying ace the Red Baron) caused them to be 'moved on' in October 1917. By the porch in the church at Zennor is a memorial to John Davey, who died in 1891, stating that he was the last person to have any great knowledge of the native Cornish language Kernuack. It is said that he remained familiar with the language by speaking it to his cat. To the southeast of the village lies the Neolithic chamber tomb, **Zennor Quoit** while, close by, is **Chysauster Ancient Village**, a Romano-Cornish village that was built around 2,000 years ago and has one of the oldest identifiable streets in the country.

ST IVES

7 miles NE of Penzance on the A3074

Now one of the most-visited places in the county, this was once one of the most important fishing centres in Cornwall, and locally mined ores and minerals were exported from the harbour (**St Ives Museum** is housed in a former mine building). St Ives is also home to **Tate St Ives**, dedicated to the work of 20th century painters and sculptures, and the **Barbara Hepworth Sculpture Garden and Museum**, housed in her former studio.

HAYLE

7½ miles NE of Penzance on the B3301

It was here in the early 1800s that the Cornish inventor Richard Trevithick built an early version of the steam locomotive and, a short time later, one of the first railways in the world was constructed here to carry tin and copper from Redruth down to the port.

MARAZION

3 miles E of Penzance off the A394

For centuries the most important settlement around Mount's Bay, this harbour town of fine old inns and residential houses that overlook the sandy beach is now a windsurfing and sailing centre. To the northwest is **Marazion Marsh**, an RSPB reserve with breeding colonies of grey herons and visiting waders and wildfowl.

Situated a third of a mile offshore and connected to Marazion by a cobbled causeway that is exposed at high tide, **St Michael's Mount** rises dramatically out of the waters of Mount's Bay. In the 11th century, Edward the Confessor founded a priory on the mount and these remains are incorporated into the marvellous **St Michael's Mount Castle**.

LAND'S END

9 miles SW of Penzance on the A30

Mainland Britain's most westerly point and one of the country's most famous landmarks, it is here that the granite of Cornwall finally meets the Atlantic Ocean in a series of savage cliffs, reefs and sheer-sided islets. Land's End has been a tourist destination since the early 19th century, and down the years an ever-expanding complex of man-made attractions has been added to the majestic scenery that nature has provided. From this headland can be seen **Longships Lighthouse**, just off shore, and **Wolf Rock Lighthouse**, seven

miles away. Just to the southeast, and protected by Gwennap Head, is **Porthcurno**, from where in 1870 the first telegraph cable was laid linking Britain with the rest of the world. Housed in a secret underground wartime communications centre is the **Porthcurno Wartime Telegraph Museum**. This interesting village is also home to the marvellous **Minack Theatre**, an open-air amphitheatre cut into the cliff that was founded by Rowena Cade in the 1930s.

ST JUST

6½ miles NW of Penzance on the A3071

The westernmost town in mainland Britain, St Just was once a thriving mining centre, and the surrounding area is littered with industrial remains. A narrow road leads westwards to **Cape Cornwall**, the only cape in England and, along the way, the road passes the last remains of Cape Cornwall Mine – its tall chimney.

St Just marks the start of **The Tinners' Way**, an ancient trackway between the town and St Ives that follows ancient moorland paths.

To the northeast lies **Pendeen**, where tin has been mined since prehistoric times. The last of 20 or so mines in this area, **Geevor Tin Mine and Heritage Centre** not only preserves the mine but also offers visitors the chance to experience the conditions that miners had to endure underground. Also close by is the mighty **Levant Steam Engine**, housed in a tiny building perched high on the cliffs.

81 PORTHCURNO TELEGRAPH MUSEUM

Porthcurno

Built in 1870, the cable station now offers an interesting experience with hands-on exhibits and demonstrations.

 see page 371

47

Cumbria

The second largest county in England, Cumbria is much more than the Lake District National Park that lies within its boundaries. It was here that the British Celts managed to preserve their independence from the Saxons and the Norse influence can still be detected in the place names here. The county town, Carlisle, lies to the north, close to the Scottish border and was for centuries a base for English soldiers who planned their attacks on Scotland from here, as well as defending Carlisle from border raids. The Lake District National Park is not only home to England's largest lake, Windermere, but also to the country's highest peak, Scafell Pike. An area of magnificent crags, isolated fells and expanses of water, this dramatic landscape has inspired Wordsworth and many other poets and artists. Of the county's coastline, the Furness Peninsula is probably the most attractive - a place of elegant and small seaside resorts and once an area of great ecclesiastical power.

FOOD & DRINK

KENDAL

The capital of south Lakeland, Kendal has royal connections: the Parr family lived at **Kendal Castle** until 1483, and it was Catherine Parr, a descendant, who became Henry VIII's last wife. Today, the castle's gaunt ruins stand high on a hill overlooking Kendal. The woollen industry, on which much of the town's prosperity was based, has long since disappeared, but there is one local product that all visitors should try: **Kendal Mint Cake**, a tasty, very sweet confection, sometimes covered in chocolate, that is cherished by climbers and walkers for its instant infusion of energy.

A number of interesting museums and galleries can be found in Kendal including the **Museum of Lakeland Life and Industry** and the **Abbot Hall Art Gallery** that includes the work of John Ruskin. At the town's Quaker Meeting House, the history of the Quaker Movement is told through a series of 77 panels that combine to form the **Quaker Tapestry Exhibition**.

AROUND KENDAL

RAVENSTONEDALE

14½ miles NE of Kendal off the A685

Known locally as Rissendale, this pretty village, clustered along the banks of Scandal Beck, lies on the edge of the **Howgill Fells**; its church, built in 1738, is one of the few Georgian churches in Cumbria.

SEDBERGH

9 miles E of Kendal on the A684

Although Sedbergh is in Cumbria it lies within the Yorkshire Dales National Park and the surrounding scenery is typical of the Dales. One spectacular local feature is **Cautley Crag**, a great cliff alongside which tumbles a beautiful

82 THE PUNCH BOWL

Barrow Green, Kendal

The **Punch Bowl** reaches out to loyal locals and Kendal's many visitors with its friendly ambience and hearty home cooking.

🍴 *see page 374*

83 BRUNT KNOTT FARM COTTAGES

Staveley, nr Kendal

Tourists, walkers and lovers of the countryside have the perfect base for a self-catering holiday at **Brunt Knott Farm Holiday Cottages**.

🛏 *see page 374*

84 ABBOT HALL ART GALLERY AND MUSEUM

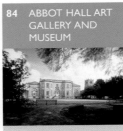

Kendal

Gallery including works by John Ruskin and George Romney.

 see page 375

85 THE COMMODORE

Grange-over-Sands

The **Commodore**, just a stone's throw from the waters of Morecambe Bay, is a good choice for a drink, a lunchtime meal or an overnight stay.

 see page 376

86 COURTYARD COTTAGE

Ulverston

Courtyard Cottage is a charming mews-style residence with two superbly appointed rooms for Bed & Breakfast.

 see page 377

narrow waterfall, Cautley Spout.

Firbank Knott, on nearby Firbank Fell, is considered to be the birthplace of Quakerism as it was here, in 1652, that George Fox gave his great sermon to inspire over a thousand 'seekers' from the whole of the north of England. The **Quaker Meeting House** is the oldest in the north of England.

KIRKBY LONSDALE

11 miles SE of Kendal on the A65

There has been a bridge over the River Lune here for at least 700 years and, for centuries, it has drawn people who come here to experience what John Ruskin described as "one of the loveliest scenes in England." The subject of a painting by JMW Turner, the **Devil's Bridge** is said to have been built by Satan in just three days.

LEVENS

4½ miles S of Kendal off the A590

To the south of the village and overlooking the Lyth valley is the superb Elizabethan mansion, **Levens Hall**, which was developed from a 14th centurypele tower. Best known for its fine furniture and unique topiary gardens, it also houses a collection of working steam engines.

MILNTHORPE

7½ miles S of Kendal on the A6

Close to this market town on the A6 is the **Lakeland Wildlife Oasis** that, since opening in 1991, has established itself as one of the county's premier attractions.

GRANGE-OVER-SANDS

12 miles SW of Kendal on the B5278

This charming town on the north shore of Morecambe Bay is the starting point of the **Cistercian Way**, an interesting 33-mile long footpath through Furness to Barrow.

To the west of Grange lies **Cartmel**, one of the prettiest villages in Furness, that is dominated by the famous **Cartmel Priory** that was founded by Augustinian canons in 1188. It was dismantled in 1537, and all that is left are the substantial remains of the 12th century **Gatehouse**.

Just to the southwest lies Cumbria's premier stately home, **Holker Hall**, one of the homes of the Dukes of Devonshire. An intriguing blend of 16th century, Georgian and Victorian architecture, the Hall is surrounded by a large estate that includes a deer park, formal gardens and the **Lakeland Motor Museum**.

NEWBY BRIDGE

10 ½ miles SW of Kendal on the A592

The bridge here crosses the River Leven that runs from the southern tip of Windermere into Morecambe Bay, and visitors to this popular tourist destination can reach the famous lake by taking a steam train on the **Lakeside and Haverthwaite Railway**. Just to the north is **Fell Foot Park**, delightful landscaped gardens and woodlands that were laid out in the late 19th century.

ULVERSTON

17½ miles SW of Kendal on the A590

Ulverston boasts England's shortest, widest and deepest canal, built by the engineer John Rennie in late 18th century. Crowning a hill to the north of the town centre is the **Barrow Monument**, a 100 feet-high replica of the Eddystone Lighthouse that was erected in 1850 to commemorate the explorer, diplomat and author Sir John Barrow. He served as a Lord of the Admiralty and it was his naval reforms that contributed to England's success in the Napoleonic Wars.

Even more famous was Stanley Jefferson, who was born in Argyle Street on 16 June 1890. Better known as Stan Laurel, he made more than 100 films in a 30-year career with his partner Oliver Hardy, and visitors can learn all about this celebrated duo in the town's **Laurel and Hardy Museum**.

BARROW-IN-FURNESS

24 miles SW of Kendal on the A590

Right up until the early 1800s, Barrow-in-Furness was just a tiny hamlet but, in just 40 years, it became the largest iron and steel centre in the world and also a major shipbuilding centre. The impressive **Dock Museum** tells the story of the town through a series of audio-visual displays and an interactive film show brings to life the people who made Barrow so successful.

Furness Abbey, a magnificent ruin of red sandstone, is the focal point of south Cumbria's monastic heritage. Another historic building nearby is **Dalton Castle**, a 14th century pele tower that provided a refuge for the monks of the abbey against Scottish raiders.

To the south of Barrow lies the **Isle of Walney**, a 10-mile long island joined to the peninsula by a bridge from Barrow that is home to two important nature reserves: **North Walney National Nature Reserve**, with a great variety of habitats, including sand dunes, heath, salt marsh and shingle; and **South Walney Nature Reserve**, the largest nesting grounds of herring gulls and lesser black-backed gulls in Europe.

BROUGHTON-IN-FURNESS

19 miles W of Kendal on the A595

Some of the Lake District's finest scenery lies within easy reach of Broughton. A couple of miles west of the town is **Swinside Circle**, a fine prehistoric stone monument, 60 feet in diameter, while, to the north, in the peaceful hamlet of **Broughton Mills**, is the **Coleridge Trail**. During his 'circumcursion' of Lakeland in August 1802, the poet stopped to refresh himself at the Blacksmith's Arms here and the inn, built in 1748, has outwardly changed little since his visit.

87 TALLY HO

Barrow-in-Furness

The **Tally Ho** is a popular local with a lively ambience and good simple food.

see page 377

88 CONCLE INN

Rampside, Barrow-in-Furness

On the very tip of the peninsula overlooking Morecambe Bay, the **Concle Inn** is a very friendly, sociable pub serving value-for-money food.

see page 378

89 THE RED LION

Dalton, nr Barrow-in-Furness

Excellent food, four regularly changing real ales and comfortable guest bedrooms are the main assets of the 17th century **Red Lion**.

see page 378

90 THE BLACK COCK INN

Broughton-in-Furness

The **Black Cock Inn** is a much-loved village hostelry serving a fine selection of drinks and excellent traditional English dishes. Also comfortable rooms for B&B.

 see page 379

91 THE GOLDEN FLEECE

Calder Bridge, nr Seascale

The **Golden Fleece** provides all-day food and en suite accommodation in a village on the A595.

 see page 380

92 LAKES HOTEL & SUPER TOURS

High Street, Windermere

Lakes Hotel is a small, friendly and comfortable 10-room hotel on the High Street. Guests can make use of the hotel's mini-coaches for touring the area.

 see page 380

93 ELIM BANK HOTEL

Bowness-on-Windermere

Elim Bank is a small, comfortable Bed & Breakfast hotel with its own car park.

 see page 380

Steam Locomotive at Ravenglass

RAVENGLASS

27 miles W of Kendal on the A595

The town's major attraction is the 15-inch narrow gauge **Ravenglass and Eskdale Railway** that runs for seven miles up the valleys of the Mite and Esk. One of the few settlements on the route of the railway is Eskdale Green and close by are a group of buildings that make up **Eskdale Mill** where cereals have been ground since 1578 and which is in full working order.

Owned by the Pennington family since 1208, **Muncaster Castle**, just east of Ravenglass, is not only famous for its many treasures - including outstanding collections of tapestry, silver and porcelain - but also for its vast and beautiful grounds, which include an Owl Centre.

A focal point for fishing, beach casting, wind surfing and water

skiing, **Seascale**, up the coast from Ravenglass, is one of the most popular seaside villages in Cumbria. Its Victorian wooden jetty was restored to mark the Millennium.

WINDERMERE

8 miles NW of Kendal on the A591

The village was originally called Birthwaite, but when the railway arrived in 1847 the Kendal and Windermere Railway Company named the station after the nearby lake even though it was over a mile away. Within a few yards of Windermere Station (now serving a single-track branch line) is a footpath that leads through woodland to one of the finest viewpoints in Lakeland – **Orrest Head**.

Just to the north of Windermere is the village of **Troutbeck**, a designated conservation area with attractive old houses and cottages grouped around a number of wells and springs that, until recently, formed the only water supply. The best-known building here is **Townend**, an enchanting example of Cumbrian vernacular architecture.

Now all but merged with Windermere, **Bowness-on-Windermere** is an attractive town right on the edge of the lake; it is from here that most of the lake cruises operate. Along with all the boating activity, the town is also home to the **Windermere Steamboat Museum** with its unique collection of Victorian and Edwardian steam launches, some of them still in working order. Just down the road from the museum is the Old Laundry Visitor Centre, the home of **The World of Beatrix Potter** where there are some fascinating re-creations of this much loved Lakeland author's books.

HAWKSHEAD

11 miles NW of Kendal on the B5285

It was in this charming little village at the head of Esthwaite Water that Beatrix Potter's solicitor husband, William Heelis, had his office; this is now **The Beatrix Potter Gallery**, which features an exhibition of her original drawings and illustrations along with details of her life. Using the royalties from her first book, *The Tale of Peter Rabbit*, Beatrix Potter purchased **Hill Top** in the village of **Near Sawrey**, having fallen in love with the place during a holiday. In accordance with her will, Hill Tophas remained just as she would

have known it and it is now full of Beatrix Potter memorabilia.

To the southwest of Hawkshead lies **Grizedale Forest**, acquired by the Forestry Commission in 1934 and famous for its 80 tree sculptures.

CONISTON

14 miles NW of Kendal on the A593

To the south of the once major copper mining centre of Coniston is Coniston Hall, the village's oldest building. But it is the **Ruskin Museum** that draws most visitors to the village. Containing many of the famous man's studies, pictures, letters and photographs, as well as his collection of geological specimens, the museum is a fitting tribute to one of its most famous residents.

Coniston Water also has tragic associations with Sir Donald Campbell who, in 1955, had broken the world water speed record here. Some 12 years later, in an attempt to beat his own record, his boat, *Bluebird*, crashed while travelling at 320 miles per hour. In March 2001 his widow was present as the tailfin of the boat was hauled to the surface after 34 years. Campbell's body was recovered later and was buried in the village cemetery on September 12th 2001 - an event overshadowed by the tragic events in New York and Washington the day before.

Today, boats on Coniston Water are limited to 10 miles per hour, an ideal speed for the wonderful old steamship, the *Gondola*, which was built in 1859

94 THE SAWREY HOTEL

Far Sawrey, nr Ambleside

The **Sawrey Hotel** is a charming family-run 18th century hostelry combining the best features of a friendly local, restaurant and hotel.

 see page 380

95 BRANTWOOD

Coniston

Once the home of John Ruskin, this beautiful house enjoys a spectacular position. Many of Ruskin's belongings can still be seen inside.

 see page 381

Coniston Water

glass being made in the traditional way and admire the restored water mill that stands next to the studio. A short walk leads to the **Armitt Museum**, dedicated to the area's history since Roman times and to John Ruskin and Beatrix Potter. **The Homes of Football** is an exhibition of football memorabilia that covers the game from the very top level right down to amateur village football. Real sporting activity takes place in the summer in the famous **Ambleside Sports**, featuring traditional sports such as carriage driving, ferret and pigeon racing, Cumberland and Westmorland wrestling (a bit like sumo but without the rolls of fat), fell racing and hound trailing. The main road leading northwards from the town climbs sharply up to the dramatic **Kirkstone Pass** that is so called because of the rock at the top (almost 1,500 feet above sea level) which looks like a church steeple.

GRASMERE
15 miles NW of Kendal on the A591

With one of the finest settings in all Lakeland, this compact rough-stone village is one of the most popular in the Lake District. Although it is the glorious scenery that draws many here, it is also its associations with Wordsworth, who lived at the tiny **Dove Cottage** from 1799 to 1808; in dire poverty he was obliged to line the walls with newspaper for warmth. Today, this place of pilgrimage has been preserved intact, and next door is an award-winning museum

---

96 THE GRASMERE HOTEL

Broadgate, Grasmere

Grasmere is at the heart of one of the most beautiful areas of Britain, and The **Grasmere Hotel** is the ideal base for discovering its delights.

🛏 *see page 382*

97 THE QUEENS HOTEL

Main Street, Keswick

Comfort, amenity and a town-centre location make the **Queens Hotel** an attractive choice for visitors.

🍴 *see page 381*

---

and was restored by the National Trust in 1980. Overlooking both the village and the lake is the great crumpled hill of the **Coniston Old Man** and from the summit there are extensive views as far north as Scotland, out to the Isle of Man and, of course, over Lakeland. From here, too, can be seen **Brantwood**, the home of John Ruskin from 1872 until his death in 1900 that lies on the opposite side of the lake from the town.

AMBLESIDE
11½ miles NW of Kendal on the A591

The centre of the town is a conservation area and contains the town's most picturesque building. **The Bridge House**, a tiny cottage perched on a packhorse bridge, is now an information centre, but in the 1850s it was the home of Mr and Mrs Rigg and their six children. Close by, at **Adrian Sankey's Glass Works**, visitors can watch dedicated to the poet's life and works.

Grief stricken after the death of their two young children, Mary and William Wordsworth moved from Grasmere to **Rydal Mount** in 1813, a handsome house overlooking tiny Rydal Water that lies just to the east of the village. The interior of the house has changed little since Wordsworth's day and it contains first editions of his works and personal possessions. The graves of Wordsworth and his sister Dorothy are in St Oswald's churchyard, while a notable occupant of the town cemetery is William Archibald Spooner, sometime Warden of New College, Oxford. He gave his name to Spoonerisms and produced gems such as *'You have hissed all my mystery lessons'* or *'Yes indeed: the Lord is a shoving leopard'*.

KESWICK

The undisputed capital of the Lake District, Keswick has been a magnet for tourists since the mid 1700s and was given a huge lift by the Lakeland poets in the early 19th century. The grandeur of the setting is the biggest draw, but Keswick also offers man-made attractions, including the fascinating **Cumberland Pencil Museum** that boasts the largest pencil in the world, and the popular **Theatre by the Lake** that hosts a year-round programme of plays, concerts, exhibitions, readings and talks. Another attraction to pencil in lies

east of the town: this is **Castlerigg Stone Circle**, some of whose 38 standing stones are 8 feet high. Close by is the charming village of **Threlkeld**, the ideal starting point for a number of mountain walks, including an ascent of **Blencathra**.

Running south from Keswick is **Borrowdale**, home to the extraordinary **Bowder Stone**, a massive cube-shaped boulder weighing almost 2,000 tons that stands precariously on one corner apparently defying gravity.

AROUND KESWICK

POOLEY BRIDGE

12 miles E of Keswick on the B5320

This charming village stands at the northern tip of **Ullswater** and there are regular cruise departures from here during the season, stopping at Glenridding and Howton. Along the northern shore of the lake is a series of waterfalls that tumble down through a wooded gorge, known collectively by the name of the largest fall, **Aira Force**. The southern end of Ullswater is overshadowed by **Helvellyn** (3,115 feet) and an assault on its summit is best tackled from Glenridding.

BAMPTON

15 miles SE of Keswick off the A6

To the south of Bampton, lies **Haweswater**, the most easterly of the lakes - actually it's a reservoir, created in the late 1930s to supply the growing needs of industrial Manchester.

98 THE FOUR IN HAND

Lake Road, Keswick

The **Four in Hand** is a popular inn serving real ales and excellent food with a smile.

see page 381

99 THE DERWENTWATER HOTEL

Portinscale, nr Keswick

The **Derwentwater Hotel** enjoys a glorious setting in grounds stretching along the lake. Also self-catering in Derwent Manor.

see page 381

100 THE SALUTATION INN

Threlkeld, nr Keswick

The **Salutation Inn** is a distinguished old pub serving generous snacks and meals and offering quality B&B accommodation.

see page 383

101 THE HORSE & FARRIER INN

Threlkeld, nr Keswick

Well-kept ales, a good selection of food and nine comfortable bedrooms have earned the **Horse & Farrier** an excellent, far-reaching reputation.

see page 383

102 THE KINGS ARMS

Main Street, Egremont

The **Kings Arms** is a fine old pub with good food, friendly ghosts and four letting rooms.

 see page 383

103 THE WESTLANDS HOTEL

Workington

The **Westlands Hotel** is a family owned and managed hotel with 70 superbly appointed en suite bedrooms.

 see page 384

104 THE SHEPHERD'S ARMS HOTEL

Ennerdale Bridge

With eight well-appointed bedrooms and a good choice of ales and food, The **Shepherd's Arms Hotel** is an ideal 'local' and a good base for touring the Lake District.

see page 384

Lake Buttermere

BUTTERMERE

8 miles SW of Keswick on the B5289

To many connoisseurs of the Lake District landscape, Buttermere is the most splendid of all the Lakes. The walk around Buttermere gives superb views of the eastern towers of Fleetwith Pike and the great fell wall made up of High Crag, High Stile, and Red Pike. Fed by both Buttermere and Loweswater, **Crummock Water** is by far the largest of the three lakes and its attractions can usually be enjoyed in solitude.

WHITEHAVEN

19 miles SW of Keswick on the A595

A handsome Georgian town which by the mid-1700s had become the third largest port in Britain, but the harbour's shallow draught halted further expansion. The harbour is now a conservation area and **The Beacon** tells the history of the town and its harbour.

To the south lies **St Bees Head**, a red sandstone bluff that forms one of the most dramatic natural features along the entire coast of northwest England. From here the 190-mile Coast to Coast Walk starts on its long journey across the Pennines to Robin Hood's Bay in North Yorkshire. St Bees Head is now an important **Nature Reserve** and the cliffs are crowded with guillemots, razorbills, kittiwakes, gulls, gannets and skuas.

Just inland is the pretty town of **Egremont**, dominated by its 12th century Castle. Its prosperity was based on its local iron ore, and jewellery made from ore can be bought at the nearby **Florence Mine Heritage Centre**.

BRAITHWAITE

3 miles W of Keswick on the B5292

This small village lies at the foot of the Whinlatter Pass, another of Cumbria's dramatic routes, with a summit some 1,043 feet above sea level. The road also runs through **Whinlatter Forest Park**, the only Mountain Forest in England and one of the Forestry Commission's oldest woodlands.

MARYPORT

17 miles NW of Keswick on the A596

Dramatically located on the Solway Firth, Maryport is a charming Cumbrian coastal town rich in interest and maritime history. Some of the first visitors to Maryport were the Romans who built a clifftop fort here, **Alauna**, which is now part of the Hadrian's Wall World Heritage Site. The award-winning **Senhouse Roman Museum** tells the story of life in this outpost of the empire.

COCKERMOUTH

10 miles NW of Keswick on the A66

A delightful market town since 1226, Cockermouth was the birthplace in the 1770s of both Fletcher Christian, who was to lead the mutiny on the *Bounty*, and William Wordsworth. The house in which the latter was born is now called **Wordsworth House** and contains a few of the poet's personal possessions.

The town is also home to the unusual **Printing House Museum**, where a wide range of historic presses and printing equipment is on display, of **Jennings Brewery** and of the excellent **Cumberland Toy & Model Museum**.

BASSENTHWAITE LAKE

4 miles NW of Keswick on the A66

Here's one for the Pub Quiz: Which is the only lake in the Lake District? Answer: Bassenthwaite, because all the others are either Waters or Meres. Only 70 feet deep and with borders rich in vegetation, Bassenthwaite provides an ideal habitat for birds - more than 70 species have been recorded around the lake.

At the northern end of the lake, at Coalbeck Farm, **Trotters World of Animals** is home to many hundreds of animals - rare breeds, traditional farm favourites, endangered species, birds of prey and reptiles.

Rising grandly above Bassenthwaite's eastern shore is **Skiddaw**, which ever since the Lake District was opened up to tourists by the arrival of the railway in the 19th century has been one of the most popular peaks to climb. Although it rises to some 3,054 feet, the climb is both safe and manageable, and from the summit, on a clear day, there are spectacular views to Scotland in the north, the Isle of Man in the west, the Pennines to the east, and to the south the greater part of the Lake District.

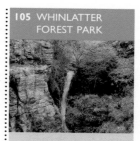

105 WHINLATTER FOREST PARK

Braithwaite, Keswick

The only mountain forest park in England, Whinlatter Forest Park offers a whole range of outdoor activities including walking, cycling and orienteering.

 see page 385

Also on the eastern shore is the
secluded **Church of St Bridget &
St Bega** which Tennyson had in
mind when, in his poem *Morte
d'Arthur*, he describes Sir Bedivere
carrying the dead King Arthur: *"to
a chapel in the fields, A broken chancel
with a broken cross, That stood on a
dark strait of barren land"*.

CALDBECK

13 miles N of Keswick on the B5299

Caldbeck is closely linked with
John Peel, the famous huntsman
who died in 1854 after falling from
his horse and is buried in the
churchyard here. His ornate
tombstone is decorated with
depictions of hunting horns and his
favourite hound. Also buried here
are John Peel's wife Mary and their
four children. Some 200 years ago
Caldbeck was an industrial village,
with corn mills, woollen mills, and a
paper mill all powered by the fast-
flowing 'cold stream' - the
Caldbeck. **Priest's Mill**, built in
1702 by the Rector of Caldbeck,
next to his church, was a stone
grinding corn mill, powered by a
waterwheel which has now been
restored to working order.

ULDALE

11 miles N of Keswick off the A591

To the northeast of Bassenthwaite
Lake stretches the area known
locally as the 'Land Back of
Skidda', a crescent of fells and
valleys constituting the most
northerly part of the Lake District
National Park.

PENRITH

The Saxon capital of the
Kingdom of Cumbria, Penrith
was sacked several times by the
Scots and by the time of the Civil
War **Penrith Castle** was in a
ruined state. Cromwell's troops
destroyed what was left but,
today, the ruins remain
impressive, standing high above a
steep-sided moat. Other
buildings in the town include the
Town Hall that is the result of a
1905 conversion of two former
Adam-style houses, one of which
was known as Wordsworth House
as it was the home of the poet's
cousin, Captain John Wordsworth.

Rheged Discovery Centre
dedicates itself to 2,000 years of
Cumbria's history, mystery and
magic.

The town is dominated by
Beacon Hill Pike, which stands
amidst wooded slopes high above
Penrith. The tower was built in
1719 and marks the place where,
since 1296, beacons were lit to
warn the townsfolk of an
impending attack. To the southeast
of the town are the substantial
remains of **Brougham Castle**
standing on the foundations of a
Roman fort.

AROUND PENRITH

LITTLE SALKELD

6 miles NE of Penrith off the A686

Close to the village are **Long Meg
and her Daughters**, a most
impressive Bronze Age site and

Long Meg and her Daughters, Little Salkeld

110 THE TUFTON ARMS HOTEL

Market Square, Appleby-in-Westmorland

Outstanding hospitality, service, food and accommodation make the **Tufton Arms Hotel** one of the finest in the region.

see page 387

second only to Stonehenge in size. There are more than 60 stones in the circle and the tallest, Long Meg, is 15 feet high.

Just to the south, in the village of **Edenhall**, is a **Plague Cross** that stands where there was once a basin filled with vinegar. This acted as a disinfectant into which plague victims put their money to pay for food from the people of Penrith.

APPLEBY-IN-WESTMORLAND

12 miles SE of Penrith on the B6260

The old county town of Westmorland, Appleby was originally built by the Norman, Ranulph de Meschines, who set it within a broad loop of the River Eden that protects it on three sides.

The fourth side is guarded by Castle Hill: at its foot is 16th century **Moot Hall** and at its head rises the great Norman keep of Appleby Castle.

Appleby is best known for its **Gypsy Horse Fair**, when hundreds of gypsies flood into the little town with their caravans and horse-drawn carts. The trade, principally in horses, and the trotting races provide a picturesque and colourful spectacle.

KIRKBY STEPHEN

21 miles SE of Penrith on the A685

Surrounded by spectacular scenery, inside the church in this old market town, is the 10th century **Loki Stone,** one of only two such carvings in Europe to have survived. Loki was a Norse God

111 THE NEW INN

Hoff, nr Appleby

Perfectly kept real ales and hearty home cooking have earned a fine reputation for the **New Inn**.

see page 386

112 THE BUTCHERS ARMS

Crosby Ravensworth, nr Penrith

A short detour from the A6/ M6 brings visitors to join the local regulars at the **Butchers Arms** and enjoy the popular home cooking.

see page 388

113 ASHLEY BANK

*Newbiggin-on-Lune,
nr Kirkby Stephen*

Two smartly refurbished
outbuildings in a beautiful,
tranquil location provide
self-catering accommodation
for up to 16 guests at
Ashley Bank.

 see page 388

114 THE KINGS HEAD HOTEL

*Ravenstonedale, nr Kirkby
Stephen*

The **Kings Head Hotel** is a
charming village inn with
Cask Marque beers, good
food and spacious en suite
accommodation.

 see page 389

115 LAKELAND BIRD OF PREY CENTRE

Lowther, Nr Penrith

A sanctuary for birds of
prey set within the grounds
of Lowther Castle.

 see page 388

and presumably Viking settlers
brought their belief in Loki to
Kirkby Stephen.

LOWTHER

4 miles S of Penrith off the A6

Lowther is the estate village to
Lowther Castle, a once grand
place that is now only a shell. It
was clearly once grand, as after
one visit Queen Victoria is reputed
to have said that she would not
return as it was too grand for her.
The grounds include the
Lakeland Bird of Prey Centre,
whose aim is to conserve birds of
prey through education, breeding
and caring for injured or orphaned
birds before releasing them back
into the wild.

SHAP

10 miles S of Penrith on the A6

In the stage coaching era Shap was
an important staging post for the
coaches before they tackled the
daunting climb up **Shap Fell** to its
summit, some 850 feet above sea
level. Much earlier, in medieval
times, the village was even more
significant because of nearby Shap
Abbey, the last abbey to be
consecrated in England (about
1199) and the last to be dissolved,
in 1540. The nearby 16th century
Keld Chapel was built by the
monks of Shap Abbey.

GREYSTOKE

5 miles W of Penrith on the B5288

According to Edgar Rice
Burroughs, Greystoke Castle was
the ancestral home of Tarzan, Lord

of the Apes, a fiction that was
perpetuated in the dismal 1984 film
Greystoke. Greystoke village itself is
a gem, its attractive houses grouped
around a trimly maintained village
green. Nearby are the stables where
Gordon Richards trained his two
Grand National winners, *Lucius* and
Hello Dandy.

CARLISLE

Carlisle was a major Roman centre
that supported the military base
that guarded the western end of
Hadrian's Wall, and today the squat
outline of 12th century **Carlisle
Castle** dominates the skyline of
this fascinating city. After the Civil
War, Cromwell's troops took the
unusual step of rebuilding the
Castle rather than demolishing it.
Although one of the smallest in
England, **Carlisle Cathedral** has
many interesting features, including
an exquisite east window that is
considered to be one of the finest
in Europe. It was here that Edward
I excommunicated Robert the
Bruce, and the bells were rung to
welcome Bonnie Prince Charlie in
1745. The award-winning **Tullie
House Museum**, close to the
cathedral, tells the fascinating story
of the notorious Border Reivers,
who occupied the lands from the
14th to the 17th century, with a law
- or rather, a lack of it - unto
themselves. Their treacherous
deeds have also added such words
as 'bereave' and 'blackmail' to the
English language. The first railway
to Carlisle opened as early as 1836

and today it is still an important centre of communications. It is also the northern terminus of the famous Settle to Carlisle Railway line, which takes in some of the most dramatic scenery that the north of England has to offer.

Located on the northwestern edge of the city, **Kingmoor Nature Reserve** occupies an area of moorland given to the city in 1352 by Edward III. In 1913, Kingmoor became one of the first bird sanctuaries in England and today provides a peaceful retreat away from the bustle of the city.

AROUND CARLISLE

BEWCASTLE

14 miles NE of Carlisle off the B6318

Now occupied by the ruins of a Norman Castle, a Roman fort once stood here, guarding the crossing over Kirk Beck. A more impressive reminder of the past stands in the village churchyard – **Bewcastle Cross**, erected around AD 670 and one of the oldest and finest stone crosses in Europe.

BRAMPTON

8½ miles NE of Carlisle on the A6071

To the east of this delightful little town, nestling in the heart of Irthing Valley, is **Lanercost Priory**, founded in 1166 by Robert de Vaux. An impressive red sandstone ruin set in secluded woodland, the priory suffered greatly in the border raids of the 13th and 14th centuries, one of them led by William Wallace. When the priory closed in 1536

116 THE FOX & PHEASANT INN

Armathwaite, nr Carlisle

Standing at the foot of a forest close to the River Eden, the **Fox & Pheasant** is equally pleasant for a drink, a meal or a leisure break.

see page 390

Lanercost Priory, Brampton

117 THE GLASS HOUSE

Wigton

The **Glass House** is a friendly meeting place for daytime snacks; also evening meals with booking.

see page 390

much of its masonry was used for local houses.

South of Brampton are **Gelt Woods**, lying in a deep sandstone ravine carved by the fast-flowing River Gelt, and close by is **Talkin Tarn**, now the focus of a 120-acre country park, which has been a popular place for watersports for over 100 years.

GILSLAND

15 miles NE of Carlisle on the B6318

Located in one of the most picturesque settings along the whole length of **Hadrian's Wall** and overlooking the River Irthing, **Birdoswald Roman Fort** is one of the best preserved mile-castles along the wall. Set high on a plateau with magnificent views over the surrounding countryside, the early turf wall, built in AD 122, can be seen along with the fort, where all the components of the Roman frontier system can still be seen.

WIGTON

10½ miles SW of Carlisle off the A596

The pleasant market town of Wigton has, for centuries, been the centre of the business and social life of the Solway coast and plain, its prosperity being based on the weaving of cotton and linen. In the Market Place is the magnificent **Memorial Fountain** that was erected in 1872 by the philanthropist George Moore in memory of his wife.

SILLOTH

18½ miles W of Carlisle on the B5300

This charming old port and Victorian seaside resort has a two-mile-long promenade that provides wonderful views of the Solway Firth and the coast of Scotland. A popular attraction is the **Solway Coast Discovery Centre**, where Michael the Monk and Oyk the Oystercatcher guide visitors through 10,000 years of local history.

Derbyshire

Derbyshire was at the forefront of modern thinking at the beginning of the Industrial Revolution, and the chief inheritor of this legacy is the county town of Derby, the home of Rolls-Royce and Royal Crown Derby porcelain. An early landmark of this new age is Richard Arkwright's mill and the associated village at Cromford. Much of the county is dominated by the Peak District National Park, the first of the ten National Parks, whose landscape changes from deep limestone valleys to bleak, desolate moorland. Along with numerous attractive villages and small towns, ancient monuments and caves, the Park is home to two of the finest stately homes not just in Derbyshire but in the whole country – Haddon Hall and Chatsworth.

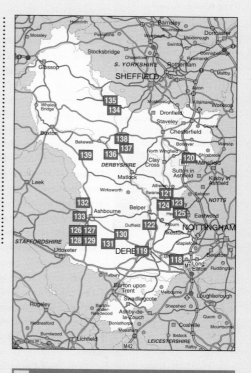

63

118 THE ROSE & CROWN

Draycott

The **Rose & Crown** is a cheerful family-run pub a short drive from Derby, serving good, freshly prepared and cooked food until 10pm Mon - Sat. Sunday carvery..

 see page 390

119 PICKFORD'S HOUSE MUSEUM

Derby

A Grade I listed building built in 1770 with a series of reconstructed rooms illustrating life in the early 19th century.

 see page 391

DERBY

This city is famously linked with two names: Rolls-Royce and Royal Crown Derby. When, in 1906, Sir Henry Royce and the Hon CS Rolls joined forces and built the first Rolls-Royce (a Silver Ghost) at Derby, they built much more than just a motor car. From the start they were considered by many to be the best cars in the world, and it was often said that the noisiest moving part in any Rolls-Royce was the dashboard clock! **Derby Industrial Museum** specialises in the history of railway engineering in the city, and also has a fine Rolls-Royce aircraft engine collection.

Guided tours round the **Royal Crown Derby** factory, museum and shop offer an intriguing insight into the high level of skill required to create the delicate flower petals, hand-gild the plates and hand-paint the superb porcelain that is instantly recognisable around the world.

The city's **Cathedral of All Saints** possesses a fine 16th century tower, the second highest Perpendicular tower in England. Its treasures include a beautiful wrought iron screen by Robert Bakewell and the tomb of Bess of Hardwick Hall - Elizabeth Talbot, Countess of Shrewsbury.

One of Derby's most interesting museums is **Pickford House**, situated on the city's finest Georgian street. Built in 1770 by the architect Joseph Pickford as a combined family home and place of work, the house offers an insight into the everyday lives of a middle-class family during the 1830s. Close by is the Industrial Museum in the beautiful old **Silk Mill**. Equally interesting is the **Derbyshire Constabulary Memorabilia Museum**, which has a display of uniforms and weapons from the 17th century to the present day.

Pride Park, the home of Derby County FC, was opened by Her Majesty The Queen in 1997.

AROUND DERBY

ILKESTON

8 miles NE of Derby on the A6007

The third largest town in Derbyshire, Ilkeston received its royal charter for a market and fair in 1252 and both have continued to the present day. Once a mining and lace-making centre, its history is told in the **Erewash Museum**.

OCKBROOK

4 miles E of Derby off the A52

In this quiet village, a **Moravian Settlement** was founded in the mid-18th century when a congregation of the Moravian Church was formed. The Settlement has several fine buildings, including The Manse, built in 1822, and the Moravian Chapel.

To the north are the ruins of Dale Abbey, founded by Augustinian monks in the 13th century. The **Church of All Saints**, at **Dale**, is surely the only church in England that shares its roof with a farm.

South of Ockbrook lies the **Elvaston Castle** estate, home of the Earls of Harrington. The magnificent Gothic castle seen today was finished in the early 19th century and stands in grounds that include Italian, parterre and old English gardens, tree-lined avenues and a large ornamental lake; the most impressive feature is the Golden Gates, erected in 1819 at the southern end of the gardens.

MELBOURNE

6½ miles S of Derby off the B587

Melbourne's most famous son is Thomas Cook, who pioneered personally conducted tours and gave his name to the famous worldwide travel company. The birthplace of the 19th century statesman Lord Melbourne, and also the home of Lady Caroline Lamb, **Melbourne Hall** is another fine building in this area of Derbyshire. The hall is surrounded by beautiful gardens, whose most notable feature is a wrought-iron birdcage pergola built in the early 1700s by Robert Bakewell.

To the south is the large Baroque mansion of **Calke Abbey** that has been dubbed the 'house that time forgot' as, since the death of the owner, Sir Vauncy Harpur-Crewe in 1924, nothing has been altered in the mansion!

REPTON

7 miles SW of Derby off the B5008

Repton, on the banks of the Trent, was established as the capital of the Saxon kingdom of Mercia in the 7th century, and a monastery founded. The parish **Church of St Wystan** is famous for its chancel and crypt, which claims to be one of the oldest intact Anglo-Saxon buildings in England.

Parts of a 12th century Augustinian priory are incorporated in the buildings of **Repton College**, founded in 1557. Two of its headmasters, Dr Temple and Dr Fisher, went on to become Archbishops of Canterbury. The gatehouse featured in the film *Goodbye, Mr Chips*.

MATLOCK

Essentially a Victorian town, Matlock nestles in the lower valley

St John's Road, Matlock

120 THE HARDWICK INN

Hardwick, nr Chesterfield

On the edge of the Hardwick Hall estate, the **Hardwick Inn** is an atmospheric setting for enjoying a drink and a meal.

 see page 392

121 THE STEAM PACKET

Swanwick, nr Alfreton

On a corner site on the B6179 in Swanwick, the **Steam Packet** attracts a loyal band with its excellent choice of real ales served all day, and food served lunchtime Thursday to Sunday.

 see page 391

122 THE HOLLYBUSH INN

Makeney

A wide choice of real ales and home-cooked lunches are the chief assets of the **Hollybush Inn**.

 see page 393

of the River Derwent and is the administrative centre of Derbyshire as well as being a busy tourist centre bordering the Peak District National Park. Matlock once had the steepest gradient tramway in the world: opened in 1893, the tramcars ran until 1927 and the Depot can still be seen at the top of Bank Street. **Peak Rail** is a rebuilt, refurbished and now preserved railway running between Matlock Riverside station to its other terminus Rowsley South.

High up on the hill behind the town is the brooding ruin of **Riber Castle**, built in the 1860s by John Smedley, a local hosiery manufacturer who became interested in the hydropathic qualities of Matlock. He constructed his own gas-producing plant to provide lighting for the lavishly decorated interior of the Castle.

To the south of Matlock lies **Matlock Bath**, which developed into a spa town and by the early 19th century had become a popular summer resort. Many buildings connected with its heyday as a spa can still be visited. Down by the riverbank is the **Peak District Mining Museum and Temple Mine** that tells the story of lead mining in the surrounding area from as far back as Roman times.

High Tor Grounds, some 400 feet above the town, offer spectacular views along with nature trails, and on the opposite side of the valley are the **Heights of Abraham Country Park and Caverns**, featuring steep rocky

gorges, vast caverns, fast-running rivers, woodland walks and refreshment areas. A cable car runs from Matlock railway station up to this unique attraction.

To the south of Matlock Bath is **Cromford**, the world famous 'model' village that was developed by Richard Arkwright into one of the first industrial towns. **Cromford Mill** and the associated buildings and attractions are now an International World Heritage Site.

The High Peak Trail, which stretches some 17 miles up towards Buxton, starts at Cromford and follows the trackbed of the Cromford and High Peak Railway.

AROUND MATLOCK

CHESTERFIELD

9 miles NE of Matlock on the A61

A friendly, bustling town on the edge of the Peak District National Park, Chesterfield grew up around a market that was established over 800 years ago. The town centre has been conserved for future generations by a far-sighted council, and many buildings have been saved, including the Victorian Market Hall built in 1857. There are also several Tudor buildings in the heart of Chesterfield, most notably the former Peacock Inn that is now home to the **Peacock Heritage Centre**. The town's most famous landmark is the **Crooked Spire** of St Mary & All Saints' Church – the magnificent spire rises to 228 feet and leans over 9 feet from its true centrepoint. The spire has eight sides, but the herringbone pattern of the lead slates tricks the eye into seeing 16 sides from the grounds.

BOLSOVER

12½ miles NE of Matlock on the A632

Above the town on a limestone ridge stands **Bolsover Castle**, a fairytale folly built for Sir Charles Cavendish during the early 1600s on the site of a ruined 12th century castle.

AULT HUCKNALL

11 miles NE of Matlock off the A617

Situated on a ridge close to the Nottinghamshire border, this village is home to the magnificent Tudor house, **Hardwick Hall**. Set in rolling parkland, the house, with its glittering tiers of windows and crowned turrets, has the letters ES carved in stone: ES, or Elizabeth of Shrewsbury, is perhaps better known as Bess of Hardwick, who married and survived four husbands. The formal gardens were laid out in the 19th century and the parkland, which overlooks the valley of the Doe Lea, is home to an impressive herd of Longhorn cattle and the ruins of **Hardwick Old Hall**.

CRICH

6 miles SE of Matlock off the A6

This large village, with its hilltop church and market cross, is the home of the **National Tramway Museum**, which provides a wonderful opportunity to enjoy a tram ride along a re-created Victorian street scene. To the east

stand the graceful ruins of the 15th century **Wingfield Manor** that held Mary, Queen of Scots prisoner under the care of the Earl of Shrewsbury on two separate occasions.

RIPLEY

8½ miles SE of Matlock on the A610

Once a typical small market town, Ripley expanded dramatically during the Industrial Revolution, and the town's Butterley Ironworks created the roof for London's St Pancras station. Close to the town is the **Midland Railway Centre** at Butterfield, with steam trains running along a line from Butterley to Riddings.

HEANOR

12 miles SE of Matlock on the A6007

This busy town is centred on its market place where the annual fair is held as well as the twice-weekly market. Away from the bustle of the market are the Memorial Gardens, while to the south is **Shipley Country Park**, on the estate of the now demolished Shipley Hall.

BELPER

8 miles SE of Matlock on the A517

In 1776, Jedediah Strutt set up one of the earliest water-powered cotton mills here, harnessing the natural power of the River Derwent to run his mills. With the river providing the power and fuel coming from the nearby South Derbyshire coalfield, the valley has a good claim to be one of the

127 CALLOW HALL COUNTRY HOUSE HOTEL & RESTAURANT

Ashbourne

The family-owned **Callow Hall Country House Hotel** offers outstanding comfort, style and service, fine food and superb accommodation in a lovely country setting.

 see page 395

128 THE GREEN MAN ROYAL HOTEL

Ashbourne

The **Green Man Royal Hotel** is a distinguished old coaching inn catering for today's visitors with well-kept ales, a wide choice of food and 18 en suite bedrooms.

 see page 394

129 TASTES RESTAURANT

Ashbourne

Fine cooking and an atmospheric cellar setting make **Tastes Restaurant** an excellent choice for a meal.

see page 395

130 THE ROSE & CROWN

Braisford, nr Ashbourne

Well-kept ales and traditional pub food are the main assets of the **Rose & Crown**, a roadside inn located between Ashbourne and Derby.

 see page 395

cradles of the Industrial Revolution. Belper's industrial heritage is explained at the **Derwent Valley Visitor Centre**.

ASHBOURNE

11 miles SW of Matlock on the A515

Originally a small settlement lying on the northern bank of Henmore Brook, Ashbourne boasts many fine examples of 18th century architecture as well as some older buildings, notably the **Gingerbread Shop** that probably dates from the 15th century. Traditional Ashbourne gingerbread is said to be made from a recipe that was acquired from French prisoners of war who were kept in the town during the Napoleonic Wars. Also worthy of a second glance is the **Green Man and Black's Head Royal Hotel**; the inn sign stretches over the St John's Street and was put up when the Blackamoor Inn joined with the Green Man in 1825.

Tissington Spires, near Ashbourne

Ashbourne was one of Dr Johnson's favourite places, and he visited the hotel so frequently that he even had his own seat – it's still there.

The area to the north is dominated by the conical hill of Thorpe Cloud, which guards the entrance to **Dovedale**. The steep sides to its valley, the fast-flowing water and the magnificent white rock formations all give Dovedale a special charm. The **Stepping Stones**, a delight for children, are the first point of interest, and further up the dale is the limestone crag known as **Dovedale Castle**.

BUXTON

At the heart of the Peak District and England's highest market town, Buxton is also a spa town, whose waters are maintained at a constant temperature of 82 degrees F (28 degrees C). **St Anne's Well** still provides water and many people coming to the town make a point of trying the pure, tepid liquid. Among the notable architectural features of the town are The Colonnade, The Crescent, The Devonshire Royal Hospital and the attractive Edwardian **Opera House** that was restored in 1979. Gertrude Lawrence, Gracie Fields and Hermione Gingold all performed here, and on one famous occasion in the 1930s Douglas Fairbanks and Mary Pickford were in the audience to watch the great Russian ballerina Anna Pavlova. **Buxton Museum and Art Gallery** has a fine collection of Ashford Marble and

Blue John ornaments, and visitors can explore the Wonders of the Peak through seven time zones. The ancient custom of well-dressing has been a part of Buxton's cultural calendar since the Duke of Devonshire provided the townsfolk with their first public water supply at Market Place Fountain. From then on, High Buxton Well and St Anne's Well were decorated sporadically, and in 1923, the Town Council set about organising a well-dressing festival and carnival that continues to this day. Every year on the second Wednesday in July, this delightful tradition is enacted.

To the west of the town lies **Axe Edge**, from where the panoramic views of Derbyshire are overwhelming; just beyond, at 1,690 feet above sea level, the Cat and Fiddle Inn is the second highest pub in England.

AROUND BUXTON

HAYFIELD

8½ miles N of Buxton on the A624

This small town below the exposed moorland of Kinder Scout, the highest point in the Peak District, is a popular centre for exploring the area and offers many amenities for hillwalkers. The town grew up around the textile industry, in this case wool weaving and calico printing, and many of the houses seen today were originally weavers' cottages.

Three miles northeast of the town is **Kinder Downfall**, the highest waterfall in the county,

131 THE RED LION INN

Hollington, nr Ashbourne

A string of awards testifies to the excellence of the cooking at the **Red Lion Inn**, which brings food-lovers from near and far to the village of Hollington.

see page 396

132 THE PEVERIL OF THE PEAK HOTEL

Thorpe, nr Ashbourne

Peace and tranquillity are bywords at the **Peveril of the Peak**, where guests can look forward to the very best in service and hospitality.

see page 397

133 THE ROYAL OAK HOTEL

Mayfield, nr Ashbourne

On the A52 near Ashbourne, the **Royal Oak** sets high standards as a free house, restaurant and hotel.

see page 398

134 THE PLOUGH INN

Hathersage

The **Plough Inn** is a family-run inn offering a warm and friendly welcome, real ales, good food and well-appointed guest accommodation.

 see page 399

135 THE LITTLE JOHN INN

Hathersage

The **Little John Inn** is a hostelry of great charm and character, catering for real ale enthusiasts and lovers of good food, and also offering a choice of guest accommodation.

 see page 398

where the River Kinder flows off the edge of Kinder Scout.

GLOSSOP

13 miles N of Buxton on the A624

At the foot of the Snake Pass, Glossop displays an interesting mix of styles, the industrial town of the 19th century with its towering Victorian mills contrasting with the 17th century village with its charming old cottages standing in the cobble streets. A little way north, at Hadfield, is the **Longdendale Trail**, which follows a former railway line and is part of the Trans-Pennine Trail.

PEAK FOREST

5 miles NE of Buxton off the A623

High on the White Peak plateau, Peak Forest takes its name from the fact that it once stood at the centre of the Royal Forest of the Peak. The **Peak Forest Canal**, completed in 1800, followed the valley of the River Goyt and had its terminal basin at Buxworth.

Within walking distance of Peak Forest is the renowned **Eldon Hole**, considered in legend to be the Devil's own entrance to Hell; thousands of pot-holers can testify to the inaccuracy of the legend that the pit is bottomless.

EDALE

8½ miles NE of Buxton off the A625

Edale marks the start of the **Pennine Way**, the long-distance footpath inaugurated in 1965 that follows the line of the backbone of Britain for some 270 miles to Kirk Yetholm, just over the Scottish

border. Not far from the village is the famous **Jacob's Ladder**, overlooking the river, and nearby are the tumbledown remains of a hill farmer's cottage, the home of Jacob Marshall, who cut the steps into the hillside leading up to Edale Cross.

CASTLETON

8 miles NE of Buxton on the A6187

Situated at the head of the Hope Valley, Castleton is overlooked by the Norman ruins of **Peveril Castle**, the only Norman castle in Derbyshire, and by Mam Tor; to the west, the road runs through the **Winnats Pass**, a narrow limestone gorge. The hills to the west of Castleton are famous for their caves and the **Blue John Mine and Caverns** are one of Derbyshire's most popular attractions. The huge vases and urns in the village's **Ollerenshaw Collection** are made of the unique Blue John fluorspar.

At the bottom of Winnats Pass lies **Speedwell Cavern**, a former lead mine that used boats on an underground canal to ferry the miners and iron ore to and from the rockface; they now ferry visitors. Peak Cavern, reached by a delightful riverside walk, has the widest opening of any cave in Europe.

EYAM

10 miles NE of Buxton off the B6521

This village, pronounced 'Eem', will forever be known as the **Plague Village**. In 1666, a tailor received a bundle of plague-infected clothing from London.

The infection soon spread and the terrified villagers prepared to flee, but the local rector, William Mompesson, persuaded the villagers to stay, and as a result most of the neighbouring villages escaped the disease. Eyam was quarantined for over a year, relying on outside help for supplies of food that were left on the village boundary. Only 83 villagers survived out of 350.

The home of the Wright family for over 300 years, **Eyam Hall** is a wonderful, unspoilt 17th century manor house that is also home to Eyam Hall Crafts Centre.

ASHFORD IN THE WATER
9 miles SE of Buxton off the A6

Developed around a ford that spanned the River Wye, this was once an important crossing place on the ancient Portway; the medieval **Sheepwash Bridge** is one of three bridges in the village and is a favourite with artists. So-called Black Marble, but actually a highly polished grey limestone, was mined nearby and, particularly during the Victorian era, it was fashionable to have decorative items and fire surrounds made from the stone. The founder of the marble works, Henry Watson, is remembered by a tablet in the great limestone **Church of the Holy Trinity**.

Ashford is perhaps most famous for its six beautifully executed well-dressings, which are held annually in early June. Rather than adhering strictly to the custom of depicting scenes from the Bible, the well-dressers of Ashford have pictured such unusual themes as a willow pattern to celebrate the Chinese Year of the Dog.

BAKEWELL
10½ miles SE of Buxton on the A6

The only true town in the Peak District National Park, Bakewell attracts many visitors, some to sample the confection that bears its name. One of the more famous guests at the Rutland Arms Hotel was Jane Austen, who stayed here in 1811; the town and the hotel feature in *Pride and Prejudice*.

Behind the large parish church is the lovely **Old House Museum**, housed in a building on Cunningham Place that dates back to 1534 and is thought to be the oldest house in Bakewell. The late 17th century Bath House is one of the few other buildings remaining from the days when Bakewell was a minor spa town.

136 HADDON HALL

nr Bakewell

A fine example of a fortified medieval manor house with a treasure trove of art works.

 see page 399

137 THE OLD SMITHY

Beeley

The **Old Smithy** is a delightful village food shop and licensed café specialising in local produce.

see page 399

River Wye, Bakewell

138 CHATSWORTH HOUSE

Bakewell

Home to the Dukes of Devonshire, Chatsworth is one of the finest stately homes in Britain.

 see page 400

139 THE OLD SMITHY TEA ROOMS & RESTAURANT

Monyash, nr Bakewell

A warm greeting and a hearty meal are keynotes of the **Old Smithy**, a friendly, popular Peak District daytime eating place.

 see page 400

Bakewell is perhaps best known as the home of the Bakewell Tart (referred to locally as a pudding). A mile to the south of Bakewell stands romantic **Haddon Hall**, thought by many to have been the first fortified house in the country, though the turrets and battlements were put on purely for show. The home of the Dukes of Rutland for over 800 years, the hall has enjoyed a fairly peaceful existence, in part no doubt because it stood empty and neglected for nearly 300 years after 1640, when the family chose Belvoir Castle in Leicestershire as their main home. The 16th century terraced gardens are one of the chief delights and Haddon's splendour and charm have led it to be used as a backdrop to numerous television and film productions including *Jane Eyre*, *Moll Flanders* and *The Prince and the Pauper*.

The gritstone landscape of **Stanton Moor**, which rises to some 1,096 feet, lies to the south of Haddon and a Bronze Age stone circle on the moor is known as the Nine Ladies. Legend has it that one Sunday nine women and a fiddler came up onto the moor to dance and, for their act of sacrilege, they were turned to stone. Also in the area is the site of an Iron Age hillfort known as **Castle Ring**.

Northeast of Bakewell, near Edensor, lies the home of the Dukes of Devonshire, **Chatsworth House**, one of the finest of the great houses of Britain. The origins of the house as a great showpiece must be attributable to the redoubtable Bess of Hardwick, one of whose husbands, Sir William Cavendish, bought the estate in 1549. Over the years, the Cavendish fortunes have continued to pour into Chatsworth, making it an almost unparalleled showcase for art treasures. The gardens of this stately home, which used the talents of Capability Brown and Joseph Paxton, also have some marvellous features, including the Emperor Fountain that dominates the Canal Pond.

ARBOR LOW
9 miles SE of Buxton off the A515

This remote Bronze Age stone circle is often referred to as the Stonehenge of the Peaks, and although many of the stones now lie on the ground it is still an impressive sight. There are several stone circles in the Peak District but none offer the same atmosphere as Arbor Low, nor the same splendid views.

LYME PARK
8 miles NE of Buxton off the A6

The ancient estate of Lyme Park was given to Sir Thomas Danyers in 1346 by a grateful King Edward III after a battle at Caen. Danyers then passed the estate to his son-in-law, Sir Piers Legh, and it remained in the family until 1946. Famous for its fantastic Palladian mansion, the work of Venetian architect Giacomo Leoni, the estate includes a late 19th century formal garden and a medieval deer park.

Devon

Known for its enchanting scenery, maritime history and bleak expanse of moorland, Devon, England's third largest county, has plenty to offer the visitor. To the southeast are the old textile towns, including Axminster that lent its name to the most luxurious of carpets, and Honiton, still famed for its lace. Here, too, lies the cathedral city of Exeter, the county capital, which has its roots firmly in Roman times. The south coast is littered with attractive and genteel seaside resorts that are particularly highly regarded for their mild climate while, in the west, is Plymouth, where Sir Francis Drake famously insisted on finishing his game of bowls before leaving to intercept the Spanish Armada. The middle of the county is dominated by Dartmoor National Park, home to the famous prison and a wealth of ancient monuments. Lastly, there is north Devon, with its spectacular coastline while, just inland, is Tarka country, the area of Devon that was made famous by Henry Williamson in his popular novel.

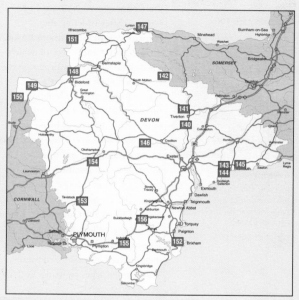

140 THE FISHERMAN'S COTTAGE

Bickleigh, nr Tiverton

The **Fisherman's Cottage** offers comfortable accommodation and a wide range of food and drink in a pleasant setting by the River Exe.

see page 400

141 THE ROSE & CROWN

Calverleigh

Just two miles from Tiverton, this picturesque inn offers a range of real ales and freshly cooked food.

see page 401

EXETER

First settled by the Romans, whose spectacular **Roman Bath House**, or Caldarium, was uncovered in the Cathedral Close in the 1970s, it was in the late 11th century that William the Conqueror took control of Exeter. After ordering the construction of Rougemont Castle, the gatehouse and tower of which can still be seen, work began on the construction of **St Peter's Cathedral**, a massive building project that was not completed until 1206. As well as being an ecclesiastical centre, Exeter was also an important port and this is reflected in its dignified 17th century Custom House that now forms the centrepiece of the **Exeter Historic Quayside**. There are some excellent museums in Exeter, and other attractions include the University Sculpture Walk, which takes in works by Barbara Hepworth and Henry Moore, and guided tours through **Exeter's Underground Passages**.

To the northeast is the large estate of **Killerton**, which is centred on a grand 18th century mansion set in parkland that contains the Dolbury Iron Age hill fort and the 15th century Marker's Cottage.

AROUND EXETER

CADBURY

8 miles N of Exeter off the A3072

Cadbury Castle is an Iron Age hill fort that claims to have the most extensive views in Devon. To the northeast lies **Bickleigh**, a charming place of thatched cottages, which is home to **Bickleigh Mill**, now a craft centre, and, Bickleigh Castle, a moated and fortified late 14th century manor house.

TIVERTON

13 miles N of Exeter on the A396

A strategic point on the River Exe, in 1106, Henry I ordered the building of **Tiverton Castle**, around which the town began to develop. The castle was later destroyed on Cromwell's orders though the remains are substantial. A few miles north of Tiverton, up the Exe Valley, is **Knightshayes Court**, a striking house that was the home of the Heathcoat-Amory family.

OTTERY ST MARY

12 miles NE of Exeter on the B3177

This small town is justly proud of its magnificent 14th century **Church of St Mary**. The vicar here during the mid 18th century was John

Knightshayes Court, near Tiverton

Coleridge, whose tenth child, Samuel Taylor, born in 1772, went on to become a celebrated poet.

A mile to the northwest of the town is **Cadhay**, a beautiful manor house that was built in 1550, while close by is **Escot Park and Gardens**, where visitors can see an arboretum and rose garden along with a collection of wildlife.

HONITON
16 miles NE of Exeter on the A30

Once a major stopping place on the great Roman road, Fosse Way, Honiton is best known for the lace that is still sought today. First introduced to east Devon by Flemish immigrants during the reign of Elizabeth I, the lace is still made here and can be bought from local shops and also seen in **Allhallows Museum**.

AXMINSTER
24 miles NE of Exeter on the A358

This ancient town on the River Axe is famous for the carpets that bear the town's name. The creation of just one carpet took so much time that each one's completion was celebrated by a procession to St Mary's Church – which naturally has its own Axminster carpet. Carpets are still manufactured here and the factory welcomes visitors, while the **Axminster Museum** dedicates some of its exhibition space to the industry.

SEATON
20 miles E of Exeter on the B3174

Once a significant port, Seaton expanded during the Victorian era as wealthy families, looking for sea air, came here and built their villas. The railway line that brought many of the Victorians here has been replaced by the **Seaton Tramway**, which links the resort with the ancient town of Colyton, three miles inland. From Seaton, the **South West Coast Path** follows the coastline eastwards to Lyme Regis in Dorset. Considered by naturalists as the last and largest wilderness on the southern coast of England, this area of unstable cliffs, wood and scrub is a haven for wildlife.

To the west of Seaton is the picturesque old fishing village of **Beer**, best known for the superb white freestone that can be seen in churches all over Devon as well as in the Tower of London and Westminster Abbey.

SIDMOUTH
13 miles E of Exeter off the A3052

It was here that the future Queen Victoria saw the sea for the first time, brought here by her proud, penniless father, the Duke of Kent. Some 50 years later, Queen Victoria presented a stained glass window to Sidmouth parish church in memory of her father.

Sidmouth Museum provides a very vivid presentation of the Victorian resort along with an interesting collection of local prints, a costume gallery and a display of lace. In 1912, Sir Joseph Lockyer founded the **Norman Lockyer Observatory** for astronomical and meteorological research.

75

145 THE DONKEY
SANCTUARY

Sidmouth

Sidmouth's **Donkey
Sanctuary**, just one of many
sanctuaries and projects
around the world, is home to
over 400 donkeys, all of
them pleased to see visitors
every day of the year.

 see page 402

Sedate Sidmouth undergoes a transformation in the first week of August each year when it plays host to the International Folklore, Dance and Song Festival.

BUDLEIGH SALTERTON

11½ miles SE of Exeter on the B3178

A famous Victorian visitor to Budleigh was the celebrated artist Sir John Everett Millais, who stayed here during the summer of 1870 in a curiously shaped house that is known as **The Octagon**. On the seafront is **Fairlynch Museum**, one of the very few thatched museums in the country.

Just to the north lies **Hayes Barton**, a wonderful E-shaped Tudor house that was the birthplace of Sir Walter Raleigh. On the banks of the River Otter stands Otterton Mill, a part medieval building, and **Bicton Park Botanical Gardens** that were laid out in the 18th century.

EXMOUTH

9 miles SE of Exeter on the A376

Situated at the mouth of the River Exe, this small fishing village was one of the first seaside resorts in Devon and was dubbed the 'Bath of the West'. On the northern outskirts of the town is one of the most unusual houses in Britain – **A La Ronde** – a unique 16-sided house that was built in the late 18th century on the instructions of two spinster cousins who were inspired by the basilica of the San Vitale at Ravenna. On the opposite bank of the river stands **Powderham**

Castle, the home of the Earls of Devon, surrounded by one of the finest parks in the county.

BARNSTAPLE

One of the most attractive buildings here is **Queen Anne's Walk**, a colonnaded arcade that has a statue of Queen Anne on top of its central doorway. Opened in 1708, it was used by the Barnstaple wool merchants who accepted that any verbal bargain they made over the Tome Stone would be legally binding.

Barnstaple is also the northern terminus of the **Tarka Line**, a wonderfully scenic 39-mile route that follows the gentle valleys of the Rivers Yeo and Taw, where Tarka the Otter had his home. Walkers, too, can discover the countryside that inspired the novel by taking the **Tarka Trail**, an unusual figure-of-eight long-distance footpath of some 180 miles that crosses over itself at Barnstaple.

AROUND BARNSTAPLE

MUDDIFORD

3½ miles N of Barnstaple on the B3230

Just to the southwest of this pretty village are **Marwood Hill Gardens** with their collections of rare and unusual trees and shrubs, while to the northeast lies **Arlington Court**, the family home of the Chichesters from 1534 until the last owner, Miss Rosalie Chichester, died in

1949. The nearby village of **Shirwell** was birthplace of the yachtsman Sir Francis Chichester, whose father was the vicar. Sir Francis died in Plymouth after being taken ill on his fourth transatlantic race; he is buried in the churchyard of St Peter, Shirwell.

COMBE MARTIN

9 miles N of Barnstaple on the A399

A popular seaside resort, with an exceptionally long main street. The village is home to a remarkable architectural curiosity, the 18th century **The Pack o' Cards Inn**, which represents a pack of cards with four decks, or floors, 13 rooms and 52 windows.

LYNMOUTH

14 miles NE of Barnstaple on the A39

This pleasant village has benefited from two great enthusiasms, romantic scenery and sea bathing, and both Coleridge and Wordsworth came here on a walking tour in the 1790s, while Shelley visited in 1812. To aid the growing tourist trade the **Lynton-Lynmouth Cliff Railway** opened in 1890, linking the town with its neighbour **Lynton**, a place of chiefly Victorian architecture. To the west lies the **Valley of the Rock** that RD Blackmore transforms into the Devil's Cheesewring in his novel *Lorna Doone*. To the southwest is one of Exmoor's most spectacular wooded valleys, **Heddon Valley**.

CREDITON

26 miles SE of Barnstaple on the A377

This sleepy market town was, in AD 680, the birthplace of Wynfrith, who went on to become one of only a few Britons to become saints - he adopted the name Boniface. It was nearly 1,200 years before the people of Crediton gave their saint any form of recognition when in 1897 an east window was installed in the town's cathedral-like **Church of the Holy Cross** that depicts scenes from his life.

GREAT TORRINGTON

10 miles SW of Barnstaple on the A386

This hilltop town has several thriving industries, including **Dartington Crystal**, where visitors can see skilled craftsmen blowing and shaping the molten glass.

Just to the south of Great Torrington and occupying a breathtaking location in the Torridge Valley is the Royal Horticultural Society's **Rosemoor**, a wonderful place that includes mature planting in Lady Anne Palmer's magnificent garden and arboretum.

BIDEFORD

8 miles SW of Barnstaple on the A386

This was once Britain's third busiest port, and evidence of this golden age can still be seen around the town in the various opulent merchants' houses that have survived. It was while staying here that Charles Kingsley wrote

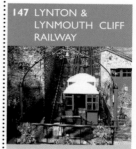
77

148 THE QUAY

Appledore

Prime Devon produce is the basis for the food served at **The Quay**, while the gallery showcases the work of local artists.

 see page 403

149 METTAFORD FARM HOLIDAY COTTAGES

Hartland

Mettaford Farm Holiday Cottages comprise eight barn conversions sleeping from 2 to 6 guests in a beautiful, tranquil setting between Clovelly and Hartland Point.

 see page 404

150 MEAD BARN COTTAGES

Welcombe, nr Bideford

Meadow Barn Cottages provide a superb year-round self-catering base in a picturesque setting near the coast.

see page 404

Westward Ho!, the swashbuckling Elizabethan story that is based around the town.

To the north, on the east bank of the River Torridge, are **Tapeley Park Gardens** – some 20 acres of gardens that have been divided into four distinctly different themed areas. Overlooking Bideford Bay is **Westward Ho!**, which developed into a resort following interest shown in Charles Kingsley's novel. **Appledore**, three miles north of Bideford, is a delightful old fishing village of narrow winding lanes and sturdy 18th and 19th century fishermen's cottages overlooking the Taw-Torridge estuary.

CLOVELLY

17 miles SW of Barnstaple on the B3237

This unbelievably quaint village, which tumbles down a steep hillside in terraced levels, is many people's idea of the typical Devonshire coastal village. Charles Kingsley lived and attended school here in the 1820s and the **Kingsley Exhibition** explores the novelist's links with the village, while the neighbouring **Fisherman's Cottage** provides an insight into what life was like in Clovelly at that time.

To the west lie **Hartland Point**, from where there are breathtaking views, **Hartland Abbey**, which houses a unique

Hartland Point

exhibition of documents that date back to 1160, and **Hartland Quay**, where a museum records the many shipwrecks that have littered this jagged coastline.

HOLSWORTHY

26 miles SW of Barnstaple on the A388

This old market town lies just four miles from the Cornish border, serving a large area of rural Devon. Each Wednesday, it comes alive with its traditional street market, and in July the town plays host to the three-day long **St Peter's Fair**, an ancient event first held here in 1185. Holsworthy's most striking architectural features are the two Victorian viaducts that once carried the railway line through to Bude. Situated high above the southern outskirts of the town, they now form part of a footpath along the old track bed and it is possible to walk across them. Housed in an 18th century parsonage, the volunteer-run **Holsworthy Museum** gives visitors an insight into local history and traditions by various themed displays.

BRAUNTON

4¼ miles NW of Barnstaple on the A361

Claiming to be the largest village in Devon, Braunton is home to one of the few remaining examples of a Saxon open field strip system that is still actively farmed, while in the dunes is the **Braunton Burrows** nature reserve. Just to the northwest lies **Croyde**, renowned for its family-friendly beach, and close by, at **Georgeham**, is the house which Henry Williamson

built and lived in after World War I, and where he wrote his famous novel, *Tarka the Otter*.

ILFRACOMBE

9½ miles NW of Barnstaple on the A361

Ilfracombe developed in direct response to the early 19th century craze for sea bathing and seawater therapies and the **Tunnel Baths** were opened in 1836, by which time a number of elegant residential terraces had been built on the hillside to the south of the old town.

TOTNES

Claiming to be the second oldest borough in England, Totnes, according to local legend, is said to have been founded by a Trojan named Brutus in around 1200 BC; the **Brutus Stone**, in the pavement of the town's main shopping street, commemorates this event. The first recorded evidence of the settlement was in the mid 10th century, when King Edgar established a mint here. There was already a Saxon castle here but the remains of **Totnes Castle** are of a once imposing Norman fortification.

Totnes Museum, housed in an Elizabethan building, remembers the town's most famous son, Charles Babbage.

AROUND TOTNES

NEWTON ABBOT

7 miles NE of Totnes on the A381

It was here in 1688, that William, Prince of Orange, was proclaimed King William III and, while here,

151 THE CHICHESTER ARMS

Mortehoe, nr Woolacombe

The **Chichester Arms** is a convivial 16th century inn serving well-kept ales and good-value home cooking.

see page 404

152 THE SMUGGLERS
HAUNT HOTEL

Brixham

The **Smugglers Haunt
Hotel** is an equally delightful
spot for a meal or an
overnight or longer stay to
explore the Devon coast and
countryside.

see page 404

he stayed at the Jacobean manor
house, **Ford House**, which had
played host to Charles I in 1625.
The whole character of this
attractive town changed in the
1850s when the Great Western
Railway made it their centre of
locomotive and carriage repair
works; it was also the junction for
the Moretonhampstead and Torbay
branch lines.

DAWLISH

14 miles NE of Totnes on the A379

From its earliest days as a seaside
resort, Dawlish has attracted many
distinguished visitors, including
Jane Austen, John Keats and
Charles Dickens, who in his novel
of the same name had Nicholas
Nickleby born near the town. To
the northeast of the town is
Dawlish Warren, a nature reserve
that is home to many species of
flowering plant, including the rare
Jersey Lily.

TEIGNMOUTH

12 miles NE of Totnes on the A379

There are two distinct sides to this
town – the popular holiday resort
with its fine Regency residences
and the working port on the
northern bank of the River Teign.

Just north of the town lies the
Shaldon Wildlife Trust breeding
centre for rare small mammals,
reptiles and exotic birds.

TORQUAY

8 miles NE of Totnes on the A379

A genteel and elegant resort that
has become known as 'The English

Naples', Torquay, which grew up
around **Torre Abbey** that was
founded in 1195, was the
birthplace, in 1890, of Agatha
Christie. It was here that she began
writing her crime novels while her
second husband was away on active
service during World War I. One
of the town's most popular
attractions is the **Agatha Christie
Memorial Room** in the Abbot's
Tower. Just inland lies **Compton
Castle**, a wonderful fortified manor
house built between the 14th and
16th centuries.

PAIGNTON

5 miles E of Totnes on the A379

The development of Torquay saw
neighbouring Paignton soon
become a resort, complete with
pier and promenade, that still
appeals to families today. Among
the main attractions are **Paignton
Zoo** and the **Paignton and
Dartmouth Steam Railway** that
follows the coastline along the
bottom of Tor Bay before
travelling through woodland to
Kingswear. Here passengers alight
and catch a ferry to Dartmouth.
Just to the south, at **Galmpton**,
lies **Greenway**, the house to
which Dame Agatha Christie
moved for the last 30 years of her
life.

DARTMOUTH

7 miles SE of Totnes on the A379

One of England's principal ports
for centuries, the town also has a
long connection with the Royal
Navy, the oldest of the British

services. Guarded by **Dartmouth Castle**, built by Edward IV after the War of the Roses, Dartmouth's harbour is home to the handsome 18th century **Custom House**, while its most famous building is the **Britannia Royal Naval College**.

On the opposite bank of the Dart estuary are the impressive remains of **Kingswear Castle** that is a twin to Dartmouth's fortification. A huge chain was strung between the two castles when there was thought to be an added threat of invasion.

Dart Estuary, View To Kingsbridge

SALCOMBE

14 miles SW of Totnes on the A381

Standing at the mouth of the Kingsbridge estuary, this delightful town enjoys one of the most beautiful natural settings in the country. The harbour throngs with pleasure craft, and its old Customs House is home to the **Salcombe Maritime and Local History Museum**.

To the south of the town lies **Overbecks**, a charming house that was built in 1913 and was the home of research chemist Otto Overbeck from 1918 to 1937. The house holds Overbeck's wide-ranging collection, including late 19th century photographs of the area, local shipbuilding tools, model boats, toys and much more. The beautiful, sheltered garden, with views out over Salcombe estuary, is planted with many rare trees, shrubs and plants, giving it a Mediterranean feel.

KINGSBRIDGE

11 miles SW of Totnes on the A381

At the head of the Kingsbridge estuary, this pretty town is a place of narrow alleys that has retained its Elizabethan market arcade, The Shambles, while its rather modest Victorian town hall has an unusual onion-shaped clock tower that adds a touch of glamour to the building.

For anyone looking to learn more about this area of Devon a visit to the **Cookworthy Museum of Rural Life** is a must. Just offshore and reached by a causeway from **Bigbury on Sea** is **Burgh Island**, which is an island only at high tide. When the tide recedes, it can be reached by walking across the sandbank or by taking an exciting ride on the Sea Tractor. The whole of this 28-acre island, complete with its 14th century Pilchard Inn, was bought in 1929 by the eccentric millionaire Archibald

81

153 MORWELLHAM QUAY

Nr Tavistock

This award-winning museum is based around the historic port and mine workings of the River Tamar.

 see page 405

154 THE PREWLEY MOOR ARMS

Sourton Down, nr Okehampton

The atmosphere is always bubbly at the **Prewley Moor Arms**, a great place to socialise, to enjoy good food or to stay in the comfortable en suite guest accommodation.

 see page 405

155 THE ANCHOR INN

Ugborough, nr Ivybridge

In a delightful South Hams village setting, the **Anchor** is equally delightful for a drink, a meal or an overnight stay.

 see page 406

Nettlefold, who built a hotel here in extravagant Art Deco style.

TAVISTOCK

This handsome old market town grew up around the 10th century Abbey and flourished following the discovery of tin on the nearby moors. The town seen today is essentially the creation of the Dukes of Bedford, who acquired the Abbey at the time of the Dissolution and remained there until 1911. While little remains of the Abbey, one of its legacies is the annual **Goose Fair**, a marvellous traditional street fair held in October. Tavistock was also permitted to hold a weekly market that, 900 years later, still takes place every Friday in the **Pannier Market**, one of the finest market buildings in the southwest.

Also on the western side of Tavistock can be found the **Tavistock-Morwellham Canal**, which was built in the early 19th century as the town and surrounding area were experiencing a copper boom. Today, **Morwellham Quay**, just south of the town, has been restored to re-create the busy atmosphere of the 1850s, when half the world's copper came through this tiny hamlet.

AROUND TAVISTOCK

LYDFORD

7½ miles NE of Tavistock off the A386

A royal borough in Saxon times, Lydford's former importance is

reflected in its austere stone fortress **Lydford Castle**. To the southwest of the village, the valley of the River Lyd suddenly narrows to form the mile and a half long **Lydford Gorge**, one of Dartmoor's most spectacular natural features. A circular walk around the gorge begins high up before passing through the enchanting riverside scenes, including the thrilling **Devil's Cauldron**. Further south again is **Brent Tor**, a 1,100 feet volcanic plug that is one of the most striking sights in the whole of Dartmoor. The **Church of St Michael of the Rocks** stands on the top of it. The fourth smallest complete church in England, St Michael's is only 15 feet wide and 37 feet long and has walls only 10 feet high but three feet thick.

OKEHAMPTON

15 miles NE of Tavistock on the B3260

The town occupies a strategic position on the main route to Cornwall, and situated on the top of a wooded hill are the remains of **Okehampton Castle**, the largest medieval castle in Devon. Housed in an ancient mill is the **Museum of Dartmoor Life** while, in the surrounding courtyard, is the **Dartmoor National Park Visitor Centre**. To the south of Okehampton are Dartmoor's greatest peaks, **High Willhays** and **Yes Tor**, which rise to over 2,000 feet.

CHAGFORD

17 miles NE of Tavistock on the B3192

An ancient settlement that was one

of Devon's four stannary towns, Chagford today is noted for the numerous ancient monuments that litter the surrounding countryside. Close by, near the pretty village of **Drewsteignton**, are two Iron Age hill forts along with the rather more modern **Castle Drogo**, designed by Sir Edwin Lutyens and built between 1910 and 1930.

PRINCETOWN

6½ miles E of Tavistock on the B3212

Situated at the heart of Dartmoor, some 1,400 feet above sea level, Princetown is the location of one of the country's best-known and most forbidding prisons – **Dartmoor Prison**, which first opened in 1809. Princetown is also home to the National Park's **Moorland Visitor Centre** that contains some excellent and informative displays about the moor. To the west lies **Widecombe in the Moor**, home to a grand old church that has been dubbed the **Cathedral of the Moors** and to a famous September fair. To the north of the village is **Grimspound**, the most impressive of all Dartmoor's Bronze Age relics, which featured in *The Hound of the Baskervilles*.

BOVEY TRACEY

21 miles E of Tavistock on the B3344

To the north of this small town lies **Parke**, the former estate of the de Tracey family and now the headquarters of Dartmoor National Park; the present house dates from the 1820s and the grounds are home to a **Rare Breeds Farm**.

Widecombe in the Moor

To the east of Bovey Tracey lies **Ugbrooke House and Park** that was built in the mid 18th century for the Clifford family and is still their home today. To the northwest is one of Dartmoor's most popular villages, **Lustleigh**, from where there are delightful walks, and **Becky Falls Woodland Park**.

BUCKFASTLEIGH

17 miles SE of Tavistock on the B3380

A former wool town on the banks of the River Mardle, Buckfastleigh is the western terminus and headquarters of the South Devon Railway, whose steam trains continue to make the seven-mile journey through the valley of the River Dart to Totnes. Another popular attraction close to the town

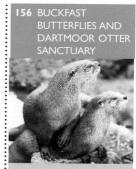

156 BUCKFAST BUTTERFLIES AND DARTMOOR OTTER SANCTUARY

Buckfastleigh

Butterflies from around the world can be seen in a tropical garden, whilst another specially landscpaed garden forms the otter sanctuary.

 see page 406

is the **Buckfast Butterflies and Dartmoor Otters**, where the exotic butterflies can be seen in a specially designed tropical rain forest environment; the three species of otter include the native British otter.

BUCKLAND MONACHORUM

4 miles S of Tavistock off the A386

Tucked away in a secluded valley above the River Tavy, 13th century **Buckland Abbey** was the last home of Sir Francis Drake, who purchased it from his rival, Sir Richard Grenville.

PLYMOUTH

11½ miles S of Tavistock on the A386

The most famous part of this historic city is undoubtedly **Plymouth Hoe**, the park and promenade overlooking **Plymouth Sound** where Sir Francis Drake was playing bowls when he was told of the approaching Spanish Armada. Just offshore, in the waters of the mouth of the River Tamar, lies **Drake's Island**, an English Alcatraz that was, in medieval times, known as St Nicholas' Island. 12 miles out in the English Channel lies the famous **Eddystone Lighthouse**.

Plymouth's oldest quarter, the **Barbican**, is today a lively area of restaurants, pubs and an innovative small theatre, while close by is **The Citadel**, a massive fortress that was built by Charles II as a defence against a seaborne invasion. Near here is a reminder that Plymouth was the departure point for the Pilgrim Fathers; the **Mayflower Stone** stands at the point where they boarded their ship.

Five miles east of Plymouth, **Plympton** is home to **Saltram House and Park**, a prestigious 18th century mansion surrounded by a large estate near the tidal creek of the Plym estuary. The **Plym Valley Railway** runs from Marsh Mills, Plympton, to the local beauty spot of Plym Bridge.

Dorset

Although Dorset is not a large county, it provides an extraordinary variety of attractions. There are the dramatic cliffs of the western coastline and the more gentle harbours and bays to the east, while inland, chalk upland and heathland supports a wealth of bird and plant life. Over the years, many of the little ports have become seaside resorts of which the most famous is Lyme Regis, with its fossils and The Cobb, but the wonderful, natural harbour of Poole continues to be a commercial port. Inland are charming, ancient market towns, many of which have their roots in Roman times and, along with the Georgian elegance of Blandford Forum, there is historic

Dorchester, one of the country's most appealing towns. It was close to the county town that Thomas Hardy was born and many of the towns and villages of the county have featured in the great writer's novels.

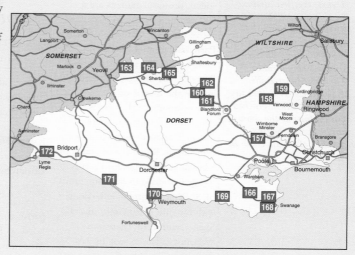

BOURNEMOUTH

Along the coast to the east of Christchurch lies the village of Mudeford, and on Hengistbury Head are the ancient ditches called the Double Dykes, an area well known for its superb walking and wonderful views. Near Double Dykes, the first airshow in Britain was staged in 1910, attracting highflyers such as Wilbur Wright, Louis Blériot and the Honourable Charles Stuart Rolls. Rolls, the first Briton to fly the Channel, crashed his biplane at the show and became the first fatality of an air crash in Britain.

At the end of the 18th century, Bournemouth hardly existed, but once the virtues of its fresh sea air were advertised it began to expand as a resort. It continued to expand during the Victorian age; the splendid pier was built in 1855 and again in 1880 when a theatre was added. Beautiful gardens are a feature of this civilised place, and above the Cliff Gardens is **Shelley Park**, named after Sir Percy Florence Shelley, son of the poet Percy Bysshe Shelley, and sometime lord of the manor of Bournemouth. Shelley House is devoted to the life and works of the poet. Shelley's ashes lie in a cemetery in Rome (he drowned off a beach in Italy), but his heart is reputedly buried in the churchyard of St Peter, Bournemouth, along with his wife Mary Wollstonecraft Shelley, author of *Frankenstein*. William Gladstone took his last communion in this church, which is notable for its brilliant Gothic

Revival interior and some Pre-Raphaelite stained glass. Among the many other places to visit are the Rothesay Museum, mainly nautical but with a collection of 300 vintage typewriters; the Teddy Bear Museum; and the Aviation Museum at Bournemouth International Airport.

AROUND BOURNEMOUTH

CHRISTCHURCH

5 miles E of Bournemouth on the A35

Situated at the junction of the Rivers Avon and Stour, Christchurch began life as a Saxon village and it was here that, in 1094, Ranulf Flambard began the construction of the magnificent **Christchurch Priory** that has ever since been used as a place of worship. Said to be the longest parish church in England, it is home to **St Michael's Loft Museum**. Christchurch is also home to the most modern of all the country's Scheduled Ancient Monuments – a World War II pillbox and anti-tank obstacles.

SANDBANKS

3½ miles SW of Bournemouth on the B3369

This spit of land, along with Studland to the southwest, almost cuts off Poole harbour from the sea, and it is these two headlands that provide the harbour with its shelter. At the top of the headland lies **Compton Acres**, a series of themed gardens that are separated by paths, steps, rock walls and terraces.

View to Christchurch Priory

POOLE

4 miles W of Bournemouth on the A350

Once the largest settlement in Dorset, Poole has a huge natural harbour and a history that goes back to Roman times. The **Waterfront Museum**, housed in an 18th century warehouse and the adjoining medieval town cellars, tells the 2,000-year story of the port. **Poole Pottery** made the famous red tiles for London Underground's stations and was the HQ of the US Navy during the Second World War.

Out in the harbour are several islands, the largest of which is **Brownsea Island**, where the heath and woodland are home to a wide variety of wildlife and where the Scout movement was born in 1907.

Just to the north of Poole lies **Upton Country Park**, a large estate of parkland, gardens and meadows that surround a handsome early 19th century manor house.

WIMBORNE MINSTER

7 miles NW of Bournemouth on the A31

A wonderful old market town, Wimborne Minster is dominated by its **Minster**, a glorious Norman building that is the best example of its kind in the county. Close by the minster is the Priest's House, a 16th century town house that is now home to the **Museum of East Dorset Life**.

Around Wimborne there are several places of interest: to the east, at **Hampreston**, is **Knoll's**

Garden and Nursery, a delightful, informal and typically English garden that was planted over 30 years ago, while further east again, is **Stapehill**, a 19th century Cistercian nunnery that is now a craft centre and countryside museum.

To the west of Wimborne lies **Kingston Lacy House**, a superb country house containing an outstanding collection of paintings that is set in attractive parkland. Elsewhere on the estate there is the Iron Age hill fort of **Badbury Rings** and 18th century **White Mill**.

BLANDFORD FORUM

An attractive market town in the Stour valley, the handsome Georgian buildings here were, mostly, designed by two talented architects, the brothers John and William Bastard, who were charged with rebuilding much of the town after a devastating fire in 1731. To mark the completion of the town's rebuilding in 1760, the **Fire Monument** was erected in front of the church and had a dual purpose – to provide water for fire fighting and for the public to drink.

To the northeast of the town lies Blandford Camp and the **Royal Signals Museum**, where there is a wealth of interactive displays on codes and code breakers, animals at war and the SAS.

157 THE COVENTRY ARMS

Corfe Mullen, nr Wimborne

The **Coventry Arms** is a superb old pub with a large following for its top-quality food.

🍴 *see page 407*

158 THE DROVERS INN

Gussage All Saints, nr Wimborne

The Drovers is a delightful old-world pub serving well-kept beers and a good variety of home-cooked food.

🍴 *see page 407*

159 FLEUR-DE-LYS

Cranborne

The **Fleur-de-Lys** is a handsome old pub in a pretty location. Produce comes from the Cranborne Estate, and the pub has 5 rooms for B&B guests.

🍴 *see page 408*

SHERBORNE

*16½ miles NW of Blandford Forum
on the A352*

In AD 705, St Aldhelm founded
Sherborne Abbey as the Mother
Cathedral for the whole of the
southwest of England and the
building that now occupies the site
features some of the finest fan
vaults in the whole country. Some
of the old buildings now house
Sherborne School, whose alumni
include Cecil Day Lewis, the poet
laureate, and the writer David
Cornwell, better known as John Le
Carré. The school has been used
as the setting for at least three
major films: *The Guinea Pig* (1948),
Goodbye, Mr Chips (1969) and *The
Browning Version* (1994).

Sherborne's best-known
resident was Sir Walter Raleigh,
who, while enjoying the favouritism
of Elizabeth I, was granted the
estate of **Sherborne Old Castle** in
1592. This stark and comfortless
residence was not to his taste, so he
built a new castle, the splendid
Sherborne Castle, which remains
today one of the grandest of
Dorset's country houses.

SHAFTESBURY

10½ miles N of Blandford Forum on the A350

This hill top town, which stands
over 700 feet above sea level, was
founded in AD 880 by King Alfred
who fortified the settlement here
and established a Benedictine abbey
for women installing his daughter as
the first prioress. Just a hundred
years later, King Edward, who was
murdered at Corfe Castle, was
buried at **Shaftesbury Abbey** and
it soon became a place of
pilgrimage. The nearby
Shaftesbury Abbey Museum
houses many of the finds from the
abbey's excavations and state of the
art, touch screen displays bring the
ancient religious house to life.

The town's most famous sight
must be **Gold Hill**, a steep cobbled
street, stepped in places and lined
with delightful 18th century
cottages. Many people who have
never visited the town will
recognise this thoroughfare as it
was made famous through the
classic TV advertisement for Hovis
bread. The cottage at the top of the
hill is home to the **Shaftesbury
Museum**. Button-making was once
an important cottage industry in the
town and some of the products can
be seen here including the
decorative Dorset Knobs, which
share their name with a famous,
also locally-made, biscuit.

TOLPUDDLE

9 miles SW of Blandford Forum off the A35

Like so many villages beside the
River Piddle, Tolpuddle's name was
changed by the Victorians from the
original – Tolpiddle. It was here in
1834 that the first trades union was
formed when six villagers, in an
attempt to escape from grinding
poverty, banded together to form
the Society of Agricultural
Labourers, taking an oath of mutual
support. The story of the martyrs
is told in the **Tolpuddle Martyrs
Museum**, housed in memorial
cottages that were built in 1934 by
the TUC.

To the west lies **Athelhampton**

House, one of the finest stone-built manor houses in England.

CERNE ABBAS

14½ miles SW of Blandford Forum on the A352

The most famous 'inhabitant' of this pretty village is the **Cerne Abbas Giant**, a colossal priapic figure cut into the chalk hillside.

DORCHESTER

After capturing the Iron Age hill fort of **Maiden Castle** in around AD 50, the Romans went on to found Durnovaia. The hill fort is one of the biggest in England and nearby is another ancient monument utilised by the Romans, who converted the Neolithic henge monument of **Maumbury Rings** into an amphitheatre.

As with so many towns in Dorset, Dorchester played host to the infamous Judge Jeffreys and here he sentenced over 70 men to death. Later, in the 1830s, the town was once again the scene of a famous trial, when in the **Old Crown Court** the Tolpuddle Martyrs were sentenced. The Old Crown Court and its cells are now open to the public. The town is also home to the **Tutankhamun Exhibition** housed in an old church.

Just to the northeast of the town, lies **Max Gate**, the house that Hardy designed and lived in from 1885 until his death in 1928. Situated on the River Cerne, on the northern outskirts of Dorchester, is the attractive village of **Charminster**, the home of

Wolfeton House, a splendid medieval and Elizabethan building surrounded by water meadows.

Just to the east of Dorchester is the village of **Stinsford** that appeared as Melstock in Hardy's *Under the Greenwood Tree*. Hardy's heart is buried in the churchyard of St Michael, beside his first wife, and his parents are buried nearby. (Hardy's official funeral was at Westminster Abbey and his ashes were placed in the south transept.) Just beyond the village is **Hardy's Cottage**, where the novelist was born in 1840 and where he continued to live, on and off, until his marriage to Emma Gifford in 1874.

Hardy's Monument on Black Downs to the southwest of Dorchester was erected in memory not of the writer but of Sir Thomas Masterson Hardy, the flag captain of *HMS Victory* at Trafalgar and the man who escorted Nelson's body home.

AROUND DORCHESTER

MORETON

7 miles E of Dorchester off the B3390

Moreton's Gothic Church of St Nicholas was wrecked by a Second World War bomb and its glass replaced with superb engraved glass by Laurence Whistler. In the cemetery is the grave of TE Lawrence - Lawrence of Arabia, Arabic scholar, traveller, soldier and man of action. To the northeast of this charming village is **Cloud's Hill**, a tiny redbrick cottage where Lawrence lived after retiring from the RAF in 1935. To the east of

164 THE TIPPLING PHILOSOPHER

Milborne Port

A warm welcome awaits visitors to the **Tippling Philosopher**, which serves a daily changing selection of home-cooked dishes. Also rooms for B&B guests.

see page 410

165 THE CROWN

Stalbridge

The Crown is an attractive old inn on the main street of Stalbridge, serving a good choice of home-cooked snacks and meals.

see page 411

166 THE CASTLE INN

Corfe Castle

The **Castle Inn** welcomes visitors with a friendly ambience and goof ood using local produce.

 see page 412

167 THE CROWS NEST

Swanage

The **Crows Nest** is a handsome Victorian pub serving classic home-cooked dishes and Cask Marque ales. Two rooms for B&B.

 see page 411

168 THE RED LION

Swanage

Town centre inn with a spacious garden. Extensive menu, real ales and 5 guest rooms for B&B.

 see page 413

Moreton is Bovington Camp, where Lawrence served as a private in the Royal Tank Corps. The camp houses the **Tank Museum**, where the collection of 300 tanks and armoured vehicles starts with Britain's first tank, Little Willie, built in 1915.

CORFE CASTLE

18 miles SE of Dorchester on the A351

This greystone village is dominated by the majestic ruins of **Corfe Castle** high on a hill. An important stronghold that protected the gateway through the Purbeck Hills, the castle was constructed in the years immediately following the Norman Conquest. Now owned by the National Trust, the castle is part of an extensive estate, with a network of footpaths taking in both the coastline and the inland heath, and encompassing important habitats for many rare species, including all six species of British reptile.

SWANAGE

20 miles SE of Dorchester on the A351

This seaside town, complete with its fully restored Victorian pier and its little exhibition, built its early fortune on Purbeck stone. The **King Alfred Column**, on the seafront, records that this was where the king fought and saw off the Danish fleet in AD 877. The column is topped by cannonballs that would, undoubtedly, have been a great help to King Alfred, had they been invented at the time. These particular cannonballs date from the Crimean War.

An attraction not to be missed is the **Swanage Railway**, which uses old Southern Region and BR Standard locomotives to pull trains on a six-mile scenic journey to Norden, just north of Corfe Castle.

To the north of Swanage lies **Studland** whose fine sandy beach stretches from Handfast Point to South Haven Point and the entrance to Poole Harbour. The heathland behind the beach is a haven for rare birds and is a National Nature Reserve. A footpath leading along the coast takes in **Tilly Whim Caves**, named after the owner, Mr Tilly, who used a whim, or wooden derrick, to load stone into barges for transportation to Swanage.

EAST LULWORTH

12 miles SE of Dorchester on the B3070

This charming little village stands on a minor road that leads down to one of the country's best loved beauty spots, **Lulworth Cove**, an almost perfectly circular bay that is surrounded by towering cliffs. **Lulworth Castle** was built as a hunting lodge in the early 17th century and played host to seven monarchs before a devastating fire in 1929 reduced it to a virtual ruin. On the MoD's Lulworth Range is the deserted village of **Tyneham**, occupied in 1943 when the range had to be expanded for the testing of increasingly powerful weapons.

WEYMOUTH

7 miles S of Dorchester on the A354

Weymouth owed its early prosperity to the woollen trade, but in the late 18th century it also began to develop as a resort; in 1789 George III came here to try out the newly invented bathing machine. An unusual painted statue of the king was erected in 1810, and close by is the colourful Jubilee Clock that was put up in 1887 to celebrate Queen Victoria's Golden Jubilee.

One of the town's most popular tourist attractions is **Brewers Quay**, with specialist shops and a museum. Not far from Brewers Quay is **Nothe Fort**, which was built as part of the defences of the new naval base that was being established at nearby Portland. The fort is now the home of the **Museum of Coastal Defence**.

Lulworth Cove

ISLE OF PORTLAND

11 miles S of Dorchester on the A354

The Isle of Portland is not, strictly speaking, an island but a peninsula that is joined to the mainland by the amazing **Chesil Beach**, a vast bank of pebbles worn smooth by the sea that stretches for 18 miles from the island westwards to Abbotsbury. The island's most famous building is **Portland Castle**, constructed by Henry VIII as part of his south coast defence. **Portland Museum** was founded by the birth control pioneer, Marie Stopes, and occupies a pair of thatched cottages.

At the tip of the island, **Portland Bill**, are two lighthouses, the older of which (1788) is now a bird observatory and field centre.

ABBOTSBURY

8 miles SW of Dorchester on the B3157

This delightful village has three main attractions that draw

holidaymakers here in their thousands each year – **The Swannery**, the **Sub Tropical Gardens** and the **Tithe Barn Children's Farm**. To the north lie several ancient monuments, among them **Kingston Russell Stone Circle**, a Bronze Age circle.

BRIDPORT

13½ miles W of Dorchester on the A35

Rope-making was an important industry here, and it also has close links with the non-conformists, with two well-appointed chapels. In the early 18th century Bridport's harbour began to silt up, so the townspeople built a new one at the mouth of the River Britt and called it **West Bay**.

LYME REGIS

22 miles W of Dorchester on the A3052

In 1588 Sir Francis Drake's fleet fought a small battle with the Spanish Armada in Lyme Bay, and in 1685 the Duke of Monmouth landed at Lyme Regis and began his

169 LULWORTH CASTLE

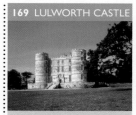

East Lulworth

The Lulworth Esatate offers a superb day out to visits the Castle, the House and the Park.

 see page 414

170 GRAINGERS GUEST HOUSE

Dorchester Road, Weymouth

Graingers Guest House provides space, comfort and modern amenities a short distance from Weymouth seafront.

 see page 414

171 ABBOTSBURY

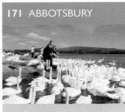

Abbotsbury

A delightful English village, home to the Swannery, the Sub-Tropical Gardens and the Tithe Barn and Childrens Farm

 see page 415

172 THE WHITE HOUSE HOTEL

Charmouth

Comfortable accommodation and superb food are the highlights of the **White House Hotel** in the heart of Charmouth.

 see page 414

unsuccessful rebellion that would lead to the Bloody Assizes of Judge Jeffreys. During the 18th century, Lyme Regis developed into a fashionable seaside resort; the town's most famous landmark is undoubtedly **The Cobb**, which was built in medieval times to protect the harbour. John Fowles set a part of *The French Lieutenant's Woman* on The Cobb, and the film of the book also used the location. Jane Austen stayed in the town writing a part of *Persuasion*, and Henry Fielding is said to have based the character of Sophie in *Tom Jones* on a local girl.

Lyme Regis is particularly famous for the fossils that were first discovered here in the early 19th century and there are fine specimens in **Lyme Regis Museum** and in the **Dinosaurland & Fossil Museum**. The fossil frenzy was fuelled by one Mary Anning, born in 1799, who with her family searched for fossils in the local cliffs and sold them to supplement the income of their carpenter father. The most famous discovery of Mary and her brother Joseph was the fossilised skeleton of an ichthyosaur; it took several years to free it from the cliff, and Mary sold it to the British Museum for £23.

The eight-mile stretch of coast to the east of Lyme Regis includes the highest cliff on the south coast, Golden Cap, and also the **Charmouth Heritage Coast Centre** that aims to further the

public's understanding and appreciation of this area's scientific wealth.

BEAMINSTER

14 miles NW of Dorchester on the A3066

As a result of a series of fires, the centre of this ancient market town is largely a handsome collection of 18th and 19th century buildings. However, some older buildings did survive the fires, including the 15th century Church of St Mary with its splendid 100ft tower from which, it is said, a number of citizens were hanged during the Bloody Assizes.

Just to the south of the town lies **Parnham House**, a beautiful Elizabethan mansion enlarged and refurbished by John Nash in the 19th century. Surrounded by glorious gardens, the house is certainly one of Dorset's finest Tudor residencies but, much more recently, in the 1970s, it came into the ownership of John Makepeace and his wife Jennie. Today, this is a showcase for the very best in modern furniture, much of which is created by John and his students at the John Makepeace Furniture Workshops that he runs from here. In the gardens, Jennie has created a magical environment with unusual plants, a lake rich in wildlife and a play area for children.

To the southeast of Beaminster, **Mapperton Gardens** surround a fine Jacobean manor house with stable blocks, a dovecote and its own church.

County Durham

County Durham is dominated by the marvellous city of Durham and, in particular, the magnificent cathedral that is now a World Heritage Site. The county's prosperity was founded largely on coal mining, and now that the industry has all but disappeared the scars it created are being swept away. County Durham's countryside has always supported an important farming industry, and Central and South Durham still retain a gentle landscape of fields, woodland, streams and country lanes.

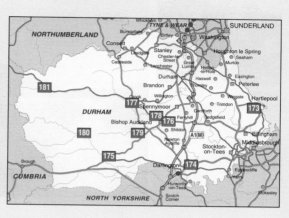

FOOD & DRINK

ACCOMMODATION

PLACES OF INTEREST

DURHAM CITY

Arriving in Durham by train, the visitor is presented with what must be one of the most breathtaking urban views in Europe. Towering over the tumbling roofs of the city is the magnificent bulk of **Durham Cathedral**, third only to Canterbury and York in ecclesiastical significance but excelling them in architectural splendour. The cathedral owes its origin to the monks of Lindisfarne, who, in AD 875, fled from Viking attacks, taking with them the coffin of St Cuthbert. In AD 980 they finally settled at this easily defended site, where the River Wear makes a wide loop around a rocky outcrop, and they built the White Church, where St Cuthbert's remains were finally laid to rest. The founder of the present cathedral was a Norman, William de St Carileph, Bishop of

93

173 HARTLEPOOL'S MARITIME EXPERIENCE

Hartlepool

One of the top Heritage and History attractions in the UK featuring a re-creation of an 18th century sea port.

 see page 416

Durham Cathedral

Durham from 1081 to 1096. He was determined to replace the little church with a building of the scale and style of the splendid new churches he had seen being built in France and in 1093 the foundation stones were laid. The result was the creation of the finest and grandest example of Norman architecture in Europe. Sharing the same rocky peninsula is **Durham Castle**, whose impregnability ensured that Durham was one of the few towns in Northumbria that was never captured by the Scots through force. The castle is now used as a hall of residence for the students of Durham University, which was founded in 1832, making it the third oldest English university, after Oxford and Cambridge.

The rest of Durham reflects the long history of the castle and cathedral it served. There are winding streets, the ancient Market Place, elegant Georgian houses and quiet courts and alleyways, churches, museums, art galleries and heritage centres.

The **Botanic Gardens**, run by the University, feature a large collection of North American trees, including junior-sized giant redwoods, a series of small 'gardens-within-gardens' and walks through mature woodland.

AROUND DURHAM

HARTLEPOOL

15 miles SE of Durham on the A179

On 16 December, 1914 Hartlepool was the first town in Britain to suffer from enemy action, when it was shelled from German warships lying off the coast. Nowadays it is a thriving shopping centre, with some outstanding tourist attractions, including the **Hartlepool Historic Quay and Museum**. Guided tours are available of *HMS Trincomalee*, Britain's oldest surviving warship, and the *PSS Wingfield Castle*, an old paddle steamer.

STOCKTON-ON-TEES

17 miles SE of Durham on the A177

Stockton-on-Tees is famous for being one end of the Stockton to Darlington railway, which opened in 1825 so that coal from the mines of South Durham could have access to the River Tees. Notable natives of Stockton include John Walker, the inventor of the humble friction match, born here in 1781; Thomas Sheraton, the furniture maker and designer, born here in 1751; and Ivy Close, who won Britain's first ever beauty contest in 1908.

DARLINGTON

17½ miles S of Durham on the A167

An ancient market town that was founded in Saxon times, Darlington's greatest claim to fame lies in the role it played, with its neighbour Stockton, in the creation of the world's first commercially successful public railway. The **Darlington Railway Centre and Museum** houses relics of the pioneering Stockton and Darlington Railway, including a replica of Stephenson's *Locomotion No 1*.

CHESTER-LE-STREET

5½ miles N of Durham on the A167

A busy market town on the River

Wear, the town's medieval Church of St Mary and St Cuthbert stands on the site of a 9th century cathedral that was established by the monks of Lindisfarne while they stayed here for 113 years before moving to Durham.

Waldridge Fell Country Park, southwest of Chester-le-Street, is County Durham's last surviving area of lowland heathland.

To the northeast lies one of the regions most popular attractions, the award-winning **North of England Open Air Museum** at **Beamish**. Set in 200 acres of countryside, it illustrates life in the North of England in the late 19th and early 20th centuries by way of a cobbled street full of shops, banks and offices, a colliery village complete with drift mine, an old engine shed, a horse yard and terraced gardens. To the northwest of Beamish is **Causey Arch**, which claims to be the world's first single-arch railway bridge; it carried the Tanfield Railway between Sunniside and Causey.

In the old part of **Washington**, northeast of Chester-le-Street, is **Washington Old Hall**, the home of the Washington family, ancestors of George Washington, the first American president. The present house was built in around 1623 and the interiors re-create a typical manor house of the 17th century. Also in Washington is the **Washington Wildfowl and Wetlands Centre**, a conservation area and bird watchers' paradise, and the **Glaxo Wellcome Wetland Discovery Centre**.

174 DARLINGTON RAILWAY CENTRE & MUSEUM

Darlington

A superb collection of engines, carriages and wagons including Stephenson's Locomotion.

 see page 416

175 THE TEESDALE RESTAURANT & COFFEE SHOP

Barnard Castle

There are seats for nearly 100 in the **Teesdale**, a popular restaurant and coffee shop serving a good variety of home-cooked British and Continental dishes.

 see page 416

176 THE TUT 'N' SHIVE

Bishop Auckland

The **Tut 'n' Shive** is a convivial town pub with super, friendly staff, changing real ales and great-value lunches.

 see page 417

177 THE FIR TREE COUNTRY HOTEL

Fir Tree, nr Crook

On the A68 close to Hamsterley Forest, the **Fir Tree** is a perfect stopping-off point for the tourist, whether pausing for refreshment or staying in the motel-style bedrooms.

 see page 417

Bowes Museum, Barnard Castle

SUNDERLAND

11½ miles NE of Durham on the A690

Sunderland is one of Britain's newer cities: the Church of St Michael and All Angels, the first minster to be created in England since the Reformation, was proclaimed Sunderland Minster in January 1998. To the south of the city centre is the **Ryhope Engines Museum**, based on a pumping station that supplied the city and surrounding area with water.

On the north side of the Wear, in the suburb of **Monkwearmouth**, is an important site of early Christianity. Glass was first made in Sunderland in the 7th century at St Peter's Church and the **National Glass Centre** is close by.

PETERLEE

10½ miles E of Durham on the A1086

Peterlee was established as a New Town in 1948 to re-house the mining families that lived in the colliery villages around Easington and Shotton. It is named after an outstanding Durham miner and county councillor, Peter Lee, who fought all his life for the well-being of the local community. **Castle Eden Dene National Nature Reserve**, on the south side of the town, is one of the largest woodlands in the North East that has not been planted or extensively altered by man.

BARNARD CASTLE

This old market town derives its name from its **Castle**, founded in the 12th century by Bernard, son of Guy de Baliol, one of the knights who fought alongside William I. The town has an especially rich architectural heritage, with handsome houses, cottages, shops and inns dating from the 17th to the 19th centuries and an impressive octagonal Market Cross.

The town is home to the extraordinary **Bowes Museum**, a grand and beautiful building styled on a French château. The fabulous collections on show include paintings by Goya, El Greco, Turner, Boudin and Canaletto, tapestries, ceramics, a wonderful display of toys (the world's first toy train set) and the breathtaking life-size Silver Swan that is an automaton and music box.

AROUND BARNARD CASTLE

BISHOP AUCKLAND

12 miles NE of Barnard Castle on the A688

Auckland Castle, still the official palace of the Bishop of Durham, began as a small 12th century manor house and was added to by successive bishops. The palace grounds contain an ancient herd of red deer.

PIERCEBRIDGE

10 miles E of Barnard Castle on the A67

The picturesque village green stands on the site of a once important Roman fort, one of a chain of forts on Dere Street. The remains of the fort, which are visible today, can be dated from coin evidence to around AD 270.

To the northwest lies **Gainford**, County Durham's most beautiful village. It sits just north of the River Tees and its core is a jostling collection of 18th and 19th century cottages and houses grouped around a green.

MIDDLETON-IN-TEESDALE

8 miles NW of Barnard Castle on the B6277

Middleton is the centre for some magnificent walks in Upper Teesdale; the most famous of these is **The Pennine Way** on its 250-mile route from Derbyshire to Kirk Yetholm in Scotland. It passes through Middleton-in-Teesdale from the south, then turns west along Teesdale, passing traditional, whitewashed farmsteads and spectacular, riverside scenery, including the thrilling waterfalls at Low Force and High Force.

IRESHOPEBURN

18 miles NW of Barnard Castle on the A689

This small village is home to the **Weardale Museum** that includes a carefully re-created room in a typical Weardale lead miner's cottage, with furnishings and costumes in period. There is also a room dedicated to John Wesley, who visited the area on more than one occasion.

To the northwest lies Killhope Mine, the focal point of what is now the remarkable **North of England Lead Mining Museum**, which is dominated by the massive 34-feet high water wheel.

178 THE SAXON INN

Escomb, nr Bishop Auckland

Good food at kind prices makes the **Saxon Inn** a firm favourite with locals and visitors.

see page 418

179 THE TRAVELLERS REST

Evenwood, Durham

The well-named **Travellers Rest** is a welcoming village inn serving popular pub dishes in convivial surroundings.

see page 418

180 THE MOORCOCK INN

Eggleston, nr Barnard Castle

The **Moorcock Inn** is a winner on all counts: great location, superb views, affable staff, cask-conditioned ales, super food and comfortable guest bedrooms.

see page 419

181 THE HARE & HOUNDS

Westgate, nr Stanhope

The **Hare & Hounds** offers good pub food in a delightful rural setting.

see page 418

Essex

Bordering the north bank of the River Thames, southern Essex has long been a gateway to London, and while it contains much heavy industry, it also encompasses some very important marshland wildlife habitats. History, too, abounds in this part of the county - Henry VIII built the riverside Block Houses at East and West Tilbury, which later became Coalhouse and Tilbury Forts. Southend-on-Sea is one of the country's best-loved venues for a family holiday or a day trip from London, and there are numerous nature reserves, the ancient royal hunting ground of Epping Forest and the yachting centre at Burnham-on-Crouch. Maldon remains famous for its traditionally produced sea salt.

Although Chelmsford is the county town, Colchester, which was first established in the 7th century BC, has the greater character. The country's oldest recorded town was the capital of Roman Britain until Queen Boudicca (Boadicea) burned the town to the ground. Other ancient towns abound in the county including Tiptree, home to the famous jam factory, Coggeshall,

which is well known for its lace, and Saffron Walden which takes its named after the Saffron crocus that was used to make dyestuffs. Along the east coast, dubbed the 'Sunshine Holiday Coast', are the resorts of Clacton-on-Sea, Frinton-on-Sea and Walton-on-the-Naze that were all developed in the 19th century. Seafaring, fishing and shipbuilding were all once the mainstays of many of the settlements along this stretch of coast and Brightlingsea has the distinction of being the only limb of the Cinque Ports outside Kent and Sussex.

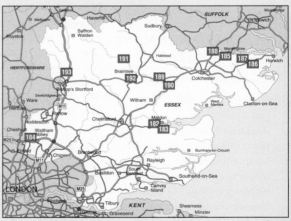

CHELMSFORD

Situated at the confluence of the Rivers Chelmer and Can, the town was first settled by Romans, who built a fort and brought Christianity to Essex. It was not until 1914 that the diocese of Chelmsford was created, though **Chelmsford Cathedral** (formerly the Parish Church of St Mary) dates from the 15th century and was built on the site of a much earlier church. The Marconi Company set up the world's first radio company in Chelmsford in 1899 and exhibits from those early days of wireless can be seen at the **Chelmsford and Essex Museum**. To the east of Chelmsford, and close to the village of **Danbury** (thought to take its name from the Danes who invaded this area in the Dark Ages), is **Danbury Country Park**, a pleasant stretch of open countryside with woodland, a lake and ornamental gardens.

At **Highwood**, three miles southwest of Chelmsford, lies **Hylands House** that was built in 1728 and has been painstakingly restored. The beautiful grounds that surround the house host a varied programme of outdoor events throughout the year.

AROUND CHELMSFORD

MALDON

9 miles E of Chelmsford on the A414

Situated on the busy Blackwater estuary, Maldon's most distinctive feature is undoubtedly the 15th century **Moot Hall**, where an ambitious tapestry commemorates the 1,000th anniversary of the Battle of Maldon. Just outside the town lies the site of one of the most decisive battles of England's early history when, in AD 991, the English leader, Byrthnoth, was killed by the invading Danes after a fierce three-day conflict. Following the defeat, the English king, Ethelred the Unready, was obliged to pay an annual tribute to his conquerors but the Danes soon tired of this arrangement and, overthrowing Ethelred, they put Canute on the throne. Maldon's **Millennium Gardens** were named in commemoration of the battle.

Sea salt has been produced here for generations, and the history of this industry is one of the topics explored in the **Maldon District Museum**. To the north, at **Langford**, is the **Museum of Power**, an ex-waterworks pumping station that houses engines, pumps and other interesting artefacts.

To the east of Maldon is **Northey Island**, a small island in the Blackwater estuary with a large area of undisturbed salt marsh; it can be reached by a causeway.

SOUTH WOODHAM FERRERS

9½ miles SE of Chelmsford on the B1012

Surrounded by the empty marshland of the Crouch estuary, South Woodham Ferrers is a successful 20th century new town that, surprisingly, boasts a traditional market square overlooked by buildings

182 THE WHITE HORSE INN

High Street, Maldon

The **White Horse Inn** enjoys a well-earned reputation for ambience, food, drink and accommodation.

see page 420

183 THE WELCOME

Fullbridge, Maldon

The **Welcome** is well named, with a wonderful ambience, home-cooked food and a weekend disco.

see page 421

constructed in the old Essex style – with brick, tile and weatherboard. To the northwest of the town, at Hyde Hall, is the **Royal Horticultural Society Garden**, which includes a woodland garden, large rose garden, ornamental ponds, herbaceous borders and the national collections of malus and viburnum.

BURNHAM-ON-CROUCH

16½ miles SE of Chelmsford on the B1012

An attractive old village that is the county's main yachting centre. On the town's bustling quay is the **Burnham-on-Crouch and District Museum** featuring agricultural and maritime exhibits relating to this ancient area of Essex.

Mangapps Farm Railway Museum on the edge of town houses an extensive collection of railway relics, historic buildings and one of the largest collections of signalling equipment. Train rides are available when the museum is open.

To the northeast of Burnham, on the northern shore of the Dengie Peninsula, lies **Bradwell-on-Sea**, a village whose name is derived from the Saxon words 'brad pall' meaning 'broad wall'. Here is the site of **Bradwell Bay Secret Airfield**, which was used during World War II by aircraft that were unable to return to their original base. The village also has what could be the country's oldest church. **St Peter's-on-the-Wall**, built by St Cedd in the 7th century, was abandoned in the 14th century and forgotten for 600 years; it has been restored and reconsecrated.

SOUTHEND-ON-SEA

17 miles SE of Chelmsford on the A127

One of the country's best loved family resorts, Southend-on-Sea has seven miles of beaches, endless amusements and the longest pleasure pier in the world, served by its own electric railway. The **Central Museum and Planetarium** is the only planetarium in the southeast outside London and it also features local history exhibits. Several museums and galleries provide ample culture, and other attractions include the **Sealife Centre** and the renowned Kursall entertainment complex. One of the

Burnham-on-Crouch

most important archaeological finds of recent years is the burial chamber of a Saxon king, unearthed near the railway line at **Prittlewell** on the western edge of Southend. The chamber, dating from the early 7th century, is remarkably intact, and among the treasures recovered are glass vessels, gilded wooden drinking cups, gold foil crosses and solid gold buckles and brooches.

Canvey Island has two unusual museums, the **Dutch Cottage Museum** with many traditional Flemish features, and the **Castle Point Transport Museum**, housed in a 1930s bus garage, with a fascinating collection of historic and modern buses and coaches.

STANFORD-LE-HOPE

15 miles S of Chelmsford on the A1014

Lying between the town and the Thames estuary are **Stanford Marshes**, an ideal location for birdwatching and also the home to various species of wildlife. Close by is **Langdon Hills Country Park**, some 400 acres of ancient woodland and meadows that is home to many rare trees and from where there are spectacular views out over the Essex countryside.

TILBURY

19 miles SW of Chelmsford on the A1089

Chosen as the site for the Camp Royal in 1588 when the threat of invasion by Spain was imminent, West Tilbury (northeast of Tilbury) remains a quiet and hidden away backwater overlooking the Thames

estuary whereas its larger neighbour is a busy, industrial centre. However, **Tilbury Fort**, the unusual 17th century building with a double moat, acts as a reminder of the past and it stands on the site of a military Block House built during the reign of Henry VIII. Close by, at the town's power station, is the **Tilbury Energy and Environment Centre** that includes a nature reserve. Another fortification, Coalhouse Fort, was constructed as a primary defence against invasion of the Thames area and it is now home to the **Thameside Aviation Museum**.

Despite the industry that lines the Thames estuary, the area around Tilbury is also rural, and the Mardyke Valley, which runs from Aveley to Orsett Fen, provides pleasant views and open spaces.

BRENTWOOD

10½ miles SW of Chelmsford on the A1016

Attractions in this town on the old pilgrim and coaching routes to and from London include a classically-styled modern cathedral, a picturesque cottage museum and a top entertainment venue. Just southeast of the town centre is **Thorndon Country Park and Hartswood**, formerly a Royal deer park. To the northwest, at **South Weald**, is the **Weald Country Park**, a former estate which was partially landscaped in the 18th century and features a lake, woodland and an ancient deer park. To the northeast of Brentwood and situated beside a Roman road is

To the west of Southend lies Leigh-on-Sea, which has managed to retain a quite distinctive character despite being encroached upon by its larger neighbour. Close by is Hadleigh Castle which was originally built for Edward III and once belonged to Anne of Cleves, Catherine of Aragon and Katherine Parr. The ruins of this once impressive castle were memorably captured by the brush of John Constable.

South Weald Country Park, Brentwood

thoroughfare, Sun Street, and is marked out on the pavement and also through the Abbey Gardens.

Gunpowder production started here in the 17th century and by the 19th century the **Royal Gunpowder Mills** employed 500 workers. The once secret buildings and the surrounding parkland are now open to the public. The town's **Dragonfly Sanctuary** is home to over half the native British species of dragonfly and damselfly. West of the town, the **Lee Navigation Canal** provides opportunities for anglers, walkers and birdwatchers, and the Lee Valley Regional Park is an important area of high biodiversity that sustains a large range of wildlife and birds.

184 ROYAL GUNPOWDER MILLS

Waltham Abbey

The Royal Gunpowder Mills offers a fascinating day out for everyone. The 300 year old gunpowder production site has been regenerated and offers a mix of history, science and beautiful surroundings.

 see page 420

Mountnessing Post Mill, a traditional weatherboarded mill dating from 1807 that was restored to working order in the 1980s.

WALTHAM ABBEY

Originally a Roman settlement and home to a hunting lodge belonging to the early Saxon kings, the town grew up around this and an Augustinian **Abbey** that was built in 1177 by Henry II. The Abbey's **Crypt Centre** explains the history of both the town and the Abbey, which was once one of the largest in the country and was the last to fall victim to the Dissolution in 1540. The Greenwich Meridian runs through the town's main

AROUND WALTHAM ABBEY

HARLOW

10 miles NE of Waltham Abbey on the A414

Though much of it is modern, Harlow has several sites of historic interest. **Harlow Museum** occupies a Georgian manor house set in picturesque gardens, while **Harlow Study and Visitors Centre** is set in a medieval tithe barn and adjacent 13th century church. At **Chingford** stands the **Queen Elizabeth Hunting Lodge**, a timber-framed building first used by Henry VIII. This unique Tudor survivor is situated in **Epping Forest**, the magnificent and expansive tract of ancient hornbeam coppice that offers miles of leafy walks and bridle paths along with some rough grazing and the occasional distant view.

CHIPPING ONGAR

8 miles SE of Harlow on the A414

In 1155, Richard de Lucy built a castle here, of which only the mound and moat remain today. However, a contemporary building, the Church of St Martin of Tours, still stands. It was here that the explorer David Livingstone spent time as a pupil pastor before beginning his missionary work in Africa.

The town is surrounded by rural Essex and several ancient villages, including **Fyfield**, home to **Fyfield Hall**, the oldest inhabited timber-framed building in England; **Blackmore**, a village that was almost totally destroyed by the plague; and **Greensted**, which became the home of several of the Tolpuddle martyrs after their sentences had been commuted. To the south of Chipping Ongar, at **Kelvedon Hatch**, a rural bungalow is the deceptively ordinary exterior of the **Kelvedon Secret Nuclear Bunker**, which was built in 1952 as a base from which the Government and military commanders could run operations in the event of a nuclear war; it is now open to the public. To the west of the town lies **North Weald Airfield Museum**, which details the history of flying in this area from 1916 to the present day.

COLCHESTER

First established in the 7th century BC and England's oldest recorded

town, Colchester was an obvious target for the Romans, and the Emperor Claudius took the surrender of 11 British kings here. However, in AD 60 Queen Boudicca took revenge on the invaders and burned the town to the ground before going on to destroy London and St Albans. The walls, the oldest in the country, still surround the ancient part of the town and **Balkerne Gate** is the largest surviving Roman gateway in the country.

A thousand years later the Normans built **Colchester Castle** on the foundations of the Roman temple of Claudius and it boasts the largest Norman keep ever built in Europe. The Castle Museum, housed in the keep, is now one of the most exciting hands-on historical attractions in the country. Located in a fine Georgian building, the **Hollytrees Museum** displays a fine collection of toys, costumes, curios and antiquities from the last two centuries; the **Natural History Museum** concerns itself with the flora and fauna of Essex; and **Tymperleys Clock Museum** in Queen Street is home to a magnificent collection of 18th and 19th century Colchester-made clocks.

Colchester is famous for its **Zoo** and even more famous for its oysters which are still cultivated on beds in the lower reaches of the River Colne – a visit to the **Oyster Fisheries** is a fascinating experience.

To the east of Colchester, at **Elmstead Market**, are the **Beth**

Downstream from Colchester, on the River Colne, is the former smugglers' haunt of Wivenhoe, where fishing and small sailing craft still line the quayside. The Fingringhoe Wick Nature Reserve encompasses both woodland and lakes along the Colne estuary, and to the west lies Abberton Reservoir and wildlife centre which is ideal for birdwatching.

Chatto Gardens that were designed and are still presided over by the famous gardener. Close by is the **Rolts Nursery Butterfly Farm**.

AROUND COLCHESTER

MANNINGTREE

7 miles NE of Colchester on the B1352

Situated on the River Stour, this ancient market town was a centre of the cloth trade in Tudor times before becoming a port serving the barges taking their wares to London. Manningtree is a centre for sailing, and from **The Walls** there are unrivalled views of the Stour estuary – a favourite subject of artists down the years.

DEDHAM

6 miles N of Colchester off the A14

This is Constable country, and the church at Dedham featured in many of the artist's paintings. Here, too, are a fascinating Arts and Crafts Centre; a Toy Museum; and **Dedham Vale Family Farm** with a comprehensive collection of British farm animals. Another artist associated with this area is Sir Alfred Munnings and, just outside the village, his former home, Castle House, now contains the **Sir Alfred Munnings Art Museum**.

HARWICH

16 miles NE of Colchester on the A120

This town has an important maritime history, the legacy of which continues through to the present day. The Elizabethan seafarers Hawkins, Frobisher and Drake sailed from here, Christopher Jones, master of *The Mayflower*, lived here and Samuel Pepys, the diarist, was an MP for the town in the 1660s.

When the town's two lighthouses, built in 1818, were aligned they indicated a safe shipping channel into Harwich harbour. The High Lighthouse is now home to the **National Vintage Wireless and Television Museum**, while the **Maritime Museum** can be found in the Low Lighthouse. Two other worthwhile museums in Harwich are the **Lifeboat Museum** and the **Ha'penny Pier Visitor Centre** on the Quay. Harwich's importance as a port in the 19th century is confirmed by **The Redoubt**, a huge grey fort similar in style to the Martello Towers, which has been opened as a museum. Another interesting building is the **Electric Palace Cinema** that dates from 1911 and is the oldest purpose-built cinema in Britain.

WALTON-ON-THE-NAZE

16½ miles E of Colchester off the B1034

A traditional resort that is focused on its **Pier**, which was first built in wood in 1830, and the Marine Parade, which dates from the same period. The **Old Lifeboat House Museum** houses an interpretative museum of local history.

The wind-blown expanse of The Naze, to the north of Walton, is constantly changing shape as it is eroded by the wind and the tide but it remains a pleasant place for walking and for picnics. The **Naze Tower** was originally built as a beacon in 1720 to warn seamen off the West Rocks just offshore.

To the southwest lies the former fishing village of **Frinton-on-Sea** that was developed as a select resort and which expanded in the 1880s into the genteel family town of today.

CLACTON-ON-SEA

13 miles SE of Colchester on the A133

First settled by hunters in the Stone Age, Clacton is another traditional family resort with a Victorian **Pier**, long sandy south-facing beach and lovely gardens, including the Clifftop Public Gardens. Close by are the ancient ruins of **St Osyth Priory** that was founded by Augustinian Canons and named after St Osytha, the martyred daughter of Frithenwald, the first Christian King of the East Angles, who was himself beheaded by the Danes in AD 653. In a Martello Tower at Point Clear is the **East Essex Aviation Museum** that contains interesting displays of wartime aviation, military and naval photographs, uniforms and other memorabilia with local and USAAF connections. To the north of Clacton is the **Holland Haven Country Park** that is an ideal place for watching the marine birds and other wildlife of this region.

BRIGHTLINGSEA

7½ miles SE of Colchester on the B1029

As well as a long tradition of shipbuilding and seafaring, Brightlingsea has the distinction of being the only limb of the Cinque Ports outside Kent and Sussex. It is also home to one of the oldest occupied buildings in Essex – the 13th century **Jacobes Hall** – that was used as a meeting hall during the reign of Henry III. There are numerous walks along Brightlingsea Creek and the River Colne which provide the opportunity to watch the birdlife on the saltings. Across the water from Brightlingsea, reached by a causeway, is **Mersea Island**, much of which is now a National Nature Reserve.

Walton-on-the-Naze

Coggeshall, nr Colchester

The Fleece is a popular old inn with well-kept beers, good home cooking and a super beer garden.

🍴 see page 423

Feering, nr Colchester

The Bell is a family-friendly inn with super hosts and an excellent chef.

🍴 see page 424

TOLLESHUNT D'ARCY

9½ miles SW of Colchester on the B1026

The birthplace of Dodie Smith, the author of *101 Dalmatians*, this modest village lies close to the **Maldon District Agricultural and Domestic Museum** at **Goldhanger**, featuring a large collection of vintage farm tools and machinery as well as printing machinery and domestic artefacts.

TIPTREE

8½ miles SW of Colchester on the B1022

This town is famous as being the home of the **Wilkin and Sons Jam Factory**, a Victorian establishment that now boasts a fascinating visitors' centre in the grounds of the original factory. Just to the east lies **Layer Marney** where a mansion to rival Hampton Court was planned but never completed. However, the massive eight-storey Tudor gatehouse was finished in 1525, and provides spectacular views out over the estate's formal gardens and across the surrounding countryside.

COGGESHALL

9½ miles W of Colchester on the A120

An ancient town whose prosperity was based on cloth and lace in the Middle Ages. Its attractions include the delightful half-timbered **Paycockes House** that dates from around 1500 and features unusually rich panelling, wood carvings and a display of Coggeshall lace. The National Trust also owns the restored **Coggeshall Grange Barn**, which dates from around

1140 and is the oldest surviving timber-framed barn in Europe.

To the south is the **Feering and Kelvedon Museum**, which is dedicated to manorial history and houses artefacts from the Roman settlement of Canonium; to the west are the **Cressing Temple Barns** which were commissioned in the 12th century by the Knights Templar and contain the timber of over 1,000 oak trees.

HALSTEAD

12 miles NW of Colchester on the A1124

Like Coggeshall and Braintree, Halstead was once an important weaving centre. The picturesque **Townsford Mill** is a reminder of the town's industrial heritage and this three-storey mill beside the River Colne, once a landmark site for the Courtauld empire. is now an antiques centre. Halstead's most famous product was once life-sized, mechanical elephants built by W Hunwicks; they could carry a load of eight adults and four children at speeds of up to 12 miles per hour!

To the east, at **Chappel**, is the **East Anglian Railway Museum**, where a comprehensive collection of period railway architecture, engineering and memorabilia can be seen. Railway enthusiasts should also visit the **Colne Valley Railway and Museum** at **Castle Hedingham**, where a mile of the Colne Valley and Halstead line has been restored to run steam trains. The village itself is dominated by its Norman Castle that was, in the 11th century, one of the country's strongest fortresses.

To the west of Halstead is the **Gosfield Lake Leisure Resort**, the county's largest freshwater lake, which lies in the grounds of Gosfield Hall, a Tudor mansion remodelled in the 19th century by its then owner, Samuel Courtauld. In the village church at **Gestingthorp** is a handsome memorial to Captain LEG Oates, who died in an attempt to save the lives of his companions on Scott's ill-fated Antarctic expedition in 1912.

SAFFRON WALDEN

This typical market town is named after the saffron crocus that was ground in the area to make dyestuffs and fulfil a variety of other uses in the Middle Ages. **Saffron Walden Museum** contains a wide range of exhibitions and displays, and among the many fascinating items are the gloves worn by Mary, Queen of Scots on the day that she died; here, too, are the ruins of historic Walden Castle. On the Common, once Castle Green, is the largest surviving **Turf Maze** in England, believed to be some 800 years old. Once the home of the 1st Earl of Suffolk and of Charles II, 17th century **Audley End House**, with its two large courtyards, was a rival in magnificence to Hampton Court. Though much of the house was demolished as it fell into disrepair, it remains one of the country's most impressive Jacobean mansions

and its distinguished stone façade is set off perfectly by Capability Brown's lake.

To the north of Saffron Walden is the village of **Hadstock** whose parish **Church of St Botolph** claims to have the oldest church door in England – it is Saxon. The village of **Hempstead** was the birthplace in 1578 of William Harvey, the chief physician to Charles I and the discoverer of the circulation of the blood, and in 1705 of the highwayman Dick Turpin, whose parents kept the Bell Inn.

AROUND SAFFRON WALDEN

THAXTED

6 miles SE of Saffron Walden on the B184

Originally a Saxon settlement, this small and thriving country town has numerous attractively pargeted and timber-framed houses along with a magnificent **Guildhall** that dates from around 1390. Built as a meeting place for cutlers, it later became an administrative centre, then part of a school. Built in 1804 by John Webb, the town's famous **Tower Windmill** remained in use until 1907 and now contains a rural life museum.

FINCHINGFIELD

10 miles SE of Saffron Walden on the B1053

A charming village of thatched cottages around a sloping village green, this is one of the most photographed villages in Essex. To the southwest lies the old market town of **Great Bardfield** whose

The jewel in Thaxted's crown is the Church of St John, one of the finest parish churches in the country. The composer Gustav Holst lived in Thaxted from 1914 to 1925 and often played the church organ.

191 THE GEORGE INN

Shalford, nr Braintree

The George is a friendly, family-run village pub serving a fine selection of real ales and a daily-changing selection of tasty home-cooked dishes.

 see page 424

---

192 BRAINTREE DISTRICT MUSEUM

Market Place, Braintree

An award-winning museum whose main displays feature the history of the wool trade, when Braintree was an important medieval centre.

 see page 425

---

193 MOUNTFITCHET CASTLE & NORMAN VILLAGE

Stansted

Reconstruction of a Norman village, together with a motte and bailey castle. A fascinating day out for all the family, it offers a rare insight into life as it was 900 years ago.

 see page 425

most notable feature is its restored windmill that goes by the name of 'Gibraltar'.

BRAINTREE

16½ miles SE of Saffron Walden on the A131

Situated at the crossing of two Roman roads, Braintree and its close neighbour Bocking were brought together by the cloth industry when Flemish and then Huguenot weavers settled here. One Huguenot, Samuel Courtauld, established a silk mill here in 1816 and the **Working Silk Museum** features demonstrations of silk production on the original handlooms. The town's magnificent former **Town Hall** is another legacy of the Courtauld family, and the **Braintree District Museum** tells the story of the town's diverse industrial heritage and traditions.

To the southwest of Braintree can be found the **Great Leighs Great Maze**, one of the most challenging in the world, while to the northwest, at **Great Saling**, is the charming Saling Hall Garden.

GREAT DUNMOW

12 miles SE of Saffron Walden on the A120

This town is famous for the 'Flitch of Bacon', an ancient ceremony that dates back to the early 12th century when a flitch, or side, of bacon is awarded to the local man who "does not repent of his

marriage nor quarrel, differ or dispute with his wife within a year and a day after marriage." In the parish church at **Broxted** a window commemorating the captivity and release of John McCarthy and the other Beirut hostages was dedicated in 1993.

STANSTED MOUNTFICHET

9 miles SW of Saffron Walden on the B1383

Though close to Stansted Airport, this village is worth a visit as it is home to a Norman Village, complete with domestic animals and the reconstructed **Mountfichet Castle**. Next to the castle is the **House on the Hill Toy Museum**, reputedly the largest in the world, with over 80,000 items on display, and nearby is **Stansted Windmill**, which dates from 1787 and is one of the best-preserved tower mills in the country. To the north, at **Widdington**, lies **Mole Hall Wildlife Park** where visitors can see a range of wild and domestic animals along with butterflies, snakes and insects; the village is also home to **Prior's Hall Barn**, a fine medieval 'aisled' barn.

Between Stansted Mountfichet and Hatfield Broad Oak lies **Hatfield Forest**, a former Royal hunting forest where many features of a medieval forest can still be seen.

Gloucestershire

For many, Gloucestershire *is* the Cotswolds, the delightful limestone hills that sweep across the county from Tetbury in the south to Chipping Campden in the north. As well as providing some of the most glorious scenery and the prettiest villages in the country, the county is also home to the historic towns of Cirencester and Cheltenham. However, Gloucestershire is not only about the Cotswolds. To the west, on the River Severn, is the ancient city of Gloucester, while further downriver is the Vale of Berkeley, and historic Berkeley Castle. On the opposite bank of the river lies the old royal hunting ground of the Forest of Dean, once an important mining and industrial area. Bounded by the Rivers Severn and Wye, the area has been effectively isolated from the rest of England and

Wales and so has developed a character that is all its own.

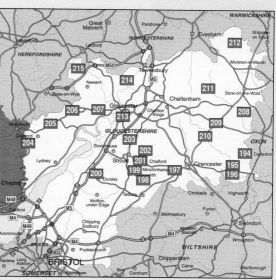

194 THE SWAN AT SOUTHROP

Southrop, east of Cirencester

The **Swan at Southrop** is a fine old village inn serving superb food and wine every lunchtime and evening.

 see page 426

195 ALLIUM

Fairford

Superb modern British/French cooking brings appreciative diners from near and far to **Allium** in a fine 18th century building.

 see page 426

196 THE EIGHT BELLS

Fairford

The **Eight Bells** is a traditional country inn where great hospitality is matched by the ales and the food.

 see page 426

197 THE TUNNEL HOUSE INN

Coates, nr Cirencester

Good food and locally brewed ales complement a lovely rural location at the **Tunnel House Inn**.

see page 427

CIRENCESTER

As Corinium Dobonnorum, this was the second largest Roman town in Britain and, although few signs remain of their occupation today, the award winning **Corinium Museum** features one of the finest collection of antiquities from Roman Britain as well as several room reconstructions.

Now dubbed the 'Capital of the Cotswolds', the Cirencester of today is a lively market town which has built upon the medieval wealth that was generated by its wool trade. One of the many legacies of this era is the magnificent **Church of St John**, perhaps the greatest of all the Cotswold 'wool churches', whose 120 feet tower dominates the town.

AROUND CIRENCESTER

FAIRFORD

9 miles E of Cirencester on the A417

Wealthy wool merchants financed the building of the splendid **Church of St Mary**, whose greatest glory is a set of 28 medieval stained-glass windows depicting the Christian faith in picture-book style.

BIBURY

7 miles NE of Cirencester on the B4425

Described by William Morris, founder of the Arts and Crafts Movement, as "the most beautiful village in England", Bibury remains a delightful place. The most photographed building here is **Arlington Row**, a superb terrace of medieval stone cottages built as a wool store in the 14th century and converted, 300 years later, into weavers' cottages and workshops. The fabric produced here was sent to nearby **Arlington Mill** for fulling and, today, the mill houses a Museum that includes pieces made in the William Morris workshops.

TETBURY

9½ miles SW of Cirencester on the A433

In the heart of this charming old wool town is the superb 17th century Market House which is connected to the old trading centre by the ancient **Chipping Stones**. Among other places of interest is **Tetbury Police Museum** in the cells of the old police station.

Just to the northwest of the town stands **Chavenage House**, a beautiful Elizabethan mansion constructed in the characteristic E-shape of the period. Still occupied by descendants of the original owners, the house contains many relics from the Cromwellian period and Cromwell himself is known to have stayed here. To the southwest of Tetbury lies **Westonbirt Arboretum**, one of the finest collections of trees and shrubs in Europe that was founded by Robert Stayner Holford and added to by his son. Now managed by the Forestry Commission, it offers numerous delightful walks along some 17 miles of footpaths.

CHIPPING SODBURY

23 miles SW of Cirencester on the A432

A pleasant market town that still retains its ancient street pattern, Chipping Sodbury once enjoyed prosperity as a weaving centre, and it was during this period that the large parish church was built. A mile or so to the east lies **Old Sodbury**, whose church contains the tomb of David Harley, the Georgian diplomat who negotiated the treaty that ended the American War of Independence. Just beyond Old Sodbury is the **Badminton Park** estate, founded by Edward Somerset, the son of the Marquis of Worcester. The house is known for its important collection of Italian, English and Dutch paintings and the estate as the venue for Badminton Horse Trials. The game of badminton is said to have started here during a weekend party in the 1860s, when the Duke of Beaufort and his guests wanted to play tennis in the entrance hall but, worried about damaging the paintings, they used a cork studded with feathers instead of a ball.

To the south of Chipping Sodbury and standing on the slope of the Cotswold ridge is **Dyrham Park**, a striking baroque mansion with a fine collection of Delft porcelain and several Dutch paintings among its treasures.

NAILSWORTH

11 miles W of Cirencester on the A46

Another town that thrived on the local wool trade, Nailsworth still has several of its old mills and associated buildings.

Just to the east of the town, in Hampton Fields, is the extraordinary **Avening Long Stone**, a prehistoric standing stone pierced with holes that is said to move on Midsummer's Eve. Another ancient monument, **Nan Tow's Tump**, a huge round barrow tomb that is said to contain the remains of a local witch, can be found to the south near **Ozleworth**.

BERKELEY

21½ miles W of Cirencester on the B4066

This small town lends its name to the fertile strip of land known as the Vale of Berkeley. Its largely Georgian centre is dominated by the Norman **Berkeley Castle**, said to be the oldest inhabited castle in Britain. Built between 1117 and 1153 on the site of a Saxon fort,

198 THE CROSS INN

Avening, nr Tetbury

The **Cross Inn** is a popular village local that also attracts plenty of outsiders with its excellent hospitality.

see page 427

199 THE HALFWAY HOUSE

Box, nr Minchinhampton

The new team who arrived in October 2005 have quickly established the **Halfway House** as one of the top food pubs in the region.

see page 428

Berkeley Castle

Cam, nr Dursley

The **Railway Inn** is a charming public house serving food Monday to Saturday lunchtimes and Friday evening; two rotating guest ales.

see page 427

Brimscombe, nr Stroud

Locals and visitors drop anchor at the **Ship Inn** to enjoy well-kept ales and a variety of home cooking.

see page 427

Eastcombe, nr Stroud

The **Lamb Inn** adds the bonus of a stunning location and lovely views to carefully kept real ales and excellent food.

see page 429

Edge, nr Stroud

Glorious views are an extra reason for visiting the **Edgemoor Inn**, which serves interesting local ales and excellent food.

see page 430

the castle has a rich and colourful history and as well as seeing the many treasures that the Berkeley family have collected over the centuries, visitors can explore the dungeons, the grounds and the medieval bowling alley.

Berkeley was also the home of Edward Jenner, the pioneering doctor and immunologist whose beautiful Georgian house, The Chantry, is now the **Jenner Museum**. At **Slimbridge** is the **Wildlife and Wetlands Centre** founded in 1946 by the great naturalist, artist, sailor and broadcaster Peter (later Sir Peter) Scott. Slimbridge has the world's largest collection of ducks, geese and swans, as well as flamingos and many other exotic wildfowl. Sir Peter died in 1989 and his ashes were scattered at Slimbridge, where he had lived for many years.

STROUD

11 miles W of Cirencester on the A419

With the surrounding hill farms providing a constant supply of wool and the several Cotswold streams which join the River Frome here supplying water power, it is not surprising that Stroud became the capital of the Cotswold woollen industry. By the 1820s there were over 150 textile mills in and around the town though only six survive today – one of these specialises in green baize for snooker tables.

To the east of Stroud lies the delightful village of **Bisley,** which stands some 780 feet above sea level and is known as 'Bisley-God-Help-Us' because of the bitter winter winds that sweep across the hillside. Below the village's impressive church are the **Seven Wells of Bisley** that are blessed and decorated with flowers each year on Ascension Day.

Just to the north of Stroud is the beautiful little wool town of **Painswick** which is known as the 'Queen of the Cotswolds'. Hidden away, to the north, amidst the magnificent Cotswold countryside is **Painswick Rococo Garden**, a unique 18th century garden that features plants from around the world along with a maze, planted in 1999, which commemorates the gardens 250th anniversary.

Further north again is **Prinknash Abbey Park** (pronounced Prinnage) to where the Benedictine monks of Caldey Island moved in 1928. Part of the abbey gardens are given over to the Prinknash Bird and Deer Park.

FRAMPTON-ON-SEVERN

17½ miles W of Cirencester off the B4071

Frampton's large village green, which incorporates a cricket ground and three ponds, was formed when the marshy land outside the gates of **Frampton Court** was drained in the 18th century. The Court is an outstanding example of a Georgian country house and has been the seat of the Clifford family ever since it was completed in the 1730s. On the opposite side of the green is Frampton Manor, also owned by the Cliffords, a much-restored medieval manor whose lovely walled garden contains many rare plants.

To the west of Frampton, on a great bend in the river, is the Arlingham Peninsula, part of the **Severn Way Shepperdine-Tewkesbury Long Distance** footpath. The land on which the village of **Arlingham** stands once belonged to the monks of St Augustine's Abbey, Bristol, and is believed to be the point where St Augustine crossed the Severn on his way to convert the heathen Welsh tribes.

COLEFORD

A former mining town, Coleford developed into an important iron-processing centre due to the availability of local ore deposits and of the ready supply of timber for the smelting process. Still regarded as the capital of the Royal Forest of Dean, Coleford is also home to the **Great Western Railway Museum**, which is housed in an 1883 goods station and numbers several steam locomotives among its exhibits. Another treat for railway enthusiasts is the Perrygrove Railway, with its narrow-gauge steam train and treasure hunt through the woods.

To the southeast lies **Parkend**, which, like many communities in the area, was once based around the extraction of minerals. At the northern terminus of the Dean Forest Railway, just west of the village, is the RSPB's **Nagshead Nature Reserve**.

Just to the south of Coleford are **Clearwell Caves**, the only remaining working iron mine in the

Frampton-on-Severn

Forest of Dean, where ochres for use as paint pigments are produced. Visitors can tour the nine impressive caverns, and several marked walks explore surface mining remains.

AROUND COLEFORD

WESTBURY-ON-SEVERN

9 miles NE of Coleford on the A48

This village is best known as the home of **Westbury Court Garden**, a formal Dutch water garden laid out between 1696 and 1705 that is home to many historic varieties of apple, pear and plum. To the west lies **Littledean Hall**, reputedly the oldest inhabited house in England, which has both Saxon and Celtic remains in its cellars and is thought to date from

204 CHERRY ORCHARD FARM

Newland, nr Coleford

Cherry Orchard Farm offers a choice of B&B rooms and a camping/caravan site in the beautiful Forest of Dean.

see page 430

205 THE SWAN INN

Brierley, Forest of Dean

The **Swan** is a splendid village inn with a fine reputation for the quality of its food.

 see page 430

206 THE YEW TREE

Longhope

The **Yew Tree** is a lovely family-run village inn serving real ales and home-cooked dishes. The beer garden is a great bonus in the summer months.

 see page 431

207 THE KINGS HEAD INN

Birdwood, nr Huntley, Glos

Easily found on the A40 west of Gloucester on the way to Ross On Wye.,The **Kings Head** is an excellent family-friendly inn with an extensive menu and well-equipped guest bedrooms. A warm welcome is extended to all

 see page 431

208 THE LAMB INN

Great Rissington, nr Cheltenham

The ambience, the service, the food and the accommodation have made **The Lamb** one of the Cotswolds' most welcoming country inns.

 see page 431

the 6th century. Westbury is an excellent place to view the famous **Severn Bore**, a tidal wave that several times a month makes its often dramatic way along the river.

LYDNEY
5½ miles SE of Coleford on the B4234

Lydney is the largest settlement between Chepstow and Gloucester, with a harbour and canal that served the iron and coal industries. The town is the southern terminus of the **Dean Forest Railway**, which operates a regular service of steam and diesel trains between here and Parkend. At **Norchard Railway Centre**, the line's headquarters, there is a railway museum, souvenir shop and details of restoration projects.

One of the key attractions in the area is **Lydney Park Gardens and Museum** on the western outskirts of the town. The gardens are not only a riot of colour, particularly in May and June, but they contain the site of an Iron Age hill fort and the remains of a Roman temple.

ST BRIAVELS
4 miles SW of Coleford on the B4228

Named after a 5th century Welsh bishop, St Briavels became an important administrative centre in the Middle Ages and was a leading manufacturer of armaments that supplied both weapons and ammunition to the Crown – in 1223 it is believed that Henry III ordered 6,000 crossbow bolts (called 'quarrels') from the village.

CHELTENHAM

This was a small, insignificant village until a mineral spring was accidentally discovered here in 1715 by a local man, William Mason, who built a pump room and began Cheltenham's transformation into one of Europe's leading Regency spa towns. In 1788, the spa received the royal seal of approval when George III spent five weeks here taking the waters with his family. As an entirely new town was planned and built on the best features of neo-classical Regency architecture there are very few buildings of any real antiquity left, but one is the **Church of St Mary** that dates back in parts to the 12th century.

The tree-lined **Promenade** is one of the most beautiful boulevards in the country, and its crowning glory is the wonderful **Neptune's Fountain** modelled on the Fontana di Trevi in Rome. Housed in Pittville Park, in the magnificent **Pump Room** overlooking gardens and lakes, is the Pittville Pump Room Museum, which uses original period costumes to bring alive the story of Cheltenham from its Regency heyday to the 1960s.

Gustav Holst was born in a terraced Regency house in Clarence Road in 1874 and this is now the **Holst Birthplace Museum and Period House**. The composer's original piano is the centrepiece of the collection that tells the story of the man and his works.

Cheltenham Racecourse, two miles north of town at Prestbury Park, is the home of National Hunt Racing and stages numerous top-quality race meetings throughout the season, culminating in the prestigious March Festival when the Gold Cup and the Champion Hurdle find the year's best steeplechaser and hurdler.

AROUND CHELTENHAM

WINCHCOMBE

5½ miles NE of Cheltenham on the B4632

The **Winchcombe Folk and Police Museum** tells the history of the town from prehistoric times, and the **Winchcombe Railway Museum and Garden** has one of the largest collections of railway equipment in the country: visitors can work signals and clip tickets and generally go misty-eyed about the age of steam. The Cotswold garden surrounding the building is full of old and rare plants.

Just to the north stands the ruins of **Hailes Abbey**, which was founded in 1246 by Richard, Earl of Cornwall and became a place of pilgrimage after a wealthy patron donated to the Cistercian monks a phial said to contain the blood of Christ.

STANTON

10½ miles NE of Cheltenham off the B4632

One of the prettiest spots in the Cotswolds, the whole village was restored by the architect Sir Philip Scott in the years before World War I; his home from 1906 to 1937 was **Stanton Court**, an elegant Jacobean residence built by Queen Elizabeth I's Chamberlain. Beyond Stanton, on the road to Broadway, is **Snowshill Manor**, an elegant mansion dating from Tudor times, which was once the home of Catherine Parr. It now contains a fascinating collection of crafts and artefacts assembled by the last private owner, Charles Paget Wade.

CHIPPING CAMPDEN

16 miles NE of Cheltenham on the B4081

The 'Jewel of the Cotswolds' and full of beautifully restored buildings, Chipping Campden was a regional capital of the wool trade from the 13th to the 16th century and much of the town dates from that era. The **Market Hall** was built in 1627 by the wool merchant, Sir Baptist Hicks; he also endowed a group of almshouses and Old Campden House, which was burnt down by Royalists to prevent it falling into the hands of the enemy.

STOW-ON-THE-WOLD

15½ miles E of Cheltenham on the A429

At 800 feet above sea level, this is the highest town in the Cotswolds and at one time held a twice-yearly sheep fair on the market square where the town stocks still stand today. In Park Street is the **Toy and Collectors Museum**, housing a charming display of toys, trains, teddy bears and dolls, along with textiles and lace, porcelain and pottery.

209 HARDING'S WORLD OF MECHANICAL MUSIC

Northleach

A superb selection of instruments and automata, both antique and modern and incorporates both a working museum and gift shop.

 see page 432

210 THE INN AT FOSSEBRIDGE

Fossebridge, nr Cheltenham

The **Inn at Fossebridge** earns high marks for location, ambience, hospitality, food, drink and accommodation.

 see page 432

211 THE FARMERS ARMS

Guiting Power, nr Cheltenham

The **Farmers Arms** is a cosy, friendly country pub serving real ales and a varied blackboard menu.

 see page 432

212 THE EBRINGTON ARMS

Ebrington, nr Chipping Campden

The **Ebrington Arms** is an 18th century country inn with blackboard menus of home-cooked dishes and three rooms for B&B.

 see page 433

Model Village, Bourton-on-the-Water

Probably the most popular of all the Cotswold villages, Bourton has the willow-lined River Windrush flowing through its centre, crossed by several delightful pedestrian bridges. Here, among the golden stone cottages, is **Miniature World – the Museum of Miniatures** that houses a unique collection of miniature scenes and models. Miniatures seem to be something of a feature here as Bourton is also home to a famous **Model Village** and a Model Railway. Those with a keen nose will want to visit the unique **Perfumery Exhibition**, where the extraction and manufacture of perfume is explained and where there is also a perfume garden.

To the north, at **Lower Slaughter**, is the **Old Mill**, a restored 19th century flour mill with a giant water wheel, while, to the southwest, near the traditional market town of **Northleach**, is the Cotswold Heritage Centre, housed in an old country prison. In the centre of the town, in a 17th century merchant's house, **Keith Harding's World of Mechanical Music** is a fascinating museum of antique self-playing musical instruments.

To the west of Northleach is **Chedworth Roman Villa**, a large, well-preserved villa that was discovered by chance in 1864. Excavations have revealed more than 30 rooms and buildings and some wonderful mosaics.

GLOUCESTER

In the 1st century AD, the Romans established a fort here to guard what was then the lowest crossing point of the River Severn; it was soon replaced by a much larger fortress and the settlement of Glevum quickly became one of the most important military bases in Roman Britain. It was at Gloucester that William the Conqueror held a Christmas parliament and also ordered the rebuilding of the abbey, an undertaking that included a magnificent church that was the forerunner of the superb Norman **Gloucester Cathedral**. The exquisite fan tracery in the cloisters of the Cathedral is the earliest and among the finest in existence and the great east window is the largest surviving medieval stained glass window in the country. It was built to celebrate the English victory at the Battle of Crécy in 1346 and depicts the coronation of the Virgin surrounded by assorted kings, popes and saints. The young Henry III was crowned at the Cathedral, with a bracelet on his little head rather than a crown.

Gloucester Docks were once the gateway for waterborne traffic heading into the Midlands and the handsome Victorian warehouses are home to several award-winning museums. The **National Waterways Museum**, which is entered by a lock chamber with running water, tells the fascinating story of Britain's canals, and the Robert Opie Collection at the **Museum of Advertising and Packaging** takes a nostalgic look at the 1940s through to the 1970s with the aid of toys and food, fashions, packaging and a continuous screening of vintage TV commercials.

In the southwestern suburbs of Gloucester are the ruins of **Llanthony Abbey**, which was moved in the 12th century from its original site in the Black Mountains of Wales - bringing with it its Welsh name - because the monks were terrified of the Welsh.

AROUND GLOUCESTER

NEWENT

5 miles NW of Gloucester on the B4215

This is the capital of an area of northwest Gloucestershire that is known as the Ryelands, home of the renowned Ryelands sheep – an ancient breed famed for the quality of its wool. Naturally, therefore, this was one of the county's principal wool trading centres and there are a number of grand merchant's houses in the town. The most distinctive building, however, is the splendid timber-framed **Market House** which was built as a butter market in the 16th century with its upper floors supported on 16 oak pillars. The **Shambles Museum of Victorian Life** is virtually a little Victorian town, a jumble of cobbled streets and alleyways with shops and even a mission chapel.

There are not a great many windmills in Gloucestershire but at **Castle Hill Farm** is a working wooden mill which provides great views from its balcony. A short distance south is the **National Bird of Prey Centre** that houses one of the largest collections of birds of prey in the world.

A couple of miles east of Newent lies **Pauntley Court** where, in 1350, Richard Whittington, the penniless orphan of the pantomime, was born. Neither poor nor an orphan, Whittington became a mercer in London, then a financier, and he

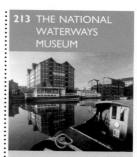

213 THE NATIONAL WATERWAYS MUSEUM

Gloucester

The Museum charts the 300-year story of Britain's inland waterways through interactive displays, touch-screen computers, working models and historic boats.

 see page 433

214 THE HAWBRIDGE INN

Hawbridge, nr Tirley

A great welcome, a superb riverside location, real ales, good food and a camping/caravan site – all in one pub, the **Hawbridge Inn**!

see page 435

215 THE BEAUCHAMP

The Village, Dymock

The **Beauchamp Arms** is a delightful parish-owned pub serving generous helpings of hospitality and tasty food.

see page 434

was indeed Mayor three times (though not Lord Mayor as that title had not yet been created).

DYMOCK

10 miles NW of Gloucester on the B4215

In the years before World War I, this village became the base for a group of writers who became known as the **Dymock Poets**. The group, which included Rupert Brooke, Wilfred Gibson, Edward Thomas and Lascelles Abercrombie and was later joined by Robert Frost, sent out its *New Numbers* poetry magazine from Dymock's tiny post office and it was also from here that Brooke published his War Sonnets, including *The Soldier*. Brooke and Thomas died in the Great War, which led to the dissolution of the group.

TEWKESBURY

A town of historic and strategic importance at the confluence of the Rivers Severn and Avon; these rivers restricted the town's lateral expansion, which accounts for the unusual number of tall buildings. Its early prosperity was based on the wool and mustard trades and

the movement of corn by river also contributed to its wealth. Tewkesbury's main thoroughfares, High Street, Church Street and Barton Street, form a Y-shape, and the area between is a marvellous maze of narrow alleyways and small courtyards hiding many grand old pubs and medieval cottages. At the centre of it all is **Tewkesbury Abbey**, one of the largest parish churches in the country, which was founded in the 8th century and completely rebuilt in the 11th. After the Dissolution, it was saved from destruction by the townspeople, who raised £453 to buy it from the Crown.

The Battle of Tewkesbury, which took place in 1471 in a field south of town, was one of the fiercest in the War of the Roses and the battle site has been known as Bloody Meadow ever since. Following the Lancastrian defeat, those who had not been slaughtered in the battle fled to the Abbey, where the killing began again. The 17-year-old son of Henry VI, Edward Prince of Wales, was killed in the conflict and a plaque marking his final resting place can be seen in the abbey.

Hampshire

Hampshire's coastal crescent, which stretches from Havant to New Milford in the west, is home to two of the country's most famous ports, Southampton and Portsmouth, and the maritime and naval traditions here remain strong. This contrasts greatly with the grand scenery in the northern part of the county and the ancient landscape of the North Downs, home to the historic towns of Winchester and Andover. On the western bank of Southampton Water lies the New Forest, the largest wild area of lowland in Britain, which William the Conqueror set aside as his own private hunting ground over 900 years ago.

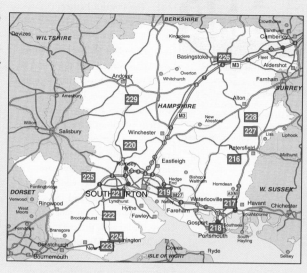

🍴 FOOD & DRINK

216	The Izaak Walton, East Meon	p 120, 435
217	Lotts General Store & Tea Room, Hambledon	p 121, 436
220	The Wheatsheaf at Braishfield, Braishfield	p 122, 437
221	The Forest Inn, Ashurst	p 123, 437
223	The Chequers Inn, Lower Woodside	p 124, 438
224	The Kings Head, Lymington	p 124, 438
225	The Royal Oak at Fritham, Fritham	p 125, 438
227	The Hawkley Inn, Hawkley	p 127, 439
229	The Mayfly, Testcombe	p 128, 440

🛏 ACCOMMODATION

222	The Watersplash Hotel, Brockenhurst	p 123, 436

🏛 PLACES OF INTEREST

218	Portsmouth Historic Dockyard, Portsmouth	p 121, 436
219	Bursledon Windmill, Bursledon	p 122, 436
226	Basing House, Basing	p 126, 439
228	Gilbert White's House, Selborne	p 127, 439

216 THE IZAAK WALTON

East Meon, nr Petersfield

Fine food and an outstanding choice of real ales are just two of the attractions of the **Izaak Walton** free house and restaurant on the main street of East Meon.

 see page 435

SOUTHAMPTON

It was from this historic port that Henry V sailed for Agincourt in 1415, the Pilgrim Fathers embarked on their voyage to the New World in 1620 and the *Titanic* steamed out into the Solent on her tragic first and last voyage. The town was an obvious target for enemy bombing during World War II, but despite the numerous attacks several ancient buildings have survived including a section of the town's medieval walls and their most impressive feature – **Bargate**. Southampton's links with the sea are never far away and the story of the luxury liners that sailed from here, along with the port, is told at the **Maritime Museum** housed in the 14th century Wool House. Along with its maritime heritage, the town was at the centre of the developing aircraft industry and this connection is explored at the

Solent Sky, where the centrepiece is the spectacular Sandringham flying boat.

On the northern outskirts of Southampton lie **Itchen Valley Country Park** and **West End**, the village to which the Captain of the liner *Carpathia*, which rescued passengers from the *Titanic*, retired. His grave lies in an old burial ground near the village's **Local History Museum**.

AROUND SOUTHAMPTON

BISHOPS WALTHAM

8 miles NE of Southampton on the B3035

This charming small town was, for nearly 1,000 years, home of the country residence of the Bishops of Winchester and at their sumptuous **Bishop's Palace** they played host to numerous monarchs. Built in 1136 by Henri de Blois, the

Teddy Bear Museum, Petersfield

palace was largely destroyed during the Civil War although the ruins remain an impressive sight.

PETERSFIELD

21 miles NE of Southampton on the B2070

The oldest building in this pleasant market town is the 12th century **Church of St Peter**. Also of interest are the town museum, the **Teddy Bear Museum**, the first of its kind in Britain, and the **Flora Twirt Gallery**.

HORNDEAN

17 miles E of Southampton off the A3

This village has a long association with brewing and the company of George Gale, founded in 1847, offers guided tours that include the techniques of brewing. To the northwest lies **Queen Elizabeth Country Park**, an Area of Outstanding Natural Beauty which contains many Roman and Iron Age sites as well as the three hills of Butser, War Down and Holt Down. Nearby, **Butser Ancient Farm** is a living, working reconstruction of an Iron Age farm.

Further northwest lies **Hambledon**, the village where the rules of cricket were laid down in 1774 and where a monument stands on **Broadhalfpenny Down**, where the early games were played.

HAVANT

18 miles SE of Southampton on the A27

Originally a Roman crossroads, the town developed into a leading manufacturing centre; the whole history of the town is explored and explained at the **Havant Museum**. To the north lies one of the south of England's most elegant stately homes, **Stansted Park**, which houses numerous treasures and stands in particularly attractive grounds. To the southeast is the picturesque village of **Emsworth**, for many years the home of the novelist PG Wodehouse.

To the south of Havant is **Hayling Island**, a traditional family seaside holiday resort with a five-mile sandy beach.

PORTSMOUTH

15 miles SE of Southampton on the A288

Portsmouth is the country's leading naval base, and **Portsmouth Historic Dockyard** is home to three of the greatest ships ever built. The most famous of all is *HMS Victory*, from which Nelson masterminded the decisive encounter with the French navy off Cape Trafalgar in 1805. Here, too, lies the *Mary Rose*, the second largest ship in Henry VIII's fleet, which foundered on her maiden voyage and was raised in 1983. *HMS Warrior*, the Navy's first ironclad warship, can also be seen. Also within the Dockyard are the **Dockyard Apprentice** and **Action Stations**, an exciting exhibition that brings the modern Navy to life. Dominating the Portsmouth skyine is the **Spinnaker Tower**, representing a billowing sail and extending some 550 feet into the sky. **Southsea**, the southern part of the city, also has much to offer: the **D. Day Museum** that commemorates the

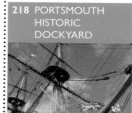

219 BURSLEDON WINDMILL

Bursledon

The last surviving working windmill in Hampshire, built in 1814, has been restored and is in full working order.

 see page 436

220 THE WHEATSHEAF AT BRAISHFIELD

Braishfield, nr Romsey

The **Wheatsheaf** is a superb country inn with a reputation for great food that has reached far beyond the local area.

 see page 437

Allied invasion of France in 1944; the **Royal Marines Museum** housed in Eastney Barracks; and **Portsmouth Sea Life Centre** which reflects the city's rich maritime history. **Southsea Castle**, built in 1545 by Henry VIII, was altered in the early 19th century to accommodate more guns and men. Just offshore lies Spitbank Fort, a huge Victorian defence that is reached by ferry from Southsea pier.

At the head of Portsmouth Harbour stands **Portchester Castle**, one of the grandest medieval castles in the country, built on the site of a Roman fort.

FAREHAM

10 miles SE of Southampton on the A27

Many aspects of this charming old town are exhibited in **Westbury Manor Museum**, housed in a 17th century farmhouse on the town's outskirts. Nearby are the Royal Armouries at **Fort Nelson** where the display of artillery, dating from the Middle Ages, is one of the finest in the world.

To the southeast lies **Gosport**, home to another of Lord Palmerston's forts, the circular Fort Brockhurst, and of the **Royal Naval Submarine Museum** located at *HMS Dolphin*, where visitors can look over several submarines. **Explosion! The Museum of Naval Firepower** is dedicated to the brave people who prepared Navy armaments from Trafalgar to the present day.

HAMBLE

5 miles SE of Southampton on the B3397

A major medieval trading port and once a centre of the shipbuilding industry on the River Hamble, this village is now famous throughout the world as a yachting centre, and some 3,000 boats have berths in the Estuary. To the south lies **Hamble Common**, an area of coastal heath with a wide range of habitats.

Just to the north lies **Bursledon**, another village with a strong maritime heritage: it was here that King Alfred's men sank 20 Viking longships, and Nelson's flagship at the Battle of Copenhagen, *The Elephant*, was built here. Close by, on a hilltop setting, is **Bursledon Windmill**, fully restored to working order. The village also has a relic of the county's industrial heritage – **Burlesdon Brickworks**, built in 1897 and after closing in 1974, restored and opened to the public.

ROMSEY

6½ miles NW of Southampton on the A3057

Romsey Abbey was founded in AD 907 by Edward the Elder, son of Alfred the Great, though most of what remains dates from the 12th and 13th centuries. Close to the Abbey stands the oldest secular building in the town, **King John's House**. Other places of interest here include **Romsey Signal Box**, home to numerous railway artefacts, and **Broadlands**, a gracious

Palladian mansion set in grounds landscaped by Capability Brown which was the family home of Lord Palmerston, three times Prime Minister in the 1850s and 1860s. The house passed to the Mountbatten family, and it was Lord Louis who first opened it to the public, shortly before his death in 1979. The Mountbatten Exhibition commemorates his life.

To the northeast lies the **Sir Harold Hillier Garden and Arboretum** which is based on the collection of this renowned gardener and now houses 11 National Plant Collections. Southeast of Romsey lies **East Wellow**, where Florence Nightingale was buried beneath the family monument on her death in 1910.

To the northwest is **Mottisfont Abbey**, which was originally an Augustinian priory but was adapted into a country mansion in the 16th century.

LYNDHURST

The only town of any size in the New Forest, Lyndhurst still remains its administrative centre. Next to the compact **Church of St Michael and All Angels** in whose churchyard is the grave of Alice Liddell, the inspiration for Alice in Lewis Carroll's novels, stands **Queen's House**. Originally a medieval hunting lodge, the house is now the Headquarters of the Forestry Commission and also home to the **Verderers' Court**, an institution dating back to Norman times that still deals with matters concerning the Forest's ancient common rights. In the High Street, the **New Forest Museum and Visitor Centre** has numerous displays covering all aspects of the forest.

To the northeast, at **Ashurst**, is the **Otter, Owl and Wildlife Conservation Park**.

To the northwest, near the picturesque village of **Minstead**, lie **Furzey Gardens**, which were laid out in the 1920s and provide excellent views over the New Forest to the Isle of Wight. Close by stands the **Rufus Stone** that is said to mark the spot where William Rufus, son of William the Conqueror, was killed by an arrow while out hunting.

AROUND LYNDHURST

BEAULIEU

7 miles SE of Lyndhurst on the B3056

Cistercian monks built an abbey by the River Beaulieu in the 13th century, and some of the abbey's buildings survive today, incorporated into a country estate now owned by Lord Montagu. The estate is most famous for its **National Motor Museum**, where over 300 historic vehicles are on display. Many Montagu family treasures can be seen in **Palace House**, the former Great Gatehouse of Beaulieu Abbey.

221 THE FOREST INN

Ashurst

The **Forest Inn** is a popular local and an ideal spot to seek out for its warm, traditional ambience and its top-notch food.

see page 437

222 THE WATERSPLASH HOTEL

Brockenhurst

Family-run and family-friendly, providing guests with a winning combination of hospitality, comfortable bedrooms and fine English food.

see page 436

123

Lower Woodside, Lymington

The **Chequers Inn** attracts a mix of locals, tourists and yachtsmen with an excellent selection of food and real ales.

 see page 438

Quay Hill, Lymington

The **Kings Head** is an outstanding old inn a short walk from the quayside, attracting customers with a special blend of conviviality and great food and drink.

see page 438

At the mouth of the River Beaulieu lies **Buckler's Hard**, a popular place for yachts and cruisers. Facing Buckler's Hard across the River Beaulieu stands **Exbury** where, in the 1920s, Lionel de Rothschild created **Exbury Gardens** with their world-renowned displays of rhododendrons, camellias and azaleas.

FAWLEY
10 miles SE of Lyndhurst on the A326

Despite the vast oil terminals and refineries of one of Europe's largest oil plants dominating the village, Fawley has retained some links with the past: the gardens of **Cadland House**, which were designed by Capability Brown,

house the National Collection of leptospermums.

To the southeast lies **Calshot**, home to RAF bases during both World Wars; at the very end of a shingle spit stands **Calshot Castle**, built by Henry VIII, now restored as a pre-World War I garrison.

LYMINGTON
8 miles S of Lyndhurst on the A337

An ancient seaport and market town, Lymington was once a major manufacturer of salt and the **St Barbe Museum** tells the story of this area, between the Solent and the New Forest, with special reference to the salt industry. Just up the River Lymington is the pretty village of **Boldre** whose charming 13th century church has

The Quay, Lymington

become a shrine to *HMS Hood* which was sunk by the *Bismarck* in 1941 with the loss of 1,400 lives.

NEW MILTON

9½ miles SW of Lyndhurst on the A332

The best-known landmark in this lively little town is its splendid **Water Tower** of 1900. A particularly striking octagonal building with a castellated parapet, it has the look of a castle rather than part of the town's water system. Just to the west of the town, the **Sammy Miller Museum and Farm Trust** holds the finest collection of fully restored machines in Europe.

To the southeast lies the unspoilt resort of **Milford-on-Sea**, from where a shingle spit extends out to sea; from its end it is less than a mile to the Isle of Wight. Here stands **Hurst Castle**, another in the chain of fortresses built by Henry VIII, while just inland are **Braxton Gardens**, with their beautiful roses and knot garden.

RINGWOOD

10 miles W of Lyndhurst on the A31

Despite extensive modernisation, this town on the western edge of the New Forest still boasts a number of elegant old buildings; notable among these are Ringwood Meeting House, now a museum, and **Monmouth House**, which both date from the early 18th century. At Crow, to the southeast, is the **New Forest Owl Sanctuary**, home to a vast collection of owls

and several pairs of breeding red squirrels.

FORDINGBRIDGE

10 miles NW of Lyndhurst on the A338

The main feature here is the medieval **Great Bridge** which has seven elegant arches and is upstream from the original ford. The town was loved by painter Augustus John and he spend much of the last 30 years of his life at Fryern Court, an austere Georgian house.

To the north lies the unspoilt village of **Breamore** and 16th century Breamore House which overlooks the Avon Valley. The house has a fine collection of 17th and 18th century paintings of the Dutch School, and the grounds are home to the **Countryside Museum** and its reconstruction of a Tudor village. Close by, on **Breamore Down**, is a mizmaze, a circular maze cut into the turf – why, nobody knows.

To the northwest is **Rockbourne Roman Villa** where excavations have revealed the remains of a large villa, with some 40 rooms, superb mosaics and part of its underfloor heating system.

WINCHESTER

Winchester was the capital of King Alfred's Kingdom of Wessex in the 9th century, and two centuries later work began on the Cathedral. **Winchester Cathedral** is filled with priceless treasures, including

225 THE ROYAL OAK AT FRITHAM

Fritham, nr Lyndhurst

The **Royal Oak** is an unspoilt New Forest pub serving a superb selection of real ales and appetising lunchtime food.

¶ see page 438

226 BASING HOUSE

Basing

Once the largest private residence in the country, the ruins of Basing House in its delightful setting, is a superb attraction.

 see page 439

copies of the Winchester Bible and Bede's *Ecclesiastical History*. The tombs of William II (Rufus), Jane Austen and Izaak Walton are among the many here, along with that of St Swithin, a 9th century bishop to whom the Cathedral is dedicated.

The area round the Cathedral holds a wealth of interest: the Deanery, occupied continuously since the 13th century; the **Pilgrims' Hall** with its marvellous hammerbeam roof; Cheyney Court, once the Bishops' courthouse; Jane Austen's House where she spent the last six weeks of her life; and the renowned College, with its beautiful chapel, founded in 1382. Here too is **Wolvesey Castle**, the chief residence of the medieval bishops, where, in 1554, Queen Mary first met Philip of Spain; the wedding banquet was held the very next day.

The only surviving part of **Winchester Castle** is its Great Hall, behind which is Queen Eleanor's Garden, a faithful representation of a medieval garden; the grounds are also the site of the Peninsula Barracks, which includes several military museums.

The story of the Red Cross in Hampshire is told at the **Balfour Museum** and, at the Historic Resources Centre there is a vast collection of historic records for this area. This centre is near the site of **Hyde Abbey**, which recent excavations have revealed as being the probable site of King Arthur's final burial place.

AROUND WINCHESTER

WHITCHURCH
11½ miles N of Winchester on the B3400

Once an important coaching stop between London and Exeter, Whitchurch has a unique attraction, **Whitchurch Silk Mill**, the last working silk mill in the south of England.

BURGHCLERE
19½ miles N of Winchester off the A34

This village is home to the **Sandham Memorial Chapel** where, in the 1920s, Stanley Spencer was commissioned to paint murals on the walls depicting scenes from World War I. The moving paintings are best seen on a bright day as the chapel has no lighting.

Southwest lies **Highclere Castle**, the largest mansion in the county, on the site of a former palace of the Bishops of Winchester.

BASINGSTOKE
17 miles NE of Winchester on the A30

Despite the extensive building work of the 1960s, there are still reminders of old Basingstoke to be seen including the evocative ruins of the 13th century **Chapel of the Holy Ghost** and the 19th century old Town Hall that is now home to the **Willis Museum**.

To the north lies **The Vyne**, a fine 16th century country house that is noted for its linenfold panelling, Gothic painted vaulting and a Tudor chapel with Renaissance stained glass. To the east of Basingstoke is **Old Basing**, a place of narrow streets and old cottages and the ruins of **Basing House**. Built on a massive scale within the walls of a medieval castle, the house was once the largest private residence in the country.

SILCHESTER
22 miles NE of Winchester off the A340

This village is home to the famous Roman site of **Calleva Atrebatum** where on-going excavations have revealed one of the most complete plans of any Roman town in Britain. East of Silchester is the estate of **Stratfield Saye House**, which was presented to the Duke of Wellington as a reward for his defeat of Napoleon at Waterloo. It is full of Wellington artefacts, including books, flags and his ornate funeral carriage, and one whole room of the house is devoted to his beloved charger, Copenhagen.

FARNBOROUGH
29 miles NE of Winchester on the A325

Famous for the **Farnborough Air Show**, the town is also home to **St Michael's Abbey** which was built in a flamboyant French style by the Empress Eugenie in honour of her husband Napoleon III.

To the south lies **Aldershot**, a little-known village until the Army established the town as the most famous military centre in the country. The **Aldershot Military Museum**, housed in the only two surviving Victorian barrack blocks, tells the history of the military town and the adjoining civilian town.

ALTON
16 miles NE of Winchester on the A339

The town's impressive double-naved **St Lawrence's Church** was the scene of a dramatic episode during the Civil War when a large force of Roundheads drove 80 Royalists into the church, killing 60 of them. Elsewhere in the town, the **Allen Gallery** contains a fine collection of porcelain and pottery including the famous Elizabethan Tichborne spoons.

Just to the south is **Chawton House**, the home of Jane Austen from 1809 until shortly before her death in 1817, and now home to the Jane Austen Museum. A little further from Alton lies the attractive village of **Selborne** which was, in 1720, the birthplace of the naturalist Gilbert White. His house, The Wakes, is now the **Gilbert White Museum**. The Wakes also contains the **Oates Museum**, which is dedicated to Francis Oates, the Victorian explorer, and his nephew, Captain Lawrence Oates, who was a member of Captain Scott's ill-fated South Pole expedition.

NEW ALRESFORD
7 miles E of Winchester on the A31

Founded in about 1200, New Arlesford has long been a world

227 THE HAWKLEY INN

Hawkley Inn, nr Liss

The **Hawkley Inn** attracts real ale connoisseurs and lovers of good food to a picturesque village in good walking country.

 see page 439

228 GILBERT WHITE'S HOUSE AND THE OATES MUSEUM

Selborne

The house contains a display of possessions of the author and naturalist, the Reverend Gilbert White. The Oates Museum is dedicated to Captain Lawrence Oates, who accompanied Scott to the Antarctic.

see page 439

Testcombe, nr Stockbridge

The **Mayfly** enjoys a wonderful setting on the banks of the River Test. Well worth seeking out also for the great ambience and super food and drink.

see page 440

centre of the watercress industry – so much so, that the railway line that carried the commodity to London was dubbed the **Watercress Line**. Now kept going by enthusiasts as a steam railway, it runs between here and Alton.

Close by is one of the finest stately homes in England, **Avington Park**, which stands on a site that was once used by the Romans. The River Itchen, renowned for its trout and watercress beds, rises close to the village of **Hinton Ampner** and here can be found **Hinton Ampner House and Gardens**.

STOCKBRIDGE

8 miles NW of Winchester on the A30

Situated on the trout-rich River Test, which flows through, under and alongside its broad main street, Stockbridge attracts visitors with its antique shops, art galleries and charming tearooms. To the south of the town lies **Houghton Lodge Gardens and Hydroponicum**, a charming 18th century cottage with glorious views over the Test Valley that also has a hydroponic greenhouse.

To the northwest is **Danbury Iron Age Hillfort** and nearby is the village of **Middle Wallop** which became famous during the Battle of Britain, when the nearby airfield was a base for squadrons of Spitfires and Hurricanes. The **Museum of Army Flying** houses an important collection that traces the development of Army flying from its beginnings during World War I.

ANDOVER

11 miles NW of Winchester on the A3057

A picturesque market town with a history going back to Saxon times, the market place is dominated by a handsome **Guildhall**; many of its coaching inns survive from the days when Andover was an important stopping place on the routes between London, Oxford and Southampton.

Just to the west of Andover, at **Weyhill**, is the **Hawk Conservancy and Country Park**, home to over 150 birds of prey from around the world. It was at the Weyhill October Fair that the future mayor, in Thomas Hardy's novel *The Mayor of Casterbridge*, sold his wife and child.

Herefordshire

With its rolling landscape, pretty villages and charming market towns, Herefordshire is a delightful place to visit and, as it has few natural resources, there are few industrial scars to mar the countryside. Apples and hops are the traditional crops of the county and cider producing remains a thriving industry. Sheep and cattle are also a familiar sight. Hereford cattle still abound and their stock are now to be found in many parts of the world.

Skirmishes with the Welsh were a common occurrence for many centuries and one of the county's best known landmarks, Offa's Dyke, was built in the 8th century as a defence against these marauders. The River Wye, which enters England at Hay-on-Wye, winds its way through some of the most glorious countryside in all the land before finally joining with the River Severn at its estuary. The whole length, which takes in many ancient villages and small towns, provides excellent walking, and the Wye Valley Walk follows the river for 112 miles, the majority in Herefordshire.

The valley is a designated Area of Outstanding Natural Beauty, while the river itself was the first to be recognised as a Site of Special Scientific Interest.

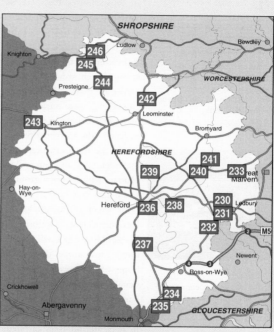

230 THE HORSESHOE INN

The Homend, Ledbury

The **Horseshoe Inn** is open all day for drinks and a good variety of lunchtime dishes. Pretty beer garden and 2 rooms for B&B.

 see page 440

231 7 SEVEN

The Homend, Ledbury

7 Seven provides a pretty 16th century setting for enjoying an all-day choice of food and drink. Also three rooms for B&B.

 see page 440

232 THE ROYAL OAK

Much Marcle

New owners are enhancing the **Royal Oak's** status as one of the top destination dining pubs in the region.

see page 441

ROSS-ON-WYE

This lovely old market town is signalled from some way out by the towering spire of St Mary's Church, which stands on a sandstone cliff surrounded by a cluster of attractive houses. Opposite the church is a row of rosy-red Tudor almshouses. In 1637, the town was visited by the Black Death and over 300 victims to the plague are buried in the churchyard, where their graves are marked by a simple cross. They were buried in the dead of night in an effort to avoid panicking the townspeople.

In the town's market square is the splendid 17th century **Market House**, with its open ground floor and pillars that support the upper floor, which is now the local Heritage Centre. Opposite the Market House is a half-timbered house (now shops) that was the home of the town's greatest benefactor, John Kyrle. A wealthy barrister who had studied law at the Middle Temple, Kyrle settled in Ross in around 1660 and dedicated the rest of his life to philanthropic works: he donated the town's main public garden, **The Prospect**; he repaired St Mary's spire; he provided a constant supply of fresh water; and he paid for food and education for the poor.

Another interesting building to look out for is **Thrushes Nest** that was once the home of Sir Frederick Burrows, a gentleman who began his working life as a railway porter and rose above his station to become the last Governor of Bengal. The town has two very different museums: the **Lost Street Museum**, which is a time capsule of shops and a pub dating from 1885 to 1935, and the **Button Museum**, which is unique as it is the only museum devoted entirely to buttons.

Ross-on-Wye is well known for its **International Festival** of music, opera, theatre, comedy and film that takes place annually in August. Among the examples of modern public art littered around the town is a mural celebrating the life of the locally born playwright Dennis Potter.

To the south of Ross-on-Wye is **Hope Mansell Valley**, one of the loveliest and most fertile valleys in the region.

AROUND ROSS-ON-WYE

BROCKHAMPTON

4½ miles N of Ross-on-Wye off the B4224

This charming village is home to one of only two thatched churches in the country. The **Church of All Saints** was designed by William Lethaby and built in 1902 by Alice Foster, a wealthy American lady, as a memorial to her parents. The Norfolk thatch is one of many lovely features of this beautifully situated church, which also has stained glass from Christopher Whall's studio and tapestries designed by Burne-Jones.

This is great walking country, and the once busy mining community of **Mordiford** is an excellent place from which to explore the Forestry Commission's Haugh Wood.

LEDBURY

11 miles NE of Ross-on-Wye on the A449

Mentioned in the *Domesday Book* as Ledeberge and granted its market status in the 12th century, this classic rural town is filled with timber-framed black and white buildings. Its most famous son was the Poet Laureate John Masefield, who wrote of his birthplace as 'A little town of ancient grace'. In the centre is the **Barrett Browning Institute** that was erected in 1892 in memory of Elizabeth Barrett Browning whose family lived at nearby Colwall. The town's symbol is the 17th century **Market House**, which stands on wooden pillars and is attributed to the royal carpenter John Abel. Another notable landmark is the Norman parish church of **St Michael and All Angels**, with a soaring spire set on a separate tower, some magnificent medieval brasses, fine monuments - and bullet holes in the door, the scars of the Battle of Ledbury.

Overlooking the Malvern Hills, just to the east of Ledbury, lies **Eastnor Castle**, a fairytale castle that has the look of a medieval fortress but was actually built between 1881 and 1924. Wanting a magnificent baronial castle, the 1st Earl Somers engaged the young architect Robert Smirke, and the result is a fine example of the great Norman and Gothic architectural revival that was taking place at that time.

SYMONDS YAT

5½ miles SW of Ross-on-Wye on the B4432

This inland resort and well-known beauty spot offers glorious views, walks, river cruises, wildlife, history and adventure including canoeing down the River Wye and rock climbing. The village is divided into east and west by the river and, with no vehicular bridge at this point, pedestrians cross by means of a punt ferry that is pulled across the river by a chain. Walking in the area is a delight, and among the many landmarks nearby are **Seven Sisters Rocks**, a collection of oolitic limestone crags; Merlin's Cave; King Arthur's Cave, where the bones of mammoths and other prehistoric creatures have been found; Coldwell Rocks, where peregrine falcons nest; **The Biblins** with a swaying suspension bridge that provides a vertiginous crossing of the river; and **Yat Rock** itself, which rises to 500 feet above sea level at a point where the river performs a long, majestic loop.

The **Jubilee Maze** is an amazing hedge puzzle created to celebrate Elizabeth II's Silver Jubilee and, on the same site, there is a Museum of Mazes and a puzzle shop.

Upriver from Symonds Yat, at the little settlement of **Kerne Bridge**, where coracles are still made, walkers can hike up to the majestic ruins of **Goodrich Castle** in a commanding position overlooking the River Wye. Built of red sandstone in the 11th century by Godric Mapplestone,

131

236 CIDER MUSEUM & KING OFFA DISTILLERY

Hereford

The Cider Museum explores the history of cider making with re-constructed cider house and coopers workshop.

 see page 442

237 THE AXE & CLEAVER

Much Birch

The **Axe & Cleaver** is a fine old country inn offering the very best local produce in excellent food served every lunchtime and evening. Camping and caravan site.

 see page 442

238 YEW TREE PUB & LEN GEE'S RESTAURANT

Priors Frome, nr Dormington

Len Gees is a delightful country pub and restaurant in a pleasant village setting with great views and walks.

 see page 443

the castle was the last bastion to fall in the Civil War when it finally gave way after a four and a half month siege.

WORMELOW

10 miles NW of Ross-on-Wye on the A466

The **Violette Szabo GC Museum** celebrates the bravery of the young woman who parachuted into Nazi-occupied France to work with the Resistance.

HEREFORD

Founded as a settlement near the unstable Welsh Marches after the Saxons had crossed the River Severn in the 7th century, Hereford grew to become an important centre of the wool trade. Fragments of the Saxon and medieval walls can still be seen today but Hereford's crowning glory is its **Cathedral**, often called the Cathedral of the Marches. Largely Norman, the Cathedral has, in its impressive New Library building, two of the country's most important historic treasures. The **Mappa Mundi** is a renowned medieval world map, drawn on vellum, which has Jerusalem as its centre and East at the top, indicating that East was the source of all things good and was religiously significant. Richard of Haldingham, its creator, was the Treasurer of Lincoln Cathedral; that explains why Lincoln appears rather more prominently on the map than Hereford. The other great treasure is the **Chained Library**, which houses 1,500 rare

books that are all chained to their original 17th century book presses.

The city's restored pumping station is now home to the **Waterworks Museum** where a wide range of Victorian technology is still very much alive in the shape of the collection of pumps along with Britain's largest triple expansion engine on display. Hereford and cider are old friends and the **Cider Museum** tells the interesting story of cider production down the ages. Also on the outskirts of the city are the Cider Mills of HP Bulmer, the world's leading cider producer, where visitors can take guided tours with tastings.

AROUND HEREFORD

HOPE UNDER DINMORE

7½ miles N of Hereford on the A49

South of the village stretch the green spaces of **Queen's Wood Country Park**, a popular place for walking that also provides panoramic views over the surrounding countryside; its arboretum has a wonderful variety of specimen trees. Adjoining the park is Dinmore Manor, where the Knights Hospitallers had their local headquarters, but today it is the manor's magnificent sheltered gardens that draw most people.

BROMYARD

13 miles NE of Hereford on the A44

This charming little market town on the banks of the River Frome is home to the **Teddy Bear Museum** housed in an old bakery. The

Bromyard Heritage Centre tells the story of the local hop growing industry and illustrates life in the town down the centuries.

ABBEY DORE

10 miles SW of Hereford on the B4347

In the 12th century a Cistercian Abbey was founded here and the building, which was substantially restored in the 17th century, is still used as the parish church. The gardens of **Abbey Dore Court**, through which the River Dore flows, are home to many unusual shrubs and perennials including a specialist collection of euphorbias, hellebores and peonies.

Another delightful garden, **Pentwyn Cottage Garden**, can be found just to the north at nearby **Bacton**.

HAY-ON-WYE

17 miles W of Hereford on the B4348

Situated on the border with Wales, Hay-on-Wye is a must for bookworms as there are nearly 40 secondhand bookshops in this small town. Richard Booth, known as the King of Wye, opened the first bookshop here more than 40 years ago and he was also instrumental in setting up the annual **Hay Book Festival** that now draws people from all over the world. However, Hay is not just bookshops - there are plenty of antique shops here, too.

A few miles southeast of the town lie the ruins of **Craswall Priory**, which was founded in the 13th century by the rare Grandmontine order and abandoned just 200 years later.

EARDISLEY

13 miles NW of Hereford on the A4111

Inside the village's **Church of St Mary Magdalene** is an early 12th century font that is decorated with figures that depict not only familiar religious themes but also two men engaged in an armed struggle. It is

Hay-on-Wye

239 THE GOLDEN CROSS INN

Sutton St Nicholas

Chargrilled Hereford steaks are a popular order at the **Golden Cross Bar & Restaurant** in a picturesque village north of Hereford.

 see page 443

240 THE FIR TREE INN

Much Cowane, nr Bromyard

The **Fir Tree** is a grand old village inn dispensing generous hospitality and good food and drink.

see page 443

241 THE GREEN DRAGON

Bishops Frome

The **Green Dragon** is everything a village local should be, with a warm, inviting feel, a good choice of real ales and tasty home cooking.

see page 444

242 THE STOCKTON CROSS INN

Kimbolton, nr Leominster

Blackboard menus offer an exceptional variety at the **Stockton Cross Inn**, using local produce and including seasonal fish and game

 see page 444

believed that these are a 12th century lord of the manor, Ralph de Baskerville, and his father-in-law, whom he killed in a dispute over land. As a penance, Ralph was ordered by the authorities to commission the extraordinary font. Outside the village, standing majestically by an old chapel, is a **Great Oak** that is thought to be some 800 years old.

Almeley Castle, just to the north east of Eardisley, was once the home of Sir John Oldcastle, who is believed to be the model for Shakespeare's Falstaff.

WEOBLEY

9½ miles NW of Hereford on the B4230

The steeple of this pretty town's parish Church of St Peter and St Paul is the second highest in Herefordshire and is a reminder that this was once a thriving market town. As well as supporting the local farming communities, one of Weobley's more unusual sources of wealth was a successful glove making industry that flourished in the early 19th century when the traditional French source of gloves was cut off due to the Napoleonic Wars. One of the town's many interesting buildings is **The Throne Inn**, where Charles I took refuge after the Battle of Naseby in 1645.

LEOMINSTER

The largest town in this part of Herefordshire, Leominster's unusual name is thought to be linked to the 7th century King of Mercia, Merewald, who was renowned for his bravery and so earned himself the nickname of 'the Lion'. The priory Church of St Peter and St Paul, which was originally King Merewald's convent, became a monastery in the 11th century and its three naves attest to its past importance. Close by, in Priory Park, is **Grange Court**, a fine timbered building that for many years stood in the Market Place. Built in 1633, the court is the work of the royal architect John Abel and displays his characteristic flamboyance in its elaborate carvings.

AROUND LEOMINSTER

ASHTON

3½ miles N of Leominster on the A49

This village is home to **Berrington Hall**, an elegant 18th century mansion designed by Henry Holland, who later became architect to the Prince Regent. The house is noted for its fine furniture and paintings, a nursery, a Victorian laundry, a tiled Georgian dairy and above all its beautifully decorated ceilings: in the drawing room is the highlight, the central medallion of Jupiter, Cupid and Venus. The surrounding parkland was laid out by Holland's father-in-law, Lancelot 'Capability' Brown.

PEMBRIDGE

6½ miles W of Leominster on the A44

The influential Mortimer family were responsible for the medieval prosperity of historic Pembridge

Grange Court, Leominster

To the east of Pembridge is the glorious village of Eardisland, a charming place on the banks of the River Arrow that is one of the most beautiful in the county. A mile outside lies Burton Court, whose centrepiece is the sumptuous 14th century Great Hall. Many additions have been made to the building down the years and the present entrance, dating from 1912, is the work of Sir Clough Williams-Ellis, the man responsible for the Italianate village of Portmeirion in North Wales.

243 HERGEST CROFT GARDENS

Kington

Four gardens for all seasons, giving year round colour and interest.

 see *page 444*

and the many handsome buildings bear witness to their patronage. The delightful 16th century **Market Hall** stands on eight oak pillars, the Old Chapel Gallery is housed in a converted Victorian chapel, and the 14th century church has a marvellous timber **Belfry**.

SHOBDON

8 miles W of Leominster on the B4362

The **Church of St John the Evangelist** is one of the most flamboyant in the whole country, its 'wedding cake rococo' interior a

jaw-dropping sight for first-time visitors. Just north of the village is a collection of Norman sculptures known as the **Shobdon Arches** that, though greatly damaged by centuries of exposure to the elements, still demonstrate the superb skills of the 12th century sculptors.

KINGTON

12 miles W of Leominster on the A44

Close to the Welsh border, Kington, like other towns in Marches, was for centuries under

135

244 YE OLDE OAK INN

Wigmore

Four well-kept real ales and excellent home cooking are two good reasons to make the short detour from the A4110 to visit **Ye Olde Oak Inn**.

 see page 445

245 WALFORD COURT

Walford, nr Leintwardine

Walford Court is an ideal spot for a relaxing break in quiet, scenic surroundings. The two superbly appointed guest rooms are in lavish period style.

 see page 444

246 THE LION HOTEL

Leintwardine

Top-class cuisine and glorious surroundings are among the attractions of the **Lion Hotel**, a delightful 18th century hostelry with a lovely riverside garden.

see page 445

threat of attack from the west. Its castle was destroyed many years ago, but outside the town, on Wapley Hill, are the earthworks of an ancient hill fort that is thought to be the site of King Caractacus' last stand. The most notable of all the defences in this border country is **Offa's Dyke**, the imposing ditch that extends for almost 180 miles from the Severn Estuary at Sedbury Cliffs to Prestatyn on the North Wales coast. Remnants of the wooden stakes unearthed down the years suggest that the dyke had a definite defensive role, rather than merely acting as a psychological barrier. This truly massive construction was in places almost 60 feet wide, and the stretch north of Kington is especially well preserved today and provides excellent and invigorating walking.

To the west of the town lies the impressive Hergest Ridge, which rises to around 1,400 feet,

and on its southern edge is **Hergest Court**, once owned by the Vaughan family. Several of these feisty Vaughans are buried in the Vaughan Chapel in Kington's parish church. **Hergest Croft Gardens** provide a dazzling display of colour from spring to autumn.

YARPOLE

3½ miles NW of Leominster off the B4361

Close to this delightful village with its jumble of cottages is **Croft Castle**, whose parkland contains many ancient oak trees and an avenue of 350-year-old Spanish chestnut trees. Behind the defensive exterior of the castle, the elegant staterooms contain rare furniture, fine plasterwork and portraits of the Croft family, who have almost continuously occupied the castle since it was built in the 14th century. Just a short walk from the castle is **Croft Ambrey**, an Iron Age fort from which there are stunning views.

Hertfordshire

Although Hertfordshire borders London, it remained essentially a rural county until the construction of the Grand Union Canal. There are still peaceful walks to be enjoyed along the canal's towpath, which flows through a gap in the Chiltern Hills on its journey to the Midlands. It was in the Edwardian era that the first Garden Cities were conceived and built here following the plans of Ebenezer Howard. Later, after World War II, several old market towns were developed as New Towns to provide pleasant housing primarily for those made homeless during London's Blitz. Further north, the countryside remains chiefly rural and there are numerous villages of timber-framed cottages and quiet market towns to explore.

Hertfordshire has its fair share of Roman remains, particularly at St Albans and Welwyn, and there are also several grand stately homes tucked away in the rolling countryside.

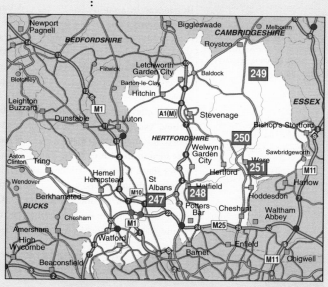

FOOD & DRINK

249	Tally Ho, Barkway	p 141, 446
250	The White Horse, High Cross	p 142, 447
251	The Red Lion, Stanstead Abbots	p 142, 448

PLACES OF INTEREST

247	St Albans Museums, St Albans	p 138, 446
248	Hatfield House, Hatfield	p 139, 446

247 ST ALBANS
MUSEUMS

St Albans

The Museum of St Albans illustrates the development of the city from a market town. At Verulamium, the museum of Roman Britain, are some amazing artefacts.

see page 446

ST ALBANS

As Verulamium, this was one of the most important major Roman cities in Britain. It was attacked and sacked by Boudicca in the 1st century and today, the remains of the rebuilt city, including the walls and the only Roman theatre in Britain, can be seen in **Verulamium Park**. Close to the park, on the banks of the River Ver, is the restored 16th century **Kingsbury Watermill** with its collection of agricultural implements.

The city's cathedral, **St Albans Abbey**, was built on the site where Alban, the first British martyr, was beheaded in the 4th century. The Abbey dates from the 11th century but was only designated a Cathedral in 1887. Among the many features inside are medieval paintings that are thought to be unique in England.

Another historic building lies in the market place – the **Clock Tower**, built between 1403 and 1412, is the only medieval town belfry in England and its original bell, Gabriel, is still in place. Also worthy of a visit are the city's two museums. The **Museum of St Albans** tells the history of the city from Roman times to the present day, and **St Albans Organ Museum** houses an amazing collection of working mechanical musical instruments.

To the north lies Redbournbury Mill, an 18th century watermill that once belonged to St Albans Abbey; it has been restored to full working order. To the southwest is one of Hertfordshire's biggest attractions, the **Gardens of the Rose**, with one of the most important rose collections in the world.

AROUND ST ALBANS

HARPENDEN

4½ miles N of St Albans on the A1081

Harpenden's High Street is lined with many listed 17th and 18th century buildings, and the whole of the town centre is a conservation area. The **Harpenden Local History Centre** is the ideal place to find out more about this charming agricultural community, and another place well worth a visit is the **Experimental Station for**

Abbey Gatehouse, St Albans

Agricultural Research housed in Rothamsted Manor. The **Harpenden Railway Museum** has a small private collection of railway memorabilia.

HATFIELD
5 miles E of St Albans on the A1057

This historic town grew up around the gateway of the palace of the Bishops of Ely but all that remains of the Royal Palace of Hatfield, where Elizabeth I spent her early life, is a single wing. This can be seen in the delightful gardens of the impressive Jacobean mansion, **Hatfield House**, which now stands on the site. The house is famous for its collection of beautiful tapestries and paintings as well as its exquisite interior and the beautiful gardens that were laid out in 1611, before the house was completed.

KING'S LANGLEY
5 miles SW of St Albans on the A4251

This historic village has a long and illustrious royal past: in the 13th century a palace was built from which Edward I governed England for a short period, while close by was a Dominican friary. Both sites are now occupied by the Rudolf Steiner School.

BERKHAMSTED
10 miles W of St Albans on the A4251

First settled by the Saxons, it was here, two months after the Battle of Hastings, that the Saxons finally submitted to William of Normandy; shortly afterwards, building work

began on a castle. **Berkhamsted Castle** had a double moat, a very necessary precaution in this low-lying situation; an important fortification up until the 15th century, the castle is now in ruins. Of the few buildings that have survived from the past is **Dean John Incent's House**, an impressive black and white timbered jettied building – Dean Incent was the founder of the original Grammar School of 1554 that is now incorporated into Berkhamsted School. Just to the north is **Northchurch** which lies on the **Grand Union Canal**. All of its length in Hertfordshire can be walked, but the towpath between Northchurch and Tring has been developed particularly for recreational use.

TRING
13 miles NW of St Albans on the A4251

This bustling market town on the edge of the Chiltern Hills has been greatly influenced by the Rothschild family. However, they are not the only people associated with Tring and, in **St Mary's Church**, lies the grave of the grandfather of the first US president, George Washington, while the 17th century **Mansion House** was reputedly used by Nell Gwynne. Another building of note is the Market House, which was built by public subscription in 1900 to commemorate Queen Victoria's Diamond Jubilee. The old **Silk Mill**, first opened in 1824, once employed over 600 people, but towards the end of the 19th

248 HATFIELD HOUSE

Hatfield

A superb Jacobean mansion containing a treasure trove of fine furniture, paintings and armour, set amid stunning gardens.

 see page 446

To the east of Tring, near Aldbury, is Ashridge Park, formerly part of the estate of Lord Brownlow and now an excellent place for walking. The focal point of the park is the Bridgewater Monument, an impressive tower erected in memory of the pioneer of canals, the Duke of Bridgewater.

century the silk trade fell into decline and Lord Rothschild ran the mill at a loss to protect his employees rather than see them destitute. From 1872 to the 1940s, the Rothschild family lived at Tring Park and their greatest lasting legacy is, perhaps, the **Walter Rothschild Zoological Museum**, first opened in 1892, which, on Walter's death in 1937, became part of the British Museum (Natural History).

Just north of Tring lies the **Tring Reservoirs National Nature Reserve**, four reservoirs built between 1802 and 1839 and declared a reserve in 1955.

MARKYATE

8 miles NW of St Albans off the A5

This quiet village of charming 18th and 19th century cottages and houses is home to a large mansion that stands on the site of **Markyate Cell**, a medieval nunnery.

STEVENAGE

Following World War II, Stevenage became the first of Britain's New Towns and it expanded as a pleasant residential town after the first houses were occupied in 1951. It was at Stevenage that the novelist EM Forster lived with his widowed mother from the age of 4 to 14 and Howards End, which featured in the book of the same name, is the house in which they lived; in the book, the village of Hilton is an adaptation of Stevenage. **Stevenage Museum** uses all the latest technology to tell the history of the town and surrounding area.

To the northeast lies one of Hertfordshire's last surviving post mills, Cromer Windmill, which dates from 1800 and ceased working in the 1920s. To the south stands **Knebworth House**, the home of the Lytton family since 1490. The present magnificent mansion was built during the 19th century and has played host to many famous visitors, including Charles Dickens, Benjamin Disraeli and Sir Winston Churchill.

Knebworth House, nr Stevenage

AROUND STEVENAGE

LETCHWORTH

5 miles N of Stevenage on the A505

Letchworth is the first garden city where the ideals of Ebenezer Howard (to create a comfortable living environment with residential, industrial and commercial areas all within easy reach) were put into practice in the early 20th century. The offices of the town's architects are now home to the **First Garden City Heritage Museum**, a unique place that traces the history and development of Letchworth.

To the southeast lies **Hitchin**, an old market town which prospered from straw that was traded here for the local cottage industry of straw plaiting. Though the market declined, many of the town's older buildings have survived, including **The Biggin**, which was built in the early 17th century on the site of a Gilbertine Priory and became an almshouse for the poor. **Hitchin Museum** is home to the largest collection of period costume in the county and it also includes the Museum of Hertfordshire Imperial Yeomanry, a Victorian chemist's shop and a physic garden.

ROYSTON

12 miles NE of Stevenage on the A10

Situated at the intersection of the Icknield Way and Ermine Street, this was a favourite hunting base for royalty, and **James I's Hunting Lodge** still stands. Just below the intersection of the two ancient thoroughfares the man-made **Royston Cave** was discovered in 1742 but its purpose remains a mystery.

BISHOP'S STORTFORD

16 miles E of Stevenage on the A120

The completion of the Stort Navigation in 1769 aided the development of the town's two industries, malting and brewing, and during the age of the stagecoach this was a major stopping point on the route between London and Norwich. The excellent **Local History Museum** brings the town's long history to life.

To the west is the unspoilt village of **Much Hadham** and the **Forge Museum and Victorian Cottage Garden**. Further west again is **Standon** where, in a field, lies the **Balloon Stone**, a giant boulder that marks the spot where, in 1784, Vincenzo Lunardi completed the first balloon flight in England.

WARE

10 miles SE of Stevenage on the A1170

Situated at the point where Ermine Street crosses the River Lea, Ware was the scene of a famous encounter between King Alfred and the Danes in AD 895. By the Middle Ages this was a market town to rival Hertford and several ancient buildings remain, including **Place House**, which is possibly one of Ware's two Domesday manor houses. The town's most interesting feature is **Scott's Grotto**, a series of passageways and

---

249 TALLY HO

Barkway, nr Royston

Each visit to the **Tally Ho** sees a different choice of real ales drawn from the barrel, to enjoy on their own or to accompany excellent home cooking.

 see page 446

Bishop's Stortford was the birthplace, in 1853, of Cecil Rhodes, who established the Kimberley Diamond Mines in South Africa. His former home, Nettleswell House, now houses the Rhodes Memorial Museum and Commonwealth Centre, which contains details of his life both here and in Africa.

250 THE WHITE HORSE

High Cross, nr Ware

A handy location on the A10 makes the **White Horse** an ideal spot to pause for a drink or a meal.

 see page 447

251 THE RED LION

Stanstead Abbots, nr Ware

The **Red Lion** attracts locals and visitors with a good choice of food and drink.

 see page 448

artificial caves built by the poet John Scott in the late 18th century.

To the south, at **Great Amwell**, are the impressive buildings of Haileybury College which was established in 1809 as a training school for the East India Company. The buildings are not open to the public, but the **Museum of Street Lighting**, with its collection of over 150 street lamps, is open by appointment.

Further south lies **Hoddesdon**, a town that dates back to Saxon times and which was a thriving market place by the 13th century. Housed in a Georgian building, the **Lowewood Museum** concentrates its collections on the region's illustrious history. In Lea Valley Park stands **Rye House Gatehouse**, where, in 1683, a plot to assassinate Charles II was formulated. The plot failed and the conspirators, including the tenant of Rye House, were executed.

HERTFORD

8½ miles SE of Stevenage on the A119

Another Saxon town on the once important waterway of the River Lea that linked the town with London. The **Hertford Nature Walk** leads through the meadows between the Rivers Lea and Beane and takes in the canal basin that is known as The Folly. Hertford is very much a mix of old and new and among its interesting buildings is the **Quaker Meeting House**, said to be the oldest purpose-built meeting house in the world – it dates from 1669.

WELWYN GARDEN CITY

8 miles S of Stevenage on the A1000

One of the two garden cities in Hertfordshire that followed the ideas and plans of Ebenezer Howard (the other is Letchworth), the land for Welwyn Garden City was acquired in 1919 and building began a year later. Just to the south of the town lies **Mill Green Museum**, housed in the workers' cottages for the adjoining mill, which displays local artefacts from Roman times to the present day. **Mill Green Mill** is a delightful watermill that has been restored to working order and stands on the site of one of the four such mills that were listed in the *Domesday Book*.

Just to the north is the historic town of **Welwyn** that grew up along the route of the Great North Road. During excavations for the new A1(M) motorway, the famous **Welwyn Roman Baths** were discovered, part of a 3rd century villa or farm that was occupied for over 150 years.

AYOT ST LAWRENCE

5½ miles SW of Stevenage off the B651

A picturesque rural village whose most famous resident was Sir George Bernard Shaw, who lived here from 1906 until his death in 1950. His house, **Shaw's Corner**, is preserved as it was in his lifetime and contains many literary and personal mementoes.

Isle of Man

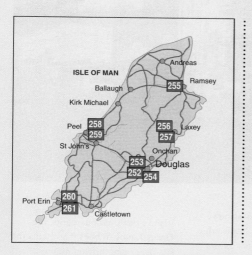

ISLE OF MAN

Andreas
Ramsey
Ballaugh
Kirk Michael
255

Peel 258
259
St John's

256 Laxey
257

Onchan
253 Douglas
252 254

Port Erin 260
261
Castletown

The Isle of Man has an unusual status as a Crown Protectorate, with the Queen as Lord of Mann represented in the Island by the Lieutenant-Governor. Best known for its motorcycle races, its tailless cats and its kippers, it has plenty to interest the visitor with a wide range of wildlife, diverse geographical features, plenty of entertainment and a rich history. The TT (Tourist Trophy) races take place in May/June, and the Manx GP in August/September.

	FOOD & DRINK	
252	The British Hotel, Douglas	p 143, 448
253	Jaks, Douglas	p 144, 449
254	The Welbeck Hotel, Douglas	p 144, 450
255	Harbour Lights, Ramsey	p 144, 448
258	The Creek Inn, Peel	p 145, 452
259	Duncans Diner & Coffee Shop, Peel	p 145, 451
260	The Falcon's Nest Hotel, Port Erin	p 146, 452

	ACCOMMODATION	
254	The Welbeck Hotel, Douglas	p 144, 450
256	The Greaves, Laxey	p 144, 448
257	Ballachrink Farm Cottages, Laxey	p 145, 451
258	The Creek Inn, Peel	p 145, 452
260	The Falcon's Nest Hotel, Port Erin	p 146, 452
261	Regent House, Port Erin	p 146, 452

DOUGLAS

The island's capital, Douglas, is a lively resort where visitors can take a leisurely ride along the promenade aboard the **Douglas Bay Horse Tramway**, a remarkable and beautiful reminder of a bygone era. Another delightful means of travel is the Victorian **Steam Railway** that runs between Douglas and Port Erin.

Following the line of the cliff tops, the memorable journey also takes in bluebell woods and steep-sided rocky cuttings. The **Manx Electric Railway**, completed in 1899, operates the oldest working tramcars in the world and runs between Douglas and Ramsey.

No trip to the island is complete without a visit to the **Manx Museum**, where the Story of Man film gives a dramatic and

252 THE BRITISH HOTEL

North Quay, Douglas

The **British Hotel** is a popular, lively pub overlooking the harbour in Douglas.

 see page 448

253 JAKS

Loch Promenade, Douglas

On Loch Promenade, with views out to sea, **Jaks** is one of the liveliest and most popular eating and drinking places on the Island.

see page 449

254 THE WELBECK HOTEL

Mona Drive, Douglas

The **Welbeck** is a family-run hotel with a long tradition of hospitality, service, comfort and good food and drink.

see page 450

255 HARBOUR LIGHTS

Peel and Ramsey

On the Promenade at Peel and in a shopping precinct at Ramsey, **Harbour Lights** serves breakfast, lunch, teas, snacks and drinks. Ramsey also open Thursday to Saturday evenings.

see page 448

256 THE GREAVES

Laxey

Superb views are a bonus at **The Greaves**, which offers home-from-home comfort for B&B guests.

see page 448

Horse Drawn Tram, Douglas

vivid portrayal of the island's unique history. On a headland overlooking the Bay is a *camera obscura* known as the **Great Union Camera**. Here, natural daylight is focused on to a white panel through a system of lenses to provide a living image of the scene outside.

AROUND DOUGLAS

RAMSEY

12 miles N of Douglas on the A18

This northernmost resort on the island is an attractive coastal town with a cosy harbour that is popular with visiting yachtsmen. Just to the north of the town stands the **Grove Rural Life Museum**, housed in a pleasantly proportioned Victorian house.

LAXEY

5 miles N of Douglas on the A2

Set in a deep, wooded valley, this village is home to one of the island's most famous sights, the **Great Laxey Wheel** that marks the site of a once thriving mining community. Known as the **Lady Isabella Wheel**, with a circumference of 228 feet, a diameter of 72 feet, and a top platform some 72 feet off the ground, it is the largest waterwheel in the world. The wheel lies in Laxey Glen, one of the island's 17 National Glens. The **Great Laxey Mine Railway**, opened in 2004, carries passengers in tiny carriages along a stretch of the line where loaded wagons once rolled.

Situated above Laxey, in a beautiful glen, are the magnificent **Ballalheanagh Gardens** while, from Laxey station, the **Snaefell Mountain Railway** carries visitors to the top of the island's only mountain. Built in 1895, the six original tram cars still climb the steep gradients to Snaefell's 2,036 feet summit from which there are outstanding views of the whole island and out over the sea to Ireland, Scotland and England.

PEEL

9 miles W of Douglas on the A1

On the western side on the island, Peel, which is renowned for its sunsets, typifies the unique character and atmosphere of the Isle of Man. It is traditionally the centre of the Manx fishing industry, including the delicious oak-smoked kippers and shellfish. Its narrow winding streets exude history and draw the visitor unfailingly down to the harbour, sandy beach, and magnificent castle of local red sandstone. The recently opened museum is well worth a visit. Peel gave its name to the only production car ever made on the Island. The three-wheel Peel was one of the tiniest cars ever made - the claim that it could carry a driver and a shopping bag was disputed by some, who thought that it was a question of one or the other!

Peel Castle, one of Isle of Man's principal historic monuments, occupies the important site of **St Patrick's Isle**. In the 11th century the castle became the ruling seat of the Norse Kingdom of Man and the Isles.

CASTLETOWN

9 miles SW of Douglas on the A7

The original capital of the island, the town's harbour lies beneath the imposing battlements of the well-preserved 12th century **Castle Rushen**. Castletown is also home to the island's **Nautical Museum**, where the displays centre on the late 18th century armed yacht *Peggy* that sits in her contemporary boathouse.

On the road between Castletown and Douglas, visitors should look out for the **Fairy Bridge**. For centuries, people on the Isle of Man have taken no chances when it comes to the little people and it is still customary to

257 BALLACHRINK FARM COTTAGES

Laxey

Ballachrink Farm Cottages comprise five beautifully appointed properties for self-catering holidays in peaceful, unspoilt countryside.

see page 451

258 THE CREEK INN

The Quayside, Peel

The **Creek Inn** is a very pleasant pub for all the family, with a fine choice of food and drink and self-catering accommodation.

see page 452

259 DUNCANS DINER & COFFEE SHOP

Michael Street, Peel

On one of Peel's busy main streets, **Duncans Diner & Coffee Shop** is open all day Monday to Saturday for a good choice of home cooking.

see page 451

Castle and Beach, Peel

260 THE FALCON'S NEST HOTEL

Port Erin

The **Falcon's Nest Hotel** offers high standards of comfort, service, food and drink in a superb setting overlooking the beach.

see *page 452*

261 REGENT HOUSE

Port Erin

Regent House is a friendly owner-run guest house on the promenade at Port Erin, with the bonus of wonderful sea views.

see *page 452*

wish the fairies, who live under the bridge, a 'Good Morning' when crossing.

Perched right on the southwestern tip of the island, **Cregneash Village Folk Museum** offers a unique experience of Manx traditional life within a 19th century crofting community. The centrepiece of Cregneash is **Harry Kelly's Cottage**. Kelly was a renowned Cregneash crofter and a fluent speaker of the Manx language who died in 1934.

PORT ERIN
16 miles S of Peel on the A5

Situated between magnificent headlands, Port Erin has its own **Arts Centre**, which since 1975 has hosted the annual **Mananan International Festival of Music and the Arts**, now recognised as one of the island's most prestigious cultural events. Port Erin also has a small steam railway museum.

CALF OF MAN
15 miles W of Douglas

This small island, situated just off the southwestern tip of the island, is a National Trust bird sanctuary. In Calf Sound, the stretch of water between the island and the Isle of Man, the largest armada of Viking longships ever assembled in the British Isles congregated before setting off to invade Ireland.

Isle of Wight

Separated from the mainland by the Solent, is the Isle of Wight, where Queen Victoria sought solitude at Osborne House after the premature death of her husband. John Keats wrote his *Endymion* (first line: *A thing of beauty is a joy for ever*) while staying on the Island. Other notable visitors have described it as the Garden Isle and England's Madeira; about half its 147 square miles have been designated Areas of Outstanding Natural Beauty.

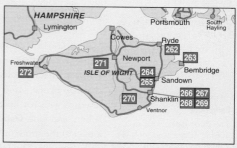

🍴 FOOD & DRINK

262	The Roadside Inn, Seaview	p 148, 453
263	The Pilot Boat Inn, Bembridge	p 148, 453
264	The Driftwood Beach Bar & Grill, Sandown	p 148, 454
265	The Ocean Deck Inn, Sandown	p 148, 453
268	Billy Bunters, Shanklin	p 149, 454
269	The Glenbrook Hotel, Shanklin	p 149, 454
270	The Worsley, Wroxall	p 150, 456

🛏 ACCOMMODATION

262	The Roadside Inn, Seaview	p 148, 453
266	The Esplanade Hotel, Shanklin	p 149, 454
267	The Channel View Hotel, Shanklin	p 149, 455
269	The Glenbrook Hotel, Shanklin	p 149, 454
271	Brockley Barns, Newport	p 150, 456

🏛 PLACES OF INTEREST

272	The Needles Park, Alum Bay	p 150, 456

COWES

East and West Cowes are linked across the River Medina by a chain ferry. West Cowes is the home of the Royal Yacht Squadron, which organises **Cowes Week**, the famous regatta that is a firm fixture in the sailing and social calendar. The links with ships and shipbuilding go back centuries and Royal Navy craft, lifeboats, flying boats and seaplanes have all been built at Cowes. The Isle of Wight's maritime history is charted at the **Cowes Maritime Museum**, which also houses a collection of racing yachts, while the **Sir Max Aitken**

Cowes

147

262 THE ROADSIDE INN

Seaview

The **Roadside Inn** is a handsome 100-year-old hostelry with popular pub dishes, daily specials and three comfortable bedrooms for B&B

 see page 453

263 THE PILOT BOAT INN

Bembridge

The **Pilot Boat**, with an outside designed to look like a boat, complete with portholes, is a friendly spot to relax with a drink or a meal.

 see page 453

264 THE DRIFTWOOD BEACH BAR & GRILL

Sandown

The **Driftwood Bar & Grill** enjoys an unbeatable location right on the beach at Sandown.

 see page 454

265 THE OCEAN DECK INN

High Street, Sandown

The **Ocean Deck Inn** is a popular pub-restaurant on the seafront at Sandown.

 see page 453

Museum has a collection of nautical paintings, instruments and artefacts. The **Isle of Wight Model Railways Exhibition** includes models spanning the whole history of railways.

On the eastern bank of the Medina lies 18th century Norris Castle, where the 12-year-old Princess Victoria stayed; she was so charmed by the island that she returned with her husband, Prince Albert, and built **Osborne House**, a mile to the south, in the style of an Italian villa. The **Isle of Wight Steam Railway** runs renovated steam trains along a preserved 5-mile track between Wootton and Smallbrook Junction. Wootton is also home to **Butterfly World & Fountain World**, which includes an indoor sub-tropical garden with hundreds of exotic free-flying butterflies.

AROUND COWES

RYDE

6½ miles SE of Cowes on the A3054

For many visitors to the island, Ryde is their arrival point. The largest town on the Island has five miles of sandy beach and with all the usual seaside attractions and a marina, it remains a popular holiday spot. One of Ryde's Victorian churches, St Thomas, is now a Heritage Centre that features the transportation of convicts to Australia - many of the unfortunates left England in ships moored off Ryde. In the middle of **Appley Park** stands Appley Tower, which houses a collection of fossils, crystals and rune readings.

To the east lies **Seaview Wildlife Encounter Flamingo Park**, whose colonies of flamingos, penguins, macaws and waterfowl are among the largest in the country, while inland from Ryde is **Brickfields Horse Country**, a centre with more than 100 animals including magnificent Shire horses and miniature ponies.

BEMBRIDGE

10½ miles SE of Cowes on the B3330

Once a thriving fishing village, Bembridge is now a popular holiday and sailing centre that maintains its maritime links through the **Maritime Museum and Shipwreck Centre**. The village is also home to the **Ruskin Gallery**, displaying an impressive collection of the 19th century artist's work. Here, too, is one of the island's best-known landmarks, the 18th century **Bembridge Windmill**.

Further along the coast lies **Sandown**, the island's leading holiday resort, which has drawn such distinguished visitors as Lewis Carroll, Charles Darwin and George Eliot. The beaches and the museums are among the attractions, and to the north, near **Brading**, is a **Roman Villa** discovered in 1880. One of the island's oldest towns, Brading is also home to the **Isle of Wight Wax Works** and the **Lilliput Museum of Antique Dolls and Toys** while, close by, are two notable historic houses. **Nunwell House**, where Charles I spent his last night of freedom, is set within a glorious garden, and 13th century **Morton Manor** features an Elizabethan sunken garden surrounded by a 400-year-old box hedge.

SHANKLIN
12 miles SE of Cowes on the A3055

To the south of Bembridge lies Sandown's more sedate neighbour Shanklin, which stands at the head of one of the island's most renowned landmarks, **Shanklin Chine**, a 300 feet deep wooded ravine. First opened in 1817 and a former refuge of smugglers, this ravine, mysterious and romantic, has long fascinated visitors with its waterfalls and rare flora. In the Heritage Centre at the top of the chine is an interesting exhibtion on the PLUTO (**Pipe Line Under the Ocean**) project for pumping fuel across the Channel to supply the troops involved in D-Day. The Chine also has a memorial to the Royal Marines of 40 Commando who used the Chine as an assault course before the disastrous assault on Dieppe in 1942.

NEWPORT
4 miles S of Cowes on the A3020

The island's capital and once a busy shipping centre on the River Medina, Newport still has many of its old riverside warehouses; one of them houses the **Classic Boat Museum**, and next door is the **Isle of Wight Bus Museum** with its impressive collection of passenger transport vehicles. In **St Thomas' Church** lies the tomb of Princess Elizabeth, Charles I's daughter, who

Ventnor

270 THE WORSLEY

Wroxall

The Worsley is a delightful village pub with a friendly welcome for all the family.

 see page 456

271 BROCKLEY BARNS

Calbourne Road, nr Newport

Brockley Barns comprise four delightful cottages (each with two or three main bedrooms) for self-catering holiday rental in the middle of the Island.

 see page 456

272 THE NEEDLES PARK

Alum Bay

Plenty to see and do here with magnificent views across The Needles Rocks and Lighthouse.

 see page 456

died of a fever while the family were held prisoner at **Carisbrooke Castle**. Here, too, a 3rd century Roman Villa has been excavated, offering an insight into the sophistication of the late Romano-British designers and builders.

VENTNOR

8 miles S of Cowes on the A3055

With much of its Victorian charm still intact, the town has much to offer today's visitors including the **Ventnor Botanic Garden** on the site of the former Royal National Chest Hospital, the **Smuggling Museum**, and the Coastal Visitor Centre dedicated to the island's marine environment. Away from the town, **St Boniface Down** provides excellent walking country as well as spectacular views across the island. Also inland lies **Appuldurcombe House**, once the grandest mansion on the island, which is now home to the **Owl and Falconry Centre** where daily flying displays and courses in the age old art of falconry are held. The **Isle of Wight Donkey Sanctuary** lies close by, as does the village of **Godshill** with its magical **Model Village** and the **Nostalgia Toy Museum**.

Nestling in the heart of the Undercliff, to the southwest of Ventnor, is the ancient village of **St Lawrence** which is home to the **Rare Breeds Waterfowl Park**. From here the coast road continues round to St Catherine's Point, the wildest part of the island, where

steps lead down to **St Catherine's Lighthouse**. On the most southerly tip of the island is **Blackgang Chine**, a Victorian scenic park that has been developed into a modern fantasy park.

CALBOURNE

9 miles SW of Cowes off the B3401

The most enchanting part of this picturesque village is Winkle Street, which has a row of charming old cottages opposite the village stream and an ancient sheepwash. Close by, in a lovely landscaped valley, is a superb 17th century Water Mill that incorporates a fascinating **Rural Museum**.

FRESHWATER

11 miles SW of Cowes on the A3054

This bustling town was the home of Alfred, Lord Tennyson, who was persuaded to move here by the pioneer photographer, Julia Cameron. Her home, **Dimbola Lodge**, houses a permanent exhibition of her work.

To the west lies the popular holiday spot of **Totland** and the famous multi-coloured sands of **Alum Bay**, and on the very western tip of the island are **The Needles**, three jagged slabs of rock with a lighthouse at the end of the most westerly.

North of Freshwater lies **Yarmouth**, a picturesque place with narrow streets, old stone quays and a castle built by Henry VIII after the town had been sacked by the French.

Kent

Kent is the first county that most cross-channel visitors encounter when visiting England (though for many the tunnel has removed the thrill of the sight of the White Cliffs of Dover), and few counties combine glorious open landscapes with such a rich history. It was here that Julius Caesar landed in 55 BC; the Vikings followed 1,000 years later and the land was widely settled by the Normans following the defeat of King Harold in 1066. Throughout the centuries there has been a threat of invasion and, with the north Kent coast situated on the Thames estuary, it is not surprising that this area became the scene of great naval activity. The World Naval Base at Chatham is centred on the historic dockyard that was established by Henry VIII, but right around the coastline of Kent there are numerous defensive structures, from medieval castles to the early 19th century Martello Towers. On the south coast, the Cinque Ports were set up in the 11th century as a commercial alliance of significant ports – but the silting up of channels over the centuries has left some of them high and dry miles from the sea.

Visitors have flocked to the seaside resorts

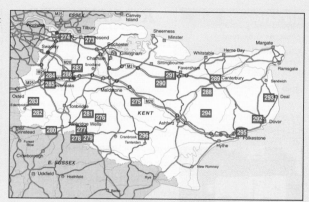

of Ramsgate, Herne Bay and Margate since Victorian times, but centuries ago Kent was a favourite place of pilgrimage as Christians made their way to Canterbury Cathedral. Royal Tunbridge Wells, too, attracted visitors who came to take the waters at this fashionable health resort in the 18th and 19th centuries.

The county's reputation as the 'Garden of England' is well earned, and green fields and orchards still abound. Rolling wooded countryside is dotted with windmills, and oast houses are still a common sight. In contrast are the remote, flat lands of Romney Marsh, sometime haunt of smugglers, and, of course, the White Cliffs of Dover, one of the most evocative sights in the land, a symbol of the country's strength that was immortalised in song by Vera (now Dame Vera) Lynn.

273 CHALK B&B

Chalk, nr Gravesend

Chalk B&B in location with easy access to M2, M25, M20, A2 and A20.

 see *page 456*

274 LADS OF THE VILLAGE

Stone, nr Dartford

The **Lads of the Village** is a lively, popular local serving a wide range of drinks and tasty lunchtime food.

 see *page 457*

ROCHESTER

The site was first settled by the Romans, but it was following the Norman invasion that William the Conqueror ordered his architect, Bishop Gundulph, to design a fortification to protect this strategic crossing point of the River Medway. Today, **Rochester Castle** remains one of the finest surviving examples of Norman architecture in the country. Bishop Gundulph was also ordered to build **Rochester Cathedral** on the site of a Saxon church that was founded in AD 604.

The city has close connections with the novelist Charles Dickens. An Elizabethan building houses the **Charles Dickens Centre, The Royal Victoria and Bull Hotel** featured in both *The Pickwick Papers* and *Great Expectations*, and **Restoration House** became Satis House in *Great Expectations*.

AROUND ROCHESTER

GRAVESEND

7 miles NW of Rochester on the A226

Gravesend marks the point at which ships entering the broad River Thames take on board a river pilot. The graveyard of St George's is thought to be the final resting place of the famous Red Indian princess, Pocahontas, who died on board ship in 1617 while she was on her way back to America, where she had reputedly saved the life of the British settler John Smith in Virginia. The precise site of her grave is not known, but there is a statue of her and two memorial windows in the church. On the A207, in **Bexleyheath**, is one of the National Trust's most recent acquisitions. This is **The Red House**, which was designed in 1859 by Philip Webb for the newly married William and Janey Morris. The interior was decorated by Webb, Morris, Burne-Jones, Madox Brown and Rossetti; William Morris described the house as 'a joyful nook of heaven in an unheavenly world'. For Dante Gabriel Rossetti it was '.....more a poem than a house - but an admirable place to live in too'.

SHEERNESS

12 miles NE of Rochester on the A249

On the **Isle of Sheppey**, this town was once the site of a naval dockyard, the first to be surveyed by Samuel Pepys as Secretary to the Admiralty in the reign of Charles II, and it was here in 1805 that *HMS Victory* docked when it brought Nelson's body back to England following the Battle of Trafalgar. It is now a busy container and car ferry port, and the **Sheerness Heritage Centre** tells the history of the dockyard and its influence on the town's development.

To the southeast lies the seaside town of **Minster** where the 15th century abbey gatehouse is home to the **Minster Abbey Gatehouse Museum**.

On the southern tip of the island is the **Swale National Nature Reserve**, home to numerous wildfowl, while to the west lies **Elmley Marshes Nature Reserve**, an area of salt marsh.

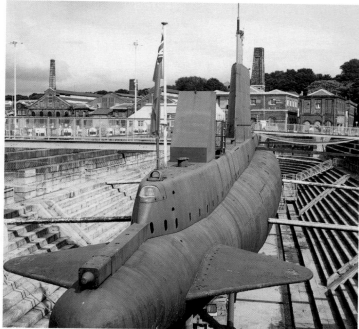
Historic Dockyard, Chatham

CHATHAM

1 mile SE of Rochester on the A229

Visitors to the historic **Chatham Dockyard** – now the **World Naval Base** – can appreciate the scale of modern fighting ships in the dry dock as well as the architecture of the most complete Georgian dockyard in the world. Rope is still made in the traditional way in the long Ropery building, and the history of lifeboats is told at the National Collection of the RNLI. The **Museum of the Dockyard** tells the 400-year-old story of the site. Close to the dockyard lies **Fort Amherst Heritage Park and Caverns**, the country's premier Napoleonic fortress that was home to a secret underground telephone exchange that co-ordinated air raid warnings during World War II.

To the east of Chatham lies **Gillingham**, the home of the fascinating **Royal Engineers Museum** where the diverse skills of this distinguished Corps are on display.

153

275 THE PEPPERBOX INN

Fairbourne Heath, nr Ulcombe

The **Pepperbox** is a cosy old country inn of abundant period charm serving real ales and a wide choice of bar and restaurant food.

 see page 457

276 THE GUN AND SPITROAST

Horsmonden

A delightful 16th century inn with inglenook spitroast. The candlelit restaurant serves a superb menu of freshly prepared home-cooked food.

 see page 458

277 THE BARNFIELD OAST

Lamberhurst

Comfort and character combine at The **Barnfield Oast**, where the oast house and two cottages offer self-catering accommodation for up to 10 guests.

 see page 458

SITTINGBOURNE

10½ miles E of Rochester on the A2

Once a stopping point for pilgrims on their way to Canterbury, Sittingbourne has developed into a thriving market town. Visitors today can also take a nostalgic ride on a steam train along the **Sittingbourne and Kemsley Light Railway**. In 1533, in nearby **Teynham**, Richard Harris, Henry VIII's fruiterer, planted England's first cherry tree along with apple trees and thus established the village as the birthplace of English orchards.

At **Milton Creek**, just north of the town centre, lies **Dolphin Yard Sailing Barge Museum**, which aims to preserve the traditional Thames barges that were built in their hundreds in boatyards around Sittingbourne.

LEEDS

11 miles SE of Rochester on the B2163

This village is synonymous with the beautiful **Leeds Castle**, which stands in glorious landscaped gardens on two islands in the middle of the River Len. Built on a site once owned by Saxon kings, the castle was immaculately modernised by the last owner, Olive Paget, later Lady Baillie. The castle contains many superb antiques and tapestries, and in one of the medieval outbuildings is an idiosyncratic Dog Collar Museum. One of the gardens is named in honour of Lady Baillie, who put so much back into the Castle unitl her death in 1974.

MAIDSTONE

8½ miles S of Rochester on the A229

Despite extensive development in modern times, Maidstone has retained many handsome historic buildings including **Chillington Manor**, a particularly fine Elizabethan residence that is now home to the **Maidstone Museum and Art Gallery**. Part of the museum's collection, The Tyrwhitt-Drake Museum of Carriage, can be found in the stables that once belonged to the Archbishops of Canterbury. Opposite the stables is the 14th century **Archbishop's Palace**, where the clergy rested while travelling between London and Canterbury, and elsewhere in the town are the College of Priests, founded in 1395, and the 13th century **Corpus Christi Fraternity Hall**.

Just north of Maidstone town centre stands **Allington Castle**, the home of Sir Thomas Wyatt, the 16th century poet who takes some credit for introducing the sonnet into English poetry.

On the opposite bank of the River Medway is Tyland Barn, a beautifully restored 17th century building that houses the **Museum of Kent Life**.

ROYAL TUNBRIDGE WELLS

Surrounded by the unspoilt beauty of the Weald, Royal Tunbridge Wells is an attractive town that

The Pantiles, Royal Tunbridge Wells

278 THE SWAN AT THE VINEYARD & VINO BEAUTY

Lamberhurst

Within the Lamberhurst Vineyard, **The Swan** is a superb 14th century inn with an inovative menu. **Vino Beauty** offers a wide range of beauty treatments.

see page 459

279 LAMBERHURST VINEYARD

The Down, Lamberhurst

Lamberhurst Vineyard offers a range of attractions, including vineyard tours, a choice of eating places, a wine shop, beauty salon, plant centre and pets corner.

see page 460

280 THE BEACON

Rusthall, nr Tunbridge Wells

The **Beacon** is one of the region's top venues for a meal, whether it's a romantic dinner for two or a large function or family gathering. Also overnight accommodation.

see page 461

developed into a fashionable health resort in the 18th and 19th centuries after the discovery of chalybeate springs in 1606. One of the most famous features of the town is **The Pantiles**, a lovely shaded walk lined with elegant shops that were, in the days of the spa, the central focus of the hectic social life arranged by the Master of Ceremonies, Beau Nash.

To the east of Royal Tunbridge Wells, close to **Goudhurst**, is a charming Georgian manor house, **Finchcocks**, which contains a magnificent collection of historic keyboard instruments. Also in this area is **Scotney Castle**, with its romantic gardens, and The Owl House, a pretty little cottage that has associations with night smugglers or 'owlers'. There are more superb gardens at nearby Groombridge Place, and to the northwest of the town there are three wonderful places that are well worth exploring. **Penshurst Place** dates back to 1341 and is surrounded by glorious gardens that are a rare survivor of the Elizabethan age. A little further on is **Chiddingstone Castle**, a traditional squire's house with the appearance of a grand castle, while, close by, is one of the county's star attractions, **Hever Castle**, the childhood home of Anne Boleyn. The estate was bought in the early 20th century by the millionaire William Waldorf Astor; his extensive restoration work has created award winning gardens along with a castle filled with fine collections of paintings, furniture, tapestries and objets d'art.

281 THE BULL OF BRENCHLEY

Brenchley, nr Tonbridge

The **Bull of Brenchley** provides friendly hospitality, good food and drink, and comfortable guest accommodation in great walking country.

 see page 461

282 THE CASTLE INN

Chiddingstone

The **Castle Inn** lives up to its superb setting by providing the very best in hospitality, food and drink.

 see page 461

283 THE FOUR ELMS INN

Four Elms, nr Edenbridge

The **Four Elms** is a traditional country pub providing the best in hospitality for the whole family, with an excellent selection of drinks and good-value food.

 see page 462

284 THE WOODMAN

Otford, nr Sevenoaks

The **Woodman** is an 18th century inn offering Shepherd Neame ales and bar and restaurant food.

 see page 462

285 THE CROWN

Otford, nr Sevenoaks

The traditional ambience of the bars makes the **Crown** a great setting for enjoying real ales and traditional home cooking.

 see page 462

SEVENOAKS

The pride of this ancient market town is **Knole House**, one of the largest private homes in the country, with 365 rooms. In 1603, Elizabeth I granted the house to the Sackville family, and it was here, in 1892, that Vita Sackville-West was born.

To the east, close to the small village of **Ivy Hatch** lies **Ightham Mote**, one of England's finest medieval houses. In the opposite direction, near the hamlet of **French Street**, stands **Chartwell**, Sir Winston Churchill's home from the 1920s until his death in the 1960s.

To the northwest is **Biggin Hill RAF Station**, whose entrance is flanked by a Spitfire and a Hurricane that act as silent reminders of the stalwart service these two aircraft, and their crews, gave during the dark days of World War II. Close to the station is **Down House**, where Charles Darwin lived for over 40 years until his death in 1882. The house is now a Museum dedicated to his life and work.

At nearby **Westerham**, a pleasant town near the Surrey border, are two statues of British heroes who had connections with the town. One is a tribute to Sir Winston Churchill, who made his home at nearby Chartwell, the other remembers General Wolfe, who defeated the French at Quebec in 1759. Wolfe was born in Westerham and his childhood home, renamed **Quebec House**, stands east of the town centre. Wolfe also has connections with nearby **Squerryes Court**, where one of the rooms has been set aside to display mementoes relating to the General.

CANTERBURY

It was here, in AD 597, that St Augustine founded an abbey which was to become the roots of Christianity in England. Lying just outside the city walls, **St Augustine's Abbey** is now in ruins, but a museum displays artefacts excavated from the site while, close by, is **St Martin's Church**, England's oldest parish church. However, both these buildings are overshadowed by the Mother Church of the Anglican Communion, **Canterbury Cathedral**, which was founded in AD 597 although the oldest part of the present building is the early 12th century crypt. Unfortunately, Canterbury Cathedral is best known as the scene of the murder of Archbishop Thomas à Becket rather than for its ecclesiastical architecture. At the **Canterbury Tales Visitor Attraction** visitors are taken back to the 14th century and can meet the Knight, the Miller and other characters that tell their stories to keep the 'pilgrims' amused.

Canterbury predates its cathedral by many centuries and was the capital of the Iron Age kingdom, Cantii, as well as being settled by the Romans. The Roman Museum centres on the remains of a Roman town house, while the **Canterbury Heritage Museum** presents a full history of the city over the last 2,000 years. In the **Kent Masonic Library and Museum** the history of freemasonry is explored.

To the south of the nearby village of Fordwich lies **Howletts Wild Animal Park** which was created by John Aspinall and is dedicated to the preservation of rare and endangered animals, including gorillas and both Indian and Siberian tigers.

AROUND CANTERBURY

HERNE BAY

7 miles NE of Canterbury on the A299

Originally a fishing village and a notorious haunt for smugglers, this chiefly 19th century town has developed into one of the main resorts on the north Kent coast. Its story is told at the **Herne Bay Museum Centre**.

East of Herne Bay is **Reculver**. The Normans built two huge towers within the remains of the Roman fort, providing sailors with a landmark to guide them into the Thames estuary. Today, **Reculver Towers and Roman Fort** is in the care of English Heritage. During World War II, the Barnes Wallace 'bouncing bomb' was tested off the coast here. Several bombs were found here on the shore in 1997 – none of them containing explosives.

GOODNESTONE

6½ miles SE of Canterbury off the B2046

Close to the village lies Goodnestone (pronounced Gunston) Park, an estate that was

Promenade Gardens, Herne Bay

290 THE CARPENTERS ARMS

Eastling, nr Faversham

The **Carpenters Arms** well deserves its reputation as a super place for good food, fine wines, quality beer and comfortable B&B rooms.

 see page 464

291 THE ALMA

Painters Forstal, nr Faversham

Long-serving hosts Mervyn and Jill Carter have made the **Alma** one of the very best pubs in the region for food and drink.

see page 464

frequently visited by Jane Austen and, today, **Goodnestone Park Gardens** are considered some of the best in the southeast of England.

STELLING MINNIS

6½ miles S of Canterbury off the B2068

Close to this village on the edge of what remains of the once great Lyminge Forest is **Davison's Mill**, a mid 19th century smock mill that is now home to a Museum of milling implements and tools.

In the heart of the Elham Valley, the **Rural Heritage Centre** at Parsonage Farm explores over 600 years of farming, while the **Elham Valley Railway Trail** provides the opportunity to observe both wildlife and plant life that have made their home along this disused track.

CHALLOCK

10 miles SW of Canterbury on the A252

Set in the dense woodlands known as **Challock Forest**, this pretty village is home to **Beech Court Gardens**, which are a riot of colour from spring through to autumn. To the north, close to the village of **Sheldwich**, lies the **National Fruit Collection** – home to what is probably the largest collection of fruit trees and plants in the world. Tucked away in the orchards and close to the village of **Throwley** is **Belmont**, a beautiful Georgian mansion house that is renowned for its impressive clock collection assembled by the 5th Lord Harris.

To the northeast, towards Canterbury, is one of the county's best-preserved villages, **Chilham**, which is often used as a film location. Built on a Roman foundation, **Chilham Castle** was originally a Norman keep but a Jacobean mansion house was added and the grounds first laid out by Charles I's gardener John Tradescant and reworked in the 18th century by Capability Brown.

FAVERSHAM

9 miles NW of Canterbury on the A2

First settled by the Romans, the town grew steadily as a market town. For 400 years it was the centre of the country's explosives industry and **Chart Gunpowder Mills** is a lasting monument to the industry based here between 1560 and 1934. Faversham boasts over 400 listed buildings, among them the 16th century Guildhall and a 15th century former inn that is now the **Fleur de Lis Heritage Centre**.

WHITSTABLE

5½ miles NW of Canterbury on the A2990

Sometimes referred to as the 'Pearl of Kent', this town, centred on its busy commercial harbour, is as famous for its oysters today as it was in Roman times. On the harbour's East Quay, the **Oyster and Fishery Exhibition** tells the story of Whitstable's connections with fishing, and **Whitstable Museum and Gallery** explores the traditions and life of this ancient seafaring community. In Whitstable's Museum will be found references to some of the 'firsts' to which the town lays claim: the first scheduled passenger train ran between Whitstable and Canterbury; the first steamship to sail to Australia from Britain left here in 1837; the diving helmet was invented in the town; and the country's first council houses were built here.

Just inland from Whitstable is **Druidstone Wildlife Park**, home to a wide variety of animals and birds including otters, owls, rheas, wallabies and parrots.

DOVER

High above the famous white cliffs of the 'Gateway to England' stands **Dover Castle**, which dates back to 1180 and is home to the Princess of Wales' Royal Regiment Museum; the remains of a Roman lighthouse and a small Saxon church can be found in the grounds. Perhaps the most spectacular attraction is the **Secret Wartime Tunnels** cut into the white cliffs.

Back in the heart of Dover is the **Roman Painted House**, an exceptionally well-preserved town house that is thought to date from AD 200. The **Dover Museum**, the area's largest and newest museum, stands opposite the **White Cliffs Experience**, where visitors can step back in time to the Roman invasion and relive the dark days of World War II.

Just inland from Dover, at **Whitfield**, is the **Dover Transport Museum**, whose exhibits include not only all forms of transport from bicycles to buses and trams,

but displays on the East Kent coalfield and the area's maritime heritage.

AROUND DOVER

MARGATE
18 miles N of Dover on the A28

Even before the coming of the railways, trippers made the journey from London by boat to enjoy the delights of sand and sea. Its pier, which was closed long ago after storm damage, was the first to be designed by the doyen of pier engineers, Eugenius Birch.

To the west is the quiet resort of **Birchington**. At All Saints Church, Birchington, is the grave of the painter and poet Dante Gabriel Rossetti; his tomb was designed by his mentor and fellow artist Ford Madox Brown.

RAMSGATE
16 miles NE of Dover on the A255

It was in Ramsgate that the architect Augustus Pugin, who designed the interiors of the Houses of Parliament, built his home, **The Grange**. He also built the Church of St Augustine next to his house, and he is buried in the family vault in a tomb-chest designed by his son. Ramsgate has an interesting Motor Museum.

Just to the south lies **Pegwell Bay**, traditionally said to be the landing place of Hengist and Horsa, who led the successful Jutish invasion of Kent in AD 449. The badge of Kent today includes a prancing white horse, the same

292 DOVER ROMAN PAINTED HOUSE

Dover

The site here has been excavated to reveal a well preserved Roman house, with under-floor heating and wall paintings.

 see page 465

image under which the Jutish warriors fought.

BROADSTAIRS

18 miles NE of Dover on the A255

A couple of miles up the coast from Ramsgate, the family seaside resort of Broadstairs still retains something of a village atmosphere and is best known for its associations with Charles Dickens. **Bleak House**, where Dickens spent 20 summers stands high up on the cliffs overlooking the popular beach at Viking Bay. The politician Sir Edward Heath was born in Broadstairs in 1916, and among the notables who made it their home were the yachtsman Sir Alec Rose, Frank Richards, creator of *Billy Bunter*, and John Buchan, author of *The Thirty Nine Steps*. The staircase on Cliff Promenade that gave him the idea for the title actually has 78 steps, a number that was halved by Buchan to provide a catchier title.

SANDWICH

9½ miles N of Dover off the A256

This was one of the original Cinque Ports and once an important naval base, but the silting up of the River Stour left Sandwich stranded a couple of miles from the coast. **Sandwich Museum**, the 16th century Guildhall, the 12th century St Bartholomew's Hospital and the 16th century Barbican Gate are all worth visiting, but to the northwest of the town lies a much older site – the impressive ruins of **Richborough Roman Fort**. Sandwich has one of the country's best-known championship golf courses, Royal St George's.

MINSTER

14 miles N of Dover off the A253

Founded in AD 670, **Minster Abbey** became part of the estate of St Augustine's Abbey, Canterbury; much of this Norman work can still be seen in the cloisters and other parts of the ruins.

DEAL

7½ miles NE of Dover on the A258

This is a delightful fishing town that, as well as being the haunt of smugglers, was also frequently visited by Nelson, who outraged local society by staying at the Royal Hotel with his mistress, Lady Emma Hamilton. The **Maritime and Local History Museum** is housed in stables that were once used to shelter army mules, while the distinctive Timeball Tower, dated 1795, stands on the site of the old naval yard. Close by is **Deal Castle**, one of a number of fortresses built by Henry VIII to protect the south coast from invasion.

Just south of Deal is the residential seaside town of **Walmer** which is best known today for its sister castle to Deal. **Walmer Castle** is now a stately home and the official residence of the Lord Warden of the Cinque Ports.

FOLKESTONE

Close to the centre of **The Leas**, a wide sweeping promenade with clifftop lawns and flower gardens, is a statue of the great physician William Harvey, who was born in the town in 1578. His greatest claim to fame is that he discovered the circulation of blood, and it is appropriate that he is holding a human heart in his hand. **The Leas Cliff Lift**, the oldest water-balanced lift in the country, carries people from the cliff top to the beach below.

Just northeast of Folkestone, close to the cliffs at Capel le Ferne, is the **Battle of Britain Memorial** commemorating the 1940 air battle that took place in the skies overhead. Close by is the **Kent Battle of Britain Museum**, the home of the country's largest collection of 1940 related artefacts on display to the public. The Channel Tunnel Terminal is at Folkestone, where cars, coaches and lorries entrain for the journey under the sea to France.

TENTERDEN

Situated right on the border between the dense woodlands of the Weald and the flatter farmland that extends to Romney Marsh, Tenterden is a charming old town that earns its nickname – the 'Jewel of the Weald'. Along with the **Tenterden and District Museum**, the town is also the home of the restored **Kent and East Sussex Railway**.

Recognised as one of the loveliest villages in the Weald, **Biddenden**, just northwest of Tenterden, has an attractive main street lined with charming half-

timbered houses that range in age from medieval through to the 17th century.

AROUND TENTERDEN

ASHFORD

9 miles NE of Tenterden on the A28

The first volunteer fire service in the country was established in Ashford in 1826, and a century later the public raised funds to acquire the first Leyland motor fire engine to see service. One of the most famous sights is a 1916 British Mark IV tank that stands proudly in St George's Square. It was presented to the people of Ashford in recognition of their splendid efforts during the two World Wars. Ashford has been a major railway centre for 150 years, and is now home to the International Station serving Eurostar trains.

APPLEDORE

5 miles SE of Tenterden on the B2080

Despite being some eight miles from the sea, Appledore was once a port on the estuary of the River Rother. The **Royal Military Canal**, which passes through the village, provides a wonderful habitat for a variety of wildlife, including dragonflies and marsh frogs.

Just to the northeast lies the village of **Small Hythe**, a little hamlet that was once a flourishing port and ship-building centre - one of Henry VIII's warships was built here. **Smallhythe Place** is a

295 THE BATTLE OF BRITAIN MEMORIAL

Capel le Ferne, Folkestone

A striking memorial in a spectacular clifftop position built to commemorate those who lost their lives in the summer of 1940.

 see page 465

296 LITTLE SILVER COUNTRY HOTEL

St Michaels, nr Tenterden

Little Silver Country Hotel is a superb family-run hotel offering top hospitality and the best in comfort and cuisine.

see page 466

161

charming 16th century half-timbered house that was the home of the famous Shakespearean actress Ellen Terry and is now a museum. Small Hythe is also home to Tenterden Vineyard.

NEW ROMNEY

13 miles SE of Tenterden on the A259

Known as the 'Capital of the Marsh', and once the most important of the Cinque Ports, New Romney is best known as the main station of the **Romney Hythe and Dymchurch Railway**, a charming one-third-scale railway that was built in the 1920s for the millionaire racing driver, Captain Howey.

In the station is a Toy & Model Museum. The very name **Romney Marsh** conjures up images of smugglers lugging their contraband across the lonely, misty landscape. Rudyard Kipling painted a charming and romantic picture of the Marsh in his poetry, but Russell Thorndyke told of a rougher side in his novel *Dr Syn*.

CRANBROOK

7 miles NW of Tenterden off the A229

Often dubbed the 'Capital of the Kentish Weald', Cranbrook grew following the introduction of wool weaving from Flanders and then developed further as a market town serving the surrounding rural communities. The tower of the Church of St Dunstan is tall, but the town is dominated by **Union Mill**, a familiar local landmark which is the tallest smock mill in England and still, wind permitting, grinds corn for sale.

A couple of miles northeast of the town lie the ruins of **Sissinghurst Castle**, famous for the lovely gardens that were created by Vita Sackville-West and her husband Harold Nicholson in the 1930s. An interesting little exhibition is housed in the estate's oast house.

Lancashire

For some, Lancashire is the brash seaside resort of Blackpool, for others a county dominated by cotton mills. However, there is much more to Lancashire than candyfloss and cotton. It is an ancient county, with many of its towns and villages dating back to Saxon times and beyond, and during the Civil War it remained fiercely loyal to the King and saw some of the bloodiest incidents of the whole bitter conflict. Away from the brash resorts, which developed to provide attractions and amenities for the mill workers who made use of the new railway network to escape for a day or even a week's holiday, there are the more genteel towns of Lytham St Anne's and Southport with its elegant mile-long main boulevard. Inland lies beautiful countryside that includes the ancient hunting ground of the Forest of Bowland and, to the south, Pendle Hill, the scene of the notorious 17th century witch hunts. Morecambe Bay, beautiful but occasionally treacherous, offers glorious views and sunsets and is an important habitat for a variety of birdlife and other wildlife.

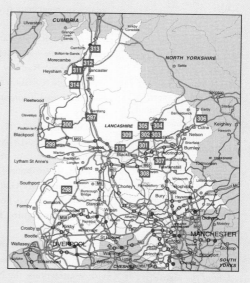

297 THE KINGS ARMS

Garstang, nr Preston

In the centre of Garstang, the **Kings Arms** is a family-friendly pub serving a good selection of lunchtime food (Mon-Sat).

 see page 467

Preston was the place where, in 1768, the single most important machine of the textile industry was invented: Richard Arkwright's water-frame cotton spinning machine. Almost overnight, the cottage industries of spinning and handloom weaving were moved from the workers' homes into factories and the entrepreneurs of Preston were quicker than most to catch on. The great days of the textile industry are long gone, but the cotton workers of the town are remembered in a statue that stands outside the old Corn Exchange.

PRESTON

Preston is strategically positioned on the highest navigable point of the River Ribble, and although the port activity has declined, the docklands, now called Riversway, have become an area of regeneration with a marina. The complex is in the **Millennium Ribble Link**, itself part of a three-mile water park. The **Ribble Steam Railway** boasts the largest single collection of standard-gauge industrial locomotives in the country.

Dominating the Market Square is a magnificent neoclassical building, reminiscent of the British Museum, which houses the **Harris Museum and Art Gallery**. Fulwood Barracks is home to the **Queen's Lancashire Regiment Museum**.

On the northern outskirts of Preston is one of its most popular visitor attractions, the **National Football Museum**.

AROUND PRESTON

GARSTANG

10½ miles N of Preston on the A6

This ancient market town dates back to the 6th century when a Saxon named Garri made his base here. At the excellent **Discovery Centre** displays deal with various aspects of the region, including the history of the nearby Forest of Bowland.

Just to the east of the town, on the top of a grassy knoll, are the remains of **Greenhalgh Castle**, built in 1490 by Thomas Stanley,

the 1st Earl of Derby. Severely damaged in a siege against Cromwell in 1645-6, the Castle was one of the last strongholds in Lancashire to hold out against Parliament. To the north, on the A6, are the remains of a 17th century tollhouse built when parts of the turnpike from Garstang to Lancaster were realigned.

CHORLEY

8 miles SE of Preston on the A6

A bustling and friendly market town, Chorley was the birthplace, in 1819, of Henry Tate, who founded the world famous sugar business of Tate and Lyle. A great benefactor, Henry gave vast sums of money to worthy causes, and endowed the art gallery that now bears his name.

The jewel in Chorley's crown is undoubtedly **Astley Hall**, built in the late 16th century and set within some beautiful parkland.

To the southeast is the charming village of **Rivington**, surrounded by moorland that forms the western border of the Forest of Rossendale. Overlooking the village, and with splendid views over west Lancashire, Rivington Pike, at 1,191 feet, is one of the area's high peaks. Just to the south of the village lies **Lever Park**, situated on the lower slopes of Rivington Moor, which was the home of William Hesketh Lever, who later became Lord Leverhulme.

LEYLAND

5 miles S of Preston on the B5253

The name is the clue: the town is best known for its associations

Lever Park, Chorley

with the manufacture of cars and lorries and the **British Commercial Vehicle Museum** is housed on the site of the former Leyland South Works, where commercial vehicles were produced for many years.

WIGAN

15 miles S of Preston on the A49

Wigan's development as an industrial town centred on coal mining, which began as early as 1450. By the 19th century, there were over 1,000 pit shafts in operation in the surrounding area, supplying the fuel for Lancashire's expanding textile industry. The Leeds and Liverpool Canal, which runs through the town, was a key means of transporting the coal to the cotton mills of Lancashire and **Wigan Pier**, the major loading bay,

remains one of the most interesting features of the waterway.

There is some fine countryside around the town, including the **Douglas Valley Trail**; **Pennington Flash**, a large lake formed by mining subsidence that is now a wildlife reserve and a country park; and **Haigh Country Park**, one of the first to be designated in England.

RUFFORD

10 miles SW of Preston on the A59

In this attractive village of pretty houses stands the ancestral home of the Hesketh family, the splendid 15th century **Rufford Old Hall**. In the outbuildings is the **Philip Ashcroft Museum of Rural Life**, with its unique collection of items that illustrate village life in pre-industrial Lancashire.

298 WWT MARTIN MERE

Nr Rufford

One of nine centres throughout the UK dedicated to the conservation of wetland areas, **WWT Martin Mere** provides a fun day out for all the family.

 see page 467

299 THE GARDEN
RESTAURANT

*World of Water, Westby,
nr Kirkham*

Quality and service are
bywords at the **Garden
Restaurant**, which is open
seven days a week for home-
cooked snacks and meals.

see page 468

300 THE WHITE BULL
HOTEL

Great Eccleston

An 18th century inn serving
a selection of real ales and
wholesome food.

see page 468

---

*To the south is Lytham St
Anne's, a quiet place that
was a small port before
the expansion of
Blackpool. However, as
its neighbour grew, this
town developed into a
genteel and elegant resort
that is famous for its
wealth of Victorian and
Edwardian architecture.
Royal Lytham and St
Anne's Golf Course is one
of the finest golf links in
the country and is a
regular host of the British
Open.*

SOUTHPORT

15 miles SW of Preston on the A565

The rise of this popular seaside
resort lies in the tradition of sea
bathing that began at nearby
Churchtown centuries ago. As the
number of people celebrating
Bathing Sunday grew, so did the
need for a more accessible beach
and a stretch of sand two miles
south of Churchtown was deemed
suitable. From the first simple hotel
Southport has grown into an elegant
and sophisticated resort that is
centred on its main boulevard, **Lord
Street**, a mile-long wide road built
between the lands of the two
neighbouring lords of the manor.
Southport's **Promenade** is bordered
by grand hotels on the land side and
a series of formal gardens on the
other. From the centre of the
promenade extends Southport's **Pier**
that, at 1,460 yards, was for a time
the longest in the country.

A unique attraction is the
British Lawnmower Museum, a
tribute to the garden machine
industry. Along the coast to the
southeast is the **Freshfield Nature
Reserve**, with a pine forest that has
one of the few colonies of red
squirrels in England.

BLACKPOOL

15 miles NW of Preston on the A583

This classic British resort, with piers,
funfairs, gardens, amusement
arcades and a promenade, was until
the middle of the 19th century little
more than a fishing village among
the sand dunes of the Fylde coast.
However, the fashion for taking day

trips and holidays, assisted by the
very expanding railway network, saw
Blackpool develop rapidly. In 1889,
the original Opera House was built
in the Winter Gardens complex and
two years later a start was made on
the world famous Tower.
Completed in 1894, **Blackpool
Tower**, modelled on the Eiffel
Tower in Paris, stands 518 feet high.
The **North Pier**, designed by the
peerless Eugenius Birch, was
opened at the beginning of the 1863
season; it soon became *the* place to
promenade and is now a listed
building. The **Pleasure Beach**,
which boasts its own railway station,
is an attraction that continues to be
extended and improved. The famous
Blackpool Trams provide
enjoyable trips along the front and
out to these less busy sides of the
town. A couple of miles inland,
Martin Mere is a Wildlife Trust
bird reserve where more than 160
species have been recorded.

POULTON-LE-FYLDE

13 miles NW of Preston on the A586

The Romans were in the area and it
was probably their handiwork that
constructed the **Danes Pad**, an
ancient trackway. The town
developed as a commercial centre
for the surrounding agricultural
communities and its Market Place
remains its focal point.

Strolling around Poulton-le-
Fylde now, it is hard to imagine that
the town was once a seaport. But
until relatively recently ships sailed
up the River Wyre to **Skippool
Creek**, now home to the Blackpool
and Fleetwood Yacht Club.

Wyre Estuary at Skippool

Along the banks of the river is the **Wyre Estuary Country Park**, an excellent place for walking and discovering the area.

FLEETWOOD

17 miles NW of Preston on the A587

The town's **Museum**, overlooking the River Wyre, illustrates Fleetwood's links with the fishing industry that suffered greatly from the Icelandic cod wars. However, Fleetwood's real claim to fame is the **Fisherman's Friend** – a staggeringly successful lozenge made from liquorice, capsicum, eucalyptus and methanol that was used by fishermen to relieve sore throats and bronchial trouble caused by the freezing conditions found in the northern Atlantic waters.

BLACKBURN

The largest town in east Lancashire, Blackburn is notable for its shopping malls, celebrated three-day market, modern cathedral, and Thwaites Brewery, one of the biggest independent brewers of real ale in the north of England. Hard though it may be to imagine today, at the height of the textile industry, Blackburn was the biggest weaving town in the world. In 1931, it received arguably its most influential visitor when Mahatma Gandhi toured the area on a study trip of Lancashire's textile manufacture. Examples of the early machines, including James Hargreaves' Spinning Jenny and his carding machine, invented in 1760, can be seen at the **Lewis Textile Museum**.

In 1926 the Diocese of Blackburn was created and St Mary's Church, built in 1826, became the **Cathedral** of the Bishop of Blackburn.

Just to the northeast of Blackburn lies the charming village of **Whalley**, home of the well-preserved 13th century **Whalley Abbey**.

301 NEW INNS

Rishton, nr Blackburn

New Inns, the **Derby Arms** at Inskip and the **Royal Oak** at Clayton-le-Dale offer the very best in British innkeeping, with outstanding food, drink and hospitality.

 see page 469

302 THE DOG INN

Whalley, nr Clitheroe

The **Dog Inn** is a popular village hostelry serving real ales (at least four always on tap) and a good variety of freshly prepared food.

see page 470

303 MARMALADE CAFÉ

Whalley, nr Clitheroe

On the main street of picturesque Whalley, **Marmalade Café** sets high standards of hospitality, service and quality of cooking.

 see page 468

304 THE OLD POST HOUSE HOTEL

King Street, Clitheroe

The **Old Post House Hotel** delivers a warm family welcome, excellent food and comfortable B&B accommodation.

 see page 470

305 THE ASPINALL ARMS HOTEL

Mitton, nr Clitheroe

A picturesque village setting by the River Ribble, fine food and drink and comfortable B&B rooms – the family-run **Aspinall Arms** has all this and more.

see page 471

306 BLACK LANE ENDS

Colne

In a scenic setting on an old drovers' road, **Black Lane Ends** tempts with an all-day selection of real ales (several from the Copper Dragon Brewery) and home cooking.

see page 471

AROUND BLACKBURN

CLITHEROE

10 miles NE of Blackburn on the A671

This old stone town, just south of the Forest of Bowland, has always been considered the forest's capital and it is also Lancashire's second oldest borough, receiving its first market charter in 1147. Clitheroe is dominated by its 800-year-old Castle, standing on a limestone crag high above the town but now little more than a ruin. The **Castle Museum** includes reconstructions of a clogger's workshop, a printer's shop, and a lead mine. Nearby **Pendle Hill** is a place rich in history and legend, famous for the tragic story of the Pendle Witches. In the early 17th century, several women of the area were imprisoned in Lancaster Castle as a result of their seemingly evil practices and, having been found guilty, were publicly hanged. To the west of the hill's summit is Apronfull Hill, a Bronze Age burial site. Also to the northeast lies **Sawley Abbey**, founded in the 13th century by the Cistercian monks of Fountains Abbey.

COLNE

14½ miles NE of Blackburn on the A6068

Before the Industrial Revolution turned this area into a valley devoted to the production of cotton cloth, Colne was a small market town that specialised in wool. In the centre of the town, next to the War Memorial, is the statue of Lawrence Hartley, the bandmaster on the ill-fated *Titanic* who heroically stayed at his post with his musicians and played *Nearer my God to Thee* as the liner sank beneath the waves of the icy Atlantic in 1912. Colne is also the unlikely home of the **British in India Museum**, where exhibits covering many aspects of the British rule over the subcontinent are housed.

To the northeast lies the **Earby Mines Museum** with a collection of lead mining tools and equipment used in the Yorkshire Dales.

ACCRINGTON

4½ miles E of Blackburn on the A680

This attractive Victorian market town is the home of the **Haworth Art Gallery**, which houses the largest collection of Tiffany glass in Europe. The collection was presented to the town by Joseph Briggs, an Accrington man, who worked with Louis Tiffany in New York for nearly 40 years.

Close by is another typical Lancashire textile town, **Oswaldtwistle**, which could be considered to be the birthplace of the industry since it was while staying here that James Hargreaves invented his famous Spinning Jenny in 1764.

BURNLEY

10 miles E of Blackburn on the A646

A cotton town rich in history and the largest in this area of east Lancashire. With the Industrial Revolution and the building of the Leeds and Liverpool Canal, Burnley grew to become the world's leading producer of cotton cloth. A walk along the towpath of the canal leads through an area known as the **Weavers' Triangle** – an area of spinning mills and weaving sheds; foundries where steam engines and looms were made; canal-side warehouses and domestic buildings. On the outskirts of town is the **Towneley Hall Art Gallery and Museum**.

To the west of Burnley is **Gawthorpe Hall**, a splendid 17th century house that was restored with a flourish of Victorian elegance during the 1850s. Beautiful period furnishings are enhanced by the ornately decorated ceilings and the original wood-panelled walls, making the perfect setting for the nationally important Kay-Shuttleworth needlework and lace collection.

DARWEN

4 miles S of Blackburn on the A666

The town is dominated by **Darwen Tower**, built to commemorate the Diamond Jubilee of Queen Victoria in 1897 and situated high on the moor. Another striking landmark is the chimney of the **India Mill**, constructed out of hand-made bricks and built to resemble the campanile (belltower) in St Mark's Square, Venice.

BOLTON

12 miles S of Blackburn on the A666

During the Civil War, the town saw one of the bloodiest episodes of the conflict when James Stanley, Earl of Derby, was brought back here by Cromwell's troops after the Royalists had been defeated. In a savage act of revenge for the massacre his army had brought on the town early in the troubles, Stanley was executed and his severed head and body, in separate caskets, were taken back to the family burial place at Ormskirk.

Impressive buildings here include 14th century **Smithills Hall** and the late 15th century **Hall-i'-th'-Wood**, a fine example of a wealthy merchant's house. One of Bolton's most recent attractions is the state-of-the-art **Reebok Stadium**, home of Bolton Wanderers FC.

Six miles east of Bolton lies **Bury**, another typical Lancashire mill town that is more famous for its inhabitants that its buildings. Over the centuries the town has given the world the Pilkington family of glassworks fame, John Kay, the inventor of the flying shuttle, and Robert Peel, the politician who repealed the Corn Laws and founded the modern police force. On the outskirts of the town lies **Burrs Country Park** which, as well as offering a wide range of activities, also has an interesting industrial trail around the historic mill site.

Further east again is **Rochdale**, another cotton town, most famous as being the birthplace of the Co-operative Movement; in carefully restored Toad Lane, to the north of the town centre, is the world's first Co-op shop, the Rochdale Pioneers.

307 THE PLOUGH HOTEL

Oswaldtwistle

The **Plough** is very much at the heart of social life in Oswaldtwistle, with entertainment almost every night, plus good food and drink lunchtime and evening.

see page 472

308 THE RED LION

Blacksnape, nr Darwen

On the edge of the West Pennine Moors, the **Red Lion** is a family-run pub with a well-earned reputation for hospitality and good food.

see page 473

309 THE WHITE BULL

Church Street, Ribchester

Prominently placed in the ancient town of Ribchester, the **White Bull** is open every day for drinks and home-cooked food. It also has three rooms for B&B.

 see page 473

310 THE MYERSCOUGH

Balderstone, nr Blackburn

The **Myerscough** is a handsome inn on the A59, with wide-ranging lunchtime and evening menus, Robinson's ales and comfortable rooms for B&B.

 see page 474

311 LANCASTER CASTLE

Lancaster

Dating back nearly 1,000 years, the castle is still in use as a prison and crown court. Guided tours include the room where the Lancashire Witches were condemned to death

 see page 475

RIBCHESTER

5 miles NW of Blackburn on the B6245

Situated on the banks of the River Ribble, the village is famous for its **Roman Fort** on the northern riverbank, first established by Gnaeus Julius Agricola in AD 79. Although little of the fort's walls remain, the granary and its hypocaust have been excavated, revealing interesting finds that can be seen in the fort's Roman Museum.

LANCASTER

The capital town of Lancashire boasts a long and interesting history. It was in the 10th century that Athelstan, the grandson of Alfred the Great, had lands in the area, and during the reign of William the Conqueror large parts of what is now Lancashire were given by the grateful king to his cousin Roger of Pitou, who made his base at Lancaster. Queen Elizabeth II retains the title of Duke of Lancaster. Within yards of the railway station lies **Lancaster Castle**, a great medieval fortress founded by the Normans to keep out Scottish invaders and strengthened by John of Gaunt, Duke of Lancaster. In Church Street stands the 17th century **Judge's Lodging**, which now houses two separate museums, the Museum of Childhood and the Gillow and Town House Museum.

The town's rich maritime

Penny Street Bridge Wharf, Lancaster

history is celebrated at **St George's Quay**, which, with its great stone warehouses and superb Custom House, is now an award-winning **Maritime Museum**. One of the first sights visitors see of the town is the great green copper dome of the impressive **Ashton Memorial**, built by the linoleum manufacturer Lord Ashton in memory of his wife and a landmark for miles around that stands on a hilltop in the centre of the splendid Edwardian Williamson Park. Pevsner described it as 'the grandest monument in England'.

AROUND LANCASTER

CARNFORTH

5 miles N of Lancaster on the A6

Not many towns are best known for their stations, but Carnforth is one of them: it was used as the setting for the 1940s film classic *Brief Encounter*. The old engine sheds and sidings are now occupied by **Steamtown**, one of the largest steam railway centres in the north of England.

Just to the north lies **Leighton Hall**, a fine early 19th century house that is now owned by a branch of the Gillow family; the fine furniture seen in the hall reflects the trade that made the family fortune.

FOREST OF BOWLAND

3 miles E of Lancaster

Designated an Area of Outstanding Natural Beauty in February 1964, this large and scenic area is a paradise for walkers and country lovers that is dotted with picturesque villages. Following the Norman Conquest, Bowland became part of the Honour of Clitheroe and the vast estates that belonged to the de Lacy family. In 1399, when the then Duke of Lancaster came to the throne as Henry IV, Bowland finally became one of nearly 100 royal hunting forests.

The remains of a Roman road can be clearly seen traversing the land and many of the villages in the area have names dating back to the Saxon period. Perhaps the most celebrated of the many routes across Bowland is the minor road from Lancaster to Clitheroe that crosses the **Abbeydale Moor** and the Trough of Bowland before descending into the lovely Hodder Valley around Dunsop Bridge.

At the heart of the Forest is **Slaidburn**, a pretty village of stone cottages and cobbled pavements whose 13th century public house **Hark to Bounty** contains an old court room where, from around 1250, the Chief Court of Bowland, or Halmote, was held. The Hark to Bounty inn was originally called The Dog, but one day in 1875 the local Hunt gathered here. A visiting squire, listening to the hounds outside, clearly made out the cry of his favourite hound rising above the others and exclaimed "Hark to Bounty!". The landlord was so impressed by this unrestrained show of delight that he changed the name of his pub there and then.

312 THE GREYHOUND HOTEL

Halton, nr Lancaster

Curries are the popular specialities at the **Greyhound**, a distinctive stone pub close to the River Lune.

see page 473

313 THE REFRESHMENT ROOM

Carnforth Railway Station, Carnforth

The **Refreshment Room** at Carnforth Station offers cakes, sandwiches and hot and cold snacks in the beautifully restored setting of the classic film *Brief Encounter*.

see page 475

314 THE DALTON ARMS

Glasson Dock, nr Lancaster

The **Dalton Arms** is a very pleasant family-run pub with a fine reputation for the quality and range of its cooking.

see page 476

MORECAMBE

3 miles W of Lancaster on the A589

Featuring prominently on the Lancashire coastline, Morecambe has long been one of the most popular seaside resorts in the North, and it can truly be said to enjoy one of the finest views from its promenade of any resort in England – a magnificent sweep of coastline and bay, looking across to the Lakeland mountains. Many buildings date from Morecambe's heyday as a holiday destination, including the Midland Hotel, built in the early 1930s to designs by Oliver Hill.

Near the Stone jetty is the **Eric Morecambe Statue** with words from the song *Bring Me Sunshine* carved into the granite steps. **Morecambe Bay**, a vast wide, flat tidal plain situated between Lancashire and Cumbria, is the home of many forms of marine life as well as being a very popular and important habitat for birds. It's also famous for a great delicacy – Morecambe Bay potted shrimps. The Bay is also very treacherous, and over the years many have fallen victim of the tides and the quicksands. In medieval times this perilous track formed part of the main west coast route from England to Scotland, and the monks of Furness would act as guides for travellers who wished to avoid the long overland route. Today, Cross Bay Walks are led by the Queen's Guide to the Sands.

Leicestershire

Rolling fields, wooded gorges and meandering waterways make Leicestershire a perfect place for exploring – on foot, by bicycle or by boat. The county is divided into two almost equal parts by the River Soar, which flows northwards into the River Trent. The Grand Union Canal threads its way through South Leicestershire, while the Ashby Canal passes close to Bosworth Battlefield, in the west of the county. Leicester, the capital, is one of the oldest towns in the country and retains outstanding monuments of almost every age of English history. Agriculture and industry go hand in hand here: the long-haired local sheep produced fine woollens, and by the end of the 17th century the now worldwide hosiery trade had been established. Loughborough has been famous for making bells for more than 100 years, while at Melton Mowbray pork pies

have been made on a commercial scale since 1830. King Richard III spent his last days in the county before his death at the Battle of Bosworth in 1485, a battle that changed the course of British history.

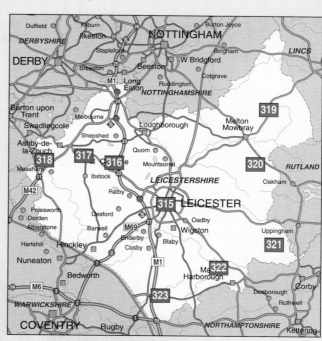

315 THE CITY GALLERY

Leicester

The City Gallery offers promotes the best in contemporary arts and crafts through a programme of continually changing exhibitions.

 see page 476

To the northwest of Leicester lies Bradgate Country Park, the largest and most popular park in the county, which was created from the ancient hunting ground and deer park of Charnwood Forest. At the centre of the park are the ruins of Bradgate House, the birthplace and early home of Lady Jane Grey (Queen for nine days in 1553).

LEICESTER

Designated Britain's first 'environment city' in recognition of its commitment to green issues, Leicester has numerous parks and open spaces but also a rich architectural heritage, with no fewer than 350 listed buildings. At the heart of Leicester's heritage is Castle Park, the old town, an area of gardens, churches, museums and other fine buildings. Here are concentrated many of the city's main attractions: **Castle Gardens** opened as a park in 1926; **Castle Motte**, a man-made mound built around 1070 by Leicester's first Norman lord; the Church of St Mary de Castro, founded in 1107 and still in use; the Great Hall of Leicester Castle built in the 12th century; and **Newarke Houses Museum**, a museum of social and domestic history contained in two 16th century houses.

Leicester's diverse cultural and religious heritage is represented by the **Jain Centre**, the **Guru Nanak Sikh Museum**; the **Jewry Wall and Museum**; and the Church of St Martin, which was in existence before 1086, was extended in the 14th and 15th centuries, restored in the 19th century and hallowed as the **Cathedral** of Leicester in

King Richards Well, Bosworth Field

174

1927. One of the very finest buildings in the city is the **Guildhall**, built around 1390 for the Guild of Corpus Christi and used as the Town Hall from the late 15th century until 1876. Across the road from the Cathedral is **Wygston's House**, a part timber-framed building, one of the oldest in the city, which now houses displays of fashion, textiles and crafts. The city's most recent and most spectacular attraction is the **National Space Centre**, where the audience can take an awe-inspiring journey through the universe and beyond.

AROUND LEICESTER

HINCKLEY

11½ miles SW of Leicester on the A47

An old town whose Fair is mentioned in Shakespeare's *Henry IV*. In Lower Bond Street, a row of restored 17th century thatched framework knitters' cottages is home to **Hinckley and District Museum**. To the east lies Burbage Common and Woods Country Park, which contains one of the largest areas of grassland in the area.

MARKET BOSWORTH

11 miles W of Leicester off the A447

This market town is most famous as the battle site for the turning point in the Wars of the Roses, when in 1485 the forces of King Richard III were routed by those of Henry Tudor, who took the throne as Henry VII. The battle was immortalised in Shakespeare's play *Richard III*, where the King is

heard to cry, *"My kingdom for a horse."* **Bosworth Battlefield** lies to the southwest of the town and the Visitor Centre has details of the Battle and numerous artefacts and displays on the Tudor period.

Market Bosworth Country Park is one of many beautiful open spaces in the area whilst another is **Bosworth Water Trust's Leisure and Water Park** to west of town. This is a 50-acre leisure park with 20 acres of lakes for sailing, boardsailing and fishing.

To the northwest of Market Bosworth lies **Twycross Zoo**, home to a wide variety of animals that include a famous primate collection, from tiny pygmy marmosets to huge Western lowland gorillas.

MOUNTSORREL

6 miles N of Leicester off the A6

Situated on the banks of the River Soar, the village is home to **Stonehurst Family Farm and Motor Museum**, where the highlights range from baby rabbits and guinea pigs in cuddle corner to an impressive collection of vintage vehicles, including Leicestershire's first motor bus.

LOUGHBOROUGH

10 miles N of Leicester on the A6

There are two attractions at Loughborough that visitors certainly should not miss. In 1858, the bell foundry of John Taylor moved here from Oxford and the **John Taylor Bell Foundry Museum** covers all aspects of bell-founding from early times. The

To the north of Market Bosworth is a village with the wonderful name of Barton-in-the-Beans. The county was apparently once known as 'bean-belly' Leicestershire, on account of the large reliance on the bean crops that formed part of the staple diet in needy times.

316 ABBOTS OAK
COUNTY HOTEL

Warren Hills, nr Coalville

Comfort, service, charm and
courtesy are bywords at the
family-run **Abbots Oak
Country Hotel** set in
extensive gardens and
woodland.

 see page 477

317 SNIBSTON
DISCOVERY PARK

Coalville

Leicestershire's dynamic
industry and science museum
with hands-on displays and
guided colliery tours.

 see page 476

318 THE SHOULDER OF
MUTTON

Oakthorpe, nr Measham

The **Shoulder of Mutton** is
an immaculate country inn
serving appetising pub
classics and dishes with a
difference in a delightful
traditional ambience.

 see page 477

Ashby Castle

town is also the headquarters of the
Great Central Railway, which
runs steam trains every weekend
and Bank Holiday, and daily in
June, July, August and local school
holidays. Tel: 01509 230726

COALVILLE
11 miles NW of Leicester on the A511

Originally called Long Lane, the
town sprang up on a bleak
common when Whitwick Colliery
was opened in 1824. **Snibston
Discovery Park**, built on the site
of the former Snibston Colliery,
provides the opportunity to
explore a unique mixture of
nature, history, art, science and
technology with the help of the
latest interactive technology. Tel:
01530 278444

To the northeast, in a beautiful
elevated position in Charnwood
Forest, is **Mount St Bernard
Abbey**, the first Catholic abbey to

be founded in England after the
Reformation.

ASHBY-DE-LA-ZOUCH
16 miles NW of Leicester on the A511

During the Civil War, **Ashby
Castle** was besieged for over a
year by the Parliamentarian Army
until the Royalists surrendered in
1646. After the war the castle was
partly destroyed to prevent its
further use as a centre of
resistance and almost wholly
forgotten until Sir Walter Scott
used the castle as the setting in
Ivanhoe for the archery competition
that Robin Hood won by splitting
the shaft of his opponent's arrow
in the bull's eye.

To the east lies the **National
Forest**, a truly accessible,
multipurpose forest providing a
full range of environmental,
recreational and social benefits for
current and future generations.

KEGWORTH

15½ miles NW of Leicester on the A6

A large village with many architectural reminders of its days as a framework-knitting centre. Topics covered at the **Kegworth Museum** include the knitting industry, saddlery, air transport and photography, and postcards of the 1920s. To the west lies Donington Park, home of the **Donington Grand Prix Collection** with over 130 exhibits in five halls covering 100 years of motor racing history.

MELTON MOWBRAY

This bustling market town is, of course, home to the pork pie, one of the most traditional of English delicacies. The Melton Hunt Cake is another local speciality and Stilton, the 'king of English cheeses', is also made here. The cheese has the longest history, dating back possibly as far as the 14th century, and the town became the market centre for Stilton.

In the town's oldest surviving bakery, **Ye Olde Pork Pie Shoppe**, visitors can watch the traditional hand-raising techniques and taste the pies and the Hunt cake. The **Melton Carnegie Museum** has displays devoted to Stilton cheese, pork pies and the history of fox hunting in the area; visitors can also learn about 'Painting the Town Red', an occasion in 1837 when the Marquis of Waterford and his pals decided to decorate the town with red paint after a night's drinking.

AROUND MELTON MOWBRAY

BELVOIR CASTLE

12 miles N of Melton off the A607

The present **Belvoir Castle**, the Leicestershire home of the Duke of Rutland, was completed in the early 19th century after previous buildings had been destroyed during the Wars of the Roses, the Civil War and in the major fire of 1816. Overlooking the lovely Vale of Belvoir, the castle's stunning interior contains notable collections of furniture and porcelain, silks and tapestries, sculptures and paintings, along with the **Queen's Royal Lancers Museum**. The grounds are as splendid as the castle and are used for medieval jousting tournaments on certain days in the summer.

WYMONDHAM

8 miles E of Melton off the B676

The six-sailed **Windmill**, dating from 1814, and partially restored, is one of only four of its kind in the country.

BURROUGH-ON-THE-HILL

5 miles S of Melton off the B6074

Burrough House, set in five acres of beautiful gardens, was a favourite meeting place of the Prince of Wales and Mrs Wallis Simpson in the 1930s. To the northeast of the village is Burrough Hill, an Iron Age hill fort.

319 THE ROYAL HORSESHOES

Waltham-on-the-Wold, nr Melton Mowbray

The **Royal Horseshoes** is a convivial food-oriented pub with a a warm welcome for the whole family and comfortable B&B rooms.

see page 478

320 THE STILTON CHEESE INN

Somerby, nr Melton Mowbray

The name of the **Stilton Cheese Inn** honours a great local speciality, which features strongly on an excellent, varied menu served every day.

see page 478

321 MEDBOURNE
GRANGE

*Nevill Holt, nr Market
Harborough*

Three en suite bedrooms at
Medbourne Grange
provide quiet, comfortable
B&B accommodation in
picturesque surroundings.

 see page 479

322 THE BLACK HORSE

Foxton, nr Market Harborough

The **Black Horse** is a
friendly country pub, affable
family tenants and a good
choice of food and drink.

 see page 479

323 THE TAVERN INN

Walcote

The **Tavern Inn** scores with
a combination of traditional
English values and
Continental flair from the
Portuguese host, with menus
to match.

see page 479

MARKET HARBOROUGH

In 1645 Charles I made Market
Harborough his headquarters and
held a council of war here before
the Battle of Naseby. The
development of turnpike roads led
to prosperity and the establishment
of coaching inns in the town, many
of them still in business. The canals
and the railways transformed
communications and manufacturing
industry became established, the
most notable company being R W
& H Symington, creators of the
Liberty Bodice. The **Harborough
Museum** incorporates the
Symington Collection of Corsetry.

AROUND MARKET HARBOROUGH

FOXTON

2 miles NW of Market Harborough off the A6

The most famous site on the
county's canals is the **Flight of
Ten Locks** on the Grand Union
Canal, one of the great engineer
Thomas Telford's most impressive
constructions. In the **Canal
Museum**, halfway down the flight,
the steam-powered boat lift of
1900 is undergoing restoration, and
there are several other buildings
and bridges of interest (including a
swing-bridge) in this pretty village.

LUTTERWORTH

*12 miles W of Market Harborough
on the A4304*

John Wycliffe was rector here
under the tutelage of John of
Gaunt. His instigation of an
English translation of the Bible into
English caused huge dissent. He
died in 1384 and was buried in the
church here, but when he was
excommunicated in 1428 his body
was exhumed and burned and his
ashes scattered in the River Swift.
Close to the church, **Lutterworth
Museum** contains a wealth of local
history from Roman times to World
War II. Lutterworth is where Frank
Whittle perfected the design of his
jet engine.

About 3 miles southeast of
Lutterworth and set in meadows
beside the River Avon, **Stanford
Hall** has been the home of the
Cave family since 1430. The
present house – pleasantly
proportioned, dignified and serene,
was built by the celebrated architect
William Smith of Warwick in the
1690s. A superb staircase was
added in around 1730, one of very
few structural alterations to the
house in its 300-year history:
another was the Ballroom, which
contains paintings that once
belonged to Bonnie Prince Charlie's
younger brother, Henry Stuart.

Lincolnshire

Although it is the second largest county in England, Lincolnshire remains relatively unknown. It is largely rural and has some of the richest farmland in the country producing, particularly, potatoes, sugar beet and flowers. The county has strong historical connections with Holland and Scandinavia and is blessed with many picturesque villages and towns including the majestic county capital Lincoln with its marvellous cathedral, historic Stamford, acclaimed as the finest stone town in England, and Grantham, the birthplace of Margaret Thatcher. Along with its extensive coastline, which boasts a number of traditional seaside resorts, Lincolnshire has also played a part in history. It is home to the world's first military air academy, RAF Cranwell; the Dambusters – 617 Squadron – were stationed near Woodhall Spa; and RAF Coningsby is home to the Battle of Britain Memorial Flight. The port of Grimsby is England's main fishing port.

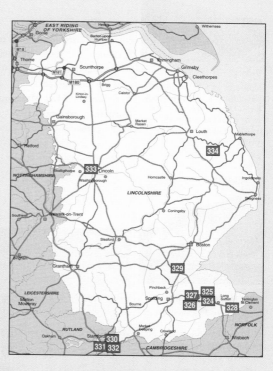

324 CHESTNUT FARM SHOP & TEA ROOM

Gedney

Motorists on the A17 should take time to stop at **Chestnut Farm Shop & Tea Room** to enjoy wholesome home cooking and to buy top-quality local produce.

🍴 see page 480

325 THE BULL

Fleet Hargate, nr Holbeach

A major-road location makes The **Bull** a convenient stop for travellers and tourists, and it also serves admirably the local community.

🍴 see page 480

326 THE STAR

Whaplode, nr Spalding

On the busy A151 between Spalding and Holbeach, the **Star** is the hub of the local community and an excellent place to seek out for a drink or a meal.

🍴 see page 481

SPALDING

This small market town is known for its annual Flower Parade, which is held in early May, when marching bands lead a succession of colourful floats through the town. Spalding is an interesting place to stroll around, and the jewel in its crown is undoubtedly **Ayscoughfee Hall Museum and Gardens**, a well-preserved medieval mansion standing in attractive riverside gardens that houses, among other displays, a permanent exhibit honouring the explorer and oceanographer Captain Matthew Flinders. On the outskirts of the town can be seen more of Spalding's heritage: the **Pode Hole Pumping Station** preserves one of the steam engines installed in 1825 to drain the local fens.

A couple of miles south of Spalding, the **Gordon Boswell Romany Museum** has a colourful collection of Romany Vardos (caravans), carts and harnesses. To the north is the Pinchbeck Engine and Land Drainage Museum, which illustrates how the South Holland Fen was drained. Also here, at **Pinchbeck**, is the **Spalding Bulb Museum** and the **Spalding Tropical Forest**.

Boston Stump

AROUND SPALDING

HOLBEACH

10 miles E of Spalding on the A151/B1168

An agreeable market town in one of the county's largest parishes. The antiquarian William Stukeley and the shot-putter Geoff Capes are sons of Holbeach.

BOSTON

13½ miles NE of Spalding on the A16

Boston's most famous landmark is the tower of the massive 14th century St Botolph's Church; it's popularly known as the **Boston Stump** – a real misnomer since it soars to 272 feet and is visible for 30 miles or more.

Another striking building is the 15th century **Guildhall** that for 300 years served as the Town Hall and now houses the town Museum. It was here, in the Guildhall cells, that the Pilgrim Fathers were held in 1607 while they tried to escape to the religiously tolerant Netherlands. The town is home to the tallest working windmill in Britain, the **Maud Foster Windmill**, which is unusual in having five sails.

CROWLAND

8½ miles S of Spalding on the B1166

Founded by King Ethelbald of Mercia in the 8th century, the ruined **Crowland Abbey** seen today dates from the 12th century and is the third to have been built on the site. The town is noted for its extraordinary 'Bridge without a River': when it was built in the 1300s, **Trinity Bridge** provided a dry crossing over the confluence of three small streams which have since dried up.

GRIMSTHORPE

12 miles W of Spalding on the A151

The village is home to **Grimsthorpe Castle**, which when viewed from the north is a stately 18th century palace; from the south, it is a homely Tudor dwelling. The Tudor part of the house was built at incredible speed in order to provide a convenient lodging place in Lincolnshire for Henry VIII on his way north to meet James V of Scotland in York. The royal visit took place in 1541 but the honour of the royal presence was tarnished by the adultery that allegedly took place here between Henry's fourth wife, Catherine Howard, and an attractive young courtier, Thomas Culpepper. A subsequently passed law declared it treason for an unchaste woman to marry the king, and both Catherine and her ardent courtier paid the ultimate price for their night of passion.

STAMFORD

An attractive market town with unspoilt Georgian streets and squares, Stamford is also noted for its rich cluster of outstanding churches. The most ancient ecclesiastical building is **St Leonard's Priory**, founded by the Benedictines in the 11th century, and a fine example of Norman architecture.

327 THE BELL HOTEL

High Street, Holbeach

On the main street of a pleasant fenland town, **The Bell** combines the virtues of a friendly local and a B&B stop for tourists and travellers.

see page 483

328 THE ANCHOR INN

Sutton Beach, nr Holbeach

Just off the A17 east of Long Sutton, the **Anchor Inn** is a friendly, cheerful pub with a welcome for everyone who visits – for a drink, a meal or an overnight stay.

see page 481

329 THE BERIDGE ARMS HOTEL

Sutterton, nr Boston

The **Beridge Arms** is a friendly, unpretentious pub and B&B close to the junction of the A16 and A17.

see page 483

330 THE CROWN HOTEL

All Saints Place, Stamford

The **Crown Hotel** offers 17th century style and 21st century standards of hospitality, service and comfort in a town centre location

see page 482

331 CENTRAL RESTAURANT

Red Lion Square, Stamford

The **Central Restaurant** tempts with breakfasts, light snacks, hot lunch dishes and excellent home baking.

see page 483

332 BURGHLEY HOUSE

Stamford

A superb example of an Elizabethan house, complete with a beautiful Capability Brown landscaped garden. An amazing ceramics collection and 17th century paintings are on display.

 see page 484

Secular buildings of note include the **Museum of Almshouse Life** and the **Stamford Museum**, which includes a display celebrating one of the town's most notable residents, Daniel Lambert, who earned a solid living by exhibiting himself as the world's heaviest man; on his death in 1809 he weighed nearly 53 stone. Other famous residents include the flamboyant conductor and Promenaders' favourite Sir Malcolm Sargent ('Flash Harry'), who lies buried in the town cemetery, and William Cecil, 1st Lord Burghley, who was Elizabeth I's Chief Secretary of State. **Burghley House** is a wonderfully opulent Elizabethan mansion that houses a magnificent collection of treasures. The **Burghley Horse Trials** are held in the glorious grounds each year at the end of August.

AROUND STAMFORD

WOOLSTHORPE-BY-COLSTERWORTH

14 miles N of Stamford off the B6403

It was at **Woolsthorpe Manor** that Isaac Newton was born in 1642 and where the Father of Modern Science made some of his greatest discoveries. A 17th century barn holds a **Science Discovery Centre** that helps to explain some of his achievements.

GRANTHAM

This ancient market town on the banks of the River Witham has some pleasing old buildings

including **Grantham House**, which dates back to around 1380, and the Angel and Royal Hotel, where King John held court and where Richard III signed the death warrant of the 2nd Duke of Buckingham in 1483. Grantham is perhaps best known as being the childhood home of Margaret Roberts, later Thatcher. **Grantham Museum** has special exhibits devoted to both Lady Thatcher and Sir Isaac Newton.

SLEAFORD

10 miles E of Grantham on the B1517

Inhabited since the Iron Age and home to a massive Roman mint, Sleaford is a busy market town with one of the oldest stone church towers in the country. Other features of interest include the **Money's Mill**, a 70 feet high tower that was erected in 1796 to allow large quantities of corn to be brought here by barge and offloaded right outside the door.

To the northwest of Sleaford is the RAF College, Cranwell, which opened in 1920 as the first Military Air Academy in the world. The **Cranwell Aviation Heritage Centre** tells the Cranwell story and that of the other RAF bases in the region.

LINCOLN

Lincoln Cathedral occupies a magnificent hilltop location, its towers soaring high above the Lincolnshire lowlands being visible for miles around. Among its many superb features are the magnificent open nave, stained-glass windows incorporating the 14th century Bishop's Eye and Dean's Eye, and the glorious Angel Choir, whose carvings include the Lincoln Imp, the unofficial symbol of the city. The imposing ruins of the **Bishops Old Palace**, in the shadow of the Cathedral, reveal the sumptuous lifestyle of the wealthy medieval bishops whose authority stretched from the Humber to the Thames.

Other notable buildings include **Lincoln Castle**, which dates from 1068 and houses one of the four original versions of the *Magna Carta*; the **Jews House**, which dates from about 1170 and is thought to be the oldest domestic building in England to survive intact; and the most impressive surviving part of the old town walls, the **Stonebow**, which spans the High Street pedestrianised shopping mall. Lincolnshire's largest social history museum is the **Museum of Lincolnshire Life** that occupies an extensive barracks built for the Royal North Lincoln Militia in 1857. The newest museum in the county, opened in 2005, is **The Collection**, a major centre of art and archaeology running alongside the Usher Gallery.

To the west of Lincoln is **Doddington Hall**, a grand Elizabethan mansion completed in 1600 by the architect Robert Smythson, and standing now exactly as then, with wonderful formal gardens, a gatehouse and a family church.

AROUND LINCOLN

MARKET RASEN

14 miles NE of Lincoln on the A631

Taking its name from the River Rase, Market Rasen was described by Charles Dickens as being *"the sleepiest town in England."* Much of the central part is a conservation area and includes two ecclesiastical buildings of some note: the Centenary Wesleyan Chapel of 1863 boasts an impressive frontage, while St Thomas's Church has a typical 15th century tower of local ironstone. Market Rasen Racecourse stages 19 National Hunt meetings throughout the year.

LOUTH

24 miles NE of Lincoln off the A16

One of the county's most appealing towns, Louth is set beside the River Lud on the eastern edge of the Wolds. The town is best known for being the home of Alfred Lord Tennyson, who lodged here with his grandmother while attending the King Edward VI School. **Broadbank**, which now houses the Louth Museum, is an attractive little building with some interesting artefacts, including some amazing locally-woven carpets that were displayed at the Paris Exhibition in 1867.

GAINSBOROUGH

15 miles NW of Lincoln on A156

Britain's most inland port is located at the highest navigable point on the River Trent for seagoing vessels. During the 17th and 18th

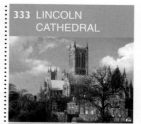

333 LINCOLN CATHEDRAL

Lincoln

A beautiful and imposing 13th century Gothic style building with a wealth of historical interest.

 see page 483

Just southeast of the city of Lincoln are the popular open spaces of Hartsholme Country Park and Swanholme Lakes Local Nature Reserve, whilst a little way further south is Whisby Nature Park that is home to great crested grebe, teal and tufted duck.

To the southwest of Louth lies Donington-on-Bain, a peaceful Wolds village on the Viking Way, the well-trodden route that runs 147 miles from the Humber Bridge to Oakham in Rutland and is waymarked by Viking helmet symbols.

Gainsborough Old Hall

William I, **Bolingbroke Castle** later became the property of John of Gaunt whose son, later Henry IV, was born at the castle in 1367. During the Civil War, Bolingbroke Castle was besieged by Parliamentary forces in 1643 and fell into disuse soon after.

Just to the south, at **East Kirkby,** is the **Lincolnshire Aviation Heritage Centre,** based in the old control tower. Exhibits include a Lancaster bomber, A Shackleton, military vehicles and a wartime blast shelter.

WOODHALL SPA

14 miles SE of Lincoln on the B1191

Woodhall became a spa town by accident when a shaft sunk in search of coal found mineral-rich water. In 1838 a pump room and baths were built, to be joined later by hydro hotels, and the arrival of the railway in 1855 accelerated Woodhall's popularity. By the early 1900s, the spa had fallen out of favour and the associated buildings disappeared one by one, but this beautifully maintained village has retained its decorous spa atmosphere.

Woodhall Spa had close connections with 617 Squadron, the Dambusters, during World War II. The Petwood House Hotel was used as the officers' mess and memorabilia of those days is displayed in the hotel's Squadron Bar.

To the southeast of Woodhall Spa lies Coningsby, the site of a major RAF Tornado base and home to the Battle of Britain Memorial Flight. In the hangars are a Lancaster, 2 Hurricanes, a Dakota and 5 Spitfires.

Also at Skegness, Church Farm Museum is home to a collection of old farm implements and machinery, a paddock of Lincoln Longwool sheep and a fine example of a Lincolnshire "mud and stud" thatched cottage brought here from the nearby village of Withern.

centuries in particular, the town prospered greatly, and although many of the lofty warehouses lining the river bank have been demolished, enough remain to give some idea of its flourishing past.

The town's most famous building is the enchanting **Gainsborough Old Hall,** one of the most striking architectural gems in the county. The hall was built in the 1470s by Sir Thomas Burgh, who entertained Richard III in the Great Hall. The hall is generally considered one of the best preserved medieval manor houses in the country.

Another notable building is **Marshall's Britannia Works,** a proud Victorian reminder of Gainsborough's once thriving engineering industry.

OLD BOLINGBROKE

22 miles E of Lincoln off the A155

Originally built in the reign of

SKEGNESS

In the early 1800s Skegness was

still a tiny fishing village but it was already becoming famous for its firm sandy beaches and bracing sea air. As late as 1871, the resident population of Skegness was only 239 but two years later the railway arrived and three years after that the local landowner, the Earl of Scarborough, built a new town to the north of the railway station. A huge pier, 1,843 feet long, was built in 1880, chosen from 44 designs submitted. The famous slogan 'Skegness is SO Bracing' was first used on posters by the Great Northern Railway in 1918 and appeared in many designs subsequently.

Natureland Seal Sanctuary on North Parade provides interest for all the family with its seals and baby seal rescue centre and numerous other animal attractions. **Gibraltar Point National Nature Reserve** is a field station among the salt marshes and dunes with hides, waymarked routes and guided tours. Yellowhammers and whitethroats nest here, and skylarks are more numerous than anywhere else in Britain.

MABLETHORPE

15 miles N of Skegness on the A52

The northernmost of the three popular Lincolnshire holiday resorts (Skegness and Sutton-on-Sea are the others) that almost form a chain along this stretch of fragile coast. Much of the original village of Mablethorpe has disappeared into the sea, including the medieval Church of St Peter. The **Seal**

Hoyles Mill, Alford

Sanctuary at North End is open every day from Easter to the end of September.

ALFORD

10 miles NW of Skegness on the A1104

Alford Manor House, built around 1660, claims the distinction of being the largest thatched manor house in England. Alford's **Five Sailed Windmill**, built of brick in 1813, stands a majestic six floors high and has five sails and four sets of grinding stones.

334 CLAYTHORPE WATER MILL AND WILDFOWL GARDENS

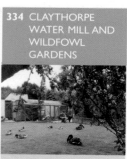

Aby, Nr Alford

Claythorpe Watermill and Wildfowl Gardens are home to over 500 birds, and with its exhibitions and delightful grounds, makes a great day out.

 see page 484

A mile or so northwest of the Hall, St Andrew's Church in the agreeable village of Burton-on-Stather contains an impressive range of memorials to the Sheffield family, the oldest of which dates back to the 1300s.

Grimsby waterfront is dominated by the 300-ft Dock Tower, built in 1852 to store water and a replica of a tower in Siena. The story of Grimsby's boom days is told in vivid detail in the National Fishing Heritage Centre in Alexandra Dock, and a popular attraction is The Fishy Tour, taking in a fish auction, a haddock breakfast, a visit to filleting and smoking houses, a tour of the Heritage Centre, and looking round a classic fishing trawler, ending with a fish & chip lunch.

SCUNTHORPE

Much of Scunthorpe's industrial and social heritage is on display at the **North Lincolnshire Museum & Art Gallery** with exhibits that include an ironmonger's cottage. The town has also created a Heritage Trail which takes visitors through three of the parks created by Victorian benefactors - Scunthorpe is proud of its parks and gardens and has claimed the title of "The Industrial Garden Town of rural North Lincolnshire".

AROUND SCUNTHORPE

NORMANBY

4 miles N of Scunthorpe off the B1430

Normanby Hall was built in 1825 for the Sheffield family and extended in 1906. The 300-acre Park has plenty to see and enjoy, including a deer park, duck ponds, an ice house in the middle of the miniature railway circuit, a Victorian laundry and a walled garden. The **Normanby Hall Farming Museum** majors on rural life in the age of the heavy horse. Near the park gates, some picturesque estate cottages bear witness to the Sheffield family's reputation as good landlords.

BRIGG

7 miles E of Scunthorpe on the A10

King John was not universally admired but one of his more popular deeds was the granting of a charter (in 1205) which permitted this modest little town to hold an annual festivity on the 5th day of August. **Brigg Fair**, along with Widdecombe and Scarborough, has joined the trio of 'Best Known Fairs in England', celebrated in a traditional song and in a haunting tone poem based on Lincolnshire folk songs, composed by Frederick Delius in 1907. 800 years later, the fair still attracts horse traders from around the country, along with all the usual fun of the fair.

GRIMSBY

According to tradition it was a Dane called Grim who founded Grimsby. He had been ordered to drown the young Prince Havelock after the boy's father had been killed in battle. Grim could not bring himself to murder the child so he fled Denmark for England. After a tempestuous crossing of the North Sea, Grim and the boy arrived at the Humber estuary where he used the timbers of their boat to build a house on the shore. They lived by selling fish and salt, thus establishing the foundations of an industry for which Grimsby would become known the world over. A statue of Grim and the infant prince can be seen at the Humberside Polytechnic.

A question for football anoraks. Why does Grimsby Town Football Club play all its games away? Answer: Because the Mariners' ground is actually in Cleethorpes, a resort which has spread northwards more or less to merge into Grimsby.

Norfolk

Norfolk is home to Britain's finest wetland areas, the Broads, which cover some 220 square miles to the northwest of Great Yarmouth. Three main rivers, the Ant, the Thurne and the Bure, thread their way through the marshes, providing some 120 miles of navigable waterways. This area is also a refuge for many species of endangered birds and plants, and during the summer and autumn the Broads are a favourite stopping off point for migrating birds. The eastern coast, from Great Yarmouth to Sheringham, is almost one continuous strip of excellent sandy beaches, dotted with charming holiday resorts such as Caister-on-Sea, Mundesley and Cromer. Inland lies the county town, Norwich, which is famous for its Norman cathedral, its castle and a wealth of other historic buildings. Norwich is also the home of mustard and its best-known producer J & J Colman.

It is surprising to find one of England's most important medieval ports, King's Lynn, at the southern end of the underwater maze of sandbanks of the Wash but then, of course, keels were shallower. King's Lynn is still a busy port today; several ancient ports along the North Norfolk coast are now holiday resorts. A little way inland is the Royal family's country estate of Sandringham.

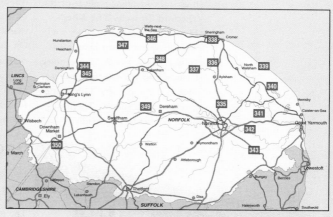

THETFORD

The town's strategic position, at the confluence of the Rivers Thet and Little Ouse, have made this an important settlement for centuries and excavations have revealed an Iron Age enclosure that is thought to have been the site of Boudicca's Palace.

In the charming heart of the town is the striking **Ancient House**, a 15th century timber-framed house that is home to a museum containing replicas of the Thetford Treasure. **The King's House** is named after James I who was a frequent visitor here from 1608-18. The town's 12th century Cluniac Priory is mostly in ruins, though the impressive 14th century gatehouse still stands. Thetford's industrial heritage is vividly displayed in the **Burrell Steam Museum**, which has full-size working steam engines, re-created workshops and vintage agricultural machinery.

To the west of the town lies **Thetford Forest**, the most extensive lowland forest in Britain, planted by the Forestry Commission in 1922. In the heart of the forest are **Grimes Graves**, the earliest major industrial site discovered in Europe. At these Neolithic flint mines, Stone Age labourers extracted materials for their axes and knives from the chamber 30 feet below ground. On the edge of the forest are the ruins of **Thetford Warren Lodge**, built in the early 15th century when the surrounding area was preserved for farming rabbits – a major element of the medieval diet.

AROUND THETFORD

WYMONDHAM

19 miles NE of Thetford on the B1172

The town is home to one of the oddest ecclesiastical buildings in the country, **Wymondham Abbey**, which was founded in 1107 by William d'Albini, butler to King Henry I.

Although many of the town's oldest houses were destroyed by fire in 1615, some older buildings escaped, including 12th century Becket's Chapel. Also of interest is The Bridewell which was built in 1785 as a model prison and reputedly served as a model for the penitentiaries established in the United States. It is now the

Ancient House, Thetford

Wymondham Heritage Museum.

The town's historic Railway Station was built in 1845 on the Great Eastern's Norwich to Ely line and, still in use, the buildings house a railway museum.

BANHAM
12 miles E of Thetford off the B1077

To the southwest of the village lies **Banham Zoo**, home to some of the world's most endangered animals including monkeys and apes – a particular concern here.

DISS
16 miles E of Thetford on the A1066

Situated on the northern bank of the River Waveney, which forms the boundary between Suffolk and Norfolk, Diss is an old market town that developed on the hill overlooking **The Mere**.

Just northeast of Diss, at **Langmere**, is the **100th Bomb Group Memorial Museum**, a tribute to the US 8th Air Force that was stationed here at Dickleburgh Airfield during World War II. Two other interesting museums can be found at **Bressingham**. The **Bressingham Steam Museum** boasts a fine collection of locomotives and traction engines. On the same site are two delightful gardens and the National Dad's Army Collection.

NORWICH

By the time of the *Domesday Book*, Norwich was the third most populous city in England and the Normans built a **Castle** here that was replaced in the late 12th century by a mighty stone fortress. Norwich Castle never saw military action and, as early as the 13th century, it was already being used as the county gaol – a role it filled until 1889. The Castle is now a lively Museum featuring a forbidding display of torture instruments.

While the castle's function has changed over the years, the **Cathedral**, consecrated in 1101, remains the focus of ecclesiastical life in Norfolk. The most completely Norman cathedral in England after Durham, this superb building has the largest Norman cloisters in the country and is noted for its 400 gilded bosses that depict scenes from medieval life. Among the cathedral's numerous treasures are the Saxon Bishop's Throne in the Presbytery, the 14th century altar painting in St Luke's Chapel and the richly carved canopies in the Choir. The vast market square is dominated by **City Hall**, which was modelled on Stockholm City Hall and opened in 1938 by George VI. No mention of Norwich is complete without telling the story of Jeremiah Colman who, in the early 1800s, perfected his blend of mustard flours and spice to produce a condiment that was smooth in texture and tart in flavour. Together with his nephew James, he founded J & J Colman in 1823 and **The Mustard Shop** commemorates the company's history.

To the south of the city are the remains of **Venta Icenorum**, the Roman town that was established

335 CITY OF NORWICH AVIATION MUSEUM

Norwich

The Museum illustrates the story of aviation history through a collection of military and civilian aircraft, as well as a comprehensive display within the main exhibition building.

 see page 485

336 THE SPREAD EAGLE

Erpingham, nr Norwich

Billie Carder's exuberant personality and her good home cooking attract a loyal band of regulars to the **Spread Eagle**.

 see page 485

337 THE DUKES HEAD

Corpusty, nr Norwich

The **Dukes Head** is a handsome 18th century village pub familiar dishes including popular Sunday roasts.

 see page 485

338 THE NORFOLK SHIRE HORSE CENTRE

West Runton, Cromer

An assortment of heavy horses and ponies have been brought together here and, together with a variety of activities on offer, the centre makes a great day out for the family.

 see page 486

here after Boudicca's rebellion in AD 61. Three miles to the north, next to Norwich International Airport, is the **City of Norwich Aviation Museum**, whose exhibits include a Vulcan bomber.

AROUND NORWICH

AYLSHAM

12 miles N of Norwich off the A140

In the churchyard of **St Michael's Church** is the tomb of one of the greatest English 18th century landscape gardeners, Humphry Repton, who created some 200 parks and gardens around the country.

One of Repton's commissions was to landscape the grounds of **Blickling Hall**, which lies just to the north of the town. Built for Sir Henry Hobart in the 1620s, the Hall is perfectly symmetrical and its most spectacular feature is the Long Gallery that extends for 175 feet and has a glorious plaster ceiling.

Within a few miles of the Hall are two other stately homes, **Mannington Hall** and **Wolterton Park**. Repton also landscaped the grounds for the latter, an 18th century mansion that was built for the brother of Sir Robert Walpole, England's first Prime Minister.

SHERINGHAM

22 miles N of Norwich on the A149

A former fishing village which still has a fleet of fishing boats that are launched from the shore, Sheringham was transformed into a seaside resort with the arrival of the railway.

Although Sheringham's railway line was closed in the 1960s, it was reopened in 1975 as the **North Norfolk Railway**; it is also known as The Poppy Line because these brilliant flowers can still be seen in the fields along the scenic five-mile route.

Just to the west of the town, footpaths lead to the lovely Repton-landscaped grounds of **Sheringham Park** from where there are grand views along the coast. Yet more glorious scenery can be found at the aptly named Pretty Corner, a particularly beautiful area of woodland.

A little further along the coast is the shingle beach known as **Weybourne Hope** (or Hoop) that slopes so steeply that an invading force could brings its ships right up to the shore. The garrison camp that defended this vulnerable stretch of beach during both World Wars now houses the **Muckleburgh Collection**, a fascinating museum of military equipment. East of Sheringham, at **West Runton**, is the highest point in Norfolk – Beacon Hill. Although only 330 feet high, it commands glorious views from the summit. Close by is the **Roman Camp**, which excavations have shown to have been an iron-working settlement in Saxon and Medieval times. The village, too, is home to the **Norfolk Shire Horse Centre** where the heavy horses give demonstrations of the valuable work they once performed on farms.

CROMER

21 miles N of Norwich on the A149

A popular seaside resort since the late 18th century, Cromer is famous for its crabs, reckoned to be among the most succulent in England. Cromer Pier is the genuine article, complete with a Lifeboat Station and theatre, and on the promenade is a museum dedicated to the coxswain Henry Blogg and 200 years of Cromer lifeboats. The newly restored **Cromer Museum** is housed in a row of restored fishermen's cottages.

Just inland from Cromer is one of Norfolk's grandest houses, **Felbrigg Hall**, a wonderful Jacobean mansion dating from the 1620s.

NORTH WALSHAM

13½ miles NE of Norwich on the A149

A busy country town with an attractive market cross dating from 1600, North Walsham was the home of Horatio Nelson, who came to the town's Paston School at the age of 10. A dual place of interest is the Cat Pottery and Railway Junk Yard, dealing in lifelike handmade pottery cats and transport memorabilia. The Norfolk Motorcycle Museum is home to more than 100 bikes from the 1920s to the 1960s, along with old pushbikes and die-cast toys.

To the west of North Walsham, near the village of Erpingham, is **Alby Crafts and Gardens** which promotes the excellence of mainly East Anglian and British craftsmanship and where there is

also a **Bottle Museum**.

To the northeast is the quiet seaside village of **Mundesley**, whose Maritime Museum in a former coastgrad lookout is believed to be the smallest museum in the country.

HAPPISBURGH

17 miles NE of Norwich on the B1159

The coastal waters of Happisburgh (pronounced Hazeborough) have seen many shipwrecks over the centuries and the victims lie buried in the graveyard of **St Mary's Church**. The large grassy mound on the north side of the church contains the bodies of the crew of the ill-fated *HMS Invincible* which was sunk on sandbanks here in 1801. On its way to join up with Nelson's fleet at Copenhagen, the ship sank with the loss of 110 sailors.

To the south, at Stalham, stands the tallest windmill in England, the 80 feet high Sutton Windmill that dates from 1789 and that finally ceased grinding in 1940. The site is also home to the **Museum of the Broads** housed in traditional buildings associated for centuries with the wherry trade.

WROXHAM

7 miles NE of Norwich on the A1151

This riverside village, linked to Hoveton by a bridge over the River Bure, is the capital of the **Norfolk Broads**, and during the high season its boatyards are full of craft of all shapes and sizes. The village is also the southern terminus of the **Bure**

339 THE HILL HOUSE

Happisburgh

A 16th century inn serving an excellent selection of bar and restaurant food and real ales.

see page 487

340 THE PLEASURE BOAT INN

Hickling

By a tying-up point on Hickling Broad, the **Pleasure Boat Inn** refreshes boaters and others with a good choice of drinks and tasty home-cooked food.

 see page 486

341 THE SHIP

South Walsham, nr Norwich

Locals and visitors to the Broads drop anchor at **The Ship** to enjoy unpretentious home cooking in convivial surroundings.

see page 488

Valley Railway, a nine-mile long steam railway that follows the course of the River Bure through glorious countryside to the market town of Aylsham.

Just to the north lies the **Wroxham Barns**, a delightful collection of beautifully restored 18th century barns that house a community of craftspeople, and to the east is **Hoveton Hall Gardens**, which offer visitors a splendid combination of lovely plants and both woodland and lakeside walks.

Further up the River Bure is the charming village of **Coltishall**, home to the **Ancient Lime Kiln**, a reminder of Norfolk's industrial heritage.

RANWORTH

9 miles E of Norwich off the B1140

A beautiful Broadland village, from where five Norfolk Broads, the sea at Great Yarmouth and the spire of Norwich Cathedral can be seen from the tower of St Helen's Church. Also to be seen is the National Trust's Horsey Mill. Along with the views, the church houses one of the county's greatest ecclesiastical treasures - an early 15th century Gothic choir screen.

GREAT YARMOUTH

18 miles E of Norwich on the A47

In Saxon times, Great Yarmouth was an island, but changes in the flow of the River Bure means that it is now a promontory. The seaward side has a five-mile stretch of sandy beach and numerous family amusements, as well as the **Maritime Museum of East Anglia** and the **Elizabethan House**, a merchant's house of 1596 which is now a museum of domestic life. Behind South Beach is the 144 feet **Nelson's Monument** crowned by a statue of Britannia.

Most of Yarmouth's older buildings are concentrated in the riverside part of the town, including the historic **South Quay** with an array of museums, including one celebrating the life and times of Horatio Nelson.

For centuries, incredible quantities of herring were landed at Yarmouth and the trade involved so many fishermen that there were more boats registered here than in London. It was a Yarmouth man, John Woodger, who developed the process to produce that great essential of a proper English breakfast – the kipper. Yarmouth's literary connections include Anna Sewell, the author of *Black Beauty*, born here in 1820, and Charles Dickens, who stayed at the Royal Hotel in 1847 to 1848 while writing *David Copperfield*.

When the Romans established their fortress, Garionnonum, now known as **Burgh Castle** a few miles west of Great Yarmouth, the surrounding marshes were still under water and the fort stood on one bank of a vast estuary commanding a strategic position. Today's ruins are impressive, its walls of alternating layers of flint and brick rising to some 15 feet in places.

To the north of Yarmouth lies **Caister-on-Sea**, a holiday resort that was an important fishing village for the Iceni tribe. The Romans built a castle here of which little remains; the **Caister Castle** seen today dates from 1432 and was built by Sir John Fastolf who distinguished himself leading the English bowmen at the Battle of Agincourt. The castle is home to a **Motor Museum** which houses an impressive collection of vintage and veteran cars, the oldest being a Panhard Levassor from 1893.

KING'S LYNN

An ancient town that is a harmonious mix of medieval, Tudor, Jacobean and Flemish architecture and with some of the finest old streets anywhere in England. It is not surprising that King's Lynn was chosen by the BBC to represent early 19th century London in their production of *Martin Chuzzlewit*. One of the most striking sights in the town is the 15th century **Guildhall of the Holy Trinity** with its distinctive chequerboard design of black flint and white stone. Next to it, in the late-Victorian Town Hall, is the **Museum of Lynn Life**, whose greatest treasure is King John's Cup, a dazzling piece of medieval workmanship. Close by, standing proudly on the banks of the River Purfleet, is the handsome **Custom House** of 1683 that was designed by the local architect Henry Bell. Other buildings of note, and there are many, include the **Hanseatic Warehouse**, the South Gate, the Greenland Fishery Building and the **Guildhall of St George**, the oldest civic hall in England and now home to the King's Lynn Arts Centre.

342 COLDHAM HALL TAVERN

Surlingham, nr Norwich

Boatmen on the River Yare tie up and find excellent refreshment at **Coldham Hall Tavern**.

see page 488

343 THE SWAN

Loddon

The **Swan** is a large and handsome redbrick village pub with a loyal local following.

see page 488

The Old Custom House, Kings Lynn

Dersingham

The royal country retreat of Sandringham is one of the many attractions close to the **Feathers Hotel**, which offers superb cooking and well-appointed guest rooms.

 see page 489

Sandringham

Sandringham is the Norfolk retreat of Her Majesty the Queen and many of the rooms used by the Royal Family are open to the public. Further possessions are displayed in the old stable block.

 see page 489

The pretty village of **Castle Rising**, just northeast of King's Lynn, is overshadowed by its massive **Castle Keep**, whose well-preserved walls rise to some 50 feet. Built in 1150 to guard what was then the sea approach to the River Ouse, Castle Rising was much more a residential building than a defensive one and it was to here, in 1331, that Edward III banished his ferocious mother Isabella who had been instrumental in his father's murder.

AROUND KING'S LYNN

DERSINGHAM

8 miles NE of King's Lynn on the B1440

A large village close to some pleasant walks through Dersingham Wood and the adjoining **Sandringham Country Park**. The Royal family's country retreat, **Sandringham House** is a relatively recent addition to the family and was purchased by the Prince of Wales, later Edward VII, as a country refuge to match the retreats his parents enjoyed at Balmoral and Osborne.

To the north of Dersingham lies **Snettisham** which is best known for its spacious, sandy beaches and the **RSPB Bird Sanctuary**

HUNSTANTON

14½ miles N of King's Lynn on the A149

A busy seaside resort, Hunstanton boasts two unique features: its cliffs of colourful layers of red, white and brown strata and its west-facing position - unique for an east-coast resort! Developed in the 1860s with the arrival of the railways, the town was assured of its social standing after the Prince of Wales, later Edward VII, came here to recover from typhoid fever and it retains a distinct 19th century charm.

To the north lies **Old Hunstanton**, a charming village at the beginning of the **Norfolk Coastal Footpath** which leads eastwards, around the coast, to Cromer. Just a little further up the coast is **Holme next the Sea**, which lies at the northern end of another long distance footpath, the 50-mile long **Peddars Way** which starts at Thetford. This village is the site of Sea Henge, a 4,500-year-old Bronze Age tree circle discovered on the beach.

To the south lies **Heacham**, the home of **Norfolk Lavender**, the largest lavender growing and distilling operation in the country. Visitors can take a guided tour around the working farm, which also contains the National Collection of Lavenders.

A few miles south of Hunstanton stands the five-storey Great Bircham Windmill, one of few in Norfolk to have found a hill to perch on, and it's still working.

BURNHAM MARKET

19 miles NE of King's Lynn on the B1155

The largest of the seven Burnhams strung along the valley of the River Burn, Burnham Market has an outstanding collection of Georgian buildings surrounding its green. To the southeast lies Burnham Thorpe, the birthplace of Horatio Nelson, whose father was the rector here for 46 years. He was born in 1758 at the now demolished Parsonage House, and both the local inn and the church contain memorabilia from his life.

WELLS-NEXT-THE-SEA

23½ miles NE of King's Lynn on the A149

Wells was a working port from the 13th century, and in 1859, to prevent the harbour silting up completely, an embankment, cutting off an area of marshland, was built; today, the harbour lies more than a mile from the sea. Running alongside the embankment, which provides a pleasant walk, is the **Harbour Railway** that runs from the small museum on the quay to the lifeboat station by the beach. This narrow-gauge railway is operated by the same company as the **Wells and Walsingham Railway** which carries passengers on the delightful ride to Little Walsingham.

Just west of the town lies **Holkham Hall**, a glorious classical mansion built by Thomas Coke that was completed in 1762. The magnificent rooms are only overshadowed by the superb collections they contain, including classical sculptures, paintings by Rubens and Van Dyck, and tapestries. A museum at the Hall has exhibits of social, domestic and agricultural memorabilia.

Further along the coast, to the east, lies the pretty village of **Stiffkey** (pronounced Stewkey) and the **Stiffkey Salt Marshes**, a National Trust nature reserve that turns a delicate shade of purple in July when the sea lavender is in bloom. Here also are found the famous Stewkey Blues – cockles that are highly regarded as a delicacy. Away from the coast can be seen the picturesque ruins of Binham Priory, founded in 1091 and once one of the most important religious houses in Norfolk.

CLEY-NEXT-THE-SEA

30 miles NE of King's Lynn on the A149

In early medieval times, Cley was a more important port than King's Lynn, a fact that is hard to believe today as the town lies a mile from the sea. The subject of thousands of paintings, **Cley Mill** was built in 1713, remained in use until 1921

Wells-Next-The-Sea

347 THE JOLLY FARMERS

North Creake, nr Fakenham

The promise of the cheerful yellow exterior is amply fulfilled inside the **Jolly Farmers**, where cask ales and super home-cooked food are served in the most delightful, friendly surroundings.

 see page 490

348 THE GREEN MAN

Little Snoring, nr Fakenham

The **Green Man** is a popular roadside inn serving real ales and an excellent choice of food on bar and restaurant menus.

see page 490

and is now open to visitors during the season.

From Cley there is a walk along the shoreline to **Blakeney Point**, a spit of land that stretches three miles out to sea and which is the most northerly extremity of East Anglia.

Another fine old mill can be found at the village of **Glandford**, which is also home to the **Glandford Shell Museum**, featuring seashells gathered from around the world, and the **Natural Surroundings Wild Flower Centre** that is dedicated to gardening with a strong ecological emphasis.

To the west of Cley is one of the most enchanting of Norfolk's coastal villages, **Blakeney**, where the silting up of the estuary has created a fascinating landscape of serpentine creeks and channels twisting their way through mudbanks and sand hills. Down the B1156 from Blakeney is **Langham Glass**, where visitors can see regular demonstrations of glass-making and walk through the 2005 Lord Nelson Maize maze.

THURSFORD GREEN
24 miles NE of King's Lynn off the A148

This village is home to one of the most unusual museums in Norfolk, the **Thursford Collection** – a fascinating collection of steam-powered traction engines, fairground organs and carousels. At the regular live music shows, the most astonishing exhibit, a 1931 Wurlitzer organ, displays its virtuosity.

To the northwest lies the village of **Little Walsingham** that still attracts pilgrims who come to worship at the **Shrine of Our Lady of Walsingham**. In 1061, the Lady of the Manor had a vision in which she was instructed to build a replica of the Holy House of Nazareth and her Holy House soon became a place of pilgrimage. In the mid 12th century, an Augustinian Priory was established to protect the shrine and, today, the largest surviving part, a stately gatehouse, can be seen on the east side of the High Street. Henry VIII went on to **Slipper Chapel**, a beautiful 14th century building at nearby **Houghton St Giles**. Other buildings of interest in this attractive village are the 16th century octagonal **Clink in Common Place**; the scant ruins of a 14th century Franciscan Friary; and the former Shire Hall that is now a museum.

FAKENHAM
20 miles NE of King's Lynn off the A148

A prosperous market town and home to a **National Hunt Racecourse**, Fakenham is a major agricultural centre for the region. An attractive town, it must be one of the few places in the country where the former gasworks have become an attraction and here they house the **Museum of Gas and Local History**. To the east of the town lies **Pensthorpe Waterfowl Park**, the home to Europe's best collection of endangered and exotic waterbirds and where over 120 species can be seen in their natural surroundings.

CASTLE ACRE

12 miles SE of King's Lynn on the A1065

William de Warenne, William the Conqueror's son-in-law, came here very soon after the Conquest and built a Castle that was one of the first, and largest, in the country to be built by the Normans. Of that vast fortress, little remains apart from the gargantuan earthworks and a squat 13th century gateway.

Much more has survived of **Castle Acre Priory**, founded in 1090 and set in fields beside the River Nar. Its glorious West Front gives a powerful indication of how majestic a triumph of late Norman architecture the complete Priory must have been.

Castle Acre village is extremely picturesque, the first place in Norfolk to be designated a Conservation Area, in 1971. Most of the village, including the 15th century parish church, is built in traditional flint, with a few later houses of brick blending in remarkably happily.

SWAFFHAM

14 miles SE of King's Lynn on the A47

A town with many handsome and interesting buildings, including the Assembly Rooms of 1817 and the elegant Butter Cross, a classical lead-covered dome standing on eight columns. Swaffham was the birthplace in 1874 of Howard Carter, who found and opened Tutankhamen's tomb.

Swaffham Museum is located

Priory Ruins, Castle Acre

in the Town Hall, and just to the southwest of the town, archaeologists have reconstructed a village from the time of Boudicca - **Cockley Cley Iceni Village and Museums**. A more recent addition to Swaffham's attractions is the **EcoTech Centre**, opened in 1998, which explores current innovations as well as technologies of the future.

Southwest of Swaffham lies **Oxburgh Hall**, a lovely moated house dating from the 15th century which was visited by Henry VII and his Queen in 1497.

DEREHAM

23 miles SE of King's Lynn off the A47

One of the most ancient towns in Norfolk, where in AD 654 St Withburga founded a nunnery. Her

349 THE WHITE HORSE

Longham, nr Dereham

The **White Horse** has a 350-year tradition of hospitality – a superb choice for a drink, a meal or an overnight or longer stay.

see page 490

Denver, Downham Market

Built in 1835 and lovingly restored to working order, visitors can take a tour right to the top of the windmill and watch flour being made.

 see page 491

name lives on in **St Withburga's Well**, which marks the place where she was laid to rest. The poet William Cowper lived here for the last four years of his life, and in the nearby hamlet of Dumpling Green, one of the country's most celebrated travel writers, George Borrow, was born. A much less attractive character connected with the town is Bishop Bonner, the enthusiastic arsonist of Protestant heretics during the reign of Mary Tudor. Rector here before being appointed Bishop of London, he lived in the exquisite thatched terrace that is known as **Bishop Bonner's Cottages**, now the home of a small Museum.

To the north of the town, at **Gressenhall**, is the **Roots of Norfolk Museum** housed in an imposing late-18th century former workhouse. The many exhibits here concentrate on the working and domestic life of Norfolk

people over the last 150 years.

DOWNHAM MARKET

10 miles S of King's Lynn off the A10

A compact little market town on the very edge of the Fens, with the River Great Ouse and the New Bedford Drain running side by side at its western edge. Of particular note here in the market place is the elegant and highly decorated cast-iron **Clock Tower** that was erected in 1878.

Just to the south, at the village of **Denver**, is the **Denver Sluice** which was built in 1651 by the Dutch engineer, Cornelius Vermuyden, as part of a scheme to drain 20,000 acres of land owned by the Duke of Bedford.

Running parallel to this is the modern Great Denver Sluice that was opened in 1964. Also here is **Denver Windmill**, built in 1835 and reopened in 2000 after being carefully restored.

Northamptonshire

Although a relatively small county, Northamptonshire has a lot to offer. The county town, Northampton, along with other local towns, is famed for its shoe industry, but outside the towns Northamptonshire remains essentially a farming county littered with ancient market towns and rural villages. Its history is as interesting as most – the decisive battle of Naseby was fought on its soil, and it was at Fotheringay Castle that Mary, Queen of Scots was executed. There are many magnificent stately homes here but the most famous now is Althorp, the country estate of the Spencer family and the last resting place of Diana, Princess of Wales. There are also some more eccentric buildings to discover, including the creations of Sir Thomas Tresham – notably the unique Triangular Lodge at Ruston.

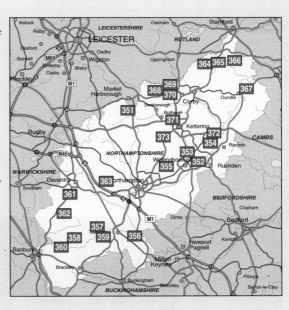

FOOD & DRINK

ACCOMMODATION

351 THE GEORGE INN AT GREAT OXENDON

Great Oxendon

Diners come from many miles around to enjoy the fine food served at The **George Inn**. Three rooms for B&B.

see page 491

NORTHAMPTON

By the 13th century Northampton was a major market town and its market square is reputed to have been the second largest in the country. The town is best known for its shoemaking and the first large order came in 1642 when 4,000 pairs of shoes and 600 pairs of boots were made for the army. The industry grew rapidly throughout the county and by the end of the 19th century 40% of the population was involved in the shoe trade. The **Central Museum and Art Gallery** has the world's largest collection of footwear, while the **Abington Museum**, set in a 15th century manor house, tells the county's military history.

There are many fine buildings here and, in particular, notably the wonderful 12th century **Church of the Holy Sepulchre**, one of only a handful of round churches in Britain. The **Welsh House**, one of the few buildings to survive a disastrous fire in 1675, recalls the time when Welsh drovers would bring their cattle to the market. The town's most prestigious building is the **Guildhall**, a gem of Victorian architecture built in 1864 by Edward Godwin.

In the south of the town stands one of the three surviving Eleanor Crosses of the original 12 that marked the journey of King Edward with his wife's body from Nottinghamshire to London.

AROUND NORTHAMPTON

ALTHORP

5 miles NW of Northampton off the A428

The home of the Spencer family since 1508, **Althorp** remains exactly that - a classic family-owned English stately home. The present house was begun in 1573, and behind the stark tiling of the exterior is a wealth of fine paintings, sculpture, porcelain and furniture. Known widely by connoisseurs for generations, Althorp is now known across the whole world since the death of Diana, Princess of Wales, in 1997;

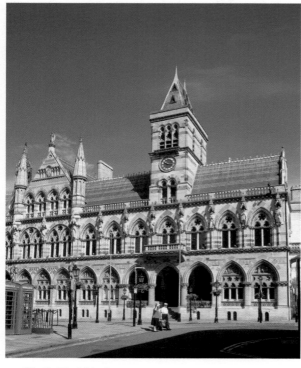

The Guildhall, Northampton

she lies at peace in the beautiful, tranquil setting of the Round Oval, an ornamental lake.

To the north is **Holdenby Hall**, which was built by Elizabeth I's Lord Chancellor, Sir Christopher Hatton, for the purpose of entertaining the Queen. At the time, it was the largest Elizabethan house in England but Elizabeth I only visited the house once. Later it became the palace and eventually the prison of Charles I, who was held here for five months after the Civil War.

Further north again is **Cottesbrooke Hall**, a magnificent Queen Anne house that is reputed to be the model for Jane Austen's Mansfield Park; close by is Coton Manor Garden, a traditional garden originally laid out in 1925 that embraces several delightful smaller gardens.

ASHBY ST LEDGERS

12½ miles NW of Northampton on the A361

From 1375 to 1605 the manor house at Ashby was the home of the Catesby family and it was in a room above the gatehouse that Guy Fawkes is said to have met Robert Catesby and hatched the **Gunpowder Plot**.

KELMARSH

12 miles N of Northampton on the A508

This village is home to **Kelmarsh Hall**, an early 18th century house that was designed by James Gibb, best known as the architect of St Martin in the Fields, London, and is surrounded by beautiful gardens, woodland and farmland. To the

southeast is another fine country house, 16th century Lamport Hall. Its grounds include the first Alpine garden and the first garden gnomes in England, along with the **Hannington Vintage Tractor Club**.

West of Kelmarsh is the site of the **Battle of Naseby**, where in 1645 Oliver Cromwell's Parliamentarian forces defeated Charles I and determined the outcome of the Civil War. The king finally surrendered in Newark some months later. **Naseby Battle and Farm Museum**, in Naseby village, contains a model layout of the battle, relics from the fight and a collection of bygone agricultural machinery.

WELLINGBOROUGH

10 miles NE of Northampton on the A509

An important market and industrial town, known for its iron mills, flourmills and tanneries, Wellingborough sits near the point where the River Ise joins the River Nene. One of many fine buildings is **Croyland Abbey**, now a Heritage Centre, and nearby is a splendid stone-walled, thatch-roofed 15th century Tithe Barn.

An attraction in the centre of town is the Millennium Rose Garden at Swanspool Gardens while to the south is **Summer Leys Nature Reserve**, a year round haven for large numbers of birds. Two miles south of Wellingborough lies **Irchester Country Park**, 200 acres of woodland walks and nature trails in a former ironstone quarry.

352 THE PUMP HOUSE CAFÉ

The Embankment, Wellingborough

The **Pump House Café** is open from 9 to 3 Monday to Saturday for a good choice of home-prepared hot and cold dishes.

 see page 491

353 THE OAK HOUSE PRIVATE HOTEL

Broad Green, Wellingborough

The **Oak House Private Hotel** is a very pleasant place to stay, with 16 comfortable en suite bedrooms.

 see page 492

354 THE HARE & HOUNDS

Great Addington

The **Hare & Hounds** is a traditional village inn that's a popular spot for food and drink, with beer gardens and off-road parking.

 see page 492

355 THE GRIFFINS HEAD

Mears Ashby

The **Griffins Head** is a popular village pub with a warm, inviting ambience and a good line in hearty home cooking.

 see page 492

CASTLE ASHBY

6 miles E of Northampton off the A428

Dating from 1574, **Castle Ashby** is a fine Elizabethan mansion on the site of a demolished 13th century castle. The surrounding parkland was landscaped by Capability Brown.

STOKE BRUERNE

6½ miles S of Northampton off the A508

This picturesque village lies on the Grand Union Canal, at the southern end of the famous Blisworth Tunnel. In addition to towpath walks and boat trips to the tunnel, the fascinating **Canal Museum**, housed in a converted corn mill, is a popular attraction.

Just south of the village is **Stoke Park**, a great house that was built by Inigo Jones in the 1630s. The main house burnt down in 1886 and only the pavilions and a colonnade remain, but they are an impressive sight.

TOWCESTER

9 miles SW of Northampton off the A43

Called Lactodorum by the Romans and situated on their major route, Watling Street, this town became an important staging post on the route between London and Holyhead. By the end of the 18th century there were 20 coaching inns in the town, servicing up to 40 coaches every day. Charles Dickens stayed here at the Saracen's Head, then called the Pomfret Hotel, and immortalised it in *The Pickwick Papers*. The parish Church of St Lawrence, on the site of a substantial Roman building, is one of the loveliest in the county, and close by is the **Chantry House**, formerly a school, founded by Archdeacon Sponne in 1447.

Towcester Racecourse is set in the beautiful parkland estate of Easton Neston, the family home of Lord Hesketh. There is racing of a different kind at nearby **Silverstone**, the home of British motor racing.

BRACKLEY

18 miles SW of Northampton on the A43

Dating back to Saxon times, the castle built here in the early 12th century is said to have been the meeting place for the rebel barons who drew up the first version of Magna Carta in 1215.

To the southwest, lies the former manor house, **Aynho Park**, a very grand 17th century country house that was originally the property of the Cartwright family, who, it is said, claimed the rents from their tenants in the form of apricots.

CANONS ASHBY

12 miles SW of Northampton off the A361

A monastery belonging to the Black Canons once stood here, but after the Dissolution some of the ecclesiastical buildings were used to create **Canons Ashby House**, one of the finest stately homes in Northamptonshire. Home of the Dryden family since the 1550s, it contains some marvellous Elizabethan wall paintings and sumptuous Jacobean plasterwork.

Sulgrave Manor

SULGRAVE

16 miles SW of Northampton off the B4525

Along with its old village stocks, the remains of a castle mound and its church, Sulgrave is home to **Sulgrave Manor**, a Tudor manor house built by the ancestors of George Washington, first President of the United States of America. Lawrence Washington, sometime Mayor of Northampton, bought the manor from Henry VIII in 1539 and the family coat of arms,

which is said to have inspired the stars and stripes design of the American flag, is prominent above the front door. The house is a treasure trove of George Washington memorabilia, including documents, a velvet coat and even a lock of his hair.

DAVENTRY

11½ miles W of Northampton on the A45

A historic town, which holds a colourful market along the High Street every Tuesday and Friday. In

360 THE WINDMILL

Badby, nr Daventry

The **Windmill** is a charming old inn with a well-earned reputation for the quality of its service, food and accommodation.

see page 495

361 THE INN

Greatworth, nr Banbury

Good honest food and well-kept Hook Norton brews bring a loyal local crowd to **The Inn**.

see page 494

362 THE FOX & HOUNDS

Charwelton

The **Fox & Hounds** offers a winning combination of warm hospitality, well-kept beers and honest, unpretentious cooking.

see page 495

203

the Market Place stands the Moot Hall, built in 1769 as a private residence; it now houses **Daventry Museum**.

Just north of the town lies **Daventry Country Park**, close by is Borough Hill, the third largest Iron Age hill fort in Britain, and to the southeast lies **Flore**, an ancient village whose wide green slopes down to the banks of the River Nene. **Adams Cottage** was the home of the ancestors of John Adams, President of the United States.

CORBY

True industry arrived at Corby only in the latter years of the 19th century with the building of the Kettering-Manton Railway. Many of the bricks used in the building of the viaduct at Harringworth were made at Corby brickworks, which closed at the beginning of the 20th century. But Corby was still essentially a small village until the 1930s, when Stewarts and Lloyds built a huge steel-making plant based on the area's known reserves of iron ore. That industry virtually stopped in 1980 but Corby remains a forward-looking modern town, with many cultural and leisure opportunities.

Just to the north lies **Rockingham Castle**, built by William the Conqueror on the slopes of Rockingham Hill overlooking the Welland valley. The grand rooms are superbly furnished, and the armour in the Tudor Great Hall recalls the Civil War, when the castle was captured by the Roundheads. Owned and lived in since 1530 by the Watson family, it was here that Charles Dickens wrote much of *Bleak House*. East of Corby lies **East Carlton Countryside Park**, with its nature trails and steel-making heritage centre.

AROUND CORBY

DEENE

4 miles NE of Corby off the A43

Originally a medieval manor, **Deene Park** was acquired in 1514 by Sir Robert Brudenell and has been occupied by the family ever since. It is surrounded by beautiful gardens filled with old-fashioned roses, and parkland containing rare trees. Close by is **Kirby Hall**, one of the loveliest Elizabethan ruins in England.

FOTHERINGHAY

11½ miles NE of Corby off the A605

The first **Fotheringhay Castle** was built in around 1100 by the son-in-law of William the Conqueror, and the second, in the 14th century, by Edmund of Langley, a son of Edward III. The future Richard III was born here, but Fotheringhay is best known as being the prison and the place of execution of Mary, Queen of Scots, who was brought here in bands of steel and beheaded in the Banqueting Hall in 1587. The castle was pulled down in 1627.

At **Nassington**, just to the north, stands **Prebendal Manor House**, dating from the early part

Fotheringhay

367 THE GEORGE INN

Oundle

The George welcomes visitors of all ages with a friendly greeting, a fully stocked bar and an impressive choice of bar and restaurant dishes.

see page 497

368 THE RED LION

*Middleton,
nr Market Harborough*

The **Red Lion** is a handsome, convivial pub with a great choice of food, guest bedrooms and an annual beer festival.

see page 498

of the 13th century and the oldest house in Northamptonshire.

OUNDLE

10 miles E of Corby on the A427

A town rich in architectural interest, with many fine 17th and 18th century buildings, Oundle is best known for the Public School that was founded by Sir William Laxton in 1556; an inscription to his memory is written above the doorway in Greek, Latin and Hebrew.

BRIGSTOCK

5 miles SE of Corby on the A6116

On the banks of a tributary of the River Nene called Harpers Brook,

this Saxon village has many delightful old cottages, a 16th century manor house, and a church with an unusual circular extension to its tower.

To the east lies **Lyveden New Bield**, a cross-shaped Elizabethan garden lodge erected to symbolise the Passion.

KETTERING

An important town standing above the River Ise, Kettering gained fame as a producer of both clothing and shoes and it was here that the missionary William Carey and the preacher Andrew Fuller founded the Baptist Missionary

369 THE ROYAL GEORGE

Cottingham, nr Market Harborough

The **Royal George** is an old-world pub with a modern restaurant serving super home-cooked food. Five rooms for B&B.

see page 498

370 BANCROFT HOUSE

Cottingham, nr Market Harborough

Bancroft House provides a quiet, secluded B&B base in three budget-price bedrooms.

see page 498

371 THE STAR INN

Geddington

Interesting beers and imaginative cooking accompany genuine hospitality at the **Star**.

 see page 499

372 THE RED LION

Cranford St John

The **Red Lion** is a very friendly, cheerful pub where an excellent varied menu is served all year round.

 see page 499

373 THE SUN INN

Broughton, nr Kettering

A quiet village location for **The Sun**, a friendly inn serving traditional home-cooked dishes.

see page 499

Society in 1792. Much of the old town has been swallowed up in modern development but there are still a few old houses in the narrow lanes. The **Heritage Quarter** around the church gives a fascinating, hands-on insight into the town's past, as does the **Manor House Museum**.

Just to the north lies **Geddington**, an attractive village that is home to the best preserved of the three surviving **Eleanor Crosses** that marked the funeral procession of Queen Eleanor, who had died at Harby in Nottinghamshire in 1290.

Just south of the village is one of the finest houses in the country, **Boughton House**, the Northamptonshire home of the Duke of Buccleuch. Originally a small monastic building, it has been transformed over the years into a magnificent mansion that holds numerous treasures, notably French and English furniture, paintings (El Greco, Murillo, 40 van Dycks) and collections of armoury and weaponry.

AROUND KETTERING

RUSHTON

4 miles NW of Kettering off the A6

Rushton Triangular Lodge is a unique folly built in 1597 and symbolising the Holy Trinity: three walls each with three windows, three gables and three storeys, topped by a three-sided chimney.

Northumberland

In the far north, beyond the city of Newcastle-upon-Tyne, Northumberland has one of the least populated and least well known of the country's 11 National Parks. An area of remote, wild and haunting landscapes, the most famous features of Northumberland National Park are the Cheviot Hills and Kielder Forest. Elsewhere in the county there are stretches of Hadrian's Wall and also border towns that were constantly under the threat of Scottish raids. However, two of the county's most dramatic castles lie on the coast – Dunstanburgh and Bamburgh. Along this coastline is also Lindisfarne, or Holy Island, that is home to one of the most famous and most evocative ecclesiastical ruins.

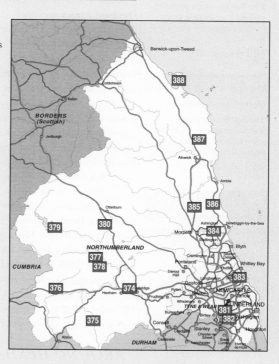

374 THE RAT INN

Anick, nr Hexham

The **Rat Inn** is an unspoilt country pub serving good food and a choice of six real ales.

 see page 499

375 THE GOLDEN LION

Market Square, Allendale

The **Golden Lion** is an imposing stone inn serving superb home cooking. Three immaculate guest bedrooms.

see page 500

376 ALD WHITE CRAIG FARM

Shield Hill, nr Hadrian's Wall and Haltwhistle

Self-catering cottages and farmhouse B&B rooms at **Ald White Craig Farm** provide an ideal base for exploring Hadrian's Wall.

 see page 499

HEXHAM

Founded in AD 674 by St Wilfrid, **Hexham Abbey** was once described as 'the largest and most magnificent church this side of the Alps'. Only the crypt of the original building survives, but the 13th century church that now occupies the site has many outstanding features, including marvellous carved stonework and a superb 16th century rood screen. The nearby early 14th century Moot Hall, built of Roman stone and once used as the courtroom of the Archbishop of York, now houses the **Border History Library**. The **Border History Museum**, housed in the 14th century gaol, tells the story of the border struggles between Scotland and England. Hexham is on the **Hadrian's Wall Path**, which runs the entire length of the Wall.

AROUND HEXHAM

BARDON MILL

10 miles W of Hexham on the A69

This former mining village is a convenient starting point for walks along **Hadrian's Wall**, particularly to the two Roman forts of Vindolanda and Housesteads nearby. Both have extensive Roman remains and accompanying exhibitions.

HALTWHISTLE

15 miles W of Hexham on the A69

The origins of the name Haltwhistle are unknown but two suggestions are the watch "wessel" on the high "alt" mound, or the high "haut" fork of two streams "twysell". It is difficult to imagine that this pleasant little town with its grey terraces was once a mining area, but evidence of the local industries remain. An old pele tower is incorporated into the Centre of Britain Hotel in the town centre.

Three miles northwest of Haltwhistle, off the B6318, is **Walltown Quarry**, a recreation area on the site of an old quarry. Today part of the Northumberland National Park, it contains laid out trails and it is possible to spot oystercatchers, curlews, sandpipers and lapwings.

KIELDER

20 miles NW of Hexham off the B6357

Kielder village was built in the 1950s to house workers in the man-made **Kielder Forest**, which covers 200 square miles of spectacularly beautiful scenery to the west of the Northumberland National Park. The forest is one of the few areas in Britain that contains more red squirrels than greys and is also home to deer and rare birds and plants. Within the forest is **Kielder Water**, the largest man-made lake in northern Europe. A pleasure cruise stops at several points of interest on the Lake, and an art and sculpture trail laid out around its shores and in the trees. To the northwest is **Kielder Castle**, once a hunting lodge for the Duke of Northumberland and now a fascinating visitor centre.

CHOLLERFORD

4 miles N of Hexham on the B6318

The remains of the Roman fort of **Chesters**, on Hadrian's Wall, include a well-preserved bathhouse and barracks and the museum houses a remarkable collection of Roman antiquities.

OTTERBURN

19 miles N of Hexham on the A696

Almost in the centre of what is now the Northumberland National Park, on a site marked by 18th century **Percy Cross**, the Battle of Otterburn took place in 1388 between the English and the Scots. This was a ferocious encounter, described by a contemporary as 'one of the sorest and best fought, without cowards or faint hearts'. **Otterburn Mill** dates from the 18th century, and on display are Europe's only original working 'tenterhooks', where newly woven cloth was stretched and dried.

North of the village are the

River Wansbeck, Morpeth

377 THE BLACK BULL HOTEL

Main Street, Wark

The **Black Bull Hotel** is a popular meeting place for locals and visitors, with a well-stocked bar, wholesome home cooking and well-appointed accommodation.

🍴 *see page 500*

378 BATTLESTEADS HOTEL & RESTAURANT

Wark

An 18th century hotel with 14 en-suite rooms and serving an excellent range of food and drinks.

🛏 *see page 500*

379 KIELDER WATER AND FOREST PARK

Kielder

A peaceful area offering a wealth of recreational activities including walking, sailing and riding.

🏛 *see page 501*

380 YELLOW HOUSE FARM

West Woodburn, nr Hexham

Yellow House is a beautiful country residence with spacious bedrooms for B&B guests.

 see page 501

209

381 THE BLACKSMITH'S TABLE

Washington Old Village

The **Blacksmith's Table** is one of the best restaurants in the region, with an impressive variety of dishes to please palates both traditional and adventurous.

 see page 501

382 THE VICTORIA

Washington

B&B rooms have been added to the amenities of the **Victoria**, which is open all day for food and drink.

 see page 502

383 THE MAGNESIA BANK

North Shields

A true Free House offering 7 cask ales, an extensive range of freshly prepared food and live music.

 see page 502

384 THE HALF MOON INN

Stakeford, nr Morpeth

The **Half Moon Inn** is an excellent choice for a drink, a bar snack, an evening meal or an overnight stay.

see page 502

remains of the Roman fort built by Julius Agricola in the 1st century.

PRUDHOE

10 miles E of Hexham on the A695

When **Prudhoe Castle** was built in the 12th century it was one of the finest in Northumberland, and a Georgian manor house in the courtyard tells its interesting story. To the west, at Mickley Square, is **Cherryburn**, the birthplace in 1753 of Thomas Bewick, the renowned illustrator and engraver.

WALLSEND

3 miles E of Newcastle on the A193

Wallsend, on the eastern edge of Newcastle, is the site of mighty shipyards and of the reconstructed **Segedunum Roman Fort**, the last outpost on Hadrian's Wall.

WHITLEY BAY

8 miles E of Newcastle on the A193

A resort at the mouth of the River Tyne, with safe beaches and spectacular views from the top of **St Mary's Lighthouse**.

SEATON SLUICE

8 miles NE of Newcastle on the A193

Inland from Seaton Sluice is **Seaton Delaval Hall**, a superb Vanbrugh mansion.

BLYTH

12 miles NE of Newcastle on the A193

This small industrial town at the mouth of the River Blyth claims its own piece of railway history with one of the country's earliest wagonways, the 17th century

Plessey Wagonway, built to carry coal from the pits to the riverside. The building, now the headquarters of the Royal Northumberland Yacht Club, was a submarine base during the Second World War.

MORPETH

28 miles NE of Hexham on the A192

Northumberland's county town has some distinguished buildings: its Town Hall was built to designs by Vanbrugh and the handsome bridge over the River Wansbeck was designed by Telford. The 13th century **Morpeth Chantry** has been over the centuries a cholera hospital, a mineral water factory and a school where the famous Tudor botanist William Turner was educated. Today, it houses a **Museum of the Northumbrian Bagpipes**, a musical instrument that is unique to the county. The 14th century Church of St Mary has some of the finest stained glass in Northumberland, and in its cemetery is the grave of suffragette Emily Davison, who died under the hooves of the King's horse Anmer at the 1913 Epsom Derby meeting.

To the east is **Ashington** and the **Wansbeck Riverside Park**, which has been developed along the embankment and offers sailing and angling facilities, plus a four-mile walk along the mouth of the River Wansbeck. The famous footballing brothers Bobby and Jackie Charlton and the England cricketer Steve Harmison are sons of Ashington.

ALNWICK

This impressive Northumberland town is dominated by the massive **Alnwick Castle**, which began as a Norman motte and bailey and was replaced in the 12th century by a stone castle. In the mid 19th century, the 4th Duke of Northumberland transformed the castle into a great country house which, still the home of the Dukes of Northumberland, contains many treasures, including paintings by Canaletto, Titian and Van Dyck. The Museum of the Northumberland Fusiliers is housed in the Abbot's Tower. The Castle is a favourite location for films, most famously doubling as Hogwart's School in the *Harry Potter* films.

The only surviving part of the town's fortifications is 15th century **Hotspur Tower**, while all that is left of Alnwick Abbey is its 15th century gatehouse. **Hulne Park**, landscaped by Northumbria-born Capability Brown, encompasses the ruins of Hulne Priory, the earliest Carmelite foundation in England (1242).

AROUND ALNWICK

WARKWORTH

6 miles S of Alnwick on the A1068

At the southern end of Alnmouth Bay, on the River Coquet, lies Warkworth Castle. The site has been fortified since the Iron Age, though what can be seen now is mainly late 12th and 13th century, including the great Carrickfergus Tower and the West Postern

Towers. An unusual and interesting walk is signposted to **The Hermitage**, along the riverside footpath below the castle, where a ferry takes you across the river to visit the tiny chapel hewn out of solid rock. It dates from medieval times and was in use until late in the 16th century.

St Lawrence's Church is almost entirely Norman, though its spire - an unusual feature on medieval churches in Northumberland - dates from the 14th century.

AMBLE

7 miles SE of Alnwick on the A1068

Amble is a small port situated at the mouth of the River Coquet, once important for the export of coal, but now enjoying new prosperity as a marina and sea-fishing centre.

A mile offshore lies **Coquet Island**, where St Cuthbert landed in AD 684. The Island had a reputation in former times for causing shipwrecks, but is now a celebrated bird sanctuary, noted for colonies of terns, puffins and eider ducks. Managed by the Royal Society for the Protection of Birds, the island can be visited by boat trips departing from Amble quayside throughout the summer.

ROTHBURY

10½ miles SW of Alnwick on the B6341

This attractive town is a natural focal point from which to explore the valley of the River Coquet. The best-known of many delightful walks leads to the **Rothbury Terraces**, a series of parallel tracks

385 THE OAK INN

Causey Park Bridge, Morpeth

A boon for travellers on the A1, the **Oak Inn** offers a warm welcome and a good variety of drinks, snacks and meals.

see page 502

386 THE WIDDRINGTON INN

Widdrington, nr Morpeth

The **Widdrington Inn** is a great favourite with the local community, with a lovely relaxing ambience and super food.

see page 503

387 THE MASONS ARMS

Rennington, nr Alnwick

The **Masons Arms** is a quiet, civilised hostelry offering great hospitality, excellent food and drink and well-appointed accommodation.

see page 503

along the hillside above the town. Just outside Rothbury is the house and estate of **Cragside**, whose owner, the industrialist and engineer Sir William Armstrong, devised a system with man-made lakes, streams and underground piping that made his home the first to be lit by hydroelectricity.

CRASTER
7 miles NE of Alnwick off the B1339

To the northeast of Alnwick is Craster, a small, unpretentious fishing village that is nationally known for its oak-smoked kippers. During the curing season visitors can sniff around the sheds where the herring are hung over smoking piles of oak chips.

EMBLETON
7 miles NE of Alnwick on the B1339

The dramatic ruins of **Dunstanburgh Castle** stand on a cliff top east of the village, on a site that was originally an Iron Age

fort. The castle, by far the largest in Northumberland, was built in 1313 by Thomas, Earl of Lancaster, and in the Wars of the Roses it withstood a siege from troops led by Margaret of Anjou, Henry VI's Queen.

BAMBURGH
13½ miles N of Alnwick on the B1340

Built on an epic scale and dominating the village, **Bamburgh Castle** dates back to the 6th century although the mighty fortress seen today was originally built in the 12th century. The tour of the Castle takes in the magnificent King's Hall, the Cross Hall, the Bakehouse, the Scullery, the Armoury and the Dungeons. The village was the birthplace of Grace Darling, the Victorian heroine, who, in 1838, rowed out with her father from the **Longstone Lighthouse** in a ferocious storm to rescue five survivors from the wreck of the steam ship *Forfarshire* which had foundered on the Farne Islands rocks. She died of tuberculosis only four years later, still in her twenties, and is buried in a canopied tomb in St Aidan's churchyard. The **Grace Darling Museum**, in Radcliffe Road, contains memorabilia of the famous rescue.

The **Farne Islands** are a group of 28 little islands that provide a sanctuary for many species

Guillemots on The Farne Islands

of sea birds, including kittiwake, fulmar, puffin, and tern. They are also home to a large colony of Atlantic Grey seals which can often be seen from the beach of the mainland. Boat trips to the islands leave from the harbour at Seahouses, down the coast from Bamburgh. It was on Inner Farne that St Cuthbert landed in AD687, and a little chapel was built in his memory.

CHILLINGHAM

11½ miles NW of Alnwick off the B6348

Chillingham is a pleasant estate village best known for the herd of wild, horned white cattle that roam the parkland of **Chillingham Castle**. They are perhaps the purest surviving specimens of the wild cattle that once roamed the hills and forests of Britain.

LINDISFARNE

18 miles NW of Alnwick off the A1

Northumberland's northern coastline is dominated by one outstanding feature – Lindisfarne, also known as Holy Island. Reached by a three-mile causeway, the island was settled in the 7th century by St Aidan and his small community of Irish monks from Iona. It was these monks who produced some of the finest surviving examples of Celtic art, the richly decorated **Lindisfarne Gospels**. St Cuthbert also came here, living on a tiny islet as a hermit before seeking further solitude on the Farne Islands.

Benedictine monks renamed Lindisfarne **Holy Island** when they came here in the 11th century and established **Lindisfarne Priory**.
Lindisfarne Castle was established in Tudor times as yet another fortification to protect the exposed flank of Northumbria from invasion by the Scots. In 1902 it was bought by Edward Hudson, the owner of *Country Life*, who employed the great Edwardian architect Sir Edward Lutyens to rebuild and restore it as a private house. It is now in the care of the National Trust and is open to the public in the summer.

BERWICK-UPON-TWEED

For centuries, this former Royal burgh of Scotland was fought over by the Scots and the English, and changed hands no fewer than 14 times until it finally became part of England in 1482. But even now, Scotland exerts a great influence. The local football team, Berwick Rangers, plays in the Scottish League, and in 1958 the Lord Lyon, who decides on all matters armorial in Scotland, granted the town a coat-of-arms - the only instance of armorial bearings being granted in Scotland for use in England.

Berwick's original medieval walls, built in the 13th century by Edward I, are regarded as being the finest preserved fortifications of their age in Europe. The walk around the walls (about 1.5 miles) provides fine views of the town and the Northumberland coastline.

Housed in the clock tower of the Hawksmoor-designed barracks

388 LINDISFARNE PRIORY

Lindisfarne

Across the causeway on Holy Island, Lindisfarne Priory is one of the Holiest sites in England. The museum depicts life as it was over a millenium ago.

 see page 504

Not far from the village of Horncliffe the River Tweed is spanned by the Union Suspension Bridge linking Scotland and England, built in 1820 by Sir Samuel Browne, who also invented the wrought-iron chain links used in its construction. The graceful structure, 480 feet long, was Britain's first major suspension bridge to carry vehicular traffic.

is the **Berwick-upon-Tweed Borough Museum and Art Gallery**, which explores the history of the town, and the **King's Own Scottish Borderers Museum**.

The Berwick skyline is dominated by the imposing **Town Hall** with its clock tower and steeple that rise to 150 feet, and which is often mistaken for a church. Guided tours in the summer enable visitors to explore the upper storeys, where there are civic rooms and the former town gaol as well as a small **Cell Block Museum**.

AROUND BERWICK-UPON-TWEED

HORNCLIFFE

4 miles W of Berwick off the A698

The village of Horncliffe, five miles upstream of Berwick, can only be reached by one road that leads into and out of the village, making it feel rather remote. Many visitors are unaware of the existence of the river, but there is nothing more pleasant than wandering down one of the paths leading to the banks to watch the salmon fishermen on a summer's evening.

DUDDO

7 miles SW of Berwick on the B6354

Close to the village are the **Duddo Stones**, one of Northumberland's most important ancient monuments. This ancient stone circle, which now consists of five upright stones over seven feet high, dates back to around 2000 BC, and

can only be reached from the village by foot.

FORD & ETAL

13 miles SW of Berwick off the B6354

The twin estate villages of Ford and Etal were built in the late 19th century. Etal is an attractive village, within which are the ruins of the 14th century castle, destroyed in 1497 by King James IV of Scotland on his way to Flodden.

Ford is a 'model' village with many beautiful stone buildings and well-tended gardens. Dating originally from the 14th century, but heavily restored in the 19th century, **Ford Castle** was the home of Louisa Ann, Marchioness of Waterford. In 1860 she built the village school and from 1862 until 1883 spent her time decorating it with murals depicting biblical scenes. As models she used local families and their children thus creating a pictorial gallery of life and work in the area at that time. Now known as **Lady Waterford Hall**, it is open to the public.

TILLMOUTH

9 miles SW of Berwick on the A698

The village of Tillmouth lies along the banks of the River Till, a tributary of the Tweed which is crossed by the imposing 15th-century **Twizel Bridge**, although a more modern structure now carries the A698 over the river. There are some lovely walks here and a well-signed footpath leads to the ruins of **Twizel Castle** and the remains of **St Cuthbert's Chapel** on the opposite bank.

Nottinghamshire

Nottinghamshire is the home of the legendary Robin Hood and various exhibitions in Nottingham tell his story. Sherwood Forest, part of a great mass of forest land that once covered much of Central England, is officially designated 'Robin Hood Country'. The Industrial Revolution saw the mechanisation of the lace and hosiery industry of which Nottingham was a centre and on which many of the surrounding towns and villages were dependant. Mills sprang up in the towns, taking the industry away from the homes, and the Nottinghamshire coalfields, which had been mined for centuries, saw their scale of operation expanded dramatically. It was into this environment that DH Lawrence was born in the late 19th century and the family's terrace house is now a museum dedicated to the novelist. One of the gems of the county is Southwell Minster, a wonderfully graceful building that is probably the least well known of England's Cathedrals. The medieval town of Newark has many reminders of the Civil War, while the ancient village of Scrooby, in the far north of the county, is closely associated with

the Pilgrim Fathers, who sailed to America on the *Mayflower* in 1620.

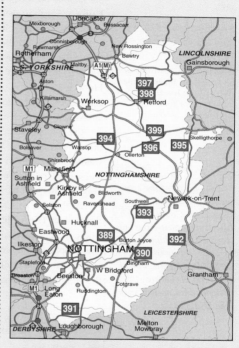

389 THE FAMOUS LORD NELSON

Burton Joyce

The **Famous Lord Nelson** offers great hospitality, well-kept ales and down-to-earth cooking at kind prices.

 see page 504

390 THE WHITE LION

Bingham

Standing at a crossroads near the centre of Bingham, the **White Lion** has a loyal local following for food, drink and genuine hospitality.

see page 504

•

To the north of the city of Nottingham lies Bestwood Country Park that encompasses part of the old royal hunting ground, while to the west is Wollaton Hall, one of the most elaborate Elizabethan mansions in the Midlands.

•

NOTTINGHAM

At the heart of the city is its **Old Market Square**, believed to be the largest market square in the country. This was the setting for the famous **Nottingham Goose Fair** that began in medieval times and continues today; it is now held at Forest Fields on the edge of Nottingham. Not far from the square, **The Tales of Robin Hood** tells the story of the celebrated outlaw who is forever linked with the city.

On a rocky outcrop high above the city centre stands **Nottingham Castle,** home now to a museum and art gallery and to the Sherwood Foresters Regimental Museum.

At the base of Castle Rock lies the famous **Trip to Jerusalem Inn**, where the crusaders are said to have stopped for a pint before setting off on their long journey to the Holy Land. Dating back to around 1189, it has claims to being the oldest pub in England; it was once the brewhouse for the castle. Close by, and set in the heart of Nottingham's historic Lace Market, is the **Museum of Nottingham Lace**, where the story of Nottingham's famous industry is told.

Nottingham is built on sandstone, and one of the many caves tunnelled down the years to provide shelter or hiding places has been left as a memorial to the black days of the Second World War.

AROUND NOTTINGHAM

RAVENSHEAD

9 miles N of Nottingham on the A60

This village is home to **Longdale Lane Rural Craft Centre**, established in the 1970s and the oldest such centre in the country.

Newstead Abbey, near Ravenshead

Just to the southwest lies **Newstead Abbey,** a magnificent 13th century ruin attached to a Victorian reworking of a Tudor mansion that is one of the county's most historic houses. The abbey was founded by Henry II in the 12th century as part of his atonement for the murder of Thomas à Becket.

BINGHAM

8 miles E of Nottingham A52

Celebrities connected with Bingham, the unofficial capital of the Vale of Belvoir, include Edward VII's mistress, Lily Langtry, who is commemorated on the chancel screen in the church. Bingham was also the third Nottinghamshire town to provide an Archbishop of Canterbury – George Abbot.

To the east lies **Aslockton,** the birthplace in 1489 of Thomas Cranmer; the church is appropriately dedicated to St Thomas, and the village school also bears his name.

RUDDINGTON

4 miles S of Nottingham on the B680

This historic village was once the home of many hosiery workers and several of their cottages still remain. There are two museums here: the **Ruddington Framework Knitters' Museum** and the **Ruddington Village Museum,** housed in the old village school building of 1852.

BEESTON

4 miles SW of Nottingham on the A6005

Lying on the outskirts of Nottingham, Beeston is the home of **Boots the Chemist,** which was started by Jesse Boot in the late 19th century. From 1880 it was also home to the Humber bicycle factory, which expanded to include motor cars before moving to Coventry in 1908.

Just to the north, in **Stapleford** churchyard, can be found the best preserved Saxon carving in the county in the form of a 10ft cross shaft that dates from the late 11th century.

EASTWOOD

8 miles NW of Nottingham on the A610

This mining town was the birthplace of DH Lawrence and the Lawrence family home, a two up, two down, terrace house at 8a Victoria Street is now the **DH Lawrence Birthplace Museum.** A place of pilgrimage for devotees of Lawrence, Eastwood also attracts those with an interest in railway history. It was at the Sun Inn in the Market Place that a group of 'Iron Masters and Coal Owners' gathered in 1832 to discuss the construction of a railway that would eventually become the mighty Midland Railway. A plaque on the wall of the inn commemorates the meeting.

The railway was formed to compete with the **Erewash Canal,** completed in 1779 and effectively

391 MANOR FARM ANIMAL CENTRE & DONKEY SANCTUARY

East Leake, Nr Ruddington

A fun day out for all the family with an assortment of animals to see and a variety of activities.

 see page 505

392 THE STAUNTON ARMS

Staunton-in-the-Vale

The 17th century **Staunton Arms** is a traditional country inn that also offers excellent food and accommodation.

see page 505

put out of business by the 1870s. Almost a century later, following years of neglect, the canal was cleared and made suitable for use by pleasure craft.

HUCKNALL

7½ miles NW of Nottingham on the A611

Hucknall attracts a constant stream of visitors who come to **St Mary Magdalen Church** to gaze not so much at the 14th century font or the Kempe stained glass but at a simple marble slab set in the floor of the chancel that marks the last resting place of Lord Byron.

Hucknall boasts another famous son, Eric Coates, who is best remembered as a composer of light music: his *Sleepy Lagoon* is immediately recognisable as the signature music of BBC Radio's long-running programme *Desert Island Discs*.

NEWARK-ON-TRENT

The market square of this elegant medieval town is lined with handsome houses and inns. The most remarkable of these is the 14th century former White Hart Inn, whose magnificent frontage is adorned with 24 plaster figures of angels and saints. Dominating one side of the square is the noble Georgian **Town Hall**, which now houses the town's civic plate and regalia and an art gallery displaying works by Stanley Spencer, William Nicholson and notable local artists.

The most glorious days of the 12th century castle were during the Civil War, when the townsfolk, who were fiercely loyal to Charles I, endured three separate sieges before finally surrendering to Cromwell's troops.

Newark possesses several other reminders of the Civil War and of the two small forts that were built to guard this strategic crossing over the River Trent only the **Queen's Sconce** has survived. Nearby is the **Governor's House**, where the governors of Newark lived during the Civil War and also where Charles I quarrelled with Prince Rupert after the prince had lost Bristol to Parliament.

With such a wealth of history inside its boundaries, Newark naturally has its fair share of museums and, along with those in the town, to the east is the **Newark Air Museum,** one of the largest privately managed collections in the country.

AROUND NEWARK-ON-TRENT

SIBTHORPE

6 miles S of Newark off the A46

All that remains above ground of a priests' college, founded here in the 14th century, is the parish church and a **Dovecote** that stands in the middle of a field. Of the three Archbishops of Canterbury born in Nottinghamshire, Thomas Cranmer is by far the best known, but Sibthorpe was the childhood home of Thomas Secker, Archbishop from 1758 to 1768.

SOUTHWELL

6 miles W of Newark on the A612

Undoubtedly one of England's most beguiling towns, Southwell is dominated by its Minster, whose twin towers, with their pyramidal Rhenish Caps, are unique in this country. Perhaps the least well-known of England's cathedrals, Southwell's history goes back to AD 956 when Oskytel, Archbishop of York, established a church here. The present building was erected in three phases between 1150 and 1290. Octagonal in design, the **Chapter House** has been hailed as the pinnacle of the Decorated period of architecture. The Cathedral stands in a delightful precinct surrounded by attractive buildings, while to the south stand the ruins of the palace of the archbishops of York built in the 14th and 15th centuries. **The Workhouse**, in the care of the National Trust, tells what life was like for 19th century paupers.

Southwell can claim to be the birthplace of the Bramley apple. The story goes that in the early 19th century, two ladies planted some apple pips in their cottage garden in the nearby village of Easthorpe. Nature took its course and one of the seedlings grew into a tree. By this time, Matthew Bramley owned the cottage and the quality of the tree's fruit began to excite public interest. Henry Merryweather, a local nurseryman, persuaded Bramley to let him take a cutting, which he subsequently propagated with enormous success.

MANSFIELD

16 miles W of Newark on the A617

The second largest town in the county, Mansfield stands at the heart of what were once the great North Nottinghamshire coalfields. That industry has now vanished but Mansfield still has the atmosphere of an industrial town although its economy is now based on a broader spread of varying businesses. The most distinctive structure in Mansfield is undoubtedly the great railway viaduct, built in 1875, which sweeps through and above the town, carried by 15 huge arches of rough-hewn stone.

LAXTON

9 miles NW of Newark off the A616

Laxton is one of the few places in the country that has managed to retain its open field farming system. Devised in the Middle Ages, this system was generally abandoned in the 18th and 19th centuries when the enclosure of agricultural land took place. The site has a Visitor Centre and Museum. Another unique feature of this interesting village is the magnificent Dovecote Inn that is owned by the Queen.

Just north of the village, along a lane close to the church, is the Norman motte, known as **Castle Mound**, which lies almost hidden beneath the trees. At the beginning of the 12th century, the stewardship of Sherwood Forest moved to Laxton and the village became the administrative centre for the forest. As a consequence,

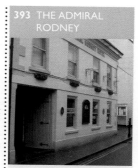

393 THE ADMIRAL RODNEY

King Street, Southwell

The **Admiral Rodney** is a distinguished old hostelry that's a great local favourite, serving lots of real ales and all-day food.

see page 506

Thoresby Park, nr Ollerton

The **Bay Tree Café Bar** is a
bright, modern licensed café
in the old stable block of
Thoresby Park, open all day
for snacks, with plenty of
hot and cold dishes at
lunchtime.

 see page 506

High Marnham, nr Tuxford

The **Brownlow Arms** is a
fine old pub serving a good
choice of drinks and home-
cooked food.

see page 507

Egmanton, nr Tuxford

An enticing variety of top-
class food has made the **Old
Plough Inn** one of the very
best dining pubs in the
region.

see page 508

220

the motte and bailey castle was one
of the biggest in this part of the
country.

OLLERTON

12½ miles NW of Newark on the A6075

Ollerton is a delightfully preserved
cluster of old houses, a charming
Georgian coaching inn, a church set
beside the River Maun and the
ancient **Ollerton Water Mill**.

To the south lies the pretty
conservation village of **Wellow**,
whose village green has the tallest
permanent **Maypole** in England,
60 feet high and colourfully striped
like a barber's pole, with a cockerel
perched on the top.

Close by lies **Rufford Country
Park**, in the grounds of Rufford
Abbey, which contain nine formal
gardens near the house along with a

display on Nottinghamshire's
history.

EDWINSTOWE

13½ miles NW of Newark on the A6075

Lying at the heart of **Sherwood
Forest**, the life of this village is still
dominated by the forest, as it has
been since the 7th century when
Edwin, King of Northumbria died
in the Battle of Hatfield in AD 632;
the village developed around the
church built on the spot where he
was slain. The **Church of St Mary**
was the first stone building in
Edwinstowe and, according to
legend it was here that the marriage
took place between Robin Hood
and Maid Marian.

Tracing the stories of Robin
Hood is a difficult task, as the tales,
which have been told for over 600

The Major Oak, Sherwood Forest

years, were spoken rather than written. Visitors still flock to see the great hollow tree that the outlaws purportedly used as a meeting place and as a cache for their supplies. The mighty **Major Oak** is located about 10 minutes walk along the main track in the heart of the forest. A little way up the road leading northwards out of Edwinstowe is the **Sherwood Forest Visitor Centre**, which houses a display of characters from the Robin Hood stories with appropriate scenes of merrymaking.

CRESSWELL

21 miles NW of Newark on the A616

Cresswell village is actually in Derbyshire but its most famous feature lies just inside the Nottinghamshire border. **Cresswell Crags** form a dramatic limestone gorge pitted with deep, dark and mysterious caves and here the bones of prehistoric bison, bears, wolves, woolly rhinos and lions twice the size of their modern descendants have been found. The Visitors' Centre contains some fascinating archaeological finds and there are some pleasant walks past the lakes to the crags.

RETFORD

Retford is actually two communities, East and West Retford, set either side of the River Idle. **Cannon Square** takes its name from a Russian cannon dating from 1855 and weighing over two tons. It was captured by British soldiers at Sebastopol and

brought to Retford at the end of the Crimean War. One of Retford's most infamous visitors was the highwayman Dick Turpin, and several historic inns still stand as a reminder of the days of stage coach travel. Another man who stood and delivered here, though in a more respectable fashion, was John Wesley, who conducted many open air meetings in East Retford. The **Bassetlaw Museum** is housed in Amcott House, an imposing late 18th century town house.

AROUND RETFORD

MATTERSEY

5 miles N of Retford off the B6045

To the east of the village lie the ruins of **Mattersey Priory**, founded in 1185 for the Gilbertine Order, the only monastic order to be established by an Englishman, Roger de Mattersey. The original priory buildings at Mattersey were destroyed by fire in 1279 so the remains seen today are of the 14th century dormitory, refectory, and the walls of the Chapel of St Helen.

NORTH WHEATLEY

4 miles NE of Retford off the A620

Famous for its strawberries that are sought after for their delicious taste and excellent quality, North Wheatley is also home to a peculiar 17th century brick house, known as the **Old Hall**, where all the external features, including the

397 THE QUEENS HOTEL

East Markham, nr Retford

Premier cask ales and good-value home cooking bring regulars from miles around to the **Queens Hotel** in the main street of East Markham.

 see page 508

398 THE BOAT AT HAYTON

Hayton, nr Retford

The **Boat at Hayton**, by the Chesterfield Canal, offers good lunches, local ales and B&B accommodation.

see page 509

399 THE GATE INN

Clarborough, nr Retford

Bar and restaurant menus offer a choice of eating at the **Gate Inn**, which enjoys a pleasant setting by the Chesterfield Canal.

see page 509

The first canal to be built in Nottinghamshire was the Chesterfield Canal that runs from Chesterfield in Derbyshire to the River Trent. Some 46 miles long, work on the canal was begun in 1771 and it took six years to complete under the supervision of John Varley, the deputy of the great canal engineer, James Brindley. During the canal's heyday in the early 1800s, it was a busy waterway and many buildings lined its route, particularly through Worksop.

vase-like decorations, are made from bricks. Just to the south is the splendid **North Leverton Windmill**, which was built in 1813 and still grinds corn today.

WORKSOP

7 miles SW of Retford on the A60

One of the major attractions of Worksop is the 14th century **Priory Gatehouse** that was originally the portal to a large Augustinian monastery; the gatehouse and the Church of St Mary and St Cuthbert are all that remain today. There is also a wayside shrine, which makes it a unique ecclesiastical attraction.

Mr Straw's House, along with an endowment of one million pounds, was bequeathed to the National Trust by William Straw in 1990. It was found that nothing in this seemingly ordinary Edwardian semi-detached house had been altered or added to since 1932, though it had been occupied by Straws until the death of the last Straw in 1990. Worksop Museum has a Pilgrim Fathers exhibition and is the start of the **Mayflower Trail** that guides visitor around the local sites connected with the Fathers.

To the southeast lies the 3,800-acre **Clumber Park**, created in 1707 when the 3rd Duke of Newcastle was granted permission to enclose part of the Forest of Sherwood as a hunting ground for Queen Anne. Only the foundations of Clumber House remain, but other buildings still stand in this lovely setting. The estate houses feature high-pitched gables and massive chimneys, and the redbrick stables are surmounted by a clocktower crowned by a domed cupola.

SCROOBY

7 miles NW of Retford on the A638

This ancient village is best known for its links with the Pilgrim Fathers and, particularly, with William Brewster. Having formed his radical ideas on religion at Cambridge and in the Netherlands, Brewster returned to England, settling in Scrooby. In 1598 he was summoned before the ecclesiastical court for poor church attendance, but he continued to maintain his battle for religious belief to be free of State control and was imprisoned for a short time before going back to Amsterdam. After some years he returned to England and became an Elder of the Separatist Church; it was a group of some 40 members of this church who, in 1620, boarded the *Mayflower* for the famous voyage which eventually landed at what is now Plymouth, New England.

Oxfordshire

A county of ancient towns and villages, whose capital, Oxford, 'that sweet city of dreaming spires', has dominated the surrounding area for centuries. The first scholars arrived at this walled Saxon town in the 12th century and, since then, this great seat of learning has influenced thinking and scientific research around the world. The southeastern part of the county is dominated by the River Thames and among the charming riverside towns and villages is Henley-on-Thames, the country's home of rowing and known worldwide for its annual Regatta. To the west lie the Vale of the White Horse and an area of downland which is littered with ancient monuments. Here, too, is Wantage, the birthplace of Alfred the Great. However, Oxfordshire's most famous feature is undoubtedly Blenheim Palace, the magnificent 18th century mansion that was the gift of a grateful queen to her loyal subject the Duke of Marlborough. A World Heritage Site, the palace is grand and opulent - it was also the birthplace of Sir Winston Churchill, whose modest room can be seen.

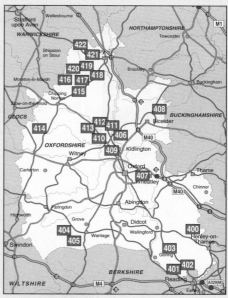

*Maidensgrove,
nr Henley-on-Thames*

The **Five Horseshoes** offers
superb home cooking in
lovely scenic surroundings.

 see page 509

Mapledurham

In a picturesque setting
visitors can tour the
Elizabethan mansion and
watch the watermill
producing flour.

see page 509

ABINGDON

One of England's oldest towns,
Abingdon grew up around a 7th
century Benedictine Abbey. Twice
sacked by the Danes, it was all but
derelict by the 10th century, but
under the guidance of Abbot
Ethwold it again prospered and in
its heyday was larger than
Westminster Abbey. Little remains
today except the late 15th century
Gatehouse.

AROUND ABINGDON

THAME

14½ miles NE of Abingdon on the A418

Founded in AD 635 as an
administrative centre for the Bishop
of Dorchester, Thame became a
market town in the 13th century

and its main street is lined with old
inns and houses. The imposing
Church of St Mary and the
Prebendal House both date from
the 13th century, while the town's
famous school was founded in
1558.

DORCHESTER

5½ miles SE of Abingdon off the A4074

All that remains of the Augustinian
Abbey, which was built on the site
of the original Saxon church, is the
**Abbey Church of St Peter and St
Paul**, whose chief glory is the huge
Jesse window showing the family
tree of Jesus.

WALLINGFORD

8 miles SE of Abingdon on the A4130

It was here that William the
Conqueror crossed the river on his

Abingdon

six-day march to London, and during the Civil War the town was a Royalist stronghold defending the southern approaches to Oxford, the site of the Royalist headquarters. Wallingford was besieged in 1646 by the Parliamentary forces under Sir Thomas Fairfax and its walls were breached after a 12-week siege; it was the last place to surrender to Parliament. The Castle, built by William the Conqueror, was destroyed by Cromwell in 1652 but substantial earthworks can still be seen and the museum tells the story of the town from earliest days.

STONOR

16 miles SE of Abingdon on the B480

The village is the home of Lord and Lady Camoys and their house, Stonor, which has been in the family for over 800 years. Set in a wooded valley and surrounded by a deer park, the house contains many rare items and a medieval Catholic Chapel.

HENLEY-ON-THAMES

19 miles SE of Abingdon on the A4155

In 1829, the first University boat race between Oxford and Cambridge took place here and, within a decade, the event was enjoying royal patronage. Today, **Henley Regatta** is a stylish as well as a sporting occasion that remains a popular annual event.

Beside the town's famous 18th century bridge is the Leander Club, the headquarters of the world famous rowing club and here, too,

is the **River and Rowing Museum**, which traces the rowing heritage of Henley.

MAPLEDURHAM

17 miles SE of Abingdon off the A4074

Hidden down a little lane that leads to the River Thames, this tiny village is home to the Elizabethan **Mapledurham House**, which has several notable literary connections. Alexander Pope was a frequent visitor in the 18th century; the final chapters of John Galsworthy's *The Forsythe Saga* were set here; and it became the fictional Toad Hall in *The Wind in the Willows*.

GORING-ON-THAMES

12 ½ miles SE of Abingdon on the B4526

Situated on a particularly peaceful stretch of the River Thames, this ancient town began to develop in the 19th century after Brunel had laid the tracks for the Great Western Railway through **Goring Gap**.

DIDCOT

5 miles S of Abingdon on the A4130

Although this town is overshadowed by the giant cooling towers of Didcot power station, it has a saving grace in the form of the **Didcot Railway Centre**, which is a shrine to the days of the steam locomotive and the Great Western Railway.

To the north lies the pretty village of **Sutton Courtenay** where, in the churchyard of the Norman church, are the graves of Herbert Asquith, the last Liberal

402 THE PACKSADDLE INN

Chazey Heath, nr Mapledurham

The **Packsaddle Inn** is a popular destination for lovers of good beer, good food and good company.

🍴 see page 510

403 THE RED LION

Woodcote

In a pleasant setting overlooking the village green and cricket pitch, the **Red Lion** is a popular choice for its excellent home cooking.

🍴 see page 510

Sparsholt

The **Star** is a 17th century country inn with good home cooking and 8 excellent guest bedrooms.

 see page 511

405 THE GREYHOUND INN

Letcombe Regis, nr Wantage

The **Greyhound** is a fine old redbrick inn serving well-kept cask ales and popular pub dishes. Six rooms for B&B.

see page 511

406 THE ROCK OF GIBRALTAR

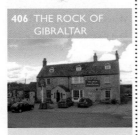

Enslow Bridge, Bletchington

A warm family welcome and a fine selection of home-cooked food awaits visitors to the **Rock of Gibraltar**, which enjoys a lovly setting by the Coventry-Oxford Canal.

 see page 512

Prime Minister, and Eric Blair, who is better known as novelist George Orwell.

WANTAGE

The birthplace of Alfred the Great in AD 849, Wantage remained a royal manor until the end of the 12th century and in the central market place is a huge statue of the King of all the West Saxons. Only the **Church of St Peter and St Paul** has survived from medieval times. Opposite the church is the **Vale and Downland Museum Centre** which is housed in a 16th century building and a reconstructed barn.

AROUND WANTAGE

UFFINGTON

6 miles W of Wantage off the B4507

This large village was the birthplace, in 1822, of Thomas Hughes, the author of Tom Brown's Schooldays, and he incorporated many local landmarks in his well-known work. The Tom Brown's School Museum tells the story of Hughes's life and works. The village is best known for the Uffington White Horse, a mysteriously abstract figure of a horse, some 400 feet long, which was created by removing the turf on the hillside to expose the gleaming white chalk beneath. Close by lies the Blowing Stone (or Sarsen Stone), a piece of glacial debris that is perforated with holes and, when blown, emits a sound like a foghorn.

BUSCOT

12 miles NW of Wantage on the A417

This small village is home to two National Trust properties: **Buscot Old Parsonage**, a William and Mary house with a small garden beside the River Thames, and **Buscot Park**, a grand late Georgian house that houses the Faringdon Art Collection, which includes paintings by Rembrandt, Rubens, Reynolds and Burne-Jones.

Just downriver from the village lies 16th century **Kelmscott Manor House**, which was the home of William Morris between 1871 and 1896. Morris is buried in the local churchyard in a grave whose ridge-shaped stone was designed by his friend and partner, the architect Philip Webb. Further along the river again is the tiny hamlet of **Radcot**, which boasts the oldest bridge across the Thames – **Radcot Bridge** dates from 1154.

OXFORD

A walled town in Saxon times, the first students arrived here in the 12th century when they were forced out of Europe's leading academic centre, Paris. The first colleges as we know them were Merton, Balliol and University. The colleges all have their own distinctive features, and one of the most beautiful is **Christ Church**, which was founded in 1525 as Cardinal College by Thomas Wolsey. The main gateway leads through the bottom of Tom Tower (designed by Christopher Wren) and into Tom Quad, the largest of the city's quadrangles, and the college's chapel is the only one in the world to be designated a cathedral; **Christ Church Cathedral** is also England's smallest.

As well as the college buildings, Oxford has many interesting places for the visitor to explore. The 18th century **Radcliffe Camera** is England's earliest example of a round reading room and this splendid building still serves this purpose for the **Bodleian Library**, which was refounded by Sir Thomas Bodley, a fellow of Merton College, in 1602. One of Oxford's most famous buildings is the magnificent **Sheldonian Theatre**, which was designed and built in the Roman style by Christopher Wren between 1664 and 1668 while he was Professor of Astronomy at the University. The ceiling has 32 canvas panels, depicting Truth descending on the Arts, and the theatre is used for such events as matriculation and degree ceremonies.

The **Ashmolean Museum**, which first opened in 1683, was originally established to house the collection of John Tredescant and his son; this internationally renowned museum is home to many treasures, including archaeological collections from Europe, Egypt and the Middle East. The Ashmolean's original building is now home to the **Museum of the History of Science** where among a remarkable

collection are Einstein's blackboard and a large silver microscope made for George III. The **Botanic Gardens** are a peaceful place, founded in 1621, a teaching garden where the plants grown were studied for their medicinal and scientific uses. The rose garden commemorates the work of Oxford's scientists in the discovery and use of penicillin. The University is also responsible for the lovely **Harcourt Arboretum** at Nuneham Courtenay, 4 miles south of Oxford.

To the southeast of the city lies the 16th century **Garsington Manor** that was the home of the socialite Lady Ottoline Morrell between 1915 and 1927. With her husband Philip she played host to a whole generation of writers, artists and intellectuals including Katherine Mansfield, Siegfried Sassoon, TS Eliot, Rupert Brooke and Bertrand Russell. Aldous Huxley based an account of a country house party in his novel *Crome Yellow* on his experiences at Garsington and, in so doing, caused a rift between himself and his hostess. DH Lawrence also fell out with Lady Morrell when he drew a less than flattering portrait of life at her house in *Women in Love*.

AROUND OXFORD

BICESTER

11½ miles NE of Oxford on the A41

Established in Saxon times, Bicester (pronounced Bister) later acquired both an Augustinian priory and a Benedictine nunnery, but much of

407 THE CHEQUERS INN

Headington Quarry, nr Oxford

The **Chequers** is a handsome and substantial inn off the A40, with good food served from 12 to 6 every day.

see *page 513*

408 THE SOW & PIGS

Poundon, nr Bicester

Bed & Breakfast accommodation is being added to good food and drink at the **Sow & Pigs**.

see *page 513*

409 ROYAL SUN

Begbroke

Excellent food is complemented by fine wines at the **Royal Sun**, where the tenants and staff have a warm welcome for all the family.

🍴 see page 514

410 THE WOODSTOCK ARMS

Market Street, Woodstock

The attractions of Woodstock are many and varied, and for those in the know the **Woodstock Arms** is *the* place to head for good food and drink.

🍴 see page 516

the old part of the town was lost during a disastrous fire in the early 18th century. The founding here of the Army's ordnance depot in 1941 brought much new development, which continued up until the 1960s in what had hitherto been a chiefly agricultural community.

EYNSHAM
6½ miles W of Oxford on the A40

To the south of this ancient market town lies **Stanton Harcourt Manor**, which dates back to the 14th century and is noted for its well-preserved medieval kitchen. It was while staying here that Alexander Pope translated Homer's *Iliad*, working in a 15th century tower that is now called Pope's Tower.

WOODSTOCK
8 miles NW of Oxford off the A44

Woodstock is known the world over and attracts visitors by the million to the magnificent **Blenheim Palace**, one of the very few sites in the country on the World Heritage List. The estate was a gift from Queen Anne to John Churchill, 1st Duke of Marlborough, for his victory at the Battle of Blenheim during the Spanish War of Succession, but the Queen's gratitude ran out before the building work was finished and the Duke had to meet the remainder of the costs himself. Designed by Sir John Vanbrugh and built between 1705 and 1722, the house is also famously associated with Sir Winston

Blenheim Palace, Woodstock

228

Bliss Tweed Mill

Churchill, who was born here in 1874, and among the grand collections, there are intimate mementoes from the great statesman's life. The surrounding parkland was landscaped by Capability Brown.

LOWER HEYFORD

12 miles NW of Oxford on the B4030

To the south of the village, which stands on the banks of the River Cherwell, is **Rousham**, a fine 17th century house built for the Dormer family, with magnificent gardens laid out by William Kent in 1738; they represent the first phase of English landscape gardening and remain the only complete William Kent garden to have survived.

CHIPPING NORTON

At 650 feet above sea level, this is Oxfordshire's highest town and was once an important centre of the wool trade. This medieval prosperity can be seen in the grandeur of the spacious Church of St Mary, which, like many other buildings in the town, endured substantial remodelling in the 19th century. To the west of the town centre is the extraordinary 19th century **Bliss Tweed Mill**, which was designed by George Woodhouse, a Lancashire architect, in the style of Versailles.

To the north, beyond **Over**

411 STURDY'S CASTLE

Tackley, nr Woodstock

In a prominent position on the Oxford-Banbury road, **Sturdy's Castle** is open all day every day for a fine selection of food and drink. Also twenty rooms for B&B guests.

see page 515

412 THE KILLINGWORTH CASTLE INN

Wootton, nr Woodstock

The **Killingworth Castle** is a 17th century coaching inn well known for its excellent food, fine ales, regular entertainment and guest accommodation.

see page 516

413 THE DUKE OF MARLBOROUGH

Woodleys, Woodstock

Major assets of the **Duke of Marlborough** include a ready welcome, fresh seasonal food, Hook Norton ales and comfortable guest bedrooms.

see page 517

229

414 THE QUART POT

Milton-under-Wychwood, nr Chipping Norton

The **Quart Pot** is a fine old village pub serving excellent food until 9 in the evening.

see page 516

415 THE MASONS ARMS

Swerford, nr Chipping Norton

For quality, variety and value for money, the **Masons Arms** is at the top of the tree among dining pubs.

see page 518

416 THE PEAR TREE INN

Hook Norton, nr Banbury

Close to the famous Hook Norton Brewery, the **Pear Tree Inn** serves excellent real ales and home-cooked pub dishes. Also 3 rooms for B&B.

see page 519

417 THE WHITE SWAN

Wiggington

The **White Swan** is a fine old pub in wonderful walking country, with Hook Norton ales and home-cooked dishes to satisfy fresh-air thirsts and appetites.

see page 519

Norton, are the **Rollright Stones** – one of the most fascinating Bronze Age monuments in the country. These great slabs of stone stand on a ridge which affords fine panoramic views.

AROUND CHIPPING NORTON

BANBURY

12½ miles NE of Chipping Norton on the A361

This historic market town has managed to preserve many of its old buildings and to retain its status as a leading livestock market. The famous **Banbury Cross** in Horsefair dates only from 1859 as the previous cross was destroyed by the Parliamentarians during the Civil War. It was erected to commemorate the marriage of Queen Victoria's oldest daughter to the Crown Prince of Prussia, and the figures around the base, of Queen Victoria, Edward VII and George V, were added in 1914. The town's other legendary claim to fame is its spicy, fruity cakes, though at one time it was also famous for its cheeses, which were only about an inch thick.

To the southwest of Banbury, in an old courthouse, is the **Bloxham Village Museum**, where the displays concentrate on the lives of Oxfordshire's rural inhabitants. Close by is the 14th century moated mansion, **Broughton Castle**, which was remodelled into a fine Tudor home in the 16th century. The castle figured prominently in the Civil War, when its secret room was used by leaders of the Parliamentary forces to lay their plans.

CHARLBURY

5½ miles SE of Chipping Norton on the B4022

Charlbury was once famous for its glove-making as well as being a centre of the Quaker Movement – the simple Friends Meeting House here dates from 1779 and there is also a Friends cemetery. Close to the Meeting House is Charlbury Museum, where the town's charters can be seen. Close by are two interesting great houses. On the opposite bank of the River Evenlode from the main town lies Cornbury Park, a large estate that Elizabeth I gave to Robert Dudley. Although most of the house now dates from the 17th century, this was originally a hunting lodge in Wychwood Forest and it had been used since the days of Henry I. Just to the west is Ditchley Park, a restrained, classical, early 18th century house with superb interiors; it was used as a weekend headquarters by Sir Winston Churchill during World War II when Chequers was thought to be unsafe.

WITNEY

10½ miles S of Chipping Norton on the A4095

Situated at the bottom of the valley of the River Windrush, Witney developed as a planned town in the early Middle Ages. Wool was the economic base of life here and Witney developed weaving and, in particular, the making of blankets. The **Blanket Hall**, which sports the arms of the Witney Company of Weavers, was built for the weighing and measuring of blankets in an age before rigid standardisation.

Just outside the town is the **Cogges Manor Farm Museum**, which tells the stories of the lives of those who have worked the surrounding land for centuries.

Just to the west of Witney lies **Minster Lovell**, one of the prettiest villages along the River Windrush and home to the once impressive 15th century manor house, **Minster Lovell Hall**. Built between 1431 and 1442, this was one of the aristocratic houses of Oxfordshire and home of the influential Lovell family. Although the hall was dismantled in the 18th century and the ruins turned into lowly farm buildings, the remains in this serene setting are extremely picturesque.

SHIPTON-UNDER-WYCHWOOD

6 miles SW of Chipping Norton off the A361

The suffix 'under-Wychwood' is derived from the ancient royal hunting forest, **Wychwood Forest**, the remains of which lie to the east of this village. Though cleared

during the Middle Ages, it was still used as a royal hunting ground until well into the 17th century; 150 years later there was little good wood left and the forest was rapidly cleared to provide arable land. The forest was one of the alleged haunts of Matthew Arnold's Scholar Gypsy.

BURFORD

11 miles SW of Chipping Norton on the A361

The site of a battle between the armies of Wessex and Mercia in AD 752, the town and surrounding area were given after the Norman Conquest to Bishop Odo of Bayeux, William the Conqueror's brother. An important centre of the wool trade for centuries, Burford saw something of a revival with the stage coaching era and many of the old inns still survive.

With an atmosphere of a small cathedral, the **Church of St John** was built on the wealth of the wool trade and has several interesting features, including possibly the first representation of a native American Indian in this country.

The town's 16th century courthouse, with its open ground floor, is now home to the **Tolsey Museum**.

418 THE ELEPHANT & CASTLE

Bloxham, nr Banbury

The **Elephant & Castle** is an atmospheric 15th century pub, family-run, with lunchtime food and 2 letting rooms for B&B.

 see page 519

419 THE SAYE & SELE ARMS

Broughton, nr Banbury

The **Saye & Sele Arms** is a super place to relax over a glass of real ale or an excellent meal.

 see page 520

420 THE LAMPET ARMS

Upper Tadmarton, nr Banbury

The **Lampet Arms** is a friendly, family-run pub with hearty home cooking and excellent B&B accommodation.

 see page 520

421 THE ROEBUCK INN

Drayton, nr Banbury

The home-made pies are just one of the tempting things on the menu at the **Roebuck Inn**.

see page 521

422 THE DUN COW

Horton

The **Dun Cow** is open Monday to Friday evenings and all day Saturday and Sunday for a very interesting selection of food and drink. Beer Festivals in February and July.

see page 520

Rutland

The motto of England's smallest county is, appropriately, 'multum in parvo' ('much in little'). It has two delightful market towns, Oakham and Uppingham, and 52 small, unspoilt villages of thatch and ironstone cottages clustered round their churches. The county's central feature is **Rutland Water**, which extends over 3,300 acres and is the largest man-made reservoir in Europe. Started in 1971 to supply water to East Midlands towns, it was created by damming the valley near Empingham. There's good walking around its 26-mile shoreline, some great bird-watching (including wild ospreys), excellent trout and pike fishing, and a wide variety of water sports.

Curiously for such a pastoral, peaceful county, it was Rutland men who were prime movers in two of the most dangerous conspiracies in England's history. In a room over the porch of Stoke Dry church, the Gunpowder Plot was hatched with the local lord of the manor, Sir Everard Digby, as one of the ringleaders. Some 75 years later, Titus Oates and his fellow conspirators hatched the anti-Catholic 'Popish Plot' at his home in Oakham.

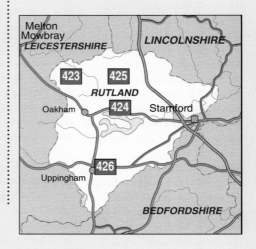

	FOOD & DRINK	
423	Slipcote, Whissendine	p 233, 521
424	Barnsdale Lodge Hotel & Restaurants, Rutland Water	p 234, 521
426	The Vaults, Uppingham	p 234, 522

	ACCOMMODATION	
424	Barnsdale Lodge Hotel & Restaurants, Rutland Water	p 234, 521
426	The Vaults, Uppingham	p 234, 522

	PLACES OF INTEREST	
425	Rutland Railway Museum, Cottesmore	p 234, 523

OAKHAM

Just off the Market Place of Rutland's county town is **Oakham Castle**, a romantic, evocative fortified manor house built between 1180 and 1190, with the earliest surviving example of an aisled stone hall in the country. One of the most unusual attractions is a collection of horseshoes presented by royalty and nobility to the Lord of the Manor. Notable natives of Oakham include the infamous conspirator Titus Oates, born here in 1649, and the famed midget Jeffrey Hudson, who worked for the Duke and Duchess of Buckingham at nearby Burley.

One of Rutland's best-known landmarks, Normanton Church, stands on the very edge of **Rutland Water**, which was formerly part of the Normanton Estate and now houses a display dedicated to the construction of the reservoir by Anglian Water and a history of the area. On the north shore of Rutland Water, the **Butterfly Farm & Aquatic Centre** contains a walk-through jungle with tropical butterflies and birds; ponds with koi carp and terrapins; an insect cave with tarantulas, scorpions and other mini-beasts; a monitor lizard enclosure; and a display of local coarse and game freshwater fish. Tel: 01780 460515.

Ospreys can be seen between May and September and the famous British Bird Watching Fair takes place in August.

To the northeast of Oakham is

Cottesmore, the home of the **Rutland Railway Museum**, a working steam and diesel museum open some weekends (Tel: 01572 813203).

UPPINGHAM

This picturesque stone-built town is the major community in the south part of the county. The town is known for its bookshops and art galleries, but whereas other places are dominated by castles or cathedrals, in Uppingham it's the impressive **Uppingham School** that gives the town its special character. The school was founded in 1584 by Robert Johnson,

423 SLIPCOTE

Whissendine

Diners come from miles around to enjoy the outstanding food served at **Slipcote** on Thursday, Friday and Saturday evenings.

see page 521

Market Square, Oakham

Normanton Church, Rutland Water

Archdeacon of Leicester, who also founded Rutland's other celebrated public school at Oakham. For more than 250 years, Uppingham was just one of many such small grammar schools, giving rigorous instruction in classical languages to a couple of dozen sons of the local gentry. Then, in 1853, the Reverend Edward Thring was appointed headmaster. During his 43-year tenure the sleepy little school was transformed.

The Old School Building still stands in the churchyard, with trilingual inscriptions around the walls in Latin, Greek and Hebrew – *Train up a child in the way he should go* is one of them. In its place rose a magnificent complex of neo-gothic buildings: not just the traditional classrooms and a (splendid) chapel, but also a laboratory, workshops,

museum, gymnasium and the most extensive school playing fields in the country.

The old school, the 18th century studies, the Victorian chapel and schoolrooms, and the 20th century great hall, all Grade I or Grade II listed, can be visited on a guided tour on Saturday afternoons in summer.

LYDDINGTON

3 miles SE of Uppingham off the A6003

A quiet village where English Heritage oversees the **Bede House,** one of the finest examples of Tudor domestic architecture in the country. This house of prayer was once part of a retreat for the Bishops of Lincoln and was later converted to almshouses. Tel: 01572 822438 for opening times.

Shropshire

The glorious border county of Shropshire hides a turbulent past, when the Marcher Lords divided their time between fighting the Welsh and each other. The remains of their fortresses can be seen in various places, and one of the finest Roman sites in the country is at Wroxeter - Viroconium was the first Roman site to be developed in this part of the country. There are ancient market towns that serve the rich farmland and some magnificent stately homes; and Shropshire saw the birthplace of the Industrial Revolution that began at Ironbridge Gorge. This stretch of the Severn Valley is now a World Heritage Centre, which ranks it alongside the Pyramids, the Grand Canyon and the Taj Mahal, and several interesting museums can be found here. Along with man-made places of interest, visitors will find spectacular scenery around Wenlock Edge, Long Mynd and Clun Forest and the extraordinary Tar Tunnel.

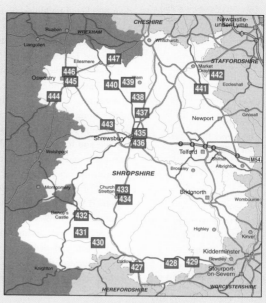

427 THE MALT HOUSE

Ludford, nr Ludlow

The **Malt House** is a delightful period cottage with three bedrooms and every amenity for a self-catering holiday in a quiet, scenic location.

 see *page 523*

428 THE PENNY BLACK INN

Knowbury

The **Penny Black Inn** is a long-hours pub in a quiet country setting, well known for its excellent, varied cuisine.

see *page 523*

429 THE KREMLIN INN

Cleehill, nr Ludlow

The **Kremlin Inn**, in a picturesque setting east of Ludlow, offers real ales, good simple home cooking and two rooms for B&B.

see *page 524*

LUDLOW

Often referred to as 'the perfect historic town', Ludlow has more than 500 listed buildings along with a medieval street pattern that remains virtually intact. **Ludlow Castle** was built on a rocky promontory above a curve of the River Teme by the Normans in the 11th century as one of a string of castles along the Marches. It has been home to many distinguished families and to royalty, including Edward V and Prince Arthur; it was also the headquarters of the Council of the Marches, which governed Wales and the border counties until 1689.

Places to seek out include the parish Church of St Laurence, one of the largest in the county, **Castle Lodge**, which was once a prison

and later the home of the officials of the Council of the Marches, the Georgian Dinham House, the Feathers Hotel and the museum.

Ever since 1960, the town has played host to the annual **Ludlow Festival**, one of the country's major arts festivals that lasts for a fortnight in June and July and the centrepiece of the event is an open-air performance of a Shakespeare play in the castle's inner bailey.

Just northwest of the town lies **Ludlow Racecourse**, a charming, rural National Hunt course, while a few miles to the southeast lies the village of **Burford**. On the banks of the River Teme stands **Burford House**, whose four acre garden is filled with well over 2,000 varieties of plants. The garden is also the home of the National Collection of Clematis.

Elizabethan Buildings, Ludlow

AROUND LUDLOW

BISHOP'S CASTLE

14 miles NW of Ludlow on the B4385

Surrounded by the great natural beauty of the border country, little remains of the castle that was built here in the 12th century for the bishops of Hereford. The **House on Crutches Museum** is situated in one of the oldest and most picturesque of the town's buildings – its gable end is supported on wooden posts that explain the unusual name. North of Bishop's Castle lie the **Stiperstones**, a rock-strewn quartzite outcrop rising to a height of 1,700 feet at the Devil's Chair. A bleak, lonely place, the ridge is part of a 1,000-acre National Nature Reserve.

CHURCH STRETTON

12 miles N of Ludlow on the A49

Just behind the High Street is the **Church of St Laurence** that has Saxon foundations and, over the aisle, is a memorial to three boys who were tragically killed in a fire in 1968. The memorial takes the form of a gridiron – the symbol of St Laurence, who was burned to death on one in AD 258. A mile from the town centre are **Carding Mill Valley** and the **Long Mynd**. The valley and the moorland into which it runs are very popular for walking and picnicking.

Just to the southwest lies the pretty village of **Little Stretton** that nestles in the Stretton Gap. The most interesting building here is the black and white timber-framed **All Saints Church**, with its thatched roof and general cottage-like appearance.

BRIDGNORTH

16½ miles NE of Ludlow on the A458

Straddling the River Severn, this ancient market town comprises Low Town and, some 100 feet up on sandstone cliffs, High Town. In 1101, Robert de Belesme built a Castle here but all that remains now is part of the keep tower.

Bridgnorth's oldest complete building is 16th century **Bishop Percy's House**, a handsome townhouse that was one of the few timber-framed buildings to survive a devastating fire in 1646. On the outskirts of the town, in the grounds of Stanmore Hall, is the **Midland Motor Museum** that holds an outstanding collection of more than 100 vehicles.

Bridgnorth is the northern terminus of the wonderful **Severn Valley Railway** but the town has another irresistible attraction in the **Castle Hill Cliff Railway**, a funicular railway built in 1892 that links the two parts of the town. John Betjeman likened a ride on this lovely little railway to a journey up to heaven.

MUCH WENLOCK

16½ miles NE of Ludlow on the A4169

Among the mellow buildings of this delightful small town are some places of real beauty, including timber-framed **Raynald's Mansion** and the magnificent 16th century Guildhall.

430 THE ENGINE & TENDER

Broome, Aston-on-Clun

The **Engine & Tender** is a 15th century pub with a good choice of real ales and food and a camping/caravan site.

see page 524

431 THE POWIS ARMS

Lydbury North

The **Powis Arms** offers period charm, local brews, fine food, en suite B&B rooms, a good garden and a caravan/camping site.

see page 524

432 CLAREMONT

Bishops Castle

Self-catering and B&B are both available at **Claremont**, in the grounds of a large Victorian house and in the house itself.

see page 524

433 THE GREEN DRAGON INN

Little Stretton

In a superbly scenic location by Long Mynd, the **Green Dragon** offers a great selection of real ales and excellent home cooking.

see page 524

434 MYND HOUSE

Little Stretton

Mynd House in a quiet setting below Long Mynd, offers comfortable accommodation and menus that feature both Western and Malaysian cuisine.

see page 525

To the south of Much Wenlock lies one of the most spectacular landmarks in the whole of Shropshire, Wenlock Edge, a limestone escarpment dating back some 400 million years that is now a paradise for naturalists and lovers of the outdoors.

The most interesting building is the **Priory of St Milburga** that was originally founded as a nunnery in the 7th century by King Merewald, who installed his daughter Milburga as head of the house. Among the remains, the Prior's Lodge, dating from around 1500, is particularly impressive, while away from the main site is **St Milburga's Well**, whose waters are reputed to cure eye diseases.

TELFORD

Telford is a sprawling modern town that absorbed several existing towns in the Shropshire coalfield. The name chosen in the 1960s commemorates Thomas Telford, whose influence can be seen all over the county.

AROUND TELFORD

IRONBRIDGE

3 miles S of Telford off the B4373

This town, at the centre of **Ironbridge Gorge**, is part of an area of the Severn Gorge where the world's first cast-iron bridge was constructed and where, over 250 years ago, the Industrial Revolution first began in earnest. In this locality, now designated a World Heritage Centre, the first iron wheels, the first iron rails and the first steam railway

The Iron Bridge, Ironbridge

locomotive were made.

The **Ironbridge Visitor Centre** offers the ideal introduction to the series of museums here, including the **Museum of Iron** at Coalbrookdale, and the neighbbouring furnace that was used by Abraham Darby when he first smelted iron with coke; the **Jackfield Tile Museum**, which houses a fine collection of wall and floor files from Victorian times through to the 1950s; and the **Coalport China Museum** with its marvellous displays of porcelain that span over two centuries.

Nearby is the extraordinary **Tar Tunnel**, which was a popular tourist attraction in the 18th century as well as being one of the most interesting geological phenomena in Britain. Further upstream from Ironbridge is one of the finest ruined abbeys in England, **Buildwas Abbey**, virtually complete, though roofless, after 850 years.

SHIFNAL

4 miles E of Telford on the A464

On the A41 at Cosford, near Shifnal, the **RAF Museum** houses an important collection of aircraft, aero engines and weapons of war from all over the world.

TONG

6 miles E of Telford on the A41

Charles Dickens set the closing chapters of *The Old Curiosity Shop* in Tong and Little Nell's home was right by the church. To the east of the village lie the ruins of **White Ladies Priory**, a 12th century

nunnery dedicated to St Leonard. Nearby is **Boscobel House**, a timber-framed building where Charles II hid after his defeat at the Battle of Worcester in 1651. The secret room where he hid can be seen, as can the Royal Oak, which was grown from an acorn taken from the original tree in which the King escaped a house search by Cromwell's men.

SHREWSBURY

Situated in a horseshoe bend in the River Severn, this lovely county town occupies, almost, an island site and it was on the two well-protected hills here that the Saxon town developed. Later, the Normans built a **Castle**, which last saw action in the Civil War, and a great Benedictine **Abbey** on the site of a Saxon wooden church. The Abbey Church remains a place of worship to this day, and the castle is now home to the **Shropshire Regimental Museum**. Close to the abbey is the **Shrewsbury Quest**, which presents the sights and sounds of medieval Shrewsbury as it grew and prospered on the wealth generated by the woollen trade.

It was at Shrewsbury that Charles Darwin was born and educated and, earlier, Robert Clive, Clive of India, lived in the town and was Mayor in 1762. His home, **Clive House**, contains mementoes from his life along with a display dedicated to Charles Darwin, whose statue can be seen opposite the castle. Just outside Shrewsbury, at **Longden Coleham**, is a museum with a difference – the

435 SHROPSHIRE REGIMENTAL MUSEUM

Shrewsbury

This superb museum tells the story of the four Shropshire Regiments, and inlcudes uniforms, medals and weaponry.

 see page 525

436 SHREWSBURY CASTLE

Shrewsbury

Dating back to 1083, Shrewsbury Castle occupies a commanding position and is home to the Shropshire Regimental Museum.

 see page 526

437 THE NEW INN

Hadnall

The **New Inn** is a handsome redbrick pub serving three real ales and a varied menu of home-cooked dishes.

 see page 527

438 THE INN AT GRINSHILL

Grinshill, nr Shrewsbury

Quality comes first at the **Inn at Grinshill** – accommodation, restaurant, pub and a warm welcome.

 see page 526

439 THE DICKIN ARMS

Loppington, nr Shrewsbury

The **Dickin Arms** is a traditional country pub open lunchtime and evening for drinks and home cooking.

 see page 527

440 THE LEAKING TAP

Cockshott

The **Leaking Tap** is a pub of wide appeal, serving good food and Banks's beers in a warm, traditional atmosphere.

 see page 527

Coleham Pumping Station – which houses the splendid Renshaw pumping engines that powered Shrewsbury's sewerage system until 1970. There are more than 30 churches in Shrewsbury and one of the finest is **St Mary's**, the town's only complete medieval church.

One of the many guided tours and suggested walks in this marvellous town leads north to a place known as the **Battlefield**. It was here, in 1403, that the armies of Henry IV and the insurgent Harry Hotspur met; in the brief but bloody battle there were many casualties, including Hotspur.

To the southeast of the town lies the village of **Atcham**, and close by is one of the finest houses in Shropshire, the splendid neo-classical **Attingham Park** with grand Regency interiors and delightful grounds that were landscaped by Humphrey Repton.

A little further from Shrewsbury lies **Wroxeter**, home to one of the most important Roman sites to have been excavated. Known as Viroconium, it was the first town to be established by the Romans in this part of the country. Six miles north of Shrewsbury on the A49 stands the village of Grinshill. This is a neat, quaint little place and the area is a walker's paradise; the hill rises to 630 feet above sea level, and its greatest asset is the substance from which it is made – sandstone. The Romans quarried it for the construction of Wroxeter, and in more recent times it was used for the door surrounds of No 10 Downing Street. The quarry has revealed many rare fossils and has accordingly been designated a Site of Special Scientific Interest.

AROUND SHREWSBURY

WEM

10½ miles N of Shrewsbury on the B5476

Although this is a peaceful place today Wem was virtually destroyed during the War of the Roses and, later, it was again attacked during the Civil War.

Fortunately some notable buildings survived the great fire that devastated much of the town in the 17th century and these include **Astley House**, the home of the painter John Astley. Another famous person associated with the town is Judge Jeffreys, of the Bloody Assizes, whose official residence was at Lowe Hall. Wem is the home of the modern sweet pea, which was developed by the 19th century nurseryman, Henry Eckford, and the **Sweet Pea Show** and carnival take place here annually.

WHITCHURCH

19 miles N of Shrewsbury on the A49

First developed by the Romans and known as Mediolanum, Whitchurch has been the most important town in the northern part of the county for centuries. The main street is dominated by the tall sandstone tower of **St Alkmund's Church**, while hidden away in the heart of the town are the Old Town Hall

Vaults, where the composer Edward German was born in 1862. Whitchurch is also the home of **Joyce Clocks**, the oldest tower clockmakers in the world.

The long distance footpath, the **Shropshire Way**, passes nearby, as does the Llangollen Canal, and nature lovers can explore the local wetland habitats at **Brown Moss**, which lies just to the south of the town.

MARKET DRAYTON
17 miles NE of Shrewsbury on the A529

Mentioned in the *Domesday Book* as Magna Draitune, Market Drayton changed its name when Abbot Simon Combermere obtained a Royal Market charter in 1245; a market continues to be held here every Wednesday.

To the east of town is the village of Moreton Say, where locally born Robert Clive, Clive of India, is buried in St Margaret's Church.

A few miles southwest of Market Drayton lies a beautiful Georgian mansion, **Hawkestone Hall**, which was the ancestral home of the Hill family from 1556 until 1906. **Hawkestone Park** is a woodland fantasy of caves, follies, grottoes and secret tunnel and pathways.

NESSCLIFFE
9 miles NW of Shrewsbury on the A5

Close to the village is **Nesscliffe Hill Country Park** where paths lead up through woodland to the hill, a sandstone escarpment, from which there are glorious views out across Shropshire and to Wales.

A short distance north of Nesscliffe is the village of **Ruyton-XI-Towns**, which acquired its curious name in medieval times when 11 communities were united into the one borough of Ruyton.

OSWESTRY
17 miles NW of Shrewsbury off the A5

This important market town takes its name from Oswald, a Saxon king who was killed in a battle in AD 642 and whose dismembered body was hung on the branches of a tree. Local legend then tells an eagle swooped down and carried off one of his arms and, where the limb fell to the ground, a spring bubbled up to mark the spot and it was around **St Oswald's Well** that the town developed while the well became a place of pilgrimage.

Due to several fires that ravaged the town's old timber-framed buildings, Oswestry's architecture is chiefly Georgian and Victorian but various fine old buildings do still remain including **St Oswald's Church**. Standing in the grounds of the church is the 15th century **Holbache House** that was once a grammar school and now houses a Heritage Centre.

In 1559, a plague killed almost a third of the town's inhabitants and the **Croeswylan Stone** commemorates this disaster as well as marking the spot to which the market was moved during the days of the infection.

Oswestry was the headquarters of the Cambrian Railway Company until it amalgamated with the Great

441 THE FALCON INN

Hinstock, nr Market Drayton

Go-ahead owners have put the **Falcon Inn** on the map as one of the best eating places in the area. Also rooms for B&B.

see page 528

442 THE FOX & HOUNDS

Cheswardine, nr Market Drayton

The **Fox & Hounds** is a convivial pub that's popular with tourists, walkers and canal-users as well as locals.

see page 528

443 THE OLD SWAN

Montford Bridge, nr Shrewsbury

The **Old Swan** is a mellow, creeper-clad hostelry with a well-deserved reputation for the quality of its food. Caravan/camping site in the grounds.

see page 529

444 THE LIME KILN

Porth y Waen, nr Oswestry

Many awards have come the way of the **Lime Kiln**, a popular country pub serving excellent home-cooked food.

see page 528

241

445 THE RED LION

Bailey Head, Oswestry

The **Red Lion** offers food, drink and B&B accommodation in the centre of Oswestry.

🍴 see page 530

446 THE WALLS

Welsh Walls, Oswestry

The Walls is a popular venue for enjoying top-class food and entertainment in spacious, stylish surroundings.

🍴 see page 530

447 THE SUN INN

Welshampton, Ellesmere

The **Sun Inn**, a former brewing house dating back 200 years, is now a convivial pub serving home-cooked food and real ales, with beer festivals in May and September.

🍴 see page 530

Western Railway in 1922 and as recently as the 1960s there were over 1,000 railwaymen in the area. One of the old engine sheds now houses the **Cambrian Museum of Transport**, where a collection of railway memorabilia, along with some old bicycles and motorbikes, is on display.

About five miles south of Oswestry lies the village of **Llanymynech** that was once a town of some standing, with a major canal and a thriving industry based on limestone. The quarried limestone was taken, after processing, to the nearby canalside wharf on the **Montgomery Canal**

that was built at the end of the 18th century chiefly for this purpose.

ELLESMERE

15½ miles NW of Shrewsbury on the A495

The most impressive building here is undoubtedly the parish church of St Mary the Virgin; built by the Knights of St John, it has an exceptional 15th century carved roof in the chapel. This church overlooks **The Mere**, the largest of several local lakes, which is home to herons, Canada geese and swans, and an ideal place for boating enthusiasts and anglers.

Somerset

As well as being home to the attractive cities of Bristol and Bath, Somerset has more than its fair share of natural beauty. The wilds of Exmoor and the ranges of spectacular hills such as the Quantocks and the Mendips add to this county's allure. In the far northwest is Exmoor, once wild hunting country: its abundance of prehistoric sites, ancient packhorse bridges and wild deer and ponies easily make it one of the more romantic and mysterious spots. As the Mendips are limestone, the hills are full of holes, and, in particular, this area is known for its caves at Wookey Hole and the spectacular Cheddar Gorge, which carves a path right through the hills as well as lending its name to the cheese. Below the hills is the charming and ancient city of Wells, from where the county's plain stretches out to Glastonbury, a place shrouded in mystery and steeped in early Christian and Arthurian legends.

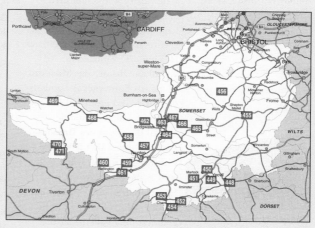

243

Union Street, Yeovil

Mulberry's Bistro, in the heart of town, is the perfect spot for anything from a working lunch to a romantic dinner or a special celebration.

 see page 531

Bishopston, nr Montacute

The **Kings Arms** is a distinguished 17th century inn combining the best features of a friendly local, a fine restaurant and a comfortable hotel.

 see page 532

Martock

Connoisseurs of real ale and lovers of good food will be pleased they stopped at the **George Inn**.

see page 532

YEOVIL

In the 1890s, James Petter, a local pioneer of the internal combustion engine, founded a business here that was to become one of the largest manufacturers of diesel engines in Britain. It later moved to the Midlands, but a subsidiary was established during World War I to produce aircraft and Yeovil became well known as the home of Westland Helicopters. Situated in Wyndham House, the **Museum of South Somerset** documents the social and industrial history of the town and surrounding area.

To the south lies **Barwick Park**, an estate that is littered with bizarre follies, while to the west is the magnificent Elizabethan mansion, **Montacute House**, which has one of the grandest long galleries in the country. Montacute village is also the home of the **TV and Radio Memorabilia Museum**. In the lanes to the southeast of Montacute and close to the village of **West Coker** is the magnificent **Brympton d'Evercy Manor House** dating from Norman times but with significant 16th and 17th century additions. In the church at **East Coker** were buried the ashes of the poet and playwright TS Eliot. This village, where his ancestors lived, is mentioned in *Four Quartets*, a poem written by Eliot, and lines from that poem are quoted on his memorial tablet.

AROUND YEOVIL

SPARKFORD
7 miles NE of Yeovil off the A303

Home to the **Haynes Motor Museum**, which holds one of the largest collections of veteran, vintage and classic cars and motorbikes in the country. Just to the east of Sparkford is **Cadbury Castle**, a massive Iron Age hill fort that is also believed by some to be the location of King Arthur's legendary Camelot.

CASTLE CARY
11½ miles NE of Yeovil on the B3152

Once the site of an impressive Norman castle, this little rural town has some interesting old buildings, including a handsome 18th century post office, a tiny 18th century lock-up called the **Round House**, and a splendid Market House that is now home to the **Castle Cary District Museum**.

WINCANTON
13 miles NE of Yeovil off the A303

This attractive old cloth-making town was also a bustling coaching town, lying almost exactly half way between London and Plymouth. Modern day Wincanton is a peaceful light industrial town whose best-known attraction is **Wincanton National Hunt Racecourse**. Also worth visiting are the beautiful **Hadspen House Gardens** that are situated to the northwest.

High Street, Castle Cary

CREWKERNE

8 miles SW of Yeovil on the A356

A thriving agricultural centre during Saxon times, Crewkerne even had its own mint in the decades that led up to the Norman invasion. The town lies close to the source of the River Parrett, from where the 50-mile long **River Parrett Trail** follows the river through some of the country's most ecologically sensitive and fragile areas. Just a couple of miles southwest of Crewkerne, close to the village of **Clapton**, are the interesting **Clapton Court Gardens**.

CHARD

15 miles SW of Yeovil on the A30

Although Chard has expanded rapidly since World War II, it still retains a pleasant village-like atmosphere; its museum is located in the attractive thatched Godworth House.

To the northwest of the town is a 200-year old corn mill, **Hornsbury Mill**, whose impressive water wheel is still in working order; to the northeast lies **Chard Reservoir Nature Reserve**, a conservation area that is an important habitat for wildlife.

451 THE WHEATSHEAF

South Petherton

Popular snacks and meals are served all day at the **Wheatsheaf**.

see page 533

Close to the county border lies **Forde Abbey**, which was founded in the 12th century by Cistercian monks. The remains of the Abbey were incorporated into the grand private house of the Prideaux family, and among the many treasures are the renowned Mortlake Tapestries brought from Brussels by Charles I. The gardens are equally superb.

ILMINSTER
13 miles W of Yeovil on the A358

On the outskirts of the ancient agricultural and ecclesiastical centre of Ilminster is the handsome part-Tudor mansion, **Dillington House**, the former home of the influential Speke family. John Speke was an officer in the Duke of Monmouth's ill-fated rebel army and, following the rebellion's disastrous defeat, Speke was forced to flee abroad, leaving his brother George to face the wrath of Judge Jeffreys and the inevitable death sentence.

MARTOCK
6 miles NW of Yeovil on the B3165

The old part of Martock is blessed with an unusually large number of fine buildings, including the **Treasurer's House,** a small two-storey house dating from the late 13th century, and a 17th century Manor House, the home of Edward Parker, the man who exposed the Gunpowder Plot.

To the east of Martock are the enchanting **Tintinhull House Gardens**.

YEOVILTON
5 miles NW of Yeovil off the A37

Here is one of the world's leading aviation museums, the **Fleet Air Arm Museum**, which contains a unique collection of aircraft.

MUCHELNEY
9½ miles NW of Yeovil off the A372

Muchelney is the location of an impressive part-ruined Benedictine monastery, **Muchelney Abbey**, thought to have been founded by King Ine in the 8th century. Opposite the parish church stands the **Priest's House**, a late medieval hall house that was built by the abbey.

WELLS

The first church here is believed to have been founded by King Ine in around AD 700 but the present **Cathedral of St Andrew** was begun in the 12th century. Taking over three centuries to complete, the treasures of this wonderful place include the 14th century **Astronomical Clock**, one of the oldest working timepieces in the world. Set in the pavement outside the Cathedral walls is a length of brass that extends over the prodigious distance leapt by local girl Mary (Bignall) Rand when she set a world record for the long jump. To the south of the cathedral's cloisters is the **Bishop's Palace**, a remarkable fortified medieval building that is surrounded by a moat fed by the springs that give the city its name.

On the northern side of the cathedral green is 14th century **Vicar's Close**, one of the oldest planned streets in Europe.

To the north of the city lies **Wookey Hole**, where the carboniferous limestone has been eroded away over the centuries to create over 25 caverns. During prehistoric times, lions, bears and woolly mammoths lived in the area.

AROUND WELLS

CHEW MAGNA

11½ miles N of Wells on the B3130

The nucleus of this former wool village is its three-sided green at the top of which is the striking early 16th century Church House while, behind a high wall adjacent to the churchyard, lies **Chew Court**, a former summer palace of the Bishops of Bath and Wells.

To the south of Chew Magna are the two reservoirs constructed to supply Bristol with fresh water but that also provide a first class recreational amenity.

NORTON ST PHILIP

15½ miles NE of Wells on the A366

The monks who founded the now-ruined Priory were also responsible for building the village's most famous landmark – the splendid **George Inn** – that was originally established as a house of hospitality for those visiting the priory.

To the west is one of the finest Neolithic monuments in the west of England, **Stoney Littleton Long Barrow** that was built over 4,000 years ago.

SHEPTON MALLET

5 miles E of Wells on the A371

From before the Norman Conquest and through the Middle Ages Shepton Mallet was at first a centre of woollen production and then a weaving town. Several fine buildings date back to those prosperous days including the 50ft **Market Cross**, which dates from around 1500, and **The Shambles**, a 15th century wooden shed where meat was traded. Each year, Shepton Mallet plays host to two agricultural shows: the Mid-Somerset Show in August and, in May, the **Royal Bath and Wells Show**.

FROME

14½ miles E of Wells on the A362

Frome's old quarter is an attractive conservation area where can be found the **Blue House** that was built in 1726 as an almshouse and a boy's school and is one of the town's numerous listed buildings.

GLASTONBURY

5½ miles SW of Wells on the A39

This ancient town of myths, legends and tales of King Arthur and the early Christians is an attractive market town dominated by the dramatic ruins of its abbey. If the legend of Joseph of Arimathea is to be believed, **Glastonbury Abbey** is the site of the earliest Christian foundation in the British Isles. However, it is the Abbey's connection with King Arthur and his wife Queen Guinevere that draws most visitors

455 BOWLISH HOUSE

Shepton Mallet

A handsome grade II* Georgian house offering stylish and comfortable accommodation and top quality food.

see page 535

456 THE NEW INN

Priddy, nr Wells

The **New Inn** is an excellent place for a drink, a meal or an overnight stay in a quiet rural setting in the Mendip Hills

see page 534

457 HESTERCOMBE GARDENS

Cheddon Fitzpaine

A superb landscaped garden with wonderful views and delightful walks.

 see page 536

458 THE RISING SUN

West Bagborough, nr Taunton

The **Rising Sun** provides history, ambience, great food and superb guest accommodation in a beautiful country setting.

see page 536

459 THE WHITE HORSE INN

Bradford-on-Tone, nr Taunton

The **White Horse Inn** is a pleasant stone-built village inn serving well-priced food, well-kept ales and decent wines.

see page 536

460 THE MARTLET INN

Langford Budville, nr Wellington

The **Martlet Inn** is a 17th century country inn serving well-kept real ales and home-cooked dishes. B&B and self-catering accommodation available.

see page 537

to Glastonbury, as this is thought by some to be their last resting place. Even the **Somerset Rural Life Museum** cannot escape from the influence of the Abbey as the impressive 14th century barn here once belonged to the Abbey.

To the east of the town lies **Glastonbury Tor**, a dramatic hill that rises above the surrounding Somerset Levels.

In the nearby village of **Street**, the Clark family began to produce sheepskin slippers in the 1820s; the oldest part of the Clark's factory is now a fascinating **Shoe Museum**.

BURNHAM-ON-SEA

15 miles W of Wells on the B3140

A large and popular seaside resort whose most distinctive landmark is the **Low Lighthouse**, a curious square structure that is raised above the beach on tall stilts. To the northeast lies **Brent Knoll**, whose 445ft summit is crowned with the remains of an Iron Age hill fort.

CHEDDAR

7½ miles NW of Wells on the A371

This sprawling village is best known for its dramatic limestone gorge, **Cheddar Gorge**, which is characterised by its high vertical cliffs, from which there are outstanding views.

This village is also renowned for its caves and, of course, its cheese. The term 'Cheddar cheese' refers to a recipe that was developed in the mid 19th century by Joseph Harding, a farmer and pioneer food scientist from near Bath who made the

first scientific investigation into cheese making.

From the nearby remote village of **Charterhouse** a footpath leads up onto **Black Down**, which at 1,067 feet is the highest point in the Mendips; from here, to the northwest, the land descends down into Burrington Combe, a deep cleft that is said to have inspired the Reverend Augustus Toplady to write *Rock of Ages*.

The Mendip Hills were once a royal hunting ground and, to the northwest of Cheddar, lies **King John's Hunting Lodge**, home to an excellent Local History Museum.

TAUNTON

Founded by the Saxon King Ine in the 8th century, Taunton, the county town of Somerset, had by Norman times grown to have its own Augustinian monastery, a Minster and a Castle – an extensive structure whose purpose had always been more as an administrative centre than as a military post. The Castle is now the home of the **Somerset County Museum** and the **Somerset Military Museum**. Somerset's famous County Cricket Ground occupies part of the priory grounds and a section of the old monastic gatehouse now houses the fascinating **Somerset County Cricket Museum**.

Taunton's attractive **National Hunt Racecourse** is one of the best country racecourses in Britain.

In the lanes to the north of Taunton lie the beautiful

Hestercombe Gardens on the south-facing foothills of the Quantocks just north of the village of **Cheddon Fitzpaine**.

AROUND TAUNTON

WELLINGTON

6 miles SW of Taunton on the A38

It was from this pleasant old market town that the Duke took his title and, to the south, stands the **Wellington Monument**, a 175ft obelisk erected to commemorate his great victory at Waterloo.

BISHOP'S LYDEARD

4½ miles NW of Taunton off the A358

This large village is the southern terminus of the West Somerset Railway, the privately operated steam railway that runs to Minehead on the Bristol Channel coast.

NETHER STOWEY

9½ miles N of Taunton on the A39

It was while staying in a friend's cottage here that Samuel Taylor Coleridge wrote most of his famous works, including *The Rime of the Ancient Mariner* and *Kubla Khan*. When not writing, he would go on long walks with his friend and near neighbour William Wordsworth. The Coleridges stayed here for three years and **Coleridge Cottage** now displays mementoes of the poet.

HINKLEY POINT

13½ miles N of Taunton off the A39

Hinkley Point is perhaps best known for its great power stations and, at the **Hinkley Point Visitor Centre**, visitors can find out just how the adjacent power station creates electricity while, the **Hinkley Point Nature Trail** leads walkers through a wide diversity of habitats.

BRIDGWATER

9 miles NE of Taunton on the A38

Situated at the lowest bridging point of the River Parrett, Bridgwater is an ancient inland port and industrial town. As the river began to silt up, Bridgwater underwent something of an industrial renaissance, as the river mud that closed the port also proved to be an excellent scourer when baked.

To the southwest, near **Enmore**, is the small redbrick country mansion of **Barford Park**, a delightfully proportioned Queen Anne house that is set in extensive grounds which incorporate a large area of woodland. Further southwest again is **Fyne Court**, which is the headquarters of the Somerset Wildlife Trust and whose grounds have been designated a nature reserve.

BURROW BRIDGE

9 miles NE of Taunton on the A361

This village on the River Parrett is home to one of several pumping stations that were built in Victorian times to drain the Somerset Levels - the **Pumping Station** is open to the public occasionally throughout the year; here, too, is the **Somerset Levels Basket and Craft Centre**.

461 THE BLUE MANTLE HOTEL

Wellington

The **Blue Mantle Hotel** is an attractive period building with eight well-appointed guest bedrooms.

see page 537

462 THE MALT SHOVEL

Bradley Green, nr Bridgwater

The **Malt Shovel** is a welcoming old inn with real ales, hearty bar food and traditional pub games.

see page 538

463 THE VOLUNTEER ARMS

Bridgwater

The **Volunteer Arms** is a popular locals pub on the Bristol side of town.

see page 538

Just west of Burrow Bridge, the **Bridgwater and Taunton Canal** winds its way through some of the most attractive countryside in the Somerset Levels and the restored locks, swing bridges and engine houses add further interest to this picturesque walk.

Just northwest of the village of **Westonzoyland** is the site of the last battle to be fought on English soil when, in July 1685, the forces of James II heavily defeated the followers of the Duke of Monmouth in the bloody Battle of Sedgemoor.

EXMOOR AND THE QUANTOCK HILLS

The characteristic heartland of the **Exmoor National Park** is a high, treeless plateau of Devonian shale carved into a series of steep-sided valleys by the prolonged action of the moor's many fast-flowing streams.

Exmoor is crisscrossed by a network of paths and bridleways,

Tarr Steps, Exmoor

which provide superb opportunities for walking and pony-trekking. Many follow the routes of the ancient ridgeways across the high moor and pass close to the numerous hut circles, standing stones, barrows and other Bronze and Iron Age remains which litter the landscape. The remarkable medieval packhorse bridge known as **Tarr Steps** lies to the north of the village of Hawkridge, near Dulverton.

MONKSILVER
13 miles NW of Taunton on the B3188

To the southwest of this pretty village of charming old houses and thatched cottages are the **Brendon Hills**, the upland area within the Exmoor National Park from where, in the mid 19th century, iron ore was mined in significant quantities and then carried down a steep mineral railway to the coast for shipment to the furnaces of South Wales.

WATCHET
15 miles NW of Taunton on the B3191

It was at Watchet that, in the 6th century, St Decuman is said to have landed from Wales with the cow that he brought along to provide sustenance. It was also from Watchet that Coleridge's imaginary crew set sail in *The Rime of the Ancient Mariner*.

To the south of Watchet, in the village of

Williton, are the diesel locomotive workshops of the West Somerset Railway and the **Bakelite Museum**. Just to the west lies **Cleeve Abbey**, the only monastery in Somerset that belonged to the austere Cistercian order.

MINEHEAD
21½ miles NW of Taunton off the A39

A popular seaside town at the foot of the wooded promontory of North Hill, now a nature reserve, Minehead is one of the county's oldest settlements. As the port declined, the town began to expand as a seaside resort and in 1962 a popular holiday camp was opened.

To the west of Minehead lies the village of Selworthy. This picturesque and much

468 THE DRAGON HOUSE HOTEL & RESTAURANT

Bilbrook, nr Minehead

The family-run **Dragon House Hotel** welcomes visitors with fine home cooking and comfortable accommodation in a pleasant setting on the edge of Exmoor.

see page 541

Church Steps, Minehead

469 THE ROYAL OAK

Porlock

The **Royal Oak** beckons with traditional hospitality, real ales and good food on the main street of a lovely old Exmoor town.

🍴 see page 542

470 ROCK HOUSE INN

Dulverton

Hilltop village pub serving a good choice of real ales and a range of appetising meals

🍴 see page 542

471 LEWIS'S TEA ROOMS

High Street, Dulverton

Lewis's Tea Rooms provide a delightful spot for enjoying a savoury or sweet snack throughout the day.

🍴 see page 542

photographed village is situated on the side of a wooded hill. Just to the northwest lies **Selworthy Beacon**, one of the highest points on the vast **Holnicote Estate**. Covering some 12,500 acres of Exmoor National Park, it includes a four-mile stretch of coastline between Minehead and Porlock Weir. **Dunkery Beacon**, the highest point on Exmoor, rises to 1,700 feet.

To the southeast lies **Dunster**, dominated by **Dunster Castle**, a medieval fortification that was remodelled in 1617 and was one of the last Royalist strongholds in the West Country to fall during the Civil War. In the castle's parkland is 18th century **Dunster Working Watermill**; little remains of Dunster Priory save its priory church and an unusual 12th century dovecote.

PORLOCK WEIR

26½ miles NW of Taunton off the A39

Once an important seaport, Porlock Weir is a picturesque place where a **Submerged Forest**, a relic of the Ice Age, can be seen at low tide. From Porlock Weir a pretty mile-long walk leads up through walnut and oak woodland to **Culbone Church**, the smallest church in regular use in England, and certainly one of the most picturesque. A true hidden treasure, measuring only 33 feet by 14 feet, this superb part-Norman building is set in a wooded combe that once supported a small charcoal-burning community and was at other times home to French prisoners and

lepers. The South West Coast Path passes this lovely secluded church.

To the west lies **Doone Valley**, a long enclosed sweep of green pasture and mature woodland that was immortalised by RD Blackmore in his classic romantic novel, *Lorna Doone*.

DULVERTON

19 miles W of Taunton on the B3222

Situated in the wooded Barle Valley on the edge of Exmoor, Dulverton is a pretty little town where the headquarters of the Exmoor national park can be found in an old converted workhouse.

BRISTOL

Situated at a strategically important bridging point at the head of the Avon gorge, Bristol was founded in Saxon times and soon became a major port and market centre. During the Middle Ages, it expanded as a trading centre and at one time was second only to London as a seaport. In the early 19th century, the harbour was expanded when a semi-artificial waterway, the **Floating Harbour**, was created by diverting the course of the River Avon to the south. Today, the main docks have moved down stream to Avonmouth and the Floating Harbour has become home to a wide assortment of pleasure and small working craft. Much of Bristol's waterfront has now been redeveloped for recreation, and several museums tell of the city's connections with the sea. The **Maritime Heritage Centre** is dedicated to the history of shipbuilding in Bristol and has a number of historic ships moored at the quayside, including Brunel's mighty *SS Great Britain*, the world's first iron-hulled passenger liner, launched in 1843.

AROUND BRISTOL

WESTON-SUPER-MARE

17 miles NW of Wells on the A370

A popular seaside resort with all the trappings, including the Edwardian **Grand Pier** (one of the last traditional iron-piled piers), the **Winter Gardens** and an Aquarium, as well as the fascinating **North Somerset Museum**. Close by is the start of the **Mendip Way**, a 50-mile long footpath that takes in the whole length of the Mendip Hills and ends at Frome.

CLEVEDON

18½ miles NW of Wells on the B3133

Clevedon Pier is a remarkably slim and graceful structure that was built in the 1860s from iron rails intended for Brunel's ill-considered South Wales Railway. When part of the pier collapsed in the 1970s, its long-term future looked bleak but, following an extensive restoration programme, the pier is now the landing stage in the summer for large pleasure steamers.

BATH

The ancient Celts were the first to become aware of the healing powers of the mysterious steaming spring here but it was the Romans who were the first to enclose the spring. The restored Roman remains centre on the **Great Bath**, a rectangular lead-lined pool that stands at the centre of the complex system of buildings. In the 8th century the Saxons founded a nunnery here but the present day **Bath Abbey** dates from the 15th century and is considered to be the ultimate example of English Perpendicular church architecture.

Bath developed into a magnificent Georgian spa resort under the influence of three gentlemen: Beau Nash, who became the Master of Ceremonies; the architect father and son, both called John Wood; and the entrepreneur Ralph Allen. Among the many fine buildings here are Queens Square; the **Royal Crescent**, the first terrace in Britain to be built to an elliptical design; the **Pump Room** completed in 1796; and the **Assembly Rooms**. Spanning the River Avon is the magnificent **Pulteney Bridge** that was inspired by Florence's Ponte Vecchio. Among the most interesting of Bath's several museums are the **Bath Postal Museum**, with its reconstruction of a Victorian sorting office, and the **Jane Austen Centre** – the novelist spent a good deal of time here.

Just to the east of the city lies the 16th century country mansion, **Claverton Manor**, now the American Museum and Gardens.

One of the Bristol's most famous features is the graceful Clifton Suspension Bridge that spans the Avon Gorge. Opened in 1864, five years after the death of its designer Brunel, it provides magnificent views over the city and the surrounding countryside.

Staffordshire

Southern Staffordshire encompasses many changing landscapes, from the busy industrial towns of Stafford and Burton upon Trent to the peace and quiet of Cannock Chase. Along with the Hednesford Hills, the Chase provides a wonderful open area of woodland and moorland that is one of the county's great recreational areas. One legacy of the Industrial Revolution and a feature throughout the whole of Staffordshire is the canal network. The motorways of their day, the network linked not only the industrial centres of the county with each other but also with the rest of the country. The northeast of the county, some of which lies in the Peak District National Park, is an area of undulating moorland that makes ideal walking and cycling country. However, the Industrial Revolution has left its mark here in the form of two great reservoirs – Rudyard and Tittesworth. Staffordshire is, of course, home to the Potteries, the area around Stoke-on-Trent that is world famous for its pottery industry. The natural resources of coal and clay found here and the foresight of such men as Wedgwood and Minton saw what began as a cottage industry explode into one of the great factory systems of the 18th century.

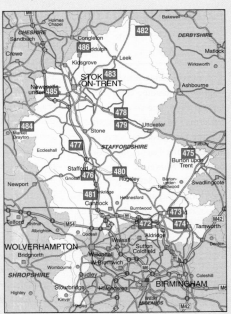

LICHFIELD

Lichfield Cathedral is particularly renowned for the three magnificent spires that dominate the city's skyline. Inside there are many treasures, including the beautiful 8th century illuminated manuscript *The Lichfield Gospels* and Sir Francis Chantrey's famous sculpture *The Sleeping Children*. The surrounding Cathedral Close is regarded by many as the most original and unspoilt in the country, and, being separated from the rest of the city by **Stowe and Minster Pools**, it is also a peaceful haven of calm.

Lichfield's most famous son is Dr Samuel Johnson, the poet, novelist and author of the first comprehensive English dictionary. The son of a bookseller, Johnson was born in 1709 in Breadmarket Street, and the house is now the **Samuel Johnson Birthplace Museum**. Another famous son is Erasmus Darwin, the doctor, philosopher, inventor, botanist and poet, and the grandfather of Charles Darwin. **Erasmus Darwin's House** has touch-screen computers to access Darwin's writings and inventions, and a garden with herbs and shrubs that would have been familiar to the good doctor.

The **Wall Roman Site**, Letocetum, has the remains of a bath house and mansion, the most substantial in the country.

AROUND LICHFIELD

ALREWAS

5 miles NE of Lichfield off the A38

The National Memorial Arboretum, to the east of this pretty village, is the first large arboretum and wildlife reserve to be created in Britain for 200 years. A substantial grant from the Millennium Commission has transformed this 150-acre former gravel quarry into a sylvan temple whose themes are remembrance and reconciliation. The central feature is the Millennium Avenue, created from cuttings from a 2,000-year-old lime tree.

BURTON UPON TRENT

11 miles NE of Lichfield on the A38

Burton has long been famous for its brewing industry that began many centuries ago - even the monks of the Benedictine Abbey, founded here in 1100, were not the first to realise that Burton well

472 ODDFELLOWS IN THE BOAT

Walsall Road, Lichfield

Oddfellows in the Boat – the cooking is as remarkable as the name, and dishes that would do credit to a top restaurant bring diners from all over the region.

🍴 *see page 543*

473 THE SWAN

Whittington, nr Lichfield

Equally popular with locals and visitors for food and hospitality, the **Swan** enjoys a delightful setting by the Coventry Canal.

🍴 *see page 543*

Lichfield Cathedral

474 THE RED LION

Hopwas, nr Tamworth

The **Red Lion** is a super redbrick inn by the A51 and the Coventry canal. Great all-day eating, wines by bottle or glass.

 see page 544

475 THE CROSS KEYS & WENDY'S RESTAURANT

Tutbury

The **Cross Keys & Wendy's Restaurant** combines the qualities of a much-loved local and an excellent little restaurant.

 see page 543

476 THE OXLEATHERS

Western Downs, Stafford

On the southwestern edge of Stafford, the uniquely named **Oxleathers** is very much the hub of the local community, with good food and drink and a long list of sporting connections.

see page 545

water was specially suited to brewing. William Bass began brewing at Burton in 1777 and by 1863 the brewery produced half a million barrels of beer each year. Now the biggest brewery site in the UK, it brews 5.5 million barrels a year. The brewery is open for tours, and the entry fee includes a tour of the **Coors Visitor Centre** in Horninglow Street.

TUTBURY
13 miles NE of Lichfield on the A511

This historic small town is dominated by the imposing remains of **Tutbury Castle**, where Mary, Queen of Scots, was imprisoned for a while. During the Civil War, Tutbury Castle remained loyal to the Crown while the town was under the control of Parliament. After a three-week siege, the castle surrendered and in the following year, 1647, Parliament ordered its destruction.

TAMWORTH
7 miles SE of Lichfield on the A51

Dominating Tamworth is the fine Norman motte and bailey **Castle** that originally dates from the 1180s. The Town Hall, built in 1701, was paid for by Thomas Guy, the local Member of Parliament, who was the founder of the London hospital that bears his name.

To the south of Tamworth lies **Drayton Manor Family Theme Park**, and further on stands **Middleton Hall**, the former home of Francis Willoughby, a 17th century naturalist and a founder member of the Royal Society.

To the northwest of Tamworth is the village of **Whittington** that is home to the **Museum of the Staffordshire Regiment** (The Prince of Wales's) at the Victorian Whittington Barracks.

BURNTWOOD
4 miles W of Lichfield on the A5190

The 700 acres of land and water known as **Chasewater Heaths** are an unexpected find in this otherwise urban setting. Criss-crossed by paths and bridleways, it supports many and varied plants and animals, some so rare that a large area has been designated a Site of Special Scientific Interest. The volunteer-run Chasewater Railway, a former colliery railway, operates passenger services behind tank engines between Brownhills West and Norton Lakeside stations.

STAFFORD

The county town of Staffordshire is Saxon in origin, though little of its early history is visible except for the extensive earthworks close to the castle and the foundations of a tiny Saxon chapel in the grounds of St Mary's Church. The grounds of the impressive Norman fortress, **Stafford Castle**, are used for historical re-enactments and also include a medieval herb garden.

One of the most interesting of the many old buildings in Stafford is **The Ancient High House**, a beautiful Elizabethan house built in 1595 that is the largest timber-framed town house in England. It now houses the Museum of the

Staffordshire Yeomanry.

Close to the High House is the **Collegiate Church of St Mary**, an unusual building that dates in part from the late 12th century and was added to in the early English, Gothic and Victorian styles. Sir Izaak Walton was baptised here on 21st September 1593 and his bust can be seen on the north wall of the nave. Each year, at a civic service, a wreath is placed around the bust to commemorate his probable birthday (9th August).

To the north of Stafford lies the ancestral home of the Earl of Harrowby, **Sandon Hall**, which was rebuilt in 1850 after the earlier house had been damaged by fire.

AROUND STAFFORD

STONE

7 miles N of Stafford on the A51

The **Trent and Mersey Canal** played a large part in Stone's early economic development and, today, it still brings work to the town through the building of holiday canal cruisers and a growing tourist trade.

UTTOXETER

12 miles NE of Stafford on the A518

Today, the town is perhaps best known for its **Racecourse**, a popular National Hunt track with 20 days of racing including the stamina-sapping Midlands Grand National held in the spring. Uttoxeter is a traditional, rural market town, with a busy livestock and street market on Wednesdays.

GREAT HAYWOOD

5 miles E of Stafford on the A51

This ancient village has the longest packhorse bridge in England. Built in the 16th century, the **Essex Bridge** still has 14 of its original 40 arches spanning the River Trent.

To the southwest lies one of the most impressive attractions in the county, **Shugborough Hall**, the 17th century seat of the Earls of Lichfield. The wonderful staterooms and former servants' quarters have been beautifully restored, and the magnificent 900-acre estate includes Shugborough Park Farm, home to rare breed animals and host to demonstrations of traditional farming.

ABBOTS BROMLEY

10 miles E of Stafford on the B5234

This delightful 13th century village in the Vale of Trent is best known for its annual **Horn Dance**, the origins of which are lost in the mists of time. In early September each year six male dancers carry the ancient reindeer horns around the village with six others and a fool, a hobby horse, a bowman and Maid Marian, the last being a man in drag.

RUGELEY

7½ miles SE of Stafford on the A51

To the west of Rugeley lies **Cannock Chase**, a surprisingly wild place of heath and woodland that has been designated an Area of Outstanding Natural Beauty. Covering some 20,000 acres, the Chase was once the hunting ground

477 IZAAK WALTON'S COTTAGE

Shallowford

Once the home of the author Izaak Walton, this delightful cottage has been carefully restored and gives an insight into his life and works.

 see page 546

478 THE DOG & PARTRIDGE

Lower Tean

The **Dog & Partridge** is a classic country pub catering admirably for the local community, with well-kept real ales and wide-ranging menus.

 see page 546

479 THE STAR

Church Leigh, nr Stoke-on-Trent

The **Star** is a picturesque, traditional pub in an equally picturesque village.

 see page 549

480 THE RED LION

Little Haywood

The **Red Lion** is a very pleasant spot for a drink or a meal, close to Cannock Chase and the National Trust's Shugborough Hall.

 see page 546

481 THE RAILWAY INN

Penkridge

Locals and visitors from further afield steam along to the **Railway Inn** to enjoy its excellent hospitality and fine food.

 see page 547

of Norman kings and, later, the Bishops of Lichfield. In the unique military cemeteries near **Broadhurst Green**, some 5,000 German soldiers from World War I lie buried. Cannock Chase was used as a training ground during that war and was the last billet for many thousands of soldiers before they left for France. The **Museum of Cannock Chase** at the Valley Heritage Centre illustrates the social and industrial heritage of the area, and there are special exhibits in the Toys Gallery and the Coal Face Gallery.

CANNOCK
9 miles S of Stafford on the A34

To the southwest of Cannock is the Elizabethan **Moseley Old Hall**, which retains much of the original panelling and timber framing. The Hall sheltered King Charles II for a short time following his defeat at the Battle of Worcester in 1651.

WESTON-UNDER-LIZARD
10 miles SW of Stafford on the A5

Situated on the site of a medieval manor house, **Weston Park** has been the home of the Earls of Bradford for 300 years. Disraeli was a frequent visitor here and on one visit presented the house with a grotesque stuffed parrot, which still enjoys the hospitality of Weston Park. Fallow deer and rare breeds of sheep roam the vast grounds that also include nature trails, a miniature railway and a **Museum of Country Bygones**.

ECCLESHALL
6½ miles NW of Stafford on the A5013

For over 1,000 years **Eccleshall Castle** was the palace of the bishops of Lichfield before becoming a family home when the Carter family moved from Yorkshire. The present simple sandstone house is typical of the best architecture of the William and Mary period and incorporates part of the 14th century castle.

A little way north of Eccleshall is Mill Meece Pumping Station, where two magnificent steam engines are kept in pristine condition. An exhibition tells the story of water and the history of the station.

Set in beautiful grounds in the tiny hamlet of **Shallowford**, to the northeast of Eccleshall, is **Izaak Walton's Cottage**, a pretty 17th century half-timbered cottage that was once owned by the famous biographer and author of *The Compleat Angler* and is now a museum.

LEEK

William Morris, founder of the Arts and Crafts movement, lived and worked in Leek for many months between 1875 and 1878 and much of his time here was spent investigating new techniques of dyeing while also reviving the use of traditional dyes. **Leek Art Gallery** has displays on the intricate work of the famous Leek School of Embroidery that was founded by Lady Wardle in the 1870s.

Leek was the home of James Brindley, the 18th century engineer who built much of the early canal network. A water-powered corn mill built by him in 1752 in Mill Street has been restored and now houses the **Brindley Water Museum**, which is devoted to his life and work.

To the northwest of Leek is the village of **Rudyard**, the name chosen for their son by Mr and Mrs Kipling in fond memory of the place where they first met in 1863. The nearby two-mile long **Rudyard Lake** was built in 1831 by John Rennie to feed the Caldon Canal. The west shore of the reservoir is also a section of the Staffordshire Way, the long distance footpath that runs from Mow Cop to Kinver Edge, near Stourbridge.

AROUND LEEK

LONGNOR

8½ miles NE of Leek on the B5053

Found on a gentle slope between the River Manifold and the River Dove, Longnor was the meeting point of several packhorse routes. The Market Square is one of the oldest in England, dating back to medieval times. The village also has some fascinating narrow flagged passages that seem to go nowhere but suddenly emerge into the most beautiful scenery.

FROGHALL

6½ miles SE of Leek on the A52

Froghall Wharf was built along the banks of the Caldon Canal to act as a trans-shipment area for limestone as it came down a railway incline from the quarries to the south of Waterhouses. Here, the limestone was tipped into narrow boats and later into railway wagons to be carried to Stoke-on-Trent. The once-busy Wharf declined after 1920 following the construction of the Manifold Valley Light Railway, which directly linked the quarries with Leek and the national railway network.

To the southeast lies **Hawksmoor Nature Reserve** and bird sanctuary that covers some 300 acres of the Churnet Valley and includes glorious landscapes, abundant natural history and industrial architecture.

CROXDEN

12 miles SE of Leek off the B5032

Tucked away in this secluded hamlet are the romantic ruins of **Croxden Abbey**, founded by the Cistercians in 1176. Although only the west front, south transept wall and a few of the eastern cloisters remain, the Abbey is well worth a visit.

CHEDDLETON

3 miles S of Leek on the A520

As well as being home to the **Churnet Valley Railway and Museum**, this village is also home to the restored Cheddleton Flint Mill, which lies in the rural surroundings of the Churnet valley. The water-powered machinery was used to crush flint that had been brought in by canal and then transported, again by water, to Stoke, where it was used in the hardening of pottery. The small

482 THE CREWE AND HARPUR ARMS

Longnor, nr Buxton

Outstanding cuisine and superb guest accommodation mark out the **Crewe and Harpur Arms** as the region's top restaurant with rooms.

see *page 548*

483 CASTRO'S RESTAURANT & LOUNGE

Cheddleton, nr Leek

Castro's Restaurant & Lounge is open Tuesday to Saturday evenings for a wide selection of dishes with a taste of Latin America.

see *page 549*

Cheddleton

484 LOGGERHEADS

Loggerheads, nr Market Drayton

The **Loggerheads** is a friendly, traditional village pub dispensing hospitality, real ales and cooked-to-order food in generous measure.

 see page 549

museum includes a rare 18th century 'haystack' boiler and a Robey steam engine, and there are also exhibits that relate to the preparation of raw materials for the pottery industry

To the south, **Consall Nature Park** is an RSPB reserve, a quiet and peaceful haven with much to delight the avid birdwatcher.

STOKE-ON-TRENT

It was the presence of the essential raw materials for the manufacture and decoration of ceramics, in particular marl clay, coal and water, that led to the concentration of pottery manufacturers in this area. Though production started in the 17th century, it was the entrepreneurial skills of Josiah Wedgwood and Thomas Minton, who brought the individual potters together in factory-style workplaces, that caused the massive leap forward in production in the 18th century. The Wedgwood and Minton factories were large, but there were also hundreds of small establishments producing a whole range of more utilitarian chinaware; production in The Potteries reached its height towards the end of the 19th century.

Among the many centres and museums telling the story of Stoke and pottery are the **Spode Museum and Visitor Centre;** the **Royal Doulton Visitor Centre**, and the **Wedgwood Visitor Centre and Museum**. **The Potteries Museum and Art Gallery** houses the world's finest collection of Staffordshire ceramics.

Etruria, to the west of the city centre, was created by Josiah Wedgwood in 1769 as a village for the workers at the pottery factory. Though the factory has gone (it moved to Barlaston in the 1940s), Etruria Hall, Wedgwood's home, is still standing in what is now the National Garden Festival site.

Stoke has a famous football team, Stoke City, and a local footballing hero, the late Sir Stanley Matthews. The city has two other famous sons – Arnold Bennett, who immortalised the five pottery towns of Tunstall, Burslem, Hanley, Longton and Stoke in his novels, and John Smith, captain of the ill-fated *Titanic*.

To the south of Stoke-on-Trent

are **Trentham Gardens** that were landscaped by Capability Brown and given a more formal style by Sir Charles Barry, whose work can be seen in the lovely Italian gardens. Although the Hall was demolished in 1911, this style can still be recognised in such buildings as the orangery and sculpture gallery.

AROUND STOKE-ON-TRENT

NEWCASTLE-UNDER-LYME

2 miles W of Stoke-on-Trent on the A53

One of Newcastle-under-Lyme's oldest buildings is the Guildhall, built in 1713 to replace an earlier timber building, which stands beside the base of a medieval cross. The **Borough Museum and Art Gallery**, set in eight acres of parkland, houses a wonderful collection of assorted items from clocks to teapots and paintings to clay pipes. A mile from the town centre, the **New Victoria Theatre** was Europe's first purpose-built 'theatre-in-the-round'.

To the southwest, on an ancient packhorse route from Newcastle-under-Lyme, is the village of **Madeley**, much of which has been designated a conservation area. Its charming focal point is **The Pool**, formed by damming the River Lea to provide waterpower for the corn mill, and now a haven for birds. Further southwest again is the **Dorothy Clive Garden** that was designed in the 1930s by Colonel Harry Clive in memory of his wife. The original garden was a woodland garden created from a gravel pit that had become overgrown with all kinds of trees.

KIDSGROVE

5 miles N of Stoke-on-Trent on the A50

Now chiefly a residential town, Kidsgrove is home to the two **Harecastle Tunnels**, major engineering feats of their time, which carry the Trent and Mersey Canal from Cheshire into The Potteries. It was Josiah Wedgwood who first dreamt of building a canal to link the area with the major Trent and Mersey navigation and thus create a waterway link right across the country from Liverpool to Hull. He fought long and hard to get the necessary Bill passed through Parliament, undaunted by the fact that a 3,000-yard long tunnel would be needed to go through Harecastle Hill. The Bill was passed and, though many scoffed at his plans, Wedgwood's canal and tunnel were built by James Brindley over an 11-year period.

BIDDULPH

5 miles N of Stoke-on-Trent on the A527

The gardens at **Biddulph Grange** are among the most unusual and remarkable in the whole country. The numerous high points include the Egyptian garden with a pyramid and clipped yew obelisks, and the Chinese garden features a joss house, a dragon parterre, a temple and a watch tower. The parterres and the Shelter House and Dahlia Walk have been restored to the way they were in the middle of the 19th century.

485 THE CREWE ARMS HOTEL

Madeley Heath, nr Keele

The **Crewe Arms Hotel** combines the best features of a friendly local, fine restaurant and comfortable hotel.

see page 550

486 BIDDULPH GRANGE GARDEN

Biddulph

Dating from the age of Victorian gardening, the visitor can go on a journey around the world with the individually themed gardens.

 see page 550

261

Suffolk

For much of its length the River Stour forms the county boundary between Suffolk and Essex, and here lies some of the county's most attractive and peaceful countryside. The beauty is largely unspoilt and those travelling through the area will come upon a succession of picturesque, ancient wool towns and villages, historic churches, stately homes and nature reserves. There is the wonderful preserved medieval town of Lavenham, the atmospheric old wool town of Long Melford and, of course, East Bergholt. This was the birthplace, in 1776, of John Constable, and two of his most famous subjects – Flatford Mill and Willy Lot's Cottage – can still be seen today looking much as they would have done in the great artist's day.

Much of inland Suffolk remains rich farmland, with ancient towns and villages along with some of the finest windmills and watermills in the country. While Suffolk has few equals in terms of picturesque countryside and settlements, it is also very much a maritime county, with more than 50 miles of coastline. The whole stretch is a conservation area, with miles of waymarked walks and cycle trails and an abundance of bird and wildlife. This coast has also been a constant source of inspiration for distinguished writers, artists and musicians. Between the major port of Ipswich in the south and the fishing port of Lowestoft in the north are some charming and popular seaside resorts, such as Southwold and Aldeburgh, which have tried their hardest to escape any brash commercialism and retain the charming and genteel atmosphere of a bygone age.

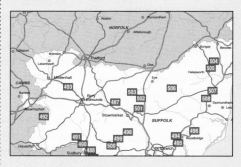

BURY ST EDMUNDS

This glorious Suffolk town takes its name from St Edmund, who was born in Nuremberg in AD 841 and came here as a young man to become the last king of East Anglia and the patron saint of England before St George. A staunch Christian, he was tortured and killed by the Danes in AD 870 and, after he was canonised in AD 910, his remains were moved to the abbey at Beodricsworth (later St Edmundsbury) where his shrine became incorporated into the Norman Abbey Church. The town grew up around the Abbey and soon became an important place of pilgrimage.

The Abbey was dismantled after the Dissolution but the imposing remains can be seen in the colourful **Abbey Gardens**. Originally the Church of St James, **St Edmundsbury Cathedral** was accorded cathedral status in 1914 and the 15th century building has been added to over the years. Work recently finished on a Millennium project to crown the Cathedral with a 140ft Gothic-style lantern tower. Also in the complex is **St Mary's Church**, whose detached tower stands just as it did when erected in the 12th century. The Abbey Visitor Centre, situated in Samson's Tower, has displays concerning the abbey's history.

Along with its fine ecclesiastical buildings, there are many other places of interest in Bury, including museums, galleries and the **Theatre Royal**. Built in 1819 by William Wilkins, who was responsible for the National Gallery, and recently magnificently restored, it is still very much a working theatre; it once staged the premiere of *Charley's Aunt*. To the southwest, near **Horringer**, stands the extraordinary **Ickworth House**. Built in 1795 by the eccentric 4th Earl of Bristol, the massive structure comprises a central rotunda and curved corridors; it was designed to house his various collections that include paintings by Titian, Gainsborough, Hogarth and Reynolds and a magnificent

Ickworth House, Bury St Edmunds

collection of Georgian silver. The house is surrounded by an Italian garden and a park landscaped by Capability Brown.

To the northwest of Bury is **Hengrave Hall**, a rambling Tudor mansion that was built between 1525 and 1538 by Sir Thomas Kytson, a wool merchant. Later owners of the house were the Gage family, one member of which imported various kinds of plum tree from France. Most of the bundles arrived labelled but one had lost its name tag and, when it produced its first crop of luscious green fruit it became known as the green Gage and the name has stuck to this day.

AROUND BURY ST EDMUNDS

IXWORTH

6 miles NE of Bury St Edmunds on the A143

This is superb walking country and **Knettishall Heath Country Park**, close to the border village of Barningham, is the official starting point of the Peddars Way National Trail. Nearby is the pretty village of **Walsham-le-Willow** with its weatherboarded and timber-framed cottages and its ancient parish church.

WOOLPIT

7½ miles E of Bury St Edmunds off the A14

Famous for its bricks, the majority of the old buildings here are faced with 'Woolpit Whites', the yellowish-white brick that looked very much like more expensive

stone. Some of the brick was used in the building of the senate wing of the Capitol in Washington DC. Red bricks were also produced and the village's **Bygones Museum** includes a brick-making display.

To the southeast is the group of villages collectively known as the **Bradfields** – St George, St Clare and Combust – that lie in a particularly delightful part of the countryside. Here, too, are **Bradfield Woods**, which have been managed by coppicing for hundreds of years.

LAVENHAM

10½ miles SE of Bury St Edmunds on the A1141

Lavenham is the most complete of all the original medieval wool towns. The medieval street pattern still exists, along with the market place and cross, and the finest of its many listed buildings is the superb 16th century timbered **Guildhall** which was originally the meeting place of the Guild of Corpus Christi, an organisation that regulated the production of wool.

Originally a 13th century home for Benedictine monks, **The Priory** is now a beautiful half-timbered house dating from around 1600 and, in the original hall, is an important collection of paintings and stained glass whilst the extensive grounds include a kitchen garden, herb garden and a pond.

John Constable went to school in Lavenham and one of his school friends was Jane Taylor, who wrote the words to *Twinkle, Twinkle Little Star*.

SUDBURY

The largest of the wool towns and once a busy port on the River Stour. Along with its three medieval churches, Sudbury is famous as being the birthplace, in 1727, of the painter Thomas Gainsborough; **Gainsborough's House** has more of the artist's work on display than any other gallery.

Northwest of Sudbury lies the attractive village of **Cavendish** where, housed in a 16th century rectory, the **Sue Ryder Foundation Museum** was opened by the Queen in 1979. Further upriver lies the medieval wool town of **Clare**, 'a little town with a lot of history' that is renowned for its **Ancient House**, a timber-framed building dating from 1473 noted for its remarkable pargeting. Another place of historical significance is **Nethergate House**, once the workplace of dyers, weaver and spinners. **Clare Castle Country Park** contains the remains of the castle and moat and has a visitors' centre in the goods shed of a disused railway line.

AROUND SUDBURY

LONG MELFORD

2 miles N of Sudbury off the A134

The heart of this atmospheric old wool town is its long and, in places, fairly broad main street filled with antique shops, bookshops and art galleries. Some of the town's houses are washed in the characteristic Suffolk pink that was originally created by mixing ox blood or sloe juice into the plaster. At the northern end of the street lies a 14-acre green and also **Holy Trinity Church**, an exuberant manifestation of the prosperity of the town in ages past. To the east of the town lies 16th century **Melford Hall**, whose attractions include the panelled banqueting hall where Elizabeth I was entertained and a Beatrix Potter room where some of her watercolours and first editions of her books are on display. She was a frequent visitor to the house as her cousins, the Hyde Parkers, were the then owners. Further north is **Kentwell Hall**, a beautiful moated Tudor mansion.

HAVERHILL

15 miles W of Sudbury on the A1307

Although fire destroyed much of the town in 1665, **Anne of Cleves House**, (where the fourth wife of Henry VIII spent the remainder of her days), escaped and has been restored. To the northeast lies **Kedington**, home to the 'Cathedral of West Suffolk', the Church of St Peter and St Paul.

NEWMARKET

The historic centre of British horse racing, Newmarket is home to some 60 training establishments, 50 stud farms, the world famous thoroughbred sales and two racecourses. The majority of the population is involved in racing in one way or another and, among the racing art and artefact shops and galleries, there are the saddlers – one even has a preserved horse on

488 GAINSBOROUGH'S HOUSE

Sudbury

The birthplace museum of the celebrated artist Thomas Gainsborough.

 see page 551

489 THE BROOK INN

Great Cornard, nr Sudbury

The Brook Inn is a 17th century country pub serving excellent food. Outside seating front and rear.

 see page 551

490 THE PERSEVERANCE

Rodbridge Hill, Long Melford

The Perseverance, known locally as The Percy, is open all day, every day for drinks, and food is served throughout the day Tuesday to Saturday. Three rooms for B&B.

 see page 552

491 THE CHERRY TREE INN

Tye Green, Glemsford, nr Sudbury

Food is served throughout the day at the **Cherry Tree Inn**, a delightful country pub opposite the village green.

 see page 552

265

492 THE THREE
BLACKBIRDS

Wooodditton, nr Newmarket

The **Three Blackbirds**
combines the essence of a
traditional English village
pub with the qualities of a
high-class restaurant.

 see page 553

493 WEST STOW
ANGLO-SAXON
VILLAGE

West Stow

An exciting reconstruction
of an Anglo-Saxon village
based on evidence found in
excavations during the late
'60s and early '70s.

 see page 552

---

display - Robert the Devil, the
runner-up in the 1880 Derby.

As far back as medieval times,
this area was popular with riders,
and in 1605 James I paused here on
a journey north to enjoy a spot of
hare coursing and so taken was he
with the town, that he moved the
royal court here. The tradition
continued with Charles I but it was
Charles II who really established the
royal sport here when he initiated
the Town Plate, a race that he won
twice as a rider and that, in a
modified form, still exists today. The
National Horseracing Museum
chronicles the history of the sport
from its royal beginnings through to
the top trainers and jockeys of
today. Close by is Palace House,
which contains the remains of
Charles II's palace, while in the same
street is **Nell Gwynn's House** that
some say was connected to the
palace by an underground tunnel.
Other places in the town associated
with horses are **Tattersalls**, where
the leading thoroughbred sales take
place between April and December;
the British Racing School; and the
National Stud that has, at one time,
been home to three Derby winners
– Blakeney, Mill Reef and Grundy.

To the southeast of Newmarket
is the pretty village of **Dalham**,
where the vast majority of the
buildings are still thatched. The
village is also the home of **Dalham
Hall** which was built in the early
18th century on the orders of the
Bishop of Ely. The home of the
Duke of Wellington for several years
it was, much later, bought by Cecil
Rhodes who, unfortunately, died

before taking up residence.

The ancient village of **Exning**,
to the northwest of Newmarket, has
been the home of Roman, Iceni,
Saxon and Norman settlers. Struck
by the plague during the Iceni
occupation, its market was moved to
the next village and thus the town
of Newmarket acquired its name.

AROUND NEWMARKET

MILDENHALL

9 miles NE of Newmarket on the A11

For an insight into the town's
heritage, the excellent **Mildenhall
and District Museum** contains a
wealth of local history exhibits,
including the artefacts from the
nearby RAF and USAAF base and
the story of the Mildenhall
Treasure, a cache of 4th century
Roman silverware found by a
ploughman in 1946 and now in the
British Museum. This parish is the
largest in Suffolk and it is fitting
that it also boasts a magnificent
parish church, dedicated to St Mary,
which dominates the heart of the
town.

In the village of **Barton Mills**,
Sir Alexander Fleming had a
country house and perhaps worked
on the discovery of penicillin in his
garden shed.

WEST STOW

9 miles NE of Newmarket off the A1101

In 1849, a Saxon cemetery was
discovered here and further
excavations have revealed traces of
a Roman settlement and the Saxon
layout of this village. Several

buildings have been constructed using 5th century tools and methods and this fascinating village is now part of the **West Stow Country Park**.

IPSWICH

A Roman port and the largest in Anglo Saxon Britain, Ipswich prospered on the exportation of wool, textiles and agricultural products. Of the great Victorian buildings here the most memorable are **Old Custom House**, the Town Hall and the splendid **Tolly Cobbold Brewery**, rebuilt at the end of the 19th century. **Christchurch Mansion** survives from an older age, a beautiful Tudor home in glorious parkland, with a major collection of works by, most notably, Constable and Gainsborough. The town's Museum displays a wealth of exhibits from natural history through to a reconstructed Roman villa, while the **Ipswich Transport Museum** concerns itself with vehicles both mechanical and self-propelled.

The town's most famous son is undoubtedly Thomas Wolsey, who was born here in 1475 and who went on to become Lord Chancellor under Henry VIII.

On the outskirts of the town lies **Orwell Country Park**, an area of wood, heath and reed beds by the Orwell estuary. The Ipswich & Gipping Valley Local Nature Reserves Management Project comprises ten nature reserves stretching up from Ipswich to Stowmarket.

AROUND IPSWICH

HELMINGHAM

8 miles N of Ipswich on the B1077

This village is home to **Helmingham Hall**, a moated Tudor house, and there's another moated hall in the nearby village of **Otley**, the home of Bartholomew Gosnold, who sailed to the New World, discovered Cape Cod and founded the settlement of Jamestown, Virginia.

WOODBRIDGE

7 miles NE of Ipswich on the A12

A market town for over 1,000 years, Woodbridge stands at the head of the Deben estuary and is a place of considerable charm, character and history. Shipbuilding flourished here and it was in a Woodbridge ship that Sir Francis Drake sailed in the 16th century.

The town's splendid Shire Hall now houses the **Suffolk Horse Museum** which is devoted to the Suffolk Punch breed of heavy working horse – the oldest such breed in the world. Other buildings of note are the town's two marvellous mills, both still in working order – **Tide Mill** dates from the late 18th century and uses the power of the sea to turn its wheels and **Buttrum's Mill**, named after the last miller, is a tower mill standing just west of the town centre.

On the opposite bank of the River Deben, lies **Sutton Hoo**, a group of a dozen grassy barrows that hit the headlines in 1939 when

494 THE CHERRY TREE INN

Woodbridge

The **Cherry Tree** is a fine old inn with CAMRA-approved ales, a wide variety of excellent food and comfortable modern accommodation.

see page 554

495 THE STATION GUEST HOUSE & WHISTLESTOP CAFÉ

Woodbridge

By the railway station in Woodbridge, the **Station Guest House & Whistlefoot Café** offers quality in both B&B accommodation and all-day snacks and meals.

see page 554

496 THE ELEPHANT & CASTLE INN

Eyke, nr Woodbridge

The **Elephant & Castle** is a 17th century pub serving popular dishes every session. Three rooms for B&B.

🍴 see page 555

497 THE WHITE HORSE

Tattingstone, nr Ipswich

The Sunday roasts are among the many excellent dishes served at the **White Horse**.

🍴 see page 555

498 THE RED LION

Great Bricett, nr Ipswich

The **Red Lion** is a family-run, family-friendly country pub open all day for drinks and excellent food.

🍴 see page 556

499 THE RED LION

Bildeston

The **Red Lion** is a lovely old village pub with a traditional ambience for enjoying real ales and good home cooking.

🍴 see page 556

excavations unearthed the outline of an 80 feet long Saxon ship filled with a great hoard of treasure. It is believed that the ship was the burial place of Raedwald, a King of East Anglia who died in about AD625. This is one of the most important archaeological sites in the country, and the National Trust provides impressive facilities for visitors.

ORFORD
16½ miles NE of Ipswich on the B1084

Although the keep is all that remains of Henry II's **Castle**, it remains an impressive sight and the climb up the spiral staircase provides some splendid views. The Castle and the grand 14th century St Bartholomew's Church are a reminder that Orford was once an important town and a thriving port until the steadily growing shingle bank of Orford Ness gradually cut it off from the sea.

Though the sea has gone the river remains and, in the summer, the quayside is alive with yachts and pleasure craft. Across the other side of the river lies **Orford Ness**, the largest vegetated shingle spit in England and home to a variety of rare flora and fauna as well as a lighthouse. Now owned by the National Trust, the Ness can be reached by ferry, and there are also boat trips to the RSPB reserve of **Havergate Island**, the haunt of avocet and tern.

FELIXSTOWE
10 miles SE of Ipswich on the A14

In the early 19th century Colonel Tomline of Orwell Park created a port here to rival Harwich and went on to develop Felixstowe as a resort. By the time of his death in 1887, most of his dreams had been realised, but he did not live to see the completion of the **Pier**. Along with all the other usual attractions for holidaymakers, there is also the **Felixstowe Water Clock**, a curious piece that is assembled from industrial bits and pieces.

The original fishing hamlet from which the Victorian town was developed is now called Felixstowe Ferry – a cluster of holiday homes, fishing sheds and a Martello Tower. The southernmost tip of this peninsula is **Landguard Point** where a nature reserve supports rare plants and migrating birds. Close by is Landguard Fort, which was built in 1718 to protect Harwich Harbour, and is now home to the **Felixstowe Museum** with its displays of local history, model aircraft and model paddle steamers.

EAST BERGHOLT
9 miles SW of Ipswich on the B1070

It was in this picturesque village that John Constable was born and, although his actual house is no longer standing, the site is marked by a plaque. Close by is Moss Cottage, which he once used as his studio, and the parish **Church of St Mary**, which contains memorials to Constable, his family and his friends.

A leafy lane leads south from the village to the River Stour and two of Constable's favourite subjects, **Flatford Mill** and **Willy Lot's Cottage**. At nearby Flatford, **Bridge Cottage** houses a Constable display.

The villages of Capel St Mary, Brantham and Stratford St Mary all have links with Constable, and it was in Stratford that Henry Williamson, author of *Tarka the Otter*, saw his first otter.

NAYLAND

14 miles SW of Ipswich on the B1087

A charming village found on a particularly beautiful stretch of the River Stour, Nayland has two fine 15th century buildings – Alston Court and the Guildhall – whilst its original 15th century wooden Abels Bridge was replaced a century later by a humped-back bridge that allowed barges to pass underneath.

HADLEIGH

8½ miles W of Ipswich on the B1070

This once prosperous wool town has a harmonious variety of architectural styles – from timber-framed buildings to elegant Regency and Victorian houses – but the gem here is the 15th century **Guildhall** with its two overhanging storeys. There are two good walks from Hadleigh: over the medieval **Toppesfield Bridge** and along the River Brett; and along the disused railway track between the town and Raydon to the south. To the northwest is the photogenic postcard village of **Kersey**, whose main street has a **Water Splash**; this and the 700-year-old Bell Inn have featured in many films.

STOWMARKET

11 miles NW of Ipswich on the A14

In the heart of Suffolk, Stowmarket enjoyed a period of rapid growth when the River Gipping was still navigable to Ipswich, and again when the railway arrived. Much of the town's history is brought to life at the **Museum of East Anglian Life** which is found surrounded by meadowland on the old **Abbot's Hall** estate, where the aisled barn dates from the 13th century. At Stonham Barns, to the east of Stowmarket, are the **Redwings Horse Rescue Centre**, with grazing for over 30 rescued horses, ponies and donkeys, and the **Suffolk Owl Sanctuary.**

ALDEBURGH

24 miles NE of Ipswich on the A1094

This is yet another town that had flourishing fishing and shipbuilding industries – Drake's *Greyhound* and *Pelican* were built at Slaughden, which was long ago taken by the sea. This village was also the birthplace, in 1754, of the poet George Crabbe, who created the character Peter Grimes, a solitary fisherman, who later became the subject of an opera by another Aldeburgh resident, Benjamin Britten. It was Britten who, in 1948, started the **Aldeburgh Festival**, a world-renowned arts festival based mainly at **The Maltings** at nearby **Snape**. One of the town's major benefactors was Newson Garrett, a wealthy businessman who was the town's first mayor. As well as developing the Maltings, he

---

500 THE RED ROSE INN

Lindsey Tye, Lindsey, nr Ipswich

The **Red Rose Inn** is a centuries-old village pub serving top-quality food.

see page 556

501 THREE BEARS COTTAGE

Middlewood Green, nr Stowmarket

Three Bears Cottage is a spacious converted barn offering comfort and privacy for up to 6 B&B or self-catering guests.

see page 556

502 THE FLEECE INN

Mendlesham, nr Stowmarket

The Fleece is an attractive 15th century village inn serving excellent home-cooked food – don't miss the pies!

see page 557

503 THE TROWEL & HAMMER INN

Cotton, nr Stowmarket

Superb food is one of the many reasons for a visit to the **Trowel & Hammer**, a country pub of character and class.

see page 557

Village Duck Pond, Alderburgh

and in the church itself is a wonderful stained glass window by John Piper depicting three Britten oratorios. The latest tribute to Britten is a huge metal clam shell designed by Maggie Hambling. It stands on the beach between Aldeburgh and the unique holiday village of **Thorpeness**. Further up the coast is the Sizewell nuclear power station, while inland the busy town of Leiston is home to the fascinating **Long Shop Museum**, once the works of the renowned Garrett engineering works. Back along the coast is what remains of the one-time capital of East Anglia, **Dunwich**, which over the centuries was claimed by the sea. Dunwich Heath is one of Suffolk's most important conservation areas, while nearby **Minsmere**, best reached through the village of Westleton, is a marvellous RSPB sanctuary.

LOWESTOFT

The most easterly town in Britain, Lowestoft's heyday as a major fishing port came during the late 19th and early 20th centuries and, although the industry has declined since World War I, it remains a fishing port, and is also a popular holiday resort. Its main attractions are its lovely golden sands, safe swimming and two piers - one of these, **Claremont Pier**, built in 1902, was a landing place for daytrippers arriving on the famous Belle steamers.

produced a remarkable daughter, Elizabeth, who was the first woman doctor in England (she qualified in Paris) and the first woman mayor (of Aldeburgh in 1908). The most interesting of Aldeburgh's older buildings is the **Moot Hall**, a 16th century timber-framed hall which has a little museum of the town's history.

Benjamin Britten's grave, along with those of his friend Peter Pears and Imogen Holst, is in the churchyard of St Peter and St Paul,

The history of the town and its links with the sea are detailed in the **Lowestoft and East Suffolk**

Maritime Museum and, nearby, the **Royal Naval Patrol Museum** remembers the minesweeping service.

Just north of the town is the largest theme park in East Anglia, **Pleasurewood Hills.** A little further afield lies **Somerleyton Hall**, one of the country's grandest and most distinctive stately homes, built in the Italian style by Samuel Morton Peto. Along with magnificent wood carvings and notable paintings, the grounds include a renowned yew-hedge maze created in 1846, a little miniature railway and, still part of the estate, Fritton Lake Countryworld. Close by is **Herringfleet Windmill**, a beautiful black-tarred smock mill which is the last survivor of the Broadland wind pumps whose job it was to assist in draining the marshes. A little way south of Lowestoft, at **Carlton Colville**, is the **East Anglia Transport Museum** where visitors can enjoy rides on buses, trams and trolleybuses. Further south again is the small resort of **Kessingland**, the home of the **Suffolk Wildlife Park**, which includes a re-creation of the Plains of Africa.

AROUND LOWESTOFT

SOUTHWOLD

10 miles S of Lowestoft on the A1095

The most interesting building at this civilised seaside resort is **Buckenham House** which, despite its classic Georgian exterior, actually dates from the mid 16th century and was built for a wealthy Tudor merchant. Many features from that age survive, including the brickwork and heavy timbered ceilings.

The town's maritime heritage is recorded in the **Museum**, which is housed in a Dutch-style cottage, and in the Sailors Reading Room.

On the other side of the River Blyth is **Walberswick** which was also once a flourishing fishing port. Today, it is best known for its bird sanctuary, **Walberswick and Westleton Heaths**. Inland lies one of the wonders of Suffolk, the **Church of the Holy Trinity** at **Blythburgh** that rises from the reed beds and is visible for miles around. Dubbed the 'Cathedral of the Marshes', its grandeur reflects the days when Blythburgh was a prosperous port until the river silted up.

HALESWORTH

14 miles SW of Lowestoft on the A144

An ancient market town, Halesworth reached its peak as a trading place when the River Blyth was made navigable as far as here in 1756. Along with some fine architecture the chief attraction here is the **Halesworth and District Museum**, housed in the town's station buildings.

FRAMLINGHAM

25 miles SW of Lowestoft on the B1119

This old market town is dominated by the **Castle** that was built by Roger Bigod, 2nd Earl of Norfolk,

507 THE GRIFFIN INN AT YOXFORD

Yoxford

The **Griffin Inn** is a fine old hostelry with an excellent restaurant and rooms for B&B guests.

 see page 559

508 PISTACHIO RESTAURANT

Kelsale, nr Saxmundham

In a lovely old thatched building, **Pistachio Restaurant** offers menus that combine classic skills with flair and imagination.

see page 559

in the 12th century. It remained the home of the Earls and Dukes of Norfolk for generations before they moved to Arundel in 1635. Still in remarkably good condition, nine of the castle's 13 towers are accessible and, on one side, the view is of a noted bird sanctuary. In the splendid **Church of St Michael** is the beautifully adorned tomb of Henry Fitzroy, the illegitimate son of Henry VIII.

On the village green at **Saxtead Green** is a particularly attractive white 18th century **Post Mill** which dates back to 1796 and is, arguably, the best example of such a mill in the world.

BECCLES

8 miles W of Lowestoft on the A145

Situated at the southernmost point of the Broads, Beccles is an ancient town that was once a major supplier of herring to St Edmundsbury Abbey. One of the few buildings to survive the fires that ravaged the town in the 16th and 17th centuries is Roos Hall, a gabled Dutch-style building dating from 1583. Another Dutch-style building houses the Beccles and District Museum, while the town's printing industry is remembered at its own Printing Museum at the Newgate works of printer William Clowes.

BUNGAY

13½ miles W of Lowestoft on the A144

An ancient town on the River Waveney, Bungay is best known for its **Castle**, which was built by Hugh Bigod, 1st Earl of Norfolk, as a rival to Henry II's castle at Orford. It was another Bigod, Roger, who came to Bungay in 1294 and built the round tower and mighty outer walls that still stand today. At **Flixton** is the **Norfolk and Suffolk Aviation Museum** which stands on the site of the USAAF Liberator base of World War II.

Surrey

Although the northern part of Surrey, which once ran all the way up to the south bank of the River Thames through the capital, has seemingly been engulfed by Greater London, this is an area rich in stately homes, notably the most magnificent royal palace of all – Hampton Court. In among this prosperous commuter land there are also several excellent racecourses, including Epsom, home of The Derby and The Oaks. The influence of London is soon lost as the countryside to the south and west gives way to leafy lanes, green fields and two famous natural features – the Hog's Back and the Devil's Punch Bowl.

Guildford, the county town of Surrey, is home to one of only two Anglican cathedrals built in England since the Reformation – the other is in Liverpool. While many travel through the county on their way to the south coast, it is well worth pausing here and taking in the quintessentially English villages, such as Chiddingfold, the old Georgian market towns of Godalming and Farnham, and the genteel Victorian towns such as Haslemere that developed with the arrival of the railway.

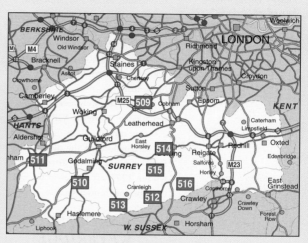

WEYBRIDGE

A surprisingly old settlement on the River Wey, this town once possessed a palace, Oatlands Park, where, in 1540, Henry VIII married his fifth wife, Catherine Howard. In 1907, the world's first purpose-built motor racing track was constructed on the nearby Brooklands estate and, although racing on this world-famous banked circuit came to an end with the outbreak of World War I, the old Edwardian clubhouse still stands, home to the **Brooklands Museum**.

Just to the southwest lies the remarkable **Whiteley Village**, a 200-acre model village founded on the instructions of the owner of a famous Bayswater department store who in 1907 left money in his will to house his retired staff.

AROUND WEYBRIDGE

RICHMOND

9 miles NE of Weybridge on the A316

Situated on a sweeping bend on the River Thames, the older part of this charming town is centred on Richmond Green, a genuine village green. Handsome 17th and 18th century houses flank the southern edges of the green, while the southwestern side was the site of 12th century Richmond Palace, where Elizabeth I died in 1603.

Richmond Hill leads upwards from the town centre and commands breathtaking views that both Turner and Reynolds have captured. A little further up the hill is an entrance to **Richmond Park** some 2,400 acres of open land on which deer roam.

On the banks of the Thames, south of Richmond, is **Ham House**, one of the best examples of a Stuart stately home in the country.

KINGSTON UPON THAMES

7 miles NE of Weybridge on the A308

Kingston was a thriving medieval market town and ancient and modern can be found side by side; close to the functional 1930s Guildhall is the **Coronation Stone**, which is said to have been used in the crowning of at least six Saxon kings.

A couple of miles southwest of Kingston lies one of the most magnificent royal residences, **Hampton Court**, which was built in 1516 by Cardinal Wolsey, Henry VIII's Lord Chancellor. After Wolsey's fall from power, the palace came into royal possession and the buildings and magnificent gardens seen today are the work of Henry VIII, Charles II and William III. The most famous feature in the 60 acres of grounds is undoubtedly the Maze, first planted in 1713.

ESHER

4½ miles E of Weybridge off the A3

The town has an excellent racecourse, **Sandown Park**, and is also home to the beautiful **Claremont Landscape Garden**, begun in 1715 and believed to be one of the earliest surviving examples of an English landscape garden. Over the years, some of the greatest names in garden history were involved in its creation, including Capability Brown, John Vanbrugh and Charles Bridgeman.

COBHAM
4 miles SE of Weybridge on the A245

A busy residential town, Cobham has a Bus Museum with the largest collection anywhere of London buses. To the north lies 19th century **Foxwarren Park**, a bizarre house with eerie gables and multi-coloured bricks, while to the west is **Painshill Park**, a white 18th century house with particularly fine grounds. Just beyond Painshill, on Chatley Heath, is a unique **Semaphore Tower** that was once part of the Royal Navy's signalling system for relaying messages between Portsmouth and the Admiralty in London.

WOKING
6 miles SW of Weybridge on the A320

Amidst the largely Victorian buildings in this commuter town is the **Shah Jehan Mosque**, the first purpose built mosque in Britain.

To the east of Woking is the Royal Horticultural Society's internationally renowned **Wisley Garden**; to the west Brookwood cemetery, the largest in the country (it once even had its own railway station) and the final resting place of John Singer Sargent, Dame Rebecca West and the murderess Edith Thompson.

Claremont Landscape Gardens, Esher

LIGHTWATER
9½ miles SW of Weybridge on the A322

For many Londoners, Lightwater represents the first taste of countryside from the metropolis. The visitor centre at **Lightwater Country Park** has a fascinating collection of exhibits about the history and natural history of this area of heath and woodland.

VIRGINIA WATER
6 miles NW of Weybridge on the B389

The water referred to here is a large artificial lake that is set within the mature woodland at the southern end of **Windsor Great Park**. The picturesque ruins on the lakeside are the genuine remains of a Roman temple that once stood at Leptis Magna in Libya and the Valley Gardens contain an unusual 100 feet totem pole that was

509 PAINSHILL PARK

Cobham

A beautiful 18th century landscape garden with many interesting walks to view all the attractions.

🏛 *see page 560*

The historic village of Compton, near Guildford, was once an important stopping place on the old Pilgrims' Way and was also the home of the 19th century artist GF Watts who, at the age of 69, married a painter and potter 33 years his junior. His wife designed the Watts' Memorial Gallery, dedicated to the artist's work, along with the Watts Mortuary Chapel, an exuberant building completed in 1904.

510 THE STAR AT WITLEY

Witley

The **Star at Witley** is a popular family-friendly pub serving a good choice of traditional pub food.

see page 562

erected here in 1958 to mark the centenary of British Columbia. Just to the west of this selected residential community is the famous **Wentworth Golf Course**, while to the north are the historic fields of **Runnymede** where King John sealed the Magna Carta in 1215.

GUILDFORD

The ancient county town of Surrey, where Henry II built a Castle on high ground, is the home of one of only two new Anglican cathedrals to have been built since the Reformation (the other is Liverpool); the impressive **Guildford Cathedral** was consecrated in 1961. A few years later, in 1968, the University of Surrey was relocated from London to Guildford and, on its pleasant, leafy hillside site, the campus contains a number of striking buildings.

Back in the city centre, **Guildford Museum** has an exhibition devoted to Lewis Carroll, who died here in 1898, and at the foot of the castle is the famous **Yvonne Arnaud Theatre**.

Just east of Guildford lies **Clandon Park**, a magnificent 18th century country mansion renowned for its superb marble hall, sumptuous decorations and fine plasterwork. Further on lies the distinctive brick house of **Hatchlands Park**, which was designed in the mid-18th century for Admiral Boscawen after his famous victory at the Battle of Louisburg.

To the west of Guildford lies a ridge, known as the **Hog's Back**, which dominates the surrounding landscape; the main road following the ridge offers fantastic views.

AROUND GUILDFORD

GODALMING
4 miles SW of Guildford on the A3100

A market town since the early 14th century, Godalming later became a centre for the local textile industry before becoming an important staging post between London and Portsmouth in the 18th century. The town's most interesting building is arguably the **Pepperpot**, the former early-19th century town hall that used to house an interesting **Museum of Local History**, which has since found new premises in Wealden House opposite. However, the town is best known for **Charterhouse**, the famous public school that moved from London to a hillside site north of the town in 1872. Among its most striking features are the 150 feet Founder's Tower and the chapel designed by Giles Gilbert Scott as a memorial to the First World War dead.

To the southeast of Godalming lies the renowned **Winkworth Arboretum**, a wooded hillside that contains a magnificent collection of rare trees and shrubs.

HASLEMERE
12 miles SW of Guildford on the A286

This genteel town owes much of its

development to the arrival of the railway in 1859 that saw it become a comfortable residential place for well-to-do commuters. However, some notable pre-Victorian buildings still exist, among them the Town Hall of 1814 and the **Tolle House Almshouses**.

The **Haslemere Educational Museum** was founded in 1888 by local surgeon and Quaker, Sir James Hutchinson.

ELSTEAD

6½ miles SW of Guildford on the B3001

An attractive village on the River Wey, Elstead is home to an 18th century watermill – Elstead Mill, standing four storeys high and topped with a Palladian cupola. To the northeast of Elstead one of the best collections of Surrey farm buildings can be seen at Peper Harrow Farm where a large early 17th century granary standing on 25 wooden pillars is a striking sight.

FARNHAM

10 miles W of Guildford on the A31

After the Norman Conquest, the Bishop of Winchester built himself a castle on a rise above the town centre. An impressive building, **Farnham Castle** remained in the hands of the Bishops of Winchester until 1927.

Other historic buildings here include a row of 17th century gabled almshouses and Willmer House, a handsome Georgian building that is now home to the **Farnham Museum**. The writer William Cobbett, best known for his *Rural Rides*, was the son of a

Farnham labourer and is buried beside his father in St Andrew's churchyard.

Just to the southeast are the atmospheric ruins of 12th century **Waverley Abbey**, the first Cistercian abbey to be built in England. Close by, near the attractive village of **Tilford**, is the **Rural Life Centre and Old Kiln Museum**, a museum of rural life covering the years from 1750 to 1960.

REIGATE

Once an important outpost for the de Warenne family, the assertive Norman rulers whose sphere of influence stretched from the south coast to the North Downs, Reigate retains an attractive mix of Victorian, Georgian and older buildings, despite its rapid postwar expansion.

Just to the northwest lies **Reigate Heath**, a narrow area of open heathland that is home to the unique **Windmill Church**, the only church in the world to be situated in a windmill.

AROUND REIGATE

LIMPSFIELD

9 miles E of Reigate off the A25

In the churchyard here lies the grave of the composer Frederick Delius, who died in France in 1934 but had wished to be buried in an English country graveyard. Sir Thomas Beecham, a great admirer of Delius, read the funeral oration and conducted an orchestra playing

511 THE BAT & BALL

Boundstone, nr Farnham

The **Bat & Ball** is tops for hospitality, food and drink – a real hidden gem a mile from Farnham.

🍴 see page 561

512 THE THREE COMPASSES

Alfold

The **Three Compasses** is a delightful traditional pub well known for its hospitality and good wholesome food.

🍴 see page 562

513 THE PUNCHBOWL INN

Oakwoodhill, nr Ockley

The **Punchbowl** is an inn of wide appeal, with good food, Cask Marque ales and an excellent wine list.

🍴 see page 563

514 HASKETTS TEA & COFFEE SHOP

South Street, Dorking

Haskett's is a traditional setting for enjoying a fine range of teas, coffees and sweet and savoury snacks.

see page 563

515 THE ROYAL OAK

Holmbury St Mary, nr Dorking

The **Royal Oak** is a delightfully welcoming pub in lovely walking country, with real ales, good food and three rooms for B&B.

see page 562

516 ZIEGLER'S GARDEN STATUARY & YA YA'S TEA ROOM

Newdigate

Ziegler's stocks a wide range of beautiful garden ornaments in stone, lead, bronze, cast iron and wood. It also has a charming little tea room.

 see page 564

works by Delius. Sir Thomas died in 1961 and was originally buried at Brookwood Cemetery near Woking. In 1991 his body was transferred to Limpsfield, where he was buried close to Delius. Also lying here are the conductor Norman del Mar and the pianist Eileen Joyce. **Detillens**, a rare 15th century hall house, contains collections of period furniture, china and militaria.

LINGFIELD

9½ miles SE of Reigate on the B2028

'Leafy' Lingfield's Church of St Peter and St Paul has been enlarged down the years to create what has become known as the 'Westminster Abbey of Surrey'. Features include a rare double nave and an exceptional collection of monumental brasses. Near the village of **Outwood**, the **Post Mill**, built in 1665, is recognised as the country's oldest working windmill.

DORKING

5½ miles W of Reigate on the A25

An ancient settlement that stands at the intersection of Stane Street and the Pilgrims' Way, Dorking owes much of its character to the Victorians.

Just to the north of the town lies **Box Hill**, whose 563 feet summit rises sharply from the valley floor.

To the northwest of Dorking is **Polesden Lacey**, a Regency villa that was extensively modified by the Edwardian hostess Mrs Ronald Greville. Four miles southwest of Dorking, **Leith Hill** is the highest point in the southeast of England, at 965 feet above sea level. On the southern slopes of the hill is a lovely rhododendron wood planted by Josiah Wedgwood, grandson of the illustrious potter.

EPSOM

7 miles NW of Reigate on the A24

The old market town of Epsom is known throughout the world as the home of the Derby. Racing was formalised in 1779 when a party of aristocratic sportsmen, led by Lord Derby, established a race for three-year-old fillies that was named after the family home at Banstead – The Oaks. This was followed a year later by a race for all three-year-olds, The Derby, which was named after the founder himself.

Polesden Lacey

Sussex

Sussex saw one of the most momentous events in England's history when, in 1066, William, Duke of Normandy landed with his army at Pevensey and went on to defeat the Saxon King Harold at Battle on the 14th of October. Battle Abbey was built on the spot where Harold fell, and both here and in nearby Hastings there are museums and exhibitions detailing this historic victory. The south coast has been no stranger to invasion and, in the days before the establishment of the Royal Navy, the confederation of Cinque Ports provided fleets of ships to defend the coast. Today, the Sussex coast is best known for the elegant and genteel resorts of Eastbourne, Bexhill, Rottingdean, Worthing and, of course, Brighton.

Inland the rolling landscape of the South Downs provides glorious walking country and the South Downs Way long distance footpath follows the crest of the hills from Winchester to Beachy Head near Eastbourne. Here there are numerous ancient market towns and a wealth of fine stately homes but Sussex is also renowned for its glorious gardens such as Wakehurst Place, Herstmonceux and Leonardslee.

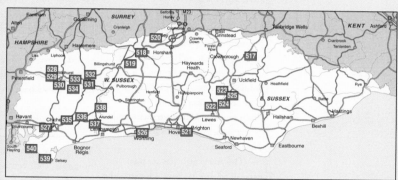

HASTINGS

This was the principal town of a small Saxon province long before William the Conqueror landed nearby but it was to Hastings that the victorious William returned after the battle that took place six miles away. The Castle he built is now in ruins, but a medieval siege tent contains a permanent display – the **1066 Story at Hastings Castle**. After the Conquest, Hastings became a leading Cinque Port, a role it played until the harbour began to silt up in Elizabethan times. However, the fishing industry has managed to survive and the tall wooden huts used for drying nets remain a familiar feature. The Church of St Nicholas is home to the **Fishermen's Museum**, where the centerpiece is the old sailing lugger *The Enterprise*.

The town also has its own version of the Bayeux Tapestry, the **Hastings Embroidery**.

Herstmonceux Castle

AROUND HASTINGS

BEXHILL
5 miles W of Hastings on the A259

This small seaside resort was founded in the 1880s by the influential De La Warr family and among the many late Victorian buildings is the striking **De La Warr Pavilion**, built in the 1930s and now a renowned centre for arts and culture. A seemingly conservative resort, Bexhill played host to the birth of British motor racing in 1902, an event that is remembered annually with the Bexhill Festival of Motoring held in May. Bexhill was also the first seaside town to allow mixed bathing on its beaches - a very daring move back in 1900!

HERSTMONCEUX
11½ miles NW of Hastings on the A271

This village is famous as being the home of 15th century **Herstmonceux Castle** - to where, in 1948, the Royal Observatory at Greenwich moved. Although the Observatory has since moved on again, the castle is now home to the Herstmonceux Science Centre.

BATTLE
6 miles NW of Hastings on the A2100

This historic settlement is renowned as being the site of the momentous battle, on 14 October 1066, between the armies of Harold, King of England, and William,

Duke of Normandy. **Battle Abbey** was built on the spot where Harold fell.

BURWASH

13 miles NW of Hastings on the A265

An exceptionally pretty village and one time centre of the Wealden iron industry, Burwash is home to Rampyndene, a handsome 17th century timber-framed house. Just outside the village stands Bateman's, a Jacobean house that was the home of Rudyard Kipling from 1902 until his death in 1936.

To the south is **Brightling**, the home of the Georgian eccentric, 'Mad' Jack Fuller. One of the first people to recognise the talents of the great painter Turner, Fuller also built several imaginative follies including **Brightling Needle**, a 40ft stone obelisk.

NORTHIAM

9 miles N of Hastings on the A28

The picturesque village of Northiam is the southern terminal for the **Kent and East Sussex Railway** that runs steam trains to Tenterden during the summer.

Just to the northwest lies **Great Dixter House**, one of the finest late medieval hall houses in the country, with superb gardens designed by Lutyens.

To the west, lies **Bodiam Castle**, begun in 1385 and one of the last great medieval fortresses to be built in England. Bodiam was once the centre of a thriving hop-growing region, served by 'The Hoppers' Line' of the Kent & East Sussex Railway.

RYE

9 miles NE of Hastings on the A259

A picturesque town and Cinque Port; its harbour gradually silted up and it now lies further down the Rother estuary. **Rye Harbour Nature Reserve**, at the river mouth, is a large area of sea, saltmarsh, sand and shingle that supports a wide range of plant, animal and bird life. A strategically important place due to its hilltop position, Rye had a substantial perimeter wall to defend its northern approaches and the Landgate, one of its four gateways, still survives. One of Rye's many interesting buildings is the handsome Georgian residence, **Lamb House** (National Trust), which was the home of the novelist Henry James (1898-1916). A later occupant was the prolific writer EF Benson, best remembered for his Mapp and Lucia novels.

To the south lies **Camber Castle** (English Heritage), a fine example of the coastal defences built by Henry VIII.

HAYWARDS HEATH

The oldest part of this town is centred on the conservation area around **Muster Green**, an open space where the 16th century Sergison Arms can be found. Modern Haywards Heath grew up around its station on the Brighton line – other local villages refused to allow the railway to run through them.

517 THE RED LION

Chelwood Gate

The **Red Lion** attracts a large and loyal following with a particularly fine selection of home-cooked dishes.

see page 564

518 THE BOARS HEAD
TAVERN

Worthing Road, Horsham

The **Boars Head Tavern** is a very friendly, convivial pub with great food and drink and the bonus of wonderful views of the North Downs.

see page 565

519 THE QUEENS HEAD

Barns Green, nr Horsham

The **Queens Head** is a splendid country inn with good food and beer and a welcome for all the family.

see page 566

520 THE STAR INN

Rusper

The **Star Inn** shines with its well-kept ales and dishes of worldwide inspiration.

see page 566

AROUND HAYWARDS HEATH

HORSHAM

10½ miles NW of Haywards Heath on the A281

An ancient town that dates back to Saxon times, Horsham's architectural gem is **The Causeway**, a tree-lined street that runs from the town hall to the Church of St Mary and the gabled 16th century Causeway House that is now home to the **Horsham Museum**. Just outside the town is the famous Christ's Hospital School, a Bluecoat school founded in London in 1552 by Edward VI that moved here in 1902.

To the southeast is the village of **Lower Beeding**, home to the beautiful **Leonardslee Gardens** that were laid out in this natural valley in the late 19th century.

CRAWLEY

8½ miles NW of Haywards Heath on the A23

One of the original new towns created after the New Towns Act of 1946, Crawley has swallowed up several ancient villages. Just to the north lies Gatwick Airport, which first opened to commercial air traffic in 1936 and where **Gatwick Airport Skyview** provides an interesting insight behind the scenes of this busy airport. To the south of Crawley, near **Handcross**, are the superb gardens of **Nymans** created by William Robinson and Gertrude Jekyll. Close by are the smaller but equally delightful High Beeches Gardens.

WEST HOATHLY

5 miles N of Haywards Heath off the B2028

A historic settlement whose most impressive building is the **Priest House**, a 15th century house that was the estate office for the monks of Lewes Priory and is now a museum.

To the southwest lies **Ardingly**, home of Ardingly College public school, the showground for the South of England Agricultural Society and, at the top of Ardingly Reservoir, **Wakehurst Place**, the Tudor home of the Culpeper family. Today, the magnificent gardens are administered by the Royal Botanic Gardens at Kew; Wakehurst is also home to the Millennium Seed Bank, a project that aims to ensure the survival of over 24,000 plant species worldwide.

EAST GRINSTEAD

9 miles N of Haywards Heath on the A22

East Grinstead was an important centre for the Wealden iron industry and a busy market town, and several buildings remaining from those prosperous days. The **Town Museum** in East Court is a fine building that was originally constructed in 1769 as a private residence; the Greenwich Meridian passes through the town at this point.

To the south lies **Standen**, a remarkable late Victorian country mansion that is a showpiece of the Arts and Crafts Movement. From near Standen, the famous **Bluebell Railway** offers a pleasant steam-powered journey through the

Sussex Weald.

To the east of East Grinstead is the old hunting settlement of **Hartfield**, which was the home of AA Milne, the creator of Winnie the Pooh. The village's 300-year-old sweet shop, Pooh Corner, is now full of Winnie the Pooh memorabilia; **Poohsticks Bridge** spans a small tributary of the River Medway.

BUXTED

10½ miles E of Haywards Heath on the A272

The village has long been dominated by the great house of Buxted Park, built along classical lines in 1725, restored after a fire by Basil Ionides and now a hotel. To the southwest, on the other side of Uckfield in the village of **Piltdown**, an ancient skull was discovered in 1912 by an amateur archaeologist that was, for a time, believed to have been the 'missing link' until exposed as a hoax. To the west lies **Sheffield Green**, home to the splendid 18th century mansion Sheffield Park whose superb Capability Brown gardens are open to the public.

SHIPLEY

12 miles W of Haywards Heath off the A272

A pleasant village which is home to Sussex's only remaining working smock mill, **Shipley Mill**. Shipley was the home of the celebrated Sussex writer, Hilaire Belloc

BRIGHTON

It was Dr Richard Russell's enthusiasm for sea bathing, taking the sea air and even drinking seawater that saw Brighton grow from an insignificant little fishing village into a popular seaside resort. But it was the patronage of the Prince Regent, who first came here in 1783, which saw the village completely transformed. Wishing to have a permanent base here, the Prince built his famous **Royal Pavilion**, and the magnificent, exotic building seen today was the creation of the architect John Nash. The gardens surrounding this early 19th century pleasure palace based on a maharajah's palace are also Nash's work.

As the Prince took up almost permanent residence in the resort a period of rapid expansion took place of which the **Royal Crescent** is probably the greatest feature. However, The Lanes, the tiny alleyways of the old village, are equally interesting with their antique shops, restaurants and smart boutiques.

The best-known features on the seafront are the **Palace Pier** which has for more than a century been one of Brighton's greatest attractions, the **Volk's Electric Railway**, the first public electric railway in Britain, and the **Sea Life Centre**, home to the longest underwater tunnel in Europe.

Just to the west lies **Hove**, a genteel place that developed alongside its neighbour. Outside the **Hove Museum and Art Gallery** stands a wooden pavilion, the **Jaipur Gateway**, which was transported here from Rajasthan in 1886. History of a different kind is on

521 THE ROYAL PAVILION

Brighton

A magnificent Regency Palace, built for King George IV and inspired by Indian architecture.

 see page 567

283

522 MILL LAINE BARNS

Offham, nr Lewes

Mill Laine Barns and the adjacent farmhouse offer a choice of self-catering and B&B accommodation in a secluded, scenic setting.

see page 567

523 THE ANCHOR INN

Barcombe, nr Lewes

Paddle-boat trips along the River Ouse are a bonus for visitors to the delightful riverside **Anchor Inn**.

see page 566

view at the **British Engineerium** which contains all manner of engines from steam powered to electric housed in a restored 19th century pumping station.

AROUND BRIGHTON

HURSTPIERPOINT

7 miles N of Brighton on the B2116

This ancient village is dominated by **Hurstpierpoint College** and its chapel while, to the south of the village lies **Danny**, the ancestral home of the Norman Pierpoint family. It was in this impressive E-shaped Elizabethan mansion that Lloyd George drew up the terms of the armistice that ended World War I. Closer to Brighton, at Poynings, is one of the greatest

natural features of the South Downs. The **Devil's Dyke** is a huge steep-sided ravine that attracts tourists, walkers and hang-gliders.

LEWES

7 miles NE of Brighton on the A27

It was in this historic settlement, the county town of East Sussex, that William the Conqueror's powerful friend, William de Warenne, constructed a Castle and founded the great Priory of St Pancras. A substantial part of the castle remains today.

HAILSHAM

18 miles NE of Brighton on the A295

A pleasant market town that was once the centre of a thriving rope and string industry. To the

Lewes High Street

southwest lies **Michelham Priory**, which was founded in 1229. Many of the priory's buildings are now incorporated into a grand Tudor farmhouse, whose rooms contain many treasures, and the gardens cover an attractive range of planting styles.

NEWHAVEN

10 miles E of Brighton on the A26

Two early visitors on the packet boat from Dieppe were the fleeing King and Queen of France, Louis Philippe and Marie Amelie. They spent a night in 1848 at the Bridge Inn (registering as Mr & Mrs Smith!) before taking a train to London, where they were met by Queen Victoria's coach and taken to Buckingham Palace.

Along the coast to the east lies **Seaford**, a once thriving port that is home to Martello Tower No 74, the most westerly of these defensive structures, which now houses the **Seaford Museum of Local History**. **Seaford Head**, a nature reserve, is an excellent place from which to view the Seven Sisters - a spectacular series of clifftop undulations.

To the west of Newhaven, in a gap in the cliffs, lies **Rottingdean** and **North End House**, the home of the artist Sir Edward Burne-Jones. Inland is the village of **Rodmell**, where **Monk's House** was the home of Virginia and Leonard Woolf from 1919 until her death in 1941. The house, now in the care of the National Trust, is filled with books and paintings and is surrounded by a lush garden.

SELMESTON

13 miles E of Brighton off the A27

Selmeston is best known as the home of the artist Vanessa Bell who shared **Charleston Farmhouse** with her husband Clive and her lover, Duncan Grant.

To the south, beyond **Alciston** with its medieval dovecote, is the beautiful village of **Alfriston**, whose splendid 14th century church is often referred to as the Cathedral of the Downs. Beside the church is the **Clergy House**, the first building acquired by the National Trust (for £10 in 1896) and a marvellous example of a 14th century Wealden hall house. To the north lies **Drusillas Park**, a child friendly zoo set in attractive gardens.

To the west of Selmeston lies **Firle Beacon** which, at 718 feet, dominates the surrounding countryside and **Firle Place**, a wonderful Tudor manor that houses superb collections of European and English Old Masters, French and English furniture and Sèvres porcelain.

EASTBOURNE

20 miles E of Brighton on the A259

A stylish and genteel seaside resort, Eastbourne's rapid growth from two small villages was instigated by the 7th Duke of Devonshire from the 1850s. Several buildings predate this expansion, including the Georgian residence that houses the **Towner Art Gallery and Museum**; Martello Tower No 73 which is home to a **Puppet**

524 THE COCK INN

Ringmer, nr Lewes

Cask-conditioned ales and dishes to suit all palates make **The Cock Inn** a popular choice with locals and visitors.

see page 568

525 THE OLD SHIP

Ringmer

Quality is the keynote at the **Old Ship Inn**, where extensive menus cater for all palates and appetites.

see page 568

285

526 THE FARMHOUSE

Durrington, Worthing

The Farmhouse is a fine modern pub with traditional standards of hospitality, food and drink.

see page 569

527 CONFUCIUS CHINESE RESTAURANT

Chichester

Confucius Chinese Restaurant regales diners with an impressive selection of authentic Cantonese, Peking and Szechuan dishes.

see page 569

528 EXSURGO RESTAURANT/BAR

North Street, Midhurst

Exsurgo Restaurant & Bar is open long hours every day for a fine variety of interesting dishes.

see page 569

529 THE BRICKLAYERS ARMS

Midhurst

Top-quality produce is the basis of the excellent food served throughout the day at the **Bricklayers Arms**.

see page 570

530 THE ROYAL OAK

West Lavington

A fine selection of food and drink is available all day at the **Royal Oak**.

see page 570

Museum; and the **Redoubt Fortress** that is now the Military Museum of Sussex. The sea has always played an important part in the life of Eastbourne and there is an RNLI Lifeboat Museum close to the lifeboat station.

To the southwest of Eastbourne lies **Beachy Head**, one of the most spectacular chalk precipices in England. This is also the end of the **South Downs Way**, a long distance bridleway established in 1972.

To the northeast lies **Pevensey**, landing place for invading Roman legions and in 1066 for William the Conqueror and his troops; it was William's half-brother, Robert de Mortain, who built **Pevensey Castle**.

Inland from Eastbourne is the **Polegate Windmill and Museum**, a superb tower mill built in 1817. Also near **Wilmington** is its famous **Long Man**, cut into the chalk of Windover Hill. At 235 feet, this is the largest such representation in Europe, and its chalk outline is so unmistakable that it was covered up during World War II lest it should act as a navigation aid to German bombers.

SHOREHAM-BY-SEA

6 miles W of Brighton on the A259

An ancient port that has suffered from the silting up of its river; its earlier importance is reflected in the construction of Shoreham Fort, which was part of Palmerston's coastal defence system. The history of Shoreham, particularly its maritime past, is explored at Marlipins Museum, while at Shoreham Airport, which first opened in 1934, is the Museum of D-Day Aviation.

WORTHING

10 miles W of Brighton on the A259

An ancient fishing community, Worthing developed into a fashionable seaside resort in the late 18th century and boasts one of the oldest piers in the country. The **Worthing Museum and Art Gallery** has a nationally important costume and toy collection along with displays on smuggling and the town riots of the 19th century.

CHICHESTER

Founded by the Romans in the 1st century, Chichester has also been an ecclesiastical centre for over 900 years and its Cathedral is unique on two counts: it is the only medieval English cathedral which can be seen from the sea, and it has a detached belfry.

One of its most distinctive modern buildings is the **Chichester Festival Theatre**, opened in 1962 and the focal point of the annual Chichester Festival.

Just east of the city are the splendid remains of **Fishbourne Roman Palace** that was built in around AD 75 for the Celtic King Cogidubnus.

Further west again is the pleasant village of **Bosham**, where legend has it that King Canute ordered back the waves.

AROUND CHICHESTER

GOODWOOD

2 miles N of Chichester off the A286

The spectacular country home of the Dukes of Richmond, **Goodwood House** was built in the late 18th century by the architect James Wyatt and, along with a fine collection of paintings, gruesome relics from the Napoleonic Wars are on display. The house is the focal point of the vast Goodwood Estate that incorporates the world famous **Goodwood Racecourse**, the venue of the fashionable 'Glorious Goodwood' meeting first held in 1814.

Nearby **Singleton** is the location of the famous **Weald and Downland Open Air Museum**, an exemplary museum with over 40 reconstructed historic rural buildings. At **West Dean** lies **Charleston Manor**, an ancient house that was originally built in 1080 for William the Conqueror's cupbearer and is now the centrepiece of a remarkable garden created by members of the Bloomsbury Group.

Just to the southwest, and overlooked by Bow Hill, is **Kingley Vale National Nature Reserve**, home to the finest yew groves in Europe – several trees here are more than 500 years old.

PETWORTH

13 miles NE of Chichester on the A285

What brings most people here is the grand estate of 17th century **Petworth House**, which has the look of a French château and is home to the National Trust's finest

531 THE OLD RAILWAY STATION

Petworth

The **Old Railway Station** is a very comfortable and atmospheric hotel, with most of the rooms in wonderful old Pullman cars.

see page 570

532 THE STONEMASONS INN

Petworth

Just across the road from Petworth House, the **Stonemasons Inn** is a delightful place for a drink, a meal or an overnight stay.

see page 571

533 THE HALFWAY BRIDGE

Petworth

Food, wine and accommodation all excel at the **Halfway Bridge**, which stands between Petworth and Midhurst close to Cowdray Park.

see page 571

Petworth House

287

534 THE FORESTERS ARMS

Graffham, nr Petworth

In fine walking country on the South Downs, the **Foresters Arms** is a great place to pause for a drink or a meal, or to stay for a night or longer.

 see page 571

535 THE BADER ARMS

Tangmere

The **Bader Arms** offers traditional hospitality in a modern setting.

 see page 572

536 WOODACRE B&B

Fontwell, nr Arundel

Woodacre provides quiet, comfortable B&B accommodation in a garden setting.

 see page 572

537 THE ARUNDEL PARK HOTEL

Arundel

The **Arundel Park** is a comfortable, family-run 15-bedroom hotel that's an ideal base for touring the region.

 see page 572

collection of art from the 15th to 19th centuries, and some superb ancient and neo-classical sculpture. To the south of the estate is the **Coultershaw Water Wheel and Beam Pump**, one of the earliest pumped water systems; it was installed in 1790 to pump water two miles to the house.

PULBOROUGH

14½ miles NE of Chichester on the A29

Situated on Roman Stane Street, Pulborough was an important staging post along the old coaching route between London and Chichester. To the southeast lies the RSPB Pulborough Brooks Nature Reserve, where a nature trail leads to views overlooking the wet meadows of the Arun Valley.

To the southwest of Pulborough, near **Bignor**, is one of the largest Roman sites in Britain – some 70 buildings surround a central courtyard and many of the fine mosaics uncovered can be seen in the Museum.

TANGMERE

2½ miles E of Chichester off the A27

This village is associated with the nearby former Battle of Britain base, RAF Tangmere, which is now home to the **Tangmere Military Aviation Museum**.

The heroic deeds of the pilots are also remembered in the local pub, the Bader Arms.

ARUNDEL

9½ miles E of Chichester on the A27

A settlement since before the Roman invasion, this peaceful town lies beneath the battlements of the impressive 11th century **Arundel Castle**. The town is also the seat of the Catholic bishopric of Brighton and Arundel; the **Cathedral of Our Lady and St Philip Howard** was originally designed by JA Hansom and Son, the inventors of the Hansom cab. Another historic site is the Maison Dieu, a medieval hospital that was founded in 1345.

To the north lies the attractive village of **Amberley** and Amberley Castle, originally a fortified summer palace for the bishops of Chichester.

BOGNOR REGIS

5½ miles SE of Chichester on the A259

A quiet fishing village with some elegant Georgian features. King George V came here in 1929 to convalesce and granted the town the title Regis. The town is best known nowadays for its annual international Birdman Rally, when competitors hurl themselves off the pier in an attempt to make the longest unpowered flight.

SELSEY

7½ miles S of Chichester on the B2145

A modest yet popular resort, whose town's most impressive building is **Selsey Windmill**, built in 1820. A Lifeboat Station was established here in 1860 and there is now an interesting **Lifeboat Museum** along with a more recent station.

The town's East Beach was the scene for smuggling in the 18th century and during World War II sections of the famous Mulberry

Harbour were gathered here before D-Day.

To the north of Selsey lies **Pagham Harbour Nature Reserve**, an area of tidal mud flats which attracts an abundance of wildfowl along with many species of animals and marine life.

WEST WITTERING

6½ miles SW of Chichester on the B2179

Situated close to the beautiful inlet that is Chichester's natural harbour, this charming seaside village is home to Cakeham Manor House, once a summer palace of the bishops of Chichester.

To the north lies **Birdham**, the setting for Turner's famous painting of Chichester Harbour, and site of the **Sussex Falconry Centre**.

SOUTH HARTING

10 miles NW of Chichester on the B2146

One of the most attractive villages on the South Downs, South Harting stands at the foot of Harting Down where the South Downs Way footpath skirts around **Beacon Hill**, one of the highest points on the Downs. The magnificent house **Uppark** lies on the crest of a hill to the south. The grounds and gardens were laid out by Humphry Repton.

538 THE BOATHOUSE BRASSERIE

Houghton Bridge, nr Amberley

Succulent roast meats and fresh dishes are among the specialities of the **Boathouse Brasserie** in a lovely riverside setting.

see page 573

539 THE SEAL BAR & RESTAURANT

Selsey

The Seal is a popular venue for a superb range of real ales, fine wines and traditional English dishes, prepared with fresh local produce.

see page 573

540 WINDRUSH HOLIDAYS

Bracklesham Bay

Windrush Holidays have a number of well-equipped self-catering chalets on a landscaped site close to the beach.

see page 574

289

Warwickshire

A rich vein of medieval and Tudor history runs through Warwickshire, and the romantic ruins of Kenilworth Castle, the grandeur of Warwick Castle and the elegance of Royal Leamington Spa set the tone for this most delightful of counties. But Stratford-upon-Avon is most visitors' focal point, a town dominated by William Shakespeare and all things Shakespearian. Another town that has found fame through one of its citizens is Rugby, as it was the young scholar William Webb Ellis who, in the early 19th century, broke the rules of football and picked up the ball and in so doing founded the game that bears the name of the town. Close by is the ancient village of Dunchurch that is often dubbed the 'Gunpowder Plot Village' as it was here that the conspirators waited to hear if their mission had been accomplished.

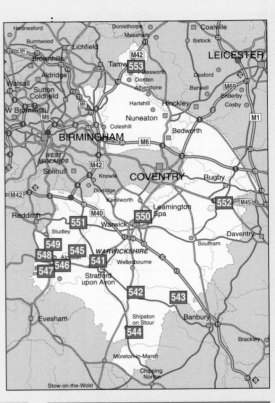

	FOOD & DRINK	
542	The White Horse, Ettington	p 291, 574
543	The Rose & Crown Inn, Ratley	p 291, 574
544	The Falcon, Shipston-on-Stour	p 292, 575
546	The Golden Cross Country Inn & Eating House, Ardens Grafton	p 292, 575
547	Broom Tavern, Broom	p 293, 576
548	Ristorante Rossini's, Alcester	p 293, 576
549	The Moat House Inn, Kings Coughton	p 293, 576
550	The Simple Simon, Warwick	p 294, 577
551	Matricardi's, Henley-in-Arden	p 295, 577
552	The Green Man, Dunchurch	p 296, 577
553	The Bird in Hand, Austrey	p 297, 578

	ACCOMMODATION	
541	Aidan Guest House, Stratford-upon-Avon	p 291, 574
542	The White Horse, Ettington	p 291, 574
544	The Falcon, Shipston-on-Stour	p 292, 575
545	Larkrise Cottage, Upper Billesley	p 292, 575
550	The Simple Simon, Warwick	p 294, 577
552	The Green Man, Dunchurch	p 296, 577

STRATFORD-UPON-AVON

It was here, in 1564, that William Shakespeare was born and having found fame in London, retired to his birthplace and lived here until his death in 1616. Few towns are so completely dominated by one man. The half-timbered house that is **Shakespeare's Birthplace** has been returned to the way it must have looked in his day and a room thought to have been his father's workshop has been re-created with the help of the Worshipful Company of Glovers. Further along, on Chapel Street, stands **Nash's House**, another half-timbered building that belonged to Shakespeare's granddaughter, Elizabeth Hall; it now contains an exceptional collection of Elizabethan furniture and tapestries,

as well as displays on the history of Stratford. Its spectacular Elizabethan-style knot garden is an added attraction.

In Old Town is one of the best examples of a half-timbered gabled house in Stratford, **Hall's Croft**, which was named after Dr John Hall, who married Shakespeare's daughter Susanna in 1607. This impressive house, along with outstanding 16th and 17th century furniture and paintings, has a reconstruction of Dr Hall's consulting room, accompanied by an exhibition detailing medicinal practices during Shakespeare's time. Outside, the beautiful walled garden features a large herb bed. In a beautiful setting by the River Avon, is 13th century **Holy Trinity Church** where Shakespeare is buried by the north wall of the chancel. The grave of his wife Anne Hathaway is close by.

Shakespeare's Birthplace

544 THE FALCON

Shipston-on-Stour

The **Falcon** offers real ales, fine food and a very comfortable base for touring an area rich in scenic and historic attractions.

 see page 575

545 LARKRISE COTTAGE

Upper Billesley, nr Stratford-upon-Avon

Larkrise Cottage is a comfortable B&B in delightful countryside yet close to Stratford-upon-Avon.

 see page 575

546 THE GOLDEN CROSS COUNTRY INN & EATING HOUSE

Ardens Grafton, nr Stratford-upon-Avon

The **Golden Cross** is a delightful country pub and eating house serving superb cuisine with modern European influences, and interesting beers and wines.

 see page 575

The town is also home to three theatres, as well as the internationally renowned Royal Shakespeare Company, and the most famous is, of course, the **Royal Shakespeare Theatre** that opened in 1879 with a performance of *Much Ado About Nothing* starring Ellen Terry and Beerbohm Tree. The Royal Shakespeare Theatre Summer House in Avonbank Gardens is home to the **Stratford Brass Rubbing Centre**, which contains a large collection of exact replicas of brasses of knights and ladies, scholars, merchants and priests.

To the west of the town is an Elizabethan farmhouse that is now known as **Anne Hathaway's Cottage**, as it was here that Shakespeare's wife was born. Another notable house connected with the Bard is that of his mother, situated in the village of Wilmcote: Mary Arden's House is a striking Tudor farmhouse that contains the **Shakespeare Countryside Museum** of farming and rural life.

AROUND STRATFORD-UPON-AVON

WELLESBOURNE

5 miles E of Stratford off the A429

The village is home to **Wellesbourne Watermill**, a brick-built working flourmill on the River Dene. Demonstrations of the art and skill of milling stoneground flour are enacted and explained by the miller and there are guided walks alongside the river.

To the southeast lies **Compton Verney Manor House**, a magnificent manor that is home to a fine art collection that includes British portraiture, European Old Masters and modern works, along with a unique collection of British Folk Art. On the other side of Wellesbourne lies 16th century **Charlecote Park**, a magnificent stately home occupying landscaped grounds overlooking the River Avon that were laid out by Capability Brown.

Used as the location for the filming of the BBC adaptation of George Eliot's *The Mill on the Floss*, 18th century **Charlecote Mill** is situated on the site of an earlier mill mentioned in the *Domesday Book*.

ILMINGTON

7 miles S of Stratford off the B4632

This pretty village at the foot of **Ilmington Downs** had its moment of history on Christmas Day 1934, when the first radio broadcast by George V was introduced by Walton Handy, the village shepherd, and relayed to the world from Ilmington Manor, the fine Elizabethan house once owned by the de Montfort family.

ALCESTER

7½ miles NW of Stratford off the A435

An ancient Roman market town built on the **Icknield Street Encampment**, Alcester boasts several very pretty cottages on Maltmill Lane and a handsome Norman church. Just to the south lies the village of **Arrow** and the 17th century home of the Marquess of Hertford, **Ragley Hall**. One of England's great Palladian country houses, it was inherited by the 8th Marquess in 1940 when he was only nine, and during World War II it was used as a hospital. Completely renovated in a style befitting its age, the Hall boasts a wonderful collection of treasures, and out in the landscaped park there are formal gardens, an impressive collection of carriages and a country trail. **Roman Alcester Heritage Centre** explores everyday life in and around Roman Alcester. At nearby Kinwarton stands the National Trust's **Kinwarton Dovecote**, a 14th century circular dovecote that still houses doves and retains its 'potence', a pivoted ladder giving human access to the nesting boxes.

WARWICK

Standing by the River Avon, Warwick is in a good defensive position and became part of Crown lands just after the Norman Conquest. Dominating the town, much of **Warwick Castle** was destroyed during the Barons' revolt in 1264, led by Simon de Montfort, and the majority of the present castle dates from the 14th century. The towers at each end are very impressive - one is known as Caesar's Tower and is shaped rather like a cloverleaf.

The castle's exterior is best viewed from **Castle Bridge**, where the 14th century walls can be seen reflected in the waters of the River Avon. There is much to explore along the ramparts and in the 60 acres of grounds, which include a re-created Victorian formal rose garden, the Peacock Gardens and an expanse of open parkland designed by Capability Brown. Events throughout the year include **Medieval Tournaments**, open-air fireworks concerts and special entertainment days.

The centre of Warwick is dominated by elegant Queen Anne architecture and there is also a wealth of museums including several honouring the county's regiments. One of the most important buildings in Warwick is St John's House, dating from 1666, which contains the Museum of the Royal Warwickshire Regiment. Two of Warwick's medieval town gateways have survived, complete with chapels and one of these, Westgate Chapel, forms part of **Lord Leycester's Hospital**, a spectacularly tottering and beautiful collection of 15th century half-timbered buildings enclosing a pretty galleried courtyard.

To the west of Warwick lies **Hatton Country World**, a uniquely charming blend of family fun and country shopping that is situated on a farm built by the descendants of Sir Richard Arkwright, the inventor of the Spinning Jenny. Along with the extensive craft village, the farm is home to the largest collection of rare breed farm animals in Britain.

547 BROOM TAVERN

Broom, nr Bidford-on-Avon

Broom Tavern is a fine old inn with a great reputation for friendliness, good food and well-kept beer.

 see page 576

548 RISTORANTE ROSSINI'S

Birmingham Road, Alcester

Rossini's is one of the top Italian restaurants in the region, with an interesting menu and well-chosen wines.

 see page 576

549 THE MOAT HOUSE INN

Kings Coughton, nr Alcester

The **Moat House Inn** is a splendid Tudor building with many original features and a wide choice of excellent home cooking

 see page 576

550 THE SIMPLE SIMON

Emscote Road, Warwick

The Simple Simon
provides a cheerful, sociable
ambience for enjoying a
drink, a meal and live music
evenings. Also B&B rooms.

see *page 577*

Warwick Castle

AROUND WARWICK

KENILWORTH

4 miles N of Warwick on the A452

Although the town was here before
the *Domesday Book* was compiled,
Kenilworth's name is invariably
linked with its castle and, today, the
remains of **Kenilworth Castle**
stand as England's finest and most
extensive castle ruins. The tales of
this great fortress, immortalised in
Sir Walter Scott's novel *Kenilworth*,
are many and varied. The
marvellous Norman keep, the
oldest part of the ruins, was built
between 1150 and 1175 and John
of Gaunt's Great Hall once rivalled
London's Westminster Hall in
palatial grandeur. The remains of
Kenilworth's Abbey can be seen
in the churchyard of the Norman
parish Church of St Nicholas in the
High Street.

ROYAL LEAMINGTON SPA

2 miles E of Warwick on the A452

This attractive town boasts a
handsome mixture of smart shops
and Regency buildings and **The
Parade** is undoubtedly one of the
finest streets in Warwickshire.
Rapidly taking advantage of the
fashion for taking the waters,
Leamington Spa developed in the
first few decades of the 19th
century and was given the title
'Royal' by the grace of the new

Queen, Victoria. The **Pump Rooms** were opened in 1814 by Henry Jephson, a local doctor who was largely responsible for promoting the spa's medicinal properties and therefore the popularisation of this elegant spa resort by the rich. Immediately opposite the spa itself are **Jephson's Gardens** containing a Corinthian temple that houses his statue.

SOUTHAM

8½ miles SE of Warwick on the A423

It was in this attractive town by the River Itchen that Charles I spent the night before the battle of Edge Hill. The Roundheads also came into the town, and Cromwell himself arrived with 7,000 troops in 1645. In the main street is the surprisingly named Old Mint Inn, a 14th century stone building that takes its name from an occurrence following the battle of Edge Hill. Charles I commanded his local noblemen to bring him their silver treasure, which was then melted down and minted into coins with which he paid his army.

SHERBOURNE

2½ miles S of Warwick on the A429

Set in lovely countryside with views across fields to the River Avon, **Sherbourne Park** is one of the very finest gardens in the county. Highlights of the gardens, which were designed by Lady Smith-Ryland in the 1950s, include a paved terrace covered by clematis, wisteria and a magnolia; an 'orchard' of sorbus trees; a box-edged, rose-filled parterre and the White Garden surrounded by yew hedges.

HENLEY-IN-ARDEN

9 miles W of Warwick on the A3400

Henley's mile-long High Street has examples of almost every kind of English architecture from the 15th century onwards, including many old timber-framed houses built from Arden oak. Little remains today of the **Forest of Arden**, the setting adopted by William Shakespeare for *As You Like It*, as its stocks were diminished in the 18th century by the navy's demand for timber. The town emerged initially under the protection of Thurston de Montfort, Lord of the Manor in 1140, and **Beaudesert Castle**, home to the de Montfort family, lies behind the churches of St John and St Nicholas, where remains of the castle mound can still be seen.

551 MATRICARDI'S

High Street, Henley-in-Arden

Contemporary Mediterranean cuisine is the speciality of **Matricardi's Restaurant** on the main street of Henley-in-Arden.

see page 577

Coughton Court

552 THE GREEN MAN

Dunchurch, nr Rugby

The family-run **Green Man** is an excellent place for real ale and home cooking, and a convenient B&B base for leisure and business visitors.

see page 577

COUGHTON

13 miles W of Warwick off the A435

The crowning glory of this village, **Coughton Court**, has been the home for almost 600 years of the Throckmorton family who were very prominent in Tudor times and were instigators of Catholic emancipation, playing a part in the Gunpowder Plot - the wives of some of the Gunpowder Plotters awaited the outcome of the Plot in the imposing central gatehouse. This and the half-timbered courtyard are particularly noteworthy, while inside there are important collections of paintings, furniture, porcelain and other family items from Tudor times to the present day. Treasured possessions include the chemise that Mary, Queen of Scots wore at her execution and the Throckmorton Coat, the subject of a 1,000 guinea wager in 1811.

SHREWLEY

5 miles NW of Warwick off the B4439

Shrewley boasts a marina on the Grand Union Canal but its well-known landmark is the **Hatton Flight** of 21 locks that stretches for a couple of miles up Hatton Hill. Just to the northwest, at **Lapworth**, the Grand Union and Stratford Canals meet and, close by, is **Baddesley Clinton**, a romantic, medieval moated manor house that has changed little since 1633.

RUGBY

Rugby's **Market Place** is surrounded by handsome buildings that act as reminders of the town's origins during the reign of Henry III. Rugby Town Trail, a two-hour walk that brings to life the town's history from its Saxon beginnings to the present day, begins at the Clock Tower in Market Place. The tower was intended to commemorate the Golden Jubilee of Queen Victoria in 1887, yet it was not completed until 1889 because over-indulgent citizens had dipped too deep into the Tower funds to feast and drink at the Jubilee. Also along the trail is the house where Rupert Brooke was born (his statue stands in Regent Place), and Caldecott Park with its beautiful floral displays, trees and a herb garden.

Rugby is bounded by two of the greatest Roman roads, Fosse Way and Watling Street, which meet just northwest of Rugby, at **High Cross**, one of the landmarks of the area.

The town is best known for **Rugby School**, founded in 1567 and moved to its present site in 1750. It was here that the game of Rugby originated when, in 1823, William Webb Ellis broke the rules during a football match by picking up the ball and running with it. The **James Gilbert Rugby Museum** is housed in the original building where, since 1842, the

Gilberts have been making their world-famous rugby footballs.

AROUND RUGBY

DUNCHURCH

2 miles SW of Rugby on the A426

On the 5th of November 1605, the Gunpowder Plot conspirators met at the Red Lion Inn, Dunchurch, to await the news of Guy Fawkes' attempt to blow up the Houses of Parliament. The Red Lion still exists today but as a private residence known as **Guy Fawkes House**.

RYTON-ON-DUNSMORE

6 miles W of Rugby off the A45

This village is home to the **Henry Doubleday Research Association** at Ryton Gardens, an organic farming and gardening organisation that leads the way in research and advances in horticulture. The grounds are landscaped with thousands of plants and trees, all organically grown. **Ryton Pools Country Park**, which opened in 1996, has a 10-acre lake that is home to great crested grebes, swans, moorhens and Canada geese. Pagets Pool, near the northeastern end of the park, is one of the most important sites in Warwickshire for dragonflies.

To the north is **Brandon Marsh Nature Centre**, 200 acres of lakes, marshes, woodland and grassland that provide a home and haven for many species of wildlife.

NUNEATON

13½ miles NW of Rugby on the A444

Originally a Saxon town known as Etone, the 'Nun' was added when a wealthy Benedictine priory was founded here in 1290. The Priory ruins are adjacent to the Church of St Nicholas, a Victorian building occupying a Norman site that has a beautiful carved ceiling dating back to 1485. **Nuneaton Museum and Art Gallery** features displays of archaeological interest ranging from prehistoric to medieval times, and there is also a permanent exhibition of the town's most illustrious daughter, the novelist George Eliot. Born at Arbury Hall in 1819, Eliot, whose real name was Mary Ann Evans, was an intellectual giant and free thinker. Situated just to the southwest of the town is **Arbury Hall** where George Eliot's father was a land agent on the estate; she portrays this, her first home, as Cheverel Manor in her novel *Mr Gifgil's Love Story*.

NEWTON REGIS

6 miles NW of Atherstone off the B5493

One of the most unspoilt villages in Warwickshire, Newton Regis has been voted Best Kept Small Village on numerous occasions. Near the Staffordshire border and between the M42 and B5453, this lovely village is built around an attractive duck pond which was once a quarry pit. The village's name is thought to derive from its former royal ownership, having once been the property of King Henry II.

553 THE BIRD IN HAND

Austrey, nr Tamworth
The **Bird in Hand** great old-world charm, a welcome for all the family, a wide choice of super food and a large garden.

see page 578

Wiltshire

A county rich in prehistoric remains, Wiltshire also has one of the highest concentrations of historic houses and gardens in the country as well as some fine downland and woodland that provide excellent walking or cycling. The industrial heritage of the county takes many forms – Brunel's Great Western Railway centred on Swindon, brewing at Devizes, carpet making at Wilton and the Kennet and Avon Canal. The jewel in Wiltshire's crown is the fine city of Salisbury with its magnificent cathedral. But it is for its ancient monuments, white horses and the intriguing crop circles that the county is best known. Along with the Stone Circles at Avebury, Silbury Hill, West Kennet Long Barrow and the White Horse at Westbury, Wiltshire is, of course, home to Stonehenge. A World Heritage Site, these massive stone blocks are one of the greatest mysteries of the prehistoric world. Close by is an even more ancient monument that is often overlooked – Woodhenge.

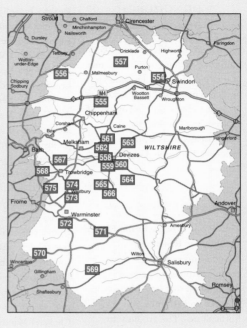

SWINDON

The largest town in Wiltshire, lying in the northeast corner between the Cotswolds and the Marlborough Downs, Swindon was an insignificant agricultural community before the railway line between London and Bristol was completed in 1835. In 1843, Isambard Kingdom Brunel, the Great Western Railway's principal engineer, decided that Swindon was the place to build his locomotive works.

Within a few years it had grown to be one of the largest in the world, with as many as 12,000 workers on a 320-acre site that incorporated the Railway Village: this was a model development of 300 workmen's houses built of limestone extracted from the construction of Box Tunnel. This unique example of early Victorian town planning is open to the public at the **Railway Village Museum**. The Great Western Railway Museum, now called **Steam**, houses a collection of locomotives, nameplates and signalling equipment along with exhibitions on the life of Brunel and of the men and women who built and repaired the rolling stock for *God's Wonderful Railway*. The site also contains the National Monuments Record Centre - the public archive of the Royal Commission on the Historical Monuments of England, with 7 million photographs, documents and texts.

On the western outskirts of Swindon is **Lydiard Park**, one of Wiltshire's smaller stately homes, which is the ancestral home of the Viscounts Bolingbroke.

Just south of the town lies **Wroughton Airfield**, a historic World War II airbase which is home to the National Museum of Science and Industry's collection of large aircraft.

AROUND SWINDON

MARLBOROUGH

10 miles S of Swindon on the A346

Marlborough College was founded in 1843 primarily for sons of the clergy. Built on the site of a Norman castle, the first mansion here was replaced in the early 18th century by a building that became the Castle Inn and is now C House, the oldest part of the college.

To the southeast of the town lies the ancient woodland of **Savernake Forest** where Henry VIII hunted wild deer.

Situated in a beautiful valley that bears its name, **Pewsey** is a charming village that was once the property of Alfred the Great. The Heritage Centre, housed in an 1870 foundry building, is well worth a visit, but the most interesting feature here lies just south of the village on Pewsey Down. The original **Pewsey White Horse** was cut in 1785 and apparently included a rider, but it was redesigned by George Marples and cut by the local fire brigade to celebrate the coronation of George VI.

554 STEAM

Swindon

Steam is an award-winning museum with superb displays and hands-on opportunities, illustrating the golden age of steam.

 see page 579

Stone Circle, Avebury

555 THE WHITE HART INN

Lyneham

A short drive from J16 of the M4, the **White Hart** is a pleasant spot for a drink, a meal or an overnight stay.

see page 579

AVEBURY

10 miles SW of Swindon on the A4361

This village is home to the **Avebury Stone Circles**, the most remarkable ritual megalithic monuments in Europe and now a World Heritage Site. Many of the archaeological finds from the site are displayed in the **Alexander Keiller Museum**, which also describes the reconstruction of the site by Keiller in the 1930s.

Avebury also has a gem from more recent times: **Avebury Manor** dates from the Elizabethan era and is surrounded by a walled garden that features a wishing well, topiary and an Italian walk.

This area abounds with ancient monuments. To the south lies **West Kennet Long Barrow**, one of the country's largest Neolithic burial tombs; on nearby Overton Hill is The Sanctuary, an early Bronze Age monument of giant standing stones. To the west of West Kennet lies the largest man-made prehistoric

mound in Europe, **Silbury Hill**, which dates from around 2800 BC and rises some 300 feet.

CRICKLADE

6½ miles NW of Swindon on the B4040

The only Wiltshire town on the River Thames, Cricklade was an important post on the Roman Ermin Street and, in Saxon times, had its own mint. There are many buildings of interest here, including the famous school founded by the London goldsmith Robert Jenner in 1651, and the elaborate Victorian clock tower. Nearby, North Meadow is a National Nature Reserve where the rare snakeshead fritillary grows.

CHIPPENHAM

An important administrative centre in King Alfred's time, Chippenham later gained prominence from the wool trade and was a major stop on the London to Bristol coaching route. In the flood plain to the east of Chippenham lies the footpath known as **Maud Heath's Causeway**, a remarkable and ingenious walkway consisting of 64 brick and stone arches that was built in the 15th century at the bequest of Maud Heath. She had spent most of her life as a poor pedlar trudging her way between the village of Bremhill and Chippenham but she died a relatively wealthy woman and her will provided sufficient funds for the construction and upkeep of the causeway.

To the south lies **Lacock Abbey**, which was founded in 1232 by Ela, Countess of Salisbury in memory of her husband William Longsword, stepbrother to Richard the Lionheart. The estate later passed into the hands of the Talbot family, whose most distinguished member was the pioneering photographer, William Henry Fox Talbot, who carried out his experiments here in the 1830s. Today, the National Trust's estate village of **Lacock** is one of the county's real treasures, with its delightful assortment of mellow stone buildings seemingly remaining unaltered over the centuries. The **Fox Talbot Museum** commemorates the life and achievements of a man who was not just a photographer but a mathematician, physicist, classicist and transcriber of Syrian and Chaldean cuneiform.

AROUND CHIPPENHAM

MALMESBURY

9 miles N of Chippenham on the B4040

England's oldest borough is dominated by the impressive remains of the Benedictine **Malmesbury Abbey**, founded in the 7th century by St Aldhelm. In the 10th century, King Athelstan, Alfred's grandson and the first Saxon king to unite England, granted 500 acres of land to the townsfolk in gratitude for their help in resisting a Norse invasion. This land is still known as **King's**

Heath and is now owned by 200 residents who are descended from those far-off heroes.

In the **Athelstan Museum** are numerous displays, including one of lace making and another of early bicycles, while a more recent piece of local history concerns the Tamworth Two – the pigs who made the headlines with their dash for freedom.

To the east lies **Easton Grey**, whose elegant 18th century manor house was used as a summer retreat by Herbert Asquith, Prime Minister between 1908 and 1916.

CALNE

5 miles E of Chippenham on the A4

Calne is a former weaving centre in the valley of the River Marden and the prominent **Wool Church** reflects the town's early prosperity; inside, is a memorial to Dr Ingenhousz, who is widely credited with creating a smallpox vaccination before Edward Jenner.

A short distance from Calne, to the west, stands **Bowood House**, which was built in 1625 and is now a treasury of Shelborne family heirlooms, paintings, books and furniture. It was in the Bowood Laboratory that Dr Joseph Priestley, tutor to the 1st Marquis of Lansdowne's son, conducted experiments that resulted in the identification of oxygen.

The **Atwell Motor Museum**, to the east of Calne, has a collection of over 70 vintage and classic cars and motorcycles from the years 1924 to 1983.

556 THE RATTLEBONE INN

Sherston

Youngs beers and country cooking bring locals and visitors to the fine old **Rattlebone Inn**.

see page 579

557 THE VALE OF THE WHITE HORSE INN

Minety, nr Malmesbury

The **Vale of the White Horse Inn** scores with an outstanding location and a wide choice of superb food and wine.

see page 580

558 THE THREE CROWNS

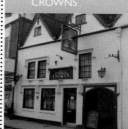

Maryport Street, Devizes

Shoppers, locals and visitors to Devizes enjoy the excellent lunches served in the **Three Crowns**.

see page 581

302

DEVIZES

9 miles SE of Chippenham on the A342

Devizes was founded in 1080 by Bishop Osmund, nephew of William the Conqueror, who built a timber castle here between the lands of two powerful manors; this act brought about the town's name, which is derived from the Latin ad divisas, or 'at the boundaries'.

After the wooden structure burnt down, the Bishop of Sarum built a stone castle in 1138 that survived until the end of the Civil War, when it was demolished.

Devizes Visitor Centre is based on a 12th century castle and takes visitors back to medieval times, when Devizes was home not just to its fine castle but also to anarchy and unrest during the

Caen Hill Locks, Devizes

struggle between Empress Matilda and King Stephen.

Many of the town's finest buildings are situated in and around the old market place, including the Town Hall and the Corn Exchange. Devizes stands at a key point on the Kennet and Avon Canal and the **Kennet and Avon Canal Museum** tells the complete story of the waterway in fascinating detail. Many visitors combine a trip to the museum with a walk along the towpath; the town really buzzes in July when the Canalfest is held at the Wharf.

TROWBRIDGE

11 miles S of Chippenham on the A361

The county town of Wiltshire and another major weaving centre in its day, Trowbridge still has a number of old industrial buildings, and an interesting waymarked walk takes in many of them. The parish **Church of St James** contains the tomb of the poet and former rector George Crabbe, who wrote the work on which Benjamin Britten based his opera *Peter Grimes*. Trowbridge's most famous son was Isaac Pitman, the shorthand man, who was born in Nash Yard in 1813.

BRADFORD-ON-AVON

10 miles SW of Chippenham on the A363

A historic market town at a bridging point on the River Avon, which is spanned by a superb nine-arched bridge with a lock-up at one end. The town's oldest building is the **Church of St Lawrence** that is believed to have been founded by

St Aldhelm in around AD 700. It 'disappeared' for over 1,000 years, during which time it was used variously as a school, a charnel house for storing the bones of the dead and a residential dwelling; it was re-discovered by a keen-eyed clergyman who looked down from a hill and noticed its cruciform shape.

Another of the town's outstanding buildings is the mighty **Tithe Barn**, which was once used to store the grain from local farms for Shaftesbury Abbey.

On the edge of the town, **Barton Farm Country Park** offers delightful walks in lovely countryside beside the River Avon and the Kennet and Avon Canal. Barton Bridge is the original packhorse bridge that was built to assist the transportation of grain from the farm to the tithe barn.

Half a mile south of the town, by the River Frome, is the Italian-style **Peto Garden** laid out between 1899 and 1933 by the architect and landscape gardener Harold Ainsworth Peto.

To the west, in the middle of the village of **Holt**, stands **The Courts**, an English country garden of mystery with unusual topiary, water gardens and an arboretum.

CASTLE COMBE

5½ miles NW of Chippenham on the B4039

The loveliest village in the region, and for some the loveliest in the country, Castle Combe was once a centre of the prosperous wool trade, famed for its red and white cloth. Many of the present

563 THE CROWN INN

Bishops Cannings, nr Devizes

The **Crown Inn** is open seven days a week for a fine selection of outstanding home cooking and cask-conditioned ales.

 see page 583

564 THE LAMB INN

Urchfont, nr Devizes

A picturesque pub in a picturesque setting – **The Lamb Inn** is very popular, particularly for its excellent home cooking.

 see page 584

565 THE BELL

Great Cheverell, nr Devizes

In a picturesque village setting, **The Bell** strikes all the right notes with an excellent variety of home-cooked dishes.

see page 584

566 THE OWL

Little Cheverell, nr Devizes

The Owl is a grand old redbrick inn offering a wide choice of food and drink, two letting rooms and two annual beer festivals.

see page 585

567 THE OLD BEAR INN

Staverton, nr Trowbridge

The **Old Bear** is a pleasant pub open every day for food and drink; the home-made desserts should not be missed!

see page 585

568 THE POPLARS INN

Wingfield, nr Trowbridge

The **Poplars** is a quintessential English village inn, complete with its own cricket pitch and known far and wide for its superb food.

see page 586

buildings date from the 15th and 16th centuries, including the covered Market Cross and the Manor House, which was built with stones from the Norman castle that gave the village its name.

SALISBURY

The glorious medieval city of Salisbury stands at the confluence of four rivers, the Avon, the Wylye, the Bourne and the Nadder. Originally called New Sarum, it grew around the present Cathedral, which was built between 1220 and 1258 in a sheltered position two miles south of the site of its windswept Norman predecessor, Old Sarum.

Surely one of the most beautiful buildings in the world, **Salisbury Cathedral** is the only medieval cathedral in England to be built all in the same Early English style – apart from its spire, the tallest in England, which was added some years later and rises to an awesome 404 feet. The Chapter House opens out of the cloisters and contains, among other treasures, one of the four surviving originals of the Magna Carta. The oldest working clock in Britain, and possibly in the world, is situated in the fan-vaulted north transept; it was built in 1386 to strike the hour and has no clock face. **The Close**, the precinct of the ecclesiastical community serving the Cathedral, is the largest in England and contains a number of museums and houses open to the public, including, in the 17th century **King's House**,

Salisbury Museum, home of the Stonehenge Gallery and **The Royal Gloucestershire, Berkshire and Wiltshire Museum**, housed in a 13th century building called the Wardrobe, which was originally used to store the bishop's clothes and documents. **Mompesson House** is a perfect example of Queen Anne architecture that is noted for its plasterwork, an elegant carved oak staircase, fine period furniture and the important Turnbull collection of 18th century drinking glasses.

There are many other areas of Salisbury to explore, and on a huge mound to the north are the ruins of **Old Sarum**, abandoned when the bishopric moved into the city. Old Sarum became the most notorious of the 'rotten boroughs', returning two Members of Parliament, despite having no voters, until the 1832 Reform Act stopped the cheating. A plaque on the site commemorates Old Sarum's most illustrious Member of Parliament, William Pitt the Elder.

AROUND SALISBURY

AMESBURY

7 miles N of Salisbury on the A345

It was here that Queen Elfrida founded an abbey in AD 979, in atonement for her part in the murder of her son-in-law, Edward the Martyr, at Corfe Castle. Henry II rebuilt the abbey's great **Church of St Mary and St Melor**, whose tall central tower is the only structure to survive from the pre-Norman monastery.

A mile to the north of the town lies **Woodhenge**, a ceremonial monument that is even older than its more famous neighbour, Stonehenge, and was the first major prehistoric site to be discovered by aerial photography.

Two miles west of Amesbury stands **Stonehenge**, perhaps the greatest mystery of the prehistoric world, one of the wonders of the world and a monument of unique importance. Stonehenge's orientation on the rising and setting sun has always been one of its most remarkable features, leading to theories that the builders were from a sun-worshipping culture or that the whole structure is part of a huge astronomical calendar.

WILTON

3 miles W of Salisbury on the A30

The third oldest borough in England, and once the capital of Saxon Wessex, Wilton is best known for its carpets and the **Wilton Carpet Factory**, on the River Wylye, continues to produce top-quality Wilton and Axminster carpets.

To the south of the town stands **Wilton House**, the home of the Earls of Pembroke that was designed by Inigo Jones in the 17th century after the original house had been destroyed by fire in 1647. Later remodelled by James Wyatt, Wilton House features the amazing Double Cube Room and a fine art collection.

To the west lies **Dinton**, a lovely hillside village that is home

to **Little Clarendon House**, a near perfect Tudor manor house, and Philipps House, a handsome early 19th century mansion that stands in the beautiful grounds of **Dinton Park**. Further west again are the ruins of **Old Wardour Castle**, a unique six-sided castle that dates from the 14th century.

STOURTON

23 miles W of Salisbury off the B3092

The main attraction of this beautiful village is **Stourhead**, one of the most famous examples of an early 18th century English landscape garden, and a place renowned for its striking vistas and woodland walks. Stourton House is a classical masterpiece dating from the 1720s and on the edge of the estate is the imposing **King Alfred's Tower**, a redbrick folly erected in 1772 that commemorates the king who reputedly raised his standard here against the Danes in AD 878.

WARMINSTER

19 miles NW of Salisbury off the A36

This historic town on the western edge of Salisbury Plain has a number of distinguished old buildings and some interesting monuments of varying age. The **Obelisk,** with its feeding troughs and pineapple top, was erected in 1783 to mark the enclosure of the parish; the **Morgan Memorial Fountain** stands in the Lake Pleasure Grounds; and *Beyond Harvest* is a statue in bronze by Colin Lambert of a girl sitting on sacks of corn.

569 OLD WARDOUR CASTLE

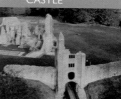

Tisbury

Built in the 14th century as a secure, luxurious home for Lord Lovel, it was damaged during the Civil War and has remained a romantic ruin ever since.

 see page 585

570 THE GEORGE INN

Mere

In the centre of Mere, the **George** offers a right royal welcome, fine food and drink and comfortable accommodation.

 see page 587

571 THE CARRIERS

Stockton, nr Warminster

The Carriers is a lovely traditional village pub serving excellent home-cooked food to please all palates.

 see page 587

572 THE BATH ARMS

Crockerton, nr Warminster

The **Bath Arms** is one of the finest dining pubs in the region, with the bonuses of local ales and superb accommodation.

 see page 588

573 THE GARDEN HOUSE HOTEL

Westbury

Resident owners ensure that guests at the **Garden House Hotel** enjoy a comfortable stay in elegant, civilised surroundings.

 see page 587

574 THE ROYAL OAK

Hawkeridge, nr Westbury

Friendly hosts provide a warm welcome, real ales and a very good variety of food at the **Royal Oak**.

see page 589

575 THE KICKING DONKEY

Brokerswood, nr Westbury

The **Kicking Donkey** reaches out to regular customers and first-time visitors with good food and Cask Marque-approved ales.

 see page 589

To the west of town, **Cley Hill** is an Iron Age hill fort with two Bronze Age barrows; it is renowned as a place for sighting UFOs. The region is also noted for the appearance of crop circles, and some have linked the two phenomena.

Just to the west of Warminster is **Longleat House**, the magnificent home of the Marquis of Bath that dates from the 1570s and is filled with a superb collection of old masters, beautiful furniture, rare books and murals by Lord Bath. The glorious grounds, landscaped by Capability Brown, are famous as the home of the Safari Park established in the 1960s.

North of Warminster is **Westbury**, a major centre of the wool and cloth trades in the Middle Ages and with many fine buildings still standing as a legacy of those prosperous days.

To the east of Westbury is the town's best known feature, the famous **Westbury White Horse** that dates from 1778 and replaces an earlier horse carved to celebrate King Alfred's victory over the Danes in AD 878. Above the horse's head are the ruins of **Bratton Castle**, an Iron Age hill fort covering 25 acres.

Longleat House

Worcestershire

The southern part of Worcestershire is dominated by the spectacular ridge of the Malvern Hills in the west, which provides excellent walking country along with breathtaking views, and the Vale of Evesham in the east, an attractive area with charming towns and villages built of the warm Cotswold stone. Most of the county's industry is centred in the northern part, where there are numerous examples of industrial archaeology to interest the historian. Canals here were once as important as roads and the area around Kidderminster and Redditch is dominated by three such waterways: the Worcester & Birmingham Canal, the Staffordshire & Worcester Canal and the Droitwich Canal. The arrival of the railways saw a rapid decline in water transport and, although this network is now much smaller than it was, the Severn Valley Railway, from Kidderminster to Bridgnorth, has survived and flourishes today as people flock here to relive the days of steam travel.

Between these two very different sections of Worcestershire lies the county town of Worcester, an ancient place that is well known for its glorious cathedral and as being the home of Royal Worcester porcelain. It was near here that one of Britain's greatest composers, Sir Edward Elgar, was born.

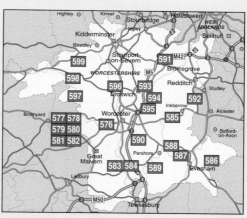

576 THE WHITEHALL INN

Rushwick

The **Whitehall Inn**, on the southwestern edge of Worcester, provides a homely ambience and traditional pub dishes.

 see page 589

WORCESTER

Situated on the River Severn, Worcester is a bustling county capital that is dominated by its **Cathedral**. Built by St Wulstan, the only English bishop not replaced by a Norman following the Conquest, the Cathedral, with its 200 feet tower and 11th century crypt, is a magnificent example of classic medieval architecture. One of the many tombs here is that of King John, adorned with a fine sculpture showing the King flanked by Bishops Oswald and Wulstan; outside is a statue of Sir Edward Elgar, who was born at nearby Lower Broadheath.

Right in the centre of the city stands a wonderful survivor from the past - **Greyfriars**, a medieval house with a pretty walled garden. By contrast, the imposing

Guildhall is a marvellous example of Queen Anne architecture that was designed by a local man, Thomas White. At the **City Museum and Art Gallery** there are displays of contemporary art and archaeology, a 19th century chemist's shop and the military collections of the Worcestershire Regiment and the Worcestershire Yeomanry Cavalry. The history of the city and its people is explored at the **Museum of Local Life**.

During the Civil War the Battle of Worcester was fought in 1651 and the Commandery, a stunning complex of buildings behind a small timber-framed entrance, was used as the Royalist headquarters. Now the **Commandery Civil War Centre** is home to a series of period rooms that offer a fascinating glimpse of the architecture and style of Tudor and Stuart times while also acting as the country's only museum devoted to the story of the Civil War.

With charming old buildings, a splendid cathedral, interesting museums and a compact National Hunt **Racecourse**, Worcester certainly has much to offer visitors, but no trip to the city would be complete without a visit to the **Royal Worcester Porcelain**

The Malvern Hills

Visitor Centre. Royal Worcester is Britain's oldest continuous producer of porcelain and the factory was founded in 1751 by Dr John Wall, who intended to create "a ware of a form so precise as to be easily distinguished from other English porcelain." Just to the southeast is **Worcester Woods Country Park**, a glorious place with ancient oak woodland, wildflower meadows and waymarked trails.

To the south of Worcester lies **Powick Bridge**, the scene of the first and last battles in the Civil War – the last, in 1651, ending with Charles II hiding in the Boscobel Oak before journeying south to nine year's exile in France.

It was at **Lower Broadheath**, just to the west of Worcester, that Edward Elgar was born in 1857, and, although he spent long periods away from the village, it remained his spiritual home. There are various Elgar Trails to follow, and the **Elgar Birthplace Museum** is housed in a redbrick cottage.

AROUND WORCESTER

MALVERN

7½ miles S of Worcester on the A449

Best known for its porcelain, annual music and drama festivals, Malvern water and Morgan cars, Malvern, beneath the northeastern slopes of the **Malvern Hills**, was a quiet and little known place with a priory at its centre before the discovery of its spring waters

started its growth. The hotels, baths and pump room were built in the early 19th century and the arrival of the railway provided easier access. The station is one of the many charming Victorian buildings, and a Regency cottage houses one source of the spring waters, **St Anne's Well**, where visitors can still sample the waters.

The centre of the town is dominated by a much older building, the priory **Church of St Mary and St Michael**, whose east and west windows (gifts from Henry VII and Richard III respectively) contain a wonderful collection of stained glass. Outside, in the churchyard, are some interesting graves including that of Jenny Lind, the 'Swedish Nightingale', who was born in Stockholm in 1820 but who died in Malvern while on a summer retreat in 1887. The 14th century Abbey Gateway still remains, now the home of the **Malvern Museum**. The town's heritage as an agricultural and market centre has not been lost, as close by is the permanent site of the **Three Counties Show**, one of the country's premier agricultural shows.

Great Malvern is the largest of the six settlements that make up the Malverns. To the south lies **Little Malvern**, where a simple headstone in the churchyard marks the grave of Sir Edward Elgar and his wife Caroline. In the churchyard at **West Malvern** is the grave of Peter Mark Roget of Thesaurus fame.

577 BREDON HOUSE

Great Malvern

A quiet, relaxed Regency/ Georgian guest house enjoying spectacular views while close to the centre of Great Malvern. Easy access to the famous hills which inspired Edward Elgar.

see page 590

578 CANNARA GUEST HOUSE

Barnards Green Road, Malvern

Cannara Guest House is a friendly home-from-home on the edge of Great Malvern, with fine views and easy access to all the local attractions.

see page 589

579 THE LAMB INN

West Malvern Road, Malvern

The **Lamb** is a cheerful, popular pub with a strong appeal for music-lovers – live sessions three times a week.

see page 590

580 THE WYCHE INN

Wyche Road, Malvern

The **Wyche Inn** is a friendly pub in great walking country, with local ales, home cooking and B&B rooms.

see page 590

581 COPPER BEECH HOUSE

Avenue Road, Malvern

Copper Beech House provides comfortable B&B accommodation in a quiet home-from-home setting.

see page 591

582 LADY FOLEY'S TEA ROOM

Great Malvern Station

Located in Great Malvern's Victorian railway station, **Lady Foley's Tea Room** is a delightfully different spot for enjoying hot and cold snacks.

see page 591

583 THE THREE KINGS INN

Hanley Castle

Super family hosts, hot and cold snacks, grills and a superb selection of real ales – no wonder the **Three Kings Inn** is so popular!

see page 591

584 THE JOCKEY INN

Baughton, nr Earls Croome

Big steaks, fresh fish, four real ales and a bungalow for overnight guests are among the attractions of the **Jockey Inn**.

see page 591

UPTON-ON-SEVERN

9 miles S of Worcester on the A4104

As one of the few bridging points on the River Severn, this unspoilt town was a Roman station and an important medieval port. It also played a role in the Civil War when in 1651 Charles sent a force to Upton to destroy the bridge; but after a long and bloody struggle the King's troops were defeated and Cromwell's men regained the town.

The Tudor House contains a museum of Upton past and present, and the 16th century White Lion Hotel was the setting for some of the scenes in Henry Fielding's novel *Tom Jones*.

Northeast of Upton, close to **Earls Croome**, lies **Croome Landscape Park**, which was Capability Brown's first complete landscape commission.

ALFRICK

6½ miles W of Worcester off the A44

The village church's claim to fame is that Charles Dodgson (better known as Lewis Carroll) once preached here but, today, it is nature lovers who are drawn to this charming village. To the northwest lies **Ravenshill Woodland Nature Reserve** where waymarked trails lead through woodland that is home to many breeding birds while, to the south, is Knapp and Papermill Nature Reserve, whose woodland and meadow are rich in flora and fauna.

To the east is the spectacular valley of **Leigh Brook**, a tributary of the River Teme, which winds its way through glorious countryside, and in the village of Leigh, in the grounds of Leigh Court, stands a massive 14th century **Tithe Barn** with great cruck beams and wagon doors.

EVESHAM

This bustling market town lies at the centre of the Vale of Evesham, an area that has long been known as the Garden of England as it produces a prolific harvest of soft fruits, apples, plums and salad vegetables. **The Blossom Trail**, which starts in the town, is a popular outing, particularly when the fruit trees are in blossom, and the waymarked trail follows a route from the town's High Street to Greenhill, where the Battle of Evesham took place.

At this point, the River Avon meanders in a loop around the town and **Abbey Park** is an excellent place for a riverside stroll although all that remains of the Abbey, which was built in around AD700 by Egwin, Bishop of Worcester, is the magnificent bell tower and the home of the Abbey Almoner that dates from around 1400. At the **Almonry Heritage Centre**, visitors can view a unique collection of artefacts that include displays showing the history of the Abbey and the defeat of Simon de Montford at the Battle of Evesham in 1265. He was buried by the high altar, and a stone marking the site was unveiled by the Speaker of the House of Commons in 1965, the 700th anniversary of his death.

AROUND EVESHAM

INKBERROW

9 miles N of Evesham on the A422

William Shakespeare stayed at the village inn, the **Old Bull**, in 1582, and it later won fame as the original of The Bull at Ambridge, the home of *The Archers*. Another handsome building in the village, the 18th century **Old Vicarage**, played host, in an earlier guise, to Charles I, while he was on his way to Naseby. Some maps that he left behind are now kept in the church.

MIDDLE LITTLETON

4 miles NE of Evesham off the B4085

Situated close to the River Avon along with the other Littletons – North and South – this village is home to a huge **Tithe Barn** that dates from the 13th century and that was once the property of the Abbots of Evesham; it is still in use as a farm building. Just to the north, in an area of fertile limestone, is **Windmill Hill Nature Reserve** while, to the southeast, near **Honeybourne**, is the **Domestic Fowl Trust and Honeybourne Rare Breeds Centre** where pure breeds of poultry, along with rare farm animal breeds, are conserved.

BROADWAY

5 miles SE of Evesham on the B4632

One of the most beautiful villages in England, this quintessential Cotswold village has a broad main street that is lined with houses and cottages built of golden Cotswold stone. It was settled as far back as 1900 BC, the Romans occupied the hill above Broadway, and the village was probably re-established after the Battle of Dyrham in AD 557 by conquering Saxons as they advanced on Worcester.

Housed in a picturesque 18th century shop on the High Street is the **Teddy Bear Museum**, where visitors of all ages will be enchanted with the numerous displays. The hall of fame tells of celebrity bears, including Paddington, Pooh and the three in the story of Goldilocks, while bears of all ages and sizes are for sale. Old bears and much-loved dolls are also lovingly restored here at – where else! – the St Beartholomew's Hospital.

On top of Broadway Beacon stands **Broadway Tower**, a folly that was built by the 6th Earl of Coventry at the end of the 18th century. Designed by James Wyatt, the tower now contains various displays and exhibitions, while the surrounding area is a delightful country park.

Just to the northwest of Broadway, near the village of **Childswickham**, is the **Barnfield Cider Mill Museum**, where visitors can see a display of cider-making down the years before sampling cider, perry or one of the wines produced from local plums and berries.

BREDON

8 miles SW of Evesham on the B4079

The most outstanding building here is undoubtedly **Bredon Barn**. This huge 14th century Cotswold stone

585 THE FLYFORD ARMS

Flyford Flavell

Great hospitality, well-kept real ales and excellent food have made the **Flyford Arms** a popular dining destination as well as a treasured 'local'.

🍴 *see page 592*

586 THE FLEECE INN

Bretforton, nr Evesham

The **Fleece** is a renowned inn owned by the National Trust, serving an interesting choice of real ales and wholesome home cooking. Now has an en suite room for B&B.

🍴 *see page 593*

587 THE GARDENERS ARMS

Charlton, nr Pershore

The **Gardeners Arms** is an outstanding inn serving excellent food in a picturesque setting.

🍴 *see page 594*

588 AVONSIDE HOTEL

Wyre Piddle, nr Pershore

Visitors to the **Avonside Hotel** enjoy lovely views, great food and excellent accommodation.

see page 593

589 THE ANCHOR INN & RESTAURANT

Eckington, nr Pershore

The **Anchor** offers excellent hotel and restaurant facilities in the picturesque Worcestershire countryside.

see page 595

590 THE MASONS

Wadborough

Outstanding cooking and a dedicated team at the helm have made **The Masons** one of the premier dining pubs in the region.

see page 596

barn has a dramatic aisled interior, marvellous beams and two porches at the wagon entrances.

To the northeast of Bredon lies Bredon Hill that dominates this area of Worcestershire and around which there are some delightful villages. Almost circular, this limestone outcrop rises to over 900 feet, and on the crest of the northern slope are the remains (part of the earthworks) of the pre-Roman settlement that is known as **Kemerton Camp**. At the top is a curious black tower called Parson's Folly that was built by a Mr Parson in the 18th century.

PERSHORE

6 miles NW of Evesham on the A44

This glorious market town, with its fine Georgian architecture, occupies an attractive location on the banks of the River Avon. Its crowning glory is undoubtedly its 7th century **Abbey**, which combines outstanding examples of both Norman and Early English architecture. Although only the choir remains of the original church, it is still a considerable architectural treasure, and the vaulting in the chancel roof is magnificent.

Pershore Bridge, which is now a favourite picnic spot, still bears the scars of damage it sustained during the Civil War.

KIDDERMINSTER

Standing on the banks of the River Stour, Kidderminster is known chiefly as a centre of the carpet-making industry that began here as a cottage

Bredon Barn

industry in the early 18th century. The introduction of the power loom instigated the move to a more industrialised method and carpet mills were built – the enormous chimneys still dominate the skyline. The industry also brought wealth to the town and surrounding area and this is reflected in the size of St Mary's Church, the largest parish church in the county, which stands on a hill overlooking Kidderminster. Outside the Town Hall is a statue to Kidderminster's best known son, Rowland Hill, a teacher, educationalist and inventor who founded the modern postal system and introduced the penny post.

The Severn Valley Railway runs from Kidderminster to Bridgnorth, in Shropshire, and at the town's station is the **Kidderminster Railway Museum**, where a splendid collection of railway memorabilia can be seen in an old Great Western Railway grain store.

AROUND KIDDERMINSTER

HAGLEY

6 miles NE of Kidderminster on the A456

In 1756, George, 1st Lord Lyttleton, commissioned the creation of what was to be the last great Palladian mansion in Britain, **Hagley Hall**, an imposing building with a restored rococo interior. In the surrounding parkland, there are temples, cascading pools and a ruined castle along with a large herd of deer.

Just to the southeast of Hagley

lie the **Clent Hills**, an immensely popular area for walking and enjoying the panoramic views. On the top of the hills are four upright stones that look as if they could be a work of modern art - in fact, they were erected over 200 years ago by Lord Lyttleton.

BROMSGROVE

8½ miles SE of Kidderminster on the A448

Along with some very handsome timber-framed buildings in the High Street, there stands a statue of AE Housman, Bromsgrove's most famous son.

Close to the town centre is the **Bromsgrove Museum** where there are displays of local crafts and industry, including the Bromsgrove Guild, an organisation of craftsmen that was founded in 1894. The skilled craftsmen of this guild designed and made the gates and railings of Buckingham Palace.

Two popular annual events are held here: the Music Festival, which hosts a wide range of musical entertainment from orchestral concerts to jazz, and the **Court Leet**, the ancient form of local administration whose annual colourful procession has been revived.

Just northeast of Bromsgrove near the village of **Burcot** is the notorious **Lickey Incline**. This stretch of railway is, at 1 in 37.7, the steepest gradient in the whole of Britain's rail network. One especially powerful locomotive, No. 58100, 'Big Bertha', the Lickey Banker, spent its days up until the late 1950s helping trains up the

591 BROMSGROVE MUSEUM

Bromsgrove

Much of the earlier history of Bromsgrove can be discovered at the museum with its interesting displays and exhibits.

 see page 597

Astwood Bank, nr Redditch

Food to cater for all tastes and appetites is served daily at **The Bell Inn**, with fresh local produce to the fore.

see page 598

bank, a task that was later performed by massive double-boilered locomotives that were the most powerful in the whole BR fleet. The steepness of the climb is due to the same geographical feature that necessitated the construction of the unique flight of locks at **Tardebigge** (to the southeast of Bromsgrove), where in the space of 2½ miles the canal is lifted by no fewer than 30 locks.

To the south of Bromsgrove is the **Avoncraft Museum of**

Historic Buildings that takes visitors on a walk through seven centuries of English history and where each building provides a snapshot of life in its particular period. Behind the museum's shop is another unique attraction, the **BT National Telephone Kiosk Collection**.

REDDITCH

14½ miles SE of Kidderminster on the A448

It was along the banks of the River Arrow that the town's famous needle-making industry was founded. Housed in one of the historic buildings in the beautiful valley is the **Forge Mill Needle Museum and Bordesley Abbey Visitor Centre** that offers a unique glimpse into a past way of life.

DROITWICH

8½ miles SE of Kidderminster on the A38

Salt deposits, a legacy from the time when this area was on the seabed, were mined here for 2,000 years, and the Romans named it Salinae, the place of salt. The natural Droitwich brine, which is pumped up from an underground lake 200 feet below the town, contains about 2½ pounds of salt per gallon – ten times that of sea water – and it is often likened to the waters of the Dead Sea. The first brine baths were built here in the 1830s and by 1876, under the influence of the 'Salt King' John Corbett, Droitwich had developed into a fashionable spa.

Many of the buildings in present day Droitwich were owned by Corbett, including the Raven

Hanbury Hall, Droitwich

Hotel, but his most remarkable and lasting monument is undoubtedly **Chateau Impney** on the eastern side of the town at Dodderhill. Designed in the style of an ornate French château by a Frenchman, Auguste Tronquois, the house has soaring turrets, a mansard roof and classical French gardens.

To the east of Droitwich lies **Hanbury Hall**, a fine redbrick mansion in William & Mary style. Along with a splendid collection of porcelain, the interior of the house is famous for its murals by Sir James Thornhill, who is perhaps best known for his frescoes in the dome of St Paul's Cathedral. The surrounding grounds include a formal garden, an orangery and an 18th century icehouse.

Leading southwestwards from Droitwich, the **Droitwich Canal**, which opened in 1771, was built by James Brindley to link the town with the River Severn at **Hawford**, where a half-timbered 16th century dovecote is sited. For some of its short length the canal passes close to the **Salwarpe Valley Nature Reserve**, one of the very few inland sites with salt water, which makes it ideal for a variety of saltmarsh plants.

STOURPORT-ON-SEVERN

3½ miles S of Kidderminster on the A451

Situated at the centre of the Worcestershire waterways, Stourport-on-Severn is a canal town of glorious Georgian buildings with an intricate network of canal basins. Prosperity and growth came quickly once the **Staffordshire and**

Worcestershire Canal had been dug, and although the commercial trade has now gone the town still prospers, as the barges laden with coal, timber, iron and grain have given way to pleasure craft.

Just to the east of the town lies **Hartlebury Castle**, a historic sandstone castle that was once owned by the Bishops of Worcester and was used as a prison for captured Royalist troops during the Civil War. It now houses the **Worcester County Museum**.

GREAT WITLEY

8½ miles SW of Kidderminster on the A443

This village is home to two remarkable buildings. Once one of the largest houses in Europe, **Witley Court** was a palatial mansion that was funded by the riches of the Dudley family but, following a devastating fire in 1937, the shell stood neglected for many years. The ruins have been made safe and accessible and along with the massive Poseidon and Flora fountains inspired by Bernini's fountains in Rome, they are a sight not to be missed. Adjacent to these haunting ruins is **St Michael's Church**, whose rather nondescript exterior does nothing to prepare visitors for the spectacularly flamboyant Baroque interior: stained glass by Joshua Price, plasterwork by Bagutti, canvas ceiling paintings by Bellucci.

BEWDLEY

3 miles W of Kidderminster on the B4190

Situated on the western bank of the River Severn and linked to its

593 THE HOP POLE

Droitwich Spa

Local ales and value-for-money lunchtime food brings a regular crowd to the **Hop Pole**.

see page 597

594 THE FIR TREE INN

Dunhampstead, Oddingley, nr Droitwich

Visitors to the **Fir Tree Inn** enjoy warm, genuine hospitality, real ales and a wide choice of popular home-cooked dishes.

see page 599

595 THE BRIDGE INN

Tibberton, nr Droitwich

By the Worcester-Birmingham Canal and just minutes from the M5, The **Bridge Inn** welcomes all-comers with an excellent choice of ales and food.

see page 600

596 THE CROWN & SANDYS

Ombersley, nr Droitwich

The **Crown & Sandys** is a distinguished old hostelry that sets and maintains high standards of food, drink and accommodation.

 see page 601

597 THE LION INN

Clifton-upon-Teme

The **Lion Inn** is a very handsome redbrick village pub with local ales, excellent food and two rooms for B&B.

 see page 599

598 THE BRIDGE

Stanford Bridge

The **Bridge** offers a scenic location in which to enjoy real ales and home cooking. Beer Festival in July.

see page 602

599 THE BELL

Pensax, nr Abberley

The **Bell** is a delightful village pub serving well-kept real ales and locally sourced food.

 see page 602

suburb, Wribbenhall, by a fine Thomas Telford bridge, Bewdley was once a flourishing port but it lost some of its importance when the Staffordshire and Worcestershire Canal was opened. It has now won fame with another form of transport, the **Severn Valley Railway**, which operates a full service of trains hauled by a variety of steam locomotives. Running from Kidderminster to Bridgnorth, the home of the railway since 1965, the route takes in several scenic attractions including the Wyre Forest and the **Severn Valley Country Park and Nature Reserve**. There are six stations along the track, each of them an architectural delight.

The **Bewdley Museum** contains exhibitions that are themed around the River Severn and the Wyre Forest and depicts local crafts such as charcoal burning, coopering and brass making. The town was the birthplace of Stanley Baldwin, Earl Baldwin of Bewdley, who was Prime Minister in 1923-1924, 1924-1929 and 1935-1937. He died at his home, Astley Hall (5 miles south of Kidderminster), opposite which is a memorial stone inscribed 'Thrice Prime Minister'. His ashes lie with those of his wife in the nave of Worcester Cathedral.

The Forestry Commission's Wyre Forest covers a vast area to the west and northwest of Bewdley and extending into Shropshire. The **Wyre Forest Visitor Centre**, just west of Bewdley, contains information on the forest, and the nearby Discovery Centre offers a wide range of holiday activities and educational programmes.

Yorkshire

The largest county in England, Yorkshire has a rich industrial and ecclesiastical heritage along with a wide diversity of countryside that helps to make it one of the most intriguing regions of England. The Yorkshire Dales National Park is an area of rich farmland, high moorland and deep valleys. The predominant limestone has given rise to a host of interesting natural features, none more so than Malham Cove, Malham Tarn and Aysgarth Falls. South of the Dales is Brontë country, an area forever associated with the tragic family, but one that also has strong links with the textile industry. The northeast of the county is dominated by the North York Moors National Park that incorporates not only the Cleveland Hills but also some spectacular coastline, including the old port of Whitby. Here, too, are elegant market towns such as Richmond and Ripon, and the famous spa town of Harrogate. Above all, there is York, a fabulous city centred on its magnificent cathedral that has a long and colourful history going back over 2,000 years.

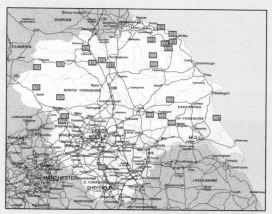

600 EASTBURN INN

Eastburn, nr Keighley

Good food, good beer and good company are all served in generous portions at the **Eastburn Inn**.

 see page 603

601 ILKLEY RIVERSIDE HOTEL

Riverside Gardens, Ilkley

Ilkley Riverside Hotel is an ideal spot for a drink, a meal or a stay in comfortable, civilised surroundings.

see page 604

HALIFAX

Halifax boasts one of Yorkshire's most impressive examples of municipal architecture, the glorious 18th century **Piece Hall**, a large quadrangle surrounded by colonnades and balconies behind which are some 40 specialist shops. Adjacent to the hall is the **Calderdale Industrial Museum**, which provides an insight into Halifax's textile heritage as well as celebrating the town's greatest contribution to modern motoring, the cats-eye. Halifax also has one of the largest parish churches in England.

On the outskirts of the town is the **Bankfield Museum**, the home between 1837 and 1886 of Edward Akroyd, the largest wool manufacturer in Britain, which now houses an internationally important collection of textiles and costumes from around the world.

To the east of Halifax lies **Shibden Hall and Park**, a distinctive timber-framed house dating from 1420, situated in 90 acres of parkland.

AROUND HALIFAX

KEIGHLEY

10 miles N of Halifax on the A650

Lying at the junction of the Rivers Worth and Aire, Keighley still retains a strangely nostalgic air of the Victorian Industrial Revolution. Several of the old mill buildings survive, and at the **Keighley Museum** is the hand-loom, complete with unfinished cloth, that was used by Timmy Feather, the last hand-loom weaver in England.

Just northeast of the town lies 17th century **East Riddlesden Hall**, which has one of the largest and most impressive timber-framed barns in the North of England that now houses a collection of farm wagons and agricultural equipment.

ILKLEY

14 miles NE of Halifax on the A65

One of the most famous West Yorkshire attractions has to be **Ilkley Moor**, immortalised in the well-known song; like any of the Yorkshire moors, Ilkley Moor can look inviting and attractive on a sunny day but ominous and forbidding when the weather is bad.

BRADFORD

6½ miles NE of Halifax on the A647

The **Bradford Industrial Museum and Horses at Work**, housed in an original worsted spinning mill complex built in 1875, re-creates life in Bradford in late Victorian times as well as offering horse-bus and tram rides. Of related interest is Britain's only **Museum of Colour**, where the fascinating story of dyeing and textile printing from Ancient Egypt to the present day is explained. The **National Museum of Photography, Film and Television** houses an IMAX, one of the largest cinema screens in the world.

HUDDERSFIELD

6½ miles SE of Halifax on the A629

Huddersfield flourished in Victorian times and its most impressive buildings date from that era: the stately railway station, the Italianate Town Hall and the lofty **Jubilee Tower**, built in 1897 to celebrate Queen Victoria's Diamond Jubilee.

HOLMFIRTH

11 miles SE of Halifax on the A635

As the location for the television comedy, *Last of the Summer Wine*, Holmfirth is familiar to millions who have never visited this little Pennine town. The town is home to the **Holmfirth Postcard Museum**, which has a comprehensive collection of the traditional saucy seaside postcard produced by Bamfords of Holmfirth in the first half of the 20th century.

HAWORTH

8 miles NW of Halifax off the A6033

Haworth is the home of the Brontë family and in its time was also a thriving industrial town. The Parsonage, built in 1777, is the focus of most Brontë pilgrimages and is now given over to the **Brontë Parsonage Museum**.

The **Brontë Way,** a 40-mile footpath with a series of four guided walks, links the places that provided inspiration to the sisters. The town is the headquarters of the **Keighley and Worth Valley Railway**, a thriving volunteer-run railway that serves six stations

Main Street, Haworth

(most of them gas-lit) in the course of its length.

SHEFFIELD

In recent years Sheffield has re-invented itself. England's fourth largest city, it is still busy with its steel, cutlery, engineering and toolmaking industries but is also a vibrant, international, multi-cultural city whose image was given a fillip

319

by the worldwide success of *The Full Monty* which was filmed in and around Sheffield.

The city's premier museum is the **Kelham Island Museum** which tells the story of Sheffield in a living museum. Sheffield's industrial heritage is celebrated in a number of museums, the most picturesque of which is undoubtedly the **Bishop's House Museum** which dates from around 1500 and is the earliest timber-framed house still standing in the city. A museum of a very different nature is the **Sheffield Bus Museum**, housed in the Tinsley Tram sheds on Sheffield Road. Sheffield also has three outstanding galleries devoted to the visual arts: the **Millennium Galleries** that not only showcase Sheffield's impressive metalware collection but also provides space to show the city's wonderful collection of paintings, drawings and natural history exhibits; the **Graves Art Gallery** with a wide-ranging collection of British art from the 16th century to the present along with European paintings and a fine collection of watercolours, drawings and prints; and the **Site Gallery**, devoted to photographic and new media exhibitions and events.

AROUND SHEFFIELD

RENISHAW

9 miles SE of Sheffield on the A616

This sizeable village gives its name to **Renishaw Hall**, home of Sir Reresby and Lady Sitwell and located about a mile or so to the northwest. The beautiful formal Italian gardens and 300 acres of wooded park are open to visitors, along with a nature trail and a Sitwell family museum, an art gallery, a display of Fiori de Henriques sculptures in the Georgian stables, and a café.

ROTHERHAM

7 miles NE of Sheffield on the A630/A631

The town's most striking building is undoubtedly the **Church of All Saints**. With its soaring tower, pinnacled buttresses and battlements, and imposing porch, it is one of the finest examples of perpendicular architecture in Yorkshire. It dates mainly from the 15th century although there is evidence of an earlier Saxon church on the site.

From the mid 18th century, the Walker Company of Rotherham was famous for cannons, their products serving to lethal effect in the American War of Independence and at the Battle of Trafalgar. They also built bridges, amongst them Southwark Bridge in London and the bridge at Sunderland. Another famous bridge builder was born here in 1901. Sir Donald Coleman Bailey invented the Bailey Bridge which proved to be of great military value, especially during World War II.

Dramatically set within the former Templeborough steelworks, **Magna** was the UK's first science adventure park.

BARNSLEY

10 miles N of Sheffield on the A61

The county town of South

Yorkshire, Barnsley stands on the River Dearne and derived its Victorian prosperity from the rich seams of coal hereabouts. It has an appropriately imposing Town Hall although the building is comparatively recent, completed in 1933. The town's most impressive museum is actually located a few miles to the west, in the village of Cawthorne. **Cannon Hall** is a magnificent 18th century country house set in formal gardens and historic parkland. It offers unique collections of pottery, furniture, glassware and paintings, along with the 'Charge Gallery' which documents the story of the 13th/18th Royal Hussars.

About a mile to the south of Barnsley is the **Worsbrough Mill and Country Park**. The Grade II listed mill dates from around 1625. A steam mill was added in the 19th century and both have been restored to full working order to form the centrepiece of an industrial museum. Another three miles to the southeast, situated in attractive South Yorkshire countryside just off the M1 (J36), the **Elsecar Heritage Centre** is an imaginative science and history centre which is fun and educational for all the family.

DONCASTER

Originally a Roman settlement, Doncaster later had one of the country's most important railway works, where steam locomotives were turned out in their thousands, including the A4 Pacifics, among which was the record-breaking *Mallard*. Doncaster is also a renowned centre of horse-racing, and the venue for the final classic of the racing year, the St Leger.

On the northwestern outskirts of Doncaster lies Cusworth Hall, home to the **Museum of South Yorkshire Life** while, a little further on, is **Brodsworth Hall**, a remarkable example of a Victorian mansion that has survived with most of its original furnishings and decorations intact.

AROUND DONCASTER

SELBY

18 miles N of Doncaster on the A63

Selby Abbey was completed in the 13th century and has suffered more than most down the centuries. It was severely damaged by Cromwell's troops during the Civil War and in 1690 the central tower collapsed. Major restoration work was carried out during the 19th century, but in 1906 a disastrous fire swept through the Abbey. Despite all this, the building is still a beautiful edifice, and the famous Washington Window that depicts the coat of arms of John de Washington, a 15th century Prior of the Abbey and a direct ancestor of George Washington, remains intact.

CONISBROUGH

5 miles SW of Doncaster on the A630

The town is best known for its 11th century Conisbrough Castle,

602 CANNON HALL MUSEUM

Barnsley

Set amid 70 acres of parkland and gardens, Cannon Hall contains collections of furniture, paintings and glassware.

 see page 602

603 THE CROSS KEYS

Thixendale, nr Malton

The **Cross Keys** is a family-run free house with well-kept beer, good home cooking and three rooms for B&B.

see page 605

which features prominently in one of the most dramatic scenes in Sir Walter Scott's novel *Ivanhoe*. The most impressive medieval building in South Yorkshire, **Conisbrough Castle** boasts the oldest circular keep in England.

PONTEFRACT

15 miles NW of Doncaster on the A639

When it was built in the 11th century, **Pontefract Castle** was one of the most formidable fortresses in Norman England. In medieval times it passed to the House of Lancaster and became a Royal Castle – Richard II was imprisoned here and murdered in its dungeons on the orders of Henry Bolingbroke, who then assumed the crown as Henry IV. The castle was a major Royalist stronghold during the Civil War, after which it was destroyed by Cromwell's troops. Today it is a gaunt ruin with only sections of the inner bailey and the lower part of the keep surviving intact.

The town is most famous for its Pontefract Cakes. Liquorice root has been grown here since monastic times and there is even a small planting of liquorice in the local park.

YORK

At the centre of this glorious city is **York Minster**, which stands on the site of an even older building, the headquarters of the Roman legions. Its stained glass windows – there are more than a hundred of them – cast a celestial light over the many treasures within. A guided tour of the Great Tower gives spectacular views across the city, while a visit to the crypt reveals some of the relics from the Roman fortress that stood here nearly 2,000 years ago.

The network of medieval streets around the Minster is one of the city's major delights. Probably most famous of these ancient streets is **The Shambles** – its name comes from 'Fleshammels', the street of butchers and slaughterhouses. Continuing to prosper into the 19th century, York became the hub of the railway system in the north at the instigation of the entrepreneur George Hudson, founder of what became the Great Northern Railway. Close to the magnificent railway station is the **National Railway Museum,** the largest of its kind in the world. One of York's most unusual attractions is the **Jorvik Centre**, an innovative exhibition of Viking York complete with authentic sounds and even smells.

AROUND YORK

MALTON

17 miles NE of York on the B1248

Malton has been the historic centre of Ryedale ever since the Romans came and built a large fort beside the River Derwent. Many relics from the site can be seen in the **Malton Museum,** along with items from the Iron Age settlement that preceded the Roman garrison.

The River Derwent has always been vitally important to Malton as it provides an essential element for what was once a major industry in Malton - brewing. In the 19th century there were nine breweries here, but now only the Malton Brewery Company survives.

Old Malton is located just to the north of the Roman Fort, an interesting and historic area on the edge of open countryside. To the north is **Eden Camp**, a themed museum dedicated to re-creating the dramatic experiences of ordinary people living through World War II, and next door is **Eden Farm Insight,** a working farm with a fascinating collection that includes old farm machinery and lots of animals.

To the southwest, lying in the folds of the Howardian Hills, stands one of the most glorious stately homes in Britain, **Castle Howard.** Well known to television viewers as the Brideshead of *Brideshead Revisited*, Castle Howard has impressed visitors ever since it was completed in the early 1700s.

SLEDMERE
22 miles NE of York on the B1253

The village is home to **Sledmere House**, a noble Georgian mansion built by the Sykes family in the 1750s. Inside, there is fine furniture by Chippendale and Sheraton; outside, gardens and parkland landscaped by Capability Brown.

Across the road from Sledmere House are two remarkable, elaborately detailed, monuments: an Eleanor Cross, modelled on those set up by Edward I in memory of his queen, and the

Waggoners Memorial, which commemorates the 1,000-strong company of men the Sykes family raised from the Wolds during World War I.

BRIDLINGTON
38 miles NE of York on the A165

The old town lies a mile inland from the bustling seaside resort, with its amusements and ten-mile stretch of sandy beach. **Bridlington Priory** was once one of the wealthiest in England but it was ruthlessly pillaged during the Reformation.

On the northern outskirts of Bridlington is **Sewerby Hall**, a monumental mansion built between 1714 and 1720. Set in 50 acres of garden and parkland, the house was first opened to the public in 1936 by Amy Johnson, the dashing,

Flamborough Head, Near Bridlington

604 THE GREY HORSE
INN

Elvington, nr York

The **Grey Horse** is a
picture-postcard village inn a
short drive from York, with
a good choice of real ales,
great home cooking and two
splendid rooms for B&B
guests.

 see page 606

605 THE FEATHERS
HOTEL

Pocklington

Dominating the market place
in Pocklington, the **Feathers**
excels both as a hotel and
restaurant.

 see page 605

606 THE RED LION

Market Weighton

Warmth and hospitality are
bywords at the **Red Lion**,
which serves good home
cooking every lunchtime.

 see page 605

Yorkshire-born pilot who captured
the public imagination with her
daring solo flights to South Africa
and Australia. The Museum here
houses some fascinating
memorabilia of Amy's pioneering
feats. Close by is **Bondville
Miniature Village**, one of the
finest model villages in the country.

A few miles north of
Bridlington is the picturesque and
dramatic scenery of **Flamborough
Head**. The Head's first, and
England's oldest surviving
Lighthouse, was built in 1674 and
its original beacon was a basket of
burning coal.

STAMFORD BRIDGE

6 miles E of York on the A166

Just a few days before the Battle of
Hastings, King Harold had clashed
at Stamford Bridge with his half-
brother Tostig and Hardrada, King
of Norway, who between them had
mustered some 60,000 men.
Harold's troops were triumphant
but immediately after this victory
they marched southwards to
Hastings and a much more famous
defeat.

DRIFFIELD

26 miles E of York on the A166

Located on the edge of the Wolds,
Driffield was once the capital of
the Saxon Kingdom of Dear, a
vast domain extending over the
whole of Northumbria and
Yorkshire. It was a king of Dear
who divided the southern part of
his realm into three parts,
'thriddings', a word which
gradually evolved into the famous

Ridings of Yorkshire.

To the northeast lies **Burton
Agnes Hall**, an outstanding
Elizabethan house with fabulous
gardens, recently voted Garden of
the Year by 25,000 friends of the
Historic Houses Association.

HORNSEA

37 miles E of York on the B1242

This small coastal town can boast
not only the most popular visitor
attraction in Humberside, **Hornsea
Pottery**, but also Yorkshire's
largest freshwater lake, Hornsea
Mere, a refuge for over 170 species
of birds. Also here, housed in a
converted 18th century farmhouse,
is the **North Holderness
Museum of Village Life**.

BEVERLEY

27 miles SE of York on the A1035

In medieval times, Beverley was
one of England's most prosperous
towns and it remains one of the
most gracious, with its great
Minster, built between 1220 and
1450, dominating the landscape.
An unusual feature of the
Guildhall is a figure of Justice with
her scales but without her
blindfold. When an 18th century
Town Clerk was asked the reason
for this, he replied, "In Beverley,
Justice is not blind."

Exhibits at Beverley's **Museum
of Army Transport** include a
wagon in which Lord Roberts
travelled during the Boer War and
the Rolls-Royce used by Field
Marshal Montgomery as a staff car
in France.

TADCASTER

9 miles SW of York off the A64

Situated on the River Wharfe, since the 14th century Tadcaster's major industry has been brewing and three major breweries are still based here: John Smiths, Samuel Smiths and the Tower Brewery, owned by Bass Charrington. The distinctive brewery buildings dominate the town's skyline and provide the basis of its prosperity.

The oldest building in Tadcaster is **The Ark**, dating back to the 1490s. During its long history, The Ark has served as many things and it now houses the Town Council offices.

WETHERBY

10 miles W of York on the A1

Situated on the Great North Road, at a point midway between Edinburgh and London, Wetherby was renowned for its coaching inns, of which the two most famous were The Angel and The Swan & Talbot. It is rumoured that serving positions at these inns were considered so lucrative that employees had to pay for the privilege of employment in them!

To the northeast, in 1644, one of the most important encounters of the Civil War, which the Royalists lost, took place on **Marston Moor**.

BOROUGHBRIDGE

16 miles NW of York on the B6265

This attractive and historic town dates from the reign of William the Conqueror and the bridge over the River Ure, from which the village takes its name, was built in 1562, forming part of an important road link between Edinburgh and London. To the west are the great **Devil's Arrows**, three massive Bronze Age monoliths, which are the most famous ancient monument in Yorkshire. Further on is one of the area's finest stately homes, 18th century **Newby Hall**, standing in magnificent gardens.

To the east of Boroughbridge is **Aldborough Roman Museum** housing relics from this once thriving Roman city.

EASINGWOLD

12 miles NW of York off the A19

Easingwold's prosperity dates back to the 18th century when it flourished as a major stage coach post. Later, it enjoyed the distinction of having its own private railway.

A little to the southeast of Easingwold is **Sutton Park,** a noble early 18th century mansion that contains some fine examples of Sheraton and Chippendale furniture.

HULL

Extensively battered by the Luftwaffe during World War II, this ancient port has risen from those ashes to be once again one of the country's busiest ports. Its most famous son is William Wilberforce, born here in 1759. After becoming the town's Member of Parliament, Wilberforce began a campaign to outlaw the slave trade, which was successful after a 30-year struggle;

607 HORNSEA FOLK MUSEUM

Hornsea

The development of village life in North Holderness is explored at the Hornsea Folk Museum and a series of restored rooms brings the Victorian age to life .

 see page 605

608 BLACKSMITHS ARMS

Lastingham

An extensive food choice, interesting real ales and comfortable accommodation makes the **Blacksmiths Arms** an excellent place to seek out at the foot of the North Yorkshire Moors.

see page 607

609 THE COACH HOUSE

Rosedale Abbey, nr Pickering

The **Coach House Inn** is a cheerful village hostelry open all day for food and drink.

see page 607

610 BIRCH HALL INN & HOLIDAY COTTAGE

Beck Hole, Goathland

In a lovely setting in the North Yorkshire moors, **Birch Hall Inn** offers well-kept ales and simple snacks. A Self Catering cottage for four is attached to the main building.

see page 607

611 THE POSTGATE INN

Egton Bridge, nr Whitby

The **Postgate Inn** is a great place for a drink or a meal, with a super selection of dishes marked up on blackboards. Also rooms for B&B.

see page 608

the **Wilberforce House Museum** presents a history of the trade and Wilberforce's efforts to eradicate it forever. Many other museums and trails tell the story of Hull's connection with the sea and fishing.

The other great point of interest here is the **Humber Bridge**, one of the world's longest single-span bridges with an overall length of 2,428 yards that was opened in 1981.

To the southeast is **Spurn Point** that leads to Spurn Head, the narrow hook of ever-shifting sands that curls around the mouth of the Humber estuary. This bleak but curiously invigorating part of Yorkshire is home to hundreds of species of rare and solitary wild fowl, playful seals, and also to the small contingent of lifeboatmen who operate the only permanently manned lifeboat station in Britain.

PICKERING

The largest of the four market towns in Ryedale and possibly the oldest, claiming to date from 270 BC, Pickering lies at the heart of the fertile Vale of Pickering. Housed in a gracious Regency mansion, the **Beck Isle Museum** has intriguing re-creations of typical Victorian domestic rooms, shops, workshops and even a pub. The town is the southern terminus of the North York Moors Railway, whose steam trains run to Grosmont.

To the south lies **Flamingo Land**, a zoo and fun park in the wooded parkland of Kirby Misperton Hall.

AROUND PICKERING

GOATHLAND

11 miles N of Pickering off the A169

A major attraction in this pleasant moorland village is **Mallyan Spout**, a 70ft waterfall locked into a crescent of rocks and trees. Just to the north is **Beck Hole**, a little village that plays host to the **World Quoits Championship**. The game, which appears to have originated in Eskdale, involves throwing a small iron hoop over an iron pin set about 25 feet away.

WHITBY

17½ miles NE of Pickering on the A171

Whitby was one of the earliest and most important centres of Christianity in England, and high on the cliff that towers above the old town stand the imposing and romantic ruins of **Whitby Abbey**. It was here in the 7th century the Synod of Whitby met and settled, once and for all, the precise date on which Easter should be celebrated. As an apprentice, James Cook, later the renowned Captain Cook, lived in Whitby, and the handsome house in Grape Lane where he lodged is now the **Captain Cook Memorial Museum**. According to Bram Stoker, Whitby was the place where Count Dracula, in the form of a wolf or large dog, came ashore from a crewless ship that had drifted into harbour.

A popular souvenir of the town is jet, a lustrous black stone that enjoyed enormous popularity

Whitby

612 THE PLOUGH INN

Sleights, nr Whitby

The Plough is a handsome stone inn with a fine reputation for good food and drink and comfortable B&B accommodation.

see page 608

613 ESTBEK HOUSE

Sandsend, nr Whitby

Situated in a pretty coastal village near Whitby, **Estbek House** offers a combination of Georgian elegance and modern amenities, with fine food, high-quality wines and superb bedrooms.

see page 609

614 THE CAPTAIN COOK INN

Staithes, North Yorkshire

Real ale devotees are in their element at the **Captain Cook Inn**, which has four bedrooms for B&B guests.

see page 610

in Victorian times when, after the death of Prince Albert, jewellery in jet was the only ornament the Queen would allow herself to wear. The **Esk Valley Line** from Whitby to Middlesbrough runs across the North York Moors on a 90-minute journey that rivals the Settle-Carlisle line in scenic splendour.

To the south of the town lies **Robin Hood's Bay**, where once smuggling was as important as fishing.

SCARBOROUGH

15½ miles E of Pickering on the A170

With its two splendid bays and dramatic cliff-top castle, Scarborough was targeted by the early railway tycoons as the natural candidate for Yorkshire's first seaside resort. Even before the advent of the railway, Scarborough had been well-known to a select few who travelled to what was then a remote little town to sample the spring water. Anne Brontë came

615 THE DOWNE ARMS

Castleton

The **Downe Arms** is a fine old moorland stone pub with a traditional ambience, an interesting menu and 5 excellent rooms for B&B.

see page 610

616 THE BAY HORSE

Crakehall, Bedale

In an attractive setting overlooking the green and cricket pitch, the **Bay Horse** serves Yorkshire ales and good home cooking.

see page 611

here in the hope that the spa town's invigorating air would improve her health, a hope that was not fulfilled. She died at the age of 29 and her grave lies in St Mary's churchyard at the foot of the castle. Built between 1158 and 1168, **Scarborough Castle** occupies the site of a Roman fort and signal station and its gaunt remains stand high on Castle Rock Headland, dominating the resort's two sweeping bays.

Down the coast from Scarborough lies **Filey**, one of the first Yorkshire resorts to benefit from the early 19th century craze for sea bathing.

COXWOLD

16½ miles SW of Pickering off the A170

At the western end of the village stands the 500-year-old **Shandy Hall,** home of Laurence Sterne, vicar of Coxwold in the 1760s. Sterne was the author of *Tristram Shandy*, a wonderfully bizarre novel which opened a vein of English surreal comedy inherited by the likes of the Goons and Monty Python.

Just to the south of Coxwold is **Newburgh Priory,** founded in 1145 as an Augustinian monastery and now a mostly Georgian country house with fine interiors and a beautiful water garden.

To the north are the lovely, cream-coloured ruins of **Byland Abbey** that was built by the Cistercians in 1177.

HELMSLEY

11 miles W of Pickering on the A170

One of North Yorkshire's most popular and attractive towns,

Helmsley lies on the banks of the River Rye at the edge of the North York Moors National Park. Founded in the early 1100s, **Helmsley Castle** was badly damaged during the Civil War and is today a romantic and picturesque ruin. Just to the west of Helmsley are the hauntingly beautiful remains of **Rievaulx Abbey**, standing among wooded hills beside the River Rye. Founded in 1131, this was the first Cistercian abbey in Yorkshire and, with some 700 people eventually living within its walls, became one of the largest.

To the southeast lies **Nunnington Hall**, a late 17th century manor house set beside the River Rye with a picturesque packhorse bridge within its grounds.

THIRSK

23 miles W of Pickering on the A61

Thirsk has become famous as the home of veterinary surgeon Alf Wight, better known as James Herriot, author of All Creatures Great and Small, who died in 1995. The World of James Herriot is housed in his original surgery in Kirkgate and offers visitors a trip back in time to the 1940s, exploring the life and times of the world's most famous country vet.

On the edge of town, the **Trees to Treske Visitor Centre** is an imaginative exhibition exploring how trees grow, the character of different woods and examples of the cabinetmaker's craft. Nearby is Thirsk **Racecourse**, known to devotees of the turf as the

'Country Racecourse'.

To the northwest is **Sion Hill Hall,** one of the last great country houses. Completed in 1913, the rooms have not altered since they were built and they are home to one of the best collections of Georgian, Victorian and Edwardian artefacts in the north of England.

HUTTON-LE-HOLE

6½ miles NW of Pickering off the A170

Long regarded as one of Yorkshire's prettiest villages, Hutton-le-Hole has a character all its own. Facing the green is the **Ryedale Folk Museum,** an imaginative celebration of 4,000 years of life in North Yorkshire; among the historic buildings is a complete Elizabethan Manor House rescued from nearby Harome.

NORTHALLERTON

27½ miles NW of Pickering on the A168

The county town of North Yorkshire, and once an important stop on the coaching route from Newcastle to London.

To the northeast is **Mount Grace Priory,** a 14th century building where a well-appointed two-storey monks' cell has been restored to give a vivid impression of what life was like in what was clearly one of the more comfortable 14th century monastic houses.

GREAT AYTON

22 miles NW of Pickering on the A173

This appealing village set around the River Leven is an essential stopping point for anyone following the **Captain Cook Country Tour,** a 70-mile circular trip taking in all the major locations associated with the great sailor. Cook's family moved to Great Ayton when he was 8 years old and he attended the little school that is now the **Captain Cook Schoolroom Museum**.

PATELEY BRIDGE

Considered to be one of the prettiest towns in the Dales, Pateley Bridge is perfectly situated as a base from which to explore Upper Nidderdale. Much of the town seen today was built in the prosperous years when it was a flourishing textile town with a local mining industry.

The **Nidderdale Museum** is housed in one of the town's original Victorian workhouses and presents a fascinating record of local folk history. To the east are **Brimham Rocks**, an extraordinary natural sculpture park where the millstone grit boulders have been formed into fantastic shapes by years of erosion.

AROUND PATELEY BRIDGE

LEYBURN

16 miles N of Pateley Bridge on the A684

The main market town and trading centre of mid Wensleydale, Leyburn is an attractive town with a broad market place lined by

617 WOODYS AT THE BLACK SWAN

Thornton-le-Moor, nr Northallerton

The owners of **Woodys at the Black Swan** have added an excellent destination restaurant to a much-loved village local.

see page 612

618 THE SWALEDALE ARMS

Morton-on-Swale, nr Northallerton

The **Swaledale Arms** is a popular village pub serving good honest English food and three real ales.

see page 611

Castle Hill, Richmond

Windsor Guest House has
ten comfortable rooms for
B&B; packed lunches and
evening meals by
arrangement.

see page 611

handsome late Georgian and
Victorian stone buildings.

To the east, and surrounded by
walled and wooded parkland, is
Constable Burton Hall, famous
for its gardens. To the south, on the
banks of the River Ure, is **Jervaulx
Abbey**, one of the great Cistercian
sister houses to Fountains Abbey,
set in beautiful gardens.

South of Leyburn lies
Middleham, an enchanting little
town with strong racing
connections. Among the illustrious
trainers based here were Sam Hall,
a master trainer on the Flat, and
Neville Crump, who trained the
winner of the Grand National on
three occasions. Rising high above
the town are the magnificent ruins
of **Middleham Castle**, a once-
mighty fortress whose finest days
were in the 15th century, when
most of northern England was
ruled from here by the Neville
family.

RICHMOND

23 miles N of Pateley Bridge on the A6108

Alan Rufus, 1st Earl of Richmond,
built the original **Richmond Castle**
in 1071 and the site, 100 feet up on
a rocky promontory overlooking
the River Swale, is both imposing
and well chosen. The first
completely Norman stone castle in
the country, it is now a ruin, though
much of the original stonework
remains intact. One of the grandest
buildings in the town is the
Culloden Tower, which was
erected in 1747 by the Yorke
family, one of whose members had

fought at the Battle of Culloden the
previous year. Richmond is also
home to England's oldest theatre,
the Georgian Theatre Royal, which
opened in the 1780s and originally
formed part of a circuit that
included Northallerton, Ripon, and
Harrogate. The **Georgian
Theatre Royal Museum** contains
a unique collection of original
playbills as well as the oldest and
largest complete set of painted
scenery in Britain.

Just outside the town lies
Easby Abbey, founded in 1155
and now a delightful monastic ruin
which looks down to the River
Swale.

MASHAM

10½ miles NE of Pateley Bridge on the A6108

Set beside the River Ure,
picturesque Masham is best known
for its beer. **Theakston's Brewery**
was founded in 1827 by two
brothers, Thomas and Robert
Theakston, and its modern visitor
centre illustrates the process of
brewing and the art of cooperage.
The **Black Sheep Brewery** is also
well worth a visit. It too offers a
guided tour and visitors get the
chance to sample the traditionally
made ale.

RIPON

10 miles NE of Pateley Bridge on the A61

This attractive city, on the banks of
the Rivers Ure, Skell, and Laver,
dates from the 7th century, when
Alfrich, King of Northumbria,
granted an area of land to the
church. Later that century, St

Wilfrid built a church on the high ground between the three rivers but the crypt is all that remains of his church; the magnificent 12th century **Cathedral of St Peter and St Wilfrid** now stands on the site.

The **Spa Baths**, opened in 1905 by the Princess of Battenberg, are a reminder of Ripon's attempt to become a fashionable spa resort. Not far from the Cathedral is the 17th century House of Correction, which now houses the **Ripon Prison and Police Museum**.

To the southwest of the city are the magnificent **Studley Royal Gardens,** created in the early 18th century. Adjoining the gardens is the glorious **Fountains Abbey**, the pride of all the ecclesiastical ruins in Yorkshire and a World Heritage Site. The abbey, which was founded in 1132, was one of the wealthiest of the Cistercian houses and its remains are the most complete of any Cistercian abbey in Britain.

Fountains Abbey, Ripon

RIPLEY

7½ miles SE of Pateley Bridge off the A61

Ripley Castle has been home to the Ingilby family for over 600 years, granted to them when Thomas Ingilby killed a wild boar that was charging at King Edward III. The castle stands in an outstanding Capability Brown landscape, and the walled garden contains the National Hyacinth Collection.

HARROGATE

10½ miles SE of Pateley Bridge on the A61

One of England's most attractive towns, Harrogate retains many of its original spa buildings including the Royal Pump Room and the Royal Baths Assembly Rooms, which in their heyday were full of rich visitors sampling the waters.

To the east lies the town of **Knaresborough** and **Mother Shipton's Cave**, the home of a Petrifying Well where the lime-rich water has seemingly turned to stone an array of objects from old boots to bunches of grapes.

SKIPTON

14 miles SW of Pateley Bridge on the A59

Skipton's origins can be traced to the 7th century, when the farmers

331

620 GRASSINGTON LODGE

Grassington

Grassington Lodge is a luxurious Bed & Breakfast for touring the beautiful Yorkshire Dales.

 see *page 613*

621 THE GOLDEN LION HOTEL

Horton-in-Ribblesdale, nr Settle

The **Golden Lion** is everything a country inn should be, with good food, good drink and comfortable accommodation.

see *page 613*

christened it Sheeptown. The Normans decided to build a castle to guard the entrance to Airedale and Skipton became a garrison town. **Skipton Castle**, home of the Cliffords, is one of the most complete and well-preserved medieval castles in England, and its most striking feature is the impressive 14th century gateway.

For many years Skipton remained just a market town, until, with the development of the factory system in the 19th century, textile mills were built and cottages and terraced houses constructed for the influx of mill workers. The **Leeds and Liverpool Canal**, which flows through the town, provided a cheap form of transport as well as linking Skipton with the major industrial centres of Yorkshire and Lancashire.

A walk around the town reveals many interesting buildings, including the Town Hall, now also the home of the **Craven Museum**. It seems appropriate that a town that was so dedicated to trade and commerce should be the birthplace, in 1851, of Thomas Spencer, co-founder of Marks and Spencer.

To the east, in a village that is part of the Duke of Devonshire's estate, are the substantial ruins of **Bolton Priory**, an Augustinian house that was founded in 1155 by monks. Upstream from the ruins is one of the most visited natural features in Wharfedale, a point where the wide river suddenly narrows into a confined channel of black rock through which the water thunders. This spectacular gorge is known as **The Strid** because, over the centuries, many heroic (or foolhardy) types have attempted to leap across it as a test of bravery.

GRASSINGTON

11 miles W of Pateley Bridge on the B6265

One of the best loved villages within the Yorkshire Dales National Park, Grassington in many ways typifies the Dales' settlement with its characteristic market square. Known as the capital of Upper Wharfedale, the historically important valley roads meet here and the ancient monastic route from Malham to Fountains Abbey passes through the village. The Upper Wharfedale Folk Museum is housed in two converted 18th century lead-miners' cottages.

To the east is the wonderful 500,000-year-old-cave at **Stump Cross Caverns**, a large show cave with a fantastic array of stalactites and stalagmites.

MALHAM

17 miles W of Pateley Bridge off the A65

Malham village was originally two settlements, Malham East and Malham West, which came under the influence of a different religious house: Bolton Priory and Fountains Abbey respectively.

To the north is **Malham Cove**, a limestone amphitheatre that is the most spectacular section of the mid-Craven fault; as recently as the 1700s, a massive waterfall that was higher than Niagara Falls cascaded over its edge! These days the water disappears through potholes at the top, called water-sinks, and reappears through the cavern mouth at Aire Head near the village. Not far away is the equally inspiring **Gordale Scar**, a huge gorge carved by glacial melt water with an impressive waterfall leaping, in two stages, from a fissure in its face. Further north of the scar is Malham Tarn, a glacial lake that, by way of an underground stream, is the source of the River Aire.

SETTLE

22½ miles W of Pateley Bridge on the B6480

This small market town is best known today as the home of the scenically unrivalled **Settle-Carlisle Railway**, a proudly preserved memento of the glorious age of steam. The line took six years to build, being completed in 1876, and incorporated 21 major viaducts and 14 tunnels. The workmen on the line endured the harshest of conditions, and many lost their lives; over 100 lie buried in the graveyard at Chapel-le-Dale. Settle is dominated by one of the huge viaducts and by the towering limestone cliffs of Castleberg Crag.

To the west, near **Giggleswick**, is the famous **Ebbing and Flowing Well**, one of many in the area that owe their unusual names to the porous limestone that causes water to be sometimes there and sometimes not.

INGLETON

30 miles W of Pateley Bridge off the A65

Ingleton Waterfalls have been delighting visitors since 1885, and along the four miles of scenic walks, the stretch of waterfalls

includes interesting names such as Pecca Twin Falls, Holly Bush Spout, Thornton Force, and Baxengill Gorge. The second principal network of caves in the area is **White Scar Caves**. Discovered in 1923, this network has been under exploration ever since. At **Ingleborough**, the peak has been used as a beacon and a fortress for 2,000 years.

RIBBLEHEAD

28½ miles NW of Pateley Bridge on the B6255

Lying close to the source of the River Ribble is an impressive structure, the 24-arched **Ribblehead Viaduct**, which was built to carry the Settle-Carlisle Railway. A bleak and exposed site, the viaduct is often battered by strong winds that can, on occasion, stop a train literally in its tracks. The regular service is worked by two-car diesel Sprinters, but there are also special excursions and charter trains.

HAWES

25½ miles NW of Pateley Bridge on the A684

One of the local industries was rope-making and at **The Hawes Ropeworkers**, next to the **Dales Countryside Museum**, visitors can see experienced ropers twisting cotton and man-made fibres to make halters, hawsers, picture cords, dog leads and clothes lines. Wensleydale's most famous product (after its sheep) is its soft, mild cheese, and at the **Wensleydale Cheese Experience** its history is told through a series of interesting displays.

622 THE OLD DAIRY FARM

Widdale, Hawes

Farm buildings in Upper Wensleydale have been converted into a secluded small hotel offering high standards of comfort, service and cuisine.

🛏 *see page 614*

623 THE MILL RACE TEA
SHOP

Aysgarth Falls

In an old mill building below
the Aysgarth Falls, the **Mill
Race Tea Shop** serves an
appetising selection of
home-made cakes, scones,
savouries and snacks.

see page 613

Just to the north and located in
a natural amphitheatre of limestone
crags, is **Hardraw Force**, the
highest unbroken waterfall in
England above ground. Because of
an undercut in the cliff, walkers can
view the water from behind, just as
Turner and Wordsworth famously
did.

AYSGARTH

18 miles NW of Pateley Bridge on the A684

The village is famous for the
spectacular **Aysgarth Falls** where
the River Ure thunders through a
rocky gorge and drops some 200
feet over three huge slabs of
limestone which divide this
wonderful natural feature into the
Upper, Middle and Lower Falls.
The Dales National Park has a
Visitor Information Centre here
and, just a short walk away, is the
**Yorkshire Museum of Horse-
Drawn Carriages**, where a
collection of nearly 60 Victorian
coaches is housed in a 200-year-old
mill overlooking the Falls.

To the northwest lies the once
important market town of **Askrigg**,

which became Darrowby in the
popular television series *All Creatures
Great and Small*. The village has been
popular with tourists since the days
of Turner and Wordsworth, many
of them coming to see the
impressive waterfalls at Whitfield Fill
Force and Mill Gill Force.

To the northeast of Aysgarth is
Bolton Castle, which has
dominated mid Wensleydale for
more than 600 years ever since the
lord of the manor, Richard le
Scrope, was granted permission to
fortify his manor house in 1379.
Today, this luxurious fortified
manor house is still occupied by a
direct descendant of the 1st Lord
Scrope and it remains an impressive
sight with its four square towers
acting as a local landmark.

REETH

23 miles NW of Pateley Bridge on the B6270

At the junction of the River Swale
and its main tributary Arkle Beck,
Reeth is home to the **Swaledale
Folk Museum**, housed in what
was once the old Methodist Sunday
School.

Accommodation, Food &Drink and Places to Visit

The establishments featured in this section includes hotels, inns, guest houses, bed & breakfasts, restaurants, cafes, tea and coffee shops, tourist attractions and places to visit. Each establishment has an entry number which can be used to identify its location at the beginning of the relevant county chapter. This section is ordered by county and the page number in the column to to right indicates the first establishment in each county.

In addition full details of all these establishments and many others can be found on the Travel Publishing website - www.travelpublishing.co.uk. This website has a comprehensive database ocovering the whole of Britain and Ireland.

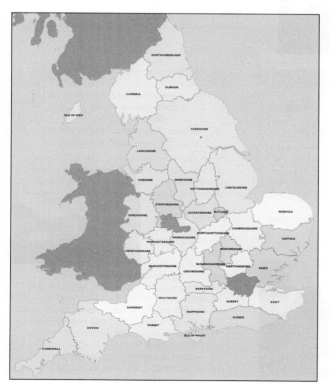

1 THE KINGS ARMS

27 London Road, Sandy,
Bedfordshire SG19 1HA
☎ 0800 2980122 Fax: 01767 691737
e-mail: sarah@foster5720.fsworld.co.uk

The **Kings Arms** combines traditional pub qualities with modern guest accommodation in the hamlet of Girtford, Sandy on the Old London Road. Tenants Sarah and martin Flynn, who took over in July 2005, have really given the old place anew lease of life, and many first-time visitors have already become regulars. Some come to enjoy a glass or two of real ale in the old-world bars, where open fires keep things cosy in the cooler months, others to sample the excellent snacks and meals served in the bars or non-smoking dining rooms.

Food is available every session except Sunday evening, and booking is recommended, particularly on

Thursday, Friday, Saturday evenings and Sunday lunch. Some come

to enjoy all the above and to relax with a short break or weekend in the motel-style accommodation to the rear of the pub. The four self-contained chalets for 2, all have en suite facilities, TV, hot drinks tray and a small fridge.

2 THE SWISS GARDEN

Old Warden Park, Old Warden,
Biggleswade, Bedfordshire SG18 9ER
☎ 01767 627666
🌐 www.bedfordshire.gov.uk

The **Swiss Garden** is set in 10 acres where visitors can wander among splendid shrubs and rare trees, at the centre of which is the Swiss Cottage. It brings together tiny follies, ornate bridges and winding ponds. Visitors can discover the breathtaking fernery and grotto, or lose themselves on the serpentine walks. In season the early bulbs and primroses, the rhododendrons and the old-fashioned
roses make wonderful displays. The Garden is open from 10am - 5pm April to October and 10am - 4pm November to March.

4 THE PLOUGH AT BOLNHURST

Kimbolton Road, Bolnhurst,
Bedfordshire MK44 2EX
☎ 01234 376274
e-mail: theplough@bolnhurst.com
🌐 www.bolnhurst.com

Set in extensive grounds on the B660 north of Bedford, the **Plough at Bolnhurst** is an outstanding pub with a fine team at the helm.
Martin and Jayne Lee with business partner Michael Moscrop have combined their talents to establish an

outstanding reputation for consistently excellent food, wine and beer, served within the relaxed and informal atmosphere of an old English pub by efficient and friendly staff. Martin is the experienced and very talented chef. His style is modern British, so inspiration comes from the world's cuisines. His creative and interesting menus change regularly to reflect the seasons and availability of the best produce. Closed Sunday evening and all day Monday.

3 THE SWAN INN

**2 Court Road, Cranfield,
Bedfordshire MK43 0DR
☎ 01234 750332**

With the M1 a short drive away, **The Swan** is a great place to take a break on a journey, whether it's for a drink, a meal or an overnight stay. Steven Meredith brought 20 years' experience in the hospitality business when he took over here in 2005, and he and his staff make all their customers feel instantly at home. Behind the substantial cream-painted façade, the inside of the inn is quite eyecatching, with a pleasing blend of traditional and contemporary elements, and the bars are open all day, seven days a week, for drinks. Up to four real ales are available, with Greene King IPA, Abbot Ale and Old Speckled Hen the usual regular brews, and there's a very good selection of other draught and bottle beers, lagers, wines, spirits and non-alcoholic drinks. Food is an important part of the swan's business, being served from noon to 9 o'clock and until 10 on Friday and Saturday. The ever-changing menu presents an across-the-board choice, and the chef

uses fresh local produce as much as possible in his dishes. Food and drink can be enjoyed inside in the bar or non-smoking restaurant, or out in the garden, where picnic benches are set out on a paved area. Booking is always advisable to be sure of a table, inside or out. For guests staying overnight, the Swan has four really excellent en suite bedrooms, one of them on the ground floor; the tariff includes a full English breakfast, with lighter options also available.

The Swan stands in the quiet village of Cranfield, east of Newport Pagnell and just inside the Bedfordshire border. It can be reached from either J13, by way of the A421, or J14, on a minor road through Mulsoe. With the motorway so handy, and the towns of Milton Keynes and Newport Pagnell close by, the Swan is a popular choice with the business community, but visitors with leisure time will find plenty to discover in the vicinity. In particular, anyone with an interest in country churches will find two splendid examples, one adjacent to the beautiful baroque Chicheley Hall, the other the Church of St Firmin at North Crawley.

5 THE NEW INN

1 Rushden Road, Wymington, nr Rushden,
Northamptonshire NN10 9LN
☎ 01933 355385

December 2005 saw the arrival of new
tenants Brian and Julie Christie at the **New
Inn**, and they lost no time in winning over
the locals from Wymington and the
surrounding area. Built as a farmhouse in the
late-18th century, it was later granted a
licence to
brew its
own beer
and
became a
pub in
the
1920s.
The New
Inn is

open all day for a minimum of three real ales,
and Brian and Julie use local produce in a
good variety of dishes served every session
except Sunday evening, and all day at the
weekend. The inn has a large, fully enclosed
garden with a children's play area.

7 THE WINTERBOURNE ARMS

Winterbourne, nr Newbury,
Berkshire RG20 8BB
☎ 01635 248200 Fax: 01635 248824
e-mail: winterbournearms@tiscali.co.uk
⊕ www.winterbournearms.tablesir.com

Overlooking the green, and very much the
hub of village life, the **Winterbourne Arms**
occupies premises dating back some 300
years. Part of it was once a bakery, and the
old ovens can
still be seen in
what is now the
pub's restaurant.
Manager Paul
Heporth and
head chef
Edouard Lelaure
take excellent

care of their customers with friendly
hospitality, a regularly changing choice of real
ales and a fine selection of traditional and
contemporary dishes based on the best local
produce. A log fire warms the bar, and
outside is a very pleasant, spacious beer
garden. The pub holds regular themed food
evenings and wine tasting dinners.

6 THE RISING SUN

Ermin Street, Stockcross, nr Newbury,
Berkshire RG20 8LG
☎ 01488 608131
e-mail: holloways@therisingsun-
stockcross.co.uk
⊕ www.therisingsun-stockcross.co.uk

The **Rising Sun** is the West Berkshire Brewery's
first pub and the first venture together for tenants
Keith and Joan Holloway. They have brought years
of individual experience in pubs and clubs, and
from the moment they arrived in December they
have put their hearts and souls into running the
place. Modernised, but still with the feel and
atmosphere of a traditional country pub, it attracts a good crowd of regulars and visitors from way
outside the immediate vicinity with its excellent hospitality, food
and drink.

Joan's menus provide an exceptional variety of first-class
English fare, from jacket potatoes, fish & chips and chicken &
mushroom pie to grilled mackerel, liver & bacon and cold
meats with bubble & squeak (a great treat – when did you last
see *that* on a menu?). One
of the favourites is a pie
with beef cooked in the
West Berkshire Brewery's
Good Old Boy ale, one
of five real ales on tap in
the bar. The enjoyment level stays high with lovely desserts
like apple crumble and treacle tart. No food Sunday or
Monday evenings. Keith and Joan are both talented working
musicians and the pub hosts regular assorted live music
evenings. Bring your maps as it is great walking country.

8   THE FIVE BELLS

Baydon Road, Wickham, nr Newbury,
Berkshire RG20 8HH
☎ 01488 657894 Fax: 01488 657143
e-mail: thefivebells@fsnet.co.uk

Standing in good walking country by the B4000, the **Five Bells** is an eyecatching inn, part thatched, with the oldest parts dating back to the 16th century. The real ales from Adnams and Ringwood have earned the pub Cask Marque recognition, and the food prepared by tenants Clive, Shirley and Graham have earned the all-

important recognition of their loyal band of regulars. It's a very popular place for food, and at peak times the trio are kept busy providing a good choice of traditional home-cooked dishes. The Five bells has a pleasant half-acre garden, and for overnight guests there's comfortable en suite room for B&B.

9   THE COACH & HORSES

Worlds End, Beedon, nr Newbury,
Berkshire RG20 8SD
☎ 01635 248743
e-mail:
info@coachandhorsesworldsend.com
🌐 www.coachandhorses.com

Still retaining the outward appearance of the private residence it once was, the **Coach & Horses** is a delightful place to drop in for refreshment on a journey, to stop for a meal or to stay overnight. Host Adrian Pearce is a countryman at heart and a lover of country pursuits,

so his customers can look forward to game birds on the regularly changing bar menus. The pub has a pleasant garden with a secure children's play area, and there are two rooms for B&B guests.

10   THE CASTLE INN

Cold Ash Hill, Cold Ash, nr Thatcham,
Berkshire RG18 9PS
☎ 01635 863232

Nick and Maggie Hex have held the lease at the **Castle Inn** since 1994, and their delightful mid-Victorian hostelry continues to win new friends. The West Berkshire Brewery's Mr Chubb's Lunchtime Bitter is one of four real ales always on tap, and Maggie's cooking ensures that everyone who eats

here leaves well filled and happy. Her homemade pies, curries and Sunday roasts are great favourites, but everything is good and fresh, and there's plenty of choice on the printed menu and blackboards. Best to book at the weekend.

HIDDEN PLACES GUIDES

Explore Britain and Ireland with *Hidden Places* guides - a fascinating series of national and local travel guides.

Packed with easy to read information on hundreds of places of interest as well as places to stay, eat and drink.

Available from both high street and internet booksellers

For more information on the full range of *Hidden Places* guides and other titles published by Travel Publishing visit our website on

www.travelpublishing.co.uk or ask for our leaflet by phoning **0118-981-7777** or emailing **info@travelpublishing.co.uk**

11 THE THREE SWANS HOTEL

117 High Street, Hungerford,
Berkshire RG17 0LZ
☎ 01488 682721 Fax: 01488 681708
e-mail: info@threeswans.net
🌐 www.threeswans.net

In the heart of Hungerford, the **Three Swans Hotel** is an impressive former coaching inn with a history going back some 700 years – the original archway that took coaches and horses into the courtyard still stands. Privately owned by brothers Steven and John

Hodges, with General Manager John Slee at the helm, it offers everything that locals and visitors could ask for.

Ales from local breweries are on tap in the convivial beamed and panelled Town Bar, and the hotel offers a choice of eating: a wide selection of dishes both traditional and contemporary in the elegant restaurant, with well-chosen wines to accompany, and less formal snacks and meals in the brasserie and bar. A full range of breakfast options is also available, to both residents and non-

residents. Sunday lunch (Best to book) is accompanied by live jazz. The guest accommodation at the Three Swans comprises 15 upstairs en suite rooms, including family rooms and a honeymoon suite, that retain the character of the old building while providing up-to-the-minute facilities such as flat-screen TV and Broadband Internet access. The Hotel is well geared up for meetings, conferences, functions and weddings, with a variety of rooms including the Cygnet Suite with a capacity of up to 55.

12 TALLY HO!

Hungerford Newtown, nr Hungerford,
Berkshire RG17 0PP
☎ 01488 682312 Fax: 01488 684690
e-mail: mike.purdue@btinternet.com

On the A338 in Hungerford Newtown, just half a mile from Junction 14 of the M4, the **Tally Ho!** is a handsome redbrick inn that's very much at the heart of village life. Hosts Mike and Ellie set very high standards in food, ale, hospitality and service, and the large open-plan bar area, with beamed oak ceiling, open fire, comfortable seats and interesting pictures on the walls, is a very agreeable spot to linger for a drink and a chat.

Ellie uses local suppliers for as many of her dishes as possible, and all the fresh meats, burgers, sausages and cheese come from the Hungerford Master Butcher. Favourites on her menu include steaks, lasagne, steak & kidney pudding, cod & mozzarella fishcakes, and warm chicken salad with a honey & mustard dressing. Ploughman's platters and ciabatta sandwiches are popular choices at lunchtime, and the Tally Ho! offers an excellent children's menu. Food is served lunchtime and evening Monday to Saturday and from 12 to 6 on Sunday; breakfast is also available by arrangement. Wadworths 6X and Henry's IPA are the resident real ales.

13 THE PHEASANT INN

Ermin Street, Shefford Woodlands,
nr Hungerford, Berkshire RG17 7AA
☎ 01488 648284 Fax: 01488 648971

The white clapboard frontage of the **Pheasant Inn** gives way to an interior of great charm and character, with flagstone floors and a wealth of interesting decorative features. This is horseracing country, and though he stopped race-riding some years ago, joint owner Charlie Brooks remain one of the best known and best loved characters in the game. His feats in the saddle are remembered in the collection of photographs,

sketches and cartoons that adorn the walls. The other joint owner is Johnny Ferrand, and between them they have made an unqualified success of the Pheasant.

Food is a major part of the business here, and there's a very talented team in the kitchen. Taking the best seasonal produce, they create a menu that presents diners with a problem but a pleasant problem: what to order, when everything is so tempting and nothing at all is run-of-the-mill. Classic combinations are given distinctive twists that elevate the dishes far above the ordinary and make every meal here an occasion to remember. The daily changing menu is served lunchtime seven days a week, and every evening except Sunday; lighter snacks are available between sessions.

For many years, the Pheasant has established itself as a terrific place to seek out for a drink and a meal, but it's now also a perfect overnight base for visitors to the area. The recent extension is a tribute to the

popularity of this outstanding inn, but the most exciting development is the bringing on stream of 11 top-of-the-range guest bedrooms. The important training centre of Lambourn is an easy drive away, and the region offers visitors a wealth of great walks and beautiful scenery. The racing connection extends to the directions printed on the Pheasant's card: 'Leave the M4 at Exit 14. Drive two furlongs towards Wantage then turn left. The pub is a furlong along on the right'. In racing parlance or any other parlance, the Pheasant is a winner!

14 THE RED LION

**5 Church Street, Theale,
Berkshire RG7 5BU
☎ 0118 930 2394**

Karen and Ian make an excellent team at the **Red Lion**, a popular pub with quality in every department. Dating from the early 19th century, it once brewed its own beer; it now keeps three real ales – Young's Bitter, Marston's Pedigree and a guest – in excellent condition, along with a good range of other draught and bottled beers and lagers, wines, spirits and non-alcoholic drinks.

The inn is open all day, seven days a week for drinks, and traditional dishes cooked by Karen are served Monday to Saturday lunchtime and evening and also for the Sunday lunchtime roasts – best to book. The Red Lion hosts live music evenings one Saturday a month, and private skittle & buffet

evenings can be booked for groups of at least 10.

When the Action Bike Bristol to London charity cycle race hits the pub on the Sunday of August Bank Holiday, you'll be sharing the bar with 500 or more thirsty cyclists!

15 THE RISING SUN

**Bath Road, Woolhampton,
Berkshire RG7 5RH
☎ 0118 971 2717 Fax: 0118 971 4691**

Woolhampton is a peaceful village set beside the Kennet & Avon Canal and its history is chronicled as far back as the Domesday Book of 1086. The **Rising Sun** shares more than 350 years of that history, and the inviting look of its cheerful yellow-painted frontage is complemented by a charming old-world interior. Beams and panelling, open fires and pictures of life on the Canal set a lovely traditional scene, while outside there are two quiet gardens and a pets corner that's guaranteed to charm more than just the children.

Hosts Dave and Sue Clinton, who came here in 1998, share the cooking with their resident chef,

keeping the customers happy with a varied choice of traditional pub food. Favourite dishes include home-made pies and puddings and succulent steaks (up to a 48oz ribeye for the really ravenous). They keep their real ales in tip-top condition and also offer an extensive wine list. The Rising Sun is open lunchtime and evening Monday to Saturday and all day Sunday. Best to book a table at the weekend.

342

16 THE POT KILN

Frilsham, nr Yattendon,
Berkshire RG18 0XX
☎ 01635 201366
e-mail: info@potkiln.co.uk
🌐 www.potkiln.co.uk

Dating back some 400 years and named after the kilns that once stood at the back, the **Pot Kiln** enjoys a pleasant rural setting with a view of fields and woods from the terrace.

Owner Mike Robinson, a well-known TV chef and pundit, heads a busy team of chefs preparing a superb, daily-changing choice of dishes of British and European inspiration. The menus are full of interest, with such dishes as razor clams with sauce vierge, rillettes of rabbit with fig chutney, smoked haddock Welsh rarebit and braised shin of beef with Madeira and wild mushrooms. Mike has made this one of the

most popular dining pubs in the whole county, and booking is strongly recommended, particularly at the weekend.

Real ales include Mr Chubb's, Maggs Mild and Brick Kiln. The Pot Kiln is open lunchtime and evening, and all day on Saturday and Sunday. Frilsham lies a mile south of Yattendon, on the other side of the M4. Drivers coming from the M4 should leave at the Chieveley Services exit.

19 THE DUKE OF WELLINGTON

27 High Street, Twyford,
Berkshire RG10 9AG
☎ 0118 934 0456
e-mail: bill@wham.fsbusiness.co.uk

The **Duke of Wellington** is the oldest pub in Twyford, with a history going back to the 1650s. It's a roomy, comfortable brick-built inn with ancient beams, period pictures and a Victorian fireplace in the bar. Outside is a very large beer garden, complete with a children's play area, and a patio with tables and chairs for sunny days.

Hosts Bill and Karen Suter took over this grand old place in 2000 and continue to bring back old friends and win new with their warm hospitality and the fine choice of real ale and real food. Every lunchtime except Sunday they serve a wide selection of bar snacks and meals, from sandwiches, jacket potatoes

and burgers to home-cooked ham, chilli with rice

(hot stuff, and a great favourite), and always some tempting daily specials. Real ale connoisseurs can choose from five brews, and the pub also keeps a good choice of wines. Functions for up to 24 can be catered for in the saloon bar. The Duke of Wellington is open lunchtime and evening and all day on Saturday and Sunday. Cash or cheque only.

17 THE SWAN

Three Mile Cross, nr Reading,
Berkshire RG7 1AT
☎ 0118 988 3674 Fax: 0118 988 4551

On the A33 3 miles south of Reading and just seconds from Exit 11 of the M4, the **Swan** has established itself as one of the very best pubs in the whole region. It stands near the Madejski Stadium, and if Reading football team has proved itself in a different class from its rivals, the same can be said of the Swan in the competitive pub league. Its success is the reward for the hard work and dedication shown by owners Vic and Jenny Harrison, who have been at the helm for almost a quarter of a century.

Their regular customers come from many miles around, and they are making new friends all the time.

The attractions of the Swan begin outside with the wonderful flower displays that have won many awards, including Best in Show, Colour & Cheer 2005 from Wokingham District Council. There are seats inside for 50, and outside for almost as many on a partly covered sun patio. Up to half a

dozen real ales are available at any one time, with Young's Bitter, Henry's IPA, London Pride and Itchen Valley Godfather all regularly featuring, and they serve food at the Swan every lunchtime and every evening. The menu sticks mainly to tried-and-tested favourites, and it's a formula that definitely works, as mealtimes are so busy that booking is always best to be sure of a table.

The Swan started life in the early 17th century as three timber-framed workers' cottages; 50 years on two of them became an ale house called the Globe Inn and in 1760 the premises were sold for £24 10s and acquired a new name, the Three Sugar Loaves. It became a well-known changing station for horses on the London-Portsmouth staging route. From Globe to Loaves to Swan, it's more popular than ever, and is a meeting place for several clubs and societies as well as favourite destination for lovers of real ale and real food. Apart from the owners, it has another distinguished resident in Jumbo, the famous Irish wolfhound who is the official mascot of the London Irish Rugby Football Club. He has been seen at the head of many processions up and down the land.

344

18 THE BULL AT RISELEY

Basingstoke Road, Riseley, nr Reading,
Berkshire RG7 1QL
☎ 0118 988 3194

The **Bull at Riseley** stands in the village of
the same name just off the A33, south of
Reading and very close to the border with
Hampshire. Lisa Hammerson is a friendly,
experienced host, and her delightful pub is
open
lunchtime
and
evening
for drinks
and every
session
except
Sunday
and

Monday evenings for food. Shepherd Neame
Masterbrew and Spitfire are the regular real
ales, and the menu and specials board provide
a good choice of dishes highlighted by meat
from a top local butcher and seasonal game.
The Bull hosts regular themed food evenings
and quiz nights.

20 LOOK OUT DISCOVERY CENTRE

Nine Mile Ride, Bracknell,
Berkshire RG12 7QW
☎ 01344 354400 Fax 01344 354422
e-mail: thelookout@bracknell-forest.gov.uk
🌐 www.bracknell-forest.gov.uk/lookout

The **Look Out Discovery Centre** is a great
day out for all ages with its exciting hands on,
interactive science and nature exhibition.
Budding scientists will spend many hours
exploring and discovering over 70 bright, fun
filled exhibits within five themed zones.
Climb the eighty eight steps of the Look Out
tower and see over the Centre towards
Bracknell and beyond.
In the surrounding
woodland, visitors can
enjoy nature walks, a
picnic area and child's
play area. In the Coffee
Shop you can relax over
a cup of tea or a hot
lunch, whilst the Gift
Shop offers a superb
range of gifts. The Look
Out is open daily from
10.00am - 5.00pm.

21 THE MAGPIE

56 Heath End Road, Flackwell Heath,
Buckinghamshire HP10 9DY
☎ 01628 523696

The **Magpie** is a handsome yellow-painted
pub standing on its own in the centre of
Flackwell Heath, on the other side of the
A40/M40 from High Wycombe. Vaughan
Passey is not only an excellent host, he's also
a very talented chef, and his spare ribs are
famous for miles around. His food is available
every
lunchtime
and until
late every
evening,
and good
choice of
drinks
headed by
Greene
King IPA
and Old

Speckled Hen is served all day, seven days a
week. Families are always made welcome, and
there's a children's play area in the garden.

22 THE RED COW

14 The Green, Wooburn Green,
Buckinghamshire HP10 0EF
☎ 01628 531344 Fax: 01628 850377

Overlooking the green in a village just off the
A40, the **Red Cow** is a 400-year-old pub with
bags of character and atmosphere. In the bar,
with its beams and wooden floors, on the
front terrace or in the secluded beer garden,
patrons can enjoy the excellent hospitality
provided
by John
Randall
and his
son Paul.
Open long
hours
every day,
the pub
offers two
real ales

among a good choice of liquid refreshment,
and a daily changing selection of home-
cooked dishes is served every lunchtime.
Booking is advisable for the traditional
Sunday roasts.

The Lees, Great Missenden,
Buckinghamshire HP16 9LZ
☎ 01494 837540 Fax: 01494 837512
e-mail: info@gianco.demon.co.uk
🌐 www.graziemille.co.uk

Hidden in the heart of the Chilterns is the delightful village of The Lees, familiar to many visitors as the filming location for a number of television programmes such as *Midsomer Murders* and *Pie in the Sky*. But who would have thought that in this quaint, out-of-the-way village there would a splendid Italian restaurant attached to a country pub?

The **Cock & Rabbit Inn and Restaurant Graziemille**, owned and run by Gianfranco Parola and his wife Victoria, is the perfect place for a relaxing lunch or elegant dinner. Surrounded by a lovely garden and sun terrace, the pub is an absolute delight. It has the appearance of a quintessential English country house, which it was when originally built, and Gianfranco arrived here in 1985 and renovated and restored it to what visitors see today. Inside are two bar areas, both with open fires that add to the welcoming atmosphere and relaxed ambience. The pub has become a very popular destination and stopping-off point for walkers, ramblers and tourists exploring the local countryside, as well as being a favourite meeting place for the local residents.

In the restaurant, food is served every lunchtime and evening, and Gianfranco is responsible for the superb menu inspired by the cuisine of the Piedmont region of Italy where he was born. His specialities, many of which use the local wild garlic, include beef carpaccio, sautéed mushrooms and toasted goat's cheese to start, followed by pasta Graziemille, chicken Contessa Rosa or salmon in a dill, cream and champagne sauce. To finish, what could be better than the

classic Italian dessert Tiramisu, made to Gianfranco's family recipe? Meals can be enjoyed in the delightful garden restaurant or in the bar. Restaurant Graziemille is well equipped to cater for weddings and other functions and to provide a wonderful location and intimate setting for dining with friends. Any vent can be catered for in inimitable Italian style. Simply let Gianfranco, Victoria and their friendly, efficient staff do all the hard work while you enjoy yourself!

24 THE RED LION HOTEL

Wendover, Buckinghamshire HP22 6DU
☎ 01296 622266 Fax: 01296 625077
e-mail: theredlionhotel.wendover
@pathfinderspubs.co.uk

Excellent food and drink are served throughout the day at the **Red Lion Hotel**, which stands in the delightful old market town of Wendover. This distinguished old hostelry with an attractive black-and-white frontage dates from the middle of the 17th century, and numbers Oliver Cromwell and Robert Louis Stevenson among its famous guests.

Today's visitors will find a choice of three real ales among a good range of drinks, and the food options on the bar and restaurant menus are many and varied, from sandwiches, jacket potatoes, eggs Benedict and a mixed mezze platter to stilton-stuffed chicken breast, swordfish steak, Provencal vegetable risotto and medallions of beef fillet with bubble & squeak and a perky horseradish and chilli hollandaise. This is good walking country, and the Red Lion, which is run in friendly style by tenant

Julia Cook, is an ideal base for exploring the countryside of the North Chilterns, or for visiting the many places of interest in the region. The 26 en suite rooms, some on the ground floor, include a family room, a romantic honeymoon suite and several other rooms with four-poster beds. Guests can book on a B&B or Dinner, B&B basis. Sunday is quiz night.

25 THE PLOUGH INN

The Common, Hyde Heath, nr Amersham, Buckinghamshire HP6 5RW
☎ 01494 783163 Fax: 01494 774408
e-mail: ploughin@gotadsl.co.uk

Chris Herring brought 30 years' experience in the hospitality business to the **Plough Inn** when he and his family took over the reins in 2004. That marked the beginning of a great relationship between Chris and Hyde Heath, and the reputation of the pub has since extended far beyond the village and its neighbours.

Overlooking the village green (where, in a typical community spirit, Chris has provided some benches, the 19th century pub is open lunchtime and evening, and all day Friday, Saturday and Sunday. London Pride and two guests cater for real ale connoisseurs, and Chris prepares a fine selection of excellent food to be enjoyed throughout opening hours until 10 o'clock in

the evening. He uses fresh local supplies as much as possible, a fact that

anyone who has a meal here will soon appreciate. Good conversation is in liberal supply in the bar, and football fans have a bonus in the big-screen TV that shows all the top matches. Hyde Heath is a pleasant village stretched out along country roads between the A143 west of Amersham and the B485 west of Chesham.

26 THE BELL

Chartridge Lane, Chartridge, nr Chesham,
Buckinghamshire HP5 2TF
☎ 01494 782878

A country road leads from Chesham to the
tiny village of Chartridge, where **The Bell** is
at the heart of the community. At the heart
of The Bell, a delightful old inn with
traditional décor and furnishings, are Philip
and Elvire Bailey, and ever since they took
over in 2003 their warm hospitality and
Philip's
cooking have
been magnets
for locals and
visitors. Philip
takes his
inspiration
from near and
far in dishes
that range

from the day's soup and chicken liver paté to
aromatic duck salad, juicy steaks, stilton-
stuffed chicken breast and kidney bean &
leek kiev with a sherry and mushroom sauce.
No food Sunday evening or Monday.

27 THE ROSE & CROWN

The Vale, Hawridge Common, nr Chesham,
Buckinghamshire HP5 2UG
☎ 01494 758944

Best approached by way of Chesham Vale,
the **Rose & Crown** lies in the tiny hamlet of
Hawridge Common. The pub, which dates
from the mid-18th century, has been run
since August
2005 by Peter
and Sandra,
who offer an
interesting
selection of
real ales and a
fine variety of
snacks and
meals. Classic

main courses typically include sausages with
bubble & squeak and onion gravy, super fish
and meat pies, succulent steaks and always
some vegetarian options. Families are very
welcome – children's meals half-price – and
the pub has a large, picturesque garden. The
Rose & Crown hosts beer festivals in April
and September each year.

28 THE WHITE HART

High Street, Stoke Goldington,
Buckinghamshire MK16 8NR
☎ 01908 551392

The **White Hart** is a traditional thatched
18th century pub that's as picturesque as the
village in which it stands. Chris and Pauline
have built up a loyal band of regulars with
their excellent hospitality, and real fires add to
the inviting ambience in the beamed bars.
Charles Wells
Eagle is the
resident real ale,
and a good
choice of freshly
prepared food is
served in the bar
and dining areas.
Traditional

roasts are added to the menu for Sunday
lunch (no food Sunday evening). The beer
garden, with picnic benches set out under
parasols, is a boon in the summer months.
Children are welcome until 9 o'clock. The
White Hart is closed Monday lunchtime
unless it's a Bank Holiday.

30 THE PHEASANT INN

39 Windmill Street, Brill, nr Aylesbury,
Buckinghamshire HP18 9TG
☎ 01844 237104
🌐 www.thepheasant.co.uk

In the quiet village of Brill, equidistant from
Aylesbury, Bicester and Oxford, the
Pheasant Inn is a 300-year-old pub with a
well-deserved reputation for the quality of its
food. Across-the-board menus offer ciabatta
sandwiches
and pub
classics at
lunchtime,
and an
interesting
main
menu
with
influences
from
home and

overseas. In a picturesque setting overlooking
the famous 17th century post mill, the inn has
three good-sized en suite letting rooms for
B&B guests.

29   THE ROBIN HOOD

Church Road, Clifton Reynes,
Buckinghamshire MK46 5DR
☎ 01234 711574
e-mail: the.robin.hood@fsmail.net
🌐 www.therobinhoodpub.co.uk

Reg and Lyn Pearson have run the **Robin Hood** since 2000, offering a friendly welcome to all their patrons. They have built up a loyal following at their fine old pub, which stands in picturesque countryside in a little village with one way in – off a minor road between the A428 west of Bedford and the A509 north of Milton Keynes – and the same way out.

Pictures of silver-screen Robin Hoods hang above the big stone hearth in the bar, where Greene King IPA and Abbot are the regular real ales. Classic English dishes – with one or two surprises – make up the menu, which is supplemented by daily specials such as pork, liver & bacon paté or a super seafood salad. A very welcome sign above the bar states that

this is a mobile phone ring-free zone – if it rings, £1 goes to a local hospice. First registered as licensed premises in the 16th century, the pub has had various names – first the Rising Sun, then the Carpenters Arms, by 1842 the Robin Hood & Little John, then Little John was dropped in 1887. Families are very welcome, and this Prince among pubs has a patio and spacious tree-fringed garden. Closed Mondays except Bank Holidays.

31   THE PUB IN CHILTON

Thame Road, Chilton,
Buckinghamshire HP18 9LX
☎ 01844 208220
e-mail: essouamah@aol.com

Food and drink are served all day, every day, at **The Pub in Chilton**, which stands off the B4011 a short drive north of Thame in the village from which it takes its name. The food options include speciality steaks, and booking is

advisable to be sure of a table on Saturday and Sunday evenings. The food is served from 12 to 9, and the ales include some less-known local brews; themed food nights with jazz are popular occasions. The Pub has a large beer garden and plenty of off-road parking.

32   THE LION INN

70 High Street, Waddesdon,
Buckinghamshire HP18 0JD
☎ 01296 651227 Fax: 01296 658894
e-mail: info@thelionwaddesdon.co.uk
🌐 www.thelionwaddesdon.co.uk

Locals and visitors alike can expect the warmest of welcomes from Annette, Peter and the team at the **Lion Inn**, a stylishly modernised pub close to the magnificent Waddesdon Manor. The Lion serves a fine selection of beers (3 real ales), wines and spirits,

and in the smart dining room the menu spans a wide range of dishes, from traditional English (fish pie, bangers & mash, steak & kidney pudding) to exotic (Thai fish cakes, chicken korma). The Queens Head at Chackmore has the same tenants.

33 THE QUEENS HEAD

Main Street, Chackmore,
Buckinghamshire MK18 5JF
☎ 01296 651227

The owners of the Lion Inn at Waddesdon also have the tenancy of the **Queens Head** on the main street of Chackmore, between Amersham and the National Trust's wonderful Stowe Gardens. Small, quaint and full of charm and character, the pub is open every lunchtime and evening for food and drink – Theakstons, Black Sheep and RG Ale are the regular real ales. The

printed menu and specials board provide a wide choice of dishes that cater for large and small appetites and plain and adventurous palates. There are seats outside at the front and back, and families are very welcome.

35 THE OLD THATCHED INN

Main Street, Adstock,
Buckinghamshire MK18 2JN
☎ 01296 712584 Fax: 01296 715375
e-mail: enquiries@theoldthatchedinn.co.uk
🌐 www.theoldthatchedinn.co.uk

In a picturesque setting in the Buckinghamshire countryside, the delightful **Old Thatched Inn** dates back more than 300 years. The welcome is warm and friendly, creating a very pleasant and relaxed atmosphere for enjoying a drink or a meal, Up to 4 real ales – hook Norton hooky and

Spitfire are the residents – are available, and in the conservatory restaurant a fine selection of excellent dishes using the very best local produce is served lunchtime and evening and all day at the weekend. The inn also scores with its accommodation: three large and luxurious en suite rooms in a converted barn.

34 THE RED LION

Buckingham Road, Little Tingewick/Finmere,
Buckinghamshire MK18 4AG
☎ 01280 848285

The **Red Lion** is situated in the tiny village of Little Tingewick, off the A421 west of Buckingham and close to the border with Oxfordshire. Leaseholders Nigel and Liz Jones have applied all their considerable skills and experience in the hospitality industry in making this one of the best and most successful dining pubs in the region.

Built in 1816 and sympathetically modernised in the 1960s, the pub is a good place to pop in for a drink (4 real ales always on the go) but it's an even better place to take time to relax and enjoy a splendid meal. Nigel has earned plaudits from inside and outside the trade for his top-class cooking, for which the start point is always

insisting on the very best seasonal produce. And when faced with a menu full of tempting things, the only problem is deciding what to choose – how about shredded oriental pork salad to start, then sea bream with bean cassoulet and mint salsa, or Padbury sirloin with chilli and olive sauce and fat chips on the side? Monday is steak night, with a special deal for 2 steaks and a bottle of house wine. The Red Lion is closed on Sunday evening in winter.

36 FARMLAND MUSEUM & DENNY ABBEY

Ely Road, Waterbeach,
Cambridgeshire CB5 9PQ
☎ 01223 860489
e-mail: f.m.denny@tesco.net
🌐 www.dennyfarmlandmuseum.org.uk

Two thousand years of history are brought fascinatingly to life in a lovely rural setting on the A10 six miles north of Cambridge. The stone-built farmhouse at the heart of the site is actually the remains of a 12th century Benedictine Abbey which at different times was home to Benedictine monks, the Knights Templar and nuns of the Franciscan order, the Poor Clares. The superb Norman interior has been beautifully preserved and restored, and visitors can see the nuns' refectory and the rooms converted for their founder, the Countess of Pembrokeshire. Displays and children's activities tell the story of how Denny has evolved down the centuries.

On the same site, and run by English Heritage as a joint attraction, is the Farmland Museum. Old farm buildings have been splendidly renovated and converted to tell visitors about the rural history of Cambridgeshire from early days to modern times. The Museum is ideal for family visits, with specially designed activities for children, and among the top displays are a village shop, agricultural machinery, a magnificent 17th century stone barn, a traditional farmworker's cottage and the workshops, which include a basket maker and a blacksmith. Special weekend events, from buttermaking demonstrations to traditional building methods, are held regularly at the Museum, which is open from noon to 5pm April to October.

38 IMPERIAL WAR MUSEUM DUXFORD

Duxford, Cambridgeshire CB2 4QR
☎ 01223 835000 Fax: 01223 837267

A branch of the **Imperial War Museum**, Duxford is Europe's premier aviation museum. It was built on a former RAF and USAF fighter base that saw that service throughout the Second World War, and the preserved hangars, a control tower and operations room retain a period atmosphere and from the historic heart of the 85-acre complex.

Over 400,000 visitors come to Duxford each year to see the biplanes and the Spitfires, the Concorde and the Gulf War jets that are among the 180 historic aircraft on show. A major exhibition on the Battle of Britain charts events of 1940, giving an insight into life at the time, and features an RAF Hurricane and a Luftwaffe Messerschmitt 109 that saw action in the Battle. An award-winning modern building designed by Lord Foster houses the American Air Museum with aircraft both on the ground and suspended from the roof as though in flight. Exhibits here range from a U2 Spyplane to a T-10 Tankbuster and the mighty B-52 Stratofortress. Tanks and artillery are on show in the exciting Land Warfare Hall, which houses 50 military vehicles and artillery pieces in a series of realistic and authentic battlefield scenes.

Major attractions are being added each year, and among the latest is an exhibition focusing on Monty and the D-Day landings. Important air shows take place several times each year, featuring resident aircraft, current military aircraft, civilian display teams and solo aerobatic performers. This wonderful museum, which lies south of Cambridge at Junction 10 of the M11, is open throughout the year apart from three days at Christmas.

39 THE SOHAM LODGE HOTEL & WINDMILL RESTAURANT

Soham, nr Ely, Cambridgeshire CB7 5DF
☎ 01353 725076 Fax: 01353 723050
e-mail: info@sohamlodge-hotel.co.uk
🌐 www.sohamlodge-hotel.com

The **Soham Lodge Hotel & Windmill Restaurant**, located in its grounds by the A142, is a pleasant place to choose for a drink, a meal or an overnight or longer stay. The building is less than 20 years old, but the ambience is one of well-established hospitality and traditional standards of service. The owner has the services of excellent General Managers in Dawn and Philip, sand they and their polite, welcoming staff ensure that every stay, no matter how short, is a real pleasure and an occasion to relish and remember.

The 15 guest bedrooms and suites, all on the ground floor, cater for all guests, from singles right up to families, and they are provided with en suite facilities, television and hot drinks trays. They offer a very comfortable, civilised base for all visitors, for business people with work in the area or with tourists discovering the sights and attractions of the region. These include the historic town of Ely, the city of Cambridge, Newmarket races, boat trips on the River Ouse, wonderful old windmills in Soham itself and at nearby Wicken, Soham's grand St Andrew's Church and the National Trust's Wicken Fen, the oldest nature reserve in the country. The hotel is also a popular spot for a meal, and in the spacious Windmill Restaurant residents and non-residents enjoy a range of meals from a full English breakfast to morning coffee, a midday buffet or lunchtime specials, afternoon tea and an evening à la carte that makes excellent use of locally sourced ingredients. The traditional Sunday carvery is always well patronised, offering roast beef and a choice of pork, turkey or gammon (no food Sunday evening).

The Soham Lodge is well geared up for meetings, conferences, banquets and special occasions and is licensed for civil wedding ceremonies. It also served as a very lively, sociable place for locals to meet, and the bar is open all day, seven days a week for drinks, including well-kept real ales. There's a regular programme of entertainment, usually on a Friday evening, throughout the year.

37 THE WHITE SWAN

Main Street, Stow-cum-Quy,
Cambridgeshire
☎ 01223 811821
e-mail: harmonyinns@aol.com
🌐 www.marionmillard@aol.com

When Marion took over the **White Swan** with Steve Smith, it was something of a homecoming, as her family ran the pub for more than 40 years until 1975, when her aunt retired. Refurbished and revitalised, it is once again very much at the heart of village life, attracting both local residents and visitors from near

and far with its CAMRA approved real ales and Marion's top-class cooking. This excellent free house is closed on Mondays except for Bank Holidays.

41 THE CHEQUERS INN

Tholomas Drove, nr Wisbech,
Cambridgeshire PE13 4SL
☎ 01945 410394

The **Chequers Inn** is a charming pub in the quiet hamlet of Tholomas Drove, reached from the A47 by way of the B1187 or through the village of Guyhirn. Hosts Annette and Michael Rolfe are rapidly raising the profile of the pub as a destination restaurant: both are talented chefs, and typical dishes on their blackboard

menu include omelettes, smoked haddock with prawn butter, baked salmon with scallops, cottage pie and grilled lamb chops. There is also an extensive a la carte menu and traditional Sunday lunch. Elgoods Cambridge and Pageant are the regular real ales, along with Old Smoothie Bitter and Mild keg ales. Closed Monday.

40 THE CHERRY TREE

8 Duck Lane, Haddenham, nr Ely,
Cambridgeshire CB6 3UE
☎ 01353 740667
e-mail: cherrytree.haddenham@tiscali.com.uk

Michael and Gill arrived to take over the **Cherry Tree Inn** in January 2006 with great plans for broadening its appeal and realising its full potential. They've already achieved a great deal, and Michael's 20+ years experience in the hospitality business at home and overseas is starting to pay dividends, winning back the local trade and attracting visitors from further afield.

The pub, which stands in the heart of the village just off the A1123, is open lunchtime and evening and all day on Friday, Saturday and Sunday. Up to four well-kept real ales are at the ready to quench thirsts in the bar, where wood features abound – on the floors, in the beams, on the panelled and half-panelled walls

and in the furniture. There are also plenty of wooden benches, chairs and tables in the pleasant beer garden.

Michael and Gill are both fine cooks, and customers can enjoy their generously-served home-cooked dishes between 12 and 2.30 and 5.30 to 8; booking is recommended on Sunday.

43 THE WHITE HORSE INN

I Market Street, Swavesey,
Cambridgeshire CB4 5QG
☎ 01954 232470 Fax: 01954 206188
e-mail: will@whitehorseswavesey.com
🌐 wwwwhitehorseswavesey.com

The **White Horse Inn** has a history going back almost 500 years. It occupies a prominent site in the village of Swavesey, off the A14 (J 27 or 28) between Cambridge and Huntingdon. In its time it has seen service as an auction house, a public health office and a meeting place for numerous local societies. It still fulfils that last role, but first and foremost it is one of the friendliest and most hospitable of village pubs. This enviable reputation is based on the popularity of the personable hosts Pat and Will Wright. When they took over, Will was returning to the village where three generations of his family had lived.

Both have a deep knowledge and strong interest in real ales and malt whiskeys, and the bar's stock of expertly kept ales has earned CAMRA recognition. Deuchars IPA is a regular, and among the frequently changing

guests are Timothy Taylor Landlord, Jack the Dragon, Adnams and Fenland Osier Cutter. During the annual May Day village festival that number increases to about 20. At any time, connoisseurs of malt whisky can take their pick from a selection of over 50. Bar lunches are served Monday to Saturday, with traditional roasts on Sunday and senior citizens specials on Tuesday. They serve evening meals Monday to Saturday, with traditional pub dishes like cod & chips, scampi, steaks, chops and grills joined by some very good vegetarian choices including popular spicy stuffed aubergines. Diners can eat in the lounge-bar or restaurant (both non-smoking) or out in the beer garden.

The bars are immensely warm and welcoming, with open log fires and exposed oak beams, and the walls provide hanging space for old photographs of the village and prints and drawings of Cambridge colleges. Outside, there's a patio and a beer garden with a children's play area. Cribbage, darts, pool (in a separate room) and bar billiards are played with enthusiasm, and Sky Sports is available, but the pub also supports rather more physical activities. Upwards of a dozen football teams have their spiritual (?) home at the White Horse, and a golfing society organises regular outings. Other clubs meeting here include an MG owners club and the Cambridge motorcycle scrambling club, and throughout the year the pub hosts charity events and musical evenings – before coming to the White Horse Will had travelled widely in the music business, being a professional drummer and sometime sound engineer with the band Slade.

42 THE RED HART

Main Road, Three Holes, nr Wisbech,
Cambridgeshire PE14 9JR
☎ 01945 773328

On the A1101 equidistant from Wisbech,
March and Downham Market, the **Red Hart**
is looking very smart after refurbishment by
tenants Lynda and Per. In a décor of pictures,
plates and assorted ornaments, customers can
enjoy Elgoods Cambridge or a guest real ale,
or sit outside
in the
landscaped
beer garden
and watch the
peacocks. Per
is Danish by
birth, and the
cuisine of his
country

features alongside traditional English pub
grub. Sunday is a carvery only (book), and in
winter the last Saturday of each month is
Danish Day. The pub, which is open
lunchtime and evening, and all day Saturday
and Sunday, has four rooms for overnight
guests.

44 THE CROWN

High Street, Earith, nr St Ives,
Cambridgeshire PE28 3PP
☎ 01487 740982

On the main street of Earith, on the A1123
east of St Ives, **The Crown** enjoys a fine
reputation both for its well-kept ales (London
Pride, Adnams Broadside and Greene King
IPA are the regular brews) and for its
excellent
home
cooking. It
also has a
very
special
additional
attraction –
a large
lawned
garden that
stretches

down to the banks of the Great Ouse. This
delightful 100-year-old pub is open lunchtime
and evening and all day on Fridays; also all
day most days in the summer.

45 THE GREYSTONES

The Green, Sawtry,
Cambridgeshire PE28 5ST
☎ 01487 831999
🌐 www.thegreystones.co.uk

The **Greystones** is a successful first team
venture for Sam and David, Sharon and
Brian, and their public house off the B1043
and short drive from the A1 has become
popular
with a
wide cross-
section of
customers
– locals,
families,
visitors
from near
and far,
motorists,

drinkers and diners. It's open all day, seven
days a week, and excellent food is served
every lunchtime and Monday to Saturday
evenings. Tuesday is curry night. The pub has
a children's room with toys, a games room
with darts and pool and plasma screen TVs.

46 THE TALBOT INN

5 North Street, Stilton, nr Peterborough,
Cambridgeshire PE7 3RP
☎ 01733 240291
🌐 www.charleswells.co.uk

In the village that gave its name to the famous
cheese that was first produced here, **The
Talbot Inn** is a popular spot with both the local
community and the many visitors who pass this
way. Its popularity is the result of the hard work
and hospitality provide by leaseholders Tony
and Ann-Marie,
managers Katherine and
Carlo and chef Jenny.
Dick Turpin was
reputedly a regular here,
but he never enjoyed
the Cask Marque ales
and the excellent Italian

home cooking, as well as traditional British
favourites, that attracts today's clientele. The
pub, which has a beer garden with a children's
play area, is open lunchtime and evening and all
day Friday, Saturday and Sunday. Food is served
every session and all day on Friday, Saturday
and Sunday.

Warrington Road, Mickle Trafford,
nr Chester, Cheshire CH2 4EB
☎ 01244 300309
🌐 www.traditional-pub-food.com

The **Shrewsbury Arms** is a superb country pub standing by the A56 Chester-Warrington road in the village of Mickle Trafford. In the 18th century the road was a notorious haunt of highwaymen, and it is recorded that in the spring of 1796 two such brigands held up and robbed a mail boy. They were captured, tried and condemned to death, and for a time their corpses were hung up on gibbets in a field close to the village. By the time of the First World War the inn formed part of the Earl of Shrewsbury's estate, and on the break-up of the estate in 1917 it was sold to the West Cheshire Brewery.

This picturesque pub, fondly known locally as 'the Shrew', has been lovingly restored to be everything a classic English pub should be, with oak beams, carpets and flagstones, comfortable chairs and sofas and a real log fire in a big brick hearth. Outside is a spacious paved area with ample seating and tables. The pub has a priceless asset in hosts Ron and Pam Crellin, who have been in the hospitality business for many years and in charge here since

2001. Their philosophy is summed up by a note on the menu that promises 'generous platefuls of delicious home-cooked food complemented by old-fashioned service and values, and the attentiveness which will take you back to days when hospitality really meant something'. The bar is open throughout the day, every day, for drinks, with up to four real ales always on tap – Black Sheep is the regular brew and the others change week by week. Fine wines are available by glass or bottle to enjoy on their own or with a meal.

The well-earned reputation for fine cuisine brings customers from near and far,

and although there are seats for 120 the popularity of the Shrew is such that booking is advisable to be sure of a table, and essential at the weekend. Local produce is used as much as possible on an extensive menu that really does have something for everyone. The tempting selection of main dishes includes traditional favourites such as lasagne, steak & mushroom pie and the Sunday roasts, as well as seasonal salads and 'Shrew Wraps' with fillings like Thai chicken or Italian vegetables. Room should definitely be left for at least one of the luscious desserts – perhaps apple pie or hot fudge cake.

Cotebrook, nr Tarporley,
Cheshire CW6 9DZ
☎ 01829 760529 Fax: 01829 760192
e-mail: info@thefoxandbarrel.com
🌐 www.thefoxandbarrel.com

In the midst of the Cheshire countryside, the **Fox & Barrel** stands in beautifully tended grounds next to the A49 in the village of Cotebrook, northeast of Tarporley. When Chris and Pamela Crossley took over the reins here in 2004 it was their first venture in the hospitality business, and what a success they have made of it! They have confirmed the pub as one of the very best eating places in Cheshire, truly a pub for all seasons offering the unbeatable combination of good food, fine wines, well-kept cask ales and great company.

The bar is a perfect spot for enjoying a convivial chat and a glass or two of real ale – 4 or 5 always available – but the best reason for a visit here is to sample the really outstanding food. Whether it's a snack or light meal from the bar selection or a full meal from the restaurant menu, the standards of preparation and presentation are uniformly high, and the enjoyment of a meal is enhanced by the relaxed, inviting atmosphere and the always friendly, helpful staff. Only the best and

freshest raw materials, much of them locally sourced, goes into the kitchen, and out of it comes a succession of superb dishes. A starter such as goat's cheese terrine, fresh salmon & smoked salmon fishcakes or a salad of fresh honeyed figs with parma ham might precede king prawns in a Thai green curry, slow-cooked lamb shank with honey-roasted root vegetables or pork steak with parmentier potatoes, peas and thyme. Desserts keep the enjoyment level sky high to the end, and the fine food is complemented by an excellent choice of

wines. For Sunday lunch, the regular menu is replaced by traditional roasts, with a vegetarian option. Sandwiches and bar snacks (burgers, ploughman's, Caesar salad, pasta) are available all lunchtimes and Sunday to Thursday evenings (sandwiches only after 7.30).

The interior is warm and traditional, and in the summer months the patio and beer garden provide very pleasant alfresco alternatives. The first Monday of the month is live jazz night, while the second Monday features pop music of the 50s and 60s.

49 THE COUNTRY MOUSE RESTAURANT

Brimstage Hall, Brimstage Lane, Brimstage,
Wirral CH63 6JA
☎ 0151 342 5382
🌐 www.countrymouse.co.uk

The **Country Mouse Restaurant** is located in the courtyard of Brimstage Hall, a medieval fortified tower that dates back to the 12th century. A converted barn makes an atmospheric setting for the restaurant, which Val and Joe have made one of the most popular daytime eating places in the region. Its success is due to the fact that just about everything is made on the premises, and Val's baking, from scones to featherlight meringues and superb cakes, is famous for many miles around.

The aroma of fresh baking wafts temptingly through the room, and the cakes on display on the Welsh dresser is very hard to resist. The savoury choice is no less delicious, from super salads to jacket potatoes, soups, baked trout with almonds, cauliflower & bacon gratin, fish pie, lasagne meat or vegetarian) and a traditional Sunday lunch. In fine weather customers can enjoy their food on the lawns, then perhaps wander round the craft and speciality shops in the courtyard.

50 THE JOLLY TAR

Nantwich Road, Wardle, nr Nantwich,
Cheshire CW5 6BE
☎ 01270 528283 Fax: 01270 528801

Five miles north of Nantwich and just across the road from the Shropshire Union Canal, the **Jolly Tar** is a cheerful, popular pub with lounge and public bars and a 50-cover restaurant. Outside is a very pleasant garden with a super children's play area. Host James Cowap offers a good choice of food and drink available lunchtime, evening and all day Saturday and Sunday. Booking is recommended to be sure of a table at the weekend.

51 YE OLDE WHITE LION

22 High Street, Congleton,
Cheshire CW12 1BD
☎ 01260 272702

With it striking black-and-white exterior, **Ye Olde White Lion** is an eyecatching landmark on the main street of town. The interior has been smartly refurbished in old-world style, and the cosy, inviting bars, where four real ales are always on tap, feature beams, brasses and a variety of ornaments. Amanda Thompson is both host and chef, and her home-

cooked dishes attract appreciative regulars at lunchtime Tuesday to Sunday. At the back of the pub is a delightful, secluded beer garden with a little menagerie.

52 THE NEW INN

Newcastle Road, Betchton, nr Sandbach,
Cheshire CW11 2TG
☎ 01477 500237

The **New Inn** is an attractive Country Inn incorporating a stylish restaurant called **'Candles'**. It is located on the A533 out of Sandbach, in the village of Betchton. Since April 2005 it has been in the capable and experienced hands of Christine and her son Mark Dickinson, who welcome visitors of all ages into a warm, friendly atmosphere.

Their chefs make excellent use of fresh, local produce, the menu choice is extensive with something for everyone. Traditional favourites like steak, ale and mushroom pie to prime fillet steak and a fresh fish board, trout, sole, salmon, seabass and many more. Traditional roasts are added to the

menu on Sundays. There is a wide variety of wines and spirits and the resident real ales are Marston's Bitter and Marston's Pedigree. Open during the week 12 to 3.30 and 5.30 to 11.00, all day Saturday and Sunday. Restaurant times: 12 to 2.30 and 5.30 to 9.30 and all day Sunday. There is a large car park, beer garden and play area. Picnic baskets available on request.

53 THE COURTYARD COFFEE HOUSE

Rear 92 King Street, Knutsford,
Cheshire WA16 6ED
☎ 01565 653974

Tucked away in its own cobbled courtyard, the **Courtyard Coffee House** is also home to the fascinating Penny Farthing Museum. The interior of the coffee house, with bicycles and a train running round the top of the walls, provides a unique ambience for enjoying high-quality food from 9.30 to 4.30 Monday to Saturday. Morning coffee comes with scones, toast and croissants, and traditional afternoon tea, with homemade scones and lovely tempting cakes, is an occasion not to be missed.

There's also a good savoury choice that includes some vegetarian options. Typical lunchtime favourites include Welsh rarebit, lamb & Puy lentil casserole, baked salmon supreme and spinach & ricotta tagliatelle. Children are welcome, and when the sun shines the outside tables are very popular. Penny Farthings were in vogue for not much more than 20 years, and the Courtyard Coffee House has already been going strong for longer than that!

54 THE DOG INN

Wellbank Lane, Over Peover, nr Knutsford,
Cheshire WA16 8UP
☎ 01625 861421 Fax: 01625 864800
e-mail: thedog-
inn@paddocksinns.fsnet.co.uk
🌐 www.doginn-overpeover.co.uk

A row of cottages built some 200 years ago
houses the **Dog Inn**, a popular choice with
both local customers and visitors from farther
afield. Behind the smart whitewashed
frontage with its
cheerful show of
flowers, the bars
and dining areas
are a particularly
cosy and inviting
setting for
enjoying well-
kept real ales

(five brews available, many more during the
annual festival in July) and a fine selection of
home-cooked dishes (best to book). For
guests exploring the many places of interest
in the vicinity or for business people needing
a quiet base, the Dog Inn has 6 very well
appointed en suite bedrooms.

55 THE CROWN INN

Crown Lane, Lower Peover,
Cheshire WA16 9QB
☎ 01565 722074

Anne West and her son Andy are the
leaseholders at the **Crown**, a splendid inn
offering its own brand of old-fashioned
hospitality. A choice of up to 7 real ales is
available in the bar, and a fine variety of
home-
cooked
food
lunchtime
and evening
Tuesday to
Saturday,
Monday
evening and
from 12 to
6.30 on

Sunday. Booking is recommended to be sure
of a table at the weekend. Among the many
attractions in and around the village are the
timber-framed St Oswald's Church and
Peover Hall, home to General Patton for a
time during World War II.

56 THE COTTAGE RESTAURANT & LODGE

London Road, Allostock, nr Knutsford,
Cheshire WA16 9LU
☎ 01565 722470 Fax: 01565 722749
e-mail:
reception@thecottageknutsford.co.uk
🌐 www.thecottageknutsford.co.uk

The **Cottage Restaurant & Lodge** is a charming
hotel owned and personally run by the Marr family.
It stands back from the main road between
Knutsford and Holmes Chapel in the village of
Allostock, at the heart of rural Cheshire. Character
abounds both inside and out, making the Cottage a
delightful place to enjoy a drink and a meal and a

very pleasant, peaceful base for a stay.

Diners can choose from à la carte and table d'hote
menus in the restaurant, where everything from the
sourcing of ingredients to cooking and presentation
receives equal care. The menus provide an impressive
choice of
meat, fish
and
vegetarian
dishes, and
a meal is an
occasion to
remember
from first

to last. The guest accommodation comprises 12
spacious, well-equipped en suite bedrooms – singles,
doubles and family rooms.

57 THE MILLBROOK

422 Huddersfield Road, Millbrook,
Cheshire SK15 3LJ
☎ 0161 338 2813

The **Millbrook** is a handsome building with a
superb traditional interior. Food is served
every lunchtime and evening
(not Monday) and all day on
Sunday. The menu provides
plenty of choice, including
grills, fish dishes, hot platters
and vegetarian options.

Explore Britain and Ireland with
Hidden Places guides - a fascinating
series of national and local travel
guides.

www.travelpublishing.co.uk

0118-981-7777

info@travelpublishing.co.uk

58 THE OLD HUNTERS TAVERN

51-53 Acres Lane, Stalybridge,
Cheshire SK15 2JR
☎ 0161 303 9477

On a corner site close to the town centre and
the canal, the **Old Hunters Tavern** is
housed within handsome redbrick premises
dating back to 1836. Anne and Derek
Wallwork have made many friends since they
took
over in
2000,
and the
welcome
they
extend
to
visitors
of all
ages is

warm and genuine. The pub is open all day,
every day for drinks (Robinson's Unicorn is
the resident real ale), and freshly prepared
food is served from the printed menu and
specials board lunchtime Monday to Friday.
Quiz Thursday, sports TV, beer garden.

59 THE CLARENCE HOTEL

Newton, nr Hyde, Cheshire SK14 4HJ
☎ 0161 368 2066

Situated in the tiny community of Newton, close to
Hyde, the **Clarence Hotel** has been run since July
2005 by Alan and Karen Crowe. This splendid mid-
Victorian pub is open all day, every day for drinks (Theakstons is the regular real ale) served in the
comfortable bar or out in the quiet beer garden at the
back. Karen is the cook, and her menu, served every
lunchtime except Tuesday, and Monday, Wednesday,
Thursday evenings, includes a selection of popular
homemade dishes. Children are welcome until 8 o'clock
in the evening.

Alan and Karen previously ran a social club in
Stockport, and they have brought a thriving social side
to the
Clarence: a
quiz
followed by
Play Your
Cards Right
on

Wednesday, live entertainment on Saturday, a pool table
and a big-screen TV for the major sporting events. The
pub is easily reached from Manchester, Stockport and
the motorway network, and among the local places of
interest are the Panhandle and the Peak District
National Park.

Church Street, Bollington, nr Macclesfield, Cheshire SK10 5PY

☎ 01625 574014 Fax: 01625 562026
e-mail: info@the-church-house-inn.co.uk
🖳 www.the-church-house-inn.co.uk

When their favourite local seemed likely to fall into decline with the departure of the incumbent landlord, a dozen friends clubbed together and bought the lease on the historic **Church House Inn** at Bollington. The prime movers behind the move and its subsequent success are Bob Gratton, Allan Sherratt, Trevor Gregory, Steve Murphy and landlord Ian King, and mention must also be made of Sue Swann, a stalwart in the kitchen for more than 20 years. The inn is a handsome 19th century stone building with a warm, welcoming atmosphere and a traditional look and feel assisted by open fires, exposed beams, pew seats and distinctive tables made from sewing machine treadles. The well-stocked bar keeps a good selection of traditional ales (Bass, Black Sheep, Greene King IPA), lagers, wines, spirits and soft drinks, and lunchtime and evening meals are served in the main bar or in the non smoking dining room. Most of the dishes are homemade, with local suppliers used

whenever possible. The meat pies and casseroles are perennially popular dishes, and among other favourites are fish & chips and lamb hotpot, with excellent desserts to finish. From the daily changing blackboard come the likes of sesame prawn toast, swordfish steak and pork with a cranberry and ginger sauce. Lighter lunchtime snacks include sandwiches, jacket potatoes and steak baguettes. An upstairs function room is a popular venue for private parties.

The pub occupies a corner site in the village of Bollington, a mile or so from the A523 and 4 miles from Macclesfield on the

edge of the Peak District National Park. Five en suite rooms (3 singles and 2 doubles) provide a very comfortable base for both business and leisure visitors, and the tariff includes a good choice for breakfast.

The rescuing of the Church House caught the imagination of the media, both local and national, and attention also focussed on the pub in October 2005 when a harvest service was conducted.

60 THE CHURCH INN

90 Ravenoak Road, Cheadle Hulme,
Stockport SK8 7EG
☎ 0161 485 1897 Fax: 0161 485 1698
e-mail: church-inn@yahoo.co.uk

Family-run and family-friendly, the **Church Inn** is Cheadle Hulme's oldest hostelry and a very popular spot well worth seeking out for a drink or a meal. The pub is open all day, every day for drinks, with Hatters and Robinson's Unicorn the resident real ales.

Food is an important part of the business, and the menu and specials board combine tried and  tested favourites such as pepper steak and tandoori chicken with daily specials like salmon cocktail, tiger prawns oriental and ham hock with bubble & squeak.

65 THE BEECH TREE INN

Runcorn Road, Barnton, nr Northwich,
Cheshire CW8 4HS
☎ 01606 77292

The **Beech Tree** is a handsome and substantial redbrick building set back from the A533 Northwich-Runcorn road. Mark Patton is carrying on a tradition of hospitality that includes excellent food, a good choice of beers and wines, a welcome for all the family and an unfailingly cheerful, convivial atmosphere. An unusual amenity is a championship standard bowling green. The inn has three well-appointed letting rooms for overnight guests.

63 THE CAT & FIDDLE

Buxton Road, Macclesfield Forest,
Cheshire SK11 0AR
☎ 01298 23364
e-mail: cat-and-fiddle@tiscali.co.uk

Midway between Buxton and Macclesfield on the A537, within Macclesfield Forest and the Peak District National Park, the **Cat & Fiddle** enjoys superb views in all directions from its lofty setting. A popular place of refreshment for walkers, cyclists, motorists and day-trippers, this renowned inn is run by Guy Danner, ably assisted by his daughter Emily. It's open every day except Thursday, serving three real ales from the Robinson Brewery: Unicorn, Olde Stockport and a changing guest. There's also a good selection of other draught and bottle beers, lagers, cider, wines, spirits and soft drinks.

Food is served all day, so no one ever goes hungry at this splendid inn. Sandwiches and jacket

 potatoes cater for smaller appetites or customers with less time to spare, but the best plan is to allow plenty of time to sit down to a first-class meal. Steaks, pies, roast beef and chicken and Cumberland sausage are just a few of the all-time hearty favourites, and other choices might include moussaka, cauliflower bake and always a selection of chef's specials and a children's menu. Booking is recommended at the weekend and for larger groups.

62 SUTTON HALL

Bullocks Lane, Sutton, nr Macclesfield,
Cheshire SK11 0HE
☎ 01260 253211 Fax: 01260 252538

Robert and Phyllida Bradshaw run an outstanding hotel, restaurant and public house at **Sutton Hall**, which stands in 14 acres of lovely grounds. Once the baronial residence of the Sutton family and more recently a convent associated with the diocese of Shrewsbury, it has been converted with great skill and at great expense into a unique 'inn of distinction', affording the traveller superb food, good ale and sumptuous accommodation.

The fully licensed lounge bar, with its original oak panelling, stained galls, log fires and eyecatching decorative features, makes a civilised, atmospheric spot for enjoying a fine range of cask-conditioned ales, wines, spirits (40+ malts!) and freshly squeezed fruit juices, and a selection of home-prepared food is available every lunchtime and evening. For a more formal occasion, the elegant dining room offers a regularly changing menu of dishes prepared from the

finest and freshest seasonal produce. In the library which is also used as a private function room accommodating up to 24 seated, guests can browse through the books and enjoy a coffee and digestif in front of the huge log fire (spot the Sutton coat of arms above the fireplace). In the summer months tables are set out on the lawn, making an idyllic setting for a drink a meal or afternoon tea.

For guests staying awhile the Hall has ten magnificent bedrooms reached by a wide, imposing oak staircase. Each room has its own individual charm and character, and the sumptuous lace-draped four-poster beds add a definite romantic feel. Rooms can be booked on a Bed & Breakfast or Dinner, Bed & Breakfast basis. Moorings can be booked on the nearby canal, and the hotel can arrange fishing, golf and other outdoor activities for guests. The hotel is a short drive from Macclesfield: southward on the A523, left into Byrons Lane signposted Langley Wincle, right just before the canal into Bullocks Lane.

64 THE BRIDGE HOTEL & RESTAURANT

Prestbury, Cheshire SK10 4DQ
☎ 01625 829326 Fax: 01625 827557
e-mail: reception@bridge-hotel.co.uk
🌐 www.bridge-hotel.co.uk

Situated in the beautiful, unspoilt village of Prestbury, the **Bridge Hotel & Restaurant** has been owned and personally run by the Grange family for more than half a century. That tradition of service and hospitality is being carried on by Norman, Elaine and their son Fraser. Standing close to the River Bollin, the building dates back to 1626; it was then a row of timbered cottages, one of which provided Bonnie Prince Charlie with a night's lodgings during his march southward at the head of his Scottish army in 1745.

Skilful conversion and the addition of a new wing created 23 guest bedrooms, all colourfully but tastefully decorated and very well equipped. All have en suite

facilities, and the rooms and all the public parts of the hotel are accessible to wheelchair users. The award-winning restaurant offers excellent classic cuisine with modern and international influences, served seven days a week in the galleried dining room, with live music adding to the atmosphere on Friday and Saturday evenings. The Bridge has two banqueting/conference rooms.

66 MARBURY COUNTRY PARK

Comberbach, Northwich,
Cheshire CW9 6AT
☎ 01606 77741

Marbury Country Park was once part of a large country estate whose history dates back to around 1200 AD. Marbury itself means a fortified or stockaded dwelling by the mere or water. The first family took the name Marbury and lived there until 1684. When the last male heir died the estate was bought by Richard Earl Rivers who never lived there. On his death in 1714 it was bought by his son-in-law James, the 4th Earl of Barrymore. It was the Barry family who shaped the park with extensive landscaping and the building of the hall.

A succession of owners and uses then followed, culminating in the hall being demolished in 1968 due to rot. In 1975, 196 acres was leased from the owners, ICI, by Cheshire County Council and restoration work was begun. Further land was later aquired and today it is managed by the Countryside Management Service to benefit wildlife and visitors.

Each habitat is carefully managed to encourage different plants and animals, so there is always plenty to see at all times of the year. In spring the woodland is covered by a spectacular carpet of wildflowers and willow warblers, chiffchaffs and blackcaps herald the arrival of summer. Autumn shows the colours of the trees off to their best and in winter, the Mere becomes a focus for many birds including goldeneye and greylag geese.

67 THE GRAPEVINE

The Courtyard, Fore Street, East Looe,
Cornwall PL13 1AE
☎ 01503 263913 Fax: 08700 520706
e-mail: info@grapevinerestaurant.co.uk
🌐 www.grapevinerestaurant.co.uk

Tucked discreetly off one of East Looe's main streets, the **Grapevine** is a real gem of a restaurant. Beyond the sign is a lovely little courtyard that's equally delightful for a lunch under parasols or dinner on a balmy summer's evening. Here and in the intimate dining room waitresses serve a tempting variety of dishes devised by Nathaniel Goss.

This hardworking owner has put his individual stamp on the cooking, which takes its inspiration from Britain, from the Mediterranean and from the Orient. The superb local seafood is showcased in delectable dishes such as pan-seared scallops, while more exotic choices are typified by crispy braised pork with soy and noodles - it's all freshly prepared, beautifully presented and of the very best quality.

69 RESTORMEL CASTLE

Off the A390 1½ miles N of Lostwithiel
☎ 01208 872687
🌐 www.english-heritage.org.uk

High on a moated mound overlooking the River Fowey, **Restormel Castle** is one of the former strongholds of the Earls of Cornwall, whose number included Edward, the Black Prince. Dating from the 11th century, it was one of the first motte and bailey castles to be raised in the West Country, and in the next century its original wooden defences were replaced with stone and a full set of domestic buildings added. In 1272 Restormel was inherited by Edmund of Almaine, Earl of Cornwall, whose builders constructed a miniature palace within its walls; this provided lavish accommodation for the Earl and his guests, who could look out on to a deer park created for their favourite pursuit.

The Black Prince stayed here in 1354 and 1365, but with the loss of Gascony soon after, most of the contents of value were removed, and the Castle fell into ruin. Today, the ruins survive in this tranquil hilltop setting. In spring the banks are covered in daffodils and bluebells, and in summer the site is one of the best picnic spots in Cornwall, boasting stunning views of the peaceful countryside.

68 THE SHIP INN

Trafalgar Square, Fowey,
Cornwall PL23 1AZ
☎ 01726 832230 Fax: 01726 834933
e-mail: aldwd@msn.com

In the heart of the lovely fishing port of
Fowey, the **Ship Inn** is a friendly, well-kept
hostelry that's equally popular with locals and
visitors. The maritime connection is strong
throughout, with sea pictures, ship's wheels
and a stained-glass window depicting the
ships of Fowey Haven putting to sea to play
their part in the defeat of the Spanish
Armada. The connection extends to the
menu, where super
fresh seafood
dishes stand
alongside snacks,
steams and
speciality sausages.
The Ship has a
number of guest
bedrooms ranging
from basic doubles
to an oak-panelled
room and a family
suite.

70 SUNRISE

Burn View, Bude, Cornwall EX23 8BU
☎ 01288 353214
e-mail: sunriseguest@btconnect.com
www.sunrise-bude.co.uk

Sunrise is a beautifully maintained Victorian
house offering style and comfort in the heart
of Bude, a short walk from two lovely
beaches. Bed & Breakfast accommodation
provided by Lesley and Bob Sharratt
comprises seven en suite rooms ranging from
a single to twins, a triple and a family room.
Guests rise and
shine to an
excellent variety
for breakfast,
and home-
cooked evening
meals can be
arranged
between
September and
June. Sunrise
offers special
deals for golfing
breaks.

71 TINTAGEL CASTLE

Tintagel, Cornwall
☎ 01840 770328
www.english-heritage.org.uk

For over 800 years the tale has been told that
Tintagel Castle was the birthplace of King
Arthur, born to the beautiful Queen Igerna and
protected from evil by the magician Merlin, who
lived in a cave below the fortress. But the history of the site goes back even further. Fragments of
a Celtic monastic house dating from the 6th century have been unearthed on the headland and
their origins certainly coincide with the activities of the Welsh military leader on which the
Arthurian legends are thought to be based. The castle was, in fact, built in the 12th century, some
600 years after the time of King Arthur, by Reginald, Earl of Cornwall, the illegitimate son of
Henry I. Whatever the truth behind the stories, the magic of this site, with Atlantic breakers
crashing against the cliffs, certainly matches that of the tales of chivalry and wizardry.

In 1998 the discovery of a 6th century
slate bearing the Latin inscription 'Artognov' -
which translates as the ancient British name
for Arthur - renewed the belief that Tintagel
was Arthur's home. The cave, found at the
foot of The Island, is known as **Merlin's
Cave** and is said still to be haunted by a
ghost. Tintagel is also of great interest to
nature-lovers: the
cliffs are at the heart of a Site of Special
Scientific Interest, providing breeding
grounds for sea birds, lizards and butterflies.
Tintagel Castle is one of over 400 historic
sites in the care of English Heritage.

72 LLAWNROC INN

33 Chute Lane, Gorran Haven,
nr St Austell, Cornwall PL26 6NU
☎ 01726 843461 Fax: 01726 844056
e-mail: llawnrocinn@onetel.com
⊕ www.llawnroc.mevagissey.com

The Llawnroc Inn is a friendly, popular village pub whose attractions include fine food and drink, comfortable hotel accommodation and glorious sea views.

It overlooks the picturesque village of Gorran Haven and the sheltered bay with fine safe and sandy beaches. The South West Coastal Path is only a stones throw away; hence it's a favourite base for walkers and anyone whom loves the great outdoors. The Llawnroc has an historic association with The Lost Gardens of Heligan and that in turn lead to the Eden project being conceived at the Inn.

There's no mistaking the cheerful, inviting feel inside, and the fisherman's bar, the lounge bar

and the non-smoking Eden restaurant, all have their own particular charms. Outside, the pleasant terraced garden beckons in the summer. The bar is well stocked with a selection of real ales, beers, wines, spirits and soft drinks. There are a variety of menus offering anything from a quick snack to a buffet and a 3 course meal. The guest bedrooms are all en-suite with attractive décor and furnishings and great sea views.

73 THE BUGLE INN

Fore Street, Bugle, Cornwall
☎ 01726 850307 Fax: 01726 850181
e-mail: bugleinn@aol.com
⊕ www.bugleinn.co.uk

The village of Bugle may not be one of Cornwall's liveliest, but **The Bugle Inn** has much to recommend it. Run by Simon and Pam Rodger, the couple have been here for ten years and have established a well-liked, friendly pub. The interior is cluttered and cosy, with a warm atmosphere and friendly staff. The chef keeps the kitchen open from 8am to 9pm each day, with a wide choice of freshly prepared un-fussy dishes, together with daily big value specials, on offer. Also five en suite guest rooms available for bed and breakfast.

74 WHEAL MARTYN CHINA CLAY MUSEUM

Carthew, St Austell, Cornwall PL26 8XG
☎ 01726 850362
⊕ www.wheal-martyn.com

Production of china clay in Cornwall has been a 250-year saga, and a visit to the **Wheal Martyn China Clay Museum** will provide a fascinating insight into this industry. Following an audio-visual introduction, the Historic Trail takes visitors through the old clay works, where the largest working waterwheel in Cornwall is an impressive sight, and other equipment includes sand and mica drags, settling pits and tanks and a linhay (clay store). Undercover

exhibitions include the great Fal Valley engine and a nature trail leads you to a viewing platform above the working modern clay pit.

75 MEUDON HOTEL

Mawnan Smith, nr Falmouth,
Cornwall TR11 5HT
☎ 01326 250541   Fax: 01325 250543
e-mail: wecare@meudon.co.uk
🌐 www.meudon.co.uk

Luxury goes hand in hand with comfort, service and value-for money at **Meudon Hotel**, a 'place of peace and beauty' standing amongst some of the delightful coastal scenery in the Southwest. Meudon takes its name from the home village near Paris of Napoleonic prisoners of war who built a farmhouse near Mawnan Smith. The hotel, based on a private late-Victorian mansion, incorporates two 17th century coastguard's cottages – a combination that provides an unusual blend of gracious Cornish country house and modern yet characterful hotel.

The hotel was developed by Mr and Mrs Harry Pilgrim, who were determined to create an oasis of calm and comfort in this beautiful part of Cornwall on the Helford River, and their son Mark is equally dedicated to maintaining and improving the very high standards set by his parents. The hotel's 29 guest bedrooms are among

the best in the whole county, with elegant décor and furnishings, superbly comfortable beds and individually controlled central heating. Among the many amenities provided are a 24-hour laundry service and a hairdressing salon. Antique furniture, sumptuous fabrics, deep carpets and fresh flowers contribute to the timeless ambience in the day rooms, and the gardens are a real joy, with rare trees and shrubs and many varieties developed on the Estate.

The cuisine matches the accommodation and the surroundings at this outstanding hotel, and fresh local produce is used as much as possible, including pork, beef, fish and shellfish and a splendid selection of Cornish cheeses, in dishes that are prepared and presented with skill and artistry. Fine wines from around the world set the seal on a memorable meal. Guests return year after year to Meudon Hotel, some to enjoy the air of total relaxation, to stroll in the grounds or to wander down to the private beach at Bream Cove, others to discover and rediscover the numerous attractions both scenic and historic that the region has to offer. Much of the land, including the Meudon Estate, is in the care of the National Trust, and the Trust's Glendurgan Garden is among the most popular family attractions in the area.

76 THE GARDENS

Tresowes, Ashton, Helston TR13 9SY
☎ 01736 763299

Owned and personally managed by Moira Cattell, **The Gardens** is the ideal B&B for people who prefer a quiet retreat while holidaying in the lovely county of Cornwall.

It has three comfortable rooms, two en suite and one with private bathroom, all stylish and reflecting the history of the house, which started off life as three 18th century miners' cottages. It is now extremely picturesque,

nestling within gardens that area riot of colour in summer.

The breakfasts are all home-cooked, and you can choose from a hearty full English or a lighter option if required.

77 NANPLOUGH FARM

Cury, nr Helston, Cornwall TR12 7BQ
☎ 01326 241088
e-mail: info@nanplough.co.uk
🌐 www.nanplough.co.uk

At the heart of the lovely Lizard Peninsula, **Nanplough Farm** welcomes visitors with a choice of both self-catering and B&B accommodation. The setting in 25 acres of wooded glades, gardens and lawns, is both beautiful and peaceful, making it an ideal base for complete relaxation or for discovering the many attractions of the region.

The well-appointed, sensitively modernised self-catering cottages, sleeping from 2 to 6, are clustered round a central courtyard that's part of the

original farm, and exposed beams and rendered walls retain their period character. The 1880s house is elegant and spacious, and its two letting bedrooms – a double and a family room – have central heating, TV, tea-making facilities and hair-dryers. A hearty breakfast starts the day, and guests have the use of a lounge with an open fire.

78 MOUNT VIEW HOTEL

Longrock, nr Penzance, Cornwall TR20 8JJ
☎ 01736 710416

In the centre of Longrock, a short drive east of Penzance, **Mount View Hotel** takes its name from the fine view originally commanded of St Michael's Mount and the bay beyond. Carpets, a big stone hearth, pictures and a modern wooden counter set the scene in the bar, where Doreen Capper ensures that the mood is always friendly and relaxed.

The bar is a popular meeting place for local customers and for the many tourists who visit this part of the world throughout the year. This free house is open all day for drinks, and the menu casts its net wide, from sandwiches and

jacket potatoes to locally-landed fish, home-made pies, steaks, chicken dishes and always a good choice for vegetarians. The list of places of interest in the vicinity, both scenic and historic, is almost endless, and Mount View's five bedrooms (three with en suite facilities) provide a very pleasant, civilised base for tourists.

81 PORTHCURNO TELEGRAPH MUSEUM

Eastern House, Porthcurno,
Penzance TR19 6JX
☎ 01736 810966
⊕ www.porthcurno.org.uk

This unique museum stands in the beautiful valley of Porthcurno. The first cable station here was built in 1870, and from that time an increasing number of undersea cables were laid, creating a communications network, which connected the village with remote and exotic parts of the world.

By the start of the Second World War, there were 14 cables and it had become the most important cable station in the world, so it was considered necessary to

build bomb-proof tunnels to protect the station from attack. These tunnels now house the major part of the museum, where regular demonstrations show working telegraph equipment from throughout the

era, as well as giving a taste of the social changes that took place.

The sights, sounds and smells here are evocative of times gone by, and there is something to interest every member of the family. There are many hands-on exhibits, as well as special activities for children, a local history exhibition and an exhibition about Brunel.

Halsetown, nr St Ives, Cornwall TR26 3NA
☎ 01736 795583

The **Halsetown Inn**, dating from 1832, is a warm, friendly local and a lot more besides. It has an elegant Regency façade, and the recently refurbished bars, with plastered walls and lots of local period pictures, have a welcoming ambience that puts visitors instantly in a relaxed mood. Open fires keep things cosy even in the coldest weather, and a splendid old Cornish range takes the eye in the lounge. Clies and Joan, customers who became hosts, provide a genuine welcome for all who pass through the doors, from familiar faces to tourists and families along with their children and dogs.

Thirsts are quenched by a wide range of beers (including 2 or 3 real ales) and a very good selection of other drinks, and a fine variety of food is served every lunchtime and evening in the summer months, and Friday and Saturday evenings and Sunday lunch in the winter. Poached salmon, smoked haddock bake, lamb shanks, beef & ale pie and sweet chilli chicken stir-fry are typical choices, and the daily specials might additionally offer pork oriental, grilled megrim sole with a white wine and prawn sauce, beef & carrot stew and a scrumptious hazelnut bake. Salads, sandwiches and lots of things with chips make up the bar, garden and lunch menu.

The inn is also an ideal base for exploring a particularly interesting part of the county, and the five pine-furnished bedrooms (three with en suite facilities) combine 19th century character with

21st century comfort and amenities. The Halsetown Inn is one of the most sociable of pubs, darts and children's games and regular quiz nights; it also fields pool and euchre teams and two soccer teams.

Halsetown takes its name from James Halse, who designed the village to house his miners; the modest price to pay in return was that they should vote for him whenever elections took place!

Gwinear, Hayle, Cornwall TR27 5JQ
☎ 01209 713931 Fax: 01209 717090

With constant expansion of both space and services offered, the Eustice family's **Trevaskis Farm** has earned its place as one of the West Country's best run and best regarded centre of top-quality farm produce in all its aspects. The family's aim is to make the farm the premier site in the Southwest offering a relaxed country retreat where visitors can learn about the production of organic fruit and vegetables, including their nutritional value and how they can be incorporated into a healthy, balanced diet.

On the 28-acre farm site they raise up to 30 different fruit and vegetable crops, many of which can be picked by visitors; guided walks can be arranged through the farm, informing visitors of the nature and properties of each crop through the guides or through educational literature. The Organic Kitchen Gardens include a demonstration area showing how to create a kitchen garden, assisting clients to set up sites, planting and maintaining it to ensure a supply of healthy food on the doorstep throughout the year.

In the Educational Growing Centre 30+ fruit and vegetable varieties are grown in small quantities, with information available on the nutritional value of each crop, its origins, history and growing patterns.

The site also offers visitors the chance to view and learn about its rare-breed animals. The Eustice family have been involved since 1890 in the breeding of British Lop pigs, Dartmoor Grey Face sheep, South Devon cattle and various breeds of poultry. All the crops grown on the farm are available in their season in the Farm Shop, along with jams and preserves, honey, chutneys, pickles and fruit juices. From the owner's butchery come the home-bred top-quality beef, pork and lamb, along with the renowned sausages made on the premises to a special recipe.

The Farmhouse Kitchen has been expanded to enable the owners to increase the services offered, and after exploring all the attractions of the farm visitors can sample the produce they have seen growing in its natural form. Food is available in the restaurant from 10 in the morning to 5 and from 6 in the evening to 10. The daytime menu ranges from sandwiches and salads to baked potatoes and pasties, while in the evening the choice typically runs from bang bang chicken, honey & mustard salmon, lasagne (beef or vegetarian) to pan-fried duck with garlic, mushrooms and leeks, steaks and sweet and sour vegetable stir fry.

82 THE PUNCH BOWL

Barrow Green, Kendal, Cumbria LA8 0AA
☎ 015395 60267
e-mail: caroline.dent@btconnect.com

After a spell on the staff of the **Punch Bowl**, Caroline Dent stepped up to take over the tenancy early in 2005. At this handsome whitewashed roadside inn, her first solo venture, her unpretentious home cooking brings an appreciative band of regulars and those in the know who make the short detour from the A65 to the south side of Kendal.

A typical list of daily specials might include battered chilli chicken, lamb rogan josh, liver & onions, scampi and roasted root vegetable bake, all served with chips (home-made, naturally), jacket potatoes, new potatoes, rice or a salad. The pub dates

from mid-Victorian times, and Caroline worked tirelessly to create the immaculate interior that greets those who pass through its doors. The pub is open from 11.30 right through the day and evening; food is served lunchtime and evening and all day on Sunday. At the back is a pleasant beer garden.

83 BRUNT KNOTT FARM HOLIDAY COTTAGES

Staveley, nr Kendal, Cumbria LA8 9QX
☎ 01539 821030 Fax: 01539 822680
e-mail: margaret@bruntknott.demon.co.uk
🌐 www.bruntknott.demon.co.uk

Tourists, walkers and lovers of the countryside will find the perfect base in **Brunt Knott Farm Holiday Cottages**. Nestled around a 17th century hill farm within the Lake District National Park, the 4 self-catering cottages command magnificent panoramic views over the Lakeland fells. They are sympathetically converted from stone and slate farm buildings and each has its own garden area and private parking. Décor is traditional, with whitewashed walls, retained beams and feature stonework. The cottages are well-equipped and fully carpeted, to ensure a comfortable, stress-free stay in relaxing surroundings all year round.

The Stables and Hayloft both sleep 2, the Bothy sleeps

4, and the Byre sleeps 4/5. Surrounded by open countryside, and with both excellent walking and cycling on the doorstep, the farm is situated a mile and a half from the village of Staveley, above the beautiful Kentmere valley, midway between Kendal and Lake Windermere. Owners William and Margaret Beck are on hand to make sure that their guests have an enjoyable and memorable stay.

Kendal, Cumbria LA9 5AL

☎ 01539 722464 Fax: 01539 722494

Abbot Hall Art Gallery forms part of a complex within Abbot Hall park and includes work by John Ruskin and the celebrated portrait painter, George Romney, who was born nearby at Dalton-in-Furness in 1734. The permanent collection also includes a wide range of 18th, 19th and 20th century British paintings and watercolours, and the Gallery hosts regular touring exhibitions.

A short walk from the Brewery Arts Centre is the **Museum of Lakeland Life and Industry** which is themed around traditional rural trades of the region, such as blacksmithing, wheelwrighting, agricultural activities, weaving, and printing. Here, too, are recreated cottage interiors, elegantly furnished period rooms and a

reconstruction of the study in which the celebrated author, Arthur Ransome, wrote the children's classic *Swallows and Amazons*.

At the other end of the town, near the railway station, is the **Museum of Natural History and Archaeology,** founded in 1796 and one of the oldest museums in the country.

Based on the collection first exhibited by William Todhunter in the late 18th century, the Museum takes visitors on a journey from prehistoric times, a trip which includes an interactive exhibit which tells the story of Kendal Castle.

The famous fellwalker and writer, Alfred Wainwright, whose handwritten guides to the Lakeland hills will be found in the backpack of any serious walker, was honorary clerk here between 1945 and 1974. Many of his original drawings are on display.

85 THE COMMODORE

Main Street, Grange-over-Sands,
Cumbria LA11 6DY
☎ 015395 32381

The charming town of Grange-over-Sands stands on the north shore of Morecambe Bay and has the unusual distinction of being a south-facing northern resort. There's plenty for the visitor to see in and around the town, including parks and gardens and good shopping, and it's also the starting point of the Cistercian Way, an interesting 33-mile footpath that runs through Furness to Barrow.

Tourists, walkers, families, business people and all-comers are very welcome at The **Commodore**, whether it's for a drink, a snack, a meal or an overnight or longer stay. It's a big, bold, white-painted building with its pub sign and other features picked out in green, and it stands close to the edge of the Bay, separated from the water by the railway line, and enjoying excellent views from its elevated position. The view of The Commodore from the Bay is the back, while the entrance is tucked away discreetly down a little alley off the main street. Ron and Terri have plenty of experience in the licensed trade, and started putting that experience to excellent use when they took command of The Commodore in the autumn of 2005.

The pub area of the hotel features lots of wood, old trade signs, brasses and mugs, making a spacious, informal setting for meeting for a drink (resident and guest real ales on tap) and a lively chat. A blackboard lists a daily selection of uncomplicated, good-value lunchtime dishes such as chicken with gravy, homemade lasagne, tuna pasta bake and tempura battered hake. For guests staying overnight, three well-priced en suite B&B rooms are available all year round. Space is in liberal supply at The Commodore, and among the amenities is a huge function suite. Friday is quiz night, and on Saturdays between Easter and October the hotel hosts live entertainment evenings.

86 COURTYARD COTTAGE

9a Queen Street, Ulverston,
Cumbria LA12 7AF
☎ 01229 581662
e-mail: info@courtyardcottage.com
🌐 www.courtyardcottage.com

The ancient market town of Ulverston is a delightful place to visit, with a number of unique attractions, and there's no more charming place to choose as a base than **Courtyard Cottage**. Tucked away off Queen Street in the heart of town, this picturesque 19th century mews-style cottage offers luxurious Bed & Breakfast accommodation in very comfortable, contemporary style.

Hospitality and a warm welcome are the cornerstone of owners Linda and Steve Weathers approach towards B&B and behind the pretty flower-decked frontage they have taken the greatest care with every detail of the décor and furnishings. The two guest rooms (soon to be three) are filled with thoughtful extras in addition to the expected amenities. Linda's

delicious breakfasts make an excellent start to the day: the 'full English' sets guests up for a day's sightseeing, and vegetarian and special diets can be catered for. Ingredients sourced locally and organic produce is used wherever possible Packed lunches can be provided, and summer barbecues are a popular 'extra'. The cottage has a laundry/drying room and guests can while away a happy hour or two with board games in the lounge.

87 TALLY HO

Wilkie Road, Barrow-in-Furness,
Cumbria LA14 5DN
☎ 01229 821221

The Bryan family – mother, father and two daughters – welcome one and all into the **Tally Ho**, their popular pub on the edge of Barrow-in-Furness. The 30-year-old building is big, bright and comfortable, a great favourite with the locals and a very pleasant place to seek out by visitors to the town (it's just seconds away from the A590).

The resident chef is kept busy preparing a good variety of tasty, down-to-earth pub favourites such as burgers, steaks, curries and the 'modern classic' chicken tikka masala. Sticky

toffee pudding, chocolate dream and baked Alaska are among the options for rounding off a meal in style. The Tally Ho is open from 11.30 right through till 2 in the morning seven days a week, and food is served between 12 and 2 and from 5 until 8 every day. The pub has a huge lounge and separate public bar, a pool table, juke box and games machines. Saturday is live music night.

88 CONCLE INN

Rampside, Barrow-in-Furness,
Cumbria LA13 0PU
☎ 01229 822319

At the very tip of the peninsula, overlooking Foulney Island and the vast expanse of Morecambe Bay, the **Concle Inn** is a fine old whitewashed pub with a particularly friendly, welcoming feel. Its popularity is due in no small part to the efforts of sociable hosts Phil and Carolyn, who keep the place spick and span, with many of the original features of its early-19th century origins retained.

An open fire keeps things cosy in the homely lounge bar, where there's a good range of drinks to enjoy on their own or to complement the value-for-money food. Freshly prepared to order, the dishes include steaks, savoury pies and fish specials. The Concle hosts a quiz every other Monday, Wednesday is cards night, and the

pool league meets on Sunday night. Neighbouring Barrow-in-Furness has plenty of interest to

discover, and the Bay and the islands also attract many visitors, but nowhere in the region will visitors find a better or warmer welcome than at Phil and Carolyn's Concle Inn.

89 THE RED LION

5 Market Street, Dalton,
nr Barrow-in-Furness, Cumbria LA15 8AE
☎ 01229 467914

Gary Thompson took over the tenancy of the **Red Lion** in February 2006, bringing fresh ideas and renewed energy to this fine old pub. Window boxes and hanging baskets make a colourful slow outside, while in the bar huge beams and a big fireplace with a roaring fire are notable features.

Four regularly changing real ales head the list of drinks, to quench thirsts or to accompany the excellent, good-value food served lunchtime and evening Tuesday to Saturday and Sunday lunch. Head chef John Jones is bringing fresh ideas to the menus, with imaginative dishes like stuffed breast of chicken wrapped in Parma ham and

served with a sweetcorn sauce sharing the menus with classics such as

steak & Guinness pie. Booking is advisable at all times and essential for Sunday lunch. The main emphasis may be on food, but the Red Lion is also an excellent place for an overnight or longer stay. Dalton and the surrounding area has a wealth of historic and scenic interest for the visitor, and the seven well-appointed guest bedrooms, four of them with en suite facilities, provide a very pleasant, civilised base.

Princes Street, Broughton-in-Furness,
Cumbria LA20 6HQ
☎ 01229 716529
e-mail: dpike91556@aol.com

The 16th century **Black Cock Inn** stands at the heart of the attractive little town of Broughton-in-Furness, within easy reach of some of the Lake District's finest scenery. Open every lunchtime and evening and all day on Saturday and Sunday, this much-loved village inn is full of history, charm and atmosphere.

In summer the black-and-white front comes alive with colourful window boxes and hanging baskets, and the inside is every bit as welcoming whatever the season. The lounge bar, with roaring log fires and low beamed ceiling, has a wonderful traditional ambience, and recent changes and a new extension have been careful to retain all the period appeal. Landlord David Pike has brought new ideas and a new vigour to the old inn, and his new chef puts his own particular stamp on a menu of Old English Fayre. Theakston's provides the resident real ale, and a superb selection of

food is available each lunchtime and until 9 o'clock in the evening.

The dining area is certainly not short of space, but such is the popularity of the inn that booking is strongly advised for all meals. The ample choice on the printed menu is supplemented by daily specials listed on the blackboard, typified by homemade meat and potato pie with mushy peas, gravy, beetroot and onions; salmon with a prawn and lemon cream sauce; minted lamb shank; and chicken breast stuffed with stilton, wrapped in parma ham and served with a white wine sauce. Children are welcome (they have their own dishes) and the inn has six very well-appointed en suite guest bedrooms, including two in the new extension. There is excellent walking country hereabouts, with plenty of history and natural features to discover, and Broughton itself is well worth taking time to explore.

The inn has a games room in the old stables, a courtyard beer garden and plenty of off-road parking.

91 THE GOLDEN FLEECE

The Square, Calder Bridge, Seascale,
Cumbria CA20 1DN
☎ 01946 841151
e-mail: thegoldenfleece@calderbridge.co.uk
🌐 www.calderbridge.co.uk

The **Golden Fleece** is a traditional village
inn with a history going back to the 1700s.
Food is served between noon and 9 o'clock,
and for overnight guests the pub has five
smartly refurbished en suite bedrooms.

Looking for:
- *Places to Visit?*
- *Places to Stay?*
- *Places to Eat & Drink?*
- *Places to Shop?*

www.travelpublishing.co.uk

---

93 ELIM BANK HOTEL

Lake Road, Bowness-on-Windermere,
Cumbria LA23 2JJ
☎ 015394 44810 Fax: 015394 48413
e-mail: hosts@elimbankhotel.co.uk
🌐 www.elimbankhotel.co.uk

Built by a local landowner in the late 19th
century, **Elim Bank Hotel** is a typical stone-
built gabled Lakeland residence. It's kept in
apple pie order by owners Brian and
Margaret Hodgkinson, and a major recent
undertaking was the rebuilding of the
conservatory in wood, accurately replicating
the
original.
The seven
guest
bedrooms
all have en
suite
facilities,
television
and
beverage tray, and the tariff includes a hearty
English breakfast. The Hotel has its own car
park.

92 LAKES HOTEL & SUPER TOURS

1 High Street, Windermere,
Cumbria LA23 1AF
☎ 015394 42751/88133
Fax: 015394 46026
e-mail: admin@lakes-hotel.com
🌐 www.lakes-hotel.com

Lakes Hotel is a small family-run hotel with
a high-street location and a well-earned
reputation for its warm, friendly ambience
and comfortable accommodation. Built in
1860 and originally a bank, this fine stone
building has
ten spacious
bedrooms,
all with
private
facilities,
central
heating,
television,
beverage
tray, fridge and hairdryer. The tariff includes
a full English breakfast, and owner Andy
Dobson runs an unusual sideline in the form
of a number of luxury mini-coaches available
for daily tours.

94 THE SAWREY HOTEL

Far Sawrey, nr Ambleside,
Cumbria LA22 0LQ
☎ 015394 43425

The **Sawrey Hotel** is a superb 18th century
inn owned and personally run by the
Brayshaw family. Standing on the B5285 a
mile from the Hawkshead Ferry, the hotel has
two fully licensed bars and 18 en suite guest
bedrooms. An extensive selection of food, all
freshly
prepared
and
cooked on
the
premises,
runs from
lunchtime
bar snacks
to a five-
course dinner served from 7 to 8.45 (open to
non-residents). The hotel is an ideal place for
touring and making the most of the vast
range of activities for which the Lake District
is renowned.

95 BRANTWOOD 🏛

Coniston, Cumbria LA21 8AD
☎ 015394 41396 Fax: 015394 41263
🌐 www.brantwood.org.uk

Brantwood is the most beautifully situated house in the Lake District and enjoys the finest lake and mountain views in England. The home of John Ruskin from 1872 until his death in 1900, Brantwood became one of the greatest literary and artistic centres in Europe. Tolstoy, Mahatma Gandhi, Marcel Proust and Frank Lloyd Wright can all be numbered

amongst Ruskin's disciples. The house is filled with Ruskin's drawings and watercolours, together with much of his original furniture, books and personal items. There is also an extensive programme of events at Brantwood, including concerts and exhibitions.

97 THE QUEENS HOTEL 🍴

Main Street, Keswick, Cumbria CA12 5JF
☎ 017687 73333 Fax: 017687 71144
e-mail: info@thequeenshotel.co.uk
🌐 www.thequeenshotel.co.uk

The **Queens Hotel** offers all the expected comfort and amenities of a pub and hotel, with the bonus of a central location in the marvellous town of Keswick. Visit the website for further details.

Explore Britain and Ireland with *Hidden Places* guides - a fascinating series of national and local travel guides.

www.travelpublishing.co.uk

0118-981-7777

info@travelpublishing.co.uk

98 THE FOUR IN HAND 🍴

Lake Road, Keswick, Cumbria CA12 5HZ
☎ 01768 772404

A central location in the undisputed capital of the Lake District is just one of the attractions of the **Four in Hand**. Tenants Debbie and Craig have a friendly welcome for all their customers at this popular, traditional hostelry, and the five real ales and the excellent food choice ensure that the smiles stay throughout a visit. Local specialities that often appear on the menu include Cumberland sausage, Derwent game pie and Borrowdale trout.

99 THE DERWENTWATER HOTEL 🛏

Portinscale, nr Keswick,
Cumbria CA12 5RE
☎ 017687 72538 Fax: 017687 71002
e-mail: info@derwentwater-hotel.co.uk
🌐 www.derwentwater-hotel.co.uk

The **Derwentwater Hotel** enjoys a marvellous setting in gardens and grounds that run stretch along the shore of the lake to the banks of the River Derwent. The original building has been much extended and modernised down the years and now offers 48 superbly appointed en suite rooms.

The Deer's Leap Restaurant serves a fine variety of dishes, and the conservatory Garden Room is a perfect spot for quiet contemplation or enjoying a snack and a drink. In the grounds stands Derwent Manor, a spacious country house converted to provide 19 luxurious self-catering apartments.

96   THE GRASMERE HOTEL

Broadgate, Grasmere, Cumbria LA22 9TY
☎ 015394 35277
e-mail: enquiries@grasmerehotel.co.uk
🌐 www.grasmerehotel.co.uk

The **Grasmere Hotel** is a delightful country house hotel and restaurant on the edge of Grasmere village in the heart of the Lake District. Built as a private residence in 1871, it first became a hotel

(The Ravenswood) in the 1930s, changing its name to The Grasmere in 1984. An acre of informal gardens and grounds, with the River Rothay running through, provides a lovely quiet setting that is complemented by the warm, friendly atmosphere within – a quality that brings guests back year after year to the hotel and the village that Thomas Gray described as "a little unsuspected paradise" and Wordsworth called "the loveliest spot that man hath ever found".

The bedrooms combine period charm and character with all the expected modern standards of comfort and amenity. Each is named after one of the writers and poets who

drew inspiration from this glorious part of the world; like each of these writers, each of the bedrooms is individual, with its own style, size, décor and furnishings. All have en suite facilities, individually controlled central heating, direct-dial telephone, tea/coffee tray, magazines and a selection of toiletries. Two rooms located on the ground floor are ideal if stairs are a problem. In the lovely bar, kept snug by a roaring fire in the cooler months, guests and non-residents can enjoy a fine variety of beers, wines, single malts and liqueurs, and there's a good supply of cards, games, puzzles and magazines in the residents' drawing room.

Owners Jan and Stuart Cardwell are perfectionists and the cooking at The Grasmere, which has earned them an AA Red Rosette for Culinary Excellence, is of the same high standard as the accommodation. A daily changing four-course menu is served each evening in the elegant restaurant, which features a fabulous chandelier suspended from its vaulted ceiling. The cooking is skilled and the food plentiful, and a 50-strong wine list from the Old and New Worlds provides a perfect match for any dish. Typical choices include cheese soufflé and smoked salmon mousseline among the starters, and main courses such as roast Cumbrian ham, Barbary duck with a honey, orange and Cointreau sauce, and pork fillet wrapped in bacon, served with an apple, cider and thyme pan gravy.

100 THE SALUTATION INN

Threlkeld, nr Keswick, Cumbria CA12 4SQ
☎ 017687 79614

Standing in the shadow of Blencathra on the old main road two miles east of Keswick, the **Salutation Inn** lives up to its name by offering the warmest of greetings to all its visitors. Dating from 1679, the inn has a genuine period charm that's assisted by low beams, wall sates in three areas divided by upright timbers, open fires, horse brasses and some interesting items of local provenance.

Jennings and Theakstons ales are on tap to quench thirsts, and heart home cooked food runs the gamut from sandwiches and light snacks to hearty main courses served lunchtime and evening. Apart from the main bar and dining areas, the pub has a games room with darts, pool and TV, a children's room and an outside seating

area. Centrally heated en suite bedrooms provide a very comfortable and civilised

base for discovering the delights of Threlkeld, for enjoying the great views, for getting rid of urban cobwebs on mountain walks (Blencathra is an excellent start!) and for venturing further afield to explore the Lake District and the Solway Coast.

101 THE HORSE & FARRIER INN

Threlkeld, nr Keswick, Cumbria CA12 4SQ
☎ 01768 779688 Fax: 01768 79823
e-mail: info@horseandfarrier.com
🌐 www.horseandfarrier.com

In the delightful Cumbrian village of Threlkeld, off the A66 east of Keswick, the Horse & Farrier is a very friendly inn with a history going back to the 17th century. Proprietor Ian Court prides himself on serving some of the best real ales in the region, and his kitchen provides a good choice that runs from lunchtime sandwiches and

snacks to hearty dishes that will satisfy the hungriest outdoor appetite. The inn's nine well-appointed guest bedrooms all have en suite facilities, TV, hairdryer and beverage tray.

102 THE KINGS ARMS

41 Main Street, Egremont,
Cumbria CA22 2AD
☎ 01946 822977
e-mail: oldear@hotmail.com

The **Kings Arms** is a fine old pub with a delightful atmosphere and an interesting variety of home-cooked food. The resident ghosts never disturb overnight guests, for whom the pub has four comfortable bedrooms.

Looking for:
• *Places to Visit?*
• *Places to Stay?*
• *Places to Eat & Drink?*
• *Places to Shop?*

www.travelpublishing.co.uk

383

103 THE WESTLANDS HOTEL

Branthwaite Road, Workington,
Cumbria CA14 4TD
☎ 01900 604544 Fax: 01900 68830
e-mail: davidwestlands@hotmail.co.uk
🌐 www.wsetlandshotel.com

Set in 6½ acres of grounds on the outskirts of Workington, the **Westlands Hotel** welcomes visitors from all over the world to the Lake District. This well-established hotel has been providing top-quality accommodation and function and business facilities for many years, developing a solid reputation for comfort, service and hospitality.

The hotel is personally owned and run by David and Iona Sale, who have been restoring the hotel to the glory days of the 1970s and 1980s, when visits from royalty, nobility and top politicians were almost an

everyday event. Open all year round, the hotel has 70 superbly appointed en

suite guest bedrooms, a number of which are on the ground floor. The hotel bar is open throughout the day and serves four resident real ales and guests, and a good selection of other beers and lagers, wines, spirits and soft drinks. Tasty traditional English meals are served lunchtime and evening, and booking is advised for the popular Sunday lunch. The adjacent Westlands Theatre stages a varied programme of entertainment.

104 THE SHEPHERD'S ARMS HOTEL

Ennerdale Bridge, Cumbria CA23 3AR
☎ 01946 861249
e-mail: shepherdsarms@btconnect.com
🌐 www.shepherdsarmshotel-
ennerdalebridge-lakedistrict.co.uk

In the centre of Ennerdale Bridge on Wainwright's famous Coast to Coast Walk, the **Shepherd's Arms** is an ideal base for touring this lovely part of the world. The hotel has eight guest bedrooms, six of them with en suite facilities, all with central heating, TV, radio alarm and hot drinks tray. Breakfast is served in the panelled Georgian dining room, where evening meals are also available. The pub also serves a good selection of bar meals and real ales.

107 THE SUN INN

Newton Reigny, nr Penrith,
Cumbria CA11 0AP
☎ 01768 867055
e-mail: dixond@tinyworld.co.uk

In a picture postcard village a few miles northwest of Penrith, the **Sun Inn** is a popular, traditional free house serving a fine selection of real ales and a good choice of appetising dishes. The Sun also has five quality en suite guest bedrooms.

Looking for:

- *Places to Visit?*
- *Places to Stay?*
- *Places to Eat & Drink?*
- *Places to Shop?*

www.travelpublishing.co.uk

105 WHINLATTER FOREST PARK

Braithwaite, Keswick, Cumbria CA12 5TW
☎ 017687 78469   Fax: 017687 78049

The only Mountain Forest in England, **Whinlatter Forest Park** is also one of the Forestry Commission's oldest woodlands, providing a whole range of outdoor activities. The best place to start is at the Visitor Centre which has a wealth of information about the work of the Lakes Forest District and staff who will be happy to help you plan your day in the forest. Visitors can also book a forest classroom or a forest discovery walk with the Rangers. There's a shop and tea room here, with a terrace overlooking the woodlands and valley, an adventure playground close by and the Centre is also the starting point for several trails suitable for the whole family. The trails are clearly waymarked to provide easily followed routes taking in some spectacular views across the fells and forests of North Lakeland. Cyclists will find many miles of forest roads with some routes offering off-road and technical sections for the enthusiastic mountain biker. And if you have never tried orienteering, Whinlatter's permanent orienteering course is the perfect place to start. For children, there are Rabbit Run and Fox Trot orienteering trails, both starting from the Visitor Centre, while for those who prefer easier terrain or are less mobile, Europe's first permanent trail orienteering course combines the navigational skills of traditional orienteering with an easy-going route along forest roads and paths.

106 THE BEEHIVE INN

Eamont Bridge, nr Penrith,
Cumbria CA10 2BX
☎ 01768 862081

On the south side of Penrith, just off the A6 and a mile-and-a-half from J40 of the M6, the **Beehive Inn** is at the buzzy heart of the small community of Eamont Bridge. Local residents, the occasional tourist and regulars down from Penrith get together to enjoy a chat, a drink and perhaps something to eat.

The pub is little changed externally from its origins as a coaching stop in the 1760s, and the bars and dining area are also delightfully traditional, with a friendly, inviting ambience created by long-standing landlord Stephen Porter and his equally affable staff. Stephen is justly proud of the food served here, which caters for light

appetites with snacks and quick bites, and for hungrier souls with hearty home-made pies and meat

dishes served with plenty of vegetables. The Beehive, which is open lunchtime and evening and all day Saturday and Sunday, has a good-sized car park and outside seating at the front, with a little area where children can run around.

385

108 THE KINGS ARMS HOTEL

Temple Sowerby, nr Penrith,
Cumbria CA10 1SB
☎ 01768 361211

Visitors exploring the delights of the lovely Eden Valley will find a friendly, civilised base at the **Kings Arms Hotel** in Temple Sowerby. Owner Ann Evans has a warm welcome for all her guests, providing a really inviting, relaxing ambience for both the local and the tourist clientele. The 300-year-old former coaching inn has ten letting rooms, seven with

en suite facilities, and in the old-world bar there's a regularly changing selection of real ales. Bar meals are served at lunchtime, and on Thursday to Monday evenings diners can choose from a wide-ranging menu in the restaurant.

109 THE LEMON GROVE

5 Bridge Street, Appleby-in-Westmorland,
Cumbria CA16 6QH
☎ 01768 354119

Lindsey Dixon has a personal welcome for all her customers at the **Lemon Grove**, a lovely little café and sandwich bar situated near the market square in Appleby-in-Westmorland. The menu includes a daily-changing soup and quiche, generously filled hot and cold baguettes and homemade meat pies, cakes and pastries. The Lemon Grove is

open from 9.30 to 4.30 Monday to Saturday, providing excellent snacking for workers, shoppers and visitors to this delightful town.

111 THE NEW INN

Hoff, nr Appleby, Cumbria CA16 6TA
☎ 01768 351317

Real ale expert Derek and talented cook Sue make a fine team at the 17th century **New Inn**, which stands neat the village of Hoff on the B6260 Tebay road south from Appleby. Four real ales in summer and two in winter are available in the bar, where the centrepiece is a huge feature fireplace.

Sue has built up a fine reputation for her honest, unpretentious cooking, and the large blackboard lists heart dishes like seafood crumble , 'fairly local' Cumberland sausage, 'very local' Westmorland sausage, chicken or vegetable kiev, steaks and the very popular lamb Henry with a minty, winy sauce. The pub is open from noon Tuesday to Sunday and

from 6 o'clock on Monday. The inn has fully earned its popularity, and Derek plans to add another string to its bow by building an extension with rooms for Bed & Breakfast guests.

110 THE TUFTON ARMS HOTEL

Market Square, Appleby-in-Westmorland,
Cumbria CA16 6XA
☎ 017683 51593 Fax: 017683 52761
e-mail: info@tuftonarmshotel.co.uk
🌐 www.tuftonarmshotel.co.uk

On the main square of the busy market town of Appleby, the **Tufton Arms Hotel** started life in the 17th century as a coaching inn. Owned and run for many years by the Milsom family, it provides a charming, relaxing destination for an enjoyable break in the heart of the beautiful Eden Valley. Guests are welcomed with a smile at reception, which sets the tone for the whole stay. The staff have a genuine desire that their guests will have a stay that's

more than just pleasant, but a time to remember. It's quite likely that visitors will quickly meet one of the owners, who speak not of guests but of 'friends who come to stay'.

Good food is a byword here, and the award-winning team of chefs seek out the best and freshest local produce, which they prepare with skill and flair to create delicious dishes with a modern twist. Dinner is served in the elegant Conservatory Restaurant overlooking the cobbled mews courtyard, and diners should allow time to peruse menus that are filled with good things. Fine food deserves fine wine, and at the Tufton Arms an expertly chosen list that runs to 200 wines provides the perfect marriage for any dish. The standards of the hospitality and the cuisine are matched by the accommodation, which caters admirably for a wide cross-section of guests, from holidaymakers and shooting/fishing parties to business and corporate individuals and groups.

Each of the 22 bedrooms has its own charm and character, and the furnishings include the occasional antique piece that belonged to the Milsom farmhouse. All the rooms have en suite facilities and all the amenities expected by today's guests; the hotel is also totally geared up to banquets and conferences, and the three purpose-designed suites combine the period elegance of the rest

of the hotel with up-to-date business requirements. Fly fishing and shooting can be arranged by the hotel, which has access to some of the best stretches of the River Eden and has its own driven and rough pheasant shoot.

Appleby, the old county town of Westmorland, is a delightful place that's well worth taking time to explore. The surrounding area, too, is rich in historic and scenic glory, with a number of important country houses and castles, and the beauty of the tranquil Eden Valley.

112 THE BUTCHERS ARMS

Crosby Ravensworth, nr Penrith,
Cumbria CA10 3JP
☎ 01931 715202
e-mail: swilson@cybermoor.org.uk

Colin and Sue Wilson are the owners of the
Butchers Arms. With Sue as chef, in the
short time
they have
been here
they have
built up a
loyal
clientele.
Well
worth
seeking
out in a
secluded
village east of Shap and a mile off the A6,
the pub has a tempting blackboard menu, that
along with a choice of Real Ales, gives the
locals exactly what they want – unpretentious,
home-cooked dishes. A childrens menu is
also available. At the back of the pub is a
very spacious beer garden. Major credit/debit
cards are accepted.

113 ASHLEY BANK

Newbiggin-on-Lune, nr Kirkby Stephen,
Cumbria CA17 4LZ
☎ 015396 23214 Fax: 015396 23214
e-mail: mail@ashley-bank.co.uk
🌐 www.ashley-bank.co.uk

Peacefully situated near the head of the
Ravenstonedale Valley, **Ashley Bank** stands
in wooded grounds that command lovely
views of the Howgill Fells. Ashley Cottage
and Beech tree sleep up to 16 in six delightful
bedrooms, and owners Iain and Nazig
Hickman
ensure that
guests have
everything
needed for
an
enjoyable
self-
catering
holiday. It's
ideal for
families or groups of friends, and the huge
garden is a great spot for a barbecues and
picnics, with plenty of romping space for
children.

115 LAKELAND BIRD OF PREY CENTRE

Lowther, Nr Penrith, Cumbria CA10 2HH
☎ 01931 712746

The centre is a sanctuary for birds of prey,
set in the walled garden and parkland of
Lowther Castle. Visitors can see over 100
eagles, hawks, falcons and owls from around
the world. The aim of the centre is to
conserve birds of prey through education,
breeding and caring for injured and orphaned
birds before releasing them back to the wild.
There is also a tearoom as well as regular
courses and lectures.

HIDDEN PLACES GUIDES

Explore Britain and Ireland with
Hidden Places guides - a fascinating
series of national and local travel
guides.

Packed with easy to read information
on hundreds of places of interest as
well as places to stay, eat and drink.

Available from both high street and
internet booksellers

For more information on the full range
of *Hidden Places* guides and other
titles published by Travel Publishing
visit our website on

www.travelpublishing.co.uk
or ask for our leaflet by phoning
0118-981-7777 or emailing
info@travelpublishing.co.uk

Ravenstonedale, nr Kirkby Stephen,
Cumbria CA17 4NH
☎ 015396 23284
e-mail: enquiries@kings-head.net
🌐 www.kings-head.net

With a history that can be traced back to the 17th century, the **Kings Head Hotel** is one of the oldest and most distinguished buildings in the quiet, unspoilt village of Ravenstonedale. Situated in the heart of the village in the foothills of the Howgill Fells in the Western Yorkshire Dales, the whitewashed premises were originally a group of three cottages; it had become a licensed public house by the end of the 17th century, and was also put to use as the local courthouse.

Behind the picture postcard exterior lies a particularly cosy interior providing customers with a warm and inviting ambience. Two open stone fireplaces set the scene, and there are wooden furnishings and rich colours throughout, as well as a collection of over 450 jugs hanging on display from the low oak beams. A major refurbishment programme in 2005 has put the pub in apple pie order, a happy mix of period and more contemporary features. Outside, the attractive beer garden stretches alongside Scandal Beck. Full of character, this charming country inn is equally popular with locals and visitors from outside the area.

Gary and Susan Kirby are friendly, outgoing hosts, assisted by equally affable staff, not forgetting Spot the dog and three amiable

resident ghosts. At the heart of the local community, the Kings Head also acts as the clubhouse for the golf, football, cricket, yacht and various other clubs. The Kirbys are also actively involved in Red Alert North West, a community-based conservation project with the aim of ensuring the long-term survival of the native red squirrel in the North West of England. The hotel has established quite a reputation for its food, and the menus range from open and close sandwiches and bar snacks to traditional English favourites and dishes with a European or more exotic inspiration. Food is served every lunchtime and evening, and booking is advisable from Friday to Sunday to be sure of a table in the candle-lit restaurant.

The Kings Head has been awarded the Cask Marque for its beers, which are headed by Black Sheep and supported by rotating guest ales. With three spacious en suite guest bedrooms, the inn is a great base for exploring the Eden Valley, starting with Ravenstonedale itself with its Georgian parish church and the remains of a 13th century abbey. Nearby Pendragon Castle claims to be the fortress of Uther Pendragon, father of King Arthur.

116 THE FOX & PHEASANT INN

Armathwaite, Cumbria CA4 9PY
☎ 01697 472400

Described by host Steven Thorpe as the 'Eden Valley's Hidden Gem', the **Fox & Pheasant** stands close to the River Eden just ten minutes from the M6 (J41 or 42) and halfway between Penrith and Carlisle. It started life in the 16th century as a coaching inn and was later extended with the addition of a former shooting and fishing lodge. In converted stables, the Stable Bar, with exposed stone, wooden beams, sandstone floors and log fires, is a great place to sample Steven's selection of between four and six real ales.

The main bar is a popular local meeting place, and in the Victorian Restaurant and Eden Lounge residents and visitors can relax and enjoy a superb meal based as far as possible on local produce. Guest accommodation is available in individually furnished bedrooms, combining period features and up-to-date amenities; they include a quaint attic room overlooking the river. Fishing can be arranged for residents, and the pub is also conveniently placed for shooting parties.

117 THE GLASS HOUSE

Wheatsheaf Square, Wigton, Cumbria CA7 8DY
☎ 01697 344458

Set back from the centre of the pleasant market town of Wigton, the **Glass House** is a friendly local meeting place for daytime coffees, teas and light meals, all made on the premises. Bistro-style evening meals are also served – bookings preferred.

118 THE ROSE & CROWN

52 Market Street, Draycott, Derbyshire DE72 3NB
☎ 01332 872531
⊕ www.roseandcrowndraycott.com

Open 4-12 Mon - Fri and all day at weekends. This is a convivial family-run pub. Freshly prepared food is cooked and served until 10pm. Carvery on Sunday 1 - 4pm. Entertainment 1st Saturday each month.

119 PICKFORD'S HOUSE MUSEUM

41 Friargate, Derby DE1 1DA
☎ 01332 255363

Pickford's House Museum is a Grade I listed building of 1770 built by Joseph Pickford, an important Midlands architect, as his home and workplace. Pickford worked on a number of architectural products throughout the Midlands including a prestigious factory and hall at Etruria for the potter Josiah Wedgwood.

Visitors today can see the comfort of the family rooms contrasting with the living and working conditions of the servants. The house is reconstructed as it might have looked when members of the Pickford family lived here.

Displays include a dining room, drawing room and servants' bedroom of about 1800, and a morning room, laundry and kitchen of about 1825.

The museum also houses a fine collection of historic costume and textiles and displays part of the nationally-important Frank Bradley collection of toy theatres. There is a lively programme of temporary exhibitions and events throughout the year.

121 THE STEAM PACKET

Derby Road, Swanwick, nr Alfreton, Derbyshire DE55 1AB
☎ 01773 602172

Leaseholder Steve Marshall has built up a strong and loyal clientele since taking over the **Steam Packet** in Millennium year. On a corner site in the former mining village of Swanwick, on the B6179 between Alfreton and Ripley, this popular pub is open all day seven days a week for drinks, and with six real ales always on tap, it's a real magnet for beer-drinkers. Regular ales are Young's, Adnams, Black Sheep and Everard's Tiger, and there are also two real ciders – Old Rosie and Addlestones.

The pub serves a frequently changing menu of traditional pub favourites between 12 and 2 Thursday to Sunday, and the choice always includes daily roasts. All are welcome to try their luck at the Tuesday and Thursday evening quizzes, and the pub hosts occasional live entertainment sessions on a Saturday and beer festivals every April and October. The Steam Packet has plenty of off-road parking.

Hardwick Park, Chesterfield,
Derbyshire S44 5QJ
☎ 01246 850245   Fax: 01246 856365
e-mail: batty@hardwickinn.co.uk
🌐 www.hardwickinn.co.uk

The **Hardwick Inn** lies on the edge of the Hardwick Hall Estate, a short drive from Junction 29 of the M1 and midway between Chesterfield and Mansfield. At the end of the 16th century, the manor house was home to Elizabeth, Countess of Shrewsbury, known throughout the land as Bess of Hardwick, whose four marriages made her one of the wealthiest women in Britain. It is thought that Bess built the present inn for one of her faithful servants on the site of an older hostelry.

The mellow yellow-gold sandstone building retains to this day many original features, including the leaded windows and handsome gables. In 1959, Hardwick Hall, its surrounding park and woodland and the inn were transferred into the care of the National Trust, which continues to be responsible for the maintenance of the estate. Steeping across the threshold of this imposing inn is like taking a

journey back in time, and the cosy, old-fashioned public rooms provide a setting for enjoying a drink or meal that is at once atmospheric and very friendly and comfortable. There are two bar areas, three separate family rooms, meeting rooms and pleasant gardens at the front and back.

The Hardwick Inn owes its success to the efforts of the Batty family, who have run the inn since 1928. The present third-generations licensees, Peter and Pauline Batty, have been here since 1982. They pride themselves on providing affable, conscientious service to all their customers, and their dedication can be seen in the large numbers of visitors who become regulars, returning time after time to this outstanding inn. The range of drinks includes plenty of real ales, together with other draught and bottled beers,

stout, lagers, ciders, spirits (more than 200 malts!) and non-alcoholic beverages. The bar menu proposes classics such as lasagne, fish pie and the renowned steak & kidney pie, as well as daily specials and afternoon teas. In the carvery restaurant (not open on Mondays) the choice includes prime roasts and grills, an excellent selection of salads and daily specials such as braised guinea fowl, sole with crab and prawns and always a choice for vegetarians.

122 THE HOLLYBUSH INN

**Hollybush Lane, Makeney,
Derbyshire DE56 0RX
☎ 01332 841729**

The **Hollybush Inn** stands next to the
church in the centre of the village of
Makeney, just off the A6 north of Derby.
The inn has a splendidly old-world look and
feel, with tiled and flagged floors, real fires
(one in a fine old range), beams, panelling and
period pictures and photographs. Six real ales,
and
another
served
straight
from the
jug, make
this a beer-
drinker's
paradise,
and
excellent

home-cooked food based as far as possible
on locally sourced ingredients brings an
appreciative crowd every lunchtime. The inn
holds an annual beer festival.

124 THE HORSE & JOCKEY

**68 Cromford Road, Ripley,
Derbyshire DE5 3FP
☎ 01773 742310**

On the outskirts of Ripley, the **Horse &
Jockey** is a cheerful family-run pub dispensing
genuine hospitality, real ales and good food.
Five brews – Greene King IPA, Abbot Ale
and Marston's Pedigree are the regulars –
provide plenty of choice for real ale
connoisseurs, and a good selection of home-
cooked dishes is served from noon to 6
o'clock every day of the week. There's never a
dull moment here: bingo on Tuesday, live
bands on Friday, karaoke on Saturday, vocalists
on Sunday, good conversation every day!

123 MOSS COTTAGE

**Nottingham Road, Ripley,
Derbyshire DE5 3JT
☎ 01773 742555 Fax: 01773 741063
e-mail: mosshotel@aol.com
🌐 www.mosscottage.net**

Located on the A610 on the edge of Ripley town
centre, **Moss Cottage** is a popular, friendly and
successful hotel, bar and restaurant. Experienced
manager Promoz Revill, Rachel and all the staff
extend a warm, genuine welcome to all their
customers, whether they've come for a drink, a
meal or an overnight or longer stay. The hotel has 14
guest bedrooms, all with en suite facilities, six of them on
the ground floor. The tariff is room only, but breakfast –
full English or Continental – can be ordered at reception.
The comfortable bar and stylish lounge, open
lunchtime and evening and all day on Sunday, provide a

very pleasant
spot to relax
with a drink:
the local Old
Trip is a
popular real
ale, and Old Rosie cider is another favourite. A variety
of different menus is available in the restaurant,
including steak nights, curry nights on Tuesday, a
carvery on Thursday evening, a long-hours Sunday
lunch and a senior citizens lunch Wednesday to Friday,
all in addition to the wide-ranging standard lunchtime
and evening menus.

125 THE THORN TREE INN

161 Church Street, Waingroves, nr Ripley,
Derbyshire DE5 9TE
☎ 01773 742014
e-mail: Michael.crookes@virgin.net

The **Thorn Tree Inn** lies in the hamlet of Waingroves, just off the A610 Ripley-Nottingham road, and only a mile from Ripley town centre. Tenants Mick and Jill Crookes have made many new friends since taking over, and they recently extended the appeal of the inn still further by creating an intimate restaurant at the end of 2005.

The inn is a great favourite with local customers and is also a popular choice for motorists to take a break and for visitors to relax over a meal. The Thorn Tree is open Monday to Friday evenings and all day Saturday and Sunday. Marstons Pedigree is the resident

real ale, accompanied by two or three rotating guests, and Mick's menu (not available on Tuesday) presents a good choice of home-cooked dishes to please all tastes and appetites. Wednesday is quiz night at this very pleasant, sociable village pub.

126 THE COCK INN

Clifton, nr Ashbourne, Derbyshire DE6 2GJ
☎ 01335 342654

Behind an attractive white exterior in the friendly village of Clifton, the **Cock Inn** is a delightful old-world country pub. With brass-bedecked darkwood beams, walls hung with old prints and a cosy fire in a brick hearth, the bar is very much the social hub of the village, and both locals and visitors from outside the region enjoy the warm hospitality of hosts Lorraine and Andrew Garside, the well-kept ales and the freshly prepared food. Children are welcome, and the pub has plentiful off-road parking and a pleasant beer garden. Closed Monday lunchtime except Bank Holidays.

128 THE GREEN MAN ROYAL HOTEL

10 St Johns Street, Ashbourne,
Derbyshire DE6 1GH
☎ 01335 345783 Fax: 01335 346613
🌐 www.gmrh.com

An equally pleasant choice for a drink, a meal or an overnight stay, the **Green Man Royal Hotel** is a grand old coaching inn with a history going back to the 17th century. Three or four real ales head the list of drinks, and a wide-

ranging choice of excellent food is served lunchtime and evening and throughout the day in the holiday season. The Green Man has 18 guest bedrooms, all en suite, providing an ideal base for exploring this lovely part of the world.

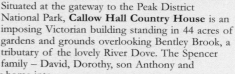

127 CALLOW HALL COUNTRY HOUSE HOTEL & RESTAURANT

Mappleton Road, Ashbourne,
Derbyshire DE6 2AA
☎ 01335 300900 Fax: 01335 300512
e-mail: reservations@callowhall.co.uk
🌐 www.callowhall.co.uk

Situated at the gateway to the Peak District National Park, **Callow Hall Country House** is an imposing Victorian building standing in 44 acres of gardens and grounds overlooking Bentley Brook, a tributary of the lovely River Dove. The Spencer family – David, Dorothy, son Anthony and daughter Emma – have transformed their family home into a hotel of great charm and character, and they and their staff provide attentive, unobtrusive service in the most gracious and comfortable surroundings.

The hotel's 16 en suite double bedrooms, some of which enjoy fine views of the beautiful countryside, are individually designed, and furnished and appointed to the highest standards. One room is a ground-floor master

suite, while another on the ground floor is equipped for disabled guests. The drawing room, with its high, ornate plastered ceiling, has a timeless traditional charm, and the elegant dining room is a perfect setting for enjoying top-class modern English cuisine complemented by an expertly compiled wine list.

129 TASTES RESTAURANT

Middle Cale, St Johns Street, Ashbourne,
Derbyshire DE6 1GP
☎ 01335 300305
🌐 www.tastesrestaurant.co.uk

The atmospheric cellars of an old grocery shop make a stylish, romantic setting for **Tastes Restaurant**. In the capable hands of Steve and Jo Rhodes, the restaurant is open Wednesday to Saturday lunchtimes and Tuesday to Saturday evenings. Steve's menus are full of temptations, and typical main courses on

the fixed-price evening menu include herb-stuffed baked sea bass, roast lamb with a redcurrant sauce and sirloin steak pizzaiola. One difficult decision that doesn't have to be taken is choosing a starter – the whole selection is put in the centre of the table for diners to choose whatever they want.

130 THE ROSE & CROWN

Main Road, Braisford, nr Ashbourne,
Derbyshire DE6 3DA
☎ 01335 360242

Standing alongside the A52 between Ashbourne and Derby, the **Rose & Crown** appeals to locals and visitors alike with its well-kept ales and traditional pub food (the Sunday roasts are particularly popular). The pub has a super beer garden and a large off-road car park.

Explore Britain and Ireland with *Hidden Places* guides - a fascinating series of national and local travel guides.

www.travelpublishing.co.uk

0118-981-7777

info@travelpublishing.co.uk

131 THE RED LION INN

Hollington, nr Ashbourne,
Derbyshire DE6 3AG
☎ 01335 360241 Fax: 01335 361209
e-mail: redlionholl@aol.com
🌐 www.redlionhollington.co.uk

A string of local and national awards testifies to the quality of the cooking at the **Red Lion Inn**, which attracts food-lovers from near and far to the village of Hollington. Reached off the A52 Ashbourne-Derby road, the inn is also top of the tree for hospitality, and leaseholder Robin Hunter and his staff make any visitor passing through the door feel like an old friend. The inn is open every lunchtime and evening and all day on Sunday for drinks, which include Marston's Pedigree and a regularly changing guest real ale. The bar is a very pleasant, civilised spot to relax and unwind, and when the sun shines the lawned area at the front comes into its own.

Robin, a talented chef with 20 years' experience, heads a kitchen team that uses the very best seasonal local produce in a succession of truly outstanding dishes, served every session except Monday lunchtime (but then, too, if it's a Bank Holiday). The ever-changing blackboard menu makes mouthwatering reading, and results on the plate never disappoint. Choices might include creamy garlic mushrooms, asparagus & parmesan salad,

crispy-roast duckling, rack of lamb, sea bass fillet on a vegetable nage with a butter sauce, and superb steaks – fillet with a three-peppercorn cream sauce, sirloin with a port and stilton sauce. Wild mushroom & goat's cheese puff pastry is a typical vegetarian option. The dishes listed on the board are flanked by a well-chosen wine selection that includes four champagnes. Bar meals provide lighter or quicker alternatives to the main menu.

The Red Lion is also a much-loved village local, and for motorists travelling along the A52, the short diversion is well worth while for a pleasant break on a journey. But first and foremost this is a destination food pub, and such is its reputation that booking is recommended for all meals, and essential at the weekend. And for motorists who drop in just for a drink, one look at the blackboard should convince them either to change their plans if it's mealtime or to make a date for a quick return visit. The last Thursday of each month brings live music from 9 in the evening.

132 THE PEVERIL OF THE PEAK HOTEL

Thorpe, Dovedale, nr Ashbourne,
Derbyshire DE6 2AW
☎ 01335 350396 Fax: 01335 350507
e-mail: frontdesk@peverilofthepeak.co.uk
🌐 www.peverilofthepeak.com

Ideally located in the heart of beautiful Dovedale, the **Peveril of the Peak** is a superlative hotel offering guests the highest standards of hospitality, service, comfort and cuisine. Set in 11 acres of gardens and grounds, it lies 3 miles from Ashbourne close to many popular sights and

attractions, including Alton Towers, Matlock Bath, Chatsworth House and Carsington Water. The hotel, which takes its name from a historical novel by Sir Walter Scott, has 45 beautifully appointed en suite bedrooms, all equipped with multi-channel television, trouser press, hairdryer and tea/coffee-making facilities. Many have private patios with chairs and a table, and room service is available at the end of the telephone.

Originally the local vicarage, the hotel is a wonderful retreat, perfect for a break amid the spectacular scenery of the Peak District National Park, or as a venue for family celebrations or any special

occasion. Families are welcome, and guests can stay on a room only, Bed & Breakfast or full board basis. In the grounds are mature, tranquil gardens and tennis courts. Peveril of the Peak is open to residents and non-residents for both food and drink. The lounge bar is stocked with real ales and a full range of other drinks, and bar snacks are served at lunchtime. In the elegant restaurant, a team of first-class chefs prepare a fine selection of dishes using the best seasonal produce in a choice of meat, fish and vegetarian dishes. The Sunday roasts are

always very popular, but booking is recommended for all meals.

Looming in the background at the hotel is the conical shape of Thorpe Cloud, which guards the entrance to Dovedale. The climb to the top is rewarded with wonderful views, but for more gentle exercise the River Dove is definitely a 'walker's river' par excellence. One of the many points of interest is the famous Stepping Stones, and this stretch of the river was famously chronicled by Sir Izaak Walton in *The Compleat Angler*.

133 THE ROYAL OAK HOTEL

Hanging Bridge, Mayfield, nr Ashbourne,
Derbyshire DE6 2BN
☎ 01335 300090
e-mail: info@royaloakhotelmayfield.co.uk
🌐 www.royaloakhotelmayfield.co.uk

Situated on the A52 a mile west of Ashbourne, the **Royal Oak Hotel** is thriving in the care of the Etheridge family, who took over the lease in April 2005. Gordon, Joan, David, Susanna and their staff have a genuinely friendly greeting for all the visitors to this versatile establishment, which combines the best features of a free house, a fine restaurant and a comfortable, well-run hotel.

Three or four real ales – Marston's Pedigree is the regular – head the list of drinks served in the bar, and a well-chosen wine list complements the freshly prepared food served lunchtime and evening, all day Saturday and

Sunday, and all day every day in the summer. The four guest bedrooms are all en suite, with televisions

and tea/coffee-making facilities. The Coach House can cater for meetings, functions and parties for up to 150 guests. Children are welcome, and the Royal Oak hosts a regular programme of theme nights, quiz nights and live music.

135 THE LITTLE JOHN INN

Station Road, Hathersage, Hope Valley,
Derbyshire S32 1DD
☎ 01433 650225 Fax: 01433 659831

Owner Stephanie Bushell has created a hostelry of great charm and character that's equally popular with locals and visitors from outside the area. The **Little John Inn** is a handsome 19th century stone building with many period features in the smartly refurbished bar, lounge and restaurant. A pleasant spot for a drink, the inn stocks a selection of real ales, plus draught bitters, stouts, lagers, ciders, wines, spirits and non-alcoholic drinks. Towards the end of the week and at weekends there are up to five rotating guest ales from micro-breweries.

It's also a perfect place to enjoy a meal, perhaps after a bracing walk on the moors, and head chef Richard Mosley creates a fine variety of dishes on a long and interesting

menu. Sandwiches, ploughman's lunches and burgers provide lighter snacks or quick

meals, while main dishes run from pub classics such as scampi or steak & kidney pie to swordfish in a Thai green sauce, ratatouille pasta bake and a mighty mixed grill to satisfy the largest fresh-air appetite. Hathersage and the surrounding area have plenty to interest the visitor, and for guests staying awhile the Little John offers a choice of five en suite rooms for B&B and two charming self-catering cottages.

134 THE PLOUGH INN

Leadmill Bridge, Hathersage,
Derbyshire S32 1BA
☎ 01433 650319 Fax: 01433 651049
🌐 www.theploughinn-hathersage.co.uk

Bob and Cynthia Emery, their son Elliott and
their staff extend a warm and friendly
welcome to customers at the **Plough Inn**,
which stands in nine acres of grounds on the
banks of the River Derwent. In summer the
garden has a wealth of flowering beds and
baskets, while in the cooler months roaring
log fires keep things cosy in the bar. The pub
serves a good choice of real ales (Theakston's
Bitter is the resident brew) and a mix of
traditional and modern European dishes
prepared from fresh local produce by the
head chef and his enthusiastic team. Three
comfortable, tastefully appointed guest rooms
are in the main building and two newly
converted
luxurious
rooms in
September
Cottage
across the
courtyard.

137 THE OLD SMITHY

Chapel Hill, Beeley, Derbyshire DE4 2NR
☎ 01629 734666

The **Old Smithy** is a delightful shop and
licensed café in the lovely unspoilt village of
Beeley, on the Chatsworth Estate. Opened by
Helen Grosvenor in May 2004, the shop
specialises in local produce with an emphasis
on 'deli' foods, as well as stocking basic
supplies. The Café provides good wholesome
country food and deli-style dishes and is
licensed to serve beer and wine with or
without a meal. The Sunday lunch is
particularly popular. The Shop and Café are
both open throughout the day, seven days a
week.

136 HADDON HALL

nr. Bakewell, Derbyshire DE45 1LA
☎ 01629 812855 Fax: 01629 814379
e-mail: info@haddonhall.co.uk
🌐 www.haddonhall.co.uk

Only a mile to the south of Bakewell down the
Matlock Road, on a bluff overlooking the Wye, the
romantic **Haddon Hall** stands hidden from the
road by a beech hedge. The Hall is thought by
many to have been the first fortified house in the
country, although the turrets and battlements were actually put on purely for show. The home of
the Dukes of Rutland for over 800 years, the Hall has enjoyed a fairly peaceful existence, in part no
doubt because it stood empty and neglected for nearly 300 years after 1640, when the family chose
Belvoir Castle in Leicestershire as their main home. Examples of work from every century from
the 12th to the 17th are here in this treasure trove.

Little construction work has been carried out on the Hall since the days of Henry VIII and it
remains one of the best examples of a medieval
and Tudor manor house. The 16th century
terraced gardens are one of the chief delights of
the Hall and are thought by many to be the most
romantic in England. The Hall's splendour and
charm have led it to be used as a backdrop to
television and film productions including *Jane
Eyre*, *Moll Flanders* and *The Prince and the Pauper*.

The Hall's chapel is adorned with medieval
wall paintings. The kitchens are the oldest extant
part of the house, and feature time-worn oak
tables and dole cupboards. The oak-panelled Long
Gallery features boars' heads (to represent
Vernon) and peacocks (Manners) in the panelling.

138 CHATSWORTH HOUSE

Bakewell, Derbyshire DE45 1PP
☎ 01246 565300 Fax: 01246 583536
e-mail: visit@chatsworth.org
🌐 www.chatsworth-house.co.uk

On the Outskirts of the village lies the home of the Dukes of Devonshire, **Chatsworth House**, known as the "Palace of the Peak", is without doubt one of the finest of the great houses in Britain. The origins of the House as a great showpiece must be attributable to the redoubtable Bess of Hardwick, whose marriage into the Cavendish family helped to secure the future of the palace.

Bess's husband, Sir William Cavendish, bought the estate for £600 in 1549. It was Bess who completed the new House after his death. Over the years, the Cavendish fortune continued to pour into Chatsworth, making it an almost unparalleled showcase for art treasures. Every aspect of the fine arts is here, ranging from old masterpieces, furniture, tapestries, porcelain and some magnificent alabaster carvings.

The gardens of this stately home also have some marvellous features, including the Emperor Fountain, which dominates the Canal Pond and is said to reach a height of 290 feet. There is a maze and a Laburnum Tunnel and, behind the house, the famous Cascades. The overall appearance of the park as it is seen today is chiefly due to the talents of "Capability" Brown, who was first consulted in 1761. However, the name perhaps most strongly associated with Chatsworth is Joseph Paxton. His experiments in glasshouse design led him eventually to his masterpiece, the Crystal Palace, built to house the Great Exhibition of 1851.

139 THE OLD SMITHY TEA ROOMS & RESTAURANT

Church Street, Monyash, nr Bakewell, Derbyshire DE45 1JH
☎ 01629 814510 Fax: 01629 810190
e-mail: smithy@monyash.com

Ed and Ruth Driscoll and their son David run the **Old Smithy Tea Rooms & Restaurant**, one of the most popular eating places in the Peak District and a great favourite with walkers and cyclists. The friendly, intimate atmosphere here, whether it's for a quiet drink (good choice of beers, wines and spirits), a snack or a full meal, is always a delight. The Tea Rooms are open all day every day, while the bistro-style restaurant is open on Saturday evenings. Popular dishes range from a hearty breakfast to Cornish pasty, omelettes and a blacksmith's lunch of cheese, pickle, salad and a bap.

140 THE FISHERMAN'S COTTAGE

Bickleigh, nr Tiverton, Devon EX16 8RW
☎ 01884 855237
e-mail: fishermanscot@ep-ltd.com
🌐 www.roomattheinn.info

A wide cross-section of locals and visitors come to enjoy the hospitality provided at the **Fisherman's Cottage**, a delightful thatched hostelry by the 14th century bridge over the River Exe. Some come for a drink, either in the bar or out in the garden overlooking the river, and to tuck into a daytime snack or a full meal. Others use the comfortable en suite accommodation as a base for exploring Devon. Suitably located between Exmoor and Dartmoor, there is plenty to see and do.

400

141 THE ROSE & CROWN

Calverleigh, nr Tiverton, Devon EX16 8BA
☎ 01884 256301 Fax: 01884 251837

For well over 200 years the picturesque **Rose & Crown** has offered its customers a warm welcome, and the tradition of hospitality is being carried on in fine style by Alec and Pam Roud and their son Nick. The wide range of real ales and freshly cooked food available would have been beyond belief to the inn's original farming customers, but the family still give a time-honoured welcome to their 'regulars' and to their many visitors from further afield. The reasonably priced menu, served every lunchtime and evening in the bar and non-smoking restaurant, runs to more then 60 choices, from light snacks to hearty, mouthwatering house specials, and head chef Mrs Roud sets great store by the finest and freshest local produce.

Among the specialities are Pork Valentine

with cream, farmhouse cider and apples, Mendip chicken casserole (promoted on TV's 'Countdown'!), traditional Sunday lunches and delicious vegetarian main courses such as hazelnut and mushroom pie.

The high standard of food has earned the Rose & Crown national recognition as runners-up in the British Food Pub of the Year competition. The inn lies two miles west of Tiverton on the 'old' Rackenford road.

142 DEER'S LEAP COTTAGES

Deer's Leap, West Ansty, Exmoor,
Devon EX36 3NZ
☎ 01398 341407
🌐 www.deersleap.com

'Paradise on the edge of Dartmoor' is a fine description of **Deer's Leap Cottages**, where guests can leave the urban bustle far behind in an idyllic setting. The five tastefully decorated cottages are fully equipped for a self-catering holiday, and apart from all the usual amenities residents Deer's Leap has a sauna, hot tub and small keep-fit facility.

Guests can wander round the garden and lake, enjoy the glorious views and watching the buzzards that have made their home here. For the more active there's a tennis court, table

tennis and a children's play area, and mountain bikes are available for hire – an ideal way to explore the quiet country lanes around the cottages. Deer's Leap is within easy reach of many attractions, including the ancient Tarr Steps, Anstey Common and Dunkerley Beacon. The Moor is home to a wealth of wildlife, including the famous ponies, red deer, foxes and badgers.

143 THE ROYAL GLEN HOTEL

Glen Road, Sidmouth, Devon EX10 8RW
☎ 01395 513221 Fax: 01395 514922
e-mail: info@royalglenhotel.co.uk
⊕ www.royalglenhotel.co.uk

The **Royal Glen Hotel** is a
distinguished Grade I listed
building with 32 bedrooms. All
vary in size, décor and
furnishings, and are well equipped and
comfortable. Bar snacks are served at lunchtime
and there's a table d'hote evening menu.

144 THE DEVORAN HOTEL

The Esplanade, Sidmouth, Devon
☎ 01395 513151
e-mail: enquiries@devoran.com
⊕ www.devoran.com

The **Devoran** is located right on
the Esplanade and its bedrooms
are warm and spacious. It has a
handsome Wedgwood dining
room and a sea-facing terrace.
The hotel is famous for its
wonderful floral displays.

146 THE OYSTER

Colebrooke, nr Crediton, Devon EX17 5JQ
☎ 01363 84576

The **Oyster** is a modern bungalow in the
scenic heart of mid-Devon. Resident owner
Pearl Hockridge has three centrally heated
rooms – two doubles and a twin – for Bed &
Breakfast guests, who also have the use of a
lounge and the spacious garden. Children and
pets are welcome at the Oyster, which is open
all year round and provides an ideal base for a
walking holiday or for discovering the many
delights of the region.

145 THE DONKEY SANCTUARY

Sidmouth, Devon EX10 0NU
☎ 01395 578222 Fax: 01395 579266
e-mail:
donkeyworld@thedonkeysanctuary.com
⊕ www.thedonkeysanctuary.org.uk

Set in unspoilt
farmland and
countryside just
outside Sidmouth,
the **Donkey
Sanctuary** is home

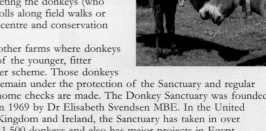

to over 400 donkeys. The majority are elderly and are kept on the
farm in order to be close to the veterinary hospital. Visitors are free
to spend as much time as they wish meeting the donkeys (who
adore the fuss and attention), taking strolls along field walks or
down to the sea, pausing at the Nature centre and conservation
area on the way.

The Donkey Sanctuary owns nine other farms where donkeys
are cared for by dedicated staff. Some of the younger, fitter
donkeys are re-homed through the foster scheme. Those donkeys

remain under the protection of the Sanctuary and regular
home checks are made. The Donkey Sanctuary was founded
in 1969 by Dr Elisabeth Svendsen MBE. In the United
Kingdom and Ireland, the Sanctuary has taken in over
11,500 donkeys and also has major projects in Egypt,
Ethiopia, India, Kenya, Mexico and Spain. It aims to prevent
the suffering of donkeys worldwide through the provision
of high-quality professional advice, training and support on
donkey welfare. Sidmouth's Donkey Sanctuary is open every
day from 9 am to dusk. Admission and parking are free.

147 LYNTON & LYNMOUTH CLIFF RAILWAY

Lynmouth, North Devon, EX35 6EP
☎ 01598 753908, Fax: 01598 752733
e-mail: enquiries@cliffrailwaylynton.co.uk
⊕ www.cliffrailwaylynton.co.uk

Visit **Lynton & Lynmouth Cliff Railway** in Exmoor National Park and discover miles of National Trust, riverside and costal walks. The railway is the South West's most popular working attraction but it is also an integral part of daily life in Lynton and Lynmouth and provides one of the world's most spectacular railway rides.

In the 19th century, the high cliffs separating the two villages were a major obstacle to economic development. Transport over land was extremely difficult and so coal, lime, foodstuffs and other essentials mostly arrived in sailing vessels, which had to be carried by packhorses or in horse-drawn carts up the steep hill to Lynmouth. A solution came with the design of the railway by a follower of Isambard Kingdom Brunel, George Marks. Sir George Newnes, a publisher with a fondness for Lynton and Lynmouth, put up most of the money and work began in 1887 and the first descent took place in 1890.

The rails are 862 feet in length and the top station is 500 feet above the first, giving a 1:1.75 incline. Each car can carry 40 passengers and the system works on a balancing principle - each car has a 700 gallon water tank, filled with water piped from the river. The drivers use pre-arranged signals to release the cars brakes. The lower driver then discharges water to make the top car heavier. The top car then rolls down the rails - at the same time pulling the lower car up. Each car has two sets of brakes which are also water operated.

148 THE QUAY

9 The Quay, Appledore, Devon EX39 1QS
☎ 01237 473355
e-mail: Richard@9thequay.co.uk
⊕ www.9thequay.co.uk

For anyone who appreciates good food in a relaxed setting, **The Quay Gallery and Restaurant** is a double delight. Owners Richard and Chris Watts use the best fresh Devon produce in the Coffee Shop and upstairs Restaurant. The Coffee Shop is open from 10 to 4.30, serving lovely made-to-order sandwiches, cakes fresh daily and super Devon cream teas.

The first-floor Restaurant is open Wednesday to

Saturday evenings (book) in the season for an always interesting selection of freshly cooked, locally sourced food typified by butternut squash and honey soup with chervil, locally made pork sausages on fennel and truffle risotto, sea

bass with a niçoise salad and grilled chicken with caramelised red onion stuffing. The gallery is a showcase for chosen local artists, whose paintings and other works form a regularly changing display.

Stunning views over the Torridge Estuary are a bonus for visitors to this excellent place.

149 METTAFORD FARM HOLIDAY COTTAGES

Hartland, North Devon EX39 6AL
☎ 01237 441249
🌐 www.mettafordfarm.co.uk

In a beautiful, tranquil setting between Clovelly and Hartland Point, **Mettaford Farm Holiday Cottages** have been skilfully converted from stone barns to provide really delightful self-catering accommodation. Totally refurbished and equipped to a very high standard, they offer modern comfort and amenities while retaining original

features such as beams and latched doors. Sleeping from 2 to 6 guests, the eight cottages (four with bedrooms and bathrooms on the ground floor) stand in 14 acres of grounds that include a nature trail, a fun golf course, a heated indoor pool and a games room and play area.

150 MEAD BARN COTTAGES

Welcombe, nr Bideford, Devon EX39 6HQ
☎ 01288 331721
e-mail: holidays@meadbarns.com
🌐 www.meadbarns.com

Mead Barn Cottages offer top-class self-catering holiday accommodation in a superb setting between Clovelly and Bude on the Devon/Cornwall border, just half a mile from the sea. Open all year for weeks and short breaks, the barns and cottages have been skilfully converted to retain all their

period charm while providing up-to-date comfort and amenities. The units have 2, 3 or 4 bedrooms and are well heated and double-glazed; ground-floor rooms are available. On site are a tennis court, games room and play area.

151 THE CHICHESTER ARMS

Mortehoe, nr Woolacombe,
Devon EX34 7DU
☎ 01271 870411

John, Marsha and Alex are the friendly hosts at the **Chichester Arms**, a quaint 16th century inn located in the village of Mortehoe. Period pictures hang in the panelled lounge and in the dining room, where a wide choice of good-value home-cooked food makes excellent use of local fish and meat. Barum Original is one of several real ales always on tap in the bar, a favourite local meeting place with pool, darts and a skittle alley. A National Trust footpath is almost on the doorstep and the golden sands of Woolacombe Beach are a short drive away.

152 THE SMUGGLERS HAUNT HOTEL

Church Hill, Brixham, Devon TQ5 8HH
☎ 01803 853050
🌐 www.smugglers-haunt-hotel.co.uk

A short walk from the harbour in the centre of Brixham, the **Smugglers Haunt** is a perfect base for exploring the many attractions of the Devon coast and countryside. The 14 guest bedrooms, all with en suite facilities, include singles, twins, doubles and family rooms, and all have television, radio,

telephone and beverage tray. The Ruffell family's hotel is also a fine place for a meal, and the kitchen makes excellent use of the rich local harvest from land and sea, including fish from the daily market on the quay.

153 MORWELLHAM QUAY

Near Tavistock, Devon PL19 8JL
☎ 01822 832766 (enquiries)
☎ 01822 833808 (information)
e-mail: info@morwellham-quay.co.uk
🌐 www.morwellham-quay.co.uk

Morwellham Quay is an award-winning, evocative museum and visitor centre based around the historic port and mine workings on the River Tamar. Here in the heart of the spectacular Tamar Valley, amidst towering cliffs and gently rolling farmland, a lost world lives again.

Costumed staff welcome visitors to the restored port and help to transport you back to the bustling 1860s when heaps of gleaming copper ore filled the quays and a forest of ships' masts lined the river. Explore the busy assay office, marvel at the over-crowded miner's cottages and stroll through the delightful, walled gardens. Authentic replica costumes are available for you to promenade through the village, while the children find out what life was really like working on the "dressing-floors" of the mine or acting as servants in the "Manager's House".

For many a highlight of the visit is the journey underground into the copper mine. Here son et lumiere displays illustrate the harsh working conditions of Victorian miners and the train drivers offer an expert commentary on the technical aspects of hard rock mining.

By way of contrast the Victorian farm and nature reserve offer you the chance to escape the hustle and bustle of 21st century life as you wander through the tranquil countryside with only the wildlife for company.

For a continually stimulating and entertaining day out, Morwellham Quay is the place to go.

154 THE PREWLEY MOOR ARMS

Church Road, Sourton Down,
nr Okehampton, Devon EX20 4HT
☎ 01837 861349

Locals, motorists, cyclists, walkers – all are welcome at the **Prewley Moor Arms**, where Lorna and Emma are the cheerful, helpful landladies. Some come for a drink, some for the excellent food, and some to stay in the comfortable en suite rooms while exploring the region. This is also very much the social hub of the village, with darts and pool teams and disco or theme nights on Friday and Saturday.

Looking for:

• *Places to Visit?*

• *Places to Stay?*

• *Places to Eat & Drink?*

• *Places to Shop?*

155 THE ANCHOR INN

1 Lutterburn Street, Ugborough,
nr Ivybridge, Devon PL21 0NG
☎ 01752 892283
e-mail: theanchorinn@btinternet.com
🌐 www.anchor-ugborough.co.uk

Many visitors fall in love with the beautiful South Hams village of Ugborough, but none have shown their affection quite as clearly as Juliano Reichert and

Ruth Kerslake – they became the landlords of the village pub, the **Anchor**. Very much the centre of village social life, the Anchor, whose origins can be traced back to the 16th century, is also popular with walkers, cyclists and holidaymakers travelling by car through Devon.

The pub has a delightful public bar with oak parquet flooring and a roaring fire, a 40-cover restaurant with oak beams and leaded windows, and an attractive outside seating area. It is one of the few places that still serves Cask Bass straight from the barrel, and also offers a variety of other beers and an excellent wine list. The extensive bar and restaurant menus combine pub classics with dishes inspired by cuisines from around the world. The Anchor is a delightful, civilised base for B&B guests with five self-contained chalet-style en suite bedrooms.

156 BUCKFAST BUTTERFLIES AND DARTMOOR OTTER SANCTUARY

Buckfastleigh, Devon TQ11 0DZ
☎ 01364 642916
e-mail: info@ottersandbutterflies.co.uk
🌐 www.ottersandbutterflies.co.uk

The tropical landscaped gardens at **Buckfast Butterflies and Dartmoor Otter Sanctuary**, with their ponds, waterfalls and exotic plants are home to a wide variety of exotic butterflies from around

the world that live, breed and fly freely. The gardens are also home to small birds and other tropical creatures such as leaf cutting ants from Costa Rica, Koi Carp and terrapins.

The complete life-cycle of the butterfly, from chrysalis to drying their wings and making their first flight, can be studied and photographed at leisure. Outside, in another specially landscaped garden is the otter sanctuary where three species of otters, including the shy native British otter, can be seen. A special underwater viewing area allows visitors to observe these playful creatures in their natural habitat and watching them during the thrice-daily feeding times is particularly amusing. Both the otters and the butterflies provide plenty of opportunity for budding wildlife photographers to hone their skills. The butterflies and otters can be seen daily between March and October. Phone for winter opening times.

157 THE COVENTRY ARMS

Mill Street, Corfe Mullen, nr Wimborne,
Dorset BH21 3RH
☎ 01258 857284
e-mail: info@coventryarms.co.uk
🌐 www.coventryarms.co.uk

The Coventry Arms is a unique and traditional free house renowned for its variety of real ale served directly from the barrel and a bistro style food menu with daily specials. Using only local quality ingredients and suppliers, dishes such as fillets of red mullet with herb cous cous, local venison,

Gressingham duck and monk fish with linguini all adorn the menu regularly.

This 15th century pub boasts splendid original features such as exposed beams, low ceilings, original stone floors and a huge open fireplace. The riverside garden is the setting for the annual beer festival and the Coventry Arms is well renowned for other culinary extravaganzas such as the Seafood Festival and French Week.

Food is served weekdays and Saturdays 12pm - 2.30pm and 6pm to 9.30pm and open all day on Sunday for traditional roasts as well as the al a carte menu or BBQ during the summer months.

158 THE DROVERS INN

Gussage All Saints, nr Wimborne,
Dorset BH21 5ET
☎ 01258 840084
e-mail: jasonanthony@btopenworld.com
🌐 www.thedroversinn.net

The Drovers Inn is a fine old village pub, part thatched, part creeper-clad, in a pretty location tucked away down country lanes 8 miles north of Wimborne. Jason and Catherine Anthony are the most affable of hosts, and they have made their pub a great favourite with the local community, as well as welcoming the many tourists who pass this way.

The two-room bar has a delightful old-world ambience, with beams, open fires, brass and copper ornaments and good-looking furnishings – the perfect spot for enjoying well-kept beers from the Ringwood Brewery and a wide range of other refreshment. Handsome wood-framed blackboards list the day's food

offerings, which range from sandwiches and ploughman's to fish & chips, smoked haddock & spring onion fishcakes, liver & bacon, curries and steaks. Vegetarians are not forgotten, with tasty options like brie, onion and olive tart. The Drovers has a pretty front lawn with lovely views across the Dorset hills, and a marquee is available for summer parties.

159 FLEUR-DE-LYS

5 Wimborne Street, Cranborne,
Dorset BH21 5PP
☎ 01725 517282

The **Fleur-de-Lys** is a handsome 16th century Grade II listed building easy to spot on the A3078 on the way into Cranborne. The landlady Amy and her staff have a friendly greeting for all of their customers, who can look forward to some of the best food in the region: all meat and dairy produce comes from the nearby Cranborne Estate.

Meals are served lunchtime and evenings. Tanglefoot, Badger Gold and K&B Sussex are on tap to quench thirsts throughout the day, and for guests staying overnight the pub has five traditional country en suite bedrooms with original 16th century features throughout.. Cranborne is a very pleasant place, well

worth taking time to explore, in a beautiful setting by the River Crane. Among the

places to see are the Manor House, on the site of a royal hunting lodge built for King John, and a fine church with some superb 14th century wall paintings, not to mention the very popular garden centre and beautiful designated walks across the Cranborne Estate.

160 THE WILLOWS TEA ROOMS

5 Blandford Road, Shillingstone, nr
Blandford Forum, Dorset DT11 0SG
☎ 01258 861167
e-mail: planet.2-cb@tiscali.co.uk

Two 18th century cob cottages in Shillingstone make up **the Willows Tea Rooms**, which is owned and run in fine style by Chris and Ray Borst. With 20 covers inside and 30 in the garden, it's a delightful spot for enjoying anything from home-made scones and cakes to traditional home-cooked dishes and the popular Sunday roasts. From May to September the tea rooms are open from 10 to 6 Tuesday to Sunday and Bank Holiday Mondays; from October to April open weekends only. The Willows also has an en suite double room for B&B guests.

161 THE OLD OX INN

Shillingstone, nr Blandford Forum, Dorset
☎ 01258 860211
e-mail: janiemartin2000@yahoo.co.uk

The **Old Ox Inn** is a whitewashed 18th century country pub in the village of Shillingstone, on the A357 2 miles north of Blandford Forum. Keith and Jane Martin have been at the helm for many years, and have recently 'reinvented' the old place with all-day opening and a choice of traditional pub grub that starts

with breakfast and includes light bites and full meals. The pub is a popular local meeting place, with entertainment provided by a pool table, a skittle alley, a Sunday quiz in autumn and winter and good conversation all year round.

Child Okeford, nr Blandford Forum,
Dorset DT11 8HD
☎ 01258 860310
e-mail: peterturner@saxoninn.co.uk
⊕ www.saxoninn.co.uk

Watch out for the signs to seek out this real "Hidden Place" and you will not be disappointed. Nestling beneath Hambledon Hill, the **Saxon Inn** is one of the most delightful and picturesque country inn you could ever encounter. Dating back some 200 years, the inn started life as a row of three cottages before being converted and opening as a pub in the 1950s. The white exterior is decorated with an impressive array of hanging baskets and at the back is a lovely garden with an abundance of trees and plants, picnic sets and a Wendy house that's guaranteed to keep the little ones busy and happy.

The interior is equally easy on the eye, with horse brasses on old beams, log fires and a warm, inviting ambience created by hosts Peter and Helen Turner. They have put their years of previous experience (ex-Scottish & Newcastle and Courage) to excellent use in making the Saxon one of the most appealing pubs for many miles around. Ringwood best and Butcombe Bitter are the regular real ales, joined by changing guests and all kept in tip-top condition – CAMRA approved of course.

The food is another good reason for a visit here. There is a wide choice of traditional pub dishes featured in the A la Carte menu, supported by a daily specials board reflecting the seasonal choices and availability of fresh fish. The food is locally sourced and predominately home cooked by Helen and her excellent kitchen team. For the lighter appetite and for those in need of a quicker alternative there is a selection of Jacket potatoes and sandwiches. Food is served lunchtime seven days a week and every evening except Sunday. There's a separate non-smoking dining area with a wood-burning stove in an impressive brick hearth. The village of Child Okeford lies off the A357 a short drive north of Blandford Forum.

Milborne Port, nr Sherborne,
Dorset DT9 5HQ
☎ 01963 250289

The latest leaseholder at the **Tippling Philosopher** is Rebecca Fairless, who is following in the footsteps of many illustrious incumbents. Rebecca and her hardworking staff make sure that every one who visits has a pleasant stay, whether it's for a drink, a snack, a meal or an overnight or longer stay. Bombardier and 6X are the regular real ales, heading a wide selection of other draught and bottle beers, lagers, wines, spirits and non-alcoholic drinks.

Food is a major part of the Tippling Philosopher's business, and in the non-smoking restaurant, everything on the menu is home cooked from the best ingredients. Most of the dishes are traditional pub favourites, as shown by gammon, egg & chips, T-bone or rump steaks, burgers or pasta with various sauces. But there are also some more unusual dishes such as seared pork loin with a red wine glaze, and the chefs come up with some exotic surprises: when kangaroo steak appeared on the menu the diners had to do a quick hop and skip to make sure they get in their order before the dish ran out!

The Tippling Philosopher is an ideal base for both business and leisure visitors, and for tourists the pub is close to many places of scenic and historic interest. There are plenty of scenic walks hereabouts, and among the attractions within a short drive are Wincanton races, the Iron Age hill fort of Cadbury Castle, the Haynes Motor Museum and the historic town of Sherborne with its 15th century Abbey, its castle – sometime home of Sir Walter Raleigh – and the famous school, the setting for classic films such as *The guinea Pig*, *Goodbye Mr Chips* and *The Browning Version*.

There are five guest bedrooms of which two have en suite facilities. In 1738, Milborne Port, which stands on the A30 about 2 miles east of Sherborne, was listed as having seven licensed victuallers and in 1753 that number had increased to nine. Among these was the Tippling Philosopher, which in 1797 was acquired by the Marquis of Anglesey, who owned most of Stalbridge and half of Milborne Port. Sometime later, the name of the pub was changed to the Kings Head in honour of a visit by King George III to Stalbridge Park, where the marquis lived. The pub passed to various other owners down the years, and at some stage the name reverted to the Tippling Philosopher, which it has retained ever since.

163 THE ROSE & CROWN

Trent, nr Sherborne, Dorset DT9 4SL
☎ 01935 850776

Tenants Sue and Mick Sellings have lost no time in making their mark at the **Rose & Crown**, a delightful, partly-thatched pub in a quiet rural setting a short drive from both Sherborne and Yeovil. There's a welcoming old-fashioned look inside, and the bar and the beer garden are both pleasant spots for

enjoying a drink. Wadworth 6X, Bishops and Henry's IPA are the regular real ales, and in the conservatory-style restaurant a good choice of home-cooked dishes includes favourites like steaks, beer-battered cod, chilli con carne and steak & ale pie. Light snacks are available throughout the day.

167 THE CROWS NEST

Ulwell Road, Swanage, Dorset BH19 1LE
☎ 01929 422651 Fax: 01929 422304
e-mail: crowsnestltd@aol.com
🌐 www.crowsnestinn.co.uk

The **Crows Nest** is a handsome Victorian pub on a busy site behind the main road into Swanage, an easy walk from the beach. The real ales (Ringwood Bitter is a favourite) have earned a Cask Marque award, and simple, delicious home-cooked food include pizzas to eat or take away and a popular carvery on Thursday lunchtimes. The Crows Nest has a lovely big garden with lawns, trees, plants and picnic sets. For overnight guests two en suite rooms with television and hot drinks trays provide comfortable B&B accommodation.

165 THE CROWN

High Street, Stalbridge, Dorset DT10 2LL
☎ 01963 362295
e-mail: ruth.panton@btconnect.com

For more than ten years Ruth Panton has been welcoming visitors to **The Crown** on the High Street of Stalbridge, a lovely little village close to the A30. for long a local favourite, it's also an ideal spot for motorists to pause on a journey or for tourists seeking to sample the excellent hospitality provided by Ruth and her staff.

Two rotating guest real ales are among the most popular thirst-quenchers, and the restaurant served god honest home-cooked dishes from 12 to 2 and 7 to 9 every day. Typical dishes – the choice changes every day – include smoked haddock pie, turkey & ham pie, liver & bacon and chicken with a perky

barbecue sauce. Sandwiches and lighter snacks are usually available throughout

the day. Pool and skittles are among the traditional pub games played in the bar of The Crown, which has a pleasant beer garden for enjoying a fair-weather tipple.

East Street, Corfe Castle, nr Wareham,
Dorset BH20 5EE
☎ 01929 480208

Mark and Laurice generate a warm, friendly atmosphere that brings customers back time and time again to the **Castle Inn**. It stands in the picturesque National Trust village of Corfe Castle, and its position on the main road (A351) brings a steady stream of visitors throughout the year. The pub's classic interior features stone slab floors and a handsome medieval fireplace – a delightful spot to relax and unwind over a glass of Wadworth 6X or Abbot Ale.

Freshly prepared home-cooked food is a major part of the Castle's business, with dishes based on locally caught fish among the favourite orders. The printed menu of classics such as steaks, cottage pie, chilli con carne and cod & chips is supplemented by a large blackboard listing interesting daily specials like haddock fishcakes, Thai-style prawns and Cajun-spiced mackerel, with a scrumptious Dorset apple cake to finish. The Castle has a large garden from which patrons can see and hear trains on the heritage Swanage Railway, which operates BR Southern Region and Standard steam locomotives on a scenic six-mile journey from Swanage to Norden just north of Corfe Castle.

There are plenty of ways of working up a thirst and appetite in the village, which is dominated by the majestic ruins of the Castle high on a hill. The Castle Museum and the amazing 1:20 scale Model Village and Garden are other attractions, and a network of footpaths through heathland and across to the coast passes important wildlife habitats. After an hour or two in the fresh Dorset air, walkers, cyclists and tourists will fine that Mark and Laurice and their staff are ready with their own special kind of hospitality. The pub, which hosts live musical entertainment on Friday and Saturday nights, has its own off-road car park, a very valuable asset in this busy, much-visited village.

63 High Street, Swanage, Dorset BH19 2LY
☎ 01929 423533
e-mail: info@redlionswanage.co.uk
🌐 www.redlionswanage.co.uk

The Red Lion offers the unusual combination of a town centre inn with a spacious garden. This friendly traditional pub is owned and run by Tim and Karen Cattle who pride themselves on serving a wide selection of real ales and ciders as well as quality wines and spirits. They also offer an extensive range of food – from snacks through to

exciting special dishes, all available every lunchtime and evening. The specials menu changes regularly but typical dishes include locally caught lemon sole; pan fried goat's cheese & cranberry; or braised lamb shank in red wine gravy. Wine is available by the glass or bottle. The fare on offer in the non-smoking restaurant also includes vegetarian and children's menus. Wednesday evening is curry night when a very reasonable inclusive price brings you a curry and a pint or small glass of wine; on Friday evenings the special deal is for two 8oz steaks with chips, onion rings, mushrooms, peas, tomatoes and side salad plus a bottle of

house wine. And on Sundays, of course, there's a traditional roast dinner. In good weather, customers can enjoy their refreshments in the large garden with its well-spaced picnic tables and children's play area (adult supervision required). Dogs are welcome.

As befits a traditional pub, there's a pool table, darts board and other pub games available and throughout the year, the Red Lion hosts a lively series of events ranging from "hot rocking bands to sublime acoustic artists" – details can be found on the inn's website.

The summer of 2005 saw another addition to the Red Lion's amenities with the conversion of the historic barn in the garden into 5 self-contained rooms for bed & breakfast guests.

Swanage itself is famous for its superb floral displays in the parks and gardens; there's a fine Blue Flag beach and old-fashioned pier; a clifftop country park and all the facilities required of a traditional seaside holiday resort. Lovers of steam railways will delight in the Swanage Railway that passes through 6 miles of lovely Dorset countryside to just north of Corfe Castle.

169 LULWORTH CASTLE

East Lulworth, Wareham,
Dorset BH20 5QS
☎ 01929 400352 Fax: 01929 400563
🌐 www.lulworth.com

Lulworth Castle was built primarily as a hunting lodge in the first decades of the 17th century and down the years has played host to no fewer than seven monarchs. It was reduced to a virtual ruin by a devastating fire in 1929, but in the 1970s restoration work was begun with the help of English Heritage. The exterior is now exactly as it was before the fire, and visitors can climb the tower to enjoy some spectacular views. A video presentation brings the history of the castle to life, and interior features including a gallery concerning the Weld family, owners of the estate since 1641, a Victorian kitchen, dairy, laundry and wine cellar. There is also a children's activity room.

Lulworth Castle House, the modern home of the Weld family, contains 18th century sculptures as well as portraits and furniture rescued from the castle fire. In the grounds of the castle are a delightful walled garden and a curious circular building dating from 1786. This was the first Roman Catholic Church to be established in Britain since Henry VIII's defiance of the Pope in 1534.

Permission to build it was given to Sir Thomas Weld by King George III. The beautifully restored chapel contains an exhibition of 18th and 19th century vestments, a collection of church silver and a wonderful Seede organ. A short walk from the Castle and Chapel are the animal farm, play area and woodland walk. The old castle stables house the licensed café serving morning coffee, light lunches and cream teas, and the courtyard shop offers a wide range of gift ideas. S Lulworth Castle Park is open all year Sunday to Friday, Lulworth Castle House on Wednesday afternoons in summer.

170 GRAINGERS GUEST HOUSE

215 Dorchester Road, Weymouth,
Dorset DT3 5EQ
☎ 01305 782362
e-mail: stay@graingers4b-b.co.uk
🌐 www.graingers4b-b.co.uk

On the A354 Dorchester Road into Weymouth, **Graingers Guest House** is a large modern house offering space, comfort and up-to-date amenities in its guest bedrooms. The seven rooms are decorated and

furnished to a very high standard, and three have en suite facilities. Resident owners

Bob and Yvonne Harding take excellent care of their guests, and the day starts with a choice of full English or a lighter breakfast. Buses on the Weymouth-Dorchester route stops right outside the house.

172 THE WHITE HOUSE HOTEL

The Street, Charmouth, Dorset DT6 6PJ
☎ 01297 560411
e-mail: ian@whitehousehotel.com
🌐 www.whitehousehotel.com

Quality is a watchword at **The White House Hotel**, which stands on the World Heritage Coastline in the centre of Charmouth. The bedrooms are elegant and comfortably equipped, and the very best produce from local farms and West Country suppliers are used for the mouthwatering dishes.

Abbotsbury Tourism Ltd, West Yard Barn,
West Street, Abbotsbury, Dorset DT3 4JT
☎ 01305 871130 Fax: 01305 871092
e-mail: info@abbotsbury-tourism.co.uk
🌐 www.abbotsbury-tourism.co.uk

Surrounded by hills, with the sea close at hand, **Abbotsbury** is one of the county's most popular tourist spots and by any standards one of the loveliest villages in England. Very little remains of the Benedictine Abbey that gives the village its name, but what has survived is the magnificent Great Abbey Barn, a tithe barn almost 250ft long that was built in the 14th century to house the Abbey's tithes of wool, grain and other produce.

The village's three main attractions, which bring the crowds flocking in their thousands to this lovely part of the world, are the **Swannery**, the **Sub-Tropical Gardens** and the **Tithe Barn Children's Farm**. The most

famous of all is Abbotsbury Swannery, which was established many centuries ago, originally to provide food for the monks in the Abbey. For at least 600 years the swannery has been a sanctuary for a huge colony of mute swans. The season for visitors begins in earnest in March, when the swans vie for the best nesting sites. From May to the end of June cygnets hatch by the hundred and from then until October the fluffy chicks grow and gradually gain their wings. Cygnets who have become orphaned are protected in special pens until strong enough to fend for themselves. By the end of October many of the swans move off the site for the winter, while other wildfowl move in. An audio-visual show is run hourly in the old swanherd's cottage, and a few lucky visitors are selected to help out at the spectacular twice-daily feeding sessions. The swans' feed includes eelgrass from the River Fleet. In May of this year the Swanherd, who has looked after the colony for 40 years, Dick Dalley, retired. When he first started the birds were still being raised for the table, but today, the 159 breeding pairs - including 2 black swans - are protected by law. Also on site are a shire horse and cart service, a gift shop and a café housed in a delightful building that was converted from Georgian kennels.

At the western end of the village, Abbotsbury Sub-Tropical Gardens, established by the first Countess of Ilchester as a kitchen garden for her nearby castle, occupy a 20-acre site close to Chesil Beach that's largely protected from the elements by a ring of oak trees. In this micro-climate a huge variety of rare and exotic plants and trees flourish, and the camellia groves and the collections of rhododendrons and hydrangeas are known the world over.

There's a woodland trail, a children's play area, visitor centre, plant nursery, gift shop and restaurant with a veranda overlooking the sunken garden. Most of the younger children will make a beeline for the Tithe Barn Children's Farm, where they can cuddle the rabbits, bottle feed the lambs, race toy tractors, feed the doves and meet the donkeys and horses. The Farm's latest attraction is the Smugglers Barn, where the little ones can learn and play at the same time.

173 HARTLEPOOL'S MARITIME EXPERIENCE

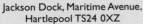

Jackson Dock, Maritime Avenue,
Hartlepool TS24 0XZ

☎ 01429 860077 Fax: 01429 867332

e-mail:
info@hartlepoolsmaritimeexperience.com

🌐 www.hartlepoolsmaritimeexperience.com

Open every day, all year round* and winner of many tourism and visitor attraction awards, **Hartlepool's Maritime Experience** is a fascinating and enjoyable day out with something to suit all ages. An authentic recreation of an 18th century seaport which tells the story of life at sea at the time of Captain Cook, Nelson and the Battle of Trafalgar. Featuring authentic reconstructions of period harbour-side shops, children's maritime adventure centre and wooden playship. A film presentation shows how two brothers were press-ganged into serving in the Royal Navy and 'Fighting Ships', an audio/visual tour which allows you to experience the noise and drama of a fierce sea battle. Costumed guides add to your experience and there are regular gun firing, cannon firing and swordfighting displays. Audio tours are available on board HMS Trincomalee, a magnificent ship launched in Bombay in 1817, the last of Nelson's Frigates. She is the oldest floating warship in Britain; restored in Hartlepool and now a major part of this attraction. Explore the Captains Cabin, Mess

Deck and Hold. Find out about life at sea in cramped and very difficult conditions. The ship and quayside have been used for many drama and documentary programmes depicting this important time in British history. The Museum of Hartlepool tells the story of the town from prehistoric times to the present day and includes exhibits such as sea monsters, a Celtic 'Roundhouse', the first 'gas illuminated lighthouse', numerous models, computer interactive displays and the paddle steam ship Wingfield Castle with on board coffee shop.
*Closed 25th, 26th and 31st December.

174 DARLINGTON RAILWAY CENTRE & MUSEUM

North Road Station, Darlington DL3 6ST
☎ 01325 460532 Fax: 01325 287746
e-mail: museum@darlington.gov.uk
🌐 www.drcm.org.uk

Experience the atmosphere of the steam railway age as you step back in time in the history of North Road Passenger Station of 1842. See Stephenson's Locomotion which hauled its

first train on the Stockport and Darlington Railway in 1825. Explore the railway heritage of North East England through a collection of engines, carriages and wagons. Open daily 10-5pm, all year except 25th and 26th december and 1st January.

175 THE TEESDALE RESTAURANT & COFFEE SHOP

Rear of 9 King Street, Galgate Car Park,
Barnard Castle, Co Durham DL12 8EP
☎ 01833 638624
e-mail: hooperhoon9f@supanet.com

The **Teesdale** has been here for 40 years, but in 2005 the premises were knocked down and rebuilt in fine traditional style. Open from 9 to 5 Sunday to Wednesday and until 11 in the evening Thursday, Friday and Saturday, the Teesdale, which is owned and run by Andrew and Christine Hooper, serves a fine selection of traditional British and Continental home-cooked food. Typical dishes include moules marinière, steaks plain and sauced, shoulder of lamb and lemon-poached salmon, and there's always a choice of main courses for vegetarians. The dessert board lists a tempting choice to round things off in style.

176 THE TUT 'N' SHIVE

Newgate Street, Bishop Auckland,
Co Durham DL14 7EQ
☎ 01388 603252

The **Tut 'n' Shive** is a convivial town pub with a super, friendly team at the helm. Tenant Michelle Walker is a real live wire, with a ready smile for all who visit her busy pub close to the shops in the town centre.

The changing selection of real ales is complemented by a good range of other draught and bottled beers and lagers, and combine with the great-value lunches served from 11 Monday to Saturday make the Tut 'n' Shive a

great favourite with the locals. Late risers can enjoy a 'full works' breakfast, and other popular dishes include jacket potatoes, fish & chips, lasagne, curries and filled Yorkshire puddings. There's plenty of neatly arranged seating in the long main public area, and in-house entertainment includes a pool table and juke box.

177 THE FIR TREE COUNTRY HOTEL

The Grove, Fir Tree, nr Crook,
Co Durham DL15 8DD
☎ 01388 762161 Fax: 01388 765255
e-mail: firtree01@btconnect.com
🌐 www.firtree-hotel.co.uk

On the main A68 Darlington-Corbridge road, the **Fir Tree** is a very pleasant small hotel with a country pub ambience. Hosts Anne and Angus Downie have been in the hospitality business for many years, and their experience in meeting the needs of their patrons has contributed to the success of this popular hotel. It's a perfect place to take a break and unwind in the friendly, welcoming surroundings of the bar and restaurant.

A full range of drinks is served in the comfortable bar and lounge, and appetites small and large are catered for with bar menus and an across-the-board à la carte menu served in the Grove Bistro. On the edge of

Weardale, with Hamsterley Forest virtually on the doorstep, the Fir Tree is an ideal base for a walking holiday, and for tourists there are many sights to discover, including Witton and Auckland Castles. The 14 motel-style bedrooms all have en suite facilities, television, radio-alarm, hairdryer and beverage tray. The hotel has facilities for meetings and small functions.

178 THE SAXON INN

**Escomb, nr Bishop Auckland,
Co Durham DL14 7SY
☎ 01388 662256**

Locals and not-so-locals enjoy the wholesome cooking, good beer and the very good wines at the **Saxon Inn**, which is set back from the A689 opposite the church in the village of Escomb. Paul Hope, the ebullient chef-patron, takes justifiable pride in the quality of the food, and in

the smart new dining extension his well-priced menus cater for all tastes. The steak pie is a favourite and other options include burgers, lasagne, steaks, curries and filled Yorkshire puddings. The inn, which dates from 1671, is at the social as well as the gastronomic heart of the community, with regular live music sessions in the summer and quiz/bingo on Sunday evenings.

179 THE TRAVELLERS REST

**Accrington Terrace, Evenwood,
Durham DL14 9QD
☎ 01388 834822**

Margaret Houghton, tenant and chef, is building a fine reputation for the food at the **Travellers Rest**, a homely pub on a corner site off the A688, a short drive southwest of Bishop Auckland. For diners in the excellent little restaurant, with an open fire, neatly laid tables, pictures, prints and Tiffany-style lamps, she prepares a fine selection of popular pub dishes, with everything freshly cooked to order. Wednesday is steak night. No credit cards.

181 THE HARE & HOUNDS

**Westgate, nr Stanhope,
Co Durham DL13 1PX
☎ 01388 517212**

On the A689 in Weardale, with wonderful countryside all around, the **Hare & Hounds** is a delightful pub dating from the end of the 18th century. Hosts Colin and Alison moved from their pub in Bridlington to take over this popular

free house, and visitors will find that it's easy to relax and unwind in the smartly refurbished bar and lounge. Tried-and-tested dishes like fish pie, chicken chasseur, lamb shanks and steaks are served in the conservatory-style restaurant overlooking the river at the back. The Hare & Hounds has a small caravan/camping site, and two rooms are available in the pub for B&B guests.

180 THE MOORCOCK INN

Hill Top, Eggleston, Barnard Castle,
Co Durham DL12 0AU
☎ 01833 650395 Fax: 01833 650052

The **Moorcock** is a charming and atmospheric stone-built country inn dating back to 1820. The address gives a clue that the location provides great views, and indeed the inn is surrounded by beautiful countryside that's a paradise for walkers and lovers of the great outdoors. Recent major refurbishment restored the pub to its pristine best in a programme that also included the creation of a new dining area. Mark, the chef, and Catherine front of house make an excellent combination, and the warm welcome and pleasant, unpretentious décor create a really delightful, congenial ambience.

A log fire keeps things cosy in the lounge bar, where a fine selection of cask-conditioned ales and malt whiskies are among the wide variety of drinks on offer. Tables on the terrace provide the opportunity to enjoy a drink or a meal while making the most of the fresh country air and the splendid views. The Moorcock's various menus provide a truly impressive choice for diners, with local produce to the fore and just about everything totally prepared and cooked in the kitchens – and what a treat to find real chips! Typifying the variety of dishes on the manus are garlic mushrooms, meat or vegetarian lasagne, roast Teesdale lamb, shepherds pie, chicken & mushroom pie, beef in orange with dumplings, smoked haddock with poached eggs, grilled sea bass with garlic and ginger, and dressed crab salad. The pub is open from 11 to 11 Monday to Saturday and from 12 on Sunday.

This is not a pub or indeed a part of the world to leave in a hurry, and for guests lucky enough to stay for a break or a holiday the Moorcock has are seven very comfortable bedrooms – four doubles, one twin and two singles. Four of the rooms have en suite facilities. Apart from the walking in the Pennines and Hamsterley Forest, the area is rich in scenic and historic attractions. Among the most notable are the dramatic High Force Waterfall, reputed to be the highest unbroken fall of water in England, and other neighbouring falls; the amazing Bowes Museum at Barnard Castle; and Raby Castle, one of the country's finest medieval castles. Even closer are Eggleston Hall Gardens, four acres of lovely gardens open to the public all year round. All this makes the Moorcock a winner on all fronts: a great location with magnificent views, congenial staff and a great atmosphere; cask-conditioned ales; super food and comfortable guest accommodation. No-one should be anywhere in the area without a visit!

182 THE WHITE HORSE INN

26 High Street, Maldon, Essex CM9 5PJ
☎ 01621 851708
🌐 www.pickapub.co.uk/
whitehorsemaldon.htm

Starting life as a coaching inn some 350 years ago, the **White Horse Inn** today enjoys an enviable reputation for its ambience, food, drink and accommodation. Run by Gary and Wendy Cooper, it's open all day for drinks, which include up to four real ales from Britain's oldest brewery, Shepherd Neame.

Forty covers throughout the pub provide very pleasant surroundings in which to enjoy Wendy's excellent freshly prepared dishes. Typical choices might include all-day breakfast fish pie, grilled plaice, liver braised in red wine, chilli con carne and roasts served in small, medium or large helpings, with old-fashioned delights like roly poly pudding or pineapple upside-down cake to round things off in style. Booking is recommended to be sure of a table for

Friday and Saturday dinner and Sunday lunch. For guests staying overnight the pub has eight bedrooms (two en suite) on upper floors, available all year round on Bed & Breakfast terms. Friday is disco night, with live music on Saturday evening and Sunday afternoon.

184 ROYAL GUNPOWDER MILLS

Powdermill Lane, Waltham Abbey,
Essex EN9 1BN
☎ 01992 767022 Fax: 01992 710341
🌐 www.royalgunpowdermills.com

The **Royal Gunpowder Mills** in Waltham Abbey is open to the general public after a 300 year history. Thanks to funding from the Heritage Lottery Fund and Ministry of Defence, this secret site which was home to gunpowder and explosive production and research for more than three centuries, has been developed to offer visitors a truly unique day out.

Gunpowder production began at Waltham Abbey in the mid 1660's on the site of a late medieval fulling mill. The gunpowder Mills remained in private hands until 1787, when they were purchased by the crown. From this date, the Royal Gunpowder Mills developed into the pre eminent powder works in Britain and one of the most important in Europe.

Set in175 acres of natural parkland and boasting 21 important historic buildings the regenerated site will offer visitors a unique mixture of fascinating history, exciting science and beautiful surroundings. Approximately 70 acres of the site, containing some of the oldest buildings and much of the canal network, will be open for visitors to explore freely. The remaining area of the site including the largest heronry in Essex has been designated as a Site of Special Scientific Interest and will be accessible to the public by way of special guided tours. Open April to September.

1 Fullbridge, Maldon, Essex **CM9 4LE**
☎ 01621 852167 Fax: 01621 851598

It would be difficult to imagine a better-named pub than **The Welcome**, where leaseholders Diane and James Round epitomise the qualities needed to turn a good pub into a really special pub. The pub stands by the River Chelmer, and when the river was tidal many years ago the pub depended on the tide and was only open when the tide allowed. When the experienced licensees took over in November 2004 the pub was once again barely keeping its head above water, very run down and in urgent need of a lot of tender loving care.

Diane and James were exactly the right people to provide it, and after closing it for a month it was ready for its renaissance in December of that year. It really buzzes now, and the perfectionist hosts still have more improvement plans in the pipeline. Welcome definitely is what it's all about, and within a short period of time the bar had become one of the most popular spots in the town for locals and visitors to chat together over a glass of beer. It has also become a favourite place to enjoy a snack or a meal, and the homely, home-cooked food is available from noon right through to 7 o'clock every day. The printed menu and the daily specials listed on cards provides a

good selection of popular pub dishes that include soups, scampi and hearty dishes such as rich minced beef or roast chicken and stuffing pudding. And if the kitchen has the necessary ingredients, they'll rustle up a dish that's not even on the menu! Diners can eat in the 30-cover non-smoking restaurant or anywhere else in the bars or out on the patio that offers views down to the river.

The Welcome has plenty more than food and drink to offer, including a disco that operates from 9 till the wee small hours on Friday and Saturday, with a super dance floor for everyone to join in the fun. And the disco

also stays in the family, as Diane and James' son is the DJ. Maldon is one of the most interesting places in the whole county, with attractions ranging from the 14th century Moot Hall to Promenade Park, the heritage centre and the magnificent old sailing barges moored at Hythe Quay. And after an hour or two unearthing the many delights of the town and the surrounding area Diane and James are ready with the renowned welcome which has become their trade mark.

185 THE SWAN INN

14-15 Brook Street, Manningtree,
Essex CO11 1DR
☎ 01206 397042
e-mail:
enquiries@theswanmanningtree.co.uk
🌐 www.theswanmanningtree.co.uk

The Swan is one of the most welcoming and sociable of pubs, with a fine reputation for hospitality. Licensees Peter and Toni (Antonietta) pride themselves on the quality of the food,
which spans
a wide range
from bar
snacks to
traditional
roasts by way
of fresh fish
landed at

Harwich, steaks, pies and Italian specialities. Six en suite rooms – singles, doubles and a family room – provide comfortable accommodation for Bed & Breakfast guests. On the social side, The Swan hosts music nights, quiz nights, golf days and a fishing club.

187 THE VILLAGE MAID

Heath Road, Bradfield, Essex CO11 2UZ
☎ 01255 870329

The **Village Maid** is a delightful country inn just off the B1352 coastal road between Manningtree and Harwich. Leaseholders Lee and Sonia welcome visitors of all ages, and their pub is open all day, seven days a week, for food
and drink.
The
printed
menu
offers
plenty of
choice,
widened
by daily
specials

such as all-day breakfast, liver & bacon, Mediterranean chicken with rice and salmon with an asparagus sauce. It's all excellent, with all the meat, eggs, dairy products and vegetables sourced locally. The pub has a secure beer garden and off-road parking.

186 THE WAGGON AT WIX

Clacton Road, Wix, nr Manningtree,
Essex CO11 2RU
☎ 01255 870279
e-mail: wixwaggon@fsnet.com

Mark and Cheryl Townley have run the **Waggon at Wix** for more than 20 years, pleasing their customers with a good selection of beers and other drinks served all day every day and an across-the-board choice of home-cooked
dishes.
They
served the
main menu
from 12 to
2 and from
6 to 9 (not
Sunday
evening),
and

sandwiches and snacks are available outside these times. It's best to book for Sunday lunch. The pub hosts live music sessions on Saturday evening and live jazz every other Wednesday.

HIDDEN PLACES GUIDES

Explore Britain and Ireland with *Hidden Places* guides - a fascinating series of national and local travel guides.

Packed with easy to read information on hundreds of places of interest as well as places to stay, eat and drink.

Available from both high street and internet booksellers

For more information on the full range of *Hidden Places* guides and other titles published by Travel Publishing visit our website on

www.travelpublishing.co.uk
or ask for our leaflet by phoning
0118-981-7777 or emailing
info@travelpublishing.co.uk

188 THE MARLBOROUGH HEAD HOTEL

Mill Lane, Dedham, nr Colchester,
Essex CO7 6DH
☎ 01206 323250

The **Marlborough Head Hotel** is a popular spot for a drink and a meal, as well as a comfortable, civilised base for tourists. This is true Constable Country, along the border with Suffolk, and the hotel, which dates back to the 15th century, is almost a tourist attraction in its own right, with an interesting history from its origins as a merchant's house.

The Marlborough Head is now in the excellent care of leaseholders Jenny and Manda, and the bar is open all day, every day, for serving drinks – Greene King IPA, Adnams Bitter and Shepherd Neame Spitfire are the regular real ales. Manda is a great chef, winning a reputation for the quality of her cooking that extends

far beyond the bounds of Constable Country. Menus that cater for all tastes mix classics like moules marinière, poached salmon, liver & bacon, sausage & mash and steaks share the list with exotic options such as Japanese-style king prawns, kangaroo and crocodile. The non-smoking restaurant has seats for 80, but such is its popularity that booking is recommended, particularly on Friday and Saturday evenings. Three en suite bedrooms are available all year round for Bed & Breakfast guests.

189 THE FLEECE

27 West Street, Coggeshall, nr Colchester,
Essex CO6 1NS
☎ 01376 561412
e-mail: info@thefleecepub.co.uk
🌐 www.thefleecepub.co.uk

The **Fleece** is a 500-year-old former coaching inn in the pleasant old cloth and lace town of Coggeshall, off the A120 east of Braintree. Hosts John and Barbara Tofts have made it a very popular port of call, both for locals as a regular place to meet for a drink and a chat and for visitors here to see Paycocke's House, the famous Grange Barn and the other nearby attractions.

Greene King IPA heads the list of well-kept ales, and Barbara produces delicious dishes served from opening time right through to 8 o'clock in the evening.

Ham, egg and chips is one of the favourite orders, along with the Sunday roasts, and there's always a good choice for vegetarians. The Fleece has a superb rear beer garden with plenty of picnic benches. No credit cards.

190 THE BELL INN

**The Street, Feering, nr Colchester,
Essex CO5 9QQ
☎ 01376 570375 Fax: 01376 572862**

Alan and Carole Nash, here since 1986, and chef-partner Keith Wilkinson make a great team at **The Bell Inn**. The 16th century pink-washed inn stands on an elevated site overlooking the green in the village of Feering, on the B1024 five miles west of Colchester. Behind the neat exterior with a steeply raked tiled roof, the place is kept in apple pie order, and the beamed lounge bar is a pleasant spot for meeting old friends or making new friends over a glass of beer – Woodforde Wherry and London Pride are among the favourite brews.

Keith and his team prepare a fine selection of dishes served every lunchtime (12 to 2) and from 6.30 to 9.30 Tuesday to Saturday. The menu mixes classics such as prawn cocktail, skate with capers and brown butter and sirloin steak with more unusual options like Thai prawns with sweet chilli dip, or lbraised lamb shank. There's always a good choice for vegetarians. Children are very welcome, and in the summer a marquee on the lawn makes a delightful venue for barbeques and parties, as well as a game of petanque.

191 THE GEORGE INN

**The Street, Shalford, nr Braintree,
Essex CM7 5HH
☎ 01371 850207
🌐 www.thegeorgeshalford.co.uk**

On the main street of Shalford, on the B1053 northwest of Braintree, **The George Inn** is very much a family affair. Owner Stuart Alderson, his brother Stephen the licensee, Stuart's son Scott and Stephen's daughter Tracey all play leading roles in the running of the pub, and although they only took over in April 2006 the word is spreading that this is one of the best places in the region for eating and drinking.

The premises date from the 15th century, and in the bar a fine old brick hearth and other brick features and a panelled serving counter contribute to the pleasant, traditional look. Five real ales, including George Bitter brewed by an Essex brewery specially for the pub, provide

an excellent choice for connoisseurs, and a blackboard announces the daily selection of freshly prepared food. A typical choice could include chargrilled ribeye steak, spinach and ricotta lasagne, chicken supreme with an asparagus cream sauce, and beer-battered plaice with hand-cut chips and petits pois. The pub is open lunchtime and evening and all day Saturday, Sunday and Bank Holidays, and food is served every session except Sunday evening.

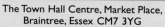

192 BRAINTREE DISTRICT MUSEUM 🏛

The Town Hall Centre, Market Place,
Braintree, Essex CM7 3YG
☎ 01376 328868 Fax: 01376 344345
e-mail: jean@bdcmuseum.demon.co.uk
🌐 www.braintree.gov.uk/museum

Housed in a beautifully converted Victorian school, **Braintree District Museum** has elegant exhibition areas and a faithfully re-created Victorian classroom, where role-play lessons are provided for schools on a daily basis. The permanent galleries tell the fascinating story of the wool trade in North Essex of which Braintree was the medieval  centre, and also of the development of engineering design. Country crafts such as straw plaiting are featured, along with the work of rural artists. A programme of changing exhibitions is a feature of the museum and a range of craft items are available for sale.

193 MOUNTFITCHET CASTLE & NORMAN VILLAGE 🏛

Stansted, Essex CM24 8SP
☎ 01279 813237 Fax: 01279 816391
e-mail:
mountfitchetcastle1066@btinternet.com
🌐 www.gold.enta.net

This historic site gives visitors a glimpse into life as it was over 900 years ago in 1066. The careful reconstruction, as it would have appeared in the Domesday era, enables the study of an 11th century motte and bailey castle and the Norman village which was enclosed within its walls. You can learn about medieval life, early fortifications, weaponry, the construction of dwellings and much more.

Many of the animals and birds to be found in the grounds are rescued and represent those which would have been kept for food by the Normans,

such as fallow deer, sheep, goats, chickens and geese. The Castle Shop carries a comprehensive range of gifts and souvenirs and is open March to November 10am-5pm daily, as is the Castle.

Also here you will find the House on the Hill Toy Museum Adventure. An impressive collection of toys, games and books can be enjoyed by children of all ages and the museum has been greatly improved by the addition of sound effects, animation and hands-on opportunities. Permanent displays of film, theatre and rock'n'roll memorabilia have been added in recent years, as has an exhibition of seaside end-of-the-pier amusements.

194 THE SWAN AT SOUTHROP

Southrop, Gloucestershire GL7 3NU
☎ 01367 850205 Fax: 01367 850517
🌐 www.theswanatsouthrop.co.ul

The **Swan at Southrop** is a fine old inn opposite the village green, located a couple of miles north of Fairford off the A417 or A361. An earlier pub, a dairy and an undertakers were combined to create the Swan, and the result is a hostelry of abundant old-world charm, with real fires, a wealth of artwork on the walls and a real home-from-home atmosphere.

The inn has built up a far-reaching reputation for the quality of both its cooking and its service, which is not a surprise, as owner Graham Williams and chef James Parkinson gained managerial and cooking experience in one of London's most illustrious restaurants, Bibendum in South Kensington. James

takes his inspiration from far and wide on mouthwatering menus that tempt with the likes of duck terrine with fig chutney, escargots de Bourgogne, fillet of halibut with aubergine curry and pork belly with bok choi, shiitake mushrooms, ginger and spring onions. A splendid wine list does full justice to the outstanding food. B&B accommodation is in the pipeline.

195 ALLIUM

No 1 London Street, Fairford,
Gloucestershire GL7 4AH
☎ 01285 712200
e-mail: restaurant@allium.uk.net
🌐 www.allium.uk.net

Housed in distinguished listed premises, **Allium** is well known for its first-class modern British/French cuisine. Book for all meals – lunch and dinner Tuesday to Saturday and for groups of 12 or more on Sunday. The top chef-patron is James Graham.

196 THE EIGHT BELLS

East End, Fairford,
Gloucestershire GL7 4AP
☎ 01285 712369

Fairford has plenty to attract the visitor, and for many visitors the **Eight Bells** is high on the list. For almost 200 years this convivial pub has been welcoming regular customers and 'outsiders', and that tradition is being carried on in fine style by Sue and Paul Wakefield. Their hospitality is second to none, complementing well-kept ales and excellent home cooking. Barbecues are held in the garden in the summer months, and traction engines puff their way round the car park and on the village green during the August Bank Holiday rally.

197 THE TUNNEL HOUSE INN

Tarlton Road, Coates, nr Cirencester,
Gloucestershire GL7 6PW
☎ 01285 770280
e-mail: info@tunnelhouse.com
🌐 www.tunnelhouse.com

The first of many attractive features of the **Tunnel House Inn** is an idyllic rural location. It nestles between the Cotswold villages of Coates and Tarlton close to the source of the River Thames, beside the Thames & Severn Canal. The famous tunnel is just a few yards away. In the delightful bar, Uley Bitter is the resident real ale, and the rotating guest ales all come from Gloucestershire breweries.

The garden is a peaceful summer retreat and a great place for children to play. The main menu of unfussy, well-cooked dishes changes regularly to make the most of seasonal variety, and all the dishes on this and the children's menu are homemade. The pub is open every session for ale, and all day Friday, Saturday and Sunday. Food is served lunchtime and evening every day,

and booking is recommended (but reservations not taken for Sunday lunch). A self-contained barn is a splendid venue for functions and special occasions.

198 THE CROSS INN

Star lane, Avening, nr Tetbury,
Gloucestershire GL8 8NT
☎ 01453 832953
e-mail: thecrossinn@tiscali.co.uk

In the village of Avening, on the B4014 east of Nailsworth, the **Cross Inn** is a popular pub with a good mix of local regulars and visitors. David and Rebecca always have two real ales available in the cosy, welcoming bar, and they

serve a good selection of food Wednesday to Saturday evenings, Saturday lunch (12-2) and Sunday roasts (12-3, best to book). The pub is closed Monday lunchtime unless it's a Bank Holiday.

200 THE RAILWAY INN

Station Road, Cam, nr Dursley,
Gloucestershire GL11 5NS
☎ 01453 543237 Fax: 01453 549192
e-mail: railway@cam.co.uk

The railway disappeared in the 1960s, but the Railway Inn is steaming along in fine style after almost 150 years. Leaseholder John Sweet always has two real ales on the go, and food is served Monday to Saturday lunchtime and Friday evening. There's an aviary and carp pond in the garden.

201 THE SHIP INN

Brimscombe, nr Stroud,
Gloucestershire GL5 2QN
☎ 01453 884388 Fax: 01453 887688

Four real ales and an across-the-board menu brings happy locals and visitors to the **Ship Inn**, which stands just off the A419 close to the Brinscombe Port and Canal Basin.

**Box, nr Minchinhampton,
Gloucestershire GL6 9AE
☎ 01453 832631**

Three miles south off the A46, the Halfway House has quickly established a reputation for serving some of the very finest pub food in the region. Dating from the early 18th century, and an inn since 1779, it was originally called the Crown & Crescent and later the Halfway Inn; the name was changed and the whole place transformed under the new team who took over in October 2005.

The food at the Halfway House is in the experienced and very capable hands of Nigel and Heather, who in the guise of their company Food for Thought have raised the cooking to new heights. The kitchen and restaurant were both totally refurbished at the time of their arrival, providing a fitting setting for the team, who have always been firm in their guiding principle of finding the very best seasonal produce. Just about everything is sourced locally, the main exception being the fish and seafood, which is express-delivered sparkling fresh from St Mawes in Cornwall. Many diners look first of all to

the fish specials, but the European/Mediterranean style of cooking provides something for everyone on menus that change every few weeks to reflect the best the seasons have to offer.

Food of this quality deserves the best wine, and with Jackie from Bona Wines, Nigel and Heather have assembled an excellent, wide-ranging list. Five real ales, including Otter form Taunton, Timothy Taylor Landlord and Wickwar Bob, are kept in A1 condition, and there's even a traditional draught cider, called Black Rat. There are seats for 72 in the stylish, uncluttered restaurant, but such is the pub's popularity that booking is always a good idea; a new, intimate 40-cover area has booth seats and its

own music system. Owner/manager Dawn and Bar manager Paul complete the main team at the Halfway House, which looks all set to take its place at the top of the dining-pub tree. The pub is closed Monday lunchtime except Bank Holidays, and there's no food Sunday evening or Monday.

Note: This Box should not be confused with the Box on the A4 east of Bath. That Box is best known for its tunnel, but it's the Halfway House that's definitely put the Gloucestershire Box on the culinary map.

Dr Crouch's Road, Eastcombe, nr Stroud,
Gloucestershire GL6 7DN
☎ 01452 770261

A stunning location with glorious views is just one of the many attractions of The **Lamb Inn**. It stands in the picturesque village of Eastcombe, east of Stroud and a mile or so north of the A419 Stroud-Cirencester road. Leaseholders Stuart and Karen Rhodes, who have lived in Gloucestershire for nine years, took over here at the end of 2004 and have greatly enhanced the appeal of the inn through hard work, enthusiasm and a real feeling for what their customers want.

The premises date back to 1820, since extended and recently smartly refurbished to retain the best period features while providing up-to-date comfort and amenities. Open every session for ale and all day on Sunday, the inn has two bars that lead down to the conservatory-style dining area.

At the back is a delightful beer garden with a section of decking raised above it. The beer garden,

the decking and part of the dining area enjoy lovely views of the countryside. Deuchars, Bombardier and Abbot Ale are kept in tip-top condition, and food is served between 12 and 2 and from 6.30 to 9 Monday to Saturday and from 12 to 3 and 7 to 9 on Sunday.

The quality of the cooking and the keen prices of food and wine have made The Lamb a very popular destination restaurant, so booking is strongly recommended on Friday, Saturday and Tuesday evenings and for the traditional

Sunday lunch. The printed menu and the daily blackboard specials offer an excellent combination of familiar favourites like lasagne (meat or vegetarian), steaks and the pie and curry of the day, and less usual choices such as tempura prawns with a sweet chilli sauce, pan-fried goat's cheese & bacon salad or Barbary duck with a garlic and orange sauce. There's always a good choice for vegetarians, and room should definitely be kept for one (at least!) of the scrumptious home-made desserts.

203 THE EDGEMOOR INN

Edge, nr Stroud, Gloucestershire GL6 6ND
☎ 01452 813576
e-mail: info@edgemoor-inn.com
⊕ www.edgemoor-inn.com

The **Edgemoor Inn** is a fine Cotswold-stone building dating back some 250 years, commanding glorious views from its location on the falloff the Cotswold escarpment. Resident owners Chris and Jill Bayes put out the welcome mat for all their

customers, whether familiar faces or first-timers, and in the cheerful bat they have excellent real ales on tap, mostly from Gloucestershire breweries. Old Spot and Cats Whiskers are the regulars, and there's usually something to sample from the Wickwar Brewery.

The daily changing blackboard menus, available every lunchtime and evening, always provide plenty of interest

with dishes such as baked camembert, leek croustade, sea bass with a lemon & herb crumb, lamb rogan josh and beef braised in red wine. When the weather is kind, the picnic tables set out on the paved terrace are in demand, with a bonus in the form of super views that stretch for miles over the trees and fields. The inn is closed on Sunday evenings in winter.

204 CHERRY ORCHARD FARM

Newland, nr Coleford,
Gloucestershire GL16 8NP
☎ 01594 832212
⊕ www.cherryorchardfarm.com

Located in the beautiful Forest of Dean, **Cherry Orchard Farm** offers Bed & Breakfast rooms or a well-equipped caravan/camping site. Ideal base for enjoying outdoor pursuits.

205 THE SWAN INN

Brierley, Forest of Dean
Gloucestershire GL17 9DQ
☎ 01594 860460

The impressive **Swan Inn** sits by the A4136 in the village of Brierley, in the heart of the Forest of Dean. Owner Shaun, who runs the pub with Karon, is a terrific chef, basing his dishes as much as possible on produce sourced within a 20-mile radius. His food is served every session except Sunday evening, and booking is

recommended for Sunday lunch. Inside there are open fires while outside decking along the front provides a pleasant spot for enjoying an alfresco drink. Barbecues are popular occasions in the summer months. The Swan is closed on Mondays in winter. A quiz is held on the first and last Sundays of the month.

206 THE YEW TREE

Monmouth Road, Longhope,
Gloucestershire GL17 0QD
☎ 01452 830355

In the village of Longhope, by the A4136
and just off the A40, the **Yew Tree** is very
much a family affair, with John, Lorraine, son
Matthew and daughter Jennifer all playing
their part. The bar is open all day, seven days
a week, for drinks (London Pride and
Wadworths 6X are the regular real ales), and
excellent home-cooked food is served every
lunchtime and evening. The bar and
restaurant have a warm, traditional appeal,
and then pub has a lovely garden at the back.

207 THE KINGS HEAD INN

Birdwood, nr Huntley,
Gloucestershire GL19 3EF
☎ 01452 750348
e-mail:
enquiries@kingsheadbirdwood.co.uk
🌐 www.kingsheadbirdwood.co.uk

Michelle and Kara are the second generation
of the Jefferies family to run the **Kings
Head Inn**. In the family for 25 years, this is
a cheerful pub with a welcome for all.
Situated by the
A40 six miles
west of
Gloucester.
Open for food
and drink all
day every day,
it's a great
place for a

meal, with a new, recently built 60 seater
dining area. They serve pub classics like
cottage pie, beef stew & dumpling as well as
steaks etc. Also popular for an overnight stay.
It has six en suite bedrooms, available all year
round. In the pub garden are ponies, goats
and a children's play area. Everyone welcome.

208 THE LAMB INN

Great Rissington, nr Cheltenham,
Gloucestershire GL54 2LP
☎ 01451 820388 Fax: 01451 820724
🌐 www.thelambinn.com

The **Lamb Inn** at Great Rissington is one of the
Cotswolds' most welcoming country inns, a 300-
year-old building of mellow Cotswold stone, with a
warm, welcoming ambience and a sunny garden.
Paul and Jacqueline Gabriel, here since 2000, have
made The Lamb a thriving hub of the community
and also a great favourite with walkers and holiday
visitors, whether it's for a drink, a snack, a full meal
or an overnight or longer stay.

The chef uses local produce as much as possible
for a truly tempting menu served in the attractive
restaurant, intimately candle-lit in the evening, with
fresh flowers in the summer, a log fire in the winter
and a collection of antique rural implements. Paul's
wide-ranging wine list complements the fine food

perfectly. Each of The Lamb's 14 en suite
guest bedrooms – five on the ground floor
– has its own character, from cosy singles
and twins in country cottage style to garden
suites and four-poster rooms. There's a
quiet lounge with plenty of books,
magazines and local information.

209 HARDING'S WORLD OF MECHANICAL MUSIC

The Oak House, High Street, Northleach,
Gloucestershire GL54 3ET
☎ 01451 860181
e-mail: keith@mechanicalmusic.co.uk
🌐 www.mechanicalmusic.co.uk

Keith Harding's love for mechanical music began 40 years ago in London, and since 1986 he has been based in a handsome period house in the main street of Northleach. Visitors of all ages will find plenty to amuse and delight them, as **Keith Harding's World of Mechanical Music** has the finest selection of musicals and automata, both antique and modern, to be found anywhere. The shop holds a large stock of musical boxes and clocks, puzzles, games and gifts of all kinds, videos and CDs and, for the collector, a large range of books on mechanical music, musical boxes and clocks. It is also a living museum of various kinds of self-playing musical instruments that were the proud possessions of former generations, from a tiny singing bird concealed in a snuff box to a mighty red Welte Steinway reproducing piano of 1907.

The instruments are introduced and played by the guides in the form of a live musical entertainment show, and the tours include demonstrations of restored barrel organs, barrel pianos, musical boxes, polyphons, automata, reproducing pianos, phonographs, gramophones and antique clocks, all in a period setting that enhances the enjoyment of a visit to this unique place. Keith Harding and his dedicated team are specialist craftsmen unrivalled in their field, and everything on show is maintained in perfect working order; customers' pieces can be restored and estimates are free. Opening times are 10 to 6 daily.

210 THE INN AT FOSSEBRIDGE

Fossebridge, nr Cheltenham,
Gloucestershire GL54 3JS
☎ 01285 720721 Fax: 01285 720793
e-mail: info@fossebridgeinn.co.uk
🌐 www.fossebridgeinn.com

The **Inn at Fossebridge** is a popular hostelry that's tops for atmosphere, location, food, drink and accommodation. The Jenkins family are the friendliest of hosts, and the quality dishes that make up their lunchtime and evening menus are among the

most interesting and varied in the region. Eight guest bedrooms with en suite bath or shower are available throughout the year. Another plus is an attractive beer garden with its own little lake.

211 THE FARMERS ARMS

Guiting Power, nr Cheltenham,
Gloucestershire GL54 5TZ
☎ 01451 850358

Robert and Dawn Dean are well established at the **Farmers Arms**, their 300-year-old pub in a village between Cheltenham and Stow-on-the-Wold. It's a cosy, friendly local with a good selection of beers, wines and spirits, a varied blackboard menu and a skittle alley that doubles as a function room.

Looking for:
- *Places to Visit?*
- *Places to Stay?*
- *Places to Eat & Drink?*
- *Places to Shop?*

www.travelpublishing.co.uk

212 THE EBRINGTON ARMS

Ebrington, nr Chipping Campden,
Gloucestershire GL55 6NH
☎ 01385 593223
e-mail: theebringtonarms@btinternet.com

The **Ebrington Arms** is a traditional country
pub dating from the 18th century and located
in a village off the B4036 east of Chipping
Campden. Jan and Iain have quickly made
their mark in this, their first catering venture,
and it's a
popular
place for
a meal,
with
local
produce
featuring
on the
blackboard
menus
of light

lunches and a full evening à la carte choice.
The pub also caters for overnight guests in
three en suite rooms – two doubles and a
family room.

213 THE NATIONAL WATERWAYS MUSEUM

Llanthony Warehouse, Gloucester Docks,
Gloucester, Gloucestershire GL1 2EH
☎ 01452 318200 Fax: 01452 318202
🌐 www.nwm.org.uk

There's so much to see and do for all ages at the
award-winning **National Waterways Museum**
located in a splendid Victorian warehouse in
historic Gloucester Docks. The Museum charts the
fascinating 300-year story of Britain's inland
waterways through interactive displays, touch-screen computers,
working models and historic boats. Visitors can find out what
made the waterways possible, from the business brains and
design genius to the hard work and sweat of the navvies, and
try their hand at designing and painting a narrow boat, building
a canal and navigating a boat through a lock.

The Museum has a working blacksmith's forge, a floor of
displays dedicated to waterway trade and cargoes, a marvellous
interactive gallery and family room where weights and pulleys,
water playareas, period costume, large jigsaw puzzles and brass
rubbings bring history to life in a way that is both instructive
and entertaining. The museum shop sells unusual gifts and
souvenirs and refreshment is provided in the café. There are
computerised information points throughout the Museum and
visitors can even take to the water themselves on a 45-minute
boat trip running along the adjacent Gloucester & Sharpness
Canal between Easter and October. The National Waterways
Museum is owned by the Waterways Trust, which preserves,
protects and promotes our waterway heritage while giving new
life to their future.

The Village, Dymock,
Gloucestershire GL18 2AQ
☎ 01531 890266

The **Beauchamp Arms** is a distinguished old inn standing in the village of Dymock, on the B4215 where it meets the B4216. It's a superb place, well worth seeking out by anyone who appreciates the virtues of a classic English village pub. The bar has an inviting, home-from-home appeal, with polished wooden furniture, a panelled serving counter and a well-chosen collection of artefacts and ornaments. Outside is a pleasant garden with a little pond, and there's plenty of off-road parking.

The pub dates in parts from the late 17th century, and in coaching inn days it was an important stop on the run from Ledbury to Newent, Gloucester and beyond. Since 1997 it has been owned by the Parish Council, and in 2003 the Council made the excellent move of installing John and Linda Griffiths as leaseholders. This friendly couple came here from running a National Trust-owned pub in Worcestershire, and their fine hospitality and Linda's cooking have won many new friends. Her menu of tried and tested pub favourites is supplemented by a daily specials board that might offer spicy

chicken baguette, chilli con carne, chicken balti or smoked haddock hotpot. Food is not served Sunday evening or Monday, otherwise 12 to 2 and 7 to 9, and booking is advisable at the weekend.

The pub has recently undergone a major refit inside and out, including an extension to the lounge bar and the creation of a new toilet block with access for wheelchair users. The early Norman Church of St Mary is well worth a look, but the main claim to fame of the village is its

poetic connections. Rupert Brooke, Edward Thomas, Wilfrid Gibson and Lascelles Abercrombie were founder members of a group known as the Dymock Poets, and were joined later by Robert frost, who sent out his poetry magazine from Dymock's tiny Post Office. Two trails visit locations associated with the poets, after which the most important trail is the one that leads to the Beauchamp Arms and its excellent refreshment.

214 THE HAWBRIDGE INN

Hawbridge, nr Tirley,
Gloucestershire GL19 4HJ
☎ 01452 780316 Fax: 01452 780896
e-mail: info@thehawbridgeinn.demon.co.uk

A wonderful welcome awaits visitors to the **Hawbridge Inn**, which enjoys a superb location on the banks of the River Severn, by the B4213 southeast of Tewkesbury. Tenants Ian and Kelly, who took over in September 2005, have really given the old place a new lease of life, making it a favourite choice both as a lively local and as a destination for motorists and tourists.

Wadworths 6X and IPA are the resident real ales, and Ian and Kelly prepare a good selection of dishes using mainly locally sourced meat, poultry and vegetables. The pub has a large beer garden (summer barbecues when the weather permits) and an adjacent

field for caravanners and campers, with toilets, showers and some electric

hook-ups. The Hawbridge Inn is open every session and all day Friday, Saturday and Sunday. Food is served lunchtime and evenings, and all day in high season.

216 THE IZAAK WALTON

High Street, East Meon, nr Petersfield,
Hampshire GU32 1QA
☎ 01730 823252
e-mail: realrestaurant@btconnect.com
🌐 www.izaak-walton.co.uk

The **Izaak Walton** is a popular free house and restaurant on the main street of East Meon. The décor is a successful mix of traditional and contemporary, with plenty of comfortable settees and chairs in the lounge bar, intimate lighting in the restaurant and a striking collection of pop art on the walls.

Chef-patron Paul sales seeks out the best local produce for his dishes, typified by bouillabaisse with fennel and saffron rouille, Meon trout and almond fishcakes, prime sirloin steaks and a scrumptious warm chocolate brownie with white chocolate mascarpone.

Everything is spot on, and it's a real pleasure to find hand-cut, home-made chips. On the drinks side, the selection of real ales is outstanding, the wine list interesting and accessible, and there's a good choice of malts. Izaak Walton, who lived in the courthouse behind the pub, is not the only distinguished resident of East Meon: Thomas Lord, founder of the cricket ground, is buried in the village churchyard.

217 LOTTS GENERAL STORE & TEA ROOM

West Street, Hambledon, Hampshire PO7 8SN
☎ 023 9263 2452

Lotts General Store & Tea Room is a delightful gem built around 1850 and once the village forge. The Tea Room is open 7.30am to 5pm seven days a week for freshly prepared sandwiches, jacket potatoes, light meals and cakes, with all the baking done on the premises. Also here is a useful village store.

218 PORTSMOUTH HISTORIC DOCKYARD

College Road, HM Naval Base, Portsmouth, Hampshire PO1 3LJ
☎ 023 9286 1533   Fax: 023 9229 5252
e-mail: mail@historicdockyard.co.uk
🌐 www.flagship.org.uk

Portsmouth Historic Dockyard, in the historic dockyard, is home port to three of the greatest ships ever built - *HMS Victory, the Mary Rose and HMS Warrior* - but has many other attractions. The latest of these is the blockbusting Action Stations, where visitors can test their skills and abilities through a series of high-tech interactive displays and simulators. Boat trips round the harbour give a feel of the soul of the city that has been home to the Royal Navy for more than 800 years.

Looking for:

- *Places to Visit?*
- *Places to Stay?*
- *Places to Eat & Drink?*
- *Places to Shop?*

www.travelpublishing.co.uk

219 BURSLEDON WINDMILL

Windmill Lane, Bursledon, Southampton, Hampshire SO31 8BG
☎ 023 8040 4999
e-mail: stensethhouse@aol.com
🌐 www.hants.gov.uk/museum/windmill

The last surviving working windmill in Hampshire was built by a Mrs Phoebe Langtry in 1814 at a cost of £800. Inactive from the time of the depression in the 1880s, the tower mill was restored to full working order between 1976 and 1991. Its sails revolve whenever a good northerly or southerly wind blows, producing stoneground flour for sale. Next to the mill is the Windmill Wood Nature Trail, a woodland habitat supporting a wide range of wildlife including woodpeckers. Open all year - phone for admission times.

222 THE WATERSPLASH HOTEL

The Rise, Brockenhurst, Hampshire SO42 7ZP
☎ 01590 622344   Fax: 01590 624047
e-mail: bookings@watersplash.co.uk
🌐 www.watersplash.co.uk

A quiet, leafy road leads to the **Watersplash Hotel**, centred on a Victorian country house and surrounded by landscaped gardens. This charming hotel, run by Robin Foster and his family, offers the very best in hospitality, and the 23 bedrooms, all with private bathroom en suite, include 3 ground-floor rooms, 4 large family rooms and 2 beautiful four-poster rooms, notably the Colonial Suite with a magnificent double Jacuzzi. The day rooms are spacious and attractive, and in the intimate dining room guests and non-residents are treated to a variety of fine English fare. The hotel's swimming pool is a great favourite with children.

220 THE WHEATSHEAF AT BRAISHFIELD

Braishfield Road, Braishfield, nr Romsey,
Hampshire SO51 0QE
☎ 01794 368372 Fax: 01794 367113
e-mail: jonesthebeer@btinternet.com
🌐 www.wheatsheafbraishfield.co.uk

Experienced hosts Peter and Jenny Jones, along with their delightful Newfoundland terrier Skye, keep the welcome mat out at the **Wheatsheaf at Braishfield**, which attracts customers from near and far with its outstanding food. Everything on the menu is well worth trying, from classics like prawn cocktail, scampi, lamb shanks and steaks, to a trio of sausages in cider and leek gravy, award-winning gumbo

(seafood, chicken or vegetarian) and pork fillet with black pudding and rhubarb compote.

Beers and wines are also serious matters here, and the five rotating real ales usually include Pride of Romsey from a local brewery. The bar areas are a real delight, with slatted wooden floors, wood panelling, beams, open fires and a wealth of prints, vintage posters, copper and brass ornaments, lamps and old farming implements.

221 THE FOREST INN

Lyndhurst Road, Ashurst,
Hampshire SO40 7DU
☎ 023 8029 2331

The **Forest Inn**, a long, low building set back from the road, is a popular country local and an ideal spot to take a break from a journey along the A35. The look and feel in the bars and restaurant is comfortably traditional, with flagstone floors, lots of wood, open fires, brick features, beams, brass and copper, ceramics and old agricultural implements.

Geoff and Mandy Hart have made their pub one of the best in the region not just for hospitality and sociability (darts teams, quiz nights, occasional live music evenings) bit also for food. Mandy and her helpers provide a fine variety of dishes, some traditional – steak & kidney pie, steaks, haddock with chips and mushy peas – others just that little bit

different, and all equally delicious. The lunchtime snack bar menu also offers sandwiches and jacket potatoes. Geoff and Mandy are planning to open a camping/caravan site for the 2006 season.

223 CHEQUERS INN

**Lower Woodside, Lymington,
Hampshire SO41 8AH**
☎ 01590 673415 Fax: 01590 679177
e-mail: enquiries@chequersinn.com
🌐 www.chequersinn.com

Simon Thoyts lived next door to the **Chequers Inn** as a youngster and worked here for many years before buying it in 1999. Simon is a keen amateur yachtsman, and the yachting fraternity are regular visitors to this convivial pub, along with locals and holidaymakers. Simon's friendly Yellow Labrador is a great favourite and always ready for a good walk.

Close to the sea in a quiet country lane, the 16th century pub has an unspoilt period charm. With beams, a wood-burning stove, rough-cast walls and a variety of wooden chairs, pews and tables. A central courtyard has its own bar, and the pub also has an award-winning garden.

Ringwood Best, Forty Niner and London Pride are the regular real ales, and the menus offer anything from a burger to a T-bone steak, with plenty in between for fish-eaters and vegetarians. Children and families welcome.

224 THE KINGS HEAD

**Quay Hill, Lymington,
Hampshire SO41 3AR**
☎ 01590 672709 Fax: 01590 688453

The **Kings Head** is a lovely 16th century inn 200 yards from the quayside in Lymington. Hanging baskets make a colourful show on the outside, while in the bar features include original beams, wood panelling and prints and photographs of old sailing vessels.

Landlord Paul Stratton, his staff and his customers provide an unfailingly cheerful, lively ambience, making it an ideal spot for enjoying a choice of real ales, excellent wines and high-quality food served every day and catering for a wide range of tastes and appetites.

225 THE ROYAL OAK AT FRITHAM

**Fritham, nr Lyndhurst,
Hampshire SO43 7HJ**
☎ 0230 812606 Fax: 02380 814066
e-mail: royaloak-fritham@btconnect.com

At the heart of the New Forest National Park, the **Royal Oak at Fritham** has been in the capable hands of Pauline and Neil McCulloch since 1997. The attractive thatched building, which stands next to the owners' 60-acre mixed farm, has three

separate rooms, each with a splendid, uncluttered old-world appeal. Real ales come straight from the barrel, to quench thirsts or to accompany food served every lunchtime in the bar, dining area or garden. Home-made pies and quiches are particular favourites. Voted Hampshire Life Country Pub of the Year in 2005 it has also been CAMRA Regional Pub of the Year 3 times.

226 BASING HOUSE

Redbridge Lane, Basing, Basingstoke,
Hampshire RG24 7HB
☎ 01256 467294
🌐 www.hants.gov.uk/museum/basingho

Built on a massive scale inside the walls of a
medieval castle, the house was once the
largest private residence in the country. The
ruins, the riverside walk, the dovecotes and
the spectacular 16th century grange barn add
up to an

attraction
of great
appeal,
and the
beauty is
enhanced
by the
re-
created
17th
century garden inside the Tudor walls. The
house was sacked by Cromwell's men, with
Cromwell himself present, after a long and
arduous siege and the ruins include the
historic Garrison gateway.

228 GILBERT WHITE'S HOUSE AND THE OATES MUSEUM

Selborne, Hampshire GU34 3JH
☎ 01420 511275 Fax: 01420 511040
🌐 www.gilbertwhiteshouse.org.uk

Gilbert White's House is a modest 18th
century country house with a glorious garden,
home of the renowned naturalist and author
of *The Natural History of Selborne*, the
Reverend Gilbert White (1720-1793). The
rooms are furnished in period style, with

many of his
possessions on
display, and
the garden has
been restored
to its 18th
century form.
Also here is
the Oates
Museum
commemorating the life and exploits of
Captain Lawrence Oates, who died on
Captain Scott's ill-fated Antarctic Expedition.
Books, gifts and plants are on sale in the
shop, and in the Tea Parlour delicious fare
based on 18th century recipes is served.

227 THE HAWKLEY INN

Pococks Lane, Hawkley, nr Liss,
Hampshire GU33 6NE
☎ 01730 827205
e-mail: nicktroth@aol.com
🌐 www.hawkleyinn.co.uk

The **Hawkley Inn** is a mid-19th century pub
in a picturesque village setting. The area is
very popular with walkers and cyclists, and
Nick Troth and his staff have built up a fine
reputation for excellent hospitality and

friendly,
courteous
service. The
choice of
real ales is
one of the
best in the
region, and
the food
selection
runs from rolls, soup and light snacks to main
courses such as Sussex beef stew, Spicy crab
cakes and Swamp donkey cider sausages. The
peaceful garden is a great asset in the
summer. Four letting bedrooms have been
opened for the 2006 season.

229 THE MAYFLY

**Testcombe, nr Stockbridge,
Hampshire SO20 6AX
☎ 01264 860283
🌐 www.themayfly.com**

The **Mayfly**, built as a farmhouse in the early
19th century, is one of the most famous of
the pubs that stand on the banks of the River
Test, probably the world's best-known trout
river. Behind the gabled exterior, old beams
and a wealth of fishing memorabilia set a

splendidly traditional scene, and when the sun shines,
tables and chairs set out by the river make a truly
wonderful setting for a drink and meal and leaving the
rest of the world far behind.

Food and drink play a vital part in the success of
the Mayfly, with real ales, excellent and numerous
quality wines by glass or bottle to accompany anything
from a light snack to a full-scale meal. The Mayfly is
an inn of immense charm, well worth seeking out for
its wonderful setting and unbeatable hospitality.

230 THE HORSESHOE INN

**The Homend, Ledbury,
Herefordshire HR8 1BP
☎ 01531 632770
e-mail: horseshoeinn@wyenet.co.uk**

Located in Ledbury's main street The
Horseshoe Inn is a traditional black and
white pub dating back to the 1700's. The cosy
Olde Worlde interior has low ceilings,
exposed beams and a real log fire. There is a
pretty secluded beer garden and heated
decked patio for outside drinking and eating.
The pub is Cask Marque accredited with
Timothy Taylors and London Pride being the
resident real ales. A
local guest ale is also
available. Good pub
food is served at
lunchtimes using
local produce where
possible. The Inn
has 2 en suite double
bedrooms and hosts
occasional live music
evenings. Dogs are
welcome.

231 7 SEVEN

**11 The Homend, nr Ledbury,
Herefordshire HR8 1BN
☎ 01531 631317 Fax: 01531 630168
e-mail: jasonhay@btconnect.com**

In a pretty 16th century building on
Ledbury's most famous street, **7 Seven** is a
delightful spot to pass a few hours or to stay
overnight. Wooden beams and open
fireplaces are in keeping with the origins of
the place, providing an intimate, atmospheric
setting for enjoying a drink or a meal. Local
produce features on an all-day menu that
caters for a wide range of tastes and
appetites, and
once a month
Ladies Night
offers pampering,
drinks, nibbles
and
entertainment. 7
Seven has three
en suite
bedrooms for
guests staying
overnight in this
historic town.

232 THE ROYAL OAK

Much Marcle, Herefordshire HR8 2ND
☎ 01531 660300
🌐 www.royal-oak-inn.com

Situated on the A449 on the Ledbury side of Much Marcle, the 200-year-old **Royal Oak** is a splendid free house serving a good selection of real ales, lagers, ciders, wines and excellent food in a very warm, homely ambience. Owners Raf and Karen Calvillo, with head chef Steve Crockett and Cindy Sadler front of house, are continuing the inn's long tradition of hospitality, having bought the pub from Mr & Mrs Stevens of Much Marcle.

High-quality home cooking at very reasonable prices provides an extensive choice of dishes, from sandwiches and jacket potatoes to classics such as breaded plaice and scampi, lasagne, steak & ale pie, cauliflower cheese and

speciality steaks. A large function room is available with seating for 100, with its own bar and facilities, and an old-fashioned wooden skittles alley. Outside is a sunny terrace with stunning views over the rolling Herefordshire countryside. The Royal Oak plays host to skittles and pool teams and provides a meeting place for several clubs and societies. B&B rooms available.

233 THE STABLES

Pitlock Farm, Cradley,
Herefordshire WR13 5LZ
☎ 01886 880273 Fax: 01886 880160

Set in the 60-acre Pitlock Farm, The **Stables** is a peaceful retreat, a place to unwind and enjoy the fresh air and the superb scenery. A barn conversion provides a superbly equipped nest for two, with everything needed for a comfortable self-catering holiday.

234 THE INN ON THE WYE

Kerne Bridge, Goodrich, Ross-on-Wye,
Herefordshire HR9 5QS
☎ 01600 890872 Fax: 01600 890592

In a beautiful location providing great views, the **Inn on the Wye** stands on the B4228 three miles south of Ross-on-Wye. This family-run 18th century inn is open every lunchtime and evening and all day in the summer months for drinks and food. Everything on the menu is freshly prepared and cooked to order, and the well-deserved popularity of the inn means that booking is recommended for all evening meals. The Inn on the Wye is a favourite choice for functions and wedding receptions, and for guests staying overnight there are ten spacious en suite rooms, including two with four-posters.

Looking for:
- *Places to Visit?*
- *Places to Stay?*
- *Places to Eat & Drink?*
- *Places to Shop?*

www.travelpublishing.co.uk

235 YE OLDE FERRIE INN

Symonds Yat West, nr Ross-on-Wye,
Herefordshire HR9 6BL
☎ 01600 890232

On a hilltop in a noted beauty spot on the
River Wye, **Ye Olde Ferrie Inn** is a favourite
place with the many tourists who come to
enjoy the spectacular scenery and the wealth
of leisure activities in the vicinity. Ray and
Julie Anthony welcome all their customers in
the delightful old-world ambience of their
pub, which is open all day for food and drink.
The chefs prepare a huge variety of dishes,
including the popular eat-all-you-want Sunday
carvery, and for guests staying overnight in
this lovely
part of
the world
the in has
seven
comfortable
en suite
bedrooms.
Moorings
and
fishing
available.

237 THE AXE & CLEAVER

Much Birch, Herefordshire HR2 8HU
☎ 01981 540203
e-mail: axeandcleaver@btconnect.com

Dating from the early-18th century, the **Axe
& Cleaver** is an attractive black-and-white
inn with a delightful old-world interior. Open
every day, home-cooked dishes are served
lunch times and evenings using prime
ingredients from local suppliers. The desserts
are not to be missed!

The inn has an attractive garden with great
views and a caravan and camping site with
full facilities.

236 CIDER MUSEUM & KING OFFA DISTILLERY

21 Ryelands Street, Hereford HR4 0LW
☎ 01432 354207
🌐 www.cidermuseum.co.uk

In the heart of the apple growing county of
Herefordshire, the **Cider Museum** explores the
history of traditional cidermaking worldwide. Visit
the reconstructed farm ciderhouse, the Champagne
Cider cellars, the Vat House, and the Cooper's Workshop. See the Herefordshire 'Pomonas'
beautiful books dating from the 19th century which illustrate the varieties of cider apples and perry
pears grown from earliest times
to the present day. Sample the
products made at our own King
Offa Distillery Cider Brandy,
Apple Aperitif and Cider
Liqueur and visit our Gift Shop
or enjoy refreshments at the
Pomona Tea Room.

A Cider making Festival is
held once a year, with various
displays, stalls and competitions,
including apple pressing for
children, Westons Shire Horse
and Dray, beekeeping display
and the Master Cooper
demonstrating the art of making
barrels and casks. Under cover
with free car and coach parking.

238 YEW TREE PUB & LEN GEE'S RESTAURANT

Priors Frome, nr Dormington,
Herefordshire HR1 4EH

☎ 01432 850467 Fax: 01432 851644

🌐 www.lengees.info

e-mail: len@lengees.info

Nestling between Mordiford and Dormington in the little community of Priors Frome, **Len Gees** excels in its dual role of country pub and restaurant. In their pretty black-and-white early-19th century premises, with great views all round, Len and Rose Gees make visitors feel instantly at home with the friendliest of welcomes and a cheerful, lively atmosphere.

Food is big business here, and the menus provide plenty of choice from sandwiches and pub classics like sausage & mash, omelettes, steak & ale pies in the bar along side the constantly changing à la carte menu with items such as 'local fallow venison chops on celeriac and potato gnocchi with red currant and damson compot' or 'baked halibut steak with sweet peppers, red onions and olives'. Naturally the à la

carte menu is also available in Len Gee's restaurant and conservatory where the

popular Carvery (4 large joints of meat and 15-20 fresh vegetables - return visits to the carvery too!) is also available on Wednesday, Thursday and Sunday lunchtimes and Saturday evenings. Children are welcome, and the pub has a garden, terrace and off-road parking. Closed all day Tuesdays.

239 THE GOLDEN CROSS INN

Sutton St Nicholas,
Herefordshire HR1 3AZ

☎ 01432 880274

🌐 www.goldencrossinn.com

Sutton St Nicholas is a picturesque village off the A49 or A465 a short 4 mile drive north of Hereford City Centre. One of the best reasons for a visit is to enjoy the hospitable ambience of the **Golden Cross**. This attractive inn has an elegant contemporary style while retaining the appeal of its early-18th century origins, providing a really super setting for a drink or a meal. Popular orders in the restaurant include chargrilled Hereford steaks and the day's fish and game specials.

240 THE FIR TREE INN

Much Cowane, nr Bromyard,
Herefordshire HR7 4JN

☎ 01531 640619 Fax: 01531 640663

The **Fir Tree Inn** is a fine old village inn located off the A465 or A4103 northeast of Hereford. Beams, whitewashed walls and panelling assist the traditional look in the bar areas, where thirsts are quenched by a good selection of drinks headed by Timothy Taylor's brews and a local real ale. The food is a

popular side of the business, and favourite dishes on the menu of pub

classics include beer-battered cod, the day's puff pastry-topped pie and a seriously hot chilli con carne. The reward awaiting anyone who can finish the mighty 32oz rump steak is a free starter or pudding. The Fir Tree is open every lunchtime and evening and all day Friday and Saturday.

241 THE GREEN DRAGON

Bishops Frome, Herefordshire WR6 5BP
☎ 01885 490607

South of Bromyard on the B4214 road to Ledbury, the **Green Dragon** is a pub of great charm and character, with public areas featuring massive old beams, flagstone floors and real fires in splendid hearths. Hosts Simon and Alison have made this a very popular spot,

where the locals come to enjoy a good choice of real ales and tasty home-cooked food. The pub is open Monday to Thursday evenings and all day Friday, Saturday and Sunday. Food is served Friday and Saturday lunches and Monday to Saturday evenings.

242 THE STOCKTON CROSS INN

Kimbolton, nr Leominster, Herefordshire HR6 0HD
☎ 01568 612509
e-mail: enquiries@stocktoncross.co.uk
🌐 www.stocktoncross.co.uk

On the A4112, just off the A49 north of Leominster, the **Stockton Cross Inn** has been an inn ever since it was built around 1570. The inn is owned and run by Stephen and Julia Walsh, who are proud of the fact that all the food served in the restaurant

is prepared in the kitchen for fresh, locally sourced ingredients. The blackboard menus offer an excellent choice for all tastes, including vegetarian and seasonal fish and game, and the food can be accompanied by some well-chosen wines or real ales. Booking is recommended at the weekend.

243 HERGEST CROFT GARDENS

Kington, Herefordshire HR5 3EG
☎ 01544 230160 Fax: 01544 232031
e-mail: gardens@hergest.co.uk
🌐 www.hergest.co.uk

Four gardens for all seasons from spring bulbs to autumn colour include an old-fashioned kitchen garden growing unusual vegetables, with spring and summer borders and roses. Brilliantly coloured rhododendrons and azaleas up to 30 feet grow in Park Wood with over 60 champion trees in one of the finest collections in the British Isles.

245 WALFORD COURT

Walford, nr Leintwardine, Shropshire SY7 0JT
☎ 01547 540570
e-mail: enquiries@romanticbreak.com
🌐 www.romanticbreak.com

Set in 20 acres of gardens and grounds, **Walford Court** is a perfect spot for a relaxing break in tranquil, scenic surroundings. The two lavishly furnished, beamed guest rooms are the Aragon Suite, with a carved oak four-poster, en suite bathroom and sitting room, and Prince Arthur's Room, with a king-size country-style wooden bed

and a large en suite bathroom. Breakfast is a real treat, with home-made muffins included, and lunches and evening meals are available by arrangement. The building dates back 500 years, but the yew tree in the garden is 100 years older!

244 YE OLDE OAK INN

Wigmore, Herefordshire HR6 9UJ
☎ 01568 770247

The village of Wigmore stands just off the A4110 Hereford to Leintwardine road, and the short detour from this road is well worth while to enjoy the hospitality provided by leaseholders Penny and Geoff at **Ye Olde Oak Inn**.

Four rotating real ales, including the local favourite Wye Valley Bitter, are on tap to quench thirsts, and in the conservatory dining area excellent traditional English food, home-cooked using locally sourced ingredients, is served every session except Sunday evening; the Sunday lunch, including a choice of roasts, is particularly popular, so booking is strongly recommended to be sure of getting a table. The 300-year-old pub hosts special food-

themed evenings to celebrate occasions like St David's Day, St Patrick's

Day and St George's Day. An even shorter detour in the other direction off the A4110 leads to the imposing ruins of Wigmore Castle, which protected the village and the surrounding area for many centuries until the Civil War.

246 THE LION HOTEL

High Street, Leintwardine,
Shropshire SY7 0JZ
☎ 01547 540203

James Johnson and Anthony Ryan have quickly made their mark at the **Lion Hotel**, a typical country pub standing by the river on the main street of Leintwardine, close to the A4113/A4110 between Ludlow and Knighton. Top-class cooking brings visitors from all over the region, and the extensive choice offers something for everyone. Battered cod with chips and mushy peas, steak & kidney pie and chicken curry are among the lunchtime favourites, while the inventive dinner menu tempts with such dishes as smoked haddock risotto, grilled salmon with stir-fried vegetables and

a port & plum sauce, and roast chicken breast wrapped in bacon with celery mash and braised lentils.

The excellent food is complemented by a well-chosen selection of wines, and three regularly changing real ales area always available. The delightful riverside garden is a definite bonus for drinkers and diners, and guests visiting the Lion have a wealth of local attractions both scenic and historic to discover at leisure.

445

247 ST ALBANS MUSEUMS

Hatfield Road, St Albans,
Hertfordshire AL1 3RR
☎ 01727 819340 Fax: 01727 837472
e-mail: history@stalbans.gov.uk
🌐 www.stalbansmuseums.org.uk

The fascinating story of historic St Albans,
from the departure of the Romans to the
present day, is told at the **Museum of St
Albans**. The range of lively displays covers
the rise of the market town that grew up
around its abbey through to its development
as a
modern
commuter
city. The
museum is
also home
to the
famous
Salaman
Collection

of trade and craft tools. Verulamium, the
Museum of everyday life in Roman Britain, is
home to some of the best Roman mosaics
and wall plasters outside the Mediterranean,
with re-created Roman rooms.

249 TALLY HO

London Road, Barkway, nr Royston,
Hertfordshire SG8 8EX
☎ 01763 848389
e-mail: info@tallyho-barkway.co.uk
🌐 www.tallyho-barkway.co.uk

Since taking over the **Tally Ho** in 1997, Paul
and Roz have won many friends with their
excellent hospitality. Three constantly
changing real ales, generally from smaller
breweries, are drawn from the barrel, and in
their time
here Paul and
Roz reckon
they've
featured
more than
3,000
different
brews. Wines
and spirits

are also very well represented, but food is a
strong point, too, and the resident chefs
produce a good choice of dishes to enjoy
every session. Plans include creating four en
suite rooms for B&B guests. The Tally Ho
has a lovely big garden with lawns and trees.

248 HATFIELD HOUSE

Hatfield, Hertfordshire AL9 5NQ
☎ 01707 287010 Fax: 01707 287033
🌐 www.hatfield-house.co.uk

Hatfield House, where Elizabethan history began,
is a superb redbrick Jacobean mansion built by
Robert Cecil, 1st Earl of Shaftesbury and Chief
Minister to King James I, in 1611. The house has
been in the Cecil family ever since, and is the home of the Marquess of Salisbury. Superb examples
of Jacobean craftsmanship can be seen throughout the house, notably in the Grand Staircase with
its elaborately carved wood and in the stained-glass
window in the private chapel. The state rooms are

treasure houses of the
finest furniture, world-
renowned paintings,
exquisite tapestries and
historic armour; they
include the fabulous
Marble Hall, the Long
Gallery and King James'
Drawing Room.
The gardens at

Hatfield House are a great attraction in their own right, laid out by
John Tradescant the Elder and planted by him with many species
never previously grown in England. The gardens, where restoration
started in Victorian times and still continues, include herb, knot and
wilderness areas

A variety of arts and crafts events are hosted throughout the
season, inlcuding gardening and flower shows.

Great Cambridge Road (A10), High Cross,
nr Ware, Hertfordshire SG11 1AA
☎ 01920 462996
e-mail: mikijor@aol.com

On the Great Cambridge Road (A10) a short drive north of ware, the **White Horse** is a perfect place to pause on a journey, but it also enjoys a growing reputation as a fine destination restaurant. Two cottages dating back to 1608 were converted a century later into this splendid country pub, where Miki Jordan is the chef-proprietor and Jacqui Thorne her business partner.

Hanging baskets make a colourful show throughout the year at the front and back, while the interior of the pub has abundant old-world appeal, with beams, brasses and mugs, real fires and country chairs set at

gleaming polished tables. Outside is a walled patio area with garden furniture and patio heaters, and beyond the car park is a grassed area with swings and a slide. Miki is a terrific chef, and her specialities include a super steak & ale pie and some scrumptious desserts. The majority of her ingredients come from local sources, and is shown in the fresh, wholesome dishes that bring in the crowds – Sunday lunch is always a full house, so booking is definitely recommended, also for Friday and Saturday evenings. Food is not served on Sunday evening or all day Monday (except Bank Holidays), otherwise from 12 to 2 (to 3 Saturday and Sunday) and 7 to 9.

To accompany the food or to quench a country thirst there are two real ales on tap (more planned), with Youngs Bitter the resident brew. Miki and Jacqui plan to make guest accommodation available, at which point the White Horse will surely become a popular spot for an overnight or longer stay, making the most of its location. The A10 ensures easy access north and south, and for motorists and business people the pub will provide a pleasant alternative to staying in a town hotel.

All are welcome to put their brains to the test at the pub quiz, which takes place on the second Thursday of each month.

251 THE RED LION

I High Street, Stanstead Abbots, nr Ware,
Hertfordshire SG12 8AA
☎ 01920 410056 Fax: 01920 421858
e-mail: mmirhosseini@msm.com

The Red Lion is open
all day for drinks and
every lunchtime and
evening (also Thursday
to Saturday evenings)
for excellent home-
cooked food.

252 THE BRITISH HOTEL

North Quay, Douglas, Isle of Man
☎ 01624 616663

Overlooking the harbour at Douglas, the
British Hotel is not a hotel but a convivial
Okells pub open all day Monday to Saturday
and lunchtime and evening on Sunday. The
three-storey brick-and-timbered pub is a
popular local, and the bar, with its long
service counter, brass bar rail and rows of
gleaming glasses, is a great place to meet for a
drink and a
chat. Snacks
and light
meals are
served all day,
and the always
sociable pub is
particularly
lively during
the live music
sessions on
Thursday to
Saturday
evenings.

255 HARBOUR LIGHTS

The Promenade, Peel, Isle of Man
☎ 01624 495157
St Paul's Square, Ramsey, Isle of Man
☎ 01624 814692

There are two **Harbour Lights** on the Isle
of Man, and they are deservedly among the
most popular café-restaurants on the island.
One is in a 19th century building on the
Promenade at Peel, overlooking the sandy
beach and close to the beautiful Castle. The
other is in modern premises in a small
shopping precinct in Ramsey a short distance
from the harbour and a working boatyard.
Both are open for breakfast, lunch, afternoon
tea, drinks and snacks, and many of the
dishes feature
Manx specialities
including fish and
shellfish, kippers,
cheese and ice
cream. The
Ramsey branch
also opens on
Thursday, Friday
and Saturday
evenings.

256 THE GREAVES

Sunnycroft, Laxey, Isle of Man IM4 7PD
☎ 01624 861500

Super views are a bonus for guests at **The
Greaves**, which offers home-from-home
comfort overlooking the village and the newly
restored Snaefell Wheel. Patsy Quirk has
many repeat visitors to her delightful
detached house, which has four comfortable
rooms, two with en suite facilities. The tariff
is based on Bed & breakfast, with evening
meals by arrangement. Ideally situated for
those wanting a walking holiday and within
easy reach of the electric trams and buses.

ISLE OF MAN

253 JAKS

43 Loch Promenade, Douglas,
Isle of Man IM1 2LZ
☎ 01624 663786 Fax: 01624 677859
e-mail: andy@jakspub.com
🌐 www.jakspub.com

Built in Victorian times as a hotel, **Jaks** is now one of the Island's most popular and liveliest pub-restaurants, as well as one of the friendliest. On a huge corner site in the heart of the town's life, both day and night, it attracts a very broad-based clientele, from among both Manx residents and the many thousands who visit the island each year.

Customers can enjoy a wide range of drinks in the open-plan ground-floor public bar; the bar stocks one of the largest selections of draught beers on the Island, a doubles bar operates every day, and there's also a happy hour every day. Traditional pub dishes are served here, including vegetarian and fish dishes and Jaks classics like the 'greasy spoon' plate of sausage, egg, chips and beans. Steps lead down to the stylishly, recently refurbished restaurant with full table service, where the main menu offers more familiar favourites as well as more unusual options such as seafood gratin, mushroom medley, Cajun chicken sizzler and grilled swordfish with lemon and parsley butter. Sunday lunch, served from 12 to 5, adds three roasts to classics like cod &

chips and sirloin and rump steaks. Scrumptious desserts like spotted dick or apple pie round things off in style. Children are always welcome, and can choose from their own menu.

Jaks is not just a place for good food and drink, it's also one of the most sociable spots on the Island. Live bands perform every Friday, and it's definitely the number one place for football fans, with several screens ensuring that no big game is missed. All the major attractions of Douglas are close at hand, including the Manx Museum and the Great Union Camera. Visitors can take a tram ride along the promenade, a steam train to Port Erin or an electric tram to Ramsey. And when they return to Douglas, they can be sure that the staff at Jaks will be ready and willing to provide the hospitality and good cheer that have made this such a popular place.

449

Mona Drive, off Central Promenade,
Douglas, Isle of Man IM2 4LF
☎ 01624 675663 Fax: 01624 661545
e-mail: mail@welbeckhotel.com
🌐 www.welbeckhotel.com

The **Welbeck Hotel** has been owned and run by the George family for over 20 years, and the warm, genuine welcome they extend to all their guests is one of the reasons for its popularity. Just off the main promenade, but 100 yards up the hill, its location is fairly quiet, yet convenient for all the shops, sights and entertainment Douglas has to offer, as well as the seafront.

The main accommodation comprises 27 en suite rooms, some with sea views, all with en suite facilities and all particularly well equipped. Centrally heated and double-glazed, they have digital TV with text, remote control and two radio stations, modem points, direct-dial telephone, hairdryer, iron, trouser press and hospitality tray. Some rooms are suitable for families, a lift serves all floors and the hotel offers a laundry service – a communal washing room is also available.

As an alternative to these rooms, the Welbeck also has seven excellent one-bedroom apartments (one of them has two bedrooms) with bathrooms, lounge-diners and partitioned kitchen areas. Top-floor

rooms enjoy sea views. Guests in the apartments can make use of all the hotel's amenities, which include a small multi-gym with steam room and shower.

In the Conservatory Restaurant, which is also open to non-residents, the chefs prepare a fine selection of excellent dishes of worldwide inspiration, traditional and contemporary, from Manx kipper pâté and steak & mushroom pie to Chinese-style spare ribs, steamed halibut steak with a sweet chilli sauce, pork loin with a devilled sauce and veal escalope with redcurrant jus. The hotel caters equally well for business

and leisure visitors, and the Rosebery Suite is a versatile function room suitable for anything from wedding receptions to conferences and staff training. The Welbeck is a very pleasant, civilised base for touring the Island, and the road and rail connections from Douglas put all the attractions within easy reach. The owners and staff are well geared up to the needs of their guests, with advice on all the Island's places of interest and making bookings for golf and riding.

257 BALLACHRINK FARM COTTAGES

Ballaragh Road, Laxey, Isle of Man IM4 7PJ
☎ 01624 862155 Fax: 01624 628520
e-mail: enquiries@iomcottages.com
⊕ www.iomcottages.com

Pretty black-and-white cottages reached up a private drive off the Ballaragh Road (B11) provide very comfortable and atmospheric self-catering accommodation. The cottages, available throughout the year, stand in five acres of pasture land overlooking Laxey Bay, with lovely views out to sea and towards the hills. The older cottages have been converted from a variety of stone barns and outbuildings, retaining original charm and character while offering every modern comfort and convenience.

All the cottages are double-glazed, with gas central heating, and the bathrooms and kitchens are fitted to the highest standards. The single-storey Cherry Cottage sleeps four; the Doll's House, with a double bedroom,

is a perfect choice for a honeymoon or romantic break; Fuchsia Cottage is also a cosy nest for two; single-storey Holly Cottage sleeps four; and Primrose Cottage is a two-storey 'upside-down' cottage, arranged with the bedrooms below the living area to take advantage of the wonderful views.

259 DUNCANS DINER & COFFEE SHOP

Michael Street, Peel, Isle of Man IM5 1HB
☎ 01624 844405

Michael Street is a narrow, winding street in the heart of Peel, and among the various shops and other outlets is **Duncans Diner & Coffee Shop**. Open throughout the day from Monday to Saturday, it's run by Heather and Brian Horne, who have made it one of the most popular eating places on the whole island.

Warm, friendly and delightfully unpretentious, Duncans serves a good choice of generously plated dishes, with fish & chips and lasagne up among the favourites. Besides the main menu there's an 'everyday pensioners special' and a children's menu for the under-

12s. Peel, traditionally the centre of the Manx fishing industry, has plenty to offer the visitor, including a newly opened museum, a historic sandstone castle, a picturesque harbour and a sandy beach. And after a stroll round town, guests can rely on Heather and Brian to provide excellent refreshment at their excellent diner.

258 THE CREEK INN

The Quayside, Peel, Isle of Man IM5 1AP
☎ 01624 842216
e-mail: jeanmcaleer@manx.net

On the quayside at Peel, with the Castle and the new museum close by, the **Creek Inn** is open all day for both food and drink. Okells and four guest real ales are kept in prime condition to quench thirsts, and a fine variety of excellent home-cooked food is served all day. The blackboard specials range from loaded

potato skins to luxury fish pie, rib-eye steak, vegetable goulash, fresh lobster, home-made Manx kipper pate and the famous Manx queenie scallops. The Creek is a pleasant family pub, and four self-catering units provide a comfortable base for touring the Island.

261 REGENT HOUSE

The Promenade, Port Erin,
Isle of Man IM9 6LG
☎ 01624 833454
e-mail: regenthouse@manx.net
⊕ regentguesthouse.co.uk

Regent House is a friendly, homely guest house on the promenade at Port Erin. The house has nine guest rooms, seven of them with en suite facilities, the others with close-at-hand private bathrooms. Resident owner Nicola Kinley offers a good choice for breakfast, and she will also provide evening meals by arrangement. On the southwestern tip of the island, Port Erin has a magnificent beach, and there are wonderful sea views from Regent House.

260 THE FALCON'S NEST HOTEL

Station Road, Port Erin,
Isle of Man IM9 6AF
☎ 01624 834077   Fax: 01624 835370
e-mail: falconsnest@enterprise.net
⊕ www.falconsnesthotel.co.uk

On the Promenade at Port Erin, overlooking a beautiful sandy beach, the **Falcon's Nest Hotel** is an impressive mid-19th century building with balconied windows and crenellated walls. Bob and Loreto Potts have created a delightful relaxed ambience, and the excellent service, first-class

bedrooms and great food appeal to a wide cross-section of visitors. Those visitors include locals and families from the Island, tourists, walkers, golfers, bike racing fans and railway buffs (there are several interesting heritage railways on the Island).

Food is big business here, with snacks and meals served in the two public bars, where there's a good choice of CAMRA

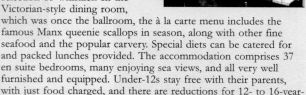

approved real ales and an amazing selection of whiskies. In the Victorian-style dining room, which was once the ballroom, the à la carte menu includes the famous Manx queenie scallops in season, along with other fine seafood and the popular carvery. Special diets can be catered for and packed lunches provided. The accommodation comprises 37 en suite bedrooms, many enjoying sea views, and all very well furnished and equipped. Under-12s stay free with their parents, with just food charged, and there are reductions for 12- to 16-year-olds. The hotel also has excellent function and meeting facilities, and can arrange free transfers to and from the airport and harbour.

262 THE ROADSIDE INN

Nettlestone Green, Seaview, nr Ryde,
Isle of Wight
☎ 01983 616969
e-mail: roadsid.hollan@btconnect.com
🌐 www.roadsideinn.co.uk

The **Roadside Inn** is a handsome and substantial 100-year-old hostelry by the road leading into

Seaview. The choice of real ales changes regularly, and snacks and light meals are served throughout the day. The menu offers popular favourites and daily specials such as lamb & spinach curry or Spanish-style pork. With three en suite guest bedrooms, the Roadside is a good holiday base for visitors to the Island, and the pleasant village of Seaview commands fine views of Spithead, the open sea and the forts built to defend the Solent and Portsmouth from the threat of invasion by Napoleon.

263 THE PILOT BOAT INN

Station Road, Bembridge, Isle of Wight
☎ 01983 874101
e-mail: michelle@pilotboatinn.com
🌐 www.pilotboatinn.com

On the eastern edge of the Island, the **Pilot Boat Inn** is surely one of the most distinctive on the Island or indeed anywhere else. It's designed to look like a boat, complete

with portholes for windows, and all is shipshape in the wooden-floored bar.
London Pride, Greene king IPA and guest ales and snacks are served all day, and the main evening menu lists classics such as steaks, scampi, chicken kiev, burgers and specials such as fish pie or sweet & sour pork. Wednesday is quiz night, and there's live music on Friday and Sunday evenings.

265 THE OCEAN DECK INN

High Street, Sandown,
Isle of Wight PO36 8AE
☎ 01983 403960

boosted by summer visitors, and both groups are made very welcome at the **Ocean Deck Inn**, one of the Island's most favourably placed refreshment spots.

This modern, purpose-built pub-restaurant overlooks the sea, and when the weather is fine, patio dining with a sea view is a treat not to be missed. The Ocean deck is very much food driven, with food served all

Sandown, with its miles of flat, safe sands, a traditional pier and abundant sports and leisure facilities, is the Isle of Wight's leading holiday resort. The resident population is considerably

day in the summer months. The Sunday carvery is particularly popular, and booking is recommended. The Ocean deck also serves a full range of beers and lagers, as well as other drinks both alcoholic and non-alcoholic.

264 THE DRIFTWOOD BEACH BAR & GRILL

Culver Parade, Sandown, Isle of Wight
☎ 01983 404004
e-mail: sean@driftwood.co.uk
🌐 www.driftwoodbeachbar.com

The **Driftwood** is one of the Island's most popular bar/restaurants, with an unbeatable location right on the beach. When the weather is fine, the tables and chairs set outside are in great demand, and when the wind blows customers can enjoy the views from the comfort of  the picture-windowed bar. The Driftwood serves an excellent selection of ales, designer beers and lagers, and food ranges from light snacks to steaks and daily specials such as fish pie or lemon chicken skewers.

268 BILLY BUNTERS

High Street, Shanklin,
Isle of Wight PO37 6JN
☎ 01983 867241
e-mail: billy.bunters@btconnect.com

On a prominent corner site on the main street of Shanklin, **Billy Bunters** has a friendly, sociable owner in Andy Campbell, who welcomes customers of all ages. It's open long hours (11am to 3am) every day of the year, serving rotating guest real ales in the summer and a choice of food – light snacks all  day in the bar and à la carte dishes such as beef Madras and chicken marinated in lemon and honey in the non-smoking upstairs restaurant.

266 THE ESPLANADE HOTEL

The Esplanade, Shanklin,
Isle of Wight PO37 6BQ
☎ 01983 863001
e-mail: bookings@esplanadeshanklin.co.uk
🌐 www.esplanadeshanklin.com

Bang on the seafront at Shanklin, the **Esplanade Hotel** is a very pleasant holiday base that caters for all ages and the whole family. Keith and Rosemary Thornton are the friendly, hardworking hosts, and the 18 guest bedrooms – ranging from singles to family rooms – all have en suite facilities, television and hot  drinks trays. Some have balconies looking out to sea. Light snacks are available on request, and the main menu includes excellent fresh fish dishes.

269 GLENBROOK HOTEL

6 Church Road, Shanklin,
Isle of Wight PO37 6NU
☎ 01983 863119 Fax: 01983 866562
🌐 www.glenbrookhotelshanklin.co.uk

Glenbrook is a small, attractive thatched hotel in the heart of Shanklin, minutes away from all the attractions that famous old town has to offer. It overlooks the Chinewaters, where guests can relax in a peaceful garden that is sunny by day and floodlit by night. Guest accommodation comprises five en suite rooms with television and tea/coffee making facilities; some have four-posters. Snacks are available all day in the  lounge bar or garden, and traditional English dishes are served by candlelight in the atmospheric Henry VIII's Kitchen Grill Lodge. Parties are catered for in the Banqueting Room.

267 THE CHANNEL VIEW HOTEL

Hope Road, Shanklin,
Isle of Wight PO37 6EH
☎ 01983 862309
e-mail: enquiries@channelviewhotel.co.uk
🌐 www.channelviewhotel.co.uk

A guest who described the **Channel View Hotel** as 'a lovely happy place' echoes the views of many who have stayed at the Gino family's hotel. It overlooks Shanklin Bay, with its sandy beaches and the safe bathing for which the Island is renowned, and most of the Island's attractions are within an easy drive.

The family owners personally oversee all aspects if this popular hotel and are justly proud of their reputation for quality with a warm welcome, efficient service, excellent food and attention to detail. All the guest bedrooms are en suite and have recently been refurbished to a very high standard. They are well appointed, beautifully decorated and tastefully furnished. Each has a full tiled bathroom with either a bath with shower over or a freestanding shower, and all are equipped with television, radio-alarm, direct-dial phone, hairdryer and welcome tray. There are three tariffs. Select Rooms are situated at the side or the rear of

the hotel, offering the hotel's excellent standards at competitive prices; Premier Rooms at either side enjoy a side view of the sea, while the top-of-the-range Premier Plus Rooms offer the luxury of front-facing sea views.

The front entrance to the hotel is reached by a flight of 20 steps, but reception can also be reached by a ramped entrance just to the side of the building. The day kicks off with a traditional English breakfast, and the three experienced chefs prepare a tempting, varied dinner menu with a selection of British, Continental and

vegetarian dishes. The hotel's amenities include an indoor heated swimming pool with integral spa, sauna and solarium. Guests can also indulge themselves with a relaxing facial, aromatherapy or reflexology massage by the well-qualified holistic therapist. In the Alverstone Room musical entertainment is provided several days a week, and the room has a large maple sprung dance floor and a well-stocked bar.

270 THE WORSLEY

High Street, Wroxall, nr Ventnor,
Isle of Wight PO38 3BW
☎ 01983 853144

David and Maxine are the enthusiastic new
hosts at **The Worsley**, and the welcome they
offer extends to visitors of all ages. This
village pub in the centre of Wroxall's main
street is a delightful spot to pause for a drink
or a meal, either in the bar or out in the beer
garden, where there's a children's play area.
The Worsley is open lunchtime and evening
and all day in the summer months.
Wednesday is quiz night. The Worsley has its
own large car park.

271 BROCKLEY BARNS

Manor Farm Lane, Calbourne Road, nr
Newport, Isle of Wight PO30 5SR
☎ 01983 537276
e-mail: mitchellbrockley@aol.com
🌐 www.brockleybarns.co.uk

Brockley Barns comprise four cottages for
holiday rental at the heart of the Island.
Bluebell, Buttercup, Daisy and Lavender, with
two or three main bedrooms, are all fully
equipped for a self-catering holiday, and in
addition to the
bedrooms
they all have
double sofa
beds in the
living area.
Cots and high
chairs can be
provided at no
extra cost, and

there's a laundry room next to the cottages.
Each has its own patio, and a barbecue area is
a shared facility. Two miles from Newport,
Brockley Barns are conveniently placed for all
the attractions of the Island, both inland and
on the coast.

272 THE NEEDLES PARK

Alum Bay, Isle of Wight PO39 0JD
☎ 0870 458 0022
🌐 www.theneedles.co.uk

Set above the world-famous sand cliffs,
overlooking The Needles Rocks and
Lighthouse, the Park offers a range of
attractions for all the family including Alum
Bay Glass Studio, Isle of Wight Sweet
Manufactory and the popular chairlift to the
beach to
view the
Island's
most
dramatic
landmark.
A variety
of gift
shops
and
places to
eat, as

well as childrens attractions, can also be
enjoyed here. Special events include 'Magic in
the Skies' fireworks finale very Thursday
throughout August.

273 CHALK B&B

8 Sutherland Close, Chalk, nr Gravesend,
Kent DA12 4XJ
☎ 01474 350819
e-mail: chalkbandb1@activemail.co.uk
www.bedandbreakfast-gravesend.co.uk

Homely, friendly, quality accommodation,
centrally heated. T/V and tea/coffee facilities
in rooms, towels/bathrobes provided. Off
street parking. Full English Breakfast.
Evening meal and laundry service by
arrangement.

274 LADS OF THE VILLAGE ¶

Elizabeth Street, Stone, nr Dartford,
Kent DA9 9AT
☎ 01322 382083

Stone, on the outskirts of Dartford, is best known for its magnificent, treasure-filled church, but many visitors to this quiet village make tracks for another destination – the **Lads of the Village**. This charming old inn was first granted a licence for selling beer in 1833 and assumed its present role in 1872.

Tastefully decorated and furnished, the bars feature an interesting collection of period local lectures and photographs, and behind the pub is a pleasant secluded garden that commands views of the Queen Elizabeth Bridge over the Thames. Host Sean Holland, here since 1978, certainly knows what his customers want, starting with a welcome that is equally warm for familiar faces and first-timers. A good range of real ales is always available, along with the usual beers, lagers, spirits and soft drinks, and a menu of tasty snacks is served every lunchtime.

275 THE PEPPERBOX INN ¶

Fairbourne Heath, nr Ulcombe,
Kent ME17 1LP
☎ 01622 842558 Fax: 01622 844218
e-mail: pbox@nascr.net

In their cosy country inn overlooking acres of farmland, Sarah and Geoff Pemble are continuing the family tradition of hospitality started by Sarah's parents nearly 50 years ago. Along with their cats and collies they welcome visitors to the **Pepperbox Inn** into

an atmospheric bar with hop-hung beams, copper pans and kettles and a variety of inviting  chairs and sofas. A good selection of real ales is always available, and the home-cooked food ranges from light snacks to bar meals and a full restaurant menu.

276 THE GUN AND SPITROAST

The Heath, Horsmonden, Kent TN12 8HT
☎ 01892 722925
e-mail: info@gunandspitroast.co.uk
🌐 www.gunandspitroast.co.uk

In the lovely village of Horsmonden with its tree-lined green at its heart, **The Gun and Spitroast**, a lovely 16th century coaching inn plays host to one of the country's few remaining inglenook spitroasts, where beef, pork and venison are cooked slowly over a large apple log fire and included on the a la carte menu, served in the oak beamed candlelit restaurant. Even the bar menu consists of

home-cooked food sourced and brought in fresh and locally where possible.

The pub is very family friendly and in the summer months benefits from a patio rose garden and a large children's play area. If you are looking for that quintessentially English country pub with roaring log fires in the winter and fragrant gardens in the summer you will always find it here at the Gun and Spitroast.

277 THE BARNFIELD OAST

Mount Pleasant, Lamberhurst,
nr Tunbridge Wells, Kent TN3 8LY
☎ 01892 890346 Fax: 01892 891246
e-mail: info@barnfieldoast.co.uk
🌐 www.barnfieldoast.co.uk

Once a familiar part of the working life of Kent, its oast houses have survived in a variety of new roles. **Barnfield Oast House**, along with Oast Cottage and Orchard Cottage, are set in 18 acres of farmland reached down a quiet country lane, providing first-class self-catering family accommodation

in the heart of Kent.

Oast Cottage (sleeps 4 to 6), Orchard Cottage (6 to 8) and the Oast House (8 to 10) are extremely well equipped, with central heating, cooker, microwave, fridge/freezer, washing machine, tumble dryer, TV and VCR, radio and CD player. Comfort, peace and tranquillity make Barnfield Oast an ideal spot for complete relaxation and gentle strolls, but the area also abounds in places of interest to discover and all sorts of sporting activities and adventures.

Lamberhurst Vineyard
The Down, Lamberhurst, Kent TN3 8EU
☎ 01892 890170
e-mail:
theswan@lamberhurstvineyards.com
🌐 www.theswanatthevineyard.com

In a beautiful Wealden setting, visitors to **Lamberhurst Vineyard** can look forward to a great family day out, touring the vineyard, taking time out at the beauty spa, meeting the animals in pets corner and enjoying a snack in the bistro or a meal at The **Swan at the Vineyard**. The Swan is a 14th century coaching inn located at the edge of

the vineyard and overlooking both the vines and The Down conservation area of Lamberhurst. Voted among the top eating pubs in the UK and featured in many publications, it has earned an enviable reputation for an innovative and out-of-the-ordinary menu complemented by an excellent wine list that showcases the outstanding products of the Lamberhurst Vineyard. The stylishly decorated dining areas and bar are cosy retreats during the cooler months, but during the summer the rear terrace,

which command outstanding views over the vineyard, provides a fantastic venue for enjoying a meal in the fresh air of the Kentish countryside. The menus cater for all tastes and appetites, and

everything from a light snack to a three-course meal receives great care in both preparation and presentation. Caramelised goat's cheese with basil mayonnaise and a red onion and cherry tomato compote is a typical sparky starter, while main courses run from traditional fisherman's pie to blue marlin steak with braised fennel, ginger, spring onion and roasted capsicums, chicken breast with bacon and brie or braised lamb shank on creamed beetroot and potato mash. Many of the wines are available by glass (two sizes) as well as bottle. The bar menu offers lighter options – open sandwiches, salads and a selection of hot dishes.

One of the many attractions besides the vines and the eating places is **Vino Beauty**, where the wide range of beauty treatments includes the Uvavita ('seed of life') skin care system from California's Napa Valley, which uses the restorative powers of grapeseed in its pampering and anti-ageing face and body treatments. Among other treatments are Dermalogica's skin care

system, Jessica's nail care products, St Tropez tanning, pedicure, 'beautiful eyes' and waxing. Vino Beauty is open 10 to 5 7 days a week. Tel: 01892 891759.

279 LAMBERHURST VINEYARD

The Down, Lamberhurst, Kent TN3 8EU
☎ 01892 890412
The Vineyard and Wine Shop, Bistro, Plant Centre and Pets Corner

Lamberhurst Vineyard was established in 1972 in a north-facing position that ensures that the harvest is a couple of weeks later than south-facing vineyards but more importantly reduces the amount of frost damage early in the growing season. The vineyard's expert viniculturist nurtures bacchus, early pinot noir, rondo, regent and Ortega among others, and an extended planting programme started in 2004 will produce its full yield in 2009. Visitors van walk round the vineyard by arrangement, or join in a guide tour that ends with a talk and wine tasting.

At the heart of the vineyard is a fully licensed **Bistro**, which offers fine, wholesome local food at very reasonable prices and the option of alfresco eating out on the terrace. The menu changes on a regular basis, always providing plenty of choice, from the popular smoked mackerel pâté to a Sunday roast with all the trimmings. For a booking at the Bistro Tel: 01892

890412. The **Vineyard Shop** sells the extensive range of the award-winning English wines from Chapel Down, as well as one of the few English lagers beers, the best of local ciders, fruit juice and liqueurs. The shop also offers a hamper service where customers can choose the contents, which are then gift-wrapped and sent to any address in the UK.

Plantbase **(Tel: 01892 891453)** has over 1,100 varieties of alpines, shrubs, perennials, trees, grasses, heathers, ferns, climbers and herbs as well as terracotta pots and other accessories. All the plants are grown at the

Vineyard in tough outdoor conditions. Australian and South American plants are a speciality, and all plants come with extensive information and advice.

Set in an orchard within sight of the Bistro terrace lies **Pets Corner**, a safe area for children to play with the friendly rabbits and guinea pigs and the recently arrived pygmy goats. All the animals are safe for children to stroke and pet, and parents can watch their little ones at play while enjoying a glass of wine or a meal on the terrace.

280 THE BEACON

Tea Garden Lane, Rusthall,
nr Tunbridge Wells, Kent TN3 9JH
☎ 01892 524252 Fax: 01892 534288
e-mail: beaconhotel@btopenworld.com
🌐 www.the-beacon.co.uk

From its position on an outcrop of
Tunbridge Wells sandstone, the **Beacon Bar
& Restaurant** enjoys truly memorable views
from the terrace. Those views have barely
altered since a Victorian guide book called it
'as beautiful as any England affords'. The
house has a wealth of interesting architectural

features, including fine stained glass and an oak-
panelled bar.

The cooking is a top attraction here, and
everything on the menu is certain to please;
seafood specials such as brill on lobster bisque,
Dover sole meunière and bream with roasted baby
vegetables are particular favourites. The Beacon is
also a good choice for a business or leisure base
with three comfortable en suite bedrooms available
all year round.

281 THE BULL OF BRENCHLEY

High Street, Brenchley, nr Tonbridge,
Kent TN12 7NQ
☎ 01892 722701

Set in great walking country east of
Tunbridge Wells, the **Bull of Brenchley**
combines the virtues of a village local and a
comfortable base for overnight guests.
Harveys London Pride and Adnams Best
Bitter head the list of drinks in the bar and
cosy snug (both warmed by open fires) and
freshly cooked traditional dishes are served in
the 16-cover restaurant every lunchtime and
evening. The printed menu is supplemented
by daily specials and light snacks.

282 THE CASTLE INN

Chiddingstone, Kent TN8 7AH
☎ 01892 870247 Fax: 01892 871420
e-mail: info@castleinn.co.uk
🌐 www.castleinn.co.uk

In one of the prettiest villages in the whole
of Kent, the **Castle Inn** is a genuine 15th
century coaching inn of classic design and
great charm. Nigel Lucas has been the owner
here for 40 years, and with his wife Janette
and their chefs has built up a fine reputation
for superb food, from all-day bar snacks to
full meals. The food is complemented by real
ales (including a local brew) and a long,
expertly compiled wine list.

461

283 THE FOUR ELMS INN

Bough Beech Road, Four Elms,
nr Edenbridge, Kent TN8 6NE
☎ 01732 700240

Dating from 1518, the **Four Elms** is a splendid country pub well situated for the M25 as well as Chartwell, Hever Castle and many other top attractions. The building has been added to down the years to create a spacious establishment where the public bar, lounge and dining room all have their individual charm and character.

The menu is largely traditional, and most of the dishes are home-cooked. Prices are kind, servings generous and as well as the main menu a selection of bar snacks is available. The well-stocked bar offers three real ales and a popular range of other drinks, and when the sun shines

food ands drink can be enjoyed in the pleasant beer garden. Cheryl and Victor Silvester and their family deserve great credit for the friendly, welcoming atmosphere they have created for visitors of all ages.

284 THE WOODMAN

2 High Street, Otford, nr Sevenoaks,
Kent TN14 5PQ
☎ 01959 522195
e-mail: shelley.wills2@tiscali.co.uk
🌐 www.thewoodmanpubotford.co.uk

The **Woodman,** standing opposite Otford pond, is a roomy, comfortable high-street pub serving real ales, draught lagers and a good variety of bar and restaurant food. Disabled access to bars and toilet facilities.

285 THE CROWN

10 High Street, Otford, nr Sevenoaks,
Kent TN14 5PQ
☎ 01959 522847

The **Crown** is a distinguished 16th century inn on the main street of Otford, opposite the famous pond. Behind the whitewashed exterior, the bars are rich in traditional character, with a mass of old ceiling beams and uprights, bare whitewashed walls and a large inglenook fireplace surmounted by a row of brasses. Jill and Jim Herring welcome locals, walkers on the Pilgrims Way and all the

many other visitors, who can look forward to real ales (CAMRA recommended) and Jim's traditional home cooking.

287 THE VIGO INN

Gravesend Road, Fairseat, nr Sevenoaks,
Kent TN15 7JL
☎ 01732 822547
e-mail: pja-9l@msn.com

Peter and Peta Ashwell, owners since 1982, follow in the footsteps of Peter's family in dispensing fine hospitality and well-kept real ales at the **Vigo Inn**, a former drovers' inn dating from the 1430s.

462

286 THE BULL HOTEL

Bull Lane, Wrotham, Kent TN15 7RF
☎ 01732 789800 Fax: 01732 886288
e-mail: bookings@thebullhotel.com
🌐 www.thebullhotel.com

Nicky Capon runs the **Bull Hotel**, a 14th century former coaching house of great charm and individuality. A refurbishment programme restored many original features while providing comfort and modern amenities. The food, all freshly prepared from mainly local ingredients, combines traditional and more innovative elements, such as grilled sea bass with tomato and sweet chilli couscous, or pan-roasted beef with stuffed artichokes and braised autumn vegetables. Besides the full lunch and evening menus, the Bull also serves morning coffee, bar lunches and afternoon teas. Eleven very well equipped en suite bedrooms provide a fine overnight base for visitors.

289 THE COACH HOUSE HOTEL

34 Watling Street, Canterbury,
Kent CT1 2UD
☎ 01227 784324 Fax: 01227 455083

Tourists visiting the historic city of Canterbury will find a friendly, comfortable and well-equipped base at the **Coach House Hotel**. This Georgian town house a short walk from the centre has four quiet, spacious en suite bedrooms and a ground-floor restaurant. This serves an extensive breakfast menu and light lunches, with home-made cakes and pastries throughout the day. Evening meals by request.

288 THE ARTICHOKE

Rattington Street, Chartham,
nr Canterbury, Kent CT4 7JQ
☎ 01227 738316
e-mail: colin.robson1@btinternet.co.uk

Signposted off the A28 3 miles out of Canterbury lies the village of Chartham. The village at the foot of the North Downs boasts a pleasant mix of old and new buildings, and one of the oldest is the **Artichoke**. Once part of a manor house, it has been in the ownership of Kent's oldest brewery, Shepherd Neame, for more than 300 years; it retains many fine original features, including beams, exposed stone walls and an ancient well that now forms part of the dining room.

Colin and Jill Robson extend the warmest of welcomes to all their customers, whether familiar faces or strangers (but not for long!), and the numerous country walks hereabouts are perfect for working up a thirst and an appetite. Jill runs the bar, while Colin is top man in the kitchen, producing excellent home-cooked English dishes every lunchtime and evening. When the sun shines, the beer garden really comes into its own.

290 THE CARPENTERS ARMS

Eastling, nr Faversham, Kent ME13 0AZ
☎ 01795 890234
e-mail: enquiries@carpentersarms.co.uk
www.carpentersarms-kent.co.uk

Sandra Dicker welcomes visitors to the **Carpenters Arms**, a pretty 14th century pub in a pleasant village south of Faversham, easily reached from the A2 and M2. Oak beams, ceilings decked with Kentish hops, inglenook fireplaces, old photos and curios set the traditional scene in the bar and restaurant, serving good food, fine wines, excellent award winning seasonal ales and beer

from the Shepherd Neame Brewery, located in Faversham.

Steak & kidney pie is a firm favourite, and other choices might include garlic prawns, Stilton-stuffed chicken breast, succulent steaks (fillet, sirloin or rump) and mushroom stroganoff. For guests staying overnight, or longer, the inn has two quiet, comfortable bedrooms with TV and tea/coffee facilities. An inclusive hearty full English breakfast makes a great start to the day at the Carpenters Arms.

291 THE ALMA

Painters Forstal, nr Faversham, Kent ME13 0DU
☎ 01795 533835
e-mail: jill@almainn.f9.co.uk

On the road that runs through the middle of the charming village of Painters Forstal, the **Alma** is a classic Kentish timbered and weatherboarded inn dating back to the 17th century. Behind the immaculate exterior, the cosy public rooms are equally neat and bright, and the husband-and-wife team of Mervyn and Jill Carter have worked hard for the past 16 years to create and maintain the marvellous ambience and reputation for which their pub is known far beyond the neighbourhood.

The bar stocks an excellent range of real ales and all the usual drinks, but what makes the Alma so outstanding is the food. Mervyn's mouthwatering menus and ever-changing specials board provide a superb choice of dishes that cater for every taste and appetite.

292 DOVER ROMAN PAINTED HOUSE 🏛

New Street, Dover, Kent CT17 9AJ
☎ 01304 203279
e-mail: kentarchaeology@aol.com

The Roman Painted House, often dubbed Britain's buried Pompeii, dates from AD 200 and, although it was demolished in 270 by the army to make way for a fortress, it has been remarkably well-preserved. Now covered by a modern building, this excavated site reveals in excellent detail the layout of the house as well as

its underfloor heating system. Originally the walls of the house were decorated with wall paintings and these have, miraculously, survived whilst the displays surrounding the excavation site not only explain the discovery of this painted house but also the development of Roman Dover.

293 THE THREE HORSESHOES ⅃⅃

139 Mongeham Road, Great Mongeham,
nr Deal, Kent CT14 9LL
☎ 01304 375812
🌐 www.threehorseshoesmongeham.co.uk

Dating from the 17th century, when it was built as a farrier's shop, the **Three Horseshoes** is a traditional English pub with a warm, welcoming feel. There's always a local brew among the real ales, and home-cooked food includes a popular Sunday roast.

295 THE BATTLE OF BRITAIN MEMORIAL 🏛

Capel le Ferne, Folkestone, Kent
☎ 01304 253286

On a spectacular clifftop position can be found the Battle of Britain Memorial that was built to commemorate those who fought and lost their lives in the summer of 1940. Taking the form of an immense three bladed propeller cut into the chalk hillside with, at its centre, the statue of a lone seated airman, this is a fitting tribute to those young men who so bravely and unselfishly served their country. The memorial was unveiled by HM Queen Elizabeth the Queen Mother in 1993 and an annual memorial day is held here on the Sunday that lies closest to 10th July, the start of the air battle.

The siting of the memorial here is particularly poignant as it was in the skies above, in the summer of 1940, that the RAF struggled to gain air supremacy over the Luftwaffe and so prevent the otherwise inevitable German invasion. The battle, that cost so many their lives, lasted until the end of October and, as well as being the last major conflict over British soil, the victory marked the turning point of World War II.

Close to the memorial, by the flagpole that originally stood at RAF Biggin Hill, is a memorial wall on which Winston Churchill's immortal words, "Never in the field of human conflict was so much owed by so many to so few", are carved. At the adjacent visitors' centre visitors can purchase a range of souvenirs and it should be remembered that this memorial and the site on which it stands relies on public donation for its maintenance. Open daily from 1st April to 30th Spetember, 11am - 5pm.

465

296 LITTLE SILVER COUNTRY HOTEL

Ashford Road, St Michaels, nr Tenterden,
Kent TN30 6SP
☎ 01233 850321 Fax: 01233 850647
e-mail: enquiries@little-silver.co.uk
🌐 www.little-silver.co.uk

Set within its own immaculate gardens and grounds in the heart of the Kentish Weald, **Little Silver Country Hotel** is Tenterden's premier hotel, where owners Christine and Oliver Johnston and their staff provide the perfect combination of friendly

hospitality, comfort and personal service. Behind the elegant Tudor-style frontage with its black-and-white timbers and tall redbrick chimneys the atmosphere is wonderfully warm and welcoming, and the spacious oak-beamed lounge with its inviting armchairs and winter fire is a perfect spot for a chat and a pre-dinner drink, or for whiling away an hour or two with a good book.

Each of the guest bedrooms is individually furnished to a very high standard; some have Jacuzzis, some four-posters, and all share the same impressive attention to detail, the high

comfort factor and the amenities, including trouser press and 8-channel television. Less mobile guests are superbly catered for, and the 'mobility' rooms provide full wheelchair access, low baths, fittings for hoists and emergency buttons. Also in the gabled wing are two very special rooms: the Platinum Room in contemporary boutique style, with separate sting and dressing areas, and the sumptuously comfortable Silver Room with a canopied bed and separate lounge.

Breakfast is served in the Victorian-style conservatory, while the evening meal is taken in the more formal surroundings of the dining room with its crisp white table linen, sparkling crystal and gleaming silver. The

excellent choice of modern British and European cuisine changes regularly and is complemented by a superb, wide-ranging wine list. The hotel is located within easy reach of the motorway network, Ashford International Station and the Channel ports, making it an ideal base for long-distance travellers as well as visitors discovering the delights of Kent.

The gardens are no less impressive than the house, and the hotel is a favoured venue for wedding receptions and other special occasions; away from the main building, the magnificent octagonal Kent Hall can seat up to 120.

294 FROGGIES AT THE TIMBER BATTS

School Lane, Bodsham, nr Ashford,
Kent TN25 5JQ
☎ 01233 750237 Fax: 01233 750176
e-mail: joel@thetimberbatts.co.uk
🌐 www.thetimberbatts.co.uk

Joël Gross, who was born in the Loire Valley
and worked in some of the top hotels in
Paris, now delights visitors to his restaurant in
the village of Bodsham. In a fine old redbrick
building, **Froggies** specialises in traditional
French cuisine, with typical dishes such as
scallops with sauce vierge, steak bordelaise,
grilled sea bream and gratin of fruits with
sabayon. Fine wines accompany the fine food,
and a selection of real ales is also on tap.

297 THE KINGS ARMS

High Street, Garstang, nr Preston,
Lancashire PR3 1EA
☎ 01995 602101
e-mail: mj3270@btconnect.com

In the centre of Garstang, just off the main
A6 between Preston and Lancaster, the
Kings Arms is very popular both with locals
and with visitors of all ages. Hosts Mick and
Jackie offer a good selection of keg bitters,
lagers, cider and stout, and excellent food is
served between 11 and 2 Monday to
Saturday. The choice includes sandwiches,
jacket potatoes, light bites, main meals
(gammon & egg, liver & onions, battered
cod) and home-made specials – steak &
mushroom pie,
chilli con
carne, lasagne,
sweet & sour
chicken. A
children's menu
is also available.
Pool and darts,
big-screen TV,
Sunday night
disco.

298 WWT MARTIN MERE

Nr Rufford, Lancashire

WWT Martin Mere is one of nine Wildfowl &
Wetlands Centres run by the Wildfowl & Wetlands
Trust (WWT), a UK registered charity. Visit WWT Martin Mere and come in close contact with
wetlands and their wildlife. You can feed some of the birds straight from your hand. Special events
and exhibitions help to give an insight into the wonder of wetlands and the vital need for their
conservation.

People of all ages and abilities will enjoy exploring the carefully planned pathways. You can go
on a journey around the world, from the Australian Riverway, through the South American Lake, to
the Oriental Pen with its Japanese gateway, observing a multitude of exotic ducks, geese, swans and
flamingos along the way. In winter, WWT Martin Mere
plays host to thousands of Pink-footed Geese, Whooper
and Bewick's Swans and much more. Visitors can see
swans under floodlight most winter evenings. Covering
150 hectares, the reserve (one of Britain's most
important wetland sites) is designated a Ramsar Site and
SSSI for its wealth of rare wetland plants.

The Wildfowl & Wetlands Trust is the largest
international wetland conservation charity in the UK.
WWT's mission is to conserve wetlands and their
biodiversity. These are vitally important for the quality
and maintenance of all life. WWT operates nine visitor
centres in the UK, bringing people closer to wildlife and
providing a fun day out for all the family.

299 THE GARDEN RESTAURANT

World of Water, Preston New Road,
Westby, nr Kirkham, Lancashire PR4 3PE
☎ 01772 687400

The **Garden Restaurant** is located within the World of Water, a garden centre speciality in watery things for the garden. It lies adjacent to the A583 at Westby, between Blackpool and Preston and a short drive up from Lytham St Anne's. Business partners Anne and Penny, with the help of husbands Trevor and Paul, run the restaurant, which is open seven days a week from 10 o'clock to 4.30 or 5, and in the evening for private parties or functions.

Quality and service are watchwords, and just about everything on the menu, from snacks to main meals, is home-made. Sandwiches are freshly prepared on white or oatmeal bread, and other choices are jacket potatoes, breakfasts (served until 11.30), great soups, scones and cakes and ice cream sundaes. The specials board widens the choice with such dishes as quiches, cannelloni, corned beef hash and minted lamb shank. Once a month on a Friday they hold a food-themed evening by bookings only – it's also wise to book for Sunday lunch.

300 THE WHITE BULL HOTEL

The Square, Great Eccleston,
Lancashire PR3 0ZB
☎ 01995 670203
e-mail: info@whitebullhotel.co.uk

The Senior family brought many years' experience in the catering and licensed trades when they took over the **White Bull Hotel** in August 2005. Overlooking the square in Great Eccleston (on the A586 between

Garstang and Blackpool), this 18th century sometime coaching inn serves an exceptional selection of real ales, with four rotating guests accompanying the resident Tetley and Black Sheep. Wholesome, freshly cooked dishes using local produce are served daily except Tuesdays, and traditional roasts are added to the menu on Sundays. A secluded beer garden provides a safe place for children to romp.

303 MARMALADE CAFÉ

73 King Street, Whalley, nr Clitheroe,
Lancashire BB7 9SW
☎ 01254 822462 Fax: 01254 822694

Marmalade Café is a splendid daytime eating place where old-fashioned standards of hospitality and quality still hold sway. With seats for 30, and a further 10 outside, the Café is a popular spot both with the local residents and with visitors to the town, and owner Enid Fitzsimmons and her chef ensure a memorable visit for one and all. Local produce is used as much as possible in the dishes, which include particularly good home-made breakfasts, soups and a super fish pie. The Café, situated on the main street of Whalley, is open from 9 to 5 Wednesday to Sunday and in the evening for private parties.

Wilpshire Road, Rishton, nr Blackburn,
Lancashire BB1 4AD
☎ 01254 243777 Fax: 01254 243888
e-mail: justinwales9@msn.com
🌐 www.mullberryvillageinn.com

New Inns is one of three excellent establishments owned by Justin Wales, each one with its own charm and character, but all with the common aim of keeping alive the tradition of British innkeeping. Very much geared to the family, they offer a warm and genuine welcome, friendly, professional staff and a fine combination of relaxing surroundings, quality and value for money. New Inns is located on the edge of Rishton, and, like the others in the Mullberry Village Inns and Dining Group, provides easy access to major conurbations main roads and the lovely Lancashire countryside. Lounge and Restaurant menus propose a mouthwatering selection of dishes to cater for all appetites and tastes and to underwrite the owner's

proud boast that his three inns are places where 'good food means the difference'. The lounge menu, served from noon to 6 o'clock, tempts with a fine selection of sandwiches available on crusty white, granary farmhouse loaf, French stick or Yorkshire pudding wrap: hot options include roast beef and melted thyme onions, and bacon with Lancashire cheese and chilli beetroot; equally mouthwatering cold choices could be pastrami with dill pickle and herb mustard or tuna with spring onion. Daily specials widen the choice, and a separate children's menu is available. The main menu, also shared with the three inns, is a super mix of time-and-tested favourites and exciting, innovative combinations – see below for examples.

The **Derby Arms**, Carrs Green, Inskip, Preston PR4 0TJ.
Tel: 01772 690326

The Derby Arms is located in the Borough of Wyre, in the northwest part of the county, with the Fylde Coast to the west, Preston to the south and the Forest of Bowland to the northeast. Bracing walks in lovely coast or countryside scenery work up an appetite that this splendid inn is more then ready to satisfy. It shares its Lounge and Restaurant menus with the New Inns above. The main menu is filled with good things, from local specialities like award-winning black pudding and Lancashire hot pot to grills and salads, aubergine caviar with hummus, beef Wellington, hake and mussel bake and macaroni cheese with roasted plum tomatoes. Food served Sun-Thur 12-9, Fri-Sat 12-9.30

The third Mullberry Inn is the **Royal Oak**, east of Preston on the Longsight Road (A59), Clayton-le-Dale BB1 9EX. Tel: 01254 813793. All three inns keep an excellent selection of drinks, including real ales and expertly chosen wines.

302 THE DOG INN

King Street, Whalley, nr Clitheroe,
Lancashire BB7 9SP
☎ 01254 823009 Fax: 01254 824090

Whalley is one of the most attractive villages in Lancashire, and among its many links with the past are the 14th century Abbey, the even older parish church of St Mary and – from the early days of the railways – the famous 48-arched Whalley Viaduct. On the main street of the village is another attraction in the shape of the **Dog Inn**, a sturdy corner-site building of local stone, with white-painted window surrounds and distinctive tall chimneys.

Norman and Christine Atty have held the lease here for 15 years, and anyone stepping inside, whether a familiar face or a first-timer, can look forward to a particularly warm and friendly greeting. The inn is open all day, seven days a week, for drinks, and in the delightfully traditional bar at least four real ales are always available, all regularly rotating

including brews from both local and national breweries. Food service starts at midday and

continues until demand falls off. The printed menu and specials board offer plenty of choice, and the ingredients are locally sourced as far as possible. The food is complemented by an extensive wine list. It's best to book to be sure of getting a table on Sunday. Children are welcome at the Dog Inn, which has a pleasant, secluded patio garden at the back.

304 THE OLD POST HOUSE HOTEL

King Street, Clitheroe, Lancashire BB7 2EU
☎ 01200 422025 Fax: 01200 423059
e-mail: rooms@posthousehotel.co.uk
🌐 www.posthousehotel.co.uk

A warm family welcome awaits visitors to the **Old Post House Hotel**, which stands in the centre of the historic town of Clitheroe in the heart of the Ribble Valley. As a Post Office (until 1928) it offered a friendly, personal service, and John and Janet provide exactly that in its incarnation as a hotel.

The guest accommodation comprises 11 en suite rooms, one of them a single in the annexe. All the rooms are equipped with TV, radio, dial-out phone, trouser press, hairdryer and beverage tray. A first-class variety of food, from snacks to three-course meals, and always with a good vegetarian and vegan

choice, is served in the popular Penny Black restaurant, which is open for

lunch every day except Thursday and for evening meals every day. The hotel has a pleasant lounge area and a fully licensed bar that's open for hotel guests and restaurant patrons.

305 THE ASPINALL ARMS

Mitton, nr Clitheroe, Lancashire BB7 9PQ
☎ 01254 826223
🌐 www.aspinallarms.co.uk

The Forster family – Simon and his parents Eileen and Bill – have recently taken over the reins at the **Aspinall Arms**, which enjoys a picturesque village setting on the B6246 close to the River Ribble. The country inn dates back to the 17th century and was built at a crossing point on the river. It was the home of the ferryman, and the old boathouse was incorporated into the structure of the present building.

The inn has a fine reputation for the quality of its cooking, and Simon, an experienced and very talented chef, has further enhanced that reputation. The food choice runs from sandwiches, jacket potatoes and bar snacks to classic main courses such as rabbit, leek and mustard pie, haddock in real ale batter, steaks and lamb Henry (with a mint and red wine sauce). There is also a specials board and many of the dishes are available in smaller portions. The menu has a separate section of 'young diners meals'. Food is served lunchtime and evening

Monday to Friday and all day Saturday and Sunday. The Aspinall Arms stocks an interesting, regularly changing choice of real ales, including a selection from the Copper Dragon Brewery and others from local breweries like Bowland and Phoenix. For guests staying overnight or longer the inn has three excellent en suite rooms for B&B; more rooms are planned for 2006/7. A bonus for visitors to the inn is a lovely enclosed garden with views of the river and a wooden play area where the children can play while you relax.

306 BLACK LANE ENDS

Skipton Old Road, Colne,
Lancashire BB8 7EP
☎ 01282 863070 Fax: 01282 870249

Black Lane Ends is a former farmhouse situated high up in scenic surroundings on an old drovers' road into Colne from West Yorkshire. Tenant Gary Schofield welcomes visitors in the traditional bar, where six real ales feature top brews from the Copper Dragon Brewery in Skipton. Home-cooked food is also served all

day, with a regular menu and a specials board proposing main courses such as pork & apple burger, lamb rump or halibut with sun-blushed tomato mash. The pub hosts a jazz evening on the second Wednesday of the month.

2 Broadfields, Oswaldtwistle,
Lancashire BB5 3RY
☎ 01254 234079

Oswaldtwistle can justifiably be considered as the heart of the traditional cotton industry, as it was here in 1764 that James Hargreaves invented his famous and revolutionary 'Spinning Jenny'. One of the mills is still working and is one of the most popular family attractions in the region. Another popular establishment in Oswaldtwistle is the **Plough Hotel**, which has been a notable landmark on Broadfields since the early 19th century. When he took over the lease in November 2005, Dave brought with him 20 years' experience in the licensed trade, and he has lost no time in reinforcing the Plough's standing as one of the favourite meeting places and the social hub of the town.

Behind the imposing stone frontage, the refurbished interior provides an atmospheric setting for relaxing with a drink or a meal. Flowers IPA and a rotating guest are the real ales here, along with a good choice of other draught and bottle beers and lagers, wines, spirits and soft drinks. Food is served between 12 and 2 at lunchtime and from 5 to 8 in the evening, and right through from 12 to 8 on Saturday and Sunday. Grills are a popular choice on the printed menu, and Cajun chicken is another dish that has won many friends. Sunday lunch centres round traditional roasts.

Entertainment features strongly in the life of the Plough. Monday is free pool night; Tuesday is drinks promotion night; Wednesday brings a live performer; on Thursday everyone is welcome for the weekly quiz; nothing formal is arranged on Friday, but there's always plenty of lively conversation; Saturday is disco or karaoke night; and on Sunday there's a variety of live entertainment once a month. The Plough is closed Monday lunchtime but open every other session, and all day on Saturday and Sunday.

308 THE RED LION

Blacksnape Road, Blacksnape, nr Darwen,
Lancashire BB3 3PN
☎ 01254 701131

The **Red Lion** is the pride of the Hargreaves family and a popular choice with both local customers and visitors to this very pleasant part of the world on the edge of the West Pennine Moors. Angela, who worked here for 20 years before taking over the tenancy in 2002, has the assistance of her son Peter (who looks after the bar) and daughter Louise (she helps in the bar and the kitchen). Together they are enhancing the pub's long-standing reputation for hospitality and good food, and regulars come from many miles around to enjoy both.

All the meals are prepared to order on a menu that spans sandwiches, toasties and barmcake snacks to pizzas, giant Yorkshire puddings and an excellent variety of main courses. These could be British classics such as steak, mushroom & ale pie, scampi, Barnsley chop, steaks

and roasts, or dishes from around the world – chilli con carne, beef

stroganoff, Indian and Chinese curries, Cantonese stir-fries. Banks's Bitter is the resident real ale, and a guest ale changes every week or two. The Red Lion is open lunchtime and evening and all day Sunday (closed Monday evening except on Bank Holiday weekends). Booking is recommended to secure a table on Saturday evenings and Sunday lunchtimes.

309 THE WHITE BULL

Church Street, Ribchester,
Lancashire PR3 3XP
☎ 01254 878303
e-mail: wbribchester@btinternet.com
🌐 www.whitebullribchester.co.uk

The **White Bull** has long been a familiar landmark in the ancient village of Ribchester. The Roman Museum is a very popular tourist attraction, and the White Bull also welcomes a steady stream of visitors as well as a loyal local clientele. Timothy Taylor Landlord is one of three real ales served in the bar, and a good choice of home-cooked food from home made soups to slow-roasted Ribble Valley lamb shoulder is available every session. Emily and Jason (he's the chef) also offer a comfortable base for B&B guests in three en suite rooms, one of them suitable for a family. All are welcome at the Sunday night quiz, the proceeds from which go to charity.

312 THE GREYHOUND HOTEL

10 Low Road, Halton, nr Lancaster,
Lancashire LA2 6LZ
☎ 01524 811356

Lisa Hughes and her friendly staff make it a real pleasure to visit the **Greyhound**, a distinctive stone inn close to the River Lune in the village of Halton. A minimum of three real ales are always available, and home cooking produces a good selection of dishes, including excellent curries spanning the temperature scale from creamy korma to the Dragon's fire. There's a special deal on curries on Wednesdays and steaks on Mondays.

Whalley Road, Balderstone, nr Blackburn,
Lancashire BB2 7LE
☎ 01254 812222
e-mail: info@themyerscough.com
🌐 www.themyerscough.com

The **Myerscough** was built as a private residence in the late-1700s and became an inn with a smithy attached in about 1830. Equally popular as a lively, convivial local and a welcome break for motorists, business people and tourists, the inn has been run since November 2005 by Adam, Alex and Tom,

who lost no time in taking the inn's already enviable and long-established reputation food and hospitality to new heights. The inn is open every session and all day on Sundays, with food served seven days a week. The lunch menu offers soup, pâté, jacket potatoes, sandwiches, baguettes and toasties, something spicy – chicken curry, chilli con carne; something filling – steak & ale cobbler, cheese & spring onion pasty; or something in a basket – scampi, chicken. Lunchers in a hurry can telephone their order before 11am (call or e-mail: order@themyerscough.com) and the food will be freshly made to eat in the

bar or to take away. The evening menu, served from 5.30 to 8.30, brings plain or sauced sirloin steak, liver & bacon, fish pie and Myerscough specials including chicken in a puff pastry basket lined with cabbage and bacon, vegetable risotto and the renowned 'baby's head' steak & kidney pudding with mushy peas. To round things off in style, perhaps home-baked apple tart, sticky toffee pudding or Huntley's Farm ice cream.

To accompany the excellent food or to quench a thirst, three real ales from the Robinson Brewery are always available, and there's a decent selection of wines. The Myerscough is a popular venue for club

meetings, small conferences and a whole range of special occasion gatherings, and regular entertainment includes charity quiz nights and themed food evenings. It's also a convenient, comfortable base for business or leisure visitors, and the three guest rooms – two doubles and a twin, all with en suite showers, television, trouser press and tea/coffee facilities – are available all year round.

From Junction 31 of the M6, take the A59 Clitheroe road and keep a careful lookout for the inn on the left, opposite BAE Systems.

474

311 LANCASTER CASTLE

Shire Hall, Castle Parade,
Lancaster LA1 1YJ
☎ 01524 64998 Fax: 01524 847914
🌐 www.lancashire.gov.uk

Lancaster Castle is owned by Her Majesty the Queen in right of her Duchy of Lancaster. For most of its history the castle has been the centre of law and order for the county, and this magnificent building is still in use as a prison and a crown court.

The castle has dominated the town for almost 1,000 years, ever since it was first established in 1093. But the hill on which it stands has a history which goes back 1,000 years further, almost to the birth of Christ. The Romans built the first of at least three military forts on the site in AD79. Little is known about Lancaster until 1093 when the Norman baron, Roger of Poitou, built a small motte and bailey castle which was replaced 50 years later by a large stone keep which still stands today as the oldest part of the castle. Throughout its long history it has witnessed many trials, including that of the Lancashire Witches of 1612, which resulted in the execution of 10 people.

Although still a working building, guided tours of the castle include the room where the witches were condemned to die; the beautiful Gillow furniture in the Grand Jury Room; the dungeons and 'Drop Room' from where the condemned went to their deaths; the Crown Court from where thousands were transported to Australia; Hanging Corner, the site of public hangings and the magnificent Shire Hall with its display of heraldic shields.

Criminals and convicts, monarchs and majesty, dungeons and death, treason and transportation, witches and martyrs, all have their place in the history of this most fascinating building.

313 THE REFRESHMENT ROOM

Carnforth Railway Station, Warton Road,
Carnforth, Lancashire LA5 9TR
☎ 01524 732432
e-mail: info@refreshmentroom.com
🌐 www.refreshmentroom.com

The **Refreshment Room** on Platform 1 at Carnforth Station passed into film history as the setting for the 1945 romantic classic *Brief Encounter*, where the central characters Laura (Celia Johnson) and Alec

(Trevor Howard) first met. The historic station buildings have been beautifully restored, and today's visitors can enjoy a generous helping of nostalgia with delicious soup, sandwiches, salads, jacket potatoes, omelettes and pastries.

The refreshment room is run by Rosie and Robert Clarke, and Robert makes all the excellent cakes and

scones that stand on display on the counter. Opening times are 10 to 4 Tuesday to Sunday, and Mondays too from May to September. Also on Platform 1, galleries tell of wartime Carnforth, local residents' memories of days on and around the railways and the heyday of steam railways.

314 THE DALTON ARMS

Ten Row, West Quay, Glasson Dock,
nr Lancaster, Lancashire LA2 0BZ
☎ 01524 751213

The Stevenson-Jones family – Carolyne, Adrian and Carolyne's parents Doreen and Harry – have put the **Dalton Arms** on the map as one of the favourite places in the area for a drink, a snack or a meal. Thwaites Original and Lancaster Bomber head the list of drinks, and the regular menu runs from lunchtime sandwiches and snacks to a full

range of classic pub dishes. The choice is supplemented by a long and interesting list of monthly specials. Such is the popularity of the pub that there are plans to open an 60-cover restaurant during 2006/7. Doreen and Harry also run the Lantern Oer Lune Café just round the corner.

317 SNIBSTON DISCOVERY PARK

Ashby Road, Coalville,
Leicestershire LE67 3LN
☎ 01530 278444   Fax: 01530 813301
e-mail: snibston@leics.gov.uk

One of the largest and most dynamic museums in the Midlands, **Snibston** is Leicestershire's all-weather science and industry museum. Visitors can get their 'hands-on' loads of fun in the popular Science Alive! Gallery or explore the County's rich heritage in the Transport, Extractives, Engineering and Textiles and Fashion Galleries. Other attractions include guided colliery tours, outdoor science and water playgrounds, sculptures and nature reserve. Open daily 10am - 5pm

315 THE CITY GALLERY

90 Granby Street Leicester LE1 1DJ
☎ 0116 223 2060
e-mail: city.gallery@leicester.gov.uk
🌐 www.leicester.gov.uk

The City Gallery promotes the best in contemporary arts and crafts through a dynamic and accessible programme of continually-changing exhibitions in three gallery spaces.

The gallery has an innovative and popular education programme, providing a wide range of interpretive events for schools, colleges and community groups of all ages. The City Gallery also runs events for the general public throughout the year, designed for all ages . Please telephone the gallery for the current events programme.

The City Gallery is located in the city centre, near to the main train station (few minutes' walk). If travelling a distance it is advisable to phone to check opening hours and for details of current shows.

There is disabled badge parking nearby and level access from the street to the Main and Craft Galleries. A chairlift is available to the Upstairs Gallery. A wheelchair accessible toilet with baby changing facilities is also available. An induction loop system is in the foyer as well as the Main Gallery Minicom on 0116 254 0595.

Opening times: Tuesday to Friday 11am - 6pm, Saturday 10am - 5pm. Sunday and Monday closed, admission free.

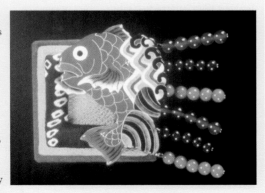

316 ABBOTS OAK COUNTRY HOTEL

Abbots Oak, Warren Hills, nr Coalville,
Leicestershire LE67 4UY
☎ 01530 832328
e-mail: admin@abbotsoak.com
⊕ www.abbotsoak.com

Abbots Oak, a fine Grade II listed building, has been the White family home for 60 years. Carolyn and her parents started offering Bed and Breakfast 12 years ago, although more recently her parents have taken a back seat and Carolyn now runs it with her husband Phil. Located on the B587 on the edge of Charnwood Forest it is a haven of courtesy, charm and genuine hospitality, and of peace, comfort and good food. The whole place is warm and convivial, a real home from home that fulfils a variety of roles: lots of business guests from Monday to Thursday, functions and special occasions at the weekend, and always a great welcome for private guests.

Public areas feature a wealth of fine oak panelling, including a splendid three-storey staircase that reputedly came from a town house owned by Nell Gwyn. The three en suite guest bedrooms are immaculately decorated and furnished in keeping with the age of the house, and each has its own individual character. Dinner is by arrangement, and in the candlelit dining room classical cuisine is served under the gaze of Elizabeth I and Sir Walter Raleigh. Guests have the use of a sauna, and the 19 acres of gardens and woodland provide quiet strolls or a game of croquet or tennis.

318 THE SHOULDER OF MUTTON

Chapel Street, Oakthorpe, nr Measham,
Leicestershire
☎ 01530 270436

The **Shoulder of Mutton** is an attractive black and white inn with lattice windows and a delightfully traditional interior. Julie Mole has held the lease here for 15 years, and down the years has built up a strong and loyal local trade. The bar is a convivial spot to meet for a chat over a glass of ale, and in the bar or restaurant wholesome, uncomplicated cooking offers all the usual favourites and a few surprises. The pub, which dates from the late 18th

century, enjoys a quiet location on the B586 Measham to Swadlincote road close to the A42/M42.

477

319 THE ROYAL HORSESHOES

**Waltham-on-the-Wold, nr Melton Mowbray,
Leicestershire LE14 4AJ
☎ 01664 464289 Fax: 01664 464022
e-mail: royalhorseshoes@btinternet.com
🌐 www.royalhorseshoes.co.uk**

Four horseshoes and the royal coat of arms on the pub sign recall the occasion when Queen Victoria stayed here when one of the horses drawing her carriage lost a shoe. The history of the **Royal Horseshoes** started (under a different name, naturally) much earlier, and the tradition of

hospitality is being carried on in great style by Audrey and Alan Noble and their hardworking, enthusiastic staff. Visitors feel the warmth of the surroundings as soon as they step inside, and the period décor and furnishings provide the ideal ambience for relaxing with a drink or a meal.

The well-lit bar is stocked with a full range of

drinks – Greene King IPA and London Pride are the resident real ales – but

for many visitors the food is the real star, and the range of dishes on offer caters for both traditional and more contemporary tastes – steak & Guinness pie is a classic here. In buildings at the back of the inn four en suite bedrooms provide spacious, well-appointed accommodation and an ideal base for touring the region.

320 THE STILTON CHEESE INN

**High Street, Somerby, nr Melton Mowbray,
Leicestershire LE14 2QB
☎ 01664 454394
🌐 www.stiltoncheeseinn.co.uk**

Stilton cheese is one of Leicestershire's great contributions to British gastronomy, so it is entirely appropriate that it should be commemorated in the name of one of the county's most famous hostelries. The **Stilton Cheese Inn**, which dates

back to the 1600s, is full of period charm and character, with beams, hops, country prints and traditional games in the convivial bar. Five real ales, including Tetley, Grainstore Ten Fifty, Marston's Pedigree and rotating guests, are always available, along with a good choice of well-priced wines and an impressive collection of malt whiskies.

The Stilton Cheese is not only a cosy spot for real pub-lovers, it's also a good place for anyone who appreciates good food. The menus list a mouthwatering selection of

dishes both traditional and more unusual, and naturally Stilton

cheese features in many of them. Carrying the flag for pub classics are sausages & mash, steaks and macaroni cheese, while specials might include crispy Cajun duck salad, Dover sole and venison & mushroom pie. Hosts Carol and Jeff Evans also offer comfortable B&B accommodation in three letting rooms – two doubles and a twin.

321 MEDBOURNE GRANGE

Nevill Holt, nr Market Harborough,
Leicestershire LE16 8EF
☎ 01858 565249 Fax: 01858 565257
🌐 www.medbournegrange.co.uk

Sally and David Beaty have a lovely
farmhouse in a beautiful, unspoilt part of
Leicestershire, with glorious views in all
directions, **Medbourne Grange** lies on the
outskirts of the picturesque village of Nevill
Holt, northeast of Market Harborough. The
farmhouse B&B accommodation comprises

two double rooms
and one twin-
bedded, all en suite,
with television,
radio, hairdryer and
tea/coffee tray. A
traditional
farmhouse breakfast
starts the day, and
guests have the use
of a peaceful lounge
and, in summer, a
heated swimming
pool.

322 THE BLACK HORSE

Main Street, Foxton,
nr Market Harborough,
Leicestershire LE16 7RD
☎ 01858 545250

Stuart, Annie and Jack greet visitors to the
Black Horse as old friends, and whatever
the weather the mood in their picturesque
country pub is always warm and sunny. A
good selection of beers and wines is served
in the bar, and the main menu in the
conservatory restaurant tempts with

favourites
like cod
& chips,
braised
lamb
shank,
lasagne
and
steak &
kidney

pie. Sunday lunch presents a choice of roasts
with all the trimmings. The pub is a short
walk from Thomas Telford's famous Flight of
Ten locks on the Grand Union Canal.

323 THE TAVERN INN

21 Lutterworth Road, Walcote,
Leicestershire LE17 4JW
☎ 01455 553338
e-mail: thetaverninn@dsl.pipex.com

The front-of-house role comes naturally to
Mario Viegas, the Portuguese host of the
Tavern Inn. He has made the inn a great

favourite with
the locals with a
combination of
traditional pub
values and a
generous dash
of Continental
flair. That
combination
applies

particularly to the food, which includes much-
loved classics such as steak & kidney pie,
exotic creations like chicken mango and
dishes from Mario's homeland.

The inn, which is open all day every day,
is located on the Lutterworth side of Walcote,
on the A4304 less than a mile from J20 of
the M1. Accommodation available.

HIDDEN PLACES GUIDES

Explore Britain and Ireland with
Hidden Places guides - a fascinating
series of national and local travel
guides.

Packed with easy to read information
on hundreds of places of interest as
well as places to stay, eat and drink.

Available from both high street and
internet booksellers

For more information on the full range
of *Hidden Places* guides and other
titles published by Travel Publishing
visit our website on

www.travelpublishing.co.uk
or ask for our leaflet by phoning
0118-981-7777 or emailing
info@travelpublishing.co.uk

324 CHESTNUT FARM SHOP & TEA ROOM

Topsgate, Gedney, Lincolnshire PE12 0BS
☎ 01406 363123

Dominating a stretch of the A17 at Gedney, **Chestnut Tea Rooms & Farm Shop** is open every day, providing visitors with excellent wholesome cooking to enjoy on the spot and a wide variety of farm and local produce to take away. The farm ceased operations and the new business evolved – and is still expanding thanks to the efforts of hardworking owners Nick and Christine Smith.

In the charming tea room, with its cosy country feel, log-burning fire and bright conservatory extension, waitress service delivers an appetising menu of snacks, light lunches, traditional desserts and cream teas. This side of the business quickly took off, and the combination of fine fresh food, value for money and attentive service has established it as a firm favourite with the local community

and increasingly with motorists and holidaymakers. Linked to the tea room is a farm shop where an abundance of produce, from fresh fruit and vegetables to chutneys, preserves and home baking, makes a tempting display. The garden centre section sells a selection of gifts, plants, pots, bird tables and bird feed and a superb range of basketware. Open from 9 to 5 seven days a week.

325 THE BULL

Old Main Road, Fleet Hargate, nr Holbeach, Lincolnshire PE12 8LH
☎ 01406 426866
e-mail: frank.round@btinternet.com

Just off the A17 east of Holbeach and close to Long Sutton, The **Bull** has a long history of serving both the local community and the numerous tourists who visit this pleasant part of South Lincolnshire. Behind the Grade II listed Georgian frontage, this handsome village pub has a delightful bar and snug and a separate 60-cover restaurant. Photos of the pub in days gone take the eye in the bar, and other memorabilia include a framed option sheet for the auction of the premises in 1832 (it fetched £50, with a few fields thrown in).

Hosts Frank and Stephen Round look after their customers from noon to midnight every day of the week, providing a good range of drinks (London Pride is the resident real ale) and well-presented, well-priced home-

cooked favourite pub dishes. Four bedrooms with 17th century wood panelling and furniture in keeping with the inn's age offer a very pleasant, civilised base for touring a region that is rich in visitor attractions. Notable among these are the Peter Scott Walk, the Butterfly & Falconry Park at Long Sutton and King John's Lost Jewels Triail. It's a great part of the world for walkers and cyclists, and country lanes to the north lead to the villages of Holbeach St Matthew and Gedny Drove and the marshland of The Wash.

326 THE STAR

High Road, Whaplode, nr Spalding, Lincolnshire PE12 6TY
☎ 01406 370521
e-mail: Helenatstar@tiscali.co.uk

In the village of Whaplode, on the busy A151 between Spalding and Holbeach, the **Star** serves the needs of the local community and of the many tourists who visit the region throughout the year. Pool and darts are played in the cosy little bar, where Tom Wood real ales are a popular order. Hosts Helen and Pete Richardson took over here in 2004 and have really made their mark, not only in providing warm, genuine hospitality and good beers, but also in expanding the food side of the business.

In the separate restaurant, the menu tempts with a mix of traditional favourites and some new ideas. The Star is open from 12 to 11 seven days a week, and food is served from 12 to 2 and from 5 to 8 (Sunday 12 to 4). This pretty little roadside pub, which dates from 1832, lies at the heart of Lincolnshire's flower and bulb-growing country, and the appeal of the area also includes a wealth of wildlife, fine fenland churches and walks on the beautiful wild marshland of The Wash.

328 THE ANCHOR INN

Sutton Bridge, nr Holbeach, Lincolnshire PE12 9SH
☎ 01406 350302

The **Anchor Inn** stands at the end of a row of houses just off the A17 east of Long Sutton, with King's Lynn to the east, Wisbech to the south and The Wash to the north. The pub dates back to 1743, and hosts Lee and Catherine keep out the welcome mat for all their customers, whether they've come for a drink in the homely, uncluttered bar or a meal in the delightful restaurant. Lee's wholesome home cooking includes excellent soups, pâtés and pies, along with super seafood specials that could include scallops. The regular food nights are very popular occasions. For Bed & Breakfast guests the Anchor has three well-priced letting rooms, and the area around the pub and the village is full of interesting things to see and do.

The region, very popular with walkers, cyclists and birdwatchers, is at the heart of the important flower and bulb-

growing industry, and the local attractions include the Peter Scott Walk. King John's Lost Jewels Trail, comprising 23 miles of quiet roads, starts at Long Sutton market place and passes Sutton Bridge, where the King is said to have lost his jewels. Another interesting feature here is the swing bridge over the River Nene, built in 1897 for the Midland & Great Northern Railway and still in use. The Anchor is open lunchtime and evening and all day on summer weekends.

481

330 THE CROWN HOTEL

All Saints Place, Stamford,
Lincolnshire PE9 2AG
☎ 01780 763136 Fax: 01780 756111
e-mail:
reservations@thecrownhotelstamford.co.uk
🌐 www.thecrownhotelstamford.co.uk

The Scottish novelist and poet Sir Walter Scott loved Stamford, calling it "the finest stone town in England". The town retains much of its period splendour, including unspoilt Georgian terraces, imposing public buildings and medieval churches. One of the town's most prestigious addresses is on All Saints Place, where the **Crown Hotel** combines 17th Century style and grace with 21st Century standards of hospitality, service and comfort. Later additions to the original building have enhanced the sandstone structure whilst adding to the amenities. Since becoming owners in 1999, Sue Olver and her brother Michael Thurlby have overseen a massive refurbishment programme that has added contemporary elements which blend in perfectly with the carefully preserved original features.

The first-class bedrooms comprise of doubles, twins and family rooms and are available in standard, superior and deluxe quality. For privacy some of the rooms are located in a nearby Georgian town house. Almost all of the rooms have an en-suite bath or shower and all are equipped with CD player, direct-dial telephone, Sky TV, hairdryer and tea/coffee making facilities. Room prices include a traditional English breakfast, with lighter options available. The high quality accommodation is complemented by first class cooking. A team of talented chefs seek out the best and freshest seasonal produce, much of it grown or reared in and around Lincolnshire. This makes for a diverse menu ranging from classic English dishes to intriguing

options inspired by the World's cuisine's. Fine food deserves fine wines and the Crown's cellar is stocked accordingly; beer drinkers will also find a varied choice including the owners homebrewed real ales. Private dining is available for select family parties or other special occasions. The hotel also caters for business needs with two conference/meeting rooms. A favourite venue to meet for a drink to chat, or for diners to enjoy a pre-dinner aperitif is the hotels newly revamped bar.

A mile south of town stands Burghley House, "the largest and grandest house of the Elizabethan Age", and home to the world famous Horse Trials. Other fine buildings like Belton House, Elton Hall, Rockingham Castle and Belvoir Castle are an easy drive away and sporting attractions include Rockingham Speedway, a variety of golf courses, sailing, fishing and cycling at Rutland Water.

482

327 THE BELL HOTEL

21 High Street, Holbeach,
Lincolnshire PE12 7DU
☎ 01406 423223
e-mail: bellhotellincs@btconnect.com

On the main street of Holbeach, the **Bell Hotel** is run by the hardworking husband and wife team of Kelvin and Janet Evans. This Elgoods pub dates back some 200 years, and behind the bold yellow frontage the pleasantly appointed interior is a very agreeable place to meet for a drink or a bar meal. Black Dog and Golden Newt are the resident real ales, and the hosts are expanding the choice of straightforward dishes on offer. For guests staying overnight, the Bell has six rooms for B&B.

All major credit and debit cards are accepted including Amex. Deep in the heart of the Fens, Holbeach is a pleasing little town with a twice-a-week market.

329 THE BERIDGE ARMS HOTEL

Station Road, Sutterton, nr Boston,
Lincolnshire PE20 2JH
☎ 01205 460272
e-mail: jacquistockwell@hotmail.com

The **Beridge Arms Hotel** is a substantial 19th century roadside hostelry in the scattered village of Sutterton, on the B1397 and close to the junction of the A16 and A17. Kevin and Jacqui Stockwell took over the lease in the middle of 2005, and the improvements they have made to the décor has pleased them and their customers – and the resident ghost no doubt approved, too! It's a very pleasant place to drop into for a drink, and the tenants are gradually expanding the food side of the business, offering wholesome, unpretentious dishes Tuesday to Sunday lunchtime and Monday to Saturday evenings. There are three letting rooms for B&B guests.

331 CENTRAL RESTAURANT

7 Red Lion Square, Stamford,
Lincolnshire PE9 2AJ
☎ 01780 763217 Fax: 01780 763230
e-mail: info@thecentralrestaurant.co.uk
🌐 www.centralrestaurant.co.uk

Visitors to the **Central Restaurant** – comprising restaurant, tea room and bakery – can look forward to an excellent snack or meal, or something tasty to buy in the bakery. In a 15th century timber-framed building overlooking Stamford's main square, breakfast is served up to 11.30, with a choice of Full English, Continental or individual items; sandwiches, salads and splendid home-baked cakes and pastries are available all day, and the lunchtime choice includes hot dishes such as Lincolnshire sausages in a rich onion gravy, the day's fish, roast and vegetarian specials and mouthwatering puddings.

333 LINCOLN CATHEDRAL

Priorygate, Lincoln LN2 1PL
☎ 01522 544544
🌐 www.lincolncathedral.com

Lincoln Cathedral is one of the finest medieval buildings in Europe. Set on a hill overlooking the city, it dominates the skyline for miles around. The Cathedral dates predominately from the 13th century when it was re-built in Gothic style, on the site of an earlier Norman cathedral, the surviving part of which is incorporated into the West Front. The library holds a valuable collection of books and manuscripts, including the Lincoln Chapter Bible (c1100), which relate stories of the people associated with the place. In order to preserve the Cathedral, a team of 30 craftspeople use traditional skills to maintain it, including stonemasons, glaziers, plumbers, carpenters, conservators and archivists.

332 BURGHLEY HOUSE

Stamford, Lincolnshire PE9 3JY
☎ 01780 752451 Fax: 01780 480125
🌐 www.burghley.co.uk

With stunning architecture, an exquisite collection of ceramics, 17th century Italian paintings, as well as beautifully maintained Capability Brown landscaped grounds, Burghley House is the largest and grandest house of the first Elizabethan Age. Built and mostly designed by William Cecil, Lord High Treasurer of England, between 1565 and 1587, the House is a family home to his descendants to this day. The State Rooms, many decorated by Antonio Verrio, house the earliest inventoried collection of Japanese ceramics in the West, rare examples of European porcelain and wood carvings by Grinling Gibbons. Four magnificent state beds stand majestically against fine examples of continental furniture and important tapestries and textiles.

An exciting new development at Burghley is the recently opened sculpture park in a reclaimed part of the gardens. This Sculpure Garden provides visitors with a tranquil setting from which to appreciate the meandering line of mature trees and the 26-acre Capability Brown Lake. Children in particular will enjoy the carved 'Teddy

Bear's Picnic' sculpture. Within the extensive grounds of the estate is a 160-acre deer park. Visitors are able to walk through the deer park, and see the original herd that was established there in the 16th century.

A visit to Burghley offers a wonderful opportunity to experience a living, breathing example of England's Elizabethan history, lavish taste and style.

334 CLAYTHORPE WATER MILL AND WILDFOWL GARDENS

Aby, Near. Alford, Lincolnshire. LN13 0DU
☎ 01507 450687 Fax: 01507 450687
e-mail: info@claythorpewatermill.co.uk
🌐 www.claythorpewatermill.fsbusiness.co.uk

Nestling at the tip of the Lincolnshire Wolds in idyllic picture postcard setting sits Claythorpe Watermill and Wildfowl Gardens which is home to over five hundred birds from exotic waterfowl, Ducks, Geese and Swans, to Crowned Cranes, Storks and Ibis. There are Peacocks and Pheasants, cheeky Cockerels, Wallabies, Goats even a Miniature Shetland Pony. In the beautiful waters of the Mill Ponds, Trout to die for swim by and leisurely feed almost from your hands.

There is a Bygone Exhibit Area, Ye Olde Bakery Shop Tableaux a Enchanted Fairy Tale Woods, and little Country Fare and Gift Shops in which to browse Several catering areas, which offer mouth watering delicacies to tempt the palette.

The Mill is open daily from 10 a.m. March till the end of October. This is a little flavour of yesteryear where you can sit and watch the world go by and feel you are in another world far from the hustle and bustle of today's lifestyle.

484

335 CITY OF NORWICH AVIATION MUSEUM 🏛

Old Norwich Road, Horsham St Faith,
Norwich, Norfolk NR10 3JF
☎ 01603 893080

Follow the brown tourist signs from the A140 Norwich-Cromer road to find the **City of Norwich Aviation Museum**, a museum dedicated to keeping Norfolk's aviation heritage alive.

Dominating the museum's collection is a massive Avro Vulcan bomber, a veteran of the Falklands War of 1982.

Eight other military and civilian aircraft are on show, and although they are the main attraction for many visitors, the most fascinating feature is the display within the main exhibition building showing the development of aviation in Norfolk. From the pioneering days of aviation to present-day civilian and military operations,

every aspect is covered in a number of displays that are constantly being revised and expanded. The major roles played by Norfolk-based aircraft during the great air battles of World War II are remembered by exhibitions on the USAAF 8th Air Force and the role of the Royal Air Force in this conflict.

A special section is dedicated to the operations of RAF Bomber Command's 100 Group which flew on electronic counter measure, deception and night intruder missions from a number of Norfolk airfields.

336 THE SPREAD EAGLE 🍴

Erpingham, nr Norwich,
Norfolk NR11 7QA
☎ 01263 761591
e-mail: billie.spreadeagle@btconnect.com
🌐 www.eateagleinn.co.uk

Tenant Billie Carder is real live wire, something of a legend in these parts, and her exuberant nature, passed on to her hospitable staff, has made the **Spread Eagle** a very popular and well-loved local. Rebuilt since its 17th century origins but retaining most of its old-world charm, it serves well-kept real ales and a good choice of dishes, from warm mackerel salad and crumb-coated mozzarella to pies, steaks and fish specials, with the likes of bread & butter pudding and treacle tart to round things off. The pub has a pleasant beer garden.

337 THE DUKES HEAD 🍴

The Street, Corpusty, nr Norwich,
Norfolk NR11 6QG
☎ 01263 587529

Michael Owen left the smoke of London for the fresh Norfolk air when he took over tenancy of the **Dukes Head**, which overlooks the village green at Corpusty on the B1149 Norwich-Holt road. Recent refurbishment has further enhanced the appeal of this delightful inn, which stands in excellent walking country close to many visitor attractions. Greene King IPA is the resident real ale, and the selection of favourite pub dishes includes popular Sunday roasts. The beer garden and the front terrace are pleasant spots fro enjoying an alfresco drink and a snack.

485

338 THE NORFOLK SHIRE HORSE CENTRE

West Runton, Cromer, Norfolk NR27 9QH
☎ 01263 837339 Fax: 01263 837132
e-mail:
bakewell@norfolkshirehorse.fsnet.co.uk
🌐 www.norfolk-shirehorse-centre.co.uk

Shires, Suffolk Punches and Clydesdales are among the stars of the show at the **Norfolk Shire Horse Centre**, and visitors can meet these wonderful, gentle giants at close quarters in the front yard stables. Two large museum sheds contain a video room and an indoor demonstration area, and also on show are carts, coaches, gypsy caravans and farm machinery of yesteryear. Next to the museum is a children's play area.

A short walk through a meadow brings visitors to the area where the small animals are kept in their sheds and pens and aviaries. This really is a paradise for animal lovers: native pony mares with their foals, donkeys, Dexter cows, pigs, goats, lambs, guinea pigs, rabbits, chipmunks, chinchillas,

cage birds. The ducks and geese have a great time in their own little pond. Twice a day the centre's proprietor, David Blakewell, accompanies demonstrations with a friendly, informative talk about the heavy horses; themes include harnessing and working the horses with the old machinery. Children can have a ride in a cart and join in the feeding of small animals. Numerous specials events are held throughout the summer, including foal days, blacksmiths days, sheepdog days, plough days and harvesting with the heavy horses. Dogs are welcome on leads; the site has a two-acre car park, a café and a gift shop.

340 THE PLEASURE BOAT INN

Hickling, Norfolk NR12 0YJ
☎ 01692 598211

The name could hardly be more appropriate, as the **Pleasure Boat Inn** is situated right next to a point on the northern edge of Hickling Broad where holidaymakers can tie up their boats. The inn was originally a farmhouse, the main part dating from the 17th century, and the later additions have not spoilt the old-world charm of the place. Darren and Julie Mayhew are the friendliest of hosts, making it a real pleasure to visit their pub at nay time of year – in summer, when the place is packed with leisure visitors, or in the quieter winter months, when a log fire keeps things cosy in the spacious bar/lounge.

Greene King IPA, Adnams Bitter and two guests please real ale connoisseurs, and simple, tasty home

cooking fills hungry stomachs with old favourites such as meat pies and lasagne – and the fresh fish specials are always in demand. Like a number of Broads pubs, the Pleasure Boat Inn easier to find by river than by road, but the effort is well worth while, and once found becomes a regular favourite with many annual visitors to the Broads. Hickling can be reached from a number of signposted points between Potter Heigham and Stalham.

The Hill, Happisburgh, Norfolk NR12 0PW
☎ 01692 650004
e-mail: clive.stockton@btconnect.com

On a site close to the Norfolk coast, the **Hill House** stands in the village of Happisburgh (pronounced 'Hazeborough'), with a church and a lighthouse as its neighbours. This family-friendly 16th century former coaching inn has been run since 1991 by Sue and Clive Stockton, who have earned a fine reputation for hospitality that extends far beyond the region and which brings visitors back time and time again – to meet them and of course to meet their equally sociable dogs – Major, a Belgian Shepherd, and Cocoa, a charming mix.

The inn offers an excellent range of food and drink to be enjoyed in the beamed bar with its woodburning stove at one end and open fire at the other, in the elegantly appointed restaurant or outside at tables at the front or in the delightful beer garden. The bar and restaurant menus provide an impressive choice of dishes both popular and original for all appetites, from toasties and ploughman's lunches to burgers in

many varieties, steaks, savoury pies and zingy-fresh locally landed fish and shellfish. There's always plenty of choice for vegetarians, and some scrumptious desserts for a fine finale. In addition to the regular lunchtime and evening menus the pub hosts very popular themed food evenings every other Friday in autumn and winter.

Real ale fans are in their element as well as lovers of good food, and the real ales on tap – usually six – include Adnams Best, Shepherd Neame Spitfire and Buffy's Elementary Ale brewed specially for the pub. Every summer solstice the pub hosts a

marvellous beer festival, with at least 40 real ales and ciders, live music and other entertainment. Close to the delights of both coast and countryside, with good walking and many places on interest nearby, the Hill House is an excellent base for tourists with four characterful guest bedrooms, two en suite. One of the rooms stands in the pub's garden in what was once a signal box. It never had to signal anything, least of all a train, as the company building the railway ran out of money before the line reached Happisburgh. The Hill House was a favourite haunt of Sir Arthur Conan Doyle, who wrote *The Dancing Men* while staying here in 1903.

341 THE SHIP

18 The Street, South Walsham, nr Norwich,
Norfolk NR13 6DQ
☎ 01603 270049
e-mail: kim.naylor@tesco.net

Kim and Giles Naylor from Yorkshire fell in love with **The Ship** as soon as they first saw it, and now as hosts they welcome a loyal band of regulars as well as visitors to the Norfolk Broads. This 18th century village inn has a very comfortable, welcoming feel, and the bar and lounge are ideal spots fro relaxing over a drink with friends old and new.

At least six real ales, with Woodfordes Wherry one of the residents, are on tap in the summer, with three or four in the winter, and fresh air appetites are satisfied with a good variety of unfussy dishes, well priced and generously served in the nice little restaurant. Typical choices include smoked haddock fishcakes, Cumberland sausage & mash,

fish & chips with mushy peas (eat in or take away), a splendid seafood platter and roasts from the Sunday carvery. Thursday is quiz night, and the Ship hosts regular live entertainment and themed food nights. South Walsham has many attractions for the visitor, but for hospitality, food and drink The Ship is definitely the place to drop anchor.

342 COLDHAM HALL TAVERN

Surlingham, nr Norwich,
Norfolk NR14 7AN
☎ 01508 538591
e-mail: stensethhouse@aol.com
🌐 www.brandestonqueenshead.co.uk

Close to a bend in the River Yare, the **Coldham Hall Tavern** is only about three miles east of Norwich as the crow flies. This is a place for walkers, birdwatchers and above all boaters on the Broads, and the place really heaves during the peak tourist season. The father and son team of

David and Colin Barnes have the services of an excellent chef, who keeps his customers happy with his cooked-to-order dishes every lunchtime and evening. A huge fireplace is a striking feature in the lounge bar.

343 THE SWAN

Church Plain, Loddon, Norfolk NR14 6LX
☎ 01508 520239

Stuart Wilson welcomes one and all to The **Swan**, a 16th century coaching inn located at Loddon, off the main Norwich to Beccles road. The substantial three-storey redbrick inn has a likeable, down-to-earth appeal, making it a very convivial place to meet for a drink – a real locals' local. Woodfordes Wherry and Greene King IPA are the regular brews, and Stuart also offers a few simple pub snacks. The pub hosts live music sessions on Saturday evenings.

344 THE FEATHERS HOTEL

Manor Road, Dersingham,
Norfolk PE31 6LN
☎ 01485 540207
e-mail: feathershotel@btclick.com
⊕ www.thefeathershotel.co.uk

Tony and Maxine Martin have built up a strong local following at the **Feathers Hotel**, a substantial mid-18th century building close to the centre of Dersingham. The interior is a merry maze of rooms and corridors, and in the cosy bar there are always three real ales on tap.

Food has long played an important part in the success of the Feathers, and the daily changing choice includes such superb dishes as sole stuffed with crab, steak & mushroom or game pie and

the popular sizzling dishes: swordfish steak with parsley butter, chicken with a cream, apple, cider and mushroom sauce, and tournedos Feathers cooked with mushrooms, onions and white wine.

There are pleasant walks to be enjoyed through Dersingham Wood and the adjoining Sandringham Country Park, and for walkers and tourists the Feathers offers five well-appointed rooms for B&B – four en suite, the other with private facilities.

345 SANDRINGHAM HOUSE

Sandringham, Norfolk PE35 6EN
☎ 01553 772675 Fax: 01553 541571
e-mail: enquiries@sandringhamestate.co.uk

Sandringham House is the charming country retreat of Her Majesty The Queen hidden in the heart of 60 acres of beautiful wooded gardens. Still maintained in the style of Edward and Alexandra,

Prince and Princess of Wales (later King Edward VII and Queen Alexandra), all the main ground-floor rooms used by the Royal Family, full of their treasured ornaments, portraits and furniture, are open to the public.

More family possessions are displayed in the Museum housed in the old stable and coach houses; these include vehicles ranging in date from the first car owned by a British monarch, a 1900 Daimler, to a half-scale Aston Martin used by Princes William and Harry.

A new display tells the mysterious tale of the Sandringham Company, who fought and died at Gallipoli in 1915, recently the subject of a television film *All the King's Men*. A free Land Train from within the entrance will carry passengers less able to walk through the grounds to the House and back.

346 THE THREE HORSESHOES

Bridge Street, Warham, nr Wells, Norfolk NR23 1NL
☎ 01328 710547

In the attractive village of Warham, just half a mile from the A149 coast road, the flint-faced **Three Horseshoes** is an excellent base for touring the North Norfolk Heritage Coast. Gas lighting, stone floors, scrubbed wooden tables, an open fire, old posters and vintage one-armed bandits paint a nostalgic scene in the bars, where real ale is served straight from the  barrel from a hole in the wall. Larger than life landlord Ian Salmon puts the emphasis on fresh seasonal ingredients in the traditional English cooking, and offers characterful B&B accommodation in the adjacent Old Post Office.

347 THE JOLLY FARMERS

1 Burnham Road, North Creake, nr Fakenham, Norfolk NR21 9JW
☎ 01328 738185
🌐 www.jollyfarmers-northcreake.co.uk

This early 19th Century Inn has a warm, homely feel assisted by mellow woods, enormous open hearths and the way the pub is divided into small rooms with bookshelves, local paintings and intimate corners. Locally sourced meat, fish, shellfish and game  are used in creating both contemporary and traditional style dishes, plus crab and lobster menus in Summer and mussel menu in Winter. Real ales from local brewers served straight from the cask.

348 THE GREEN MAN

Little Snoring, nr Fakenham, Norfolk NR21 0AY
☎ 01328 878227
e-mail: info@snoringgreenman.co.uk
🌐 www.snoringgreenman.co.uk

The Green Man is a traditional inn on the main A148 Holt road, a short drive east of Fakenham. Equally popular with locals and the many tourists who visit this lovely part of Norfolk,  the pub serves a selection of real ales and a good variety of value-for-money homemade food. The bar menu is ideal for lighter appetites, and there's an extensive à la carte menu, daily specials and a Sunday lunch menu that offers a choice of four roasts and a vegetarian option. All dietary requirements are catered for and the menu carries symbols to indicate vegetarian, vegan, wheat-free and dairy-free options. Regular entertainment in the bar includes karaoke, quiz and live music evenings.

349 THE WHITE HORSE

Longham, nr Dereham, Norfolk NR19 2RD
☎ 01362 687464 Fax: 01362 687484
e-mail: barry@longhamwhitehorse.co.uk

Home-cooked food, a fine range of ales, wines and spirits and superb guest accommodation brings visitors from near and far to the **White Horse** in a quiet village five miles from Denham. Barry and Chrissie White and their excellent staff make it a pleasure to tarry awhile in this quintessentially English inn, whether it's to enjoy a glass of real ale, a meal based on fresh local  produce, or an overnight or longer stay in one of the seven supremely comfortable and well-appointed en suite bedrooms. The White Horse is an ideal base for exploring a really delightful part of the Norfolk countryside.

350 DENVER WINDMILL

Denver, Downham Market,
Suffolk PE38 0EG
☎ 01366 384009 Fax: 01366 388665
e-mail:
enquiries@denverwindmill@fsnet.co.uk
🌐 www.denvermill.co.uk

Denver Windmill was built in 1835 and continued to grind corn using wind power for over one hundred years until in 1941 the sails were struck by lightning. It has since been lovingly restored to full working order and is now the only working windmill in Norfolk.

Visitor facilities provide the opportunity to explore the whole site with a guided tour going right to the top of the windmill tower. Visitors can see flour being made in the traditional way (wind permitting!) while the visitor centre tells the story of windmills, corn milling, and the people who lived and worked in these wonderful buildings. A tearoom and bakery within the site sells a tempting range of goodies, with bread and cakes baked daily using the mill's own flour.

351 THE GEORGE INN AT GREAT OXENDON

Great Oxendon,
Northamptonshire LE16 8NA
☎ 01858 465205
🌐 www.thegeorgegreatoxendon.co.uk

The **Georege Inn at Great Oxendon** lies just two minutes' drive from Market Harborough, but regulars come from much further to enjoy the hospitality, the fine food and the well-chosen wines. Chef-patron David Dudley, in the business since 1964 and here since 2004, oversees the kitchen, where everything on the varied, interesting menu from the bread to the ice cream is made on the premises. The public rooms at

this 500-year-old inn are warm and inviting, and for overnight guests there are three en suite rooms in an adjacent outbuilding. The inn is closed Sunday evening.

352 THE PUMP HOUSE CAFÉ

6 Nene Court, The Embankment,
Wellingborough,
Northamptonshire NN8 1LD
☎ 01933 440088

Follow the landmark Embankment, with the river and abundant wildlife close by, to find the **Pump House Café** located in – what else? – an old redbrick pumphouse that was once part of the town's water system. Run in fine style by Suzanne Darby and her daughter Elizabeth, the café is open from 9 to 3 Monday to Saturday for a good

choice of unfussy home-cooked dishes listed on the blackboard. Breakfast is served from opening time to 11.30. 50 seats inside, 20 more in the upstairs gallery and 20 outside.

353 THE OAK HOUSE PRIVATE HOTEL

8/9 Broad Green, Wellingborough,
Northamptonshire NN8 4LE
☎ 01933 271133

In a pleasant location convenient for the town's amenities, the **Oak House Private Hotel** is very professionally run by resident owner Gayle O'Sullivan. A warm welcome awaits all her visitors, and the 16 well-appointed en suite bedrooms, all double-glazed and centrally heated, include six on the ground floor and some suitable for families. A terrific breakfast

sets guests up for the day, and an evening meal, served at 6 o'clock, is available for residents.

354 THE HARE & HOUNDS

Main Street, Great Addington,
Northamptonshire NN14 4BJ
☎ 01536 330521

In an attractive village close to the A6, A45 and A14, the **Hare & Hounds** is a popular spot for food and drink, with beer gardens and off-road parking. No food Sunday evening or Monday lunchtime. Themed food evenings Wednesday and Thursday.

355 THE GRIFFINS HEAD

Wilby Road, Mears Ashby,
Northamptonshire NN6 0DX
☎ 01604 812945

The **Griffins Head** is a substantial redbrick free house with a large and loyal local following. Behind the ornate windows and hanging baskets the open-plan bar/lounge/restaurant is very cheerful and inviting, with a big open fire contributing to the homely ambience.

Jumbo cod in the special house beer batter is a popular choice for diners, and cod might also appear as a special wrapped in prosciutto with garlic tomatoes; meaty options could be hearty gammon with eggs and chips, or a chunky chicken casserole.

356 WATERWAYS COTTAGE

Bridge Road, Stoke Bruerne, nr Towcester,
Northamptonshire NN12 7SD
☎ 01604 863865
e-mail: waterwayscottage@btinternet.com
🌐 www.waterwayscottage.co.uk

The picturesque village of Stoke Bruerne lies on the Garnd Union Canal, at the southern end of the famous Blisworth Tunnel. **Waterways Cottage** is just feet from the water. House-proud Kath Allum keeps the thatched cottage absolutely spotless, and the three en suite bedrooms

– Red, Blue and Green – offer abundant comfort and character. Two of the rooms have spa baths. A fine breakfast starts the day, and there are several eating places nearby for other meals.

2 Helmdon Road, Weston, nr Towcester,
Northamptonshire NN12 8PX
☎ 01295 760310
e-mail: thecrown-weston@tiscali.co.uk

Robert Grover is a young, go-ahead landlord who has assembled around him a fine team that includes an excellent head chef. Together they have made the **Crown** a pub well worth seeking out for its warm welcome and genuine hospitality, as well as its well-kept real ales and great-value food.

The pub, which is reached off the A43 or B4525, is equidistant from Brackley and Towcester; it dates from 1593, and its long and interesting history is detailed on a framed chart in the bar. Greene King IPA, Hook Norton Best, Black Sheep and two guests provide plenty of choice for real ale connoisseurs, and the tile-floored bar with its huge stone-faced fireplace is a great spot to enjoy it. In the elegant little restaurant area, diners reap the rewards of the chef's insistence on using only the best locally sourced ingredients, including outstanding meat and seasonal game.

The Crown is open every evening from 6 o'clock to midnight, and from 12 to 3 at lunchtime every day except Monday and Tuesday. Food is served these lunchtimes and from 6 to 9.30 in the evenings. Everyone is welcome for the regular quiz, which takes place on the second Wednesday of the month. But any time is a good time to visit this outstanding old inn, which excels in its inviting, unpretentious ambience, in its hardworking, motivated landlord and staff, and in its well-priced food and drink.

357 SLAPTON MANOR

Slapton Manor, Chapel Lane, nr Towcester,
Northamptonshire NN12 8PF
☎ 01327 860344
e-mail: slapton.manor@abthorpe.net
🌐 slapton.manor@abthorpe.net

On a 250-acre working farm next to medieval
St Botolph's Church, Barbara Smith welcomes
guests into her peaceful, period home, 12th
century Slapton Manor. The accommodation,
in a sympathetically converted period
carthorse stable block and hay loft with own

entrance
adjoining the
farmhouse,
comprises
three rooms
for Bed &
Breakfast and
converted
cowbyres used
as self-
catering

studios. This is excellent walking country, and
Stowe, Canons Ashby, Sulgrave Manor, Stoke
Bruerne and Silverstone are all within an easy
drive.

359 THE NEW INN

Silver Street, Abthorpe, Towcester,
Northamptonshire NN12 8QR
☎ 01327 857306
e-mail: jane.costall@abthorpe.net

Tucked away in a corner of a pretty village
close to the historic town of Towcester and
the Silverstone motor racing circuit, the **New
Inn** is a delightful pub dating back to the
17th
century.
This
Hook
Norton
pub
features all
that
brewery's
ales,
which the

regulars and the many visitors to the locality
enjoy in the warm, traditional surroundings
of the bar – made even warmer and more
cheerful by the splendid open fire. Warming,
too, are good simple dishes such as steak &
ale pie. Closed Monday lunch.

360 THE INN

Chapel Road, Greatworth, nr Banbury,
Oxfordshire OX17 2DT
☎ 01295 710976
e-mail: theinn.greatworth@btinternet.com

Marie Mollington is the hands-on hostess at **The
Inn**, and the rapport she has established with her
local clientele is one that any pub would envy. The
pub, which started life in the early 18th century as a
roadhouse, stands in the village of Greatworth, east
of Banbury, north of Brackley, reached from the A422 (leave at Farthinghoe) or the B4525.

The pub is kept in an excellent state of repair
by the owners Hook Norton Brewery, whose fine
brews can be enjoyed in the comfortable bar with
its cheerful open fire. Food is an important side
of the business, and the good honest pub grub,
with everything freshly prepared on the premises,
is as unpretentious as the pub's name. Typical

dishes on the
daily specials
board are tuna
pasta bake,
herby lamb
casserole,
beef curry
and steak &
ale pie. The
Inn is open every lunchtime and evening, and food is served
every session except Sunday evening.

361 THE WINDMILL

Main Street, Badby, nr Daventry,
Northamptonshire NN11 3AN
☎ 01327 702363 Fax: 01327 311521
e-mail: info@windmillinn-badby.com
🌐 www.windmillinn-badby.com

The **Windmill** is a well-known landmark on the main street of Badby, south of Daventry just off the A361 Banbury road. Dating from 1673, the mellow stone and brick building has small-paned windows and a thatched roof, and features in the beamed bars and snug lounge include sturdy country furnishings, flagstones, a white-tiled inglenook and pictures and prints with cricket and rugby themes.

John Freestone and Carol Sutton have made their superbly maintained inn a very popular place, so visitors should book for all meals to be sure of a table in the bright restaurant. The food choice runs from bar meals to a full menu that offers traditional pub classics and dishes that are just a little bit different; the pie of the day is the choice of many regulars, and salmon with dill mayonnaise

and loin of lamb with a red wine jus are other typical dishes. Well-kept real ales and keenly-priced wines accompany the excellent food, and friendly, efficient service sets the seal on a very enjoyable meal. The Windmill is also a great place for an overnight stay, with ten bedrooms in a sympathetic modern rear extension and two more in a cottage next door. All rooms have en suite bath or shower, direct-dial phone, satellite TV and hot drinks tray.

362 THE FOX & HOUNDS

Banbury Road, Charwelton,
Northamptonshire NN11 3YY
☎ 01327 262358

The **Fox & Hounds** is a handsome former coaching inn standing on the main A361 Daventry-Banbury road. The promise of the redbrick exterior, with its white-framed bay windows, is amply fulfilled inside, where the décor and furnishings have an unpretentious traditional appeal. Open fires keep things cosy even in the coldest spells, and Andy and his staff provide helpful, attentive service with a smile.

Locals, leisure visitors and motorists needing a break on their journey combine to provide convivial company in which to enjoy a glass of beer (Bass and Hook Norton are the resident real ales), a snack or a

meal. The main menu sticks in general to tried and tested pub classics such as steak & ale pie (a big favourite with the regulars), and the blackboard snack menu lists baguettes and jacket potatoes, juicy burgers served in a sesame seed bun, chicken or steak in pitta bread and a breakfast-style brunch. The pub is open 11.30 to 3 and from 5.30 Monday to Friday, and all day Saturday and Sunday.

363 THE ROYAL OAK

**High Street, Flore,
Northamptonshire NN7 4LL
☎ 01327 341340**

The Williams family have recently taken over at the **Royal Oak**, a distinguished old building on the main street of Flore, just off J16 of the M1. The décor and furnishings are a pleasing mix of traditional and more modern, providing a very agreeable ambience for enjoying a drink or a meal. The blackboard bar menu lists a variety of options, from sandwiches and jacket potatoes to cottage pie, home-cooked ham, steaks and lasagne.

364 THE BLUE BELL

**90 High Street, Gretton,
Northamptonshire NN17 3DF
☎ 01536 770404
e-mail: thebluebell.inn@btconnect.co.uk**

Jim and Barbara Caulfield were managers at the **Blue Bell** before they bought it, so many of their regular customers are old friends. But everyone is equally welcome at this find old inn (the oldest parts date from 1547), where Greene King IPA and Abbot Ale and two guests provide a choice for real ale fans. Honest, unfussy pub food is served Saturday and

Sunday lunchtimes and Thursday, Friday and Saturday evenings. Gretton lies close to the River Welland off the A43 or A6003 north of Corby.

365 THE QUEEN'S HEAD

**Main Street, Bulwick,
Northamptonshire NN17 3DY
☎ 01780 450272
e-mail: queenshead-bulwick@tiscali.co.uk**

Friendly licensees Geoff and Angela have really put the **Queen's Head** on the map since taking over in 2003. One of the main reasons for their success is the range and quality of the food, and the chef has developed a following that reaches far beyond the surrounding communities. Lunchtime brings bar snacks as well as more substantial dishes, while the evening menu sees the chef's full talents in superbly executed creations such as red gurnard and Cornish crab risotto with wood-roasted pepper, fennel and spinach. Seasonal game, simply and expertly prepared appears in terrific dishes like roast pheasant or woodcock wrapped in prosciutto, or saddle of wild venison.

The stone-floored two-bam bar

is delightfully traditional, with beams, fires at each end and time-honoured pub games. In the summer, the garden terrace is a perfect spot to enjoy an alfresco drink. The setting is quiet and picturesque, in a village just off the A43 Kettering-Duddington road. The pub is open for food and drink lunchtime and evening every day except Monday.

366 THE MALTINGS COTTAGE & 19 WEST STREET

19 West Street, Kings Cliffe,
Peterborough PE6XB
☎ 01780 470365 Fax: 01780 470623
e-mail: howarddixon@btconnect.com
🌐 www.kingjohnhuntinglodge.co.uk

In a village off the A43 and A47, close to the Cambridgeshire, Northamptonshire and Lincolnshire boundaries, **The Maltings Cottage & 19 West Street** offer a choice of Bed & Breakfast and self-catering accommodation, both 4-Star rated, very comfortable and full of period charm.

At the mid-18th century Maltings Cottage at 18 West Street, Jenny and Howard Dixon have a self-catering cottage for two, with wooden floors, central heating, an inglenook fireplace, a well-equipped kitchen, and a quiet courtyard garden. Breakfast can be arranged with the B&B at 19 West Street

across the road. This period property has three guest bedrooms – a single, a twin and a double, all with private bathrooms. Both properties operate a strict no smoking, no pets policy. Both 18 and 19 West Street are available all year round.

367 THE GEORGE INN

91 Glapthorn Road, Oundle,
Peterborough PE8 4PR
☎ 01832 272324 Fax: 01832 274679
e-mail: georgeinn@dsl.pipex.com

Since taking over **The George Inn**, John and Dawn have enhanced the reputation of this fine hostelry as a very pleasant family pub with a friendly, inviting atmosphere. The fully stocked bar is a lively, sociable place for enjoying a chat and a drink (JHB and John Smiths Cask are the regular real ales with changing Guest Ales) and when the weather is fine the large patio and the beer garden, with its bouncy castle and life-size model animals, are where the action is and where the children are in their element.

Food is big business here, with all tastes and appetites catered for on menus that range from bar

snacks and do-it-yourself sandwiches (the fillings are presented on a plate with brown or white bread, baguettes or tortilla wraps, coleslaw, crisps and a salad garnish) to calves' liver with garlic mushrooms, steaks, salmon with lemon & herb butter and a Mediterranean vegetable pancake.

The George is a great favourite with the local community, and darts, pool and skittles are among the traditional games played in the bar. The pub hosts a quiz every other Thursday and holds regular themed evenings.

368 THE RED LION

**7 The Hill, Middleton,
nr Market Harborough,
Leicestershire LE16 8YX
☎ 01536 771268**

The **Red Lion** is an outstanding village inn with everything that locals and visitors could want. Located in good walking country between Corby and Market Harborough, this classic 1930s inn has spacious, comfortable public rooms and an enormous garden that's full of colour in spring and summer and has a safe, secure children's play area. Two or three real ales (Bombardier and Old Speckled Hen are the regulars) are always available, with up to a dozen, plus music and a good time all round, during the Beer Festival held every June.

Hosts David and Julie also keep their customers happy with an excellent variety of dishes served in the lounge and restaurant. Among the favourites are fajitas filled with beef, chicken or both, chilli con carne, barbecued rack of ribs and steak pie. A blackboard lists a tempting selection of hot and cold

desserts, and senior citizens can enjoy a bargain lunch Monday to Friday. Booking is advisable for Saturday evening and Sunday lunch. The Red Lion is a great place to stay, and the three upstairs en suite bedrooms, including a family room, can be booked on a Room Only, Bed & Breakfast or Dinner, Bed & Breakfast basis. The pub is open lunchtime and evening and all day Saturday and Sunday, with a late licence at the weekend.

Food is served from 12 to 3 and 6 to 9.30 and all day Saturday.

369 THE ROYAL GEORGE

**Blind Lane, Cottingham, nr Market
Harborough, Leicestershire LE16 8XE
☎ 01536 771005
🌐 www.royalgeorge-cottingham.co.uk**

In the heart of the pleasant village of Cottingham, the **Royal George** is one of its most venerable buildings. While most of the pub retains its splendid old-world look, the newly completed restaurant is

smartly contemporary. With outstanding home cooking the menu ranges from light snacks to three-course meals. Three real ales are always on tap. Five en suite bedrooms are available throughout the year for guests staying overnight.

370 BANCROFT HOUSE

**34 Bancroft Road, Cottingham, nr Market
Harborough, Leicestershire LE16 8XA
☎ 01536 770799
e-mail: judy@bancroft88.fsnet.co.uk
🌐 www.bancrofthouse.co.uk**

Judy and Gordon Evans provide a comfortable, economical base for discovering the Welland Valley in their home in the quiet village of Cottingham. Three bedrooms in their detached redbrick **Bancroft House**, with central heating, washbasin, TV and beverage tray, share a bathroom across the landing. Good choice for breakfast; garden with country views. Bancroft House is a strictly non-smoking establishment.

498

371 THE STAR INN

2 Bridge Street, Geddington,
Northamptonshire NN14 1AD
☎ 01536 742386 Fax: 01536 742386
🌐 www.star-inn-geddington.com

The **Star** is a much-loved locals' pub standing
opposite the Eleanor Cross in the village of
Geddington, on the A43 north of Kettering.
Alister, Angela and Jean are the friendly
threesome at the helm, dispensing traditional
hospitality
and serving
an
interesting
variety of
real ales and
real food.
Blackboards
announce
the beers

(among them several from smaller local
breweries) and the specials, which include a
pie of the week and other main courses such
as grilled salmon fillet topped with a lobster
and prawn sauce, Moroccan lamb or beef
tikka masala kebabs.

373 THE SUN INN

126 High Street, Broughton, nr Kettering,
Northamptonshire NN14 1NQ
☎ 01536 790284

In the quiet village of Broughton, tucked
away off the A43, **The Sun** is popular with
all who visit it for its warm, friendly
atmosphere. Carole and Gordon Jones have
established themselves as very likeable and
welcoming hosts, and Carole's cooking is
another reason for the pub's success. Her
menus range from sandwiches and light
snacks to hearty main dishes such as scampi
and chips or Yorkshire pudding with
Cumberland sausage. Pub games include darts
and table skittles.

372 THE RED LION

42 High Street, Cranford St John,
Northamptonshire NN14 4AA
☎ 01536 330663

The **Red Lion** at Cranford is a very
distinctive yet traditional village pub,
welcoming visitors into its warm and cheerful
ambience and is located just half a mile from
J11 of the A14. Open lunchtime and evening,
and all day in summer and at the weekend,
the pub serves four real ales, great wines and
a particularly interesting variety of home-
cooked dishes and traditional snacks. Terrace,
beer garden and children's play area, complete
the offering.

374 THE RAT INN

Anick, nr Hexham,
Northumberland NE46 4LN
☎ 01434 602814

The **Rat Inn,** with it's traditional bar,
charming garden and
lovely views is a magnet
for real ale connoisseurs,
with no fewer than six
always on tap. Food
options run from light
snacks to main meals.

376 ALD WHITE CRAIG FARM

Shield Hill, nr Hadrian's Wall, Haltwhistle,
Northumberland NE49 9NW
☎ 01434 320565
e-mail: whitecraigfarm@yahoo.co.uk

Ald White Craig Farm comprises a
farmhouse with two rooms for B&B and five
self-catering cottages splendidly converted
from the old smithy and barns. Sleeping from
2 to 6 guests, they are equipped with
everything needed for a comfortable stay in a
lovely rural location close to Hadrian's Wall.

375 THE GOLDEN LION

Market Square, Allendale,
Northumberland NE47 9BD
☎ 01434 683225

Michael and Margaret Stonehouse continue a major programme of refurbishment at the **Golden Lion**, where every customer, whether face or a first-timer, is greeted with the warmest of welcomes. The superb home cooking is a big attraction at this imposing stone inn, and much of the produce is sourced

from local farms, including top-quality lamb, beef, pork and home-made icecream. The Golden Lion is a good base for exploring Allendale and the many scenic and historic attractions of the surrounding area.

378 BATTLESTEADS HOTEL & RESTAURANT

Wark, Hexham, Northumberland NE48 3LS
☎ 01434 230209 Fax: 01434 230039
e-mail: info@battlesteads.com
🌐 www.battlesteads.com

Proprietors: Richard & Dee Slade
Originally built as a farmstead in 1747, this stone-built Inn and Restaurant features a cosy open fire, beer garden, excellent bar meals and a la carte menus using

fresh, local produce, good choice of wines and three cask ales.

A friendly , family run hotel, it has 14 en-suite bedrooms, including ground floor rooms with disabled access, and is ideally placed for exploring Hadrian's Wall, Kielder and Border Reiver country, wether by car, cycle or on foot.

377 THE BLACK BULL HOTEL

Main Street, Wark,
Northumberland NE48 3LG
☎ 01434 230239
e-mail:
Raymond@raymondcarr.wanadoo.co.uk

The **Black Bull** is a fine old inn dating back to the 17th century. It stands in the heart of the village of Wark close to the edge of the Northumberland National Park between

Hexham and Otterburn, and within easy reach of Kielder Water and Hadrian's Wall. Farmers use the inn as an unofficial headquarters, and they, along with other locals and visitors, make for an excellent convivial atmosphere.

A handsome greystone building with a huge sign on its slate-tiled roof, the hotel has a well-stocked bar and a lovely bright lounge with a separate restaurant section. Here, hearty country appetites are satisfies by a good, well-balanced choice of wholesome, unfussy dishes prepared and presented with care.

Food is available lunchtime and evening seven days a week. The hotel has a pleasant garden and plenty of off-road parking. And for anyone planning a stay in this glorious part of the country, the Black Bull offers comfortable accommodation in five guest bedrooms, all with en suite facilities, television and hospitality tray.

379 KIELDER WATER AND FOREST PARK

Kielder, Northumberland
☎ 01434 220643 (Bellingham Tourist Information Centre)
🌐 www.kielder.org

In a land of astonishing beauty, **Kielder Water and Forest Park** perfectly captures the mood of Northumberland. An inspirational and romantic place where you can escape the trials of everyday life and experience pure tranquility in a truly stunning environment.

Kielder, the North Tyne Valley and nearby Wild Redesdale offers a wealth of choice and experiences within an environment where freedom to be tranquil, adventurous or in touch with nature is yours for the taking.

A wide range of recreational opportunities are available, providing something for everyone, whether you are a skilled outdoors enthusiast or looking to absorb the intoxicating sights and sounds at a more sedate pace.

The many activities include walking, cycling, sailing, riding and fishing, and around the park you can find a variety of places to eat and drink, shop, swim or play miniature golf. There is ample parking and several picnic sites.

An 80 seater motor cruiser will take you on a trip around the lake and on board you have use of a bar, shop, lounge and toilets.

380 YELLOW HOUSE FARM

West Woodburn, nr Hexham, Northumberland NE48 2RA
☎ 01434 270070
e-mail: avril@yellowhousebandb.co.uk
🌐 www.yellowhousebandb.co.uk

Yellow House is a beautiful stone-built residence where spacious bedrooms provide the perfect base for discovering the many local. A Northumbrian breakfast starts the day.

Explore Britain and Ireland with *Hidden Places* guides - a fascinating series of national and local travel guides.

www.travelpublishing.co.uk

0118-981-7777

info@travelpublishing.co.uk

381 THE BLACKSMITH'S TABLE

The Green, Washington Old Village, Tyne & Wear NE38 7AB
☎ 0191 415 1788
🌐 www.blacksmithstable.com

Opened in 1988 on the green at Washington Old Village, the **Blacksmith's Table** has earned a reputation as one of the top restaurants in the North, with food, wine, service and ambience all of the highest standard. Head chef Marc Crook and his talented team take their inspiration

from the world's great cuisines on menus that are truly amazing in their variety. Familiar meats, poultry and game are joined by exotic choices such as crocodile (served with a 'snappy' chilli dip) and kangaroo, and there are separate early evening and Sunday lunch menus. The Old Dairy Farm in Upper Wensleydale has the same owners.

382 THE VICTORIA

Fatfield Road, Washington,
Tyne & Wear NE38 7DS
☎ 0191 417 2526
e-mail: carling2@aol.com
🌐 www.victoriapub-washington.co.uk

For the past five years Chris and Lynda
Carling have been wooing the locals with
their own special brand of hospitality at the
Victoria. In their spacious modern pub near
the Galleries shopping mall they serve a good
range of
drinks and
a selection
of good
honest pub
dishes at
kind
prices.
Very much
a favourite
with the

locals, the Victoria is expanding its appeal
with the creation of several rooms for B&B
guests. Wednesday and Thursday are quiz
nights, with karaoke sessions at the weekend.

383 THE MAGNESIA BANK

1 Camden Street, North Shields,
Tyne & Wear
☎ 0191 257 4831
🌐 www.magnesia.com

Situated high on the bankside overlooking the
River Tyne, the award-winning **Magnesia
Bank** is a true Free House with no brewery or
pubco ties. It is a family-run business with a
reputation for consistency and quality, offering
a spacious bar with 7 cask ales, real coal fire,
live music three nights per week and regular
Blues weekends. The Garden Restaurant seats
up to 50, and the food policy is to provide
locally sourced 'restaurant quality food at pub
prices'. Extensive chalkboard menus featuring
Northumbrian lamb, Angus beef and fish from
nearby Fish Quay, change weekly and all food
is freshly
prepared.
Open 7 days
a week with
meals and
snacks
available all
day.

384 THE HALF MOON INN

Half Moon Street, Stakeford, nr Morpeth,
Northumberland NE62 5TT
☎ 01670 853258
e-mail: tony43@wanadoo.co.uk

In the village of Stakeford, close to Morpeth,
Ashington and Newbiggin-on-Sea, the **Half
Moon** started life in the 15th century as a
coach house, and recent refurbishment has
created a very pleasant, comfortable
environment for enjoying a drink and a meal.

A bar
operates in
the daytime,
with a full à
la carte
menu in the
evening, and
many of the
dishes are

highlighted by the use of fresh local produce.
This is very much an inn for the whole
family, and guests staying overnight have the
choice of four en suite rooms in the main
building and self-catering chalets. The inn has
a games room with pool and darts and hosts
regular quiz and bingo sessions.

385 THE OAK INN

Causey Park Bridge, Morpeth,
Northumberland NE61 3EL
☎ 01670 787388
e-mail: northarm@supanet.com

Duncan, Maggie and staff keep out the
welcome mat at the **Oak Inn**, which enjoys
the distinction of being the only hostelry for
miles on the A1. It draws its custom from
near and far, from local residents, families
with children
and dogs and
motorists
looking for a
break, to coach
parties and
shooting parties.
The bar and

conservatory restaurant are warm and
inviting, and excellent dishes prepared from
local ingredients run from bar snacks to
three-course meals. Very much geared to the
family, the Oak has a large car park and an
outside area where children can romp in
safety. Accommodation is available at their
sister pub 'The Northumberland Arms' which
is 4 miles away.

386 THE WIDDRINGTON INN

Widdrington Village, nr Morpeth,
Northumberland NE61 5DY
☎ 01670 760260
e-mail: billyshaw15@aol.com

The **Widdrington Inn** stands proudly on its own just off the village green in the village of the same name, north of Morpeth on the road that leads up to Amble and beyond. Built 100 years ago, it has a private garden, a good-sized car park and picnic benches at the front and on the green. Inside, the theme is oak – for the floor, the bar counter, the tables and the chairs – and the whole place is kept in excellent order by tenants Billy and Julia.

Food is an important part of the business, and Billy's accomplished cooking can be enjoyed from 11.30 to 3 and from 5 to 9 every day (no food Sunday evening). The bar stocks a selection of real ales, but for many of the regular customers the favourite tipple is John Smiths Smooth. Tenants and staff work really hard to create a delightfully

relaxed, friendly atmosphere that attracts a good cross-section of the local

community, who come to enjoy the company, the food and the drink, and perhaps a game of pool. The inn has recently undergone a major refurbishment programme that included an extension to the bar and dining area. Open all day, the inn is a short drive inland from Druridge Bay on a beautiful stretch of coast.

387 THE MASONS ARMS

Stamford, Rennington, nr Alnwick,
Northumberland NE66 3RX
☎ 01665 577275
e-mail: bookings@masonsarms.net
🌐 www.masonsarms

In the heart of England's beautiful Border Country, the **Masons Arms** is a handsome 200-year-old country inn with a fine restaurant. Situated 4 miles from Alnwick and 3½ miles from the A1 on the B1340 road to Seahouses, the inn is an ideal base for exploring the natural beauty and the historic heritage of Northumberland's countryside and coast.

The inn's tastefully decorated bedrooms, all en suite, are a mixture of doubles, twins and family rooms. Four rooms, including two family rooms, are in the converted stable block, and six 'superior' rooms, two with sitting rooms, are in the DeLuxe annexe. The first-floor annexe

rooms open on to balconies, the ground-floor rooms on to a secluded patio garden. All rooms have TV, central heating, hairdryer, beverage tray and ironing facilities. Owners Bob and Alison Culverwell take excellent care of guests old and new, and the beamed bar is a convivial spot for enjoying a drink – perhaps a traditional ale from a local brewery or a malt whisky. In the dining rooms, meals are cooked to order using the very best seasonal local produce whenever possible.

388 LINDISFARNE PRIORY

Lindisfarne, Northumberland
☎ 01289 389200

Lindisfarne Priory is one of the Holiest Anglo-Saxon sites in England. When you cross the dramatic causeway to Holy Island, you journey into our spiritual heritage. Few places are as beautiful or have such special significance. The corpse of St. Cuthbert was found undecayed in 698AD, and this became one of the most sacred shrines in Christendom. For 1300 years it has been a place of pilgrimage and still is today.

Here you can learn about the Monastery's fantastic wealth and walk in the grounds where brutal Viking raiders plundered the priory, forcing Monks to refuge on the mainland. It is advisable to have a tide table with you when you visit Lindisfarne - at high tide the causeway linking Holy Island to the Northumbrian coast is submerged, cutting the Island off.

There is a sculpture on show entitled "Cuthbert of Farne" which was created by local artist Fenwick Lawson. This sculpture depicts a comtemplative Cuthbert reflecting on his religious life and desire for solitude. His interlaced hands echo the stillness and peace he sought.The Museum features is lively and atmospheric and explains what life was like more than a millenium ago. Open daily except Christmas and New Year, the facilities include parking, toilets, gift shop, souvenir guide and exhibition.

389 THE FAMOUS LORD NELSON

Chestnut Grove, Burton Joyce, Nottinghamshire NG14 5DN
☎ 0115 931 3263

The **Famous Lord Nelson** is a convivial pub on a corner site in the shadow of the church in Burton Joyce, close to the A612 Nottingham-Southwell road. Phil Webb, host and chef, keeps an excellent selection of real ales (Theakston's Best, Greene King IPA and Marston's Pedigree plus guests)

and offers good honest pub food served in generous platefuls at kind prices. The pub has a spacious lounge/restaurant, a smaller public bar and a beer garden with a children's play area. The River Trent runs at the back of the pub, which is open from 12 to 11 seven days a week. Food served Wednesday to Sunday.

390 THE WHITE LION

Nottingham Road, Bingham, Nottinghamshire NG13 8AT
☎ 01949 875541

Bingham, the unofficial 'capital' of the Vale of Belvoir, is a medieval market town with a fine 13th century church. It also has a fine old pub and a hub of the local community, the **White Lion**, where hands-on tenant Sue Boardman has struck up a terrific rapport with her customers. Standing at a busy crossroads near the town centre, the pub is open long hours every day for

a full range of drinks, and an interesting variety of food is served every session except Saturday and Sunday lunches. Typical dishes could include Thai duck and hoisin spring rolls, meat & potato pie and Mediterranean vegetable & cheese Wellington.

391 MANOR FARM ANIMAL CENTRE & DONKEY SANCTUARY

Castle Hill, East Leake, nr Loughborough,
Nottinghamshire LE12 6LU
☎ 01509 852525

Manor Farm Animal Centre & Donkey Sanctuary is a fun day out for all the family, with an amazing variety of activities on offer. As well as the assortment of animals to see, there is a nature trail, pond dipping, a wild flower meadow and a living willow village to stroll around.

Young children are very well catered for with an adventure playground, straw maze and an art &

craft activity centre and for those a little older, donkey and pony rides as well as quad bikes, are available. The facilities here make it easy to stay all day with a cafe, gift shop, picnic area, toilets, free parking and disabled access.

392 THE STAUNTON ARMS

Staunton-in-the-Vale,
Nottinghamshire NG13 9PE
☎ 01400 281062 Fax: 01400 282564
e-mail: trevorwalker@stralyns.fsnet.co.uk
⊕ www.staunton.co.uk

Nestling in the Vale of Belvoir a short drive from the Long Bennington turn-off from the A1, the **Staunton Arms** excels in a variety of ways. It's a traditional country inn dispensing warm hospitality and well-kept real ales that have earned CAMRA recognition. It's a destination food pub serving a selection of carefully prepared unpretentious dishes on snack and restaurant menus – the suet puddings are renowned for miles around! It's a comfortable, civilised base for the exploring the lovely Vale of Belvoir, with nine en suite rooms available all year round.

The 17th century building is in classic traditional style; its name commemorates one of England's oldest

families, whose coat of arms graces the pub sign and whose family tree is on

display in the bar. Last, but definitely not least, is the super atmosphere generated by Trevor, Jennifer and Adrian Walker. They provide the warmest of welcomes, friendly service and a genuine wish that first-time visitors become regulars.

393 THE ADMIRAL RODNEY

**King Street, Southwell,
Nottinghamshire NG25 0EH**
☎ 01636 812292
🌐 www.admiralrodney.com

Neil McKechan is a Southwell man through and through, and he has made the **Admiral Rodney** a great favourite not just with fellow Southwellians but with the many visitors who come to Southwell whether to explore the town's history or to try their luck at the races. A huge roaring fire in a big brick hearth greets visitors in the bar, where real-ale connoisseurs are spoilt for choice – Abbot Ale, London Pride, Timothy Taylor landlord and three regularly changing guests. The pub is open long hours every day, and good wholesome dishes at very reasonable prices, served all day, range from club sandwiches and melts to burgers, pasta, scampi, surf 'n' turf and a hearty beef and Abbot Ale pie.

The Admiral Rodney dates back to the middle of the 18th century, and before it another pub, the White Lion, and its associated brewery stood on the site. The pub's name remembers George Brydges, later Admiral Rodney, who played major roles in West Indies conflicts in the early 18th century and in the American War of Independence. A beam from the warship HMS Rodney was incorporated into the building, as was a beam from Southwell Minster, and in 1985 a well was discovered beneath the lounge, one of many in the locality which perhaps explains the town's name. Monday is quiz night.

394 THE BAY TREE CAFÉ BAR

**The Courtyard, Thoresby Park, nr Ollerton,
Nottinghamshire NG22 9EP**
☎ 01623 825225

Part of the old stable block in the grounds of Thoresby Park is now the **Bay Tree Café Bar**, a bright modern licensed café with a fine reputation for its fresh, wholesome cooking. Owner Adam Valintine has made this a warm, welcoming place, well decorated and furnished, with 40 seats inside and 40 more in the courtyard.

Croissants, bagels and pastries are served throughout the opening hours (10 to 4 seven days a week, a little later on warmer evenings), while lunchtime brings a much wider selection of hot and cold dishes. The printed menu and the daily changing blackboard lists range from club sandwiches, salads, quiches and jacket potatoes to

platters of mixed cheese, charcuterie and smoked fish, haddock & spring onion fishcakes, curries, chilli con carne, lasagne and moussaka. The grand mansion in the park (the largest park in the county) is Thoresby Hall, a Victorian mansion designed by Anthony Salvin and now a private hotel.

395 THE BROWNLOW ARMS

High Marnham, nr Tuxford,
Nottinghamshire NG23 6SG
☎ 01636 822505
🌐 www.thebrownlowarms.co.uk

The **Brownlow Arms** is a handsome brick and stone building with a red-tiled roof, standing just yards from the River Trent in the village of High Marnham. The main building is Grade II listed and dates from the 17th century, The old stables and other outbuildings still stand, and the whole place retained many fine original features in a full restoration in the 1990s.

Hosts Malcolm and Fiona make everyone feel instantly at home in the cosy bar and lounge, where the walls are hung with mementos and prints of the local area in days gone by, and the shelves are laden with brass and copper ornaments. Outside, there is a pleasant enclosed garden, with a terrace along the front of the building, with views over the River Trent. It's a real pleasure to relax with a glass of ale – Greene King IPA and Abbot Ale are the regulars – to quench a thirst or to decide what to eat, either in the bar or in the lovely little restaurant. Combos for two to share are a great idea – the seafood version has scampi, king prawns and scallops, garlic bread, jacket wedges, sauces and a salad garnish. There are curries at all temperature levels, from kindly korma to fiery vindaloo, and a terrific specials board tempts with such dishes as steak & Guinness pie, guinea fowl with marsala sauce, and three-cheese pasta and broccoli bake. They employ a full-time cook here, and Fiona also takes a great interest in what goes into the kitchen, and what comes out!

Opening hours at the Brownlow Arms are 12 to 2 and 5 to 11 Monday to Thursday, 12-12 Friday and Saturday and 12 to 11 Sunday. The inn is located on a minor road between the A1 (leave at the Tuxford roundabout) and the A1133. it can also be reached from the A57 Lincoln-Worksop road. The area round the pub has plenty of good walking and places to explore, and for anyone looking for a convenient base, the pub has an adjacent caravan and camping site.

396 THE OLD PLOUGH INN

Main Street, Egmanton, nr Tuxford, Nottinghamshire NG22 0EZ
☎ 01777 872565
🌐 www.oldploughinn.co.uk

Leaseholders, business partners and professional chefs Mark and Matthew have established a fine reputation for the hospitality and cuisine at the **Old Plough Inn**. Just minutes from the A1 at Toxford, the inn is open all day seven days a week for drinks (John Smiths Cask and Black Sheep are the regulars), and Mark and Matthew serve their super food from noon to 9 o'clock every day except Monday.

The printed menu, the grills board and the regularly changing specials board deliver an enticing choice for the pub's happy patrons, from sandwiches and burgers to mussels (with wine, herbs and cream or Thai-style), smoke haddock & spring onion fishcakes, braised lamb shank, and liver & bacon on a black pudding mash. The traditional Sunday lunch always brings a full house, and booking is also recommended for the monthly theme nights based on cuisines from around the world.

397 THE QUEENS HOTEL

High Street, East Markham, nr Retford, Nottinghamshire NG22 0RE
☎ 01777 870288

In spite of its name, The **Queens Hotel** is not a hotel at all but a very popular pub that's the hub of village life. In their 15 years as tenants, Chris and Barbara Russon have made this a great favourite not just with the locals but with regulars who come from many miles around to enjoy the ready welcome and the home-from-home atmosphere in the bar. And with the A1 close by, it's a very pleasant place to pause on a journey.

Well-kept real ales – Everards Beacon and Tiger and Adnams Southwold are the residents – have earned the CAMRA seal of approval, and good honest pub food,

from salads, snacks and sandwiches to steaks and pies and curries is served either in the bar or out in the beer garden every day except Monday. The Queens is open from 2 o'clock on Monday and all day every other day.

398 THE BOAT AT HAYTON

Main Road, Hayton, nr Retford,
Nottinghamshire DN22 9LF
☎ 01777 700158

In a picturesque setting the
Boat at Hayton is a
pleasant old inn serving
Hardy & Hansons ales and
an across-the-board menu.
Six bedrooms, four of them
en suite, are in a smartly
converted outbuilding.

Explore Britain and Ireland with
Hidden Places guides - a fascinating
series of national and local travel
guides.

www.travelpublishing.co.uk

0118-981-7777

info@travelpublishing.co.uk

399 THE GATE INN

Smeath Lane, Clarborough, nr Retford,
Nottinghamshire DN22 9JW
☎ 01777 703397

A pleasant setting by the Chesterfield Canal,
off the A620 northeast of Retford, is one of
the chief assets of the **Gate Inn**, which is
run in fine style by Karen and Daniel Bull.
Open lunchtime and evening and all day
Saturday
and
Sunday, the
pub offers
a good
choice of
drinks and
a choice of
bar and
restaurant
menus.

Inside, a big brick hearth is an eye-catching
feature, while outside, seats by the canal are
in demand when the sun shines. Wednesday is
quiz and bingo night, and the bar bounces to
the sounds of karaoke on the first Friday of
the month.

400 THE FIVE HORSESHOES

Maidensgrove, nr Henley-on-Thames,
Oxfordshire RG9 6EX
☎ 01491 641282 Fax: 01491 641086
e-mail: admin@thefivehorseshoes.co.uk
🌐 www.thefivehorseshoes.co.uk

The **Five Horseshoes** enjoys a scenic
location with stunning views, 4 miles north
of Henley and best reached from the B480
signed at Stonor. Tenant Nataliina and
experienced chef Jamie are really putting the
place on the
map as
somewhere
well worth
seeking out for
its ambience
and fine food.

Jamie's classic skills are evident in terrific
dishes like ham hock terrine, rump of lamb
with haricot beans, grease-free fish & chips
and a marvellous pork pie served with
piccalilli, cheese and rustic bread. And how
about treacle tart or chocolate truffle cake to
finish? The pub has two gardens where hog
roasts and BBQs take place in the summer.

401 MAPLEDURHAM ESTATE

Mapledurham, near Reading,
Oxfordshire RG4 7TR
☎ 01189 723350 Fax: 01189 794016
e-mail: Mtrust1997@aol.com
🌐 www.mapledurham.co.uk

Mapledurham House and Water-mill
nestle on the banks of the River Thames in
the beautiful south Oxfordshire countryside.
Visitors can watch the working watermill in
action – still producing flour – and tour the
Elizabethan mansion. Cream teas are a
speciality here and can be eaten in the Old
Manor tearooms or
on the lawns sloping
down to the Thames.
Arrival can also be
by boat from nearby
Caversham – a
delightful way to
start the afternoon.
Open in the
afternoons at
weekends and Bank
Holidays from Easter
to the end of
September.

509

402 THE PACKSADDLE INN

Chazey Heath, Mapledurham,
Oxfordshire RG4 7UD

☎ 0118 946 3000 Fax: 0118 947 4676

e-mail: enquiries@thepacksaddleinn.co.uk

🌐 www.thepacksaddleinn.co.uk

The **Packsaddle Inn** is set back from the A4074 northwest of Reading – at the Mapledurham Village turn off. Paul and Irene McCrystal, who took over this true hidden gem in September 2004, have made it a very popular place to visit for its winning combination of a friendly, mellow ambience, well-kept real ales and outstanding cuisine.

Open every session and all day Friday, Saturday and Sunday, it serves five real ales – Wadworth IPA, 6X, JCB, Bishops Tipple and a rotating guest. Regularly changing printed and blackboard menus tempt with a something-for-everyone selection of dishes, from whitebait and coarse chicken liver paté for starters to seafood pancakes,

cod in batter or with a Mornay sauce, field mushrooms topped with minced steak & cheddar or creamed leeks & stilton, Thai green curries and a steak & kidney pudding that's 'a legend in its own mealtime'. Sunday lunch brings four succulent roasts, with topside of beef always among them. Children are very welcome, and there's a secure play area in the garden.

403 THE RED LION

Goring Road, Woodcote,
Oxfordshire RG8 0SD

☎ 01491 680483

e-mail: sally-and-maurice@hotmail.com

🌐 www.theredlionwoodcote.co.uk

The **Red Lion** enjoys a very pleasant setting overlooking the green and cricket pitch in the village of Woodcote, off the A4074 between Reading and Wallingford. Dating from 1845, it has a warm, inviting feel that is reinforced by the welcome from landlords Sally and Maurice Cook.

The front of the pub is a blaze of colour from tubs and hanging baskets in spring and summer, and there are seats outside on the front terrace and rear patio.

Greene King IPA and Abbot Ale are the regular real ales, and in the kitchen Sally and the resident chef prepare a fine selection of dishes, including star-quality home-made pies, for the various menus. A Modest

Appetite Menu offers smaller portions of the main meals at lunchtime; Sunday sees brunch (11 to 4) and traditional roasts (12 to 2); Tuesday is curry night, from 6 to 9, to eat in or take away; and on most nights main courses can be bought to take way up to 11 o'clock. The Red Lion is closed Monday lunchtime, otherwise open every session and all day Saturday and Sunday. No food Sunday evening or Monday.

404 THE STAR INN

Watery Lane, Sparsholt,
Oxfordshire OX12 9PL
☎ 01235 751539
e-mail: info@starinnsparsholt.co.uk
🌐 www.starinnsparsholt.co.uk

The **Star** is a splendid 17th century country pub in red brick layered with stone, its roof slate-tiled, located in the village of Sparsholt just off the B4507 west of Wantage. The bar is particularly warm and inviting, with a log fire and some interesting old pictures, and locals and visitors meet to chat (often about horseracing – this is training territory) over a glass or two of cask ale; Courage Best is the resident brew.

The present owners, who took over the reins in January 2006, are maintaining the pub's long tradition of hospitality, and their chefs produce an excellent variety of dishes to enjoy every session except Sunday evening and Monday lunchtime (the pub is closed Monday lunchtime in

winter). Wednesday is fish night, Friday steak night, both with dishes at special

prices. This is good walking country – the Ridgeway Path is a mile-and-a-half away – and there are many places of scenic and historic interest in the vicinity. The Star makes an excellent base for exploring the region with eight en suite rooms in a converted barn with their own dedicated parking slots. Five of the rooms are on the ground floor; one is a family room.

405 THE GREYHOUND INN

Main Street, Letcombe Regis, nr Wantage,
Oxfordshire OX12 9JC
☎ 01205 771093 Fax: 01205 770905

The **Greyhound Inn** is a Grade II listed redbrick building in Letcombe Regis, a short distance from Wantage off the B4507. Leaseholders Frank and Hilary are maintaining the pub's tradition of hospitality in fine style, and Hilary caters for all appetites with a good choice of tasty home-prepared dishes, from jacket potatoes and generously filled sandwiches to burgers, steaks, fish & chips, curries and lasagne. Well-kept cask ales include

Morlands Original and Everards Original. For guests staying overnight the Greyhound has six comfortable bedrooms, including singles, doubles, twins and an en suite family room. The pub is open lunchtime and evening and all day Friday, Saturday and Sunday. Book for Sunday lunch; no food Sunday evening.

511

**Enslow Bridge, Bletchington,
Oxfordshire OX5 3AY
☎ 01869 331373**

The **Rock of Gibraltar** enjoys a splendid setting by the Coventry-Oxford Canal at Enslow Bridge, on the A4095 a few miles north of Oxford. The Canal was once busy with boats and barges plying their commercial trade, but is mow almost exclusively the domain of pleasure boaters. The inn was built around 1780 to house the navvies working on the Canal; it was then called the Waterways Inn, but now, as the Rock of Gibraltar, it is well placed for visitors to relax and unwind in the most pleasant of surroundings.

The restaurant has recently been redecorated, bringing a fresh, light look while retaining all the traditional character and appeal. Tenants Faith and Stamatis Trivizas have played a key part in the current popularity of the pub. Charming, friendly and hardworking, they make an excellent partnership, with Stamatis in charge of the bar and Faith the main force in the kitchen. Along with their sons John and Tim, they have generated a warm family atmosphere that imparts itself to visitors as soon as they cross the threshold into the traditional bar. Three real ales are kept in tip-top condition, and when

the weather is kind a drink or a meal can be enjoyed in the outdoor decking area by the Canal. Faith is a great cook, and she insists on seeking out the best and freshest seasonal produce for her menus. A blackboard lists the lunchtime selection, which includes sandwiches, ploughman's platters and popular hot and cold dishes. The evening brings the main à la carte choice of mainly traditional English dishes, typified by rack of lamb, chicken in white wine,

duck breast with a red wine and cherry sauce, and the always popular steaks. Sunday lunch sees a main-course choice of two roasts, a fish dish and a vegetarian dish.

This splendid place is very popular throughout the year, but it positively heaves on warm summer days, with boaters tying up to slake their thirsts and satisfy their appetites, and motorists who come from a wide catchment area. Children and dogs are welcome, and there's a safe play area in the garden.

407 THE CHEQUERS INN

17a Beaumont Road, Headington Quarry,
nr Oxford, Oxfordshire OX3 8JN
☎ 01865 762543

Located just north of Oxford, the **Chequers Inn** is well worth the short detour from the A40 to enjoy the excellent hospitality offered by Katerina and Mark, who took over the tenancy in June 2005.

The handsome and substantial early-19th century inn is open all day, seven days a week for real ales and a good array of keg bitters, lagers, stouts and ciders as well as wines, spirits and non-alcoholic drinks.

Food is available from 12 to 6 daily – good simple pub dishes served in generous platefuls, with filled giant Yorkshire puddings a speciality. Children are welcome until 9 in the evening, and the pub has a large beer garden and ample off-road parking space. Cash and cheque only. About the address: a major quarry once covered much of this area, and the beer garden of the Chequers once marked one of the quarry's edges.

408 THE SOW & PIGS

Main Street, Poundon, nr Bicester,
Oxfordshire OX27 9BA
☎ 01869 277728

Bar and restaurant menus provide an excellent choice for diners at the **Sow & Pigs**, a popular pub with parts going back to the 17th century. In the main street of Poundon, reached by a minor road east of Bicester, the pub has excellent hosts in the experienced Shirley and Chris Bamber and a fine chef in Fraser Gunn.

The kitchen's repertoire runs from simple classics like hot filled baguettes or basket meals, fish & chips and steaks to imaginative creations such as black pudding & spring onion fritters with chilli and mango salsa, or roast duck with sweet potato dauphinoise and a red cherry jus. Brakspears Bitter and two guest ales

head the list of drinks served lunchtime and evening and all day Saturday and Sunday.
Food is not available Sunday evening or Tuesday lunchtime. Sunday lunch is a popular carvery. The pub is closed Monday lunchtime except when it's a Bank Holiday. During 2006 the Sow & Pigs will have a new dining room and four rooms for B&B guests.

409 THE ROYAL SUN

2 Woodstock Road West, Begbroke,
Oxfordshire OX5 1RZ
☎ 01865 372231

2005 saw a change of owners and a major refit at the **Royal Sun**, which first saw the light of day as long ago as 1664. Closed for a month by the incoming team of Sheena Town, Angela and chef Matthew, it emerged spick and span after a top-to-toe refurbishment programme that gave the old place a fresh look while losing nothing of its traditional appeal.

Matthew and his assistants in the kitchens insist on the finest quality ingredients, and almost everything is sourced locally. Mussels steamed with white wine or a classic chicken and duck liver pâté might start a meal, followed perhaps by salmon hollandaise, a plain grill, the day's curry or, for vegetarians, three-cheese pasta and broccoli bake. The enjoyment level stays high to the end with scrumptious desserts such as treacle sponge, spotted dick or – wait for it! – lumpy bumpy chocolate cheesecake. Lighter lunchtime options include sandwiches, baguettes and wraps, jacket potatoes, burgers and meat or vegetable lasagne. The same high standards that distinguish the food also apply to the drinks: real ales and lagers are kept in tip-top condition, and the wine list offers something to provide a perfect marriage for any dish on the menu. The bar and dining areas have a neat, uncluttered appeal, with solid oak tables and chairs on wooden floors. The Royal Sun is open lunchtime and evening, and throughout the day during the summer months.

Begbroke lies on the A44 five miles northwest of Oxford. Woodstock, Blenheim Palace, the Churchill family grave at Bladon, the Roman Villa at North Leigh, and the Bus Museum at Long Hanborough are among the many and varied places of interest in the region, and visitors to the area who've built up a thirst and appetite looking at the sights know that the staff at the Royal Sun are ready and waiting with refreshment and hospitality.

Banbury Road, Tackley,
Oxfordshire OX5 3EP

☎ 01869 331328 Fax: 01869 331686
e-mail: enquiries@sturdyscastle.com
🌐 www.sturdyscastle.com

Continuity is the key to success at **Sturdy's Castle**, where the same family proprietors have maintained high consistently standards for more than 30 years. In a prominent position on the A4260 Oxford-Banbury road, it provides the ideal base for the business traveller or for touring the many sights and places of interest of Oxford and Oxfordshire. Still immaculate after recent refurbishment, Sturdy's has a traditional bar, an 80-cover restaurant and a separate accommodation block.

The inn is open all day, seven days a week, and food and drink are served throughout the day in the bar and restaurant. The lunchtime and à la carte menus, supplemented by daily specials, provides abundant choice for all tastes and appetites, and in the summer months the large beer garden is a delightful spot for drinking (Hook Norton Cask Ale and a guest cask bitter always on tap) or dining while enjoying the Oxfordshire air. The separate accommodation block close to the restaurant

has 20 smartly decorated and furnished bedrooms, all with en suite facilities, television, telephone and hot beverage tray. Ten of the rooms are located on the ground floor, two of the twin rooms are suitable for disabled guests and four of the doubles can sleep families of up to four. Interconnecting rooms are available.

A traditional full English breakfast starts the day, but it's also possible to book on a room only basis. Sturdy's Castle has a separate function room that is available for private hire. Any type of function can be catered for, and the room has its own skittle alley. With this facility and ample off-road car parking, it's the perfect venue for a business meeting or conference, and anything from buffets to full meals can be arranged for participants. For leisure guests, the Castle offers easy access to the numerous attractions that bring visitors from all over the world: Woodstock, the magnificent Blenheim Palace and the Churchill family grave are only two miles away, and it's less than ten miles to the almost endless sights of Oxford.

410 THE WOODSTOCK ARMS

8 Market Street, Woodstock,
Oxfordshire OX20 1SX
☎ 01993 811251
e-mail: sylvia.lodge@btinternet.com
🌐 www.woodstockarms.co.uk

There's never a shortage of things to see and do in and around Woodstock, including the magnificent Blenheim Palace, and one place on many visitors' itineraries is the **Woodstock Arms**. Old beams and open fires paint a traditional scene in the bar, and outside is a pleasant courtyard garden. Greene King IPA, Abbot Ale and Old

Speckled Hen are on tap for real ale enthusiasts, and hosts Sylvia and Alan offer a fine selection of freshly prepared food, including super fish specials, from noon until 9 o'clock (5 o'clock on Sundays).

414 THE QUART POT

3 High Street, Milton-under-Wychwood, nr
Chipping Norton, Oxfordshire OX7 6LA
☎ 01993 830589

In the heart of a village off the A361 north of Burford, the **Quart Pot** is enjoying great popularity under go-ahead tenants Sharon and John Smith. Sharon is the chef, and in the 30-cover restaurant dishes like her fish pie and minted lamb shanks keep a smile on the face of her customers. The pub has garden with a barbecue,

and ample off-road parking. The Quart Pot is close Sunday evening and Monday lunchtime, otherwise open lunchtime and evening and all day on Friday and Saturday.

412 THE KILLINGWORTH CASTLE INN

Glympton Road, Wootton, Woodstock,
Oxfordshire OX20 1EJ
☎ 01993 811401
e-mail: wiggiscastle@aol.com
🌐 www.killingworthcastle.co.uk

On the edge of the village of Wootton, the **Killingworth Castle Inn** beckons locals and visitors with fine ales, imaginative food, a regular programme of jazz and folk music and comfortable Bed & Breakfast accommodation. Add in the handsome surroundings of the 17th century former coaching inn and the welcome from hosts David and Sue Wiggins, and you have all the ingredients of an outstanding country inn.

Morland Original, Greene King IPA and Abbot Ale are the regular real ales, and a blackboard lists Sue's excellent home-cooked dishes. The 4 guest bedrooms, 2 on the ground floor, are in a converted barn next to the pub.

Woodleys, Woodstock,
Oxfordshire OX20 1HT
☎ 01993 811460 Fax: 01993 810165
e-mail: sales@dukeofmarlborough.co.uk
🌐 www.dukeofmarlborough.co.uk

Nobody exploring the historic sights of Woodstock and Blenheim Palace should leave the area without a visit to the **Duke of Marlborough**. Set beside the main A44 Oxford to Stratford road, this is a delightful 18th century coaching inn with an abundance of charm and character. It's named after the great military commander for whom a grateful nation built the magnificent Blenheim Palace and who was an ancestor of Winston Churchill.

The pub is on top form under the tenancy of Derek and Jan Allan, and the standards of hospitality, cuisine and accommodation are impressively high. A great deal of thought goes into the menus, starting with an emphasis on procuring the very best seasonal produce, and as a result the Duke of Marlborough has become one of the most successful dining pubs in the whole county. There's a really excellent choice throughout the meal.

Starters might include deep-fried Somerset Brie with a cranberry compote, warm duck salad or Thai-style prawns, followed perhaps by mushroom tortellini, chicken or seafood paella, or one of the popular steaks or beef specialities. Beef Marlborough is medallions of fillet topped with bacon and Stilton, served with a red wine sauce; Beef Blenheim is fillet filled with spinach, glazed with mozzarella and served with a horseradish cream sauce. There's always an excellent choice for vegetarians, and a children's menu that treats children as little grown-ups rather than big babies. Sandwiches and bar snacks are available for quicker/lighter meals.

A fine selection of wines complements the food, and two real ales are on tap. The Duke of Marlborough has two distinct restaurant areas, one traditional with oak-clad and exposed stone walls, oak beams and a roaring log fire, the other with modern décor and furnishings, imposing prints, vaulted ceilings and splendid views over the gardens. The beer garden comes into its own during the summer months, either for a drink or for a meal. The accommodation here maintains the high standard that obtain throughout. The 13 en suite rooms are beautifully furnished and decorated, and supplied with television, telephone and hospitality tray. Seven of the rooms are on the ground floor, one of them fully equipped for disabled guests, and there are two Executive rooms. Guests can stay on a Room Only, B&B or Dinner B&B basis.

415 THE MASONS ARMS

Banbury Road, Swerford,
nr Chipping Norton, Oxfordshire OX7 4AP
☎ 01608 683212   Fax: 01608 683105
e-mail: themasonschef@hotmail.com
⊕ www.masonsarms.co.nr

Bill Leadbeater, who runs the **Masons Arms** with his wife Charmaine and business partner Tom Aldous, spent a year looking for the right pub in the region of Oxford and the Cotswolds. His efforts were rewarded when he found this classic stone-built roadside inn, which ticked all the right boxes, including a good car park, a large garden with potential and the ability to attract passing trade.

The new team took over in September 2003, since when they have put the Masons Arms on the map as one of the leading destination dining pubs in the region, crowded most of the time with a wide cross-section of regulars in the know and first-timers delighted with the hospitality and the superb cooking. Bill has been in the catering and hospitality trade for 25 years, mostly as a chef, and his experience with such luminaries as Gordon Ramsay and Marco Pierre White, as well as four years in France, have given him a deep understanding of ingredients combined with the skills to produce top-class dishes. Seeking out the best seasonal produce, locally sourced as much as possible, he and his staff make everything on the

premises, including bread, terrines, pies, pasties, pastries and desserts. All the meat is fully traceable: beef from Shorthorn cattle, Oxford Down lamb, Gloucester Old Spot pork, local free-range poultry. Bill puts a modern, personal twist on old-fashioned cuts of meat such as shin of beef, lamb shanks, pig's cheek, belly of pork and ox tongue. His individual approach is apparent everywhere: fish fingers become salmon goujons (all the seafood is delivered fresh daily), chips become chunky fries, beans become mixed bean stew. The printed menu is supplemented by a huge choice on the

blackboard, where the mouthwatering options might include diver-caught scallops with scallop terrine and a sweet & sour sauce; haunch of venison two ways – casserole and steak; smoked duck breast with blackberries and wild mushrooms; and fried basil risotto balls with basil mayonnaise and an artichoke mayonnaise dip.

For quality, variety and value for money, the Masons Arms is a place to return to time and time again – many happy customers do just that, so it's always best to book. The pub has seats for 80 in the restaurant and extension and a pleasant lawned garden with splendid views.

416 THE PEAR TREE INN

Scotland End, Hook Norton, nr Banbury,
Oxfordshire OX15 5NU
☎ 01608 737482

The **Pear Tree Inn** is an outstanding old public house in the heart of Hook Norton and just a stone's throw from the renowned brewery. In the trade since 1972, the experienced Ian and Linda run the Pear Tree, a former grain store and cottages dating from the mid-18th century. The pub is open all day every day for drinks, which include most of the real ales from the Horton Brewery and a changing guest, along with a good choice of wines by glass or bottle.

Food served every session except Sunday evening offers classic pub dishes both traditional and modern: cod & chips, Old English fish pie, salmon fishcakes,

sausage & mash, faggots, steaks, lamb chops, chilli con carne, lasagne. The Pear Tree and the village are places to linger, and for guests staying overnight or longer the pub has 3 excellent en suite rooms – a double, a twin and a family room. The tariff includes a good hearty breakfast.

417 THE WHITE SWAN

Pretty Bush Lane, Wiggington,
Oxfordshire OX15 4LE
☎ 01608 737669

The **White Swan** is a fine old pub in wonderful walking country, and a walk in the bracing Oxfordshire air is sure to generate a thirst and appetite that hosts Dave and Carol can satisfy in splendid style. Three Hook Norton real ales are on tap to quench thirsts, and blackboards list the day's bill of fare, typified by classics such as

steak & kidney pie, casseroles and the Sunday lunchtime roasts. Close Monday lunch except when it's a Bank Holiday. The White Swan lies off the A361 between Banbury and Chipping Norton.

418 THE ELEPHANT & CASTLE

Bloxham, nr Banbury,
Oxfordshire OX15 4LZ
☎ 01295 720383
🌐 www.elephantandcastle.tableserve.com

The **Elephant & Castle** is a fine old village pub purpose-built in the 15th century and located just off the A361 a few miles south of Banbury. Charles Finch and his son Simon represent the family who have been for more than 30 years, and visitors can look forward to their warm and genuine hospitality, along with well-kept real ales and a good choice of freshly prepared

lunchtime food. And for guests staying overnight the pub has two en suite bedrooms – the tariff includes Continental breakfast.

519

419 THE SAYE & SELE ARMS

Main Road, Broughton, nr Banbury,
Oxfordshire OX15 5ED
☎ 01295 263348 Fax: 01295 272012
e-mail: mail@sayeandselearms.co.uk
🌐 www.sayeandselearms.co.uk

The **Saye & Sele Arms** is located on the
B4035 at Broughton, 3 miles west of
Banbury. Danny and Liz McGeehan took
over in May 2005 and quickly imbued the old
place with their special brand of hospitality.
The immaculate public area, with original
stone walls,
sturdy beams,
open fire,
mugs, jugs
and other
ornaments, is
a lovely
setting for
enjoying
well-kept

cask ales and first-class cooking. The day's
fresh fish dish and the day's savoury pie are
just a few of the temptations, and no meal is
complete without sampling one of Danny's
delicious desserts. No food Sunday evening.

420 THE LAMPET ARMS

Main Street, Upper Tadmarton, nr Banbury,
Oxfordshire OX15 5TB
☎ 01295 780070 Fax: 01295 788066
e-mail: lampet@btinternet.com
🌐 www.lampetarms.com

It's always a pleasure to visit the **Lampet
Arms**, whether it's for a drink, a meal or an
overnight stay. This friendly pub is in the
excellent care of Dawn and Mike Francis,
who put
visitors
instantly at
ease in the
spotless,
homely bar.
Up to four
real ales are
on tap, and
top produce,
sourced from

within the county as far as possible, is used
for the dishes on the nicely varied menu.
Closed Monday until 4, otherwise open all
day every day, this fine public house also
offers excellent guest accommodation in four
en suite rooms in the converted coach house.

422 THE DUN COW

West End, Horton, Oxfordshire OX15 6DA
☎ 01295 670524 Fax: 01295 678516
e-mail: vitiswines@hotmail.com
🌐 www.drunkenmonk.co.uk

In the lovely village of Horton, a short drive
northwest of Banbury, the **Dun Cow** is a delightful
17th century country pub. Part thatched, part slate-
roofed, the pub has a warm and welcoming interior
that's an ideal ambience for enjoying traditional ales,
unusual bottled beers, meads and wines, including fruit and country wines. Hook Norton Best and
Charles Wells Bombardier are the resident real ales, accompanied by changing guests and many
more brews during the February and July Beer Festivals.

Food is an equally important part
of the business at Martin and Gwyneth
Gelling's splendid pub, and the menus
really do offer something for everyone.
Gwyneth's steak & kidney pudding has
achieved superstar status in the region,
and the pub is one of the regular
meeting places of the Banbury Steak &
Kidney Pudding Club. Families are
welcome, and there's a separate
children's play area. The pub is open
Monday to Friday evenings and all day
on Saturday and Sunday. The Dun Cow
and a nearby field are frequently visited
by groups practising for historical battle
re-enactments.

421 THE ROEBUCK INN

Stratford Road, Drayton, nr Banbury,
Oxfordshire OX15 6EN
☎ 01295 730542

On the A422 a mile or so out of Banbury on the Stratford Road, the **Roebuck Inn** is a fine early 17th century hostelry serving excellent food lunchtime and evening. Nick and

Angie Saul, together in the trade since 1978, came here in June 2004 and really put the place on the map with their expertise and fine hospitality. The real ales are from the Hook Norton Brewery, and the food choice includes terrific home-made pies or dishes such as breast of chicken in a cream & stilton sauce. Booking is recommended at the weekend.

424 BARNSDALE LODGE HOTEL & RESTAURANTS

The Avenue, Rutland Water, nr Oakham,
Rutland LE15 8AH
☎ 01572 724678   Fax: 01572 724961
e-mail: enquiries@barnsdalelodge.co.uk
🌐 www.barnsdalelodge.co.uk

Barnsdsale Lodge is a 17th century farmhouse in stone and Collyweston slate in a prime position overlooking Rutland Water and open countryside. The 45 bedrooms, all with en suite facilities, are furnished in a mixture of styles, from Edwardian to contemporary. There's a great deal to see and do in the vicinity of the hotel, whether

it's exploring the historic sights and buildings, walking, cycling, indulging in the water-born activities on Rutland Water or just relaxing and unwinding in the hotel and its extensive, mature gardens and grounds. In the hotel restaurant, locally sourced produce is put to excellent use as the basis of daily changing menus.

423 SLIPCOTE

39 Main Street, Whissendine,
Rutland LE15 7ES
☎ 01664 474333
e-mail: slipcote@fsmail.net

Barry Knight front of house and chef Keith Harris at the stoves make a fine team at **Slipcote**, combining to provide a memorable dining experience in stylish contemporary surroundings, with the opportunity to eat al fresco. Served from 7 o'clock on Thursday, Friday and Saturday evenings, the à la carte menu is filled with good things.

Keith's considerable talents shine through in wonderful dishes like mixed seafood tartlet; fillet of plaice with mushrooms and prawns; breast of Gressingham duck with a black rice vinegar sauce and fillet steak with a cassis jus and crispy onion rings. To finish, perhaps world-class sticky toffee pudding with butterscotch sauce or chocolate fondue with fresh fruit, amaretti and marshmallows. A simpler three-course table d'hôte menu is available, with two choices for

each course.

This excellent restaurant is enrolled in the Gourmet

Society, a fine dining club for the East Midlands. Next to the restaurant is their coffee shop and deli selling Slipcote's soups, together with cheese and other prime foodstuffs. The charming medieval village of Whissendine, off the A606 between Oakham and Melton Mowbray, was one famous for producing a soft cheese called Whissendine Slipcote, the recipe for which has been lost.

Market Place, Uppingham,
Rutland LE15 9QH
☎ 01572 823259 Fax: 01572 820019
🌐 www.rutnet.co.uk/vaults

The picturesque stone-built town of Uppingham is the major community in the south part of Rutland, with a long and handsome main street and a fine market place. The town's best-known building is the famous Uppingham School, but for many visitors the first place to head for is **The Vaults**. Standing on a corner of the market place next to the old church, this much-loved establishment is equally popular with the residents of Uppingham and with the many travellers and tourists who visit this interesting region every year.

The owner of The Vaults, John Pearson, is himself something of an institution, one of the town's best-known characters and a constant presence here for more than 40 years. The bar is a convivial meeting place with a particularly warm, traditional ambience – a perfect spot for exchanging local news, putting the world to rights and enjoying a glass or two of beer. Marston's Bitter and Pedigree are the resident real ales, joined by a regularly changing guest; Happy Hour is 5 to 7 on Monday to Friday evenings.

Food is also a big attraction at The Vaults. The lunchtime menu includes filled baguettes, jacket potatoes, light snacks/starters, grills and time-honoured favourites like scampi, lasagne, shepherd's pie and chicken curry. The restaurant is open in the evening for full à la carte meals from a wide-ranging menu. Among the dishes listed on the specials board might be cod, chips & peas, sausage casserole, sweet & sour prawn balls and Mediterranean vegetable tart, and once a week it's steak & curry night, when the price of a main course includes a pint or a glass of wine. For Sunday lunch, the regular menu is supplemented by traditional roasts. Opening hours are 11.30 to midnight every day, with food served from 12 to 2 and 6 to 9.

Uppingham and the surrounding area are well worth taking time to explore, and there's no more convenient or friendly base than The Vaults. The three twin-bedded rooms and a family room are all en suite, with television and tea/coffee-making facilities.

425 RUTLAND RAILWAY MUSEUM

Ashwell Road, Cottesmore, Oakham,
Rutland LE15 7BX
☎ 01572 813203

Located in the pleasant countryside of the ancient county of Rutland, four miles from Oakham, the Museum is dedicated to telling the story of railways in industry, especially local ironstone quarrying. It goes back to the days before mass road transport when most freight was carried by rail and factories, works and quarries had their own railway systems.

The Museum's open air steam centre hosts a large collection of steam and diesel locomo-tives, wagons, vans and coaches, together with other related items and artefacts. Train rides and demonstrations are a regular feature of steam days - part of the ongoing development and restoration of the Museum site by volunteer members.

You can relax in comfort at the Visitor Centre where light refreshments are available and the Centre's souvenir shop has a variety of books, videos, souvenirs and low priced children's items on sale. Or why not enjoy a walk in pleasant country alongside the Museum's demonstration line. Watch the trains go by as you walk or picnic, and see the remains of the old Oakham Canal. A leaflet is available giving details of features of natural interest along the way. There are regular displays and exhibitions and the locomotives can be seen being repaired or painted.

427 THE MALT HOUSE

Long Meads, Lower Barns Road, Ludford,
Ludlow, Shropshire SY8 4DS (Bookings)
☎ 01584 873315
e-mail: jean@mellings.freeserve.co.uk
🌐 www.shropshirecottage.co.uk

A delightful period cottage with three double bedrooms and every amenity needed for a self-catering holiday. Quiet, scenic setting.

428 THE PENNY BLACK INN

Hope Bagot Lane, Knowbury, Ludlow,
Shropshire SY8 3LL
☎ 01584 890589
🌐 www.thepennyblackinn.co.uk

The cheerful orange paintwork makes it easy to spot the **Penny Black Inn**, which enjoys a quiet location in the secluded village of Knowbury, off the A4117 east of Ludlow. Since taking over in the summer of 2004, Peter and Sharron have really put their stamp on the inn, notably in the varied menus that range from light lunches and the Sunday carvery to a main menu featuring

prime meat from local butchers and some terrific fish specials. There are plenty of pleasant local walks to build up a thirst and appetite, some of them starting from the pub's car park. Open long hours every day.

429 THE KREMLIN INN

Cleehill, nr Ludlow, Shropshire SY8 3NB
☎ 01584 890950
e-mail: brianadshead@tiscali.co.uk

The **Kremlin Inn** is a 100-year-old former
quarrymaster's house in the picturesque village
of Cleehill, by the A4117 4 miles east of
Ludlow. Lesley and Brian Adshead took over
the pub in November 2005 as their first
venture into this type of business, and their
popular pub is open all day for ale and for
good, unpretentious home-cooked food. Two
spacious en suite rooms are available all year
round. The Kremlin Inn is the highest located
public house in Shropshire, and on a clear day
the views stretch over seven counties.

431 THE POWIS ARMS

Lydbury North, Shropshire SY7 8AU
☎ 01588 680254

The **Powis Arms** is a centuries old traditional
Coaching Inn. Inside you will find a warm
ambience in period surroundings.
The Bar serves Local Real Ales to perfection
complimenting the freshly made Bar Meals
and Snacks. The Restaurant, set in Baronial
surroundings, offers Traditional British home
cooked food using
local produce and
a wide selection of
wines to tempt
your palate.
B&B is provided
in 4 spacious
double en-suite

rooms tastefully decorated. One room is
suitable as a family room.
Outside there is a Beer Garden and a secure
Children & Family Area There is also a
Caravan & Camping Site with full Electric
and Water Hook-ups plus a well appointed
new amenity Building. Central for Fishing,
Walking, Cycling, Horse Riding and other
country pursuits.

430 THE ENGINE & TENDER

Broome, Aston-on-Clun, Craven Arms,
Shropshire SY7 0NT
☎ 01588 660275   Fax: 01588 660808

Bar snacks, a full à la carte and a children's
menu provide plenty of eating choice at the
15th century **Engine & Tender**. Three
locally brewed real ales include the pub's own
Engine Oil. The pub has a camping/caravan
site with an amenity block and electric hook-
ups.

432 CLAREMONT

Bull Lane, Bishops Castle,
Shropshire SY9 5DA
☎ 01588 638170
e-mail: info@priceclaremont.co.uk
🌐 www.priceclaremont.co.uk

Set in the grounds of a large Victorian house,
Claremont offers comfortable self-catering
accommodation in skilfully converted
properties sleeping from 2 to 6 guests. B&B
available in the main house.

433 THE GREEN DRAGON INN

Ludlow Road, Little Stretton,
Shropshire SY6 6RE
☎ 01694 722925

The **Green Dragon Inn** enjoys a lovely
scenic location in a village by the lower slopes
of Long Mynd. Built 400 years ago as an ale
house, it has an excellent host in Gary
Medlicott, who regales his customers with a
fine choice of real ales (including some less
well known local brews) and an extensive
selection of food. Plans include the opening
of B&B rooms, which will provide a perfect
base for walkers on the paths that cross the
Long Mynd over ancient hills and moorland.

434 MYND HOUSE

Ludlow Road, Little Stretton,
Shropshire SY6 6RB
☎ 01694 722212
e-mail: info@myndhouse.co.uk
🌐 www.myndhouse.co.uk

Mynd House, awarded 4 Stars by Visit Britian, is a very pleasant, civilised base for exploring the Stretton Hills and the surrounding area, whether by car, by bicycle or on foot.

Standing in its own grounds in the shadow of Long Mynd, the guest house, owned and run by Nigel and Theresa Rogers, has eight comfortable en suite bedrooms, each with its own character, including a family room and a four-poster room with a spa bath. It's also a great place for a meal, and Theresa's varied menu offers a choice of Western and Malaysian/Chinese/Nonya cuisine.

435 SHROPSHIRE REGIMENTAL MUSEUM

Shrewsbury Castle, Shrewsbury,
Shropshire SY1 2AT
☎ 01743 358516
e-mail: museum@shrewsbury.gov.uk
🌐 www.shrewsburymuseums.com

Housed in Shrewsbury Castle the **Shropshire Regimental Museum** tells the proud story of the four Shropshire Regiments – King's Shropshire Light Infantry, Shropshire Yeomanry, Shropshire Royal Horse Artillery and 4th Battalion King's Shropshire Light Infantry TA. On display are the colours bearing hard-won battle honours, now beautifully restored and hung around the Great Hall, the splendid regimental silver and china, the exotic uniforms and badges, weapons ranging from sword to machine gun, and medals gained in campaigns around the world, including three Victoria Crosses. Copious exhibits trace the history of the regular regiments as they helped to carve out and then garrison a world-wide empire, and of the territorial regiments at home ready for any crisis that might threaten the nation.

Of particular interest amongst the many treasures on display are the Standard of the Harford Dragoons, seized from the American Army outside Washington in 1814; the Croix de Guerre presented by the French nation to the 4th Territorial Battalion KSLI for their gallantry at the Battle of Bligny in 1918; and the baton of Grand Admiral Doenitz, Hitler's successor, taken in 1945. The last figure visitors see as they leave wears the uniform of the 5th Battalion The Light Infantry – today's volunteers and inheritors of the long tradition of service in Shropshire.

436 SHREWSBURY CASTLE

Castle Street, Shrewsbury,
Shropshire SY1 2AT
☎ 01743 358516

Noted for its commanding position and fantastic views, **Shrewsbury Castle** dates back more than 900 years to its founding in 1083. That was when Roger de Montgomery, a kinsman of William the Conqueror, was granted Shrewsbury and much of Shropshire as a reward for his loyalty. The fortress was part of the Normans' attempts to control the lawless border with Wales but by the time of Elizabeth I it had become a virtual ruin with no military significance. Of that Norman structure only the gateway remains along with one side and two corner towers from the 13th century.

During Elizabeth's reign the castle was used as a private residence but it saw action again during the Civil War when a small Parliamentary force captured the castle and town with little bloodshed. Two centuries passed and then the young Thomas Telford remodelled the castle, inside and out, for Sir William Pulteney. In 1924, Shropshire Horticultural Society bought the castle and presented it to the Corporation of Shrewsbury. It is now in the care of their successors, Shrewsbury and Atcham Borough. The castle has returned to a military role, in a peaceful way, by becoming home to the Shropshire Regimental Museum.

438 THE INN AT GRINSHILL

The High Street, Grinshill, nr Shrewsbury,
Shropshire SY4 3BL
☎ 01939 220410
e-mail: info@theinnatgrinshill.co.uk
🌐 www.theinnatgrinshill.co.uk

The **Inn at Grinshill** offers high standard accommodation, tailor-made dining and a traditional pub. It has been entirely re-furbished by the owners, Kevin & Victoria Brazier who have brought this country inn back into the 21st century whilst keeping its 18th, 19th and 20th century features. Six ultra-chic en-suite bedrooms offer sumptuous decor and furnishings but also up-to-date facilities such as broadband technology, LCD mirrored televisions, telephone facilities and luxury bathrooms that include sunken baths and power showers. 3 additional en-suite bedrooms are currently being planned. The modern and elegant Grinshill Garden Restaurant where Jeremy Stone, a top-class chef, and his team prepare mouthwatering meals in a kitchen

that is open to the restaurant. The cosy and inviting Elephant & Castle pub offers real ales, classic pub food and a welcoming fire that dominates the room, perfect for anybody passing by wanting a drink and a pub meal. Bookings are essential for Friday and Saturday evenings and Sunday lunch; Sunday evening meals by prior arrangement only.

437 THE NEW INN

Shrewsbury Road, Hadnall,
Shropshire SY4 4AE
☎ 01939 210249

On the A49 a few miles north of
Shrewsbury, the **New Inn** is a handsome
redbrick inn dating from 1864. Inside, the
public areas are comfortable and traditional,
and three real ales are on tap to quench
thirsts or to accompany the home-cooked
food ranging from light snacks to full meals,
served every lunchtime and evening. Gill and
Rob greet all their customers as old friends,
making every trip here a real pleasure.

439 THE DICKIN ARMS

Loppington, nr Shrewsbury,
Shropshire SY4 5SR
☎ 01939 233471
e-mail: dickinarms@hotmail.com

Close to the church in Loppington, the
Dickin Arms is a warm, hospitable inn dating
back over 300 years. It's open every lunchtime
and evening for guest ales, well-chosen wines
and home cooking including super sweets.
Book for a table at the weekend.

Looking for:
- *Places to Visit?*
- *Places to Stay?*
- *Places to Eat & Drink?*
- *Places to Shop?*

www.travelpublishing.co.uk

---

440 THE LEAKING TAP

Shrewsbury Road, Cockshott,
Shropshire SY12 0JQ
☎ 01939 270636 Fax: 01939 270746
⊕ www.theleakingtap.co.uk

Through a combination of hard work and
enthusiasm, Nick and Jennie have turned the
Leaking Tap into a pub of wide appeal both for
their regular customers and for visitors to the area.
The 400-year-old Grade II listed whitewashed
building on the A528 southeast of Ellesmere has a
homely, traditional interior of wood and beams and
hops, providing a delightful ambience for relaxing and
enjoying entertaining company and a glass of real ale –
Banks's Bitter and original are the residents.

Jennie is the queen of the stoves, and her à la carte
menu and
specials
board
provide an
excellent
choice that's
available
every
session

except Sunday evening. The name of the pub might
seem appropriate to the name of the village, but actually
it was inspired by the fact that Nick was a plumber for
many years.

441 THE FALCON INN

Wood Lane, Hinstock, nr Market Drayton, Shropshire TF9 2TA
☎ 01952 550241 Fax: 01952 550765
e-mail: info@falcon-inn-hinstock.co.uk
🌐 www.falcon-inn-hinstock.co.uk

If you live in an area that's short of good eating places, one answer is to open one. That's exactly what Rachel, John and Neil did when they took over the redbrick **Falcon Inn** in August 2005. They've made a great success of the venture, and their three chefs

are kept on the go preparing dishes for the interesting daily changing menus, which show a winning combination of classic and contemporary elements. For guests staying overnight, the Falcon has six bedrooms for B&B – two singles, a double and three twins, including one suitable for families.

442 THE FOX & HOUNDS

High Street, Cheswardine, nr Market Drayton, Shropshire TF9 2RS
☎ 01630 661227

The **Fox & Hounds** stands in the shadow of Cheswardine's magnificent church in an area that's popular with walkers and boating folk – the Shropshire Union Canal is close by. The pub, the first venture for Lee and Alan, is open Monday to Friday evenings and all day Saturday, Sunday and Bank Holidays for drinks; Tetleys and a guest real ale head the list of drinks,

and Guinness is also a great favourite with the regulars. The hosts have gradually been introducing food, starting with Sunday lunch and now extending to the evenings.

444 THE LIME KILN

Porth y Waen, nr Oswestry, Shropshire SY10 8LX
☎ 01691 831550
e-mail: bookings@thelimekiln.net
🌐 www.thelimekiln.net

Local and regional awards testify to the high standards set by John and Christine Hanby at the **Lime Kiln**, a former Quarry Pub and Count House that was once called the

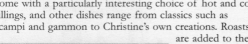

Red Lion. Christine's excellent, creative cooking is the major contributor to the success story, and the dishes on her blackboard are based as far as possible on local, seasonal produce. Lunchtime sandwiches and baguettes come with a particularly interesting choice of hot and cold fillings, and other dishes range from classics such as scampi and gammon to Christine's own creations. Roasts are added to the Sunday selection –

booking is recommended for Sunday lunch and all evenings.

Well-kept real ales include Banks's Bitter and Marston's Pedigree, and there's a good choice of good-value wines. The interior of the pub features lots of wood, including stripped pine panels, pine tables and some comfortable pew seating. Outside, picnic benches are set out in the garden, and visitors can enjoy an alfresco drink and a game of boules. The Lime Kiln stands by the A495 between the village and the junction with the A483.

Montford Bridge, nr Shrewsbury,
Shropshire SY4 1EB
☎ 01743 850750
e-mail: mail@theoldswan.com
🌐 www.theoldswan.com

In the picturesque village of Montford Bridge, just off the main A5 3 miles north of Shrewsbury, **The Old Swan** is a pub of great appeal for the whole family. Parts of the pub, which was previously called the Wingfield Arms, dated back some 400 years, and behind the mellow, yellow-painted, part creeper-clad exterior the public areas feature some interesting brickwork.

Business partners and good friends Frank and Denise, Stephen and Julie own and run the pub, which is open lunchtime and evening, all day Saturday and Sunday and all day every day in summer for drinks and light bites such as burgers and baguettes. Three real ales are always on hand to quench thirsts or to accompany the fine food that has contributed in great part to the pub's success.

The printed menu offers a good choice of manly tried and tested favourites: chicken liver pâté, garlic mushrooms, lasagne, liver & bacon

with onion gravy, steaks, steak & ale pie, beer-battered cod. The daily-changing specials provides further choice with the likes of 'Supreme Salmon' wrapped in smoke bacon and puff pastry served with cream and tomatoe sauce or venison topped with caramelised red onions. Sunday lunch is a carvery only, and food is not available Sunday evening or Monday. Booking is recommended at all meal times to be sure of a table in the restaurant.

Caravanners and campers can avail themselves of the large area at the back, which has 23 hardstandings, showers, toilets and

electric hook-ups. The owners hope soon to offer Bed & Breakfast rooms at the pub, which will make it a super base for both leisure and business visitors. The Old Swan has fishing rights along a three quater of a mile stretch of the River Severn and there are many pleasant walks to take and villages to explore in the area, and the town of Shrewsbury is as rich in historic interest as almost any in the country.

Two other points of interest at the Old Swan: the pub holds a mixed auction every other Tuesday – view by day, bidding from 6.30; and a park-and-ride bus for Shrewsbury stops outside.

529

445 THE RED LION

Bailey Head, Oswestry,
Shropshire SY11 1PZ
☎ 01691 656077

Centrally located in the historic market town
of Oswestry, the **Red Lion** serves both as a
cosy, friendly local with real ales and home
cooking, and a B&B base with five en suite
rooms.

446 THE WALLS

Welsh Walls, Oswestry,
Shropshire SY11 1AW
☎ 01691 670970 Fax: 01691 653820
⊕ www.the-walls.co.uk

Geoffrey and Kate continue to enhance the
reputation of **The Walls** as the top place in
Oswestry for food and entertainment. The
dining areas in this former school building are
nothing if not impressive – a spacious,
comfortable setting for enjoying superb,
award-winning cooking, from much-loved
classics to more elaborate or exotic dishes.
The Walls hosts regular live music evenings,
often featuring big-name performers.

Looking for:
- *Places to Visit?*
- *Places to Stay?*
- *Places to Eat & Drink?*
- *Places to Shop?*

www.travelpublishing.co.uk

447 THE SUN INN

Welshampton, Ellsemere,
Shropshire SY12 0PH
☎ 01948 710637 Fax: 01948 710812
e-mail: thesuninn@tiscali.co.uk
⊕ www.thesuninnwelshampton.co.uk

Formerly a malthouse and drying house dating back
some 200 years, the **Sun Inn** is the hub of the
community of Welshampton, on the A495 between
Oswestry and Whitchurch. Stuart and Shirley
Thomas have held the tenancy since 2002, pleasing
their

regular customers and visitors alike with their fine brand
of hospitality. Black beams ands rich red half-panelling are
striking features in the public areas, which comprise a main
bar, lounge and family room.

Three real ales – Tetley's Bitter and Mild and a
rotating guest – are always available, and another ten are

added during
the weekend-
long beer
festivals the Sun
hosts each May
and September. Local produce, including home-grown
vegetables in the summer, are the basis of the home-
cooked food served lunchtime and evening Monday to
Friday and all day on Saturday and Sunday. Tuesday is
quiz night, and there's live music most Fridays. Picnic
benches are set out in the large beer garden and seperate
childs play area at the rear, where there's also a small site
for caravans, with electric hook-ups.

448 MULBERRY'S BISTRO

9 Union Street, Yeovil, Somerset BA20 1PQ
☎ 01935 434188 Fax: 01935 434188
e-mail: mulberrysbistro@aol.com

The good folk of Yeovil, a historic market town on the River Yeo, are lucky indeed to have in **Mulberry's Bistro** an eating place to rival the best in the region. But the reputation of this outstanding bistro has spread far beyond the confines of the town, and its popularity is founded on the very best of reasons – the excellence of the cooking. This intimate, relaxed restaurant was established in 1992 by Kevin Green, who runs it with his wife Michele, and in Liam Pople they have a chef who combines classical skills and innovation at a very high level. His main passion is French cuisine, and his experience includes a spell with the doughty Billy Reid at the Vineyard in Stockbridge. Liam's repertoire covers a wide variety of flavours and textures, and his lunch menus range from garlic field mushrooms and Thai fish cakes to super homemade burgers, sizzling steaks, lamb shanks and calves' liver. In the evening he gives full rein to his skills on a menu that offers British and French classics, imaginative variations on meat and poultry and always an excellent choice for fish-eaters and vegetarians. One of Liam's signature dishes is memorable pan-seared brill with a tomato ratatouille and beurre blanc. Everything if freshly cooked to order, and the quality of the ingredients, much of them local, shines through each and every dish. The desserts keep

the enjoyment level high to the end, and a well-chosen, wide-ranging wine list complements perfectly the outstanding food.

First-time visitors soon become regulars at Mulberry's Bistro, which is a perfect choice for anything from a business lunch to a romantic dinner for two and a celebration of a birthday or other special occasion. There are 56 covers in the downstairs room and 20 in an upstairs private room. Mulberry's is open from 10 to 2.45 and from 6.45 to 10.30 (later by arrangement) Monday to Saturday; closed Sunday.

531

449 THE KINGS ARMS INN AND RESTAURANT

Bishopston, nr Montacute,
Somerset TA15 6UU
☎ 01935 822513 Fax: 01935 826549
e-mail: kingsarmsmont@aol.com
🌐 www.thekingsarmsmontacute.co.uk

Resident owners Chris and Carol Millward
welcome visitors old and new to the **Kings
Arms Inn and Restaurant**, which stands
next to the church in the attractive village of
Montacute. Built of the distinctive local
hamstone in the 17th century, the inn retains

many original features, and blazing log fires add to
the inviting ambience in the lounge bar.

In the summer months, the beautiful gardens
are a great asset. In the restaurant, the chefs
prepare an excellent choice of dishes that use the
very best local suppliers of Meat, fish, dairy and
vegetable produce; a separate snack menu is also
available. For guests wanting to explore the many
places of interest in the area the Kings Arms has
15 comfortable en suite bedrooms available
throughout the year.

450 THE GEORGE INN

Church Street, Martock, Somerset TA12 6JL
☎ 01935 822574

Thousands of visitors pass through the little town
of Martock each year, and those who choose to
break their journey are rewarded with a wealth of
interesting places to see. The former abbey church, the Treasurer's House and the Old Court house
are among the many distinguished buildings, but those in the know add **The George Inn** to the
list.

This 15th century stone hostelry, with many
original features still intact, is in the excellent care of
Philip behind the bar and Angela in charge of culinary
matters. In the classic old-world bar area with its low-
beamed ceiling, four or more real ales are always on tap,
and in the elegant restaurant diners can choose from an

impressive
selection of
home-cooked
dishes. The
steak & ale
pies

disappear as quickly as the kitchen can serve them up,
and the long list of blackboard specials might include
spicy Thai fish or chicken cakes, locally made faggots in a
rich onion gravy, pork in an orange and cinnamon sauce,
beer-battered cod and tagliatelle dolcelatte. A senior
citizens lunchtime special is served Tuesday to Friday.
Mondays senior citizen special is a 2 course roast lunch.

451 THE WHEATSHEAF

Silver Street, South Petherton,
Somerset TA13 5AN
☎ 01460 240382
e-mail:
stevewheatsheaf@btopenworld.com
🌐 www.thewheatsheafontheweb.co.uk

With food served from noon till 9 every day, the **Wheatsheaf** is definitely the place to head for with a hunger. The bar menu and specials board provide an excellent choice of pub favourites, from baguettes, burgers and

jacket potatoes to battered cod, scampi, chilli, steaks and pies, plus daily specials such as lamb hotpot and there's always a good choice of vegetarian dishes.

Stephen Wainwright has kept his customers happy for many years at his no-nonsense little sandstone pub, where thirsts are quenched by a variety of well-kept real ales.

453 THE KINGS HEAD

Church Street, Chard,
Somerset TA20 2DW
☎ 01460 63206

Colin and Lucinda Foster are the friendly hosts at the **Kings Head**, a well-established pub in the centre of Chard. Equally popular with regulars and first-timers, the pub has a splendidly, traditional ambience, with slate

floors and wood-burning stove. Real ales and ciders accompany a menu of pub favourites

that include daily specials and Sunday roasts; Thursday is steak night. On the social/sporting side the Kings Head offers darts, pool and skittles and is the HQ of rugby and cricket teams.

452 GABRIELS B&B

Fore Street, Winsham, nr Chard,
Somerset TA20 4BY
☎ 01460 30936
e-mail: info@staygabriels.co.uk
🌐 www.staygabriels.co.uk

Gabriels, a period village house with a secluded garden and easy access to the Dorset coast and East Devon, has recently been transformed into a luxury B&B. Each of

the three bedrooms is fresh and airy, with super-comfortable beds, new duvets, a supply of books, and extras such as

fresh fruit bowl, fresh milk for morning tea, books and magazines. The en suite bathrooms are generously supplied with lotions and potions, and guests have the use of a quiet drawing room. The breakfast choice includes fresh fruit salad, yoghurts, kedgeree, kippers, and scrambled eggs with smoked salmon. Evening meals are available.

454 THE GOLDEN FLEECE

Perry Street, South Chard,
Somerset TA20 4QH
☎ 01460 220285
e-mail: goldenfleece2003@hotmail.com

Located on the B3167 close to Forde Abbey, the **Golden Fleece** is a grand 17 th century pub that offers delightful hospitality in a peaceful, relaxed atmosphere. The walls of the restaurant are hung with paintings by the well-known local artist Dick Sturgeon.

Carol presides over the kitchen, where local produce features as much as possible in a variety of dishes served lunchtime and evening. Lamb shanks, steak & ale pie and the varied vegetarian menu are among the favourite orders, along with succulent steaks and a traditional Sunday lunch. A children's menu is also available, along with lighter options for lunch.

Behind the pub is a patio, a large car park

and a 2-acre camp site that offers beautiful views and a well located base for touring the region.

456 THE NEW INN

Priddy Green, Priddy, nr Wells,
Somerset BA5 3BB
☎ 01749 676465
e-mail: Pauline.groome@btconnect.co.uk

On the green in the little village of Priddy, the **New Inn** enjoys a quiet rural setting in the Mendip Hills, close to Cheddar gorge, Wookey Hole and the cathedral city of Wells. Pauline and Michael assure all their guests of the warmest and most genuine of welcomes, and the atmosphere in the bar and lounge is invariably cosy and friendly. The fully stocked bar offers a good selection of real ales, other beers and lagers, spirits, fine wines and soft drinks, and also serves a variety of tasty bar snacks and light meals.

In the separate conservatory-style restaurant, an excellent choice of home-cooked food is available lunchtime and evening; everything is fresh and

appetising, and the fish specials are definitely not to be missed.

There's plenty to explore in the vicinity of the inn, which provides an ideal B&B base for tourists in tastefully furnished and decorated bedrooms equipped with television and tea/coffee-making facilities.

455 BOWLISH HOUSE

Wells Road, Shepton Mallet,
Somerset BA4 5JD
☎ 01749 342022
e-mail: info@bowlishhouse.com
🌐 www.bowlishhouse.com

Bowlish House, in historic Shepton Mallet, is just 10 minutes drive from the cathedral city of Wells, the old world charms of Glastonbury, and within easy travelling of unique landmarks such as Glastonbury Tor, Cheddar Gorge, Wookey Hole Caves and Longleat House & Safari Park.

Bowlish House is the ideal place to get away from it all with friends and family. Its unique grade II* Georgian House setting provides an interesting and peaceful location in which to escape and enjoy top quality food at reasonable prices. Originally built by a prosperous clothier, one of several who built large houses along the valley of the River Sheppey, ownership passed to the Anglo Bavarian Brewery in the mid 1800s. The proprietors, Jason Goy and Darren Carter, are implementing a gradual restoration of the interior of the building, creating a natural blend of Georgian architecture with contemporary art providing truly stylish yet charming surroundings where everyone is made to feel

welcome.

Open for morning coffee as well as lunch and dinner, the menus make the most of seasonal produce and are creative whilst ensuring there is something for every palate.

Choose from lighter meals such as sea bass served on a bed of lemon and ginger couscous or more robust dishes like rack of English lamb with a Roquefort and nutmeg breadcrumb served with turnip mash and a rich red wine jus. And for desserts - you'll just be spoilt for choice, from sticky toffee and bread and butter pudding to the famous cheeseboard, something for everyone.

For information on sample menus, rooms and other facilites visit the website. Open for morning coffee from 10am, for lunch noon-2pm and for dinner Monday to Saturday 7pm-9pm.

535

457 HESTERCOMBE GARDENS 🏛

Cheddon Fitzpaine, near Taunton,
Somerset TA2 8LG
☎ 01823 413923 Fax: 01823 413747
e-mail: info@hestercombegardens.com
🌐 www.hestercombegardens.com

On the southern slopes of the Quantocks,
Hestercombe Gardens lie on an estate that
goes back to Saxon times but, from the 14th
to the late 19th centuries it was owned by one
continuous family and it was Coplestone
Warre Bampfylde who designed and laid out
the magnificent landscaped garden. In 1872,
the estate was acquired by the 1st Viscount
Portman and his grandson, Hon Edward
Portman commissioned sir Edwin Lutyens in
1904 to create a new formal garden that was
planted by
Gertrude
Jekyll. A walk
around this
wonderful 40-
acre garden will
include lakes,
temples and
magnificent
views.

459 THE WHITE HORSE INN ⚑

Regent Street, Bradford-on-Tone,
nr Taunton, Somerset TA4 1HF
☎ 01823 461239
e-mail: donna@pmccann1.wanadoo.co.uk

Donna and Philip McCann have been
proprietors at the **White Horse Inn** for
more than five years now. This handsome old
pub in a quiet village is equally popular with
locals,
walkers
and
tourists
alike.
The
interesting
menus
provide
traditional
dishes
as well
as fine

A la Carte, and there is a selection of fine
wines to accompany your meal.. Selected by
CAMRA for their well-kept ales, they pride
themselves on quality and tradition.

458 THE RISING SUN ⚑

West Bagborough, nr Taunton,
Somerset TA4 3EF
☎ 01823 432575
e-mail: rob@theriser.co,uk
🌐 www.theriser.co.uk

In the heart of the lovely Quantock Hills, the
Rising Sun is a fine pub that's equally delightful to
visit for a drink, a meal or a break away from the
hubbub of city life. The inn was re-created from
virtually bare bones after a devastating fire in 2002,
and risen from the ashes it combines rescued or
replaced original features (walls, oak windows,
panelling, flagstones) with 21st century style and
comfort.

Five real ales from local breweries are always on
tap, and top-notch head chef Guy Horley creates
menus for all tastes: superb, imaginative dishes such as
breast of
Quantock
duck on
basil-crushed
potatoes with
a Courvoisier
and plum
sauce or

salmon a bed of crab and leeks stand alongside all-time
pub classics and lighter bar meals. The guest
accommodation comprises two superbly appointed
bedrooms, one in Tudor style with a four-poster bed, the
other in French farmhouse style.

460 THE MARTLET INN

Langford Budville, nr Wellington,
Somerset TA21 0QZ
☎ 01823 400262 Fax: 01823 401555

In a delightful setting off the B3187 north of Wellington, the **Martlet Inn** commands lovely views of the Blackdown Hills. The inn, which was built as a farmhouse some 400 years ago, is adorned with beautiful hanging baskets and window boxes, and the award-winning front and rear gardens feature superb planting and lots of pots and tubs, as well as a children's play area – and a child-free zone! Inside, flagstone floors, exposed beams, inglenook fireplaces and locally made farmhouse pine furniture paint a traditional scene, and collections of rural and agricultural antiques hang on the walls and ceilings.

Vic and Paulette Bigg are the proprietors, Paulette the queen of the kitchen and Vic running the bar and cellar. Well-kept real ales include three local brews, and there's a varied list of wines from around the world. A wide-ranging menu featuring as much local produce as possible offers mainly traditional British dishes, all prepared on the premises by Paulette. This is great walking and cycling country, and the Martlet Inn has en suite rooms for B&B guests. Also available are a self-catering cottage and self-catering apartment.

461 THE BLUE MANTLE HOTEL

2 Mantle Street, Wellington,
Somerset TA21 8AW
☎ 01823 662000
e-mail: bluemantlehotel@aol.com

Wellington is the pleasant old market town from which the Duke took his title, and south of town an obelisk 175 feet high was erected to commemorate his great victory at Waterloo. Back in the main street of town, another landmark is the **Blue Mantle Hotel**, a pretty period building painted in light blue, with small-paned windows framed in white.

Chris and Kathleen Towle, whose interests and skills range from languages and arts and crafts to natural therapies, printing production and cooking. They are also the friendliest and most civilised of hosts, and they have a genuine desire to make their guests feel instantly at home. The guests cover a wide spectrum of backgrounds and interests and include regular visits from students at the nearby international school

and their parents. The guest accommodation comprises eight well-appointed bedrooms, all but one with en suite facilities. Non-residents are welcome to drop in for breakfast, tea, coffee and cakes.

462 THE MALT SHOVEL

Blackmore Lane, Bradley Green,
nr Bridgwater, Somerset TA5 2NE
☎ 01278 653432

In the small village of Cannington, off the A39 west of Bridgwater, the **Malt Shovel** has a genuine country appeal that's enhanced by the warm welcome provided by Tracy, Malcolm and their staff.

Much loved by the local community, it's also perfect spot to pause on a journey, and many a motorist on the busy A39 has been grateful for the fine hospitality that is always on offer. Butcombe Bitter, Exmoor Fox and two guests provide a choice for real ale connoisseurs to

enjoy in the atmospheric old-world bar and snug.
Hungers are satisfied with good honest cooking in the best English tradition, with a carvery available Sundays. Families are always welcome, (children can choose from their own menu). In the summer months, the picnic benches in the garden come into their own.

463 THE VOLUNTEER ARMS

Union Street, Bridgwater,
Somerset TA6 4BY
☎ 01278 422780
e-mail: dannyvolunteerarms@yahoo.co.uk

February 2006 saw the arrival of Danny Bull at the **Volunteer Arms**, and in his first venture into the licensed trade he is proving to be a very popular landlord. This is first and foremost a locals pub, with a regular following drawn from all age groups, but visitors to the ancient inland port and industrial town of Bridgwater are always welcome.

Located on the outskirts of town on the A38 Bristol road, the pub has a spacious, comfortable interior that's looking spick and span after Danny and his helpers spent a lot of effort into putting it in order. Old Speckled hen and Otter are the regular real ales, and Danny has started

serving popular pub dishes.
Bridgwater's most famous son was the celebrated military leader Robert Blake, who was an important officer in Cromwell's army. The museum that commemorates his life is one of the many places of interest in the town, and after a visit to this and the other attractions the best plan is to head for the Volunteer Arms to enjoy Danny's hospitality.

**Huntworth, nr Bridgwater,
Somerset TA7 0AQ
☎ 01278 662473**

Coming off the M5 at junction 24 you will find the small village of Huntwoth. Just over the canal bridge The **Boat & Anchor,** a 120-year-old hostelry, nestles alongside the picturesque Taunton-Bridgwater Canal. The setting and the views are a real delight, and the inn is an ideal spot to pause on a journey to or from Devon and Cornwall.

The welcome from owners and staff is warm and genuine, and the wide choice of food and drink provides something to please everyone. Baguettes, ploughman's platters and jacket potatoes are favourite lunchtime fare, with steaks, sizzlers and seafood specials popular choice from the main menu. The pub serves real ales among a fine selection of other draught and bottled beers, lagers, wines, spirits and soft drinks. It also provides a delightful base for touring Somerset, with 11 comfortable en suite bedrooms. A versatile function suite caters for all kinds of celebrations, get-togethers, meetings and conferences. The Toby at nearby Chilton Polden has the same owners.

THE TOBY

**Chilton Polden, nr Bridgwater, Somerset TA7 9AH
01278 722202**

On the A39 Glastonbury road east of Bridgwater, 5 miles from junction 25 off the M5, **The Toby** is a purpose-built modern pub with state-of-the-art amenities and smart contemporary styling. Food is a big part of the business here, and there's always an excellent choice of Greek and other Mediterranean dishes, grills and seafood specials. The Toby and the sister establishment the Boat & Anchor both have very talented chefs, and their friendly rivalry keeps standards commendably high at both. The seven guest bedrooms in roadhouse style combine superb comfort with practicality; one of the rooms has been adapted for disabled guests, and the bar and restaurant are also accessible to wheelchair users.

Ashcott, nr Bridgwater, Somerset TA7 9QQ
☎ 01458 218282

On the A39 west of Street and Glastonbury and east of Bridgwater, the **Ashcott Inn** is a fine old hostelry that has been welcoming visitors since the 17th century. Sarah Shaw heads the family team at the helm, and their warmth and hospitality make this a particularly pleasant place to pause on a journey. Smart black shutters and hanging baskets take the eye on the pub's stone frontage, and the inside is no less appealing. A woodburning stove in a huge inglenook hearth warms the popular stripped stone public bar, and the lounge is an equally convivial spot for enjoying a drink.

The décor includes some fascinating old portraits and a wealth of brass and copper ornaments. At least three real ales are always available, and there's also a good selection of wines to enjoy on their own or as an accompaniment to the food. And food is an increasingly important part of the Ashcott's business. Sarah's husband is the head chef, and the cooking has taken a dramatic turn for the better since he took over the kitchens, so 'Famous for Food' on the huge sign on the outside of the pub really does mean what it says. And whether you're a 'traditionalist' or a 'modernist', there's plenty to choose from on the wide-ranging menus in the restaurant that overlooks the garden.

The chef sets great store by the best local produce, which features in hearty dishes like Somerset pork with apple mash, roast chicken and stuffing suet pudding, or braised Glastonbury lamb. One of the chef's signature dishes is Ashcott Wellington – fillet on a bed of pâté, with a puff pastry crust, served on a bed of potato with a creamy stilton sauce. The Sunday roast, with a choice of beef, pork or lamb, is a real bargain, with roast and new potatoes, Yorkshire pudding, a selection of fresh vegetables and a dessert included in the price. Fish eaters could choose from the likes of classic cod, chips and mushy peas, smoked haddock rarebit, or salmon with tarragon and lemon butter. For more exotic tastes, the choice might be Peking chicken kebabs, Thai green curry or sweet & sour pork. Vegetarians are certainly not forgotten, and there are some scrumptious desserts to round things off in style. In the summer, sandwiches can be ordered outside main meal times.

The inn is open all day in the summer, when the tables on the terrace come into their own. This is very much a place for all the family, and children can have fun and use up surplus energy in the adventure play area.

467 THE KNOWLE INN

**Bath Road, Bawdrip, nr Bridgwater,
Somerset TA7 8PN
☎ 01278 683330
e-mail: peter@matthews3.wanadoo.co.uk**

Peter Matthews in the bar and Christina at the stoves are the busy husband-and-wife team who run the **Knowle Inn**. On the A39 east of Bridgwater and a short drive from Junction 23 of the M5, the inn started life as far back as the 16th century, and the tenants have enhanced the old-world appeal by adding their own personal touches in the quaint public bar, the side lounge and the elegant adjoining restaurant.

The choice of real ales here is one of the very best in the region, with some smaller local breweries featured, but the food provides an equally good reason for a visit. Local ham served with egg, chips & peas,

lasagne, steak & ale pie and chicken breast with mushrooms, bacon and melted cheese all have their supporters, but many of the regulars cast their eyes in the direction of the seafood specials board, which tempts with superb dishes such as John Dory or Gurnard with lemon butter, Smoked Haddock in a stilton sauce, or a Mixed Seafood Platter that can be ordered as a starter or main course. Sandwiches and jacket potatoes provide lighter or quicker meals.

468 THE DRAGON HOUSE HOTEL & RESTAURANT

**Bilbrook, nr Minehead,
Somerset TA24 6HQ
☎ 01984 640215
e-mail: info@dragonhousehotel.co.uk**

The **Dragon House Hotel**, stands on the very edge of Exmoor on the A39 midway between Watchet and Minehead. Set in two acres of grounds that include a black poplar thought to be one of the oldest and largest in the land, the main house dates from the late 16th century.

The bar and restaurant have a traditional appeal that's enhanced by rich oak panelling, creating a very mellow and inviting ambience for enjoying a drink and a meal. Prime fresh produce is the basis of dishes that range from classics such as prawn cocktail, duck in orange sauce or succulent steaks to more unusual offerings typified by swordfish poached in white wine, lime and chilli chicken or Mediterranean vegetable risotto. The hotel's nine en suite bedrooms are quiet, comfortable and well appointed, with telephone, TV, tea/coffee tray and hairdryer.

469 THE ROYAL OAK

High Street, Porlock, Somerset TA24 8PS
☎ 01643 862798
e-mail: oakroyalmo@aol.com

The **Royal Oak** stands on the main street of
Porlock, an ancient settlement that's now a
popular riding and holiday centre. It lies at
the foot of Porlock Hill in the heart of
Exmoor
National Park,
and after a
walk in the
country or
around
Porlock's
lovely old
streets the
Royal Oak is
definitely the
place to head
for. Dating

from 1740, it provides a delightfully
traditional setting for enjoying good home
cooking, including fish specials, steaks and
home-made pies. Three real ales are on tap,
and the pub has a family seating area, a skittle
alley and a function room.

470 ROCK HOUSE INN

1 Jury Road, Dulverton,
Somerset TA22 9DU
☎ 01398 323131

With its hilltop location the **Rock House
Inn** is one of the highest buildings in the
picture postcard village of Dulverton. Built in
the mid-1800s as a row of tiny dwellings, this
is a true village pub and since early 2003 has
been run by brothers Dave and Ian Bartlett.
Ian looks
after the
bar where
you'll find
an
excellent
choice of
real ales;
Dave is in
charge of
the

kitchen where he produces an appetising
selection of honest-to-goodness pub grub at
value-for-money prices. Food is served
Thursday to Sunday from noon until 2.30pm,
and from 6.30pm to 9pm.

471 LEWIS'S TEA ROOMS

13 High Street, Dulverton,
Somerset TA22 9HB
☎ 01398 323850

Dulverton is an attractive little town on the edge of
Exmoor in the wooded Barle Valley. It's home to
the headquarters of the Exmoor National park, and
after a wander round the town a pause for
refreshment in **Lewis's Tea Rooms** is always a pleasure to look forward to. A pair of 18th
cottages on Dulverton's High Street make up
the tea rooms, where a fine selection of
wholesome snacks and light meals, both
savoury and sweet, is served.

Fires in stone hearths keep the cold at bay
in the cooler months, while in the summer the
flower-filled courtyard comes into its own.
Fresh flowers are set on the tables in the
primrose-painted room, and various items,
including pottery, paintings and dried flowers,
are on display and for sale.

The savoury options include rarebits,
quiches, p□ tés, pies and jacket potatoes, and a
sweet treat not to be missed is afternoon tea
with home-made scones, strawberry jam and
clotted cream, accompanied by one of the
speciality lose-leaf teas.

472 ODDFELLOWS IN THE BOAT

Walsall Road, Lichfield,
Staffordshire WS14 0BU
☎ 01543 361692
e-mail: info@oddfellowsintheboat.com
🌐 www.oddfellowsintheboat.com

The name suggests something a little bit different, and **Oddfellows in the Boat** is certainly far from ordinary. Local and national awards mark it out as one of the very best dining pubs in the region, a reputation firmly established by owner Ann Holden and her team of talented professional

chefs. The menu and the kitchen skills would certainly do credit to many a top restaurant, and the comfortable, stylish surroundings set the seal on a memorable meal at this outstanding inn, which stands by the main A5 a few seconds east of the Muckley Corner roundabout.

475 THE CROSS KEYS & WENDY'S RESTAURANT

29 Burton Street, Tutbury,
Burton-on-Trent DE13 9NQ
☎ 01283 813677

The **Cross Keys** is open for drinks every session and all day Wednesday to Friday, while **Wendy's Restaurant** serves excellent home cooking every session except Sunday evening.

Explore Britain and Ireland with *Hidden Places* guides - a fascinating series of national and local travel guides.

www.travelpublishing.co.uk

0118-981-7777

info@travelpublishing.co.uk

473 THE SWAN

Burton Road, Whittington, nr Lichfield,
Staffordshire WS14 9NR
☎ 01543 432264
🌐 www.theswanwhittington.co.uk

Whittington is probably best known as the home of the Museum of the Staffordshire Regiment (the Prince of Wales's) in the Victorian barracks. But there's a splendid country pub that's also long been a landmark in the village. Dating back to the early 19th century, The **Swan** enjoys a picture-postcard location alongside the Coventry Canal on a country road between Lichfield and Tamworth.

Leaseholder Victoria Goodacre, who took over in the summer of 2005, has lost no time in enhancing the popularity of the pub, with both local patrons and visitors from near and far. Jamie is the assistant manager and chef, and her dishes provide an excellent choice for both lunch

and dinner. Much of the produce that goes into her kitchen is sourced locally, and

traditional roasts are added to the menu for Sunday lunch. Wednesday is curry night (eat in or take away), when up to 5 main- course curries are available between 6 and 9. It's best to book for this occasion, especially in the summer. The Swan has a huge beer garden leading down to the canal. Sunday night is quiz night.

474 THE RED LION

Lichfield Road, Hopwas, nr Tamworth, Staffordshire B78 3AF
☎ 01827 62514

The big bold red lion rampant on the pub sign matches the rich red brickwork of this impressive Victorian building by the A51 two miles west of Tamworth. The **Red Lion** is a family pub par excellence, and its owner John Runcorn, who took over the pub in 2001, is a man who has many years' experience in the business and a passion for food, and knows exactly what his customers want. Inside, the look is smartly contemporary but still with the welcoming feeling of a traditional country pub. Outside there are benches on decking and a lawned area by the Coventry Canal.

The Red Lion offers a wide range of food, available for longer hours a day, every day, than almost any pub (or indeed restaurant) in the region. And quality is the watchword throughout. The day starts with breakfast, served from 10 o'clock till noon, which could be anything from scrambled eggs on toast to a full English plateful, and an equally generous vegetarian version. The lunch menu is available from noon to 5.30 Monday to Friday and from noon to 5 on Saturday and Sunday. Panini, with a choice of ten tasty fillings and an accompaniment of 'herbie' diced potatoes and a salad garnish,

are a very popular order, and other options include baguettes and sandwiches, baked jacket potatoes, salad bowls, pasta bowls and beef or chicken burgers. The centrepiece of Sunday lunch is a choice of four roasts.

The front of the main menu bears the motto 'serving your needs and fancies' and indeed the choice should satisfy the smallest and the largest appetites and tastes ranging from staunchly traditional to more exotic and adventurous. Sirloin, rump, T-bone and fillet steaks come plain or with a choice of speciality sauces; there are ten ways with chicken, from plain grilled to spicy Cajun, Thai red curry and stir-fried with a choice of sauces, and there's always a good selection of fish and vegetarian dishes. The specials board extends the choice still further with mouthwatering dishes like cod and bacon with a red pepper sauce or kidneys turbigo (a super dish and a real classic – when did you last see that on a menu?)

Good food deserves good wine, and at the Red Lion a well-annotated list proposes wines from around the world, all available by bottle and two sizes of glass. Families are very welcome, and a special menu is available for small children; there's also a safe area for kids to play in the garden. There are seats for 60 in the restaurant, with up to 200 more in the garden. Booking is recommended at the weekend and for larger groups. John Runcorn is also the leaseholder of the Bird in Hand at Austrey, on the other side of Tamworth.

476 THE OXLEATHERS

Sundown Drive/Cape Avenue, Western
Downs, Stafford, Staffordshire ST17 9FL
☎ 01785 223741

The **Oxleathers** is a substantial redbrick pub
standing by the A518 Newport road on a corner
site at Western Downs, in the southwest suburbs of
Stafford. The name is unusual, perhaps unique
among British pubs, and the pub has earned a unique place among the local community, not only
for its outstanding hospitality and good food and drink, but also for the regular entertainment and
the host of sporting connections and events.

Simon Hyde
took over the
reins (or should
that be the
leathers?) in
March 2005, and
with the
assistance of a
dedicated,
hardworking team
has confirmed the
pub as one of the
favourite spots
where visitors of
all ages can be
sure of having a
good time. The
pub is open all
day, seven days a week, for drinks, headed by Banks's Bitter and Original and supported by several
lagers. Food is served from noon to closing time, ranging from sandwiches to steaks. This is very
much a place for the family; picnic benches are set out on the lawn at the back, and in summer
there's a bouncy castle in the play park. There's always something going on at the Oxleathers, and
if it's not an entertainment evening or a sporting occasion it's convivial company and lively
conversation.

This most sociable of pubs supports three adult and one under-16s football teams; a cribbage
team; a dominoes
team; two pool teams;
one Sunday pool
team; one men's and
two ladies' darts
teams; and a fishing
team.

All the favourite
pub games are played,
and entertainment
includes karaoke on
Friday and a disco on
Saturday. A much-
visited attraction near
the pub is Stafford
Castle on the site of a
Norman fortress; the
grounds are used for
regular historical re-
enactments.

545

477 IZAAK WALTON'S COTTAGE

Worston Lane, Shallowford, Near Stone,
Stafford ST15 0PA
☎ 01785 760278 (Apr - Oct)
or 01785 619619 (Nov - Mar)
e-mail:
izaakwaltonscottage@staffordbc.gov.uk

Stafford's rural heritage is embodied in **Izaak Walton's Cottage**, the charming 17th century home of the celebrated author of 'The Compleat Angler.' The thatched, half-timbered cottage is set in the heart of the Sow Valley at Shallowford, and gives a fascinating insight into the history of angling and the life of a writer whose

work remains 'a unique celebration of the English countryside.' Izaak Walton, the son of a Stafford alehouse keeper, purchased the property in 1654, which today is a registered museum and fully restored to reflect its famous heritage.

478 THE DOG & PARTRIDGE

Uttoxeter Road (A522), Lower Tean,
Staffordshire ST10 4LN
☎ 01538 722468 Fax: 01538 724601
e-mail: info@dogandpartridgetean.co.uk
⊕ www.dogandpartridgetean.co.uk

The **Dog & Partridge** started life in the 18th century as a coaching inn with its own smithy. Catering admirably ever since for discerning diners it has all the best features of a traditional country inn: a cosy, relaxing interior, well-kept real ales, and an excellent choice of food. A full à la carte menu is served in the conservatory restaurant, and a bistro was created in 2004 to provide lighter options. Add to all this the welcome from Malcolm and Hazel, and you have the perfect country pub! The Dog

& Partridge is closed Monday to Wednesday lunchtime except in December. A spacious, attractive function room is available.

480 THE RED LION

Main Road, Little Haywood,
Staffordshire ST18 0TS
☎ 01889 881314

The **Red Lion** stands on the main street of the pretty village of Little Haywood, just off the A51, a mile from the junction with the A513 and a short drive from Rugeley. The handsome red lion of the pub sign matches the rich redbrick exterior of the pub, which is open every session in summer, from 4.30 Monday to Friday in winter and all day on Saturday and Sunday throughout the year.

In the warm, welcoming bar, where tenants Robert and Lin greet all their customers as old friends, Banks's Bitter and Marston's Pedigree are the resident real ales, with two others

changing on a rotating basis. Well-priced food from the printed menu and specials board are served from 12 to 3 and from 5 to 8

except Monday and Tuesday (unless it's a Bank Holiday). The Red Lion is a very pleasant stopping place for motorists and for tourists taking in the local attractions. Cannock Chase and the Hednesford Hills provide wonderful open areas of woodland and moorland that form one of the county's great recreational centres. Also close by is the National Trust's Shugborough Hall, the 17th century seat of the Earls of Lichfield.

2 Clay Street, Penkridge,
Staffordshire ST19 5AF
☎ 01785 712685

The **Railway Inn** stands in the centre of Penkridge adjacent to the A449 and a short drive from the M6 (Junction 12 or 13). Michael and Joan Stanton and their daughters Liz and Laura have won many friends since taking over the lease in 2004. It's their first venture together, but Liz has 20 years' experience in the business and Laura nearly as many years. Hospitality is key here, and the warmth of the welcome is unmistakable.

The décor is a pleasing mix of traditional and more contemporary elements, including some railway memorabilia, and the home-from-home ambience makes visitors feel instantly relaxed. The pub is open every session and all day Friday, Saturday and Sunday for a wide range of drinks: Abbot Ale, Old Speckled Hen and Black Sheep are the regular real ales, and the bar also stocks a good selection of keg bitters, mild, stout, lagers and ciders.

The inn is close to the Hednesford Hills on the edge of Cannock Chase, and a bracing walk enjoying the scenery and the wildlife is a good way of working up a thirst and appetite. Food is served lunchtime and evening Monday to Saturday and from 12 to 5 on Sunday. Joan and Liz are both dab hands in the kitchen, and their dishes are based as far as possible on local produce. Typical dishes on the regular menu run from jacket potatoes to cod & chips, scampi, poachers chicken, lamb shanks, a splendid medley of cod, haddock, salmon and plaice, and two particular hearty favourites – lamb & mint suet pudding and steak pie

cooked with Abbot Ale. It's best to book at the weekend, and definitely recommended for the popular Sunday carvery.

The pub has a large, secluded rear garden and patio where hog roasts are a very popular attraction throughout the summer months. A separate function room makes a very pleasant venue for a special celebration. All are welcome for the Tuesday evening jam session – bring along an instrument or a voice, or just come along and enjoy the fun!

Longnor, nr Buxton,
Staffordshire SK17 0NS
☎ 01298 83205 Fax: 01298 83689
e-mail: enquiries@creweandharpur.co.uk
🌐 www.creweandharpur.co.uk

In the village of Longnor, close to the Derbyshire border, the **Crewe and Harpur Arms** provides up-to-date standards of comfort and service in a splendid Georgian setting. Owners Mark Bennison and Fraser Mitchell, friends and former colleagues in the RAF, have transformed it into one of the very finest restaurants with rooms in the whole region, combining as it does the very best in cuisine with superb accommodation and outstanding hospitality.

From the outset, the owners have adhered to the principle of providing excellent service in a friendly, relaxed ambience, and the Crewe and Harpur Arms continues to fulfil the role of much-loved local as well as catering for tourists, walkers and anyone who appreciates great food. Marstons Bitter and Pedigree are the regular real ales among the four (rising to eight in the summer) that are available in the bar. Diners can look forward to a memorable eating experience in the wood-panelled dining room, savouring the talents of an enthusiastic kitchen team led by head chef Neil Smith and sous chef James Catling. Local produce

features as much as possible in dishes that show equal attention to detail in both preparation and presentation. Typical lunchtime dishes could include salmon & dill fish cakes, pepper steak and

millefeuille of brioche, marinated field mushrooms and brie. The evening menu also caters admirably for carnivores, fish-eaters and vegetarians with the likes of tenderloin of pork en croute, halibut with fennel and apricot risotto and open lasagne of chargrilled asparagus. Desserts like fresh fruit pavlova or chocolate and plum bread & butter pudding keep up the enjoyment level to the end, and to complement the splendid cooking Mark has compiled an outstanding wine list.

The bedrooms are exceptional – stylish and spacious, each one equipped with the latest technology including 30" flat-screen TVs and free internet connection. The Italian-style bathrooms feature sumptuous fittings and underfloor heating. In addition to the eight rooms there are three comfortable cottages available on either a B&B or a self-catering tariff. Longnor stands high up in the Staffordshire moorland, and the Crewe and Harpur's lofty position commands beautiful views of the countryside, including the upper parts of the Dove and Manifold valleys. As well as providing one of the best dining experiences in the region, it's an excellent base for walking, cycling or touring the Peak District and its many scenic and historic attractions.

479 THE STAR

Park Hall Lane, Church Leigh,
nr Stoke-on-Trent, Staffordshire ST10 4PT
☎ 01889 502002
e-mail: scohel@btconnect.com

The **Star** is a picturesque old inn, open every
evening, plus lunchtime Thursday and Friday
and all day Saturday and
Sunday. Real ales and bar
food is served Thursday to
Saturday evenings and
Sunday lunch.

Looking for:

- *Places to Visit?*
- *Places to Stay?*
- *Places to Eat & Drink?*
- *Places to Shop?*

www.travelpublishing.co.uk

484 LOGGERHEADS

Eccleshall Road, Loggerheads,
nr Market Drayton, Staffordshire TF9 4NX
☎ 01630 672224 Fax: 01630 674230
e-mail: theloggerheadshotel@lesley-
neal.wanadoo.co.uk

The village and the pub are both called
Loggerheads, but the mood is always warm
and friendly. The black-and-white timbered
building was well-known in coaching inn
days, and it remains a popular spot for taking
a break. Lesley Wilkinson and her staff
dispense genuine hospitality, four real ales and
cooked-to-order food lunchtime and evening,
and all day Saturday and Sunday. The huge
well-kept gardens are another plus.

483 CASTRO'S RESTAURANT & LOUNGE

11 Cheadle Road, Cheddleton, nr Leek,
Staffordshire ST13 7HN
☎ 01538 361500
e-mail: enquiries@castros-restaurant.co.uk
🌐 www.castros-restaurant.co.uk

'A Taste of Latin America that's closer then
you think.' That's what they offer at **Castro's**,
splendid restaurant and lounge by the A520
and alongside the Caldon Canal. Very much
the creation of Jamie, Nikki and Thom (he's
the chef),
Castro's is
open from
6pm every
evening,
except
Sundays &
Mondays, for
an impressive
range of

dishes with a Latin kick, from nachos, fajitas
and chimichangas to tiger prawns wrapped in
bacon, creamy tequila chicken and fillet steak
stuffed with mozzarella and fresh chillies.
Visitors are welcome to come just for a drink
and to listen to the Latino music.

HIDDEN PLACES GUIDES

Explore Britain and Ireland with
Hidden Places guides - a fascinating
series of national and local travel
guides.

Packed with easy to read information
on hundreds of places of interest as
well as places to stay, eat and drink.

Available from both high street and
internet booksellers

For more information on the full range
of *Hidden Places* guides and other
titles published by Travel Publishing
visit our website on

www.travelpublishing.co.uk
or ask for our leaflet by phoning
0118-981-7777 or emailing
info@travelpublishing.co.uk

485 THE CREWE ARMS HOTEL

Wharf Terrace, Madeley Heath, nr Keele,
Staffordshire CW3 9LP
☎ 01782 750392 Fax: 01782 750587
e-mail: info@thecrewearmshotel.co.uk
🌐 www.tehcrewewarmshotel.co.uk

In the Staffordshire village of Madeley Heath, the **Crewe Arms Hotel** combines the best elements of a much-loved local rendezvous, a fine restaurant and a well-appointed hotel. Another major asset is the unfailingly friendly welcome and professional service offered by Derek and Ann Cornish, their daughter Amanda and her husband Eric. It's a super place to drop into at any time for drink, and the bar and lounge with their log fires and designated no smoking areas provide a warm, civilised ambience for a chat and a glass of real ale.

Eric is the chef, and he features as much local produce as possible for his menus, which are available

every session in the bar or Tudor-style panelled restaurant. A special menu including roasts replaces the bar menu Sunday lunchtime. The hotel is an excellent base both for business people – Newcastle-under-Lyme and Stoke-on-Trent are a short drive away – and for leisure visitors, with a number of places of interest nearby. The ten recently refurbished bedrooms are all en suite, and half are on the ground floor.

486 BIDDULPH GRANGE GARDEN

Grange Road, Biddulph,
Stoke on Trent ST87SD
☎ 01782 517999

Biddulph Grange Garden, near Stoke on Trent, is a series of picturesque gardens, each with its own character and set of growing conditions. It is one of the most exciting survivals of the great age of Victorian Gardening. A visit will take you on a journey of discovery around the world, through tunnels and winding pathways. Search for the beauty and tranquillity of China, the magnificence of an Egyptian court and the cool splendour of a Scottish Glen. Unusual and rare plants, mythical beasts and eccentric follies ensure surprises around every corner.

The National Trust owned property is open on Wednesday, Saturday, Sunday and Bank Holiday Monday from April to October and Saturdays and Sundays only during November and December (phone for up to date details and prices). The tearoom offers a wonderful Victorian themed menu with hot and cold lunches, afternoon teas and homemade cakes and biscuits and the shop is full of excellent range of gardening books,gifts and plants.

487 THE FOX

**Station Road, Elmswell,
nr Bury St Edmunds, Suffolk
☎ 01359 244594**

Toyah Glennon and her mother Mariesa run **The Fox**, a friendly, lively 19th century pub by the station at Elmswell, a mile off the A14 midway between Bury St Edmunds and Stowmarket. It's open lunchtime and evening and all day Friday and Saturday for drinks, and in the smart wood-floored dining area they serve an across-the-board menu of home-cooked dishes (no food Sunday or Monday evenings). The Fox welcomes visitors of all ages, and there's a children's play area in the superb beer garden.

488 GAINSBOROUGH'S HOUSE

**46 Gainsborough Street, Sudbury,
Suffolk CO10 2EU
☎ 01787 372958   Fax: 01787 376991
e-mail: mail@gainsborough.org
🌐 www.gainsborough.org**

Gainsborough's House is the birthplace museum of Thomas Gainsborough (1727-1788), one of England's most celebrated artists. An exceptional collection of his paintings, drawings and prints is on display in this charming town house with a Georgian façade built by the artist's father. Around 25 oil paintings are on show, including a miniature of his wife.
Among his personal belongings are his swordstick and pocket watch. Two galleries and the garden showcase contemporary art and craft.

489 THE BROOK INN

**241 Bures Road, Great Cornard, nr
Sudbury, Suffolk CO10 0JQ
☎ 01787 373166**

The Brook Inn is the heartbeat of the village of Great Cornard, which lies a short drive south of Sudbury on the B1508 Colchester road. Barbara and Mark Whitehart have been in the hospitality business for many years, but this was their first tenancy together when they took over in January 2006.

They are already making their mark, bringing back the locals and attracting business from Sudbury and further afield. In the welcoming bar, with wood panelling and polished wooden furniture, they serve Greene King IPA, Old Speckled Hen and a guest real ale, and diners can enjoy a fine selection of excellent

food chosen from the printed menu and the daily changing specials board. Sunday lunch is roasts only, and booking is advisable (no food Sunday evening). Outside seating is available front and rear. The Brook Inn is open Monday to Friday evenings (all day in the summer) and all day Saturday and Sunday all year round. No credit cards.

490 THE PERSEVERANCE

Rodbridge Hill, Long Melford, nr Sudbury,
Suffolk CO10 9HN
☎ 01787 3758
e-mail: melfordpercy@aol.com

Known locally as The Percy (that's even what the sign says!), **The Perseverance** is a pinkwashed mid-Victorian pub open all day every day for drinks. Experienced leaseholders Alan and Paula Bond serve good home-cooked food from noon to 7 o'clock Tuesday to Saturday, and they also provide excellent

guest accommodation in converted outbuildings to the side of the inn. It comprises one double and two twin rooms, and the tariff includes breakfast. The Percy has a nice little beer garden and off-road car parking. No credit cards.

491 THE CHERRY TREE INN

Tye Green, Glemsford, nr Sudbury,
Suffolk CO10 7RG
☎ 01787 281812

The **Cherry Tree Inn** stands opposite the village green in the hamlet of Tye Green, near Glemsford, reached off the A1092, B1065 or B1066. Owners Don and Gerry Carter have created a very warm and welcoming ambience for enjoying Greene King IPA or one of two guest real ales, and a good variety of

food is served every day until 10 in the evening. They offer special 2-for-1 meals lunchtime Monday to Saturday. Tuesday is quiz night, and a DJ does his stuff on the last Friday of each month.

493 WEST STOW ANGLO-SAXON VILLAGE

The Visitor Centre, Icklingham Road,
West Stow, Bury St Edmunds,
Suffolk IP28 6HG
☎ 01284 728718 Fax: 01284 728277
🌐 www.stedmundsbury.gov.uk/
weststow.htm

Between 1965 and 1972 the low hill by the River Lark in Suffolk was excavated to reveal several periods of occupation, but in particular, over 70 buildings from an early Anglo Saxon village. There was also information from about 100 graves in the nearby cemetery. It was decided that such extensive evidence about these people should be used to carry out a practical experiment to test ideas about the buildings that formed the elements of the original village.

Part of the Anglo Saxon Village has been reconstructed, on the site where the original (inhabited from around AD420 - 650) was excavated, over a period of more than 20 years. Each of the eight buildings is different, to test different ideas, and each has been built using the tools and techniques available to the early Anglo Saxons. Exploring the houses is an excellent way of finding out about the Anglo Saxons who lived at West Stow. Costumed "Anglo Saxons" bring the village to life at certain times, especially at Easter and during August. The new Anglo Saxon Centre is an exciting addition to the site, housing the original objects found there and at other local sites. Many of the objects have never been seen by the public before. The displays show aspects of village life and the focal point is a series of life size reconstructions of costume, based upon the grave finds.

Ditton Green, Woodditton, nr Newmarket,
Suffolk CB8 9SQ

☎ 01638 730811   Fax: 01638 730162

🌐 www.threeblackbirds.com

The **Three Blackbirds** in Woodditton is a traditional thatched pub that dates back as far as 1642. It retains the air of a large country cottage, with a spacious front garden and a truly welcoming ambience. Two separate bars lead off the main entrance: the bar to the right leads through to the extensive rear dining area. This has an unusual upstairs room that can be used for private functions. Low beams and open fires add to the charming traditional atmosphere. Seating is primarily at discreet and cosy four-person 'cubicles'.

The proximity of the village to the horseracing centre of Newmarket is reflected in the many fine paintings and prints of equestrian scenes that adorn the walls. The village itself gives its name to a long-established stakes race at Newmarket. Chef/proprietor Paul Lange, widely travelled and with a wealth of knowledge and experience, creates superb menus of dishes that combine classical skills with touches of imagination using the very best of seasonal ingredients. It's best to book to be sure of a table, particularly for the traditional Sunday roasts. Fine food deserves fine wine, and the extensive list at the Three Blackbirds has something to provide the perfect accompaniment to every dish. The pub also stocks a range of top-quality real ales. Paul also operates a successful patisserie business at the back of the pub.

The pub is very much at the heart of village life, and visitors interested in the history of the village can buy a book at the pub that's written by the villagers themselves. Paul has put the Three Blackbirds firmly on the map as the quintessence of the traditional village pub, its marvellous ambience supplemented by top-quality food and drink.

494 THE CHERRY TREE INN

73 Cumberland Street, Woodbridge,
Suffolk IP12 4AG
☎ 01394 384627
e-mail: info@thecherrytreepub.co.uk
🌐 www.thecherrytreepub.co.uk

The **Cherry Tree** is a traditional Suffolk inn (Grade II listed) close to the A12. Sheila and Geoff Ford have been at the helm since 2001 and continue to make new friends with their fine hospitality and the quality of beer, food and accommodation. The pub is listed in the CAMRA Good Beer Guide and is known for its seven real ales, offering a full range of Adnams beers, as well as regularly changing guest beers.

The food makes a major contribution to the Cherry Tree's success, with fine home cooking starting with breakfast, served from 7.30 to 10.30, and the main menu coming on stream at noon and continuing right through until 9 o'clock. The guest bedrooms in a converted Suffolk barn overlooking the gardens are named after Adnams brews. Broadside sleeps up to four, Explorer is a double and Regatta is a twin with wheelchair access. All have TV with DVD and VCR and broadband access. The inn, which is open all day, every day, has a large car park, a safe garden with a children's play area, and modern accessible facilities.

495 THE STATION GUEST HOUSE & WHISTLESTOP CAFÉ

Station Road, Woodbridge,
Suffolk IP12 4AU
☎ 01394 384831

Amber Cross and her daughter Carla run the **Station Guest House & Whistlestop Café**, where they offer quality B&B accommodation and some of the best informal eating in the region. The unusual setting is the railway station at Woodbridge, on the Ipswich-Lowestoft line.

Three of the four en suite bedrooms look out over the Deben river, providing a very comfortable base for exploring the many attractions of Woodbridge and the surrounding area. The café is open from 7 in the morning right through to 5 o'clock (from 9 at the weekend), and the printed menu and specials board offer a mouthwatering selection of cakes and pastries,

sandwiches, hot and cold savoury dishes and hot and cold drinks, including a fine range of speciality coffees. There are seats for 30 inside, and a further 50 outside in the station forecourt.

496 THE ELEPHANT & CASTLE INN

**The Street, Eyke, nr Woodbridge,
Suffolk IP12 2QG
☎ 01394 460241**

On the main street of Eyke, on the A1152 northeast of Woodbridge, the **Elephant & Castle** was already 100 years old when it became an inn at the beginning of the 18th century. It's the first venture into ownership for Barbara and Sally, but they brought plenty of related experience when they took over in March 2006 and they have lost no time in putting the old inn back on the map.

The bar is open all day, seven days a week, for drinks, with Adnams Bitter and Explorer the resident real ales, and the bar, with its wood-panelled servery and a wood-burning stove in a huge brick hearth, is a delightful place to relax and unwind. Popular pub

dishes are served every lunchtime and evening, and for guests staying overnight in this pleasant part of the world the pub has three en suite upstairs rooms for Bed & Breakfast. Children are welcome, and the pub has a beer garden and off-road car parking.

497 THE WHITE HORSE

**White Horse Hill, Tattingstone, nr Ipswich,
Suffolk IP9 2NU
☎ 01473 328060**

The **White Horse** is an attractive old slate-roofed pub off the A137 in a village 4 miles south of Ipswich. Black beams, brick features, a log-burning stove and a bench seat in the inglenook fireplace paint a delightfully traditional picture in the bar, creating a warm, inviting ambience for enjoying a drink or a meal.

It's run in fine style by Kevin and Samantha (Sam), and Sam's cooking is a major reason for the pub's popularity. Blackboards lunchtime and evening and an additional printed menu in the evening offer an excellent variety of hearty dishes typified by cottage pie, fish pie, beef stew and hickory chicken;

sandwiches, ploughman's and jacket potatoes provide lighter or quicker alternatives. Booking is recommended for the Sunday roasts. A good range of wines includes third of a bottle (two glass) size. The White Horse is a regular meeting place for several clubs and societies, and a field at the back, beyond the beer garden, is available all year round for tents and caravans. Cash and cheques only.

498 THE RED LION

Green Street Green, Great Bricett, nr
Ipswich, Suffolk IP7 7DD
☎ 01473 658492
e-mail: jwe4607264@aol.com
🌐 www.redlionracing.co.uk

John and Colette Weaver and their son Mark
run the **Red Lion**, a mid-19th century pub
off the B1078. It's open all day for drinks,
and John prepares a fine selection of tried-
and-tested pub favourites such as cod &
chips,
lasagne and
liver &
bacon.
Customers
can enjoy his
dishes from
noon to 9
Monday to
Saturday and

from 12 to 4 on Sunday (breakfast is also
served on Sunday from 9 to noon). The Red
Lion has a large beer garden with a children's
play area. Quiz night is the first Sunday on
the month, with an impromptu jamming
session on the last Sunday.

499 THE RED LION

High Street, Bildeston, Suffolk
☎ 01449 740476
e-mail: kevbyford@btinternet.com

On the main street of Bildeston, between
Sudbury and Stowmarket, the **Red Lion**
started life in the 16th century as a smithy. It
is now a lively village pub where first-time
leaseholders Kevin and Denise Byford are
making
many new
friends. The
beamed and
panelled bar
has a
welcoming
traditional
ambience
for enjoying
a drink, and

Kevin prepares a wide choice of dishes on
his printed menu and the daily specials board.
The pub is close Tuesday lunchtime,
otherwise open lunchtime and evening and all
day Saturday, Sunday and Bank Holidays.

500 THE RED ROSE INN

Lindsey Tye, Lindsey, nr Ipswich,
Suffolk IP7 6PP
☎ 01449 741424 Fax: 01449 744988
🌐 www.redroseinn.co.uk

Centuries old, the **Red Rose Inn** offers well
kept real ales, a roaring fire in winter and one
of the prettiest beer gardens in Suffolk. The
Leith trained chef proprietor uses local
organic meats and everything including
stocks, pastas,
breads and
chutneys is
home made.
Vegetarian
dishes are
always available
and most food
allergies are

catered for. All this in an atmospheric inn
where cyclists, walkers (and their dogs) are
made particularly welcome. The food is
served throughout opening hours – lunch and
dinner Wednesday to Saturday and lunchtime
Sunday. Lindsey Tye is signposted off the
A1141 Hadleigh-Monks Eleigh road.

501 THREE BEARS COTTAGE

Mulberry Tree Farm, Blacksmiths Lane,
Middlewood Green, nr Stowmarket,
Suffolk IP14 5EU
☎ 01449 711701
e-mail: gbeckett01@aol.com
🌐 www.aristoclassics.com

Ideally situated for touring Suffolk, **Three
Bears Cottage** is a spacious, self-contained
converted barn offering comfort and privacy
for up to six guests. Long-time owners Sue
and Greg
Beckett,
who live in
the adjacent
farmhouse,
provide a
continental
breakfast
and ensure
that their
guests have

all they need for a very relaxing holiday. An
indoor swimming pool and sauna are available
by arrangement. The cottage can be hired on
a Bed & breakfast or self-catering basis

502 THE FLEECE INN

61 Front Street, Mendlesham, nr
Stowmarket, Suffolk IP14 5RX
☎ 01449 766511

The Fleece is a 15th century pub in a village off the A140 north of Stowmarket. A huge brick hearth decorated with horse brasses and harnesses takes the eye in the bar, where Greene King IPA and Abbot Ale are the resident real ales.

Keith and Sheila Mangan took over The Fleece in 2004, and Sheila's cooking has earned a reputation that has spread far beyond the neighbourhood. Her pies, especially the steak & ale pie, have acquired a loyal and large following, but everything is first-class; booking is advised for Friday and Saturday evenings, Sunday lunch and the special pensioners lunch served on Wednesdays.

One room is dedicated to the airmen of the 34th Bomb Group, which was stationed at Mendlesham airfield in 1944/45. The Fleece has a pretty lawned garden with picnic sets under sunshades.

503 THE TROWEL & HAMMER INN

Mill Road, Cotton, nr Stowmarket,
Suffolk IP14 4QL
☎ 01449 781234 Fax: 01449 781765

Superb food is just one of the many attractions that make the **Trowel & Hammer** a very special place. In the village of Cotton, off the B1113 north of Stowmarket, the 15th century inn oozes character and class, and in Sally Burrows, who was born two villages away, it has a hands-on owner who really cares about her pub and her customers. Four real ales – Greene King IPA and Abbot and Adnams Bitter and Broadside – head an impressive list of drinks served all day in the bar.

The top-quality food can be enjoyed anywhere – in the main bar, in the non-smoking dining room or outside on warm days. The menus and the specials

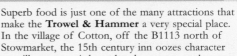

board offer a mix of dishes from Britain and around the world, with the 'home side' including much-loved but sometimes forgotten classics such as kedgeree or toad-in-the-hole. Tapas are served throughout opening hours. The garden is truly spectacular, with an African theme, a heated pool and a charming house that is an ideal spot for a private party. The pub hosts a regular programme of weekend entertainment all year round.

557

504 THE RACEHORSE INN

Westhall, nr Halesworth, Suffolk IP19 8RQ
☎ 01502 575706
e-mail:
racehorse@westhall1810.fsbusiness.co.uk

The Racehorse Inn has long been the social heartbeat of village life, with pool and darts teams playing in the local leagues and always plenty of lively conversation. Inside, beams, an open fire darkwood furniture and traditional décor make a pleasant setting for enjoying a glass of real ale – the choice includes a beer from Tindalls, a small local brewery.

Outside, there's a small garden at the front and a larger rear garden with terrace seats for 40. Jerry and Bella Aldred take excellent care of their pub and their customers, and no one leaves hungry or thirsty. Jerry produces a wide and interesting variety of dishes based as far as possible on local

produce, and Bella sets the seal on a fine meal with her scrumptious desserts. Booking is recommended for the popular Sunday roasts. The Racehorse is open lunchtime and evening and all day Saturday, Sunday and Bank Holidays. Food is served every session except Sunday evening.

505 EDWARDS RESTAURANT

59a The Thoroughfare, Halesworth, Suffolk IP19 8AR
☎ 01986 873763

Small, cosy and inviting, **Edwards Restaurant** is a lovely spot for enjoying traditional English cuisine. Lovely cakes and pastries, sandwiches and toasted treats are served from 9 to 4 Monday to Saturday, joined at lunchtime by tried-and-tested favourites such as fish & chips, lasagne, steak & kidney pie, omelettes, chilli and curries. Traditional extends to delicious sweets like pancakes, fruit crumble and treacle sponge.

506 THE KINGS HEAD INN

Laxfield, Suffolk IP13 8DW
☎ 01986 798395
e-mail: geoff.puffett@virgin.net

When the tenancy of the **Kings Head** became available in March 2006, Geoff and Ros jumped at the chance to run this marvellous, unspoilt thatched 15th century inn. The bar is delightfully traditional, with scrubbed tables, old prints and traditional pub games, and the beer – Adnams Best, Broadside and guests – is tapped straight from barrels in the taproom. A

good variety of excellent food is served lunchtime and evening, which can be enjoyed in the non-smoking restaurant, in the bar or out in the garden, which has a vine-covered arbour and a small pavilion. Guest accommodation is contained in a holiday cottage for two in a converted barn.

507 THE GRIFFIN INN AT YOXFORD

High Street, Yoxford, Suffolk IP17 3EP
☎ 01728 668229 Fax: 01728 667040
e-mail: enquiries@thegriffin.co.uk
🌐 www.thegriffin.co.uk

On the main street of Yoxford, just off the A12 4 miles north of Saxmundham, the **Griffin Inn** started life in the 14th century as a Manorial Court for the local Lord of the Manor. It became a hostelry in the 16th century, and behind its black-and-white, slate-roofed exterior it retains an old-world look with timbered walls and lofty ceilings, a log fire and church pew seating in the bar. Once reputedly the haunt of smugglers, it now attracts a wide cross-section of visitors, from locals here for a drink and a chat to diners and tourists.

Adnams real ales are on tap to quench thirsts, and the food options run from sandwiches and snacks in the bar to a full menu in the restaurant, where typical dishes might

include cod in beer batter; gammon and beef steaks; cannelloni; mushroom, red onion and cheddar tartlets, and a super steak, kidney and mushroom pie cooked in Adnams ale. Hosts Trevor and Claire also have three beamed bedrooms for guests looking for an ideal base for exploring the many nearby attractions of coast and countryside.

508 PISTACHIO RESTAURANT

Main Road (A12), Kelsale, nr Saxmundham, Suffolk IP17 2RF
☎ 01728 604444
🌐 www.pistachio-restaurant.com

Pistachio Restaurant (1 Rosette AA Awarded) is located in a lovely little whitewashed, thatched building just off the main road (A12) at Kelsale. Dating from the 16th century, it has a wonderful old-world appeal, with beams, rafters and an open fire, and outside there's a beautiful garden with a pagoda.

Owner-chef Graham Ball has really put this wonderful place on the map with his top-class cooking. His style is traditional English with many contemporary touches, resulting in ever-changing menus that make deciding what to order a pleasant problem. Every dish is prepared and presented with great care, and typical choices run from a timbale of blue swimming crab with

an oyster sauce dressing to loin of pork with leeks and tomatoes, lemon

sole with prawns and guinea fowl with a root mash and crispy pancetta. The best bet to end a memorable meal is the platter of seven mini-desserts. The wine list is as expertly conceived as the menus, with house wines available by glass (2 sizes) or bottle. Pistachio is open for morning coffee and afternoon teas as well as main meals. Closed Sunday evening and all day Monday.

509 PAINSHILL PARK

Portsmouth Road, Cobham,
Surrey KT11 1JE
☎ 01932 868113 Fax: 01932 868001
e-mail: info@painshill.co.uk
⊕ www.painshill.co.uk

This once barren heathland was transformed by the celebrated plantsman and designer, the Hon Charles Hamilton, into one of Europe's finest 18th Century landscape gardens. **Painshill** was one of the earliest 'naturalistic' gardens ever created, Hamilton conjured up a mysterious and magical place in which to wander- the equivalent of a 20th century theme park - where fashionable society could wander through a landscape theatre, moving from scene to scene. Staged around a huge serpentine lake with surprises at every turn. A Gothic Temple, Chinese Bridge, Ruined Abbey, a Grotto, Turkish Tent, Gothic Tower and the most magnificent waterwheel all disappear and reappear as the walk proceeds.

But Hamilton eventually ran out of money and to discharge his debts sold the estate in 1773. Since then it has been in the possession of many owners but was eventually fragmented and sold off in lots in 1948 and the gardens, which had been well-maintained for nigh on two centuries, were allowed to deteriorate. By 1981 they lay derelict and overgrown and it seemed that what had been a national treasure would be lost for all time. However Elmbridge Borough Council, conscious of the importance of Painshill, purchased 158 acres and formed the Painshill Park Trust with a view to restoring the gardens and opening them to the public. The subsequent ongoing restoration has been one of the great success stories of garden conservation. Most of the principal features of the garden are open for viewing and the restored planting schemes are steadily maturing. The restoration has been a slow process. It's not simply a matter of clearing undergrowth and repairing features. Lots

of detailed and painstaking research is required. Archaeological excavation, documentary research and the identification and dating of trees, tree stumps and historic paths. From this, detailed plans and maps are created to show what the estate would have looked like in the 18th century and all the later stages to the present day.

Now there are a variety of walks which allow visitors to explore Hamilton's idyll. The historic circuit is a signposted two-mile long route that an 18th century visitor would have followed to view all the attractions of the garden. A shorter path round the lake passes delights such as the ruined abbey, boat house and crosses the Chinese bridge. A vineyard flourished at Painshill from 1740 to 1812. This has been replanted with Pinot noir, Chardonnay and Seyval blanc grapes and once again wine is being produced at Painshill. Painshill is not allowed to call their sparkling white wine champagne but when Charles Hamilton was making wine here in the 18th century the French ambassador of the day, mistook Hamilton's product for the champagne of his native land. In a tribute to the man who made it all possible, the Painshill trust have named the new visitor centre restaurant Hamilton's. It's open from early morning serving breakfasts, coffee, light lunches and splendid afternoon teas. The shop is a cornucopia for present and souvenir buyers containing everything from trugs and dibbers to umbrellas, food, china, books, honey and beeswax candles and, of course, Painshill wine. Open March to October Tuesday to Sunday and Bank Holidays 10.30am - 6.00pm; November - February: Wednesday to Sunday and Bank Holidays 11.00am - 4.00pm. Closed Christmas Day.

511 THE BAT & BALL

Bat & Ball Lane, Boundstone, nr Farnham,
Surrey GU10 4SA
☎ 01252 792108 Fax: 01252 794564
e-mail: info@thebatandballfarnham.co.uk
🌐 www.thebatandballfarnham.co.uk

The **Bat & Ball** is a delightful free house owned and run in fine style by the experienced husband and wife team of Kevin and Sally Macready. Both have long connections with the licensed trade that go back more than 25 years. Their son and three daughters are all involved in some way in the running of the pub, which is somewhat tucked away in the dip of the valley of the River Bourne at Boundstone, a mile southwest of Farnham town centre. A little tricky to find first time, perhaps, but the return visits that will certainly follow will be much easier! Turn south off Shortheath Road down Sandrock Hill Road, and after the dip in the road take the second left into Upper Bourne Lane, then second left down Bat and Ball lane – the pub is at the bottom, with plenty of off-road parking available.

The Bat & Ball is a great favourite with the local community and is regularly used as a meeting place by the Cricket Club and Golfing Society. The pub also attracts aplenty of walkers, being situated at a point where five public footpaths converge. Dating back some 150 years, it was originally surrounded by hop fields, and in days gone by the hop-pickers were paid in the front room of the pub. In those days the beer was delivered in barrels to the bottom of a nearby road, then put into the stream of the Bourne and dragged the rest of the way by donkey power! The inside of the pub is warm and welcoming, with oak beams, wooden furniture, terracotta tiles on the floor of the main bar, a roaring log fire in the cooler months – and of course cricket memorabilia including pictures, prints and even bats and balls.

This is definitely a pub that serves good food rather than a restaurant that serves beer.

Patrons can eat and drink throughout the pub or outside on the patio area, and there's a spacious non-smoking area. Typical dishes include British stalwarts such as steaks and puff pastry-topped pies, and dishes from around the world like Sri Lankan chicken curry, rich Hungarian vegetable goulash and cod steak with a pesto and parmesan crust. The pub offers a choice of six real ales at any one time. The garden ahs a children's play area and a lovely vine-topped pergola that backs onto the Bourne stream.

510 THE STAR AT WITLEY

Petworth Road, Witley, Surrey GU8 5LU
☎ 01428 684656
e-mail: star@dcs-uk.net

The **Star at Witley** is a well-loved, family-friendly pub serving traditional pub dishes. Favourite choices include burgers, bangers, lasagne, chilli, scampi, fish & chips and shepherd's pie. When the summer sun shines, the beer garden and children's play area are very popular spots, but outside or in the bar this is a delightful place to spend an hour or two. The Star is open lunchtime and evening and all day Friday, Saturday and Sunday. Food is served every session except Sunday and Monday evenings.

512 THE THREE COMPASSES

Dunsford Road, Alfold, Surrey GU6 8HY
☎ 01483 275729

The **Three Compasses** lies off the B2133 just south of its junction with the A281 Horsham-Guildford road, and adjacent to the restored Wey & Avon Junction Canal. Visitors come from all points of the compass to enjoy the hospitality, well-kept ales and good wholesome food provided by leaseholder Tony Davis and his affable staff. Real fires, beams and ample country character create the  ideal ambience for relaxing with a drink and a chat or settling down to a meal. Familiar favourites are the mainstay of the menu, which is served lunchtime and evening and all day on Sunday. The pub has a large beer garden and ample off-road parking.

514 HASKETTS TEA & COFFEE SHOP

86b South Street, Dorking,
Surrey RH4 2EW
☎ 01306 885833
e-mail: Margaret.garrett@ukgateway.net

Haskett's is one of the most delightful places in the region for enjoying a wide range of teas, coffees, cakes and hot and cold savoury dishes. A really charming, traditional tea & coffee shop.

515 THE ROYAL OAK

Felday Road, Holmbury St Mary, nr Dorking,
Surrey RH5 6PE
☎ 01306 730120
e-mail: the.royaloak@btconnect.com

Walkers, cyclists, motorists and local residents all appreciate the hospitality offered by Ian and Dawn at the **Royal Oak**, a 200-year-old inn with a traditional interior, a large beer garden to the front and an enclosed family garden to the rear. Four real ales are always on tap, and familiar pub dishes are  served lunchtime and evening. The menu has a special section for young diners, and bar snacks are available all day. For guests staying overnight the Royal Oak has three smartly decorated en suite rooms; breakfast is served in the pub's dining room. The Royal Oak is a popular venue for small functions and has full wireless internet access throughout.

513 THE PUNCHBOWL INN

Oakwoodhill, nr Ockley, Surrey RH5 5PU
☎ 01306 627249   Fax: 01306 628186

Close to the A29 Billingshurst road 7 miles south of Dorking, the **Punchbowl Inn** started life in the 16th century as a classic Hall House. It later became two cottages before being converted into a tavern in the early 19th century. Behind its tile-hung exterior under a Horsham stone roof opposite Oakwoodhill Cricket Club, the large bar-dining area has flagstone floors, beams, a broad inglenook fireplace with a log fire, kitchen-style tables, pew benches and an assortment of other seating, pictures, jugs, china and horse brasses. A separate dining room, small and cosy, with carpets and candlelight, is an intimate spot for enjoying a meal. Outside is a paved area set with tables and chairs, with a lawned garden and abundant greenery.

Wendy and Phillip Nisbet took over the pub in 2001, having run the Cider house at Shackleford, and they have made the Punchbowl one of the most popular destination dining pubs in the area. The dishes on the menu, all home-cooked, include both traditional pub favourites and some less usual options, and a meal ends in fine style with a choice of delicious home-made desserts and luscious ice creams in a dozen flavours. Cask Marque ales include Badger gold and Tanglefoot, and Phillip is responsible for compiling an excellent wine list.

The pub is a popular venue for cyclists and walkers, as well as a great place to pause on a journey; but above all this is a place to allow plenty of time to relax over an enjoyable meal. There are plenty of opportunities to work up a thirst and appetite in the vicinity, including Oakwood Hill and the Sussex Border Path walk. The Punchbowl is also a very sociable pub. Rolls Royce, Bentley, Morgan and Saab owners' clubs regularly meet here, and it's very popular with anglers. On Boxing Day the Surrey Union Hunt gathers here before a d ay in the field. The pub is easily reached from the A29 and is also only a short drive from the A24 Dorking-Horsham road.

516 ZIEGLER'S ORNAMENTAL GARDEN STATUARY & YA YA'S TEA ROOM

Village Street, Newdigate, nr Dorking,
Surrey RH5 5DH
☎ 01306 631287
e-mail: nina@zieglers.co.uk
🌐 www.zieglers.co.uk

Ziegler's supplies ornamental statuary to clients all over the world with gardens large and small. Nina Ziegler's double-fronted 15th century building has a patio at the front and a garden at the back. The interior and the garden display a marvellous range of statues, fountains and garden collectables in

bronze, lead, cast iron, stone and wood. Ziegler's also has a small tea room called Ya Ya's, open for morning coffee, light lunches and afternoon tea, and featuring excellent home baking and home cooking. Ziegler's is open Tuesday to Friday 9.30am-5pm. Saturday & Sunday 10am-4pm.

HIDDEN PLACES GUIDES

Explore Britain and Ireland with *Hidden Places* guides - a fascinating series of national and local travel guides.

Packed with easy to read information on hundreds of places of interest as well as places to stay, eat and drink.

Available from both high street and internet booksellers

For more information on the full range of *Hidden Places* guides and other titles published by Travel Publishing visit our website on

www.travelpublishing.co.uk
or ask for our leaflet by phoning
0118-981-7777 or emailing
info@travelpublishing.co.uk

517 THE RED LION

Lewes Road, Chelwood Gate,
West Sussex RH17 7DE
☎ 01825 740265

Standing by the A275 just below the junction with the A22, the **Red Lion** is a strong magnet for lovers of good food. The inn, which dates back to the 17th century, is in the excellent care of Ian and Karen Perry, who welcome all the family (and their dogs) and continue to make new friends both from the local community and from the many motorists and tourists who pass this way. The bar has a lovely traditional appeal, and the pub's menus really do offer something for everyone.

The talented team in the kitchen does justice to every dish on the list, from baguettes, ploughman's platters and jacket potatoes to a wide range of meat,

fish and vegetarian dishes. Meaty options could include liver

& bacon, steaks and beef curry, while favourites among the superb fish dishes include king scallops and monkfish. There are always plenty of daily specials, typified by grilled plaice, sea bass with lyonnaise potatoes, stir-fried squid with tiger prawns and red snapper with a red pepper sauce.

518 THE BOARS HEAD TAVERN

Worthing Road, Horsham,
West Sussex RH13 0AD
☎ 01403 254353 Fax: 01403 218114
e-mail: Richards.4@hotmail.co.uk
🌐 www.boarsheadtavern.co.uk

The **Boars Head Tavern** is a very friendly and convivial pub located at the corner of Worthing Road and Tower hill on the southern edge of Horsham. David and Fiona Richards, tenants since the autumn of 2003, have a warm welcome for all their customers, many of them regulars from Horsham and the surrounding area but also visitors to the area and motorists needing a break on their journey. In the small, cheerful bar they serve a good range of beers, usually including King & Barnes Sussex, Badger, Tanglefoot and something a little out of the ordinary such as Fursty Ferret, as well as draught lagers. The choice is even wider during the 10-day beer festival held at the end of April. In the summer months, the pub's two delightful patios come into their own, one of them providing glorious views over the North Downs.

Bar and restaurant menus provide plenty of choice for diners, with soup, jacket potatoes, sarnies, salads and hot and cold snacks for quick/light meals and a regularly changing list of dishes served in the 48-cover non-smoking restaurant. All the familiar favourites (burgers, liver & bacon, curries, chicken, ham & leek pie) appear on the printed menu and specials board, along with the likes of aubergine and two-cheese melt; crab-filled mushrooms; smoked haddock & spring onion or cod & pancetta fish cakes; pan-fried sea trout; and the ever-popular Sunday roasts. To accompany the fine food is an excellent wine list including a super selection of well-priced house wines.

A pub has been on this site since 1761, and from the time of the granting of its beer licence in 1830 until 1971 it was called the Fox & Hounds. It is open lunchtime and evening Monday to Thursday, all day Friday and Saturday and from noon to 8 on Sunday. It has a thriving golf society, and a big following among the rugby crowd, who can watch all the big matches on a big-screen TV.

519 THE QUEENS HEAD

Chapel Road, Barns Green, nr Horsham,
West Sussex RH13 0PS
☎ 01403 730436
e-mail: BrendaCMcFadyen@ aol.com
🌐 www.cottageguide.co.uk/hollytreehouse

Two 18th century cottages that were once the home of smugglers are fulfilling a much more public-spirited role as a splendid country pub. In a village a short drive south of Horsham, the **Queens Head** is a pure delight inside and out. Flowers make a colourful show on the façade, and there's a pleasant patio at the front and a lawned garden at the back with a children's play area. Inside, low ceilings, heavy black beams, an inglenook fireplace and a variety of pew benches, settees and comfortably upholstered seats create an inviting, old-world ambience.

Hosts John and Lucy Pullinger dispense hospitality and

good cheer in generous measure, with three real ales and a regularly changing menu of home-cooked dishes. Among the favourite choices are the weekend fish specials and their homemade pies. Booking is advisable on Friday and Saturday evenings, for the Sunday carvery and for the regular themed food evenings.

520 THE STAR INN

Horsham Road, Rusper,
West Sussex RH12 4RA
☎ 01293 871264

The **Star Inn** is a charming country pub in a secluded village of tile-hung and timbered cottages north of Horsham. The bars and dining areas have an inviting, traditional appeal, with heavy ceiling beams and pillars, wooden floors, rustic furniture and a big brick hearth. Up to four real ales are kept in tip-top condition, earning a CAMRA recommendation. Excellent food served lunchtime and evening and all day on Sunday combine old favourites with specials such as wild boar sausages, pepperpot beef, chicken dhansak and spinach & Roquefort gratin.

523 THE ANCHOR INN

Anchor Lane, Barcombe, nr Lewes,
East Sussex BN8 5BS
☎ 01273 400414 Fax: 01273 401029
e-mail: maharris@ukonline.co.uk
🌐 www.anchorinnandboating.co.uk

The **Anchor Inn** is located off the A275 in a lovely unspoilt part of rural Sussex on the west bank of the River Ouse. Built in 1790, it has two cosy bars serving a good selection of real ales, lagers, wines and freshly prepared traditional pub dishes. Visitors can make the most of the riverside setting by hiring a paddle boat for a trip to the Fish-Ladder Falls, which takes a leisurely two hours. Back on land, comfortable accommodation is available in individually decorated bedrooms with fine country views.

566

521 THE ROYAL PAVILION

Brighton, East Sussex BN1 1EE
☎ 01273 292822 Fax: 01273 292821
e-mail: visitor.services@brighton-hove.gov.uk
🌐 www.royalpavilion.org.uk

The Royal Pavilion is one of the most exotically beautiful buildings in the British Isles. Indian architecture contrasts with interiors inspired by China in this breathtaking Regency palace. Built for King George IV the Pavilion was also used by William IV and Queen Victoria. Originally a farmhouse, in 1787 architect Henry Holland created a neo-classical villa on the site. It was transformed into Indian style byJohn Nash between 1815 and 1822.

A £10 million restoration scheme has returned the palace to its full Regency splendour with lavish decorative schemes. The centrepiece of the Banqueting Room is a huge chandelier held by a silvered dragon illuminating a table laid with dazzling Regency silver gilt. The Music Room is equally stunning, with lotus-shaped lanterns hanging from a high domed gilded ceiling.

The Pavilion is open daily, except 25th and 26th December and has a good range of facilities including a tea room and gift shop.

522 MILL LAINE BARNS

Offham, nr Lewes, East Sussex BN7 3QB
☎ 01273 475473
e-mail: harmer@farming.co.uk
🌐 www.milllainebarns.co.uk

Mill Laine Barns and the adjacent farmhouse offer a choice of self-catering and Bed & Breakfast accommodation in a secluded setting at the foot of the beautiful Sussex Downs, off the A275 a mile north of Lewes. Mill Laine is a 600-acre working farm producing arable crops and prize-winning Sussex cattle and Southdown sheep. Mill Laine Barns have been converted into four well-equipped self-catering holiday homes accommodating 2, 4, 6 and 6 guests. Each has an en suite bathroom and family bathroom, well-provided kitchen, central heating, wood-burning stove and living area with TV/video, DVD and CD player. All are 4/5 star ETB. The Old Wash House is an 18th century brick-and-flint building sympathetically converted into a self-contained, well-equipped B&B cottage

retaining several original features. It comprises a bedroom with a double or twin beds (a Z-bed is available for a child), kitchen, living area and shower room. The South Downs Way passes nearby, and the owners welcome walkers, cyclists and horse riders as well as tourists, business people and families on holiday.

524 THE COCK INN

Uckfield Road, Ringmer, nr Lewes,
East Sussex BN8 5RX
☎ 01273 812040
e-mail: matt@cockpub.co.uk
🌐 www.cockpub.co.uk

The Ridley family – father Ian, mother Val, sons Matt and Nick and daughter Caroline – pride themselves on the excellent hospitality they offer at **The Cock Inn**. On the A26 between Lewes and Uckfield, the Cock Inn is a 16th century coaching inn – a cock horse was a spare horse kept ready at the foot of a hill to help another horse with a heavy load up the hill. The bar features original oak beams, a flagstone floor and an inglenook fireplace where a log fire blazes a welcome in the cooler months.

On fine days the gardens and the patio come into their own, the former commanding unobstructed views across open fields to the South Downs. Harveys Best Bitter, Old and Mild alternate with the seasons and are the regular real ales, enhanced further with guest beers. A good selection of wines is available to enjoy on their own or to accompany a meal. A fine selection of dishes is served lunchtime and evening and all day on Sundays, ranging from pub favourites such as battered cod and steak & ale pie to venison sausages, salmon with a cream and watercress sauce, and chicken breast in a cheese and spinach sauce. Reservations are recommended and especially for Friday evenings, lunch and dinner Saturday and Sunday lunch.

525 THE OLD SHIP

Uckfield Road, Ringmer,
East Sussex BN8 5RP
☎ 01273 814223
🌐 www.oldship.co.uk

Michael Burdass heads the family team who run the lovely **Old Ship Inn**, which lies just outside the village of Ringmer on the Uckfield Road (A26). The pub dates back to the 17th century and once served an important coaching route. Today's customers come from near and far to enjoy the fine hospitality and the excellent choice of home-cooked dishes, all prepared in house from the best ingredients by Michael's son Ben.

Quality is the keynote throughout Ben's dishes, served every day from noon to 9.30. Familiar favourites like whitebait, fish & chips, sausage & mash, burgers, steaks and lasagne share the menus with fajitas, tacos and nachos, and super specials such as marinated spare ribs and asparagus & shallot tagliatelle, with a lovely cider & apple crumble to

finish. Sandwiches and lighter meals are served until 6 o'clock. The bar and restaurant have a delightfully traditional look, and the lawned garden is a pleasant spot for enjoying an alfresco drink. The Old Ship is a popular choice with locals, walkers and cyclists and is increasingly earning a reputation as a fine destination dining pub.

526 THE FARMHOUSE

Fulbeck Avenue, Durrington, Worthing,
West Sussex BN13 3RS
☎ 01903 261997

In this 2002 conversion of a period
farmhouse and adjoining barn 3 real ales are
served in a modern bar with traditional
touches. There is a bright conservatory style
lower bar and high ceiling restaurant with
outside decking area overlooking the duck
pond. A fine selection of home cooked food
is served daily and the lower bar, restaurant
and disabled toilets are accessible to
wheelchair users from the reserved parking
bays.

528 EXSURGO RESTAURANT & BAR

Rothermere, North Street, Midhurst,
West Sussex GU29 9DJ
☎ 01730 810011   Fax: 01730 817206
e-mail: exsurgo@supanet.com
🌐 www.exsurgo.co.uk

A small 17th century cottage developed in
subsequent centuries into the handsome
building now occupied by **Exsurgo
Restaurant & Bar**. Restoration has revealed
many of the older features, and owners
Darren and
Tiffany have
given the
place a new
lease of life
as a fine
restaurant.
Along with
Annie (front
of house)
and Steve
(head chef),

they have made it one of the most popular
eating places for many miles around, open
long hours every day offering various menus
of worldwide inspiration.

527 CONFUCIUS CHINESE RESTAURANT

2 Cooper Street, off South Street,
Chichester, West Sussex
☎ 01243 783158

Owner Gordon Lee has enjoyed great support
since opening **Confucius Chinese Restaurant** in
a quiet Chichester location in 1993. This converted
cottage has a very comfortable interior with a bar
and two dining areas, with seats covered in dark green velvet, matching green linen, sparkling
glasses and ornamental Chinese wall decorations.

The long menu puts the emphasis on Cantonese,
Peking and Szechuan cuisine, offering all the favourite
dishes that have made this such a popular place for a
relaxing meal served by friendly, efficient staff. The
main menu runs to some 150 dishes, supplemented by

set menus
from two or
more and a
short non-
Chinese
section. The
house

specials, the choice of many customers for a spectacular
start to a meal, are deep-fried crispy aromatic duck and
barbecued Peking duck, both available in quarter, half and
full duck servings. The Confucius Chinese Restaurant is
open from 12 to 2 and 6 to 11 Monday to Saturday.
Gordon Lee also owns the Boathouse Brasserie at
Houghton bridge, near Amberley.

529 THE BRICKLAYERS ARMS

Wool Lane, Midhurst,
West Sussex GU29 9NB
☎ 01730 812084 Fax: 01730 812047
e-mail: bricklayers-arms@bt.com

Centrally located in Midhurst, the **Bricklayers Arms** dates back some 550 years. Tenant Paul Blackmun, assisted by Jenny and Adam, have made this one of the best-loved pubs in the region, and the bars have a delightful old-world look and feel. Food is served from opening time right through to 9.30, and since the owners also own the local butchers and fishmongers, the quality and freshness of the dishes is guaranteed. Other produce comes from the nearby Goodwood Estate.

530 THE ROYAL OAK

Chichester Road, West Lavington,
West Sussex GU29 0EP
☎ 01730 814611

The **Royal Oak** is a tile-roofed brick building set back from the A286 a short drive south of Petworth. Brothers and leaseholders Rossi and Matt Cinquemani are very popular and welcoming hosts, and there's invariably a good atmosphere in the bar. The pub is open all day, seven days a week, for a good selection of drinks, and Rossi's excellent cooking is available from noon every day. The Royal Oak has a lovely beer garden with a children's play area.

531 THE OLD RAILWAY STATION

Station Road, Petworth,
West Sussex GU28 0JF
☎ 01798 342346 Fax: 01798 343066
e-mail: info@old-station.co.uk
🌐 www.old-station.co.uk

Set in two acres of gardens and grounds, the **Old Railway Station** started life serving railway passengers in 1894. It is now a Grade II* listed building of great elegance and style, a perfect retreat for a relaxing break and a romantic setting that recalls the luxury and style of days gone by.

Two of the bedrooms are in the station building, while the rest are in three wonderful old Pullman carriages dating from between 1912 and 1923.

Period furnishings add to the appeal, and all have private bathrooms. The impressive former waiting room, with its 20ft vaulted ceiling and original ticket

office windows, is now the breakfast room and lounge. In winter, breakfast is

taken by the fire, while in the summer months it can be served on the platform with no trains or commuters to disturb the peace. No children under 10; no smoking except on the platform.

532 THE STONEMASONS INN

North Street, Petworth,
West Sussex GU28 9NL
☎ 01798 342510 Fax: 01798 342515
e-mail: stonemasons@onetel.com
🌐 www.thestonemasonsinn.co.uk

Leaseholders Arjen Westerdijk and Michael
Huntley have quickly made their mark at the
Stonemasons Inn, which started life in the
15th century as a row of cottages. They have
retained all the best traditional aspects of the
building, and the bar and restaurant are
delightful spots for enjoying the home-
cooked fare
that is served
every
lunchtime
and evening.
Four real ales
are available,
along with an
interesting
wine list compiled by Michael, who is also a
wine merchant. For guests staying awhile, five
impressive en suite bedrooms combine old-
world character with modern amenities.

533 THE HALFWAY BRIDGE

Halfway Bridge, Petworth,
West Sussex GU28 9BP
☎ 01798 861281
e-mail: hwb@thesussexpub.co.uk
🌐 www.thesussexpub.co.uk

Personal service is a strong point at the
Halfway Bridge, which lies on the A272
between
Petworth and
Midhurst and
very near
Cowdray Park.
Paul and Sue
Carter, Head
chef Paul
Butcher and a
hard-working
team take excellent care of their customers,
whether they've popped in for a quick drink
(Betty Stoggs is the resident real ale) or to
enjoy an excellent meal or an overnight stay.
The pub is well known for its first-class food
and wine, but the Jewel in the Crown has to
be the accommodation – six superbly
appointed bedrooms in a converted 250-year-
old traditional Sussex barn.

534 THE FORESTERS ARMS

Graffham, nr Petworth,
West Sussex GU28 0QA
☎ 01798 867202
🌐 www.foresters-arms.com

The rolling chalk hills of the South Downs are a
magnet for walkers and lovers of the great
outdoors, and the South Downs Way passes close
to the **Foresters Arms**. An ideal place to pause for
a drink, to
settle down to a snack or a meal, or to stay for a night or
longer, the inn dates back to the 16th century. The old beams
and the open fire create a warm, welcoming ambience in
which to enjoy a glass or two of real ale in the bar.

Leaseholders Serena and Nick Bell are the most affable
of hosts, and Nick, a talented professional chef, produces an
across-the-board menu to please one and all; the day's fish

special is always a
popular choice,
and other
favourites include
a tasty beef & ale
pie and the traditional roasts that are added to the
Sunday choice. Children are welcome, and for B&B
guests the inn has two en suite rooms next to the main
building; the tariff includes breakfast in the form of a
luxury hamper. The Foresters is easily reached from the
A285 south of Petworth, from the A286 south of
Midhurst and from the A272 between the two.

535 THE BADER ARMS

Malcolm Road, Tangmere,
West Sussex PO20 2HS
☎ 01243 779422

The Bader Arms is a modern pub offering traditional standards of hospitality. Mementoes of the eponymous hero adorn the walls. The pub fields football and pool teams.

536 WOODACRE B&B

Arundel Road, Fontwell, nr Arundel,
West Sussex BN18 0QP
☎ 01243 814301 Fax: 01243 814344
e-mail: wacrebb@aol.com
🌐 www.woodacre.co.uk

Four rooms, one en suite, 2 ground floor, provide quiet, comfortable B&B at **Woodacre**, a handsome 100-year-old house set in a lovely garden.

537 THE ARUNDEL PARK HOTEL

The Causeway, Arundel,
West Sussex BN18 9JL
☎ 01903 882588 Fax: 01903 883808
e-mail: info@arundelparkhotel.co.uk
🌐 www.arundelparkhotel.co.uk

Close to the railway station and a five-minute walk from the entrance to the Castle, the **Arundel Park Hotel** is an excellent choice for anyone discovering the many attractions of Arundel and the surrounding towns, villages and countryside. Charming hosts Prajay and Punita Patel provide a warm, genuine family welcome for all their guests, who come from all over the UK and elsewhere to enjoy the delights of this lovely part of the world.

The accommodation comprises 15 individually decorated en suite bedrooms, all non-smoking, some with views of the Downs, all with television and tea/ coffee making facilities. Wireless Internet facilities are available in the bedrooms and in the bar, which is a very pleasant spot for meeting friends over a drink. Breakfast

is served in the conservatory restaurant or out on

the patio, and the lunch and dinner menus are available for both residents and non-residents. The chefs produce some very interesting dishes for the main menu, typified by sea bass with a vanilla pod dressing, Thai-style prawn and cod fishcakes and breast of chicken with a leek and mustard stuffing. The hotel is geared up to cater for a range of functions and special occasions, and there's ample free parking for patrons.

538 THE BOATHOUSE BRASSERIE

**Houghton Bridge, nr Amberley,
West Sussex BN18 9LR**

☎ 01798 831059 Fax: 01798 831063
e-mail: confuciuslee@hotmail.co.uk

Succulent roast meats from the carvery and lovely fresh fish dishes are among the specialities that make the **Boathouse Brasserie** such a popular place. Gordon Lee and his wife Yvonne, both Hong Kong-born, took over the Brasserie in December 2005 and, with their talented chefs Danny and Gary, have built up a loyal and growing clientele at their riverside restaurant. Blackboards display the day's fish specials, which might include poached salmon, halibut Mornay and black bream fillets. There's also a good selection for meat-eaters, with choices typified by steaks served plain or with a variety of sauces and medallions of pork with an intriguing Drambuie and mushroom sauce.

The wine list includes plenty by the half-bottle and house wines by the glass. The non-smoking bar and restaurant are adorned with nautical bric-a-brac, including a canoe and anglers' yellow wellies and sou'westers. Both enjoy views of the River Arun, and when the weather is kind the decking tables on the patio are in demand. The Brasserie is closed on Sunday evenings. Gordon Lee also owns the Confucius Chinese Restaurant in Chichester.

539 THE SEAL BAR & RESTAURANT

**6 Hillfield Road, Selsey, Chichester,
West Sussex PO20 0JX**

☎ 01243 602461 Fax: 01243 606091
e-mail: bookings@the-seal.com
⊕ www.the-seal.com

The Seal has been established for 35 years and is one of the area's most popular public houses serving a wide range of traditional Real Ales, continental lagers and traditional English food. The Seal is located just south of Selsey town centre and is within 10 minutes walk of the beach.

A wide range of locally caught fish including bass, skate, and bream, as well as crab and lobster are always on the menu, all served with fresh local produce procured from the extensive local farming community. Fresh traditional English and continental desserts are made on the premises to complete your meal.

You will always find something to complement your meal from the extensive wine list which includes wines from Europe, Australia, South Africa and South America. Regular wine tasting evenings also take place where you can sample some of the wines.

The Seal is well known for providing a wide selection of the cask conditioned English Ales, from major breweries as well as micro-breweries found locally and around the country, and is one of the best places in the area to sample them. Regular ale sampling nights take place throughout the year.

Early in 2006 The Seal underwent a major refurbishment to improve its facilities. The Seal now provides disabled access and has a disabled toilet. A new kitchen, cellar and bar have been added and the pub has been finished in a traditional Victorian style in keeping with the building. There is a large front patio and smaller patio area to the rear. The Seal can cater for small wedding parties, private dinner parties and functions and is also a meeting place for many local societies.

540 WINDRUSH HOLIDAYS (BRACKLESHAM BAY, WEST SUSSEX)

Windrush Farm Rd, Bracklesham Bay, West Sussex PO20 8JT
☎ 0845 644 0717 Fax: 0870 766 2713
e-mail: enquiries@windrush-holidays.com
www.windrush-holidays.com

Situated on a pleasant landscaped site in Bracklesham Bay, 1 and 2 bedroom self-catering chalets, sleeping up to six. The chalets are either wooden, brick or rendered; individual

details vary, but all are equipped to ensure a comfortable, relaxed holiday. On-site facilities include an outdoor pool, tennis courts, a play area and a small shop; the beach is 3-minute walk away. Other holiday accommodation available.

541 AIDAN GUEST HOUSE

11 Evesham Place, Stratford-upon-Avon, Warwickshire CV37 6HT
☎ 01789 292824 Fax: 01789 269072
e-mail: eve@aidanhouse.wanadoo.co.uk
⊕ www.aidanhouse.co.uk

A quiet, relaxing base for visitors, close to the town centre, it has six guest bedrooms, all with en suite showers, and the car park at the rear is a major asset. A good breakfast starts the day.

Explore Britain and Ireland with *Hidden Places* guides - a fascinating series of national and local travel guides.

www.travelpublishing.co.uk

0118-981-7777

info@travelpublishing.co.uk

542 THE WHITE HORSE

Banbury Road, Ettington, nr Stratford-upon-Avon, Warwickshire CV37 7SU
☎ 01789 740641
⊕ www.whitehorseettington.co.uk

Originally built as three farm cottages, the **White Horse** is a traditional Cotswold pub offering real ales, good food and comfortably appointed accommodation. Kirk and Ali Waller have a warm welcome for all their customers, whether old faces or new, locals or visitors who come to this part of the country from all over the world. The Wallers are members of the

British Institute of Innkeeping, so the ales, beers and lagers are always in tip-top condition. The food, too, is outstanding, with locally sourced produce to the fore, fish specials on Tuesday evenings and game in season. The White Horse has four excellent en suite rooms for B&B guests.

543 THE ROSE & CROWN INN

Church Lane, Ratley, Warwickshire OX15 6DS
☎ 01295 678148

Run in fine style by Mary Houguez and her daughter Laura, the **Rose & Crown** is a charming old redbrick inn with a steeply-raked roof and distinctive tall chimneys. The inside is equally delightful, with real old-world feel assisted by a real fire in a vast stone hearth. Five real ales – Charles Wells Eagle and Bombardier, Greene King Abbot and St Austells Tribute are the residents – provide an exceptional choice for connoisseurs, and Laura's various menus cater for a wide cross-sections of tastes and appetites. Booking is recommended at the weekend; no food Sunday evening or Monday (the pub is closed Monday lunchtime).

544 THE FALCON

Church Street, Shipston-on-Stour,
Warwickshire CV36 4AS
☎ 01608 664414
e-mail: tutt@skippy48freeserve.co.uk
🌐 www.the-falcon-hotel.com

In the delightful little town of Shipston-on-Stour, the **Falcon** is a three-storey Georgian-fronted building with a strong following among both locals and visitors. The mellow bar is a pleasant spot for relaxing with a chat over a glass of real ale, and the pub has earned a fine reputation

for the quality of its food. The choice is extensive, with plenty of home-cooked dishes for meat-eaters, fish-eaters and vegetarians. The Falcon's five bedrooms (three en suite) offer a spacious, civilised base for visitors to a region rich in scenic and historic interest.

545 LARKRISE COTTAGE

Upper Billesley, Wilmcote, nr Stratford-upon-Avon, Warwickshire CV37 9RA
☎ 01789 268618
🌐 www.larkrisecottage.co.uk
e-mail: alanbailey17@hotmail.com

Larkrise Cottage has two spacious, comfortable B&B rooms that offer rural tranquillity, lovely views and easy access to all the attractions of Stratford-upon-Avon.

546 THE GOLDEN CROSS COUNTRY INN & EATING HOUSE

Ardens Grafton, nr Stratford-upon-Avon,
Warwickshire B50 4LG
☎ 01789 772420
e-mail: info@thegoldencross.co.uk
🌐 www.thegoldencross.net

The **Golden Cross** is a delightful stone-built country inn and eating house set among open fields off the A46 or B439 a few miles west of Stratford-upon-Avon. Owners Steve and Pat Wainwright have refurbished the whole place to a very high standard, putting the inn firmly back on the map as one of the most attractive and comfortable inns in the area as well as one of the best for a drink or a meal. The public rooms are very warm and welcoming, and when the sun shines the garden, also recently refurbished, provides a very pleasant alfresco alternative.

There are three interesting real ales and excellent wines to enjoy, either on their own or to accompany a bar snack or a

meal. Everything is freshly prepared on the premises throughout the menus, which feature fresh seasonal ingredients in dishes with English or modern European influences: home-cured beetroot and vodka gravad lax; terrine of chicken, sunblush tomatoes and baby spinach wrapped in prosciutto; baked sea bass on harissa potatoes; slow-braised lamb shank on smoked cheddar mash; lemon tart with fruit compote.

547 BROOM TAVERN

High Street, Broom, nr Bidford-on-Avon, Warwickshire B50 4HL
☎ 01789 773656 Fax: 01789 772983
e-mail: sdsmngmnt@btinternet.com
🌐 www.broomtavern.co.uk

Behind its Grade II listed frontage the redbrick **Broom Tavern** has abundant charm and character, along with a delightfully warm ambience and a well-earned reputation for friendliness. The tradition of hospitality is being carried on in fine style by Steve, Katrina and their affable, hardworking staff, and it is thanks to their efforts that their pub, which stands just off the A46 Evesham-Warwick road, has built up a very substantial band of regular customers. In the sympathetically modernised bars three well-kept real ales – Timothy Taylor, Black Sheep, Greene King IPA – are always available, along with other draught and bottle beers and lagers and keenly priced wines, including ten house wines.

Fresh seasonal produce, much of it local, goes into the kitchen, and out comes a good variety of wholesome

dishes of worldwide inspiration, from deep-fried brie, Thai fish cakes and duck spring rolls to excellent home-made pies, grilled cod with a prawn sauce and hunter's chicken. Darts, cribbage and dominoes are the favourite games, and the pub hosts regular charity events. At the back is a large garden where the story goes that William Shakespeare once fell asleep under a tree after losing a drinking contest.

548 RISTORANTE ROSSINI'S

50 Birmingham Road, Alcester, Warwickshire B49 5EP
☎ 01789 762764

One of the top Italian restaurants in the county, **Rossini's** has been a magnet for lovers of good food for more than 25 years. The menus tempt with all the classic Italian dishes and much more – the specials board always includes seafood and game dishes such as Dover sole, monkfish veneziana and pheasant alla Toscana. Wines from an expertly chosen list accompany the fine food.

549 THE MOAT HOUSE INN

Kings Coughton, nr Alcester, Warwickshire B49 5QF
☎ 01789 762984
🌐 01789 762984

The **Moat House Inn** is a delightfully traditional inn by the A435 just north of Alcester. This is David and Deborah Bailey's first venture into the licensed trade, and the inn's superb cooking attracts customers from far beyond the neighbourhood. The Lounge Menu emphasises much-loved classics such as fish & chips, curries, lasagne,

braised lamb and sausages & mash, while the Cavalier Menu offers additional choices typified by Thai-style chicken and halibut steak with a tomato salsa. The Moat House is a relaxing, welcoming place – even the resident ghost wears a smile!

550 THE SIMPLE SIMON

105 Emscote Road, Warwick,
Warwickshire CV34 5QY
☎ 01926 400333

Two bars provide a lively, convivial ambience
at **The Simple Simon**,
where the attractions include
four real ales, home-cooked
food and regular live music
evenings. The pub has two
rooms for B&B guests.

552 THE GREEN MAN

Daventry Road, Dunchurch, nr Rugby,
Warwickshire CV22 6NS
☎ 01788 810210
e-mail: sjbennettrugby@aol.com

The Bennett family – father, son and
daughter – are all involved in the running of
the **Green Man**, which stands opposite Guy
Fawkes' House in the centre of the village.
Six rotating brews provide a great choice for
real ale fans, and the excellent new chef
prepares a
good variety
of traditional
dishes every
lunchtime and
evening. The
Green Man's
four letting
bedrooms, all
with shower
en suite,
provide a
useful base for
both leisure
and business
visitors.

Looking for:
- *Places to Visit?*
- *Places to Stay?*
- *Places to Eat & Drink?*
- *Places to Shop?*

www.travelpublishing.co.uk

551 MATRICARDI'S

High Street, Henley-in-Arden,
Warwickshire B95 5AT
☎ 01564 792135
e-mail: enquiry@matricardis.co.uk
⊕ www.matricardis.co.uk

Contemporary Mediterranean cuisine brings lovers
of good food to **Matricardi's**, an attractive black-
and-white building opposite the police station on
Henley-in-Arden's main street. Behind the
traditional frontage, the bar-lounge and dining area
have been
tastefully modernised, providing a very stylish, comfortable
setting for relaxing over a drink, a snack or a meal.

Specialities on the interesting à la carte menu include dill-
marinated Scotch salmon, chilli spaghetti, beef cannelloni
wrapped in home-made frittatine, boeuf bourguignon and
honey and sherry-glazed breast of Gressingham duck. Fish-
lovers look to the
daily-changing list of
seafood specials
typified by scallops
sautéed in garlic and
chilli, served on a
bed of rocket, or grilled halibut fillet in a white wine,
cream and dill sauce. Sandwiches and snacks provide
lighter lunchtime options. The dining area looks out on
to an attractive garden that offers a pleasant venue for
an alfresco drink or meal in the balmy summer months.
Matricardi's is open every session except Sunday
evening, and the bar is open all day, every day.

Main Road, Austrey, North Warwickshire CV9 3EG
☎ 01827 830260

The **Bird in Hand** is an old-fashioned inn of great charm and character, standing next to the church in the village of Austrey, reached from the A444 Nuneaton-Burton road or the B5493 Tamworth-Measham road. It's also a short drive from junction 10 or 11 of the M42.

The inn is a thatched property dating back some 300 years and was at one time a monastery. The appeal of the outside is more than matched within, where low ceilings, beams, brasses and decorative plates set a splendidly traditional and welcoming scene in the bar. Leaseholder has made a great success of the Red Lion at Hopwas, on the other side of Tamworth, and when he took over the Bird in Hand in August 2005 he laid down similar high standards of hospitality, service, quality and value for money. He has installed excellent managers in Jane and Paul Compton, and the pub's many patrons, both regulars from local towns and

villages and visitors from further afield, are certain to leave contented after enjoying Jane's cooking.

The menus really do provide something for everyone, whatever their taste and whatever their appetite. For those who like their steaks and their chicken dishes, the meat/sauce combinations come to quite a few dozen, and there's always plenty of choice for fish-eaters and vegetarians. For many regular customers, Sunday lunch is a treat not to be missed, with up to four roasts as the centrepiece of the meal. Other lunches see a

wide choice of mainly lighter options, from sandwiches and salads to jacket potatoes, salads, pasta and burgers. The fine food is complemented by wines, available by glass or bottle, from a well-annotated list.

The bar stocks a wide range of drinks, including Marston's Pedigree and two rotating guest real ales. When the weather is kind, demand soars for a seat in the garden, which contains a children's play area. The Bird in Hand is open lunchtime and evening, and all day at the weekend. There is plenty to see and do in the area, including the family attraction of Twycross Zoo.

554 STEAM

Kemble Drive, Swindon, Wiltshire SN2 2TA
☎ 01793 466646
🌐 www.steam-museum.org.uk

The award-winning **STEAM,** the Museum of the Great Western Railway, is located in a beautifully restored building at the heart of Swindon Railway Works, where for nearly 150 years thousands of men and women worked for the Great Western Railway. The main activity was the building of great steam locomotives, the last being 92220 *Evening Star*, one of a fleet of powerful 2-10-0 freight engines which were destined to have all too short a working life. The star of the show in the Museum is 6000 *King George V*, which stands in a platform at the head of the 'Bristolian' express. Visitors can climb aboard the footplate of this marvellous thoroughbred and relive the glory days. Visitors can also walk underneath *Caerphilly Castle* as it stands in its inspection pit.

The sounds, sights and smells of the railway works live on in the workshops, where locomotives and carriages are restored, and one section of this fascinating place contains GWR accessories and road vehicles, including the famous Scammell 'mechanical horse', which could turn on a sixpence. The story of the great engineer, Isambard Kingdom Brunel, is told together with that of the thousands of other workers, from the navvies to drivers, signalmen and station masters. There are many hands-on opportunities to relive the action and special events and family activities are held regularly throughout the year.

All areas are wheelchair accessible, and a cafe and gift shop make your visit complete.

555 THE WHITE HART INN

Chippenham Road, Lyneham,
Wiltshire SN15 4BP
☎ 01249 890243

The **White Hart Inn** is an 18th century former coaching inn located on the outskirts of Lyneham, a short drive from Junction 16 of the M4. It's the first venture into the licensed trade for Kevin and Jayne Witts, who offer popular home-cooked dishes between 11 at lunchtime and from 5 to 9 in the evening. The pub is open all day seven days a week, with a late licence

on Friday and Saturday evenings. The White Hart is an excellent choice for locals, walkers and anyone looking for a break on a journey, and for visitors touring the area four ground-floor bedrooms in an adjacent outbuilding provide comfortable B&B accommodation.

556 THE RATTLEBONE INN

Church Street, Sherston,
Wiltshire SN16 0LR
☎ 01666 840871
e-mail: eat@therattlebone.co.uk

The **Rattlebone Inn** is a lovely old village pub with beams, stone walls, a log fire and plenty of old-world charm. Real ales include Youngs brews, and the kitchen provides a good selection of classic country cooking 'with a twist'. The inn is very the social hub of the community, with two boules pitches, pool and

other pub games, a skittle alley and a Sunday quiz. It stands in the centre of Sherston on the B4040 Malmesbury to Chipping Sodbury road.

557 THE VALE OF THE WHITE HORSE INN

Minety, nr Malmesbury,
Wiltshire SN19 9QY
☎ 01666 860175
e-mail: enquiries@vwhi.net
🌐 www.vwhi.net

The **Vale of the White Horse Inn** is a very handsome and substantial historic building located on the eastern side of the village of Minety, on the B4040 six miles east of Malmesbury and about eight miles south of Cirencester. Built from blocks of natural stone, floored in oak, set in large grounds and overlooking its' own lake, there's no more pleasant a place to dine in summer than sat on the terrace overlooking the lake and surrounded by the abundant floral displays. Equally attractive are the garden and lawn areas around the lake where light meals, snacks or simply a quiet drink can be enjoyed. Inside, there is choice of three dining areas and two bars, each offering a different ambience.

The Main Dinning Room has two open fires and French doors leading onto the terrace. In this atmospheric stone-walled restaurant with high-backed cushioned chairs and immaculately laid tables, fine lunchtime and evening meals are served seven days a week. The four international chefs take their inspiration from near and far: Locally reared beef, game and other fresh produce are a speciality. English classics such as beer-battered haddock & chips or steak, stilton & mushroom steamed suet pudding share the menu with more exotic choices like moules marinière, oriental-style tuna and prawn fishcakes, spicy chicken or beef and noodle stir-fry with a sweet chilli and soy sauce. A special fixed-price menu – booking required a day in advance – is available Monday to Saturday lunchtimes and Sunday to Thursday evenings. Under-12s have a special menu. Vegetarian dishes are always available and there is large interesting wine list.

The Village Bar, again with an open fire and French doors leading outside, dispenses five local real ales, six wines by the glass and a selection of sandwiches, ploughman's platters, tortillas, pizzas and the ever-popular Sunday lunchtime roasts.

The Garden Room, except when being used as part of the large event venue, operates as a brasserie style restaurant offering light meals and snacks.

The Lakeside Rooms are a series of large bright airing rooms with enormous arched windows and more French doors overlooking the lake. These rooms have been cleverly designed to provide either; one large venue for wedding parties, conferences and the like, or a series of separate rooms for private dinning. The Lakeside Bar offers, a skittle alley and sports room with a 7-foot screen. Other recreational facilities on site include a squash court, pool and football tables and a fully equipped dancing room.

Luxurious Guest Bedrooms are due on-stream later this year and the Vale of the White Horse Inn will be a superb base for touring an area with a wealth of places to visit.

The Vale of the White Horse Inn is owned and run by a highly motivated professional team, who started their first restaurant in London in 1987 before moving to Wiltshire in 2002. The chefs are clearly both very talented and highly imaginative. The popularity this establishment enjoys is richly deserved!

558 THE THREE CROWNS

**26 Maryport Street, Devizes,
Wiltshire SN10 1AG
☎ 01380 722688**

There's plenty to see in Devizes, including the Kennet & Avon Canal Museum, and after a walk along the canal towpath visitors can reward themselves with a drink and a meal at the **Three Crowns**. Centrally located, with its own car park at the back, the pub dates back to the early 17th century, and original beams contribute to the traditional look in the bar and restaurant. Outside, the courtyard is a mass of colour in spring and summer.

Tenants Mick and Gale take excellent care of their customers, with Wadworth 6X, Henry's IPA and a seasonal special drawn from the wood, and a bar menu served from 10 to 2 Monday to Saturday and from 12 to 2 on Sunday. They are planning to serve meals also in the evenings, and Wednesday has already become popular as fish & chip night, to eat in or take away.

Booking is best for this evening, and also for the Sunday carvery with a choice of three roast meats.

559 ROSEMUNDY COTTAGE

**London Road, Devizes, Wiltshire SN10 2DS
☎ 01380 727122 Fax: 01380 720495
e-mail: info@rosemundycottage.co.uk
🌐 www.rosemundycottage.co.uk**

Rosemundy Cottage enjoys a delightful setting with gardens leading down to the Kennet & Avon Canal. Tony and Zita's picturesque cottage offers very quiet, comfortable Bed & Breakfast accommodation in double rooms, all with bath or shower en suite, television with freeview and DVD, hairdryer and hot drinks tray. One room has a four-poster bed, and a ground-floor room is available with level access from the car park. The sitting room has plenty of games, books, magazines and travel guides, and the enclosed rear garden has a heated swimming pool. Guests can make use of the barbecue on the patio on warm summer evenings. No smoking; no pets.

560 THE ARTICHOKE INN

**The Nursery, Bath Road, Devizes,
Wiltshire SN10 2AA
☎ 01380 723400**

John, Sue and right-hand lady Caroline greet visitors to the **Artichoke Inn** with ready smiles and warm, genuine hospitality. The interior is inviting and traditional, with handsome polished wood to the fore, while outside is a pleasant little suntrap patio. The printed menu and specials board provide an excellent choice of favourite pub dishes such as steaks, liver & bacon and chicken & mushroom pie, with traditional roasts for Sunday lunch. Families are welcome, and the Artichoke has three good upstairs en suite rooms for B&B guests.

581

561 THE OLIVER CROMWELL

71 St Edith's Marsh, Bromham, Wiltshire
☎ 01380 850293 Fax: 01380 859620
e-mail: BrendaCMcFadyen@ aol.com
🌐 www.cottageguide.co.uk/hollytreehouse

The **Oliver Cromwell** is a 17th century former coaching inn standing on the A342 Devizes to Chippenham road. In their six years at the helm, Bob and Pam have made this one of the region's most popular places to visit for a drink or a meal.

The cream-painted frontage, with its slate roof and colourful flower troughs, gives way to an equally delightful interior, where black beams, exposed stone walls, a massive stone hearth topped by a portrait of Cromwell and old implements and armoury create an inviting and very traditional atmosphere.

The pub is open all day, seven days a week, for drinks – Wadworth 6X, Doom Bar and a rotating guest are the three real ales – and lunchtime and evening Monday to Friday and

all day Saturday and Sunday for food. Pam and the chef prepare an across-the-board variety of dishes that include old favourites such as liver & bacon, steak & kidney pie and faggots with mash & mushy peas, and new favourites like Thai curries and chilli con carne. There are seats for 36 in the restaurant and extra room in the old stable, which has a skittle alley and is a popular venue for functions and parties. The pub has a lovely garden with a children's play area and a view to the distant Roundway Hill, the scene of a violent battle in 1643 which was won decisively by the Royalists.

562 THE CROSS KEYS AT ROWDE

High Street Rowde, Devizes,
Wiltshire SN10 2PN
☎ 01380 722368 Fax: 01380 725758
e-mail: pub@crosskeysrowde.com
🌐 www.crosskeysrowde.com

In a village on the A342 a couple of miles from Devizes, the **Cross Keys at Rowde** is a handsome pub that was built on the site of a previous ancient thatched pub that burnt down in 1939. Sarah and Julian, who came here in the autumn of 2005, have already made this a very popular place that's open lunchtime and evening, and all day Saturday and Sunday in the summer. Sarah runs front of house and also oversees the kitchen, where Shane is the talented head chef.

Bar and restaurant menus and a daily changing specials board provide plenty of choice, and the food is complemented

by a quality wine list, as well as a minimum of two real ales – Wadworth 6X and Henry's IPA are the regulars. The food is served every lunchtime and evening, and it's always best to book, especially for Sunday lunch. The Cross Keys is not only a popular dining pub, it's also one of the most sociable, with a wide variety of entertainment and events, from themed food evenings to quizzes, pub games, folk music, discos, karaoke and skittles. The pub has plenty of off-road parking and a beer garden with a children's play area.

**Chandlers Lane, Bishops Cannings,
nr Devizes, Wiltshire SN10 2JZ**

☎ **01380 860218**

e-mail: thecrown@bishopscannings.com

⊕ www.thecrown.bishopscannings.com

The **Crown Inn** is a top-of-the-range establishment standing on Crown land in the picturesque village of Bishops Cannings, just off the A361 4 miles northeast of Devizes. Tanya Wynyard, a local lady, took over the tenancy of this late-Victorian hostelry in 2005, and Tanya, assistant manager Jackie and chef Claire make a particularly fine team.

The pub is open lunchtime and evening and all day on Sunday, and food is served every session. Claire makes a point of procuring as many of the raw materials for her kitchen as possible from local growers or suppliers, and her printed menu is supplemented by an impressive list of daily changing blackboard specials. Farmer's, poacher's and fisherman's platters, hot and cold sandwiches and jacket potatoes are popular lunchtime orders, while the main menu tempts with sausage, chips & peas, lasagne (beef or vegetarian), cod, scampi,

chicken breast in a Dijon mustard or sweet & sour sauce, trout with almonds and steaks served plain or with a choice of sauces. From the blackboard come dishes that show the full range of Claire's repertoire: typical choices could include Thai-style prawns with a plum sauce; ham & mushroom carbonara; turkey & leek pie; salmon in horseradish sauce under a herb crust; and moussaka – a wonderful dish seen all too rarely on pub menus. To round off a meal in style the board proposes hard-to-resist desserts like spotted dick, jam sponge, fruit crumble or treacle tart. A note on the menu reads 'Families, muddy boots

and dogs with well-behaved owners are most welcome' – a typical lighthearted touch at this most friendly of country pubs.

To accompany the food or to enjoy on their own are cask-conditioned ales and well-chosen wines. The Crown has a spacious beer garden with a children's play area, and ample off-road parking. The pub stands in the shadow of the spire of the Church of St Mary; the Bishops of Salisbury once owned a manor here and built this very grand church even before work started on the Cathedral.

564 THE LAMB INN

**The Green, Urchfont, nr Devizes,
Wiltshire SN10 4QU
☎ 01380 848848
e-mail: marc.salazar@virgin.net**

The **Lamb Inn**, parts of which date back as far as the 15th century, is located in the picturesque village of Urchfont, four miles south of Devizes. Built of red brick, part pink-washed, topped with a steeply raked thatched roof, the pub is equally attractive within, providing a really delightful ambience in which to relax and enjoy a drink – Wadworth 6X and Henry's IPA are the regular real ales – and a snack or a meal.

The Lamb is in the tender care of Jacqui and Marc Salazar, and it's their first venture in the business after Marc had completed 23 years as a Flight Engineer in the RAF.

They both cook, and they and their chef are all kept busy at peak times turning out a good variety of dishes for the

printed menu and daily changing specials board. Booking is advisable for the popular Sunday lunchtime roasts. The pub hosts regular themed food evenings, wine tasting evenings and live music evenings – ring for details and times of future events. The Lamb has a good beer garden and plenty of off-road parking.

565 THE BELL

**57 High Street, Great Cheverell, nr Devizes,
Wiltshire SN10 5TH
☎ 01380 813277
e-mail: gillc@clara.co.uk
🌐 www.thebellgreatcheverell.co.uk**

The **Bell** is situated in the picturesque village of Great Cheverell off the A360/B3098 south of Devizes. The setting is a definite plus, but The Bell has many other assets, including the delightful owners Gill Currie and her daughter Sara. The inn dates back as far as 1730, and the excellent first impression of the long, whitewashed building with shutters and ornamental cartwheels continues into the very traditional bar and dining areas.

The Bell is open every session except Sunday evening and Monday lunchtime. Food is served in all of these sessions except Monday evenings. Virtually everything on the menu is home-made, and the food is a major contributor to the pub's popularity. Lunchtime

fare includes ploughman's platters, freshly

baked baguettes, doorstop sandwiches and old favourites such as ham & eggs, beef & ale pie, scampi and curries. The main menu continues the theme and also offers some often neglected: lamb's kidneys, served here with a mushroom & onion sauce; beef or mushroom stroganoff; and chicken with a classic Normandy prune and Calvados sauce. The Bell has a lovely secluded garden reached through the bar.

584

566 THE OWL

Low Road, Little Cheverell, nr Devizes, Wiltshire SN10 4JS
☎ 01380 812263

The Owl is a grand old redbrick inn set in pleasant rural surroundings south of Devizes. Paul and Jamie, who took over here in 2001, quickly made their mark by updating the pub's amenities, which include two en suite rooms for B&B guests. A wide selection of dishes caters for lunchtime and evening appetites, and the choice of real ales is supplemented by many more during the two annual beer festivals hosted by the pub. Families are always welcome at The Owl,  which has a splendid decked seating area overlooking the garden. A charity quiz is held on the first Wednesday of each month.

569 OLD WARDOUR CASTLE

Tisbury, Wiltshire SP3 6RP
☎ 01747 870487
🌐 www.english-heritage.org.uk

One of the most romantic ruins in England, **Old Wardour Castle** was built in the late 14th century for John, 5th Lord Lovel and its six-sided design, with many rooms for guests, is unique in this country. Lord Lovel had been inspired by the castles then being built in France and was determined to copy the style for his new home. As well as providing security, the castle was a place for luxurious living. Besieged twice during the Civil War, the castle was badly damaged in 1644, and was never restored. When the new castle was built in the 1770s, the old castle was left as an ornamental feature. It is a venue for regular special events during the summer.

567 THE OLD BEAR INN & SAMUELS RESTAURANT

Staverton, nr Trowbridge, Wiltshire BA14 6PB
☎ 01225 782487 Fax: 01225 783623
e-mail: enquiries@theoldbear.co.uk
🌐 www.theoldbear.co.uk

The **Old Bear Inn** is an impressive hostelry located in Staverton, between Bradford-on-Avon and Trowbridge. Four weavers' cottages were long ago woven seamlessly into this fine pub, where Mike Phillips has been the leaseholder since 2003.

Using the best local suppliers for the raw materials, the kitchen produces an interesting selection of dishes listed on the printed menu and the blackboard. The food is hearty, wholesome and generously served, and the speciality home-made desserts make a memorable ending to a fine meal. Sunday lunch is a carvery operating between 12 and 2.30 in the 65-cover Samuels Restaurant at the back of the pub.

The Old Bear is open every lunchtime and evening for drinks and very session except Sunday evening for food. Four real ales are available – Bass, Wadworth 6X and two changing guests.

568 THE POPLARS INN

Shop Lane, Wingfield, nr Trowbridge,
Wiltshire BA14 9LN
☎ 01225 752426 Fax: 01225 766206
e-mail: poplarswingfield@tesco.net

Log fires in winter, village cricket in the summer, well-kept ales, fine wines, great home cooking, fast, friendly service in a pleasantly relaxed atmosphere – the **Poplars Inn** is the perfect example of the quintessential English country pub. Built originally as a farmhouse, it first received its alcohol licence in 1929.

Family owners Bernard and Carol, daughter Ria and her partner James, along with their excellent staff, share the very best qualifications for the job: they are members of the British Institute of Innkeeping, and three of the chefs are members of the prestigious Guild of Master Chefs. The pub is open every lunchtime and evening for food and drink; Wadworth 6X and Henry's IPA are the resident real ales, and food is served from 12 to 2 and from 7 to 9 – a little longer on Saturday and Sunday, and it's best to book at all times. The menu offers an

exceptional choice that caters for all tastes and appetites. For traditional palates there are steaks plain or sauced and cod with chips and mushy peas, while the more adventurous might take their steak with garlic and crayfish tails. Other typical choices from a truly mouthwatering list could be brie and cranberry filo parcels; mushrooms poached in red wine and filled with goat's cheese; crab cakes with a sweet chilli sauce; pan-fried lamb with spring onion mash and a rosemary sauce; and sea bass in white wine with a strawberry sauce.

The Poplars stages themed food evenings about four times a year, and it's a popular venue for wedding receptions and other special occasions. Outside is a raised patio where's there's a regular programme of live entertainment between June and September – events include live bands to accompany barbecues and World War II Days complete with visits by military vehicles. Wingfield is located on the A356/B3109 a couple of miles west of Trowbridge and very close to the border with Somerset.

570 THE GEORGE INN

The Square, Mere, Wiltshire BA12 6DR
☎ 01747 860427
e-mail: rob.binstead@btconnect.com
🌐 www.thegeorgeinnmere.co.uk

In the heart of Mere, on the B3092 and just seconds from the A303, the **George Inn** is a lovely old hostelry with real character and atmosphere. Rob and Jennie Binstead have made many new friends since becoming tenants in December 2004, and anyone who crosses the threshold into the warm, traditional bar can be sure of the friendliest of welcomes.

The menu offers an across-the-board selection of dishes, from sandwiches, salads and jacket potatoes to classics such as home-cooked ham, crispy-battered cod and lasagne to chargrilled steaks, the day's puff pastry-topped pie, a trio of lamb cutlets and the renowned Mere trout. The popular Sunday carvery operates both

lunchtime and evening. To accompany the food or enjoy on their own

are three real ales and well-chosen wines. The Church of St Michael the Archangel in High Gothic style and the local museum are both well worth a visit, but in Mere the George is definitely the tops for lovers of quality food and well-kept beer. And it's also an ideal base for exploring the local sights, with seven well-appointed guest bedrooms available on a B&B or Dinner, B&B basis.

571 THE CARRIERS

Stockton, nr Warminster,
Wiltshire BA12 0SQ
☎ 01985 850653 Fax: 01985 850335
e-mail: Kathy@thecarriers.co.uk
🌐 www.thecarriers.co.uk

The Carriers is a real gem of a pub, very warm and traditional, with beams, log fires, pictures, prints, horse brasses, trophies and country furniture.

It's an ideal place to relax and enjoy the excellent hospitality provided by owners Kathy and Ian and their experienced chef Mike. Three real ales are always available at this free

house, and Mike's repertoire runs from light snacks to fish specials and a signature dish of chicken in a sauce of mussels, prawns, tomatoes, tarragon, white wine and brandy, served on a bed of spaghetti. Book for the Sunday roasts. The Carriers is closed Sunday evenings and winter Mondays but always open on Bank holidays.

573 THE GARDEN HOUSE HOTEL

26 Edward Street, Westbury,
Wiltshire BA13 3BD
☎ 01373 859995 Fax: 01373 858586
e-mail: reception@thegardenhotel.co.uk
🌐 www.thegardenhotel.co.uk

Resident owners Ashley and Rachael turned the long-neglected Westbury Post Office into a luxury small hotel catering for both leisure and business guests. The eight bedrooms of the **Garden House Hotel** are comfortable and well equipped with power shower and spa bath.

The high quality décor and furnishings adds to the pleasure of a stay here, with bar and lounge perfect

spots to relax and unwind. Fine dining is offered in the elegant Mulberry Restaurant. No smoking throughout.

Clay Street, Crockerton, nr Warminster,
Wiltshire BA12 8AJ
☎ 01985 212262 Fax: 01985 218670
e-mail: batharmscrockerton@hotmail.co.uk

The **Bath Arms**, a 17th century Grade II listed building, is an absolutely outstanding pub with a equally outstanding chef-patron in Dean Carr. Immaculate inside and out, this is a pub worth more than just the traditional detour, and indeed many of the regular patrons travel many miles to enjoy the hospitality and fine food provided by Dean and his staff.

One look at the menu tells diners that is a place where food is taken very seriously. Familiar ingredients, all of the best quality, are prepared in often unexpected combinations to produce dishes that are probably not to be found on any other menus, whether pubs or restaurants. Roast scallops are served with cauliflower cheese; the signature fish cake combines Cornish crab and broad beans; haddock is served with squash tortellini and sage butter; pork loin steak is complemented with a fennel and tarragon salad; grilled

ribeye steak is accompanied by blue cheese fritters and rocket pesto. Plainer dishes are also available, and Sunday brings both brunch and traditional roasts. The superb food is matched by an equally fine selection of drinks, headed by three or four CAMRA approved real ales including Crockerton Classic and Naughty ferret, both brewed within half a mile of the pub.

The Bath Arms is open every session and all day in the summer months. Booking is recommended Thursday to Sunday to be sure of a table. A large field behind the pub is a venue for regular events such as jazz lunches and beer festivals. Off the A350 Shaftesbury

road just outside Warminster, Crockerton is close to many places of interest, including the National Trust's Cley Hill, a renowned sighting place for UFOs; the Arn Hill Nature Reserve, Shearwater Lakes and the magnificent house and Safari Park at Longleat. And for a spot of exercise there are plenty of forest walks and cycle trails. For a combination of comfort, peace and accessibility, the Bath Arms has few equals in the region, and the two large guest bedrooms have en suite facilities, superior décor and furnishings, plasma screen TVs and other up-to-the-minute amenities.

574 THE ROYAL OAK

**Hawkeridge, nr Westbury,
Wiltshire BA13 4GA
☎ 01373 826270
e-mail: theroyaloak40@btinternet.com
🌐 www.theroyaloakhawkeridge.co.uk**

John and Mich Stratton took over the reins of **The Royal Oak,** a 16th century redbrick, tile-roofed pub, in November 2005 and lost no time in winning new friends in the area. The well-stocked bar offers a good selection of real ales,

and appetites large and small are satisfied by a fine range of snacks and main dishes. Mich cooks familiar favourites like steaks, steak & kidney pie, pork chops, cod, scampi, lasagne and Cajun chicken, with plain and toasted sandwiches and jacket potatoes for quicker meals. The pub has a pleasant garden with a children's play area.

575 THE KICKING DONKEY

**Brokerswood, nr Westbury,
Wiltshire BA13 4EG
☎ 01373 823250 Fax: 01373 865685**

Having one sampled the delights of the **Kicking Donkey,** customers return time and again to the little village of Brokerswood west of Westbury. Nicky and her chef satisfy country appetites with hearty home cooking (steaks are a speciality) and cater for fresh-air thirsts

with four real ales – Butcombe Bitter, Doom Bar, Wadworth 6X and Bath Ales Gem – plus Thatchers cider on draught. The Kicking Donkey has Cask Marque recognition. Across the road from the pub is a beer garden with an outstanding children's play area.

576 THE WHITEHALL INN

**Bransford Road, Rushwick,
Worcestershire WR2 5TA
☎ 01905 422660
e-mail: thewhitehallinn@tiscali.co.uk**

When Ron and Fiona Goldsby took over the tenancy of the **Whitehall Inn,** they soon set about a major refurbishment programme to restore its best features. Close to the A44, A4103 and the Worcester ring road, the inn has a

homely, traditional appeal, and the tried-and-tested pub dishes are served on Friday, Saturday and Sunday. Boddingtons and Flowers IPA are the favourite locals' tipple. The pub is closed Monday lunchtime, otherwise open lunchtime and evening and all day Friday, Saturday and Sunday.

578 CANNARA GUEST HOUSE

**147 Barnards Green Road, Malvern,
Worcestershire WR14 3LT
☎ 01684 564418
e-mail: info@cannara.co.uk
🌐 www.cannara.co.uk**

Tourists, walkers, cyclists and business people will all find a friendly home-from-home at **Cannara**, a family-run guest house on the edge of Great Malvern. Comfort is paramount in the four en suite bedrooms, each with its own style and character and all handsomely furnished and luxuriously appointed. A

whirlpool spa bath is available to guests, who also have the use of a spacious lounge. A multi-choice breakfast is served in the dining room. The guest is ideally placed for both business and leisure visitors, with Qinetiq and the Science Centre, the Malvern Hills and Three Counties Showground all a short drive away.

577 BREDON HOUSE

34 Worcester Road, Great Malvern,
Worcestershire WR14 4AA
☎ 01684 566990 Fax: 01684 577530
e-mail: rayella@bredonhouse.co.uk
🌐 www.bredonhouse.co.uk

AA
◆◆◆◆
Guest
Accommodation

A quiet relaxed family run guest house enjoying spectacular views yet only 100 yards from the town centre which offers a choice of shops, restaurants and pubs as well as the acclaimed Malvern Theatres and Cinema complex. From the front door walk up the famous Hills or drive to the many local attractions. The Three Counties Showground is just 10 minutes away by car.

The 10 well appointed bedrooms are all en-suite with TV, radio, tea/coffee facilities, telephone and internet access. Relax and enjoy a drink and the views of Bredon Hill from the elegant lounge or the peaceful garden. Pets and Children are made very welcome.

579 THE LAMB INN

West Malvern Road, Malvern,
Worcestershire WR14 4NG
☎ 01684 577847

The **Lamb** is a popular pub with a friendly, convivial atmosphere and a wide following among music-lovers as well as anyone who appreciates good ale and good conversation. Walking in the Malvern Hills is a good way to work up a thirst, and a selection of real ales rotates in the cheerful bar, where an eyecatching feature is a display of

the flags of some 30 nations. Owner Colin Robinson is passionate about music and a noted brass session player, and his love is reflected in the jazz, folk, blues and other live music evenings that take place three times a week. Skittles is a favourite game in the bar, which has a big-screen TV for major sporting events.

580 THE WYCHE INN

74 Wyche Road (B4218), Malvern,
Worcestershire WR14 4EQ
☎ : 01684 575396
e-mail: reservations@thewycheinn.co.uk
🌐 www.thewycheinn.co.uk

The **Wyche Inn** is a traditional English country hostelry with a warm welcome from hosts Eric and Viv, local ales, home cooking and well-appointed accommodation in double rooms or self-contained flats. The lounge bar is open all day for drinks (Hobsons and the local Malvern Hills are the resident cask ales), and lunchtime and evening menus

offer a selection of hearty home-cooked dishes. Tuesday is steak night. The inn is reputedly the highest located in the county, and the setting and the views make it a popular choice with tourists and walkers.

581 COPPER BEECH HOUSE

32 Avenue Road, Malvern,
Worcestershire WR14 3BJ
☎ 01684 565013
e-mail:
enquiries@copperbeechhouse.co.uk
🌐 www.copperbeechhouse.co.uk

In leafy Avenue Road a short walk from the
railway station **Copper Beech House,**
(graded 4 Star by Visit Britain), provides a
delightful home

from home for
Bed & Breakfast
guests. Built as a
private residence
in 1898, it has
been carefully
updated while
retaining period
charm and
warmth, and the seven bedrooms all have en
suite bath or shower, television, hairdryer and
hot drinks tray. Resident owner Phil Butler
provides an excellent breakfast to start the
day, and guests have the use of a cosy lounge
and a tranquil garden.

582 LADY FOLEY'S TEA ROOM

Great Malvern Station, Imperial Road,
Malvern, Worcestershire WR14 3AT
☎ 01684 893033

Lady Foley's Tea Room is located in the
Victorian railway station. Margaret Baddeley
and her daughter Melissa
prepare and serve an all-day
menu including sandwiches
and salads, soup, baked
potatoes, toasted snacks,
quiches, cakes and scones.

Explore Britain and Ireland with
Hidden Places guides - a fascinating
series of national and local travel
guides.

www.travelpublishing.co.uk

0118-981-7777

info@travelpublishing.co.uk

583 THE THREE KINGS INN

Hanley Castle, Worcestershire WR8 0BL
☎ 01684 592686

Just off the B4211 Upton-Malvern road, the
Three Kings Inn is a free house with origins
going back 500 years. The Roberts family are
delightful hosts, providing a welcoming
ambience for enjoying lively conversation, hot
and cold snacks and grills, and a superb choice
of real ales – always at least five, with Hobsons
and Butcombe Bitters the regulars. The guest
ales change all the time, and anyone lucky
enough to drop in every day in 2005 could
have sampled 420 different brews!

584 THE JOCKEY INN

Baughton, nr Earls Croome,
Worcestershire WR8 9DQ
☎ 01684 592153 Fax: 0870 127 8311
🌐 www.thejockeyinn.com

When Colin and Carol Clarke took over the
reins at the **Jockey Inn**, they brought with
them over 30 combined years in the business,
along with
the
invaluable
assistance
o f
daughter
Nicola and
son-in-law
Simon.
Four real
ales are
headed by

John Smiths and Directors Bitter, and the
printed menu and several blackboards
provide great home-cooked food (big juicy
steaks and fresh fish among the specialities).
Next to the inn is a self-contained bungalow
with a double room available for B&B, dinner
or self-catering.

Old Hill, Flyford Flavell,
Worcestershire WR7 4DA
☎ 01905 381890

Standing on the edge of the village of Flyford Flavell, on the A422 road between Worcester and Inkbarrow, the **Flyford Arms** started life in 1787. Formerly called The Union, it has recently been smartly refurbished, enhancing its appeal as a much-loved local (its hospitality is second to none) as well as a place to seek out for the quality of its cooking.

The main bar area has a variety of seating, including inviting leather armchairs and sofas, a huge brick hearth at one end, topped by a row of horse brasses, and a traditional range at the other. It's a very pleasant setting for enjoying a glass of real ale – four are always on tap, including Admans Broadside and the pub's own Flyford Ale. The pub has been in the excellent care of the Jewell family – James and Bridget, son Philip (the head man in the kitchen) and daughter Anne Louise, who assists in the restaurant and bar.

Philip has played a major role in making this one of the top places to drive out to for a meal. All tastes and appetites are catered for, and among the most popular of the meat dishes are chilli con carne and Flyford steak & ale pie. Flyford Terracotta pots – more than a light bite, less than a main course – are perfect for smaller appetites or for anyone with limited time to enjoy more of Philip's repertoire. Booking is recommended for Saturday dinner, the Sunday roast lunch and the occasional food or music themed evenings (phone for details). Children are welcome, either inside or out in the beer garden.

The Jewell family plan to add another amenity to the Flyford Arms by opening guest accommodation. When that happens, the pub will be not just one of the best for food and hospitality but a very pleasant, civilised base for touring the region. There are some lovely scenic walks in the vicinity, and Worcester to the west and Stratford-upon-Avon to the east are both within easy reach for motorists. The pub is closed Monday lunchtime (unless it's a Bank Holiday) otherwise open lunchtime and evening and all day Friday, Saturday, Sunday and Bank Holidays. Food is served every session except Sunday evening and Monday (unless it's a Bank Holiday).

586 THE FLEECE INN

The Cross, Bretforton, nr Evesham,
Worcestershire WR11 7JE
☎ 01386 831173
e-mail: Nigel@thefleeceinn.co.uk
🌐 www.thefleeceinn.co.uk

The **Fleece Inn** is a renowned public house owned by the National Trust. A quintessentially English inn, the lovely half-timbered building was originally a farmhouse and was first licensed in 1848. Set in the equally attractive village of Bretforton, just east of Evesham, the Fleece has a charming and extremely atmospheric interior, with low black-beamed ceilings, stone walls, small-paned lattice windows and log fires in large open hearths. At the rear is an excellent beer garden.

The inn is run in fine style by Nigel Smith, who offers a choice of six real ales, including Hook Norton Best, Pigs Ear from the Uley Brewery and regularly rotating guests. There's even hand-pumped local scrumpy. Cooking is modern British in style, expert and imaginative, using seasonal local produce

in dishes such as faggots with mushy peas, and desserts include scrumptious ice cream made in the village as well as all-time favourites like apple crumble or bread & butter pudding. An asparagus festival, including two auctions, is held here at the end of May, and a special menu based round the wonderful Evesham Vale asparagus adds to the options. New for 2006 is a guest bedroom with en suite shower, created in the oldest (15th century) part of the building.

588 AVONSIDE HOTEL

Wyre Piddle, nr Pershore,
Worcestershire WR10 2JB
☎ 01386 552654 Fax: 01386 554843
e-mail: avonsidehotel@tiscali.co.uk

Owner Peter Freeman has invested considerable time and resources into refurbishing the **Avonside Hotel** and adding many new amenities. He has made it a really outstanding Restaurant with Rooms, with two excellent chefs preparing superb dishes

that include British classics and some Thai specialities. The seven beautifully appointed en suite bedrooms offer all the modern comforts, and guests have the use of a heated outdoor swimming pool. The landscaped grounds lead down to the River Avon, and the hotel has moorings and fishing rights.

HIDDEN PLACES GUIDES

Explore Britain and Ireland with *Hidden Places* guides - a fascinating series of national and local travel guides.

Packed with easy to read information on hundreds of places of interest as well as places to stay, eat and drink.

Available from both high street and internet booksellers

For more information on the full range of *Hidden Places* guides and other titles published by Travel Publishing visit our website on

www.travelpublishing.co.uk
or ask for our leaflet by phoning
0118-981-7777 or emailing
info@travelpublishing.co.uk

The Strand, Charlton, nr Pershore,
Worcestershire WR10 3JZ
☎ 01386 860388
e-mail: info@gardenersarms.wanadoo.co.uk

Always an inn, and always called the **Gardeners Arms**, this outstanding hostelry is on top form under hosts Denise and Tony. It enjoys a picture-postcard setting in the village of Charlton, which lies between the A44 and B4084 a couple of miles west of Evesham and about five miles east of Pershore. Handsome on the outside, it's delightfully traditional within, with wood or quarry-tiled floors, beams, a big open hearth, bygone pictures and a brick-fronted bar with an impressive parade of bottles ready for duty. A minimum of three real ales are always available (Flowers IPA is a regular) along with a hand-pulled cider from the Thatcher brewery. Denise has a quarter of a century's experience in the business, so she knows exactly how to please her customers.

Her cooking is the pub's strongest magnet, drawing regular customers from a wide area as well as tourists in this very attractive part of the world. Well-loved British stalwarts are well to the fore, as in cod & chips;

chicken, ham & leek pie; faggots in rich onion gravy; apple pie and bread & butter pudding. There's also a good choice of sandwiches and hot ciabatta melts with interesting fillings like steak, mushroom & stilton, Mediterranean vegetables with tomato sauce and mozzarella, and smoked bacon with brie & grapes. Sunday lunch – served from 12 to 5, but best to arrive in good time – includes three roasts, with children's portions available. The evening menu tempts with some more tried-and-tested favourites such as ham & eggs, classic prawn cocktail, Cajun chicken and home-made beefburgers. A note on the menu sums up the

hosts' philosophy of serving good food not fast food, freshly prepared for full enjoyment. If they know a customer is in a hurry, they'll do their best to serve as quickly as possible, and with notice they will do their best to accommodate special dietary requirements.

Live music evenings are held one Sunday a month..The pub is open lunchtime and evening Tuesday to Saturday, with extended hours during the summer months. It's open all day on Sundays and 'special occasions' and closed Mondays except Bank Holidays.

Eckington, nr Pershore,
Worcestershire WR10 3BA
☎ 01386 750356
e-mail: anchoreck@aol.com
🌐 www.anchoreckington.co.uk

The **Anchor** is a charming traditional inn with hotel facilities and an excellent restaurant. Dating in part from the 17th century, it stands 5 miles south of Pershore 150 yards from the B4080 Tewkesbury road, the main road through the quiet village of Eckington. The interior of the inn is comfortable and traditional , with original timber beams, feature stone pillars, a large open fireplace, barrel stools, brass ornaments, pictures of days gone by and collections of beer mats and badges.

A minimum of four real ales usually includes Bass, Marstons Pedigree and Piddle, and home-cooked food is served every lunchtime and evening). The cooking is traditional British with some imaginative touches and the lounge bar and à la carte menus cater for all palates and pockets with anything from bar snacks to three-course meals. A well-stocked wine cellar provides a fine complement to the food. Thursday is steak night, there's live music every other Friday and a quiz is held one Tuesday a month.

As well as satisfying hunger and thirst, the Anchor also provides very comfortable guest accommodation in tastefully decorated rooms with en suite shower, television and hot drinks tray.

It's an ideal place for exploring a region that offers a wealth of scenic and historic interest. Eckington itself was founded in AD172 as a Roman settlement on land belonging to the British Duboni tribe. It's a village of pretty black-and-white cottages, with a Norman church and a 15th century bridge over the River Avon. Footpaths lead to Bredon Hill, where on the crest of its northern slope are the remains of a pre-Roman settlement known as Kennereton Camp; on the summit of the hill is an 18th century brick tower folly. Tewkesbury, Evesham, Pershore are all nearby, and Worcester, Gloucester and Cheltenham are within an easy drive.

Station Road, Wadborough,
Worcestershire WR8 9HA
☎ 01905 840524

In the picturesque village of Wadborough, **The Masons** is well worth seeking out for its excellent hospitality and top-class cuisine. Three adjacent properties – the oldest dates from the mid-Victorian age – were combined to create the pub, and in the bar and dining areas wooden beams and uprights, half-panelling and gleaming white walls paint a traditional scene. Outside is a canopied area with seats for up to 30 that can be used for most of the year.

Experienced licensee and chef Matthew Ace became the owner of The Masons in the summer of 2005, and his flair and hard work and the assistance of an equally dedicated staff has made this one of the top destination dining pubs in the county. Its reputation has spread quickly far beyond the immediate area, and booking is strongly recommended for all meals to be sure of getting a table. The menu combines British with some Continental influences, and many of the dishes show individual, often unusual treatment of ingredients. Camembert comes not

as the usual deep-fried cubes but baked in the box, served 'hot and runny' with warm dipping bread; roast chicken might be accompanied by a damson sauce, or the breast stuffed with banana and drizzled with a spicy jam sauce; chargrilled fillet steak is topped with a mushroom and stilton sauce. Even the sandwiches are special – how about bacon, goat's cheese, red onion and mango chutney, or smoked salmon and crayfish tails? The sandwiches come with a small salad and crispy fried potatoes to make a perfect quick lunch. The menus change every session, so each visit brings the same pleasant problem – what to order when it's all so tempting! Children are welcome, and there's a play house and slide in the garden.

The Masons, a non-smoking establishment, is situated west of the B4084 a couple of miles out of Pershore. It's also a short drive from the M5 (leave at Junction 7, take the B4084 and turn right at Stoulton). The pub is closed Sunday evening and all day Monday.

591 BROMSGROVE MUSEUM

**26 Birmingham Road, Bromsgrove,
Worcestershire B61 0DD
☎ 01527 577983**

Much of the earlier history of Bromsgrove
can be seen at **Bromsgrove Museum**, which
contains exhibits of the glass, salt and nail
industries, and of the Bromsgrove Guild. It
also contains an attractive range of shop
windows, which feature costumes, toys,
cameras and much more. The building is the
former Coach House of Davenal House, built
in 1780. On the front of the Museum the
wrought iron balcony
that originally
adorned the
stationmasters house
at Bromsgrove can
be seen. It is said
that, in 1848,
Stephenson, the great
engineer, stood on it.
The Museum is open
Monday to Saturday,
10.30am-12.30pm
and 1pm-4.30pm.

593 THE HOP POLE

**Friar Street, Droitwich Spa,
Worcestershire WR9 8ED
☎ 01905 770155
⊕ www.thehoppoleatdroitwich.co.uk**

Owner Tim, Bar Manager Chris and Queen of the
Kitchen Lyn are the energetic threesome who run
the **Hop Pole**, which was converted and extended
from a row of cottages that date back to the 1700s.
The pub is open all day, seven days a week, for ale,
with Wye Valley's Butty Bach and Hereford Pale Ale
joined by a guest ale that changes each month.
Complementing the great beer, kept by Chris in perfect
condition, the Hop Pole satisfies lunchtime appetites
with a varied selection of dishes that offer excellent
value for money (cash and cheques only).

Children are welcome inside if lunching with

adults, but
everyone
has the use
throughout
opening
times of a
pleasant

rear garden with a delightful summer surprise in the
shape of a little swimming pool. The go-ahead tenants
are always looking for ways to add to the already
considerable appeal of the Hop Pole, the most
important being a Beer Festival planned for the summer
of 2006.

592 THE BELL INN

Astwood Bank, Evesham Road, Redditch,
Worcestershire B96 6AX
☎ 01527 894290

The Bell is an early-19th century inn standing on the A441 at Astwood Bank, 4 miles south of Redditch. Another pub, long since demolished, stood next door on land that is now The bell's beer garden, a popular spot in warm weather with plenty of space for children to romp and a bouncy castle in the summer months.

Experienced licensees Jeff and Sarah took over here in September 2005 and made changes that put their own individual stamp on the place. The changes clearly ring the right bells with their customers, as the inn has gone from strength to strength. The main reason for the success is the quality and variety of the cooking, and the owners' policy of buying the finest, freshest local produce available enables the chefs to cook all the dishes to the highest possible standards. The main à la carte menu is wide in choice, with eight or so starters and up to 30 main

courses, including plenty for fish-eaters and vegetarians as well as meat-lovers; and some scrumptious desserts to round things off. One of the most popular of the traditional dishes is chilli con carne, and a footnote to the dish asks "Why not try the atomic chilli – the water's free". The bar snack menu includes a range of fajitas – beef, chicken, king prawn and vegetarian – and there's another section for smaller appetites. The 4oz steak is perfect for the less peckish, but only the truly ravenous will order the Bell's Bully 50oz rump steak (the 24 hours notice required is presumably to alert the local butcher!). The reward for finishing this awesome plateful is a free dessert and a

free drink, and the hosts ring the pub's bell to let everyone know about the feat.

Note for the mathematically minded: the chargrill section of the menu lists eight grills, a choice of five vegetables, eight sauces, seven toppings and four butters. This means that diners can order 8,960 different combinations before starting all over again.

The pub is open lunchtime and evening Monday to Friday and all day Saturday and Sunday. Food hours are 12 to 2.30 and 6 to 10, Sunday 12 to 9; booking is advisable for all meals.

594 THE FIR TREE INN

Trench Lane, Dunhampstead, Oddingley, nr
Droitwich, Worcestershire WR9 7JX
☎ 01905 774094
e-mail: firtreeinn@btinternet.com

The **Fir Tree Inn** is the social heartbeat of the little village of Dunhampstead, which stands in the parish of Oddingley, a short drive northeast of Worcester. Martyn and Tracy Perrins have many years' in the licensed trade, and they have made their pub a favourite place not only with a loyal local clientele but with walkers, cyclists, motorists and holidaymakers exploring the neighbouring Worcester-Birmingham Canal.

Dating back around 200 years, the pub has recently seen a major refurbishment that has added contemporary touches without in any way compromising the period appeal. The inn is open for drinks lunchtime and evenings and all day on Saturdays and Sundays. Hook

Norton Bitter and Timothy Taylor are the resident real ales, with one other that changes regularly. Food, served every session, provides a choice of baguettes, jacket potatoes and hot dishes such as beer-battered cod and steak & kidney pie served in the bar with a full a la carte menu available in the non-smoking restaurant. Booking is advisable at the weekend.

597 THE LION INN

Clifton-upon-Teme,
Worcestershire WR6 6DH
☎ 01886 812975

Overlooking the green in the picturesque village of Clifton-upon-Teme, the **Lion Inn** is a very handsome redbrick inn with the oldest parts dating back more than 700 years. The main feature inside is a huge open fireplace between the bar and dining areas, and a roaring fire keeps both parts cosy in the cooler months.

Alan and Linda are the leaseholders, and Linda's cooking is one of the pub's major assets – 'We don't served fast food, we serve good food' reads the message above the bar counter. Linda seeks out local produce for as many dishes as possible, and her dishes keep the smiles on

her customers' faces every session. The upstairs guest bedrooms, both with en suite facilities and one suitable for a family, are available all year round. The rooms can be booked on a B&B or room only basis. The Lion has a beer garden and off-road car parking space.

595 THE BRIDGE INN

Plough Road, Tibberton, nr Droitwich,
Worcestershire WR9 7NQ
☎ 01905 345874
e-mail: darren.magor@btconnect.com
🌐 www.spanglefish.com/TheBridgeInn

When Darren and Jacqueline arrived just before Christmas 2005, they brought with them 20 years combined experience in the catering business, Darren as a manager of licensed premises, Jacqueline as a chef. The Bridge is located by the Worcester to Birmingham Canal, and is a five-minute drive from Junction 6 of the M5.

There's a cosy, friendly atmosphere in this traditional inn, and the interior features panelling and beams. Two open fires keep the place snug even during the long, cold winter, while in the

warmer months the large lawned beer garden, with a children's play area, is the place to be. Banks's Bitter and Original, Marston's Pedigree and a regularly changing guest keep real ale enthusiasts happy. The printed menu and specials board add up to a very wide and varied selection of freshly prepared, home cooked dishes which use local produce when ever possible. Sandwiches, baguettes and snacks are available Monday to Saturday lunchtimes, with roasts the centrepiece of Sunday lunch. Options on the main menu include beer-battered cod, sausages with chips or mash, fish cakes, lasagne and a choice of steaks, fresh fish and vegetarian options. There are also daily seasonal specials such as game pie and whole sea bass.

The pub is open lunchtime and evening, and all day on Saturday, Sunday and Bank Holidays. It's closed on Mondays in January and February. Food is served every lunchtime and evening, and booking is recommended at the weekend and on Bank Holidays and special days. The main areas are accessible to wheelchair users, and baby changing facilities are available at this fine pub, which truly caters for all ages. It is equally popular as a much-loved local, a destination restaurant and a place of general refreshment for tourists, ramblers, cyclists, dog walkers, escapers from the bustle of Droitwich and Worcester....everyone is welcome!

Main Road, Ombersley, nr Droitwich,
Worcestershire WR9 0EW
☎ 01905 620252 Fax: 01905 620769
e-mail: enquiries@crownandsandys.co.uk
🌐 www.crownandsandys.co.uk

In a prime location in the picturesque village of Ombersley, the **Crown & Sandys** is a distinguished gabled building with a history that traces back to 1566. The leaseholders since 1998 are Richard and Rachel, from a family who have been closely connected with village life and trade for over a century.

The inn is open every lunchtime and evening and all day on Saturday and Sunday, and visitors who appreciate a good glass of real ale can choose from at least four: the residents are Marston's Bitter and Pedigree, Burton Bitter and the locally brewed Sadlers Ale. The food, as well as the beer, brings a loyal band of regulars to the Crown & Sandys, and there are no fewer than 150 covers in the three separate restaurant areas; even so, such is the pub's popularity that booking is advisable on Friday, Saturday and Sunday. Local produce features strongly on a good variety dishes, and the printed menu is supplemented by daily specials. Seats are set outside in the summer months on the impressive front patio, and there's plenty of off-road car parking space.

The standard of the accommodation certainly lives up to all the offerings at this outstanding hostelry, and the five luxuriously appointed double rooms all have en suite facilities. Ombersley, very traditional and very English, is well worth taking time to explore at leisure, and the Crown & Sandys is the ideal base. In its early days the inn was called simply The Crown, until the local Lord of the Manor added his name. The Sandys family lived at Ombersley Court, a splendid Georgian mansion now in other private hands, and in the Church of St Andrew visitors can see family memorials and the capacious family pew.

598 THE BRIDGE

Stanford Bridge, Worcestershire WR6 6RU
☎ 01886 812771

The **Bridge** is an eye-catching pub in a scenic location on the B4203 close to the banks of the River Teme. Tim and Bex have put the pub backing apple pie order since they took over in November 2005, creating a smart, cosy  ambience for enjoying a drink and a meal. Worcestershire produce features strongly in the food, which is served lunchtimes Thursday to Sunday and every evening. Up to four real ales are available at any one time, with many more during the annual July Beer festival. The pub has a secluded rear patio garden.

599 THE BELL

Pensax, nr Abberley,
Worcestershire WR6 6AE
☎ 01299 896677

John and Trudy Greaves offer a friendly greeting, fine ales and home-cooked food at The **Bell**, a handsome redbrick inn with half-timbering and a steeply raked red-tiled roof. Built in 1883 as a hunting lodge for nearby Abberley Hall, this family-friendly pub has a spacious interior divided into several areas, each with an open fire to create a warm,  inviting atmosphere throughout. Hobsons is the regular brew among at least five real ales always available (CAMRA commended). Local ingredients, including organic produce from a farm across the road, are used to form the basis of the dishes listed on the blackboard menu.

602 CANNON HALL MUSEUM

Bark House Lane, Cawthorne, Barnsley,
South Yorkshire S75 4AT
☎ 01226 790270
e-mail: cannonhall@barnsley.gov.uk

Set in 70 acres of historic parkland and gardens, **Cannon Hall Museum** provides an idyllic and tranquil setting for a day out. For 200 years Cannon Hall was home to the Spencer-Stanhope family. From the  1760s the architect John Carr of York was commissioned to extend and alter the house while the designer Richard Woods was hired to landscape the park and gardens. Over 40 varieties of pear trees still grow in the historic walled garden, as well as peaches and nectarines. The famed Cannon Hall vine grows in one of the greenhouses. The park provides an ideal setting for a picnic, outdoor activities and games. Cannon Hall was sold by the family in the early 1950s to Barnsley Council and was first opened as a museum in 1957. The Hall now contains collections of furniture, paintings, glassware and pottery, much of which is displayed in period settings. It also houses Charge, the Regimental Museum of the 13th/18th Hussars.

The Victorian Kitchen Cafe near the gardens is open each weekend and during the school holidays for home-made light refreshments in the traditional setting of the original kitchens and servant's hall. The Museum also has a shop stocking a range of greetings cards, local history books, confectionery and giftware. Off the A635 Barnsley to Huddersfield Road. Easy access from junctions 37 or 38 of the M1.

Main Road, Eastburn, nr Keighley,
West Yorkshire BD20 7SN
☎ 01535 653000

In Airedale, off the A629 between Keighley and Skipton, the **Eastburn Inn** is one of the most popular and certainly one of the most sociable inns in the whole region. Until recently it was called the White Bear, and it emerged with its new name in December 2005 after a major top-to-toe refurbishment.

Leaseholders Karen and Lee are continuing a long tradition hospitality, good food and well-kept ale, and there's no mistaking the warmth of the welcome they and their staff provide, whether it's for familiar faces or first-timers. Strangers soon become friends in the relaxing surroundings of the bar, where two or three real ales head a wide selection of drinks. The inn is open from 5 o'clock on Mondays, otherwise all day, seven days a week, and the printed menu and specials board list a good range of dishes, many of them highlighting prime fresh local produce. Everything is good and tasty, but for many of the regulars it just has to be her speciality mixed grill. Families with children are always welcome, and there's a secure play area in the garden, where there's also a barbecue and a space for dancing the evening away.

This is not a place for popping in and out in a hurry, it's somewhere to relax and unwind, to enjoy the convivial atmosphere and to join in the lively chat. And most days of the week some sort of entertainment is laid on. On Tuesday the quiz starts at 9 o'clock; on Wednesday and Sunday nights there's the popular game 'Open the Safe'; Friday is karaoke or disco night; and there's live musical entertainment on occasional Saturdays. The inn also has a pool table, and sports fans can catch the big events on Sky TV.:

Riverside Gardens, Bridge Lane, Ilkley,
West Yorkshire LS29 9EU
☎ 01943 607338
e-mail: enquiries@ilkley-riversidehotel.com
🌐 www.ilkley-riversidehotel.com

In a quiet, picturesque location by the River Wharfe, the **Riverside Hotel** is the perfect spot to take a break, whether it's for a drink, a snack, a meal or an overnight or longer stay. No one knows more about the hospitality business than Kristine and Kelvin Dobson, who have been here for more than 35 years, and there's no mistaking the warmth of the welcome and the friendly atmosphere that puts visitors at ease the moment they walk through the door.

The bar – open all day, seven days a week – serves hand-pulled ales (Tetleys, Samuel Smith and Copper Dragon from the Skipton Brewery) that have earned it a top CAMRA award for 2005, and a large selection of other drinks to enjoy by a log fire in the chillier months or out on the patio when the sun shines. An extensive menu, served from 12 to 7 daily and until 8.30 in season, really does cater for every palate and appetite, with a choice that runs from traditional favourites like steak & Guinness pie to haute cuisine dishes of worldwide inspiration. Attached to the main building is the Riverside Kabin, a favourite family spot that's open all day for fish & chips and award-winning ice creams.

The hotel's 11 guest bedrooms are en suite, with Sky TV and hot drinks trays, and all enjoy views of the river, the gardens or the moor. The Riverside is the ideal spot for both business and leisure visitors. The town centre is only a few minutes away, and the tranquil setting makes it easy to unwind after the business or pleasure of the day. And that pleasure could be a walk on the Dalesway or Ilkley (with or without a hat!), a game of golf or tennis, or discovering the many places of interest in the locality.

603 THE CROSS KEYS

Thixendale, nr Malton,
North Yorkshire YO17 9TG
☎ 01377 288272

The **Cross Keys** is a real hidden gem, an 18th century farmhouse that long ago became a cosy one-roomed pub. This delightful family-run free house is open every session for real ales and home cooking, and when the sun shines the picnic benches on the hedge-flanked lawn come into their own. For guests staying overnight the Cross Keys has

three good bedrooms in the old stable block – a double and two twins, all with en suite facilities.

605 THE FEATHERS HOTEL

Market Place, Pocklington,
East Yorkshire YO42 2AH
☎ 01759 303155 Fax: 01759 304382
e-mail: info@thefeathers-hotel.co.uk
🌐 www.thefeathers-hotel.co.uk

Dominating the market place in the historic town of Pocklington, the **Feathers** has earned an enviable reputation as both hotel and restaurant. The bedrooms, all spacious and well equipped, comprise six in the main building (including a four-poster room and a family room) and ten in chalet style set round the rear courtyard. A full English breakfast is served in the attractive restaurant, pub meals are served

in the fully licensed bar, and fresh local produce is also the basis of the 1-, 2- and 3-course evening meals, accompanied by an extensive list of wines by glass or bottle.

606 THE RED LION

High Street, Market Weighton,
East Yorkshire YO43 3AH
☎ 01430 872452

Tenants Christine and Jim Bytheway have been in charge of the **Red Lion** since 1990, welcoming old friends and new throughout the day. For seven of the last ten years they've won the top award from the Chamber of Trade for the lovely flower displays that adorn the frontage, and the inn is equally delightful inside. Black Sheep, Tetleys and John Smiths Cask are the resident real ales, to enjoy with a chat or to accompany the excellent lunchtime food. The printed menu is supplemented by a daily special, and on Sunday it's roasts only – booking advisable.

607 HORNSEA FOLK MUSEUM

11 Newbegin, Hornsea,
East Yorkshire HU18 1AB
☎ 01964 533443

The excellent award-winning **Hornsea Folk Museum** occupies a Grade II listed former farmhouse. Village life in North Holderness is explored as it has changed over the centuries and features the characters who influenced the development of the area. Human evolution is illustrated from the early 1700s to post second world war and meticulously restored rooms are brimming with furniture, decorations, utensils and tools of the Victorian period. The kitchen, parlour and bedroom have fascinating displays of authentic artefacts, and the museum complex includes a laundry, workshop, blacksmith's shop and a barn stocked with vintage agricultural implements.

604 THE GREY HORSE INN

Main Street, Elvington, nr York,
North Yorkshire YO41 4AG
☎ 01904 608335 Fax: 01904 608338
🌐 www.elvington.net/pub

Opposite the green on the main street of Elvington, the **Grey Horse Inn** is a picture-postcard village inn dating back to the 17th century. Hanging baskets and window boxes adorn the whitewashed frontage, and picnic tables are set outside in the summer. The interior is equally charming, with a wealth of wood, subtle lighting and plenty of cosy seating enhancing the welcoming ambience. The lounge area has plush leather sofas, and upstairs, the Hayloft, with its warm yellow walls, watercolours and palewood furniture, provides a bright, stylish venue for functions and special occasions. The abundance of memorabilia on display throughout includes old photographs of village life.

Run by David Forster and Jason Butler, the inn, winner of a CAMRA (Yorkshire Branch) Country Pub of the Year Award and regional winner of The Pub Shine awards for drinking experience, serves up to five real ales (Black Sheep, John Smith, Timothy

Taylor Landlord and guests) together with a good range of other beers and stouts, lagers, wines, spirits and non-alcoholic drinks. The Grey Horse is also a great place for a meal, and the regular menu and specials board offers a wide and tempting choice served until 9 o'clock (but not on Monday). Typical classic pub dishes such as scampi, lasagne, steaks and steak & ale pie are expertly prepared and well presented, and locally sourced ingredients are used whenever possible.

The inn lies just six miles southeast of York on the B1228, and for visitors exploring this marvellous city the Grey Horse provides a pleasant and convenient base in two en suite bedrooms – a double and a family room – with superb comfort and full facilities. Even closer, just over a mile away, is one of the most interesting museums in the whole region – the Yorkshire Air Museum, with its unique collection of over 40 aircraft and numerous displays, located on one of the very few original wartime bomber bases open to the public. For opening times check the website which also has plenty of other useful information and images. Thursday is quiz night, and there's a music quiz every Sunday.

606

608 THE BLACKSMITHS ARMS

Front Street, Lastingham,
North Yorkshire YO62 6TL
☎ 01751 417247
e-mail: pete-
hils@blacksmithsarmslastingham.co.uk

Adjoining the ancient church where three roads meet, the **Blacksmiths Arms** is a warm, convivial wayside inn. Lastingham, signposted off the A170 west of Pickering, lies at the foot of the North Yorkshire Moors, and Peter and Hilary Trafford's neat stone inn naturally attracts walkers, anglers, sportsmen and holidaymakers discovering the natural and historic delights of the North East Dales.

In the cosy, old-fashioned bar, with its beams, log fire, local photographs and assorted mugs, tankards and harnesses, thirsts can be quenched with an interesting of real ales featuring smaller breweries. Home-cooked food

served in the bar or restaurant also offers an interesting choice that runs from familiar favourites like fish pie or steaks to evening specials that might include Mediterranean-style grilled sardines, herb-crumb-crusted salmon with a fresh tomato coulis and a very tasty lamb & apricot goulash. The en suite guest accommodation, including a splendid four-poster room, is available all year round.

609 THE COACH HOUSE INN

Rosedale Abbey, nr Pickering,
North Yorkshire YO18 8SD
☎ 01751 417208
e-mail: info@coachhouseinn.co.uk
🌐 www.coachhouseinn.co.uk

Starting life 100 years ago as a garage, the **Coach House** has been an inn for a quarter of that time. It's now looking very smart after recent refurbishment, and visitors can look forward to a very friendly reception from hosts Howard and Daphne Hebron. Mars Magic from the Woldtop Brewery is an interesting real ale, and the food caters for all appetites, from baguettes, jacket

potatoes and burgers to warm chicken salad, fish & chips, chicken tikka masala, grilled pork chops and a hunger-busting Desperate Dan steak pie. The pub hosts regular charity quizzes and live entertainment evenings. Children are welcome until 9.30.

610 BIRCH HALL INN & HOLIDAY COTTAGE

Beck Hole, Goathland, nr Whitby,
North Yorkshire YO22 5LE
☎ 01947 896245
e-mail: glenys@birchhallinn.fsnet.co.uk
🌐 www.beckhole.info

For many years Glenys and Neil Crampton have owned and run the **Birch Hall Inn**, and they have made it one of the best-known and best-loved inns in the whole county. In a stunning location on the route of the North Yorkshire Moors Railway, its two rooms provide a delightful, homely

setting in which to enjoy a glass or two of ale, a simple, tasty snack or a slice of the excellent beer cake. Attached to the main building is a self-catering cottage for four.

611 THE POSTGATE INN

**Egton Bridge, nr Whitby,
North Yorkshire YO21 1UX**
☎ 01947 895241
e-mail: thepostgateinn@ukonline.com
🌐 www.postagteinn.co.uk

Enough blackboards to supply the local school announce the day's dishes at the **Postgate Inn**, which stands in the heart of the North Yorkshire moors opposite the railway station in Egton Bridge. The pub is open lunchtime and evening and all day Saturday and Sunday for drinks, with Black Sheep and Camerons Ruby the resident real ales.

Food, served every session, makes excellent use of prime local produce in dishes such as smoked haddock, Whitby cod with lemon butter served on parsley mash with a prawn Mornay sauce, griddled monkfish wrapped in bacon on mixed peppers, steaks and beef

stroganoff. Booking is recommended at the weekend. Three en suite bedrooms are available all year round for Bed & Breakfast guests. The inn takes its name from Nicholas Postgate, born in the village in 1596, who was martyred for ministering to those loyal to the Catholic faith at a time when it was banned.

612 THE PLOUGH INN

**180 Coach Road, Sleights, nr Whitby,
North Yorkshire YO22 5EN**
☎ 01947 812410
e-mail: theploughsleights@tiscali.uk

On the A169 three miles south of Whitby, the **Plough Inn** is well placed for discovering all the many attractions of the North Yorkshire coast and countryside. This large, handsome former coaching inn is rustic and comfortable, homely and relaxed, with convivial hosts in Miranda and Dennis Jackson. It's open lunchtime and evening, and all day Easter to October and Sundays throughout the year.

Three real ales and a draught lager are ready to quench thirsts, and food is served from noon to 9 o'clock in the summer, and lunchtime and evening in the winter. Miranda is a very talented cook, and her

customer-pleasing repertoire runs from hearty meat dishes like Ryedale lamb chops or pork oysters with a stilton sauce to fish specials and always something interesting for vegetarians, perhaps a butternut squash filo tart. Bed & Breakfast is available.

613 ESTBEK HOUSE

East Row, Sandsend, nr Whitby,
North Yorkshire YO21 3SU

☎ 01947 893424   Fax: 01947 893625
e-mail: reservations@estbekhouse.co.uk
🌐 www.estbekhouse.co.uk

On the edge of the North Yorkshire Moors coastline, with the Cleveland Way in front and the National Park boundary to the rear, **Estbek House** enjoys a glorious setting in one of England's prettiest villages. The house is Georgian, built around 1750, and hands-on owners David Cross and Tim Lawrence have made it one of the finest restaurants with rooms in the whole county.

The food here is absolutely outstanding, with chef James and his team combining skill and flair at the highest level and putting their personal stamp on every dish. Estbek's signature dish, and its most popular fish dish, is fillet of fresh local halibut, pan-seared and served with a wine sauce or a crab and crayfish sauce. The seafood selection, usually including snapper, sea bass, red mullet and Nile perch, served with a King scallop on a bed of crayfish tails, is a dish fit for a king, and other options – the list is long and mouthwatering! – include a classic steak au poivre, seared duck fillet with a honeyed cherry reduction, and superb vegetarian dishes such as a trio of spiced bean cakes or couscous stuffed mixed vegetables.

They're as passionate at Estbek about wine as about food, and the selection includes a connoisseur list and a range of excellent quality wines by the glass. There are two dining areas – one in bistro style, the other more traditional, just right for a romantic candlelit dinner. The guest accommodation at the house is also top-class, comprising three doubles and a twin, all with flat-screen TV, CD player, alarm clock, hairdryer, tea & coffee making facilities and a complimentary bathroom guest pack. The double rooms have en suite showers, while the twin is fitted with a whirlpool spa bath. Each room has pictures by local artists, most of local scenes.

The house was built for the manager of the local alum works that once dominated the coastline, producing a substance that was more valuable than gold; its main use was for fixing colours in fabrics. Sandsend nestles between the coast and the Mulgrave Woods, with glorious sandy beaches only 10 yards away and the two fantastic Mulgrave castles a short walk away. It stands on the A174 a short drive or a pleasant walk along the beach to Whitby.

614 THE CAPTAIN COOK INN

60 Staithes Lane, Staithes,
North Yorkshire TS13 5AD
☎ 01947 840200
⊕ www.thecaptaincookinn.co.uk

At the top of a bank above the fishing village of Staithes, the **Captain Cook Inn** is a delightful place to visit for a drink, a meal or a short break or holiday. Built in Victorian times as the station hotel (the railway has long gone), it is an ideal base for exploring the North York Moors National Park and TV's *Heartbeat* country).

Landlord Trevor Readman is a real ale devotee, and his customers can enjoy a constantly changing selection of brews – at least five, and more during the beer festival he organises each August. Trevor is expanding the food side of the business, adding more variety to the snacks and meals available. Packed lunches can be organised for residents. Two

of the four guest bedrooms have en suite facilities, and all have television and beverage tray. Why Captain Cook? At the age of 17, James Cook, later Captain Cook RN, came and worked as a grocer's apprentice in Staithes, and the Cook connection is strong throughout the region.

615 THE DOWNE ARMS

3 High Street, Castleton,
North Yorkshire YO21 2EE
☎ 01287 660223
e-mail: info@thedownearms.co.uk
⊕ www.thedownearms.co.uk

A warm welcome, classic pub décor, great food and drink, super staff, top-class accommodation – the **Downe Arms** offers all this and more. South of the A171 in the heart of the North Yorkshire Moors, the premises started life in the early 18th century as three cottages and later became an important stop on the York-Stockton coaching route.

Picture-postcard pretty, with great moor views and old-world décor and furnishings, it's a perfect spot that's open all day, seven days a week for drinks; Timothy Taylor Landlord and Black Sheep are the regular real ales, with a changing guest adding to the choice. Tradition lives on in this excellent pub, but it also moves with the times. This is amply demonstrated in the menus, which combine tried and tested

restaurant classics such as lamb shanks, roast duck and beef stroganoff with

unusual and exotic offerings like sea bass with a vanilla butter vinaigrette or a 'Safari kebab' with zebra, bluebook, springbok, impala, kudu, wildebeeste and rattlesnake served on citrus couscous – surely one of the most intriguing dishes ever seen on a British menu! The recently created guest accommodation comprises five superbly fitted en suite rooms.

616 THE BAY HORSE

**The Green, Crakehall, Bedale,
North Yorkshire DL8 1HP
☎ 01677 422548
🌐 www.crakehall.org.uk**

In a picturesque location across from the village green stands the **Bay Horse**, home of the cricket club and very much the heartbeat of village life. The tile-roofed building started life in the 17th century as a

smithy selling ale; it was first licensed a century later, and is now run by John and Dianne Shephard, whose customers can look forward to a warm welcomes, well-kept Yorkshire ales and good honest home cooking. Food is served lunchtime and evening every day except Monday, and it's always best to book in the summer holiday period. Another attraction in Crakehall is the 17th century Water Mill.

619 WINDSOR GUEST HOUSE

**9 Castle Hill, The Bar, Richmond,
North Yorkshire DL10 4QP
☎ 01748 823285
e-mail: mike-sheila@tiscali.co.uk**

Sheila and Mike offer a friendly family welcome at **Windsor Guest House**, a Grade II listed building with ten letting bedrooms. The tariff is on B&B terms, but packed lunches and evening meals are available by arrangement.

618 THE SWALEDALE ARMS

**Morton-on-Swale, nr Northallerton,
North Yorkshire DL7 9RJ
☎ 01609 774108
e-mail: lane594@msn.com**

Morton-on-Swale is a pretty village on the A684 Northallerton-Bedale road, and Laura and Mark have made a big impact here since taking over the **Swaledale Arms** in August 2005. They've made it a very popular place, not just with the locals abut also with tourists and motorists who find the short detour from the A1 at Leeming very worth while.

The pub is closed on Mondays in winter, but otherwise open all day, every day for serving drinks – John Smiths Cask, Theakstons Best and Black Sheep are the resident real ales. Good English cooking is a big part of the pub's appeal, served every lunchtime and

evening. Customers can eat in the bar, the snug or the bistro, with Rafters Restaurant

available as an overflow or for private parties. Booking is recommended on Friday and Saturday evenings and Saturday and Sunday lunches. Families with children are very welcome, and plans include creating a children's play area in the garden.

617 WOODYS AT THE BLACK SWAN

Thornton-le-Moor, nr Northallerton,
North Yorkshire DL7 9DN
☎ 01609 774117 Fax: 01609 774444
e-mail: woodys@thornton-le-moor.co.uk
🌐 www.thorntonlemoor.co.uk

After creating, opening and running a very successful restaurant in Northallerton, Peter and Angela Wood brought their skills and experience to Thornton-le-Moor. They also oversaw a superb refurbishment programme, adding a fine destination restaurant to a much-loved village local, so **Woodys at the Black Swan** offers the best of both worlds.

It remains a great place for a drink (John Smith Cask is the regular real ale), but the best plan is to book a table and relax over a splendid, leisurely lunch or dinner. For food is definitely king here, and the menus are full of good things. Steaks are perennial favourites, and other meat options could include chicken breast in a cranberry, red wine and orange sauce, lasagne, beef stroganoff and venison sausages. Fish-eaters can go traditional with deep-fried haddock & chips or opt for something a little more unusual like sea bass with a cracked pepper and lemon sauce, or seafood casserole in a mild, creamy curry, apricot and almond sauce. Vegetarians are certainly not forgotten, with typical dishes such as deep-fried goat's cheese with beetroot and cherry tomatoes, or meatless moussaka. Pasta comes in three sizes – starter, medium and main. The lunchtime menu offers filled ciabatta and rustic rolls, jacket potatoes and warm salads.

Children are very welcome, and can choose from their own menu. There are seats outside, and plenty of off-road parking. At the rear of the pub there's a certified caravan site with some electric hook-ups. Open lunchtime and evening (closed Sunday evening and Monday lunch). Woodys stands in the village of Thornton-le-Moor, just off the A168 Thirsk-Northallerton road.

620 GRASSINGTON LODGE

Wood Lane, Grassington,
North Yorkshire BD23 5LU
☎ 01756 752518
e-mail: relax@grassingtonlodge.co.uk
🌐 www.garssingtonlodge.co.uk

Built as a private residence in 1898, **Grassington Lodge** has now been providing guest accommodation for over 50 years, and standards have never been higher than since Tim and Diana Lowe acquired the property in April 2004. Just 100 yards from the village square in beautiful Wharfedale – one of the most spectacular and varied of the Yorkshire Dales – the lodge has ten superb bedrooms with en suite bath or shower, luxurious Egyptian cotton bedding, high-quality toiletries and TVs with DVD players (free loan of DVDs).

A multi-choice breakfast gets the day off to a

perfect start, and the lodge has two lounges where guests can plan their days. The patio area has barbecue facilities, and there's ample private parking. Tim and Diana can organise various activity breaks, including guided walks, climbing, caving, canoeing and riding.

621 THE GOLDEN LION HOTEL

Horton-in-Ribblesdale, nr Settle,
North Yorkshire BD24 0HB
☎ 01729 860206
e-mail: tricia@goldenlionhotel.co.uk
🌐 www.goldenlionhotel.co.uk

The **Golden Lion** is a distinctive green-painted building on the B6479 in the Ribblesdale Valley, north of Settle and not far from the spectacular Ribblesdale Viaduct. Resident owners Michael and Trisha Johnson have run this 16th century hostelry for 20 years, and it's everything a country inn should be, with quality to the fore in

food, drink, accommodation and service. Excellent food is served from opening time until 9.30 every day, and five upstairs en suite bedrooms are warm and comfortable; for groups of up to 15 walkers or cyclists bunk room is a budget-price alternative. Food served 12-2pm and 7pm-9pm.

623 THE MILL RACE TEA SHOP

Yore Mill, Aysgarth Falls, Aysgarth,
North Yorkshire DL8 3SR
☎ 01969 663446
e-mail: millraceteashop@aol.com

The **Mill Race Tea Shop** is housed in a lovely 18 th century building on the bridge by the channel ('Race') that brings water down from the upper Aysgarth Falls. The food served is all home made, with bread, cakes, scones and savouries among the chief delights.
Takeaway picnic food and drinks are available, and a small shop on the premises sells a selection

of local foodstuffs. The Mill Race is a great favourite with walkers, cyclists and tourists visiting the spectacular Falls.

622 THE OLD DAIRY FARM

Widdale, Hawes, North Yorkshire DL8 3LX
☎ 01969 667070
🌐 www.theolddairyfarm.co.uk

The **Old Dairy Farm** is the latest enterprise of restaurateurs Paul and Pam Cajiao, owners of the acclaimed Blacksmiths Table Restaurant in Washington Old Village, Tyne & Wear. Having opened as recently as October 2005, the quaint Upper Wensleydale farm buildings have been tastefully converted into a luxurious 'get-away-from-it-all' small hotel.

The guest accommodation comprises three double rooms with beautiful executive-style en suite facilities, and the farm itself is set within five acres of farmland, with excellent access and lovely views. The property is ideally located to tour the Dales either by car or on foot, or to visit the Lake District. The cuisine, as would be expected from the experienced restaurateurs, is superb. Pam oversees the evening meal, which usually consists of three courses plus coffee, with choices per course, served in the exquisite beamed lounge/dining room. Breakfast is always hearty but with lighter alternatives available. Paul's knowledge of wine is very apparent in the list, and a wide selection of bottled beers and lagers, spirits and liqueurs is also to hand.

The Old Dairy Farm has links with the Wensleydale Creamery and was once owned by Kit Calvert, the man responsible for the development of Wensleydale cheeses. Guests can visit the Creamery, which is only three miles away, for conducted tours. The Old Dairy Farm has impressed with its excellent, friendly service, prompting the General Manager of an international hotel chain to comment: 'As a professional of some 38 years, I can think of no global offering to outperform the Old Dairy Farm in its niche market'.

Tourist Information Boards

CUMBRIA TOURIST BOARD

Cumbria and The Lake District
Ashleigh Holly Road
Windermere
Cumbria LA23 2AQ
Tel: (015394) 44444
Fax: (015394) 44041

EAST OF ENGLAND TOURIST BOARD

Cambridgeshlre, Essex Hertfordshire, Bedfordshire, Norfolk, Suffolk and Lincolnshire
Toppesfield Hall
Hadleigh
Suffolk IP7 5DN
Tel: (01473) 822922
Fax: (01473) 823063

HEART OF ENGLAND TOURIST BOARD

Derbyshire, Gloucestershire, Hertfordshire, Leicestershire, Northamptonshire, ottinghamshire, Rutland, Shropshire, taffordshire, Warwickshire, Worcestershire, The West Midlands and representing the districts of Cherwell and West Oxfordshire
Woodside
Larkhill Road
Worcester WRS 2EF
Tel: (01905) 763436
Fax. (01905) 763450

LONDON TOURIST BOARD

Greater London
6th Floor,
Glen House
Stag Place
London SW1E 5LT
Tel: (0207 932 2000
Fax: (0207 932 0222

NORTHUMBRIA TOURIST BOARD

Durham, Northumberland the Tees Valley and Tyne & Wear
Aykley Heads
Durham   OH 1 5UX
Tel: (0191) 3753000
Fax: (0191) 3860899

NORTH WEST TOURIST BOARD

Cheshire, Greater Manchester, Lancashire, Merseyslde and the High Peak District of Derbyshire
Swan House
Swan Meadow Road
Wigan Pier
Wigan WN3 5BB
Tel: (01942)821222
Fax: (01942) 820002

SOUTH EAST ENGLAND TOURIST BOARD

East Sussex; Kent Surrey and West Sussex
The Old Brew House
Warwick Park
Tunbridge Wells
Kent TN2 5TU
Tel: (01892) 540766
Fax: (01982) 511008

SOUTHERN TOURIST BOARD

Berkshire, East and North Dorset, Hampshire,Isle of Wight, Bucklnghamshire and Oxfordshire
40 Chamberlayne Road
Eastleigh
Hampshire S050 5JH
Tel. (01703) 620006
Fax: (01703) 620010

WEST COUNTRY TOURIST BOARD

Bath, Bristol, Cornwall and the Isles of Scilly, Devon, Dorset, Somerset and Wiltshire
Woodwater Park
Pynes Hill
Rydon Lane
Exeter EX2 5WT
Tel: (01392) 425426
Fax: (01392) 420891

YORKSHIRE TOURIST BOARD

Yorkshire, North Lincolnshire and North East Lincolnshire
312 Tadcaster Road
York Y02 2HF
Tel: (01904) 707961
Fax: (01904) 701414

Towns, Villages and Places of Interest

VISIT THE TRAVEL PUBLISHING WEBSITE

Looking for:

- *Places to Visit?*
- *Places to Stay?*
- *Places to Eat & Drink?*
- *Places to Shop?*

Then why not visit the Travel Publishing website...

- Informative pages on places to visit, stay, eat, drink and shop throughout the British Isles.

- Detailed information on Travel Publishing's wide range of national and regional travel guides.

www.travelpublishing.co.uk

HIDDEN PLACES GUIDES

Explore Britain and Ireland with *Hidden Places* guides - a fascinating series of national and local travel guides.

Packed with easy to read information on hundreds of places of interest as well as places to stay, eat and drink.

Available from both high street and internet booksellers

For more information on the full range of *Hidden Places* guides and other titles published by Travel Publishing visit our website on

www.travelpublishing.co.uk
or ask for our leaflet by phoning **0118-981-7777** or emailing **info@travelpublishing.co.uk**

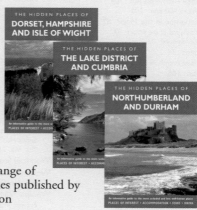

TRAVEL PUBLISHING ORDER FORM

To order any of our publications just fill in the payment details below and complete the order form. For orders of less than 4 copies please add £1.00 per book for postage and packing. Orders over 4 copies are P & P free.

Name:

Address:

Tel no:

Please Complete Either:

I enclose a cheque for £ _____ made payable to Travel Publishing Ltd

Or:

Card No:

Expiry Date:

Signature:

Please either send, telephone, fax or e-mail your order to:

Travel Publishing Ltd, 7a Apollo House, Calleva Park, Aldermaston, Berkshire RG7 8TN
Tel: 0118 981 7777   Fax: 0118 940 8428   e-mail: info@travelpublishing.co.uk

	Price	Quantity
HIDDEN PLACES REGIONAL TITLES		
Cornwall	£8.99	....
Devon	£8.99	....
Dorset, Hants & Isle of Wight	£8.99	....
East Anglia	£8.99	....
Lake District & Cumbria	£8.99	....
Northumberland & Durham	£8.99	....
Peak District	£8.99	....
Yorkshire	£8.99	....
HIDDEN PLACES NATIONAL TITLES		
England	£11.99	....
Ireland	£11.99	....
Scotland	£11.99	....
Wales	£11.99	....
HIDDEN INNS TITLES		
East Anglia	£7.99	....
Heart of England	£7.99	....
South	£7.99	....
South East	£7.99	....
West Country	£7.99	....

	Price	Quantity
COUNTRY PUBS AND INNS		
Cornwall	£5.99	....
Devon	£7.99	....
Sussex	£5.99	....
Wales	£8.99	....
Yorkshire	£7.99	....
COUNTRY LIVING RURAL GUIDES		
East Anglia	£10.99	....
Heart of England	£10.99	....
Ireland	£11.99	....
North East	£10.99	....
North West	£10.99	....
Scotland	£11.99	....
South of England	£10.99	....
South East of England	£10.99	....
Wales	£11.99	....
West Country	£10.99	
OTHER TITLES		
Off the Motorway	£11.99	....

Total Quantity:

Post & Packing:

Total Value:

READER REACTION FORM

The *Travel Publishing* research team would like to receive reader's comments on any visitor attractions or places reviewed in the book and also recommendations for suitable entries to be included in the next edition. This will help ensure that the *Hidden Places series of Guides* continues to provide its readers with useful information on the more interesting, unusual or unique features of each attraction or place ensuring that their visit to the local area is an enjoyable and stimulating experience. To provide your comments or recommendations would you please complete the forms below and overleaf as indicated and send to:

The Research Department, Travel Publishing Ltd,
7a Apollo House, Calleva Park, Aldermaston, Reading, RG7 8TN.

Your Name:

Your Address:

Your Telephone Number:

Please tick as appropriate:

Comments ☐   Recommendation ☐

Name of Establishment:

Address:

Telephone Number:

Name of Contact:

READER REACTION FORM

COMMENT OR REASON FOR RECOMMENDATION:

....
....
....
....
....
....
....
....
....
....
....
....
....
....
....
....
....
....
....
....
....
....

READER REACTION FORM

The *Travel Publishing* research team would like to receive reader's comments on any visitor attractions or places reviewed in the book and also recommendations for suitable entries to be included in the next edition. This will help ensure that the *Hidden Places series of Guides* continues to provide its readers with useful information on the more interesting, unusual or unique features of each attraction or place ensuring that their visit to the local area is an enjoyable and stimulating experience. To provide your comments or recommendations would you please complete the forms below and overleaf as indicated and send to:

**The Research Department, Travel Publishing Ltd,
7a Apollo House, Calleva Park, Aldermaston, Reading, RG7 8TN.**

Your Name:

Your Address:

Your Telephone Number:

Please tick as appropriate:

Comments ☐   Recommendation ☐

Name of Establishment:

Address:

Telephone Number:

Name of Contact:

READER REACTION FORM

COMMENT OR REASON FOR RECOMMENDATION:

....

....

....

....

....

....

....

....

....

....

....

....

....

....

....

....

....

....

....

....

....

READER REACTION FORM

The *Travel Publishing* research team would like to receive reader's comments on any visitor attractions or places reviewed in the book and also recommendations for suitable entries to be included in the next edition. This will help ensure that the *Hidden Places series of Guides* continues to provide its readers with useful information on the more interesting, unusual or unique features of each attraction or place ensuring that their visit to the local area is an enjoyable and stimulating experience. To provide your comments or recommendations would you please complete the forms below and overleaf as indicated and send to:

**The Research Department, Travel Publishing Ltd,
7a Apollo House, Calleva Park, Aldermaston, Reading, RG7 8TN.**

Your Name:

Your Address:

Your Telephone Number:

Please tick as appropriate:

Comments ☐   Recommendation ☐

Name of Establishment:

Address:

Telephone Number:

Name of Contact:

READER REACTION FORM

COMMENT OR REASON FOR RECOMMENDATION:

....

....

....

....

....

....

....

....

....

....

....

....

....

....

....

....

....

....

....

....

Index of Advertisers

ACCOMMODATION

FOOD AND DRINK

INDEX OF ADVERTISERS

PLACES OF INTEREST

INDEX OF ADVERTISERS